AP* WORLD HISTORY:
AN ESSENTIAL COURSEBOOK

By Ethel Wood

WoodYard Publications, Reading, Pennsylvania

*AP and Advanced Placement are registered trademarks of the College Entrance Examination Board wich was not involved in the production of and does not endorse this book.

AP* World History: An Essential Coursebook

Published by WoodYard Publications
P.O. Box 3856
Reading, PA 19606 U.S.A.
Ph. 610-207-1366
Fax 610-372-8401
worldhistap@comcast.net

http://worldhistap.home.comcast.net/

ISBN 978-0-9743481-4-8

TABLE OF CONTENTS

Other Books by Ethel Wood

American Government: A Complete Coursebook

AP Comparative Government and Politics: A Study Guide (editions 1-3)

AP Human Geography: A Study Guide

The Immigrants: An Historical Reader (editor)

Introduction to Sociology, A Nextext Coursebook

Multiple-Choice and Free-Response Questions in Preparation for the AP United States Government and Politics Examination (editions 1-5)

Multiple-Choice and Free-Response Questions in Preparation for the AP World History Examination

Teacher's Guide - AP Comparative Government and Politics

The Best Test Preparation for the Graduate Record Examination in Political Science

The Presidency: An Historical Reader (editor), *A Nextext Reader*

A note of thanks goes to Katherine Wood for her time and effort in editing this book. Her intelligence and skill contributed greatly to the finished product, and her comments and suggestions were invaluable to me.

Ethel Wood
May 2008

INTRODUCTION

> "Learning without thought is labor lost.
> Thought without learning is intellectual
> death."

> Confucius (551-479 B.C.)

No doubt you have heard of the man quoted above, since his legendary wisdom has played a significant role in shaping the beliefs and events of human lives for many centuries. It is appropriate, then, that we begin this journey through the course of world history with his thoughts, even though the traditional ways that history has been taught and learned have not always been based on his advice. History is sometimes seen as an assortment of facts that students must memorize in order to pass an endless series of tests, a procedure that we might describe as "learning without thought," and surely as "labor lost." Yet thought must also reflect learning in order to escape "intellectual death." How does a student achieve both learning *and* thought? That is the challenge of history well learned, and the curriculum of the AP World History course offers a balance between the two that provides a framework for thoughtful learning.

"World history" covers a lot of ground, both in terms of land space and time. How can one learn all of the history of humankind in one school year? Clearly that is an impossible task. However, it is possible to learn the broad "story" of humanity by using some tools that help to connect the parts of the story from beginning to end (or present). Once you know the plot, you are in a good position to learn the sub-plots that in turn help make sense of all the facts that support the overall story. This kind of learning with thought enables a life-long expansion of knowledge that gives history meaning that enriches the present and shapes the future.

TOOLS FOR LEARNING HISTORY

What are these magical tools that transform the study of history? We will begin with these:

1) Think About the Big Picture – Just when did world history begin? With the first civilization? With the first written records? With the first human beings? Or maybe with the creation of the earth…or even the universe! Really "big history" dwarfs the importance of our own era if we put it within the context of the history of the universe. Even though it is rather arbitrarily agreed that history begins with written records, that limited time line still means that the "story" of history is very big. It is important to identify **"marker events"** that make a difference in the course of history, and to distinguish them from the myriad of details that can make us feel that history is just a bunch of unrelated facts.

A COSMIC CALENDAR: DECEMBER

Sunday	Monday	Tuesday	Wednesday	Thursday	Friday	Saturday
1	2	3	4	5	6	7
8	9	10	11	12	13	14
15 Cambrian Explosion (burst of new life forms)	16	17 Emergence of first vertebrates	18 Early land plants	19	20 First four-limbed animals	21 Variety of insects begin to flourish
22	23	24 First dinosaurs appear	25 First mammalian ancestors appear	26	27 First known birds	28
29 Dinosaurs wiped out by asteroid or comet	30	31				

31 - 10:15 AM - Apes appear
9:24 PM - First human ancestors to walk upright
10:48 PM - Homo erectus appears
11:54 PM - Anatomically modern humans appear

11:59:45 PM - Invention of writing
11:59:50 PM - Pyramids built in Egypt
1 second before midnight - Voyage of Christopher Columbus.

A Cosmic Calendar. Astronomer Carl Sagan was the first person to explain the history of the universe in one year as a "Cosmic Calendar" in his television series, *Cosmos.* He started New Years Day with the "Big Bang," to give his viewers some idea of how old the universe is. Even our "big picture" view of human history is dwarfed by Sagan's perspective.

Reference: http://school.discoveryeducation.com; *An Exploration with the American Museum of Natural History*

2) Think about themes – An important tool in organizing and understanding history is thinking about themes, or unifying threads, that may be separated, even though they often intertwine. The themes in the AP World History curriculum that may be followed throughout history are humans and the environment, cultures, political structures and power (government and politics), economic systems, and social structures.

3) Think about chunks – The study of world history becomes more manageable if you "chunk it" into different time periods, a process called **periodization.** History textbooks usually chunk content into regions, but periodization is much more than that. It requires a student to think cross-culturally about a time period and analyze interactions among societies, as well as changes in political, economic, or social arrangements within societies. Even though history is broken up into periods, you are still seeing the big picture because you are concerned with broad patterns and **"marker events"** that change the course of world history. Big picture events and trends that make one period distinct from another are generally cross-cultural in that they impact several areas of the world, and they also often create change in more than one theme area. For example, an international war (such as World War II in the 20th century) that not only challenges government structures and officials, but also brings about major economic and social class changes is likely to be a marker event. The AP World History curriculum chunks history into five periods, although many other periodization patterns are possible.

AP WORLD HISTORY THEMES

Theme One: **Humans and the** **Environment**	This theme emphasizes demography (the science of human populations) as people migrate, settle, spread disease, and alter the environment through technology. Human interactions with their environment have impacted the course of world history in many ways.
Theme Two: **Culture**	This theme focuses on cultural influences that have shaped societies throughout history, including belief systems (such as religion, philosophies, and ideologies), science and technology, and the arts and architecture.
Theme Three: **Government and** **Politics**	This important theme throughout world history investigates government in various forms, including empires, nations, and regional and global organizations. It also includes a study of politics, or who wields power and how.
Theme Four: **The Economy**	A study of economic systems includes the many ways that people have made a living throughout history, such as agriculture, pastoralism, trade, commerce, and industry. This theme also investigates labor systems, and economic ideologies such as socialism and capitalism.
Theme Five: **Social Structures**	Social structures include gender roles, family and kinship, race, ethnicity, and social classes. These social structures have impacted the course of world history in very different ways than politics and economics, but their influence is equally as important.

AP World History Themes. Organizing history by themes helps you to follow continuities and changes over time and to compare different societies or regions within one time period.

4) Think comparatively – Another way to think thoughtfully about history is to analyze through comparison that makes use of the big picture, themes, and chunks (#1,2, and 3 above). For example, you may be interested in comparing social class (a theme) in India and China between 600 and 1450 C.E. (chunk). If you think about how social class in the two societies is different as well as similar, you gain a better understanding of both than you would if you just learned about them separately. You may compare many categories in history: societies or regions, belief systems (such as Buddhism and Hinduism), economic systems (such as capitalism and communism), revolutions (such as the American and French revolutions), or demographic patterns (such as different migrations of people from one area to another).

PERIODIZATION IN THE AP* WORLD HISTORY COURSE

Foundations: 8000 B.C.E. - 600 C.E.

600 C.E. - 1450

1450 - 1750

1750 - 1914

1914 - Present

5) Think about change over time – To approach history as a story necessarily means that you must think about change over time. What happens in the beginning of the story? What events occur that makes the story change? What happens in the middle of the story that is caused by something that occurred earlier? How do all the events and characters that interact throughout the story influence the ending? Every time you tell a story, you are making connections among its various parts. In the same way, history is much more meaningful if you make connections across time periods. What happened in Latin America during the period from 1450 to 1750 that shaped the events of the 19th century? What happened in the 19th century that shaped the 20th century? How have events and people during all three time periods interacted to help explain modern day news stories from Latin America?

6) Think Like an Historian – We will never know all the events that have occurred in the past because knowledge of most of them has not passed on to later generations. No one thought to tell their children about these occurrences, and so remembrance of them ceased when individuals died. However, some people, places, and events are remembered, sometimes through stories told around the fire at night, occasionally by paintings on cave walls, or often through written records. Historians look at all kinds of evidence in order to reconstruct the past, including physical evidence left behind, such as remnants of buildings, pottery, and clothing. In order to find out what really happened, an historian (or history student) needs many skills, including the ability to analyze **perspective**, or point of view. The slave's view is usually different from the slaveholder's, and the conqueror usually doesn't see things the same way as the conquered. If an historian finds a letter from a 16th-century European nobleman that praises his king, the historian must take into account the nobleman's point of view. To an historian, history is not a collection of static facts, but is an exciting, dynamic puzzle that must be interpreted and analyzed.

NECESSARY SKILLS (OR HABITS OF MIND) FOR HISTORIANS

1) **Evaluation based on evidence** – In evaluating occurrences or influences from the past, historians must carefully use factual evidence to back their arguments. Or as Confucius implies, thought must be accompanied by specific learning.

2) **Analysis of primary documents and data** – Historians must be able to interpret information provided in documents from the time period, paying particular attention to point of view.

3) **Comparison and continuity and change over time** – Historians are better able to interpret the past if they are able the compare societies, trends, and events across societies, and if they understand how the topic they are studying has changed over time.

4) **Understanding of both global and local events** – Patterns that occur across the globe are often reflected in local events, and local events may stimulate global developments. Historians need to see the connections between them. Likewise, some ideas, beliefs, values, and norms are shared across cultures; others are unique to particular areas.

5) **Understanding of how the past impacts the present and future** – We may debate the old truism of whether or not history repeats itself, but one pattern is clearly important: the past shapes the present and future.

These tools are emphasized throughout this book to build your knowledge of world history as you read, and to make the connections that will help you to remember the ever-changing but always interconnected story of the world.

THE AP WORLD HISTORY EXAM

The College Board administers AP exams each May during a two-week period. The AP World History Exam is offered during this time, with a total testing time of 3 hours and 5 minutes. The questions are based on the themes identified on page 8 of this book, and will require you to make use of the skills listed on page 10. The exam is weighted so that half the exam grade is determined by the number of multiple-choice questions that are correctly answered out of a total of 70 questions, and half the exam grade is based on the student's scores on 3 free-response questions.

Section I: Multiple-Choice Questions

The 70 multiple-choice questions test student knowledge of the five chronological periods of the curriculum, with a number of questions being cross-chronological; however, all periods are fairly equally represented, with slightly more questions based on the 600-1450 C.E. period. The questions are challenging. Some points to keep in mind about the multiple-choice section are:

- On the exam, the College Board subtracts one-fourth of the number of questions answered incorrectly from the number of questions answered correctly. So if you have no idea how to answer a question, it is usually better to leave the answer blank. However, if you can eliminate one or more of the answer choices, it is probably advantageous to guess from among the remaining choices.

- Some are based on charts, photographs, and maps, so it is important to carefully consider the visual information provided, including the title and the two axes of a chart or graph. Sometimes these questions just require that you read the chart correctly, but sometimes you must also have some content knowledge in order to answer correctly.

- Be prepared for EXCEPT, NOT, and LEAST questions, such as "Which of the following was NOT a political leader in a river valley civilization?" These are sometimes called "reverse multiple-choice questions," and they require you to identify the only *incorrect* answer. These questions take practice because you must reverse your thinking in order to answer them correctly.

THE AP WORLD HISTORY EXAM

Question Type	Percentage of Exam	Time
Section I: Multiple-Choice (70 Questions)	50%	55 minutes
Section II: Free-Response	50%	130 minutes for all 3 questions
1) Document-Based	(1/3 of 50%)	50 minutes (includes 10-minutes for reading)
2) Change Over Time	(1/3/ of 50%)	40 minutes
3) Comparative	(1/3 of 50%)	40 minutes

- Questions on the exam rarely require you to know exact chronological dates, but they may ask you to place events or trends within a particular time period. Questions may also test your knowledge of the proper order of events, so that you know what happened first, last, and in between.

This book provides many multiple-choice questions throughout that will help prepare you for Section I of the exam.

Section II: Free-Response Questions

Section II consists of 3 free-response questions that must be answered in 130 minutes. Since you can allocate your time in any way you wish during this time period, it is important to not get bogged down too long in any one of the questions. Otherwise, you will not have enough time to properly answer the 3rd question. Part A is a document-based question (DBQ) that includes a 10-minute period for reading the documents and a 40-minute writing period (50 minutes); Part B is an essay question that deals specifically with continuity and change over time over at least one of the five time periods (40 minutes); and Part C is an essay the compares similarities and differences in at least two societies (40 minutes). You do not have to answer the questions in order; the most important consideration is to allow enough time for each.

The highest score for each free-response question is a "9."

Part A: The Document-Based Question (DBQ)

The DBQ is designed not to test your content knowledge, but to measure your skills as an historian. The question is presented first, and is followed by a set of primary documents that must be read before the question can be answered. For example, look ahead to page 133 to see the DBQ for Unit One. The question reads, "Using the documents, analyze the tensions between nomadic and sedentary people during the period before 600 C.E. Identify one additional type of document and explain briefly how it would help your analysis." Since you haven't read Unit One yet, don't worry if you can't answer the question yet, but look at how it is worded. The question is followed by seven documents, each written by an individual from the time period. Some DBQs may include photographs, paintings, charts, maps, or graphs about the particular topic. Your task is to come up with a thesis, and then back it with specific evidence from the documents. Imagine that you are an historian deeply involved in seeking the truth. Documents shed light on the truth, but each is only a small piece of the answer. How can you put them all together to come up with a solid thesis that provides insightful answers to the mysteries of the past? The DBQ exercise is meant to simulate the historian's methods for interpreting the past.

Your response will be assessed according to a rubric with these basic guidelines:

1) **Thesis** – Answer the question, don't just repeat it. A good thesis requires some judgment and interpretation of the evidence, and it must be squarely focused on the question. For example, in Unit One's question, your thesis should not just read, "Tensions existed between nomadic and sedentary people during the period before 600 C.E." A strong thesis would give an overview of what the tensions were (positive, negative, great, small), and supporting paragraphs would provide the details of the nature of the tensions.

2) **Use of all documents** – You must make use of ALL the documents in your response. You may refer to each document in any way you like, but it must be clear to the reader which one you are addressing. For example, you may refer to documents by number (Document 1), by author, or by a brief description. You must demonstrate understanding of the documents, but you may misinterpret one of them and still get this point.

3) **Supporting evidence** – The documents must be used to support the thesis. You may use a particular quote from the document, or simply describe which part of the document you are using to support your thesis. Do not quote extensively from the documents because it is too

time consuming; just make sure that your references are clear. You will receive either 1 or 2 points for your supporting evidence – 2 points for appropriate evidence from all or all but one document, or 1 point for appropriate evidence from all but two documents (see chart on page 15).

4) **Point of view** – You must analyze the author's point of view in at least TWO documents. This point is at the heart of the historian's necessary skills. Look carefully at who wrote the document and when it was written, and critically evaluate how objective the author might be. For example, the documents for the DBQ for Unit One (pp. 133-135) includes one document by a Chinese historian, a member of a sedentary society, and another document by a chieftain of the Xiongnu, a nomadic society. You would expect the two men to see the tensions between nomads and settled people quite differently. Clearly, all writers have their own points of view, so what they write will always be affected, even though what they have to say is usually still important to consider. Historians often look for evidence from different points of view to be sure that their analysis approximates what actually happened. Remember, you are seeking the truth, and documents should be evaluated for their reliability.

5) **Grouping documents** – Don't just list the documents and comment on each. You must group them in whatever ways make sense to you based on the question asked. Generally, there is no one formula for grouping. Instead, there is a range of possibilities. You may group chronologically, or you may group by region or culture or by theme. You may also group by authors that agree with one another. For example, for the Unit One question, you could do two simple groups: one for documents written by people who lived in sedentary societies and one for documents written by people who lived in nomadic societies. Then you might do another group based on region: writers from the Mediterranean area and writers from Asia. Another division might be between positive and negative points of view in the documents. There is no one way to organize groups, but it is important that your groups are clearly identified. Again, imagine an historian separating documents into piles according to their point of view, or according to what aspect of the issue they are commenting on. For the DBQ, you must group in TWO or THREE ways, depending on the question.

6) **Additional documents** – This one is easy to forget, but don't. You must identify at least ONE type of additional document or source and explain why that document would help you to answer the question. Again, imagine the historian's dilemma – many documents may be available,

but you can't quite understand the issue because you need something else – another point of view or another type of document. These are the "if onlys" of history – "If only I knew how the peasants felt about this!" or "If only I had an accurate map from the time!" Remember you must explain *why* you need the document in order to answer the question more fully.

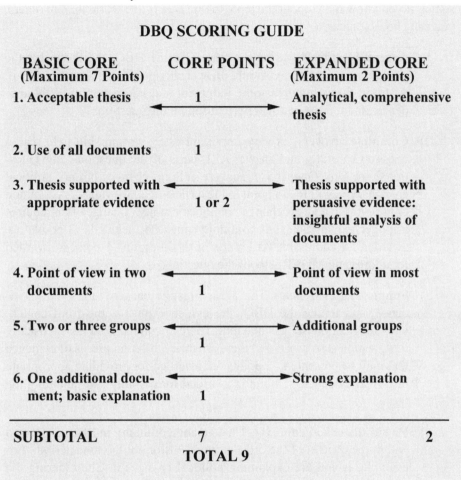

DBQ SCORING GUIDE

BASIC CORE (Maximum 7 Points)	CORE POINTS	EXPANDED CORE (Maximum 2 Points)
1. Acceptable thesis	1	Analytical, comprehensive thesis
2. Use of all documents	1	
3. Thesis supported with appropriate evidence	1 or 2	Thesis supported with persuasive evidence: insightful analysis of documents
4. Point of view in two documents	1	Point of view in most documents
5. Two or three groups	1	Additional groups
6. One additional document; basic explanation	1	Strong explanation
SUBTOTAL	**7**	**2**

TOTAL 9

The scoring guide is divided into a "basic core" of 7 points that a student MUST get before any points will be awarded for the "expanded core" of 1 or 2 points. If any 1 point is missed in the basic core, the maximum score would be a "6." Notice how most of the ways to demonstrate "excellence" in the expanded core match points in the basic core. Instead of "acceptable" it is "analytical," or instead of "appropriate," it is "persuasive."

Part B: Continuity and Change Over Time Essay

This essay question requires you to analyze both changes and continuities over the course of at least one time period in the curriculum and sometimes more than one. You will generally have to explain how one aspect (theme) of a society or region changed and/or stayed the same from one point in history to another. For example, look at Question 2 for Unit One on Page 135. The question reads, "Analyze the cultural and political changes and continuities in ONE of these civilizations during the early classical era from 1000 to 1 B.C.E." The choices are Rome and China.   Often these questions allow choices in regions, so that if you know more about the topic in one area of the world than in others, you can choose that area.

1) **Acceptable thesis** – Like the thesis for the DBQ, the thesis for the change over time essay should answer the question, not just repeat it. A strong thesis requires some judgment and interpretation of the evidence, and it must be squarely focused on the question.

2) **Complete answer** – A very important essay-writing skill is to read a question carefully and answer ALL parts of the question. For Question 2 for Unit One, if you analyze cultural changes but not political changes, you will lose a point in the basic core of the rubric. A common omission is to address change but not continuity. Change often requires a longer explanation, but continuity must be included. 2 points are awarded for addressing ALL parts of the question. 1 point is awarded for addressing MOST parts of the question.

3) **Supporting evidence** – The thesis must be backed with specific evidence, and unlike the DBQ, the evidence must come from content knowledge of the subject at hand. There are no required facts – usually the question is so broad that there are many different pieces of evidence that may be presented. 2 points are awarded for providing appropriate historical evidence. 1 point is awarded for partially substantiating the thesis.

4) **World historical context** – Change and continuity must be explained within the context of the broader world history of the time period. For example, if you are explaining political changes in China during the early classical era, you must put China within the context of the era. What contacts did China have with other civilizations that affected its politics? Was China isolated or connected to others? Your focus should be on China itself, but create a context for the changes and continuities.

5) **Analysis of the process of continuity and change** – In order to get this point, you must not only describe, or tell about, a change or continuity. You must also determine how various factors or parts of the topic relate to the change or explain the continuity. Using political change in China

during the classical era, your answer must demonstrate *why* political change occurred. For example, you might identify Shi Huangdi's use of legalism as a reason why political authority became more centralized. As with the DBQ, there are usually many ways to answer the question, and there is no one piece of historical evidence that is absolutely essential to use.

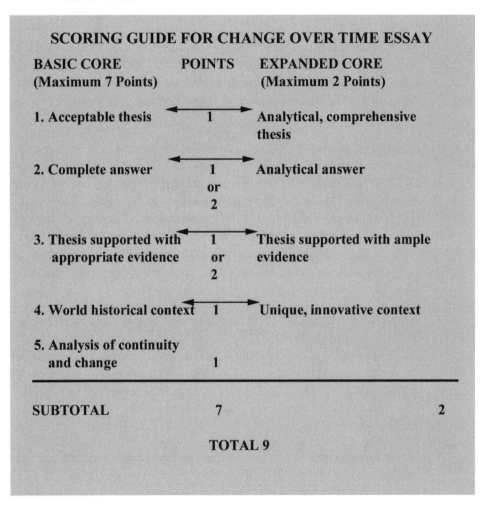

SCORING GUIDE FOR CHANGE OVER TIME ESSAY

BASIC CORE (Maximum 7 Points)	POINTS	EXPANDED CORE (Maximum 2 Points)
1. Acceptable thesis	1	Analytical, comprehensive thesis
2. Complete answer	1 or 2	Analytical answer
3. Thesis supported with appropriate evidence	1 or 2	Thesis supported with ample evidence
4. World historical context	1	Unique, innovative context
5. Analysis of continuity and change	1	
SUBTOTAL	7	2

TOTAL 9

The scoring guide is divided into a "basic core" of 7 points that a student MUST get before any points will be awarded for the "expanded core" of 1 or 2 points. If any 1 point is missed in the basic core, the maximum score would be a "6." Notice how most of the ways to demonstrate "excellence" in the expanded core match points in the basic core. Instead of "acceptable" it is "analytical," or instead of "appropriate," it is "ample."

Part C: The Comparative Essay

This essay requires the student to compare at least two societies or regions in terms of one of the major themes, such as interactions between societies, economic systems, belief systems, or political organizations. The question usually asks for both similarities and differences, and often some choice of societies or regions is allowed. For example, the comparative question for Unit One on page 135 reads, "Compare and contrast the reasons for and the outcomes of the fall of TWO of the following classical civilizations: The Roman Empire, Han China, and Gupta India."

Your response will be graded according to a rubric with these basic points:

1) **Acceptable thesis** – Like the thesis for the DBQ and the change over time essay, the thesis for the comparative essay should answer the question, not just repeat it. A strong thesis requires some judgment and interpretation of the evidence, and it must be squarely focused on the question.

2) **Complete answer** – A very important essay-writing skill is to read a question carefully and answer ALL parts of the question. If a question asks you to discuss both similarities and differences, be sure that you discuss both. The Unit One question asks you to "compare and contrast," so you should discuss both similarities and differences. A common omission is to address differences but not similarities. Differences often require a longer explanation, but similarities must be included. 2 points are awarded for addressing ALL parts of the question. 1 point is awarded for addressing MOST parts of the question.

3) **Supporting evidence** – The thesis must be backed with specific evidence, and unlike the DBQ, the evidence must come from content knowledge of the subject at hand. There are no required facts – usually the question is so broad that there are many different pieces of evidence that may be presented. 2 points are awarded for providing appropriate historical evidence. 1 point is awarded for partially substantiating the thesis.

4) **Direct comparison** – A common mistake that students often make on this essay is to present both societies ("Here's Rome, Here's China") without *directly* pointing out differences or similarities between the societies. If you are comparing the reasons for the fall of classical civilizations, for example, you need to make some statements such as, "Unlike in Rome, Chinese society was held together by Confucianism…" You can avoid this problem by organizing your essay by topic, rather than by country or society.

5) **Reason for a similarity or difference** – For this point, you need to explain *why* the two societies are different or similar. For example, differences in outcomes of the fall of Rome and India might be explained by the unifying influence of Hinduism in India and the lack of a comparable unifying influence in Rome. This explanation must be made within the context of a *direct* comparison.

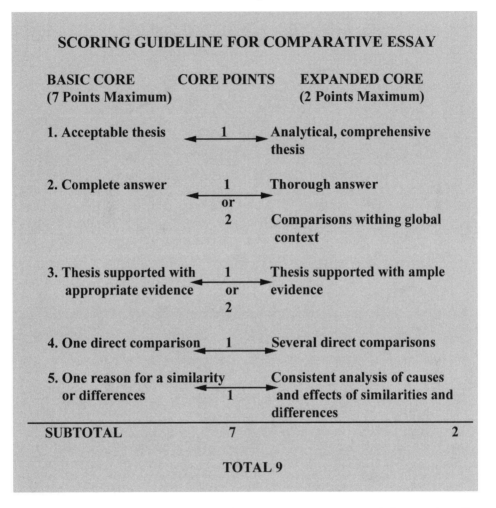

SCORING GUIDELINE FOR COMPARATIVE ESSAY

BASIC CORE (7 Points Maximum)	CORE POINTS	EXPANDED CORE (2 Points Maximum)
1. Acceptable thesis	1	Analytical, comprehensive thesis
2. Complete answer	1 or 2	Thorough answer / Comparisons withing global context
3. Thesis supported with appropriate evidence	1 or 2	Thesis supported with ample evidence
4. One direct comparison	1	Several direct comparisons
5. One reason for a similarity or differences	1	Consistent analysis of causes and effects of similarities and differences
SUBTOTAL	7	2

TOTAL 9

The scoring guide is divided into a "basic core" of 7 points that a student MUST get before any points will be awarded for the "expanded core" of 1 or 2 points. If any 1 point is missed in the basic core, the maximum score would be a "6." Notice how most of the ways to demonstrate "excellence" in the expanded core match points in the basic core. Instead of "acceptable" it is "analytical," or instead of "appropriate," it is "ample."

For all the free-response questions, it is important to plan your answers carefully and to be sure that you answer ALL parts of the question. Once you know what to expect on the exam, the best preparation for the exam is to know your stuff. The questions do require reading and writing skills, but the surer you are of the material, the more likely you are to answer the questions correctly. This book provides the concepts and information, as well as plenty of practice questions that will prepare you for the exam.

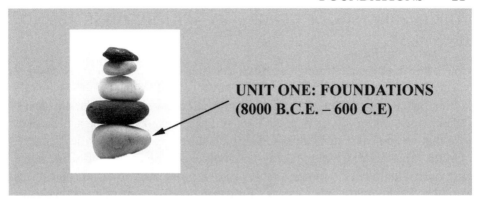

**UNIT ONE: FOUNDATIONS
(8000 B.C.E. – 600 C.E)**

The first historical period of the AP World History curriculum is called "Foundations," a name that describes the importance of the era for shaping virtually all events and trends that followed. It is by far the longest of the five time periods of the course, encompassing some 8600 years. As a result, we will divide (or periodize) Foundations into three big "chunks" to make it more manageable:

1) **Development of Agriculture and Early Agricultural Communities** (8000 B.C.E. – about 3500 B.C.E.)

2) **Early "River Valley" Civilizations** (about 3500 B.C.E. – about 1200 B.C.E.)

3) **Classical Civilizations** (about 1000 B.C.E. – 600 C.E.)

The dates of these eras are flexible, and historians disagree about exactly when each one began and ended, but the categories help to make the story of early human settlements and civilizations a little easier to follow. Part of the problem with fixing exact dates for eras is that we have only a limited knowledge of the eras, particularly the first two, and archaeologists regularly discover new evidence that changes our previous conceptions about them. Another problem in fixing dates, particularly for **"marker events"** that change the course of history, is that interactions among groups of human beings were very limited, so that change in one area might not occur in another part of the world till much later. For example, the invention of agriculture did not occur at one time all over the world. The first agricultural settlements probably appeared about 8000 B.C.E. (setting the beginning year for the Foundations Period), but they did not quickly spread to other areas of the world. Instead, agriculture seems to have been independently invented by many different, widely dispersed groups of people around the globe.

THE IMPORTANCE OF GEOGRAPHY AND THE PHYSICAL ENVIRONMENT

Have you ever looked through an historical atlas of the world to study changes in civilizations and their borders? If you have, you know that change is the rule rather than the exception. The world in 4000 C.E. looks very similar physically to our world today. If you pick out the familiar land and water shapes you realize that geological history moves at a much slower pace than political history. On the other hand, try to trace any nation in existence today, and while some are older than others, you don't have to go very far back in history to find its origins. Yet no matter what time period you choose over the past 6000 years or so, the political imprint of human beings is there, and political change occurs much more rapidly than geological change.

Study the map on the opposite page by concentrating on the physical features of the earth's surface that it reveals. Notice the land shapes and the lakes, seas, and oceans. Larger scale maps of different regions would of course show many more physical features that are very similar to those that our ancestors in ancient times were familiar with. Before people began transforming the landscape with their cultural imprints, physical geography shaped and limited their activities. These alterations became apparent first as people settled into agricultural communities, and grew more profound with the growth of cities and eventually industry. In even the earliest civilizations, people devised and used maps that not only represented physical geography but their cultural transformations (such as cities and roads) as well.

The Cultural Perspective

If we are to successfully travel backward through time to try to understand what life was like during the Foundations period, it is important to focus on **perspective**, or point of view. All of us see our surroundings through the lens of our own time period and culture, even though we seldom realize it. For example, did you notice that the map on the opposite page has one cultural construct? It is divided into continents. Think objectively about this. Why does one continent begin in one place and end in another? Certainly, physical geography has something to do with the divisions, but not always. For example, look at the areas where Europe, Asia, and Africa intersect. For most of us, cultural images shape those dividing lines, so that we think of "Europeans" in one way, "Asians" in another, and "Africans" in yet another. In ancient times, people made cultural distinctions, too, but not the same ones that we do in modern times. So our task is to adjust our cultural perspectives as we go through time, realizing that cultural meanings from one era impact those of later eras and that change has been continual.

The Myth of Continents. Dividing the world into basic chunks called "continents" is a cultural construction loosely based on physical geography, but more importantly on our conceptions of cultural differences.

Demography

The study of population is called **demography,** a term derived from the ancient Greek words "demos", meaning population or people, and "graphe", meaning to describe. Demography is of interest to many social science disciplines including geography, with its special emphasis on spatial organization: the location of places, people, and events, and the connections among places and landscapes. For historians, changes in population are an important part of the human mosaic that has shaped the story of the world. Population increases and decreases have caused people to move from one place to another, bringing them in contact with other ways of life and causing many political, social, and economic changes.

Migrations are permanent moves to new locations that have occurred on local, regional, and global levels. There are countless reasons why people voluntarily migrate, but most of them are economic. A **push factor** encourages people to move from the region that they live in, and a **pull factor** attracts them to a new region. For example, push factors force refugees to migrate from their homes because of persecution based on religion, race, nationality, or political opinions. Pull factors for these refugees may bring them to an area that has better jobs and a more democratic government. Environmental factors influence migrations greatly, sometimes as **intervening obstacles**, or physical features that halt or

PERSPECTIVES:
The Myth of Continents

The Myth of Continents is a book by Martin W. Lewis and Karen E. Wigen that focuses on the unexamined spatial assumptions that we all make, starting with the idea that the world is somehow divided into "continents." They comment on "our tendency to let a continental framework structure our perceptions of the human community...Each continent is accorded its own history, and we locate its essential nature in opposition to that of the other continents...An obsolete formulation, this framework [continents] is now wholly inadequte for the load it is routinely asked to carry." They conclude that only by examining our commonplace notions can we develop a "sophisticated understanding of global geography." Lewis and Wigen's perspective is an important one to consider in the study of world history.

Reference: Lewis, Martin W. and Karen Wigen, *The Myth of Continents*. Berkeley, CA: University of California Press, 1997.

slow migration from one place to another. Over time, these obstacles may have different meanings: an ocean that separated lands no longer prevents migrations once the technology to cross the ocean develops.

With population movement, people spread their cultures to new areas through a process called **cultural diffusion**, including innovations, technology, religion, language, food and clothing styles, and disease. Throughout history diseases have spread as human interactions have increased. Famous examples include the 14th century plague that spread from Asia to Europe, and the contagious diseases that spread rapidly through the Native American populations that came into contact with Europeans in the New World during the 15th and 16th centuries. During prehistoric times, human beings migrated to many parts of the globe, setting the stage for human domination of other species on earth. Although we cannot pin these prehistoric migrations to a single "marker event" because they took place gradually over long periods of time, without them humans might not have survived those early years.

THE BIG PICTURE: FOUNDATIONS
(8000 B.C.E. - 600 C.E)

Be sure to keep up with these broad trends and themes for the Foundations Period:

1) Interactions among different groups of people on the planet were usually limited to groups that were geographically nearby, but interactions increased steadily throughout the time period, both in frequency and distance.

2) Physical geography and the natural environment interacted with human activities to shape changes and continuities during the time period.

3) Foundations is made up of three time periods that are distinguished by big changes in human life styles, including "marker events": the development of agriculture and early agricultural communities, the early river valley civilizations, and classical civilizations.

IMPORTANT TERMS AND CONCEPTS

cultural diffusion
demography
intervening obstacles
"marker events"
migrations
The Myth of Continents
periodization
perspective
push and pull factors

CHAPTER ONE: AGRICULTURAL DEVELOPMENT AND EARLY AGRICULTURAL COMMUNITIES

"History" is usually defined as the study of the past beginning with the first systematic written records, sometime in the 4th millennium (4000-3000 B.C.E.). However, some important developments occurred earlier that greatly influenced the course of world history. One important "marker event" was the development of agriculture and agricultural communities.

HUMAN LIFE BEFORE 8000 B.C.E.

Exactly when the first human beings appeared is debatable, but they existed on earth for millions of years before the beginning year for the AP World History curriculum (8000 B.C.E.). Archaeologists (scientists who study prehistoric and ancient peoples) currently believe that the decisive differentiation between humans and apes occurred between 6 and 8 million years ago. New discoveries are being made every day, but the general trend has been to push the date further and further back into prehistory. One distinction between humans and other mammals is **bipedalism**, or the preference for walking erect on two limbs rather than four. DNA analysis of bone fragments that are millions of years old indicates that the earliest known bipedal creature was *Ardepithecus ramidus,* discovered in Ethiopia in 2001. From there, many different species of humans developed, but all disappeared except for *homo sapiens*, which appears to have become the only surviving human species somewhere between 50,000 and 10,000 years ago.

In the long period of time before people began keeping written records, **primary sources** (original evidence from the time period) did not take the form of documents but included objects, artifacts, and skeletal remains. Some objects made of stone and bone have survived, so that we know that hominids used refined tools by the time that the **Paleolithic Age (or Old Stone Age)** began some 70,000 years ago. The Paleolithic Age extended until about 8000 B.C.E., by which time humans inhabited all the continents except Antarctica. *Homo sapiens* had several advantages over other species, including forelimbs freed from walking and opposable thumbs, with both features allowing them to manipulate objects as tools or weapons. Perhaps the most significant advantage, however, was the development of a large brain, especially well developed in the frontal regions where conscious and reflective thought takes place. Humans were not as strong as many other species, but they were able to figure out how to thrive, even in colder climates, by devising effective ways to solve the problems of survival.

PRIMARY SOURCES: LUCY

A very important milestone in the development of early humans was the discovery in 1974 of the hominid "Lucy," so named because the researchers celebrated by loudly playing the old Beatles' song "Lucy in the Sky with Diamonds" in their camp the evening after they found her. Lucy's species was named *Australopithecus afarensis*, a bipedal creature that lived in eastern Africa more than three million years ago. Lucy was a hybrid between modern humans and apes that was able to walk upright for small distances. Lucy's species, like all other hominids except *homo sapiens,* eventually became extinct.

Hunting and Gathering

During the Paleolithic Age humans survived by foraging for their food: hunting wild animals and gathering edible plants. They traveled in small groups (probably about thirty to fifty members) and had to constantly keep moving in order to follow the herds of animals and to find new areas where edible plants grew.   Their movement kept them from accumulating possessions and from developing any sense of property ownership. Although some people undoubtedly emerged as leaders, hunting and gathering groups were marked by very few status differences since they did not accumulate wealth. The basic division of labor was based on sex, with the men usually responsible for hunting and the women for gathering. However, it appears as if they made no judgment that one activity was more important than the other, so many scholars believe that one sex did not dominate the other. Meat was highly prized, as was the hunter, but the groups could not have survived without the gathering skills of women.

The survival of hunters and gatherers depended on a thorough understanding of their natural environment. Older women, in particular, had an extensive knowledge of which plants were edible and which were poisonous, and they passed their skills down to younger women, who were able to gather with young children strapped to their bodies. Hunters had to devise clever ways of catching animals that were often larger and faster than they were, and they wore disguises, carefully coordinated their movements, set traps, and created distractions in order to snare their prey.

The Importance of Tools

Homo sapiens and some of their ancestors created special tools, such as sharp knives, bows and arrows, and spears. Early tools were made from wood, bone, and stone, although no wooden tools and few bone tools survive. The earliest stone tools were made by breaking off the edges of stone cores to create points or cutting surfaces. Later they sharpened flakes broken off the core stone. Humans used tools to help them build huts of branches, stones, bones, skins, and leaves, and some 26,000 years ago they began to weave cloth. Tools also eventually allowed them to invent and sustain agriculture as early as 8000 B.C.E.

Paleolithic Culture

Little is known about Paleolithic culture since few artifacts have survived to modern day. Perhaps the best known remainders of culture that we have today are the cave paintings in Europe and North Africa, the oldest being created about 32,000 years ago. The paintings show food animals, such as wild oxen, reindeer, and horses, as well as people dressed in animals skins, smeared with paint. A newly discovered cave near Pont d'Arc in the Ardeche region of France shows panthers, bears, owls, rhinoceros, and a hyena. Some cave art also indicates that Stone Age people had well-developed religions, and at several Neanderthal (a people first found in the Neander valley in southwestern Germany) sites, there are signs of careful, ritualistic burials. In some, survivors placed flint tools and animal bones in and around the graves of the dead. Cro-Magnon people wore necklaces, bracelets, and beads, and also decorated their furniture.

The life styles of prehistoric people are often characterized as violent, uncertain, and exhausting, but many scholars believe that hunters and gatherers in areas abundant with game and plants, such as the African grasslands, probably only spent from three to five hours a day tending to their survival. In such areas, people would have had plenty of time to make tools, create art, and socialize with others in their group.

THE INVENTION OF FIRE: A PALEOLITHIC MARKER EVENT

Long before the time period of *homo sapiens,* human ancestors made the important discovery of fire, probably borrowed from flames caused by lightning or lava flows. Eventually they learned to start their own fires, and the control of fire led to many improvements in their lives. For example, it made a much wider range of foods edible, particularly animal flesh. Cooked meat is not only easier to digest; it may be stored and preserved more easily. Also, fire frightened off predatory animals, hardened wooden weapons and tools, and warmed body and soul. Even though no one knows exactly who or when the discovery of fire was first made, it is one of the first "marker events" that changed early human prehistory.

THE NEOLITHIC REVOLUTION

The term **Neolithic (or Agricultural) Revolution** refers to the changeover from food gathering to food producing that serves as a "marker event" to begin the Foundations period in history (8000 B.C.E.). However, the term is deceiving because the revolution was not a single event but instead occurred at different times in different parts of the world. Even as the "agricultural revolution" took place in one place, it usually happened gradually over the course of several generations. Slowly, hunting and gathering gave way to sowing, harvesting, and keeping domesticated animals. Usually **agriculture** (the deliberate tending of crops and livestock in order to produce food and fiber) was adopted a little at a time to supplement the needs of hunters and gatherers. Some members of the group hunted while other experimented with planting seeds from wild plants, usually grasses, and eventually agriculture became the primary economic activity. When that event occurred, the revolution was complete for that group, as the sequence of events continued to evolve for other groups.

Early Horticulture and Pastoralism

Horticulture may be distinguished from agriculture in that horticulturists used only hand tools, such as hoes and digging sticks to plant seeds and cultivate crops. Horticulture developed earlier than agriculture that made use of animals and plows to speed up and otherwise greatly improve the process. **Pastoralists** were the first domesticators of animals, and they remained semi-nomadic, leading their herds to fresh grazing lands. Horticulturists were the first to settle in one place, and eventually were able to integrate domesticated animals into their communities. Agriculturists could cultivate fields vastly larger than the garden-sized plots worked by horticulturists, and plows turned and aerated soil to increase fertility. As a result, their communities grew larger and their surpluses rose.

The Domestication of Grains

In the Middle East, the region with the earliest evidence of agriculture, humans transformed wild grasses into higher-yielding domesticated grains called emmer wheat and barley. According to Jared Diamond, author of *Guns, Germs, and Steel,* the development of agriculture was mainly dependent on the availability of grains and animals in the area that were domesticable. Another factor may have been the availability of food that could be hunted and gathered, and hunger may have necessitated invention in areas where readily available food was scarce. Plants domesticated in the Middle East spread to nearby areas through **cultural diffusion** as nearby people learned from those already practicing farming, but agriculture probably rose as an **independent invention** (no cultural diffusion involved) in many other areas. Domestic rice originated in southern China, Southeast Asia, or northern India; maize (corn) was grown in Mesoamerica; and potatoes, squash, tomatoes, and peppers were grown in the Andes Mountain areas of Peru.

The Domestication of Animals

As agriculture developed, many areas also domesticated animals. It makes sense that as people settled down, they had to free themselves from following the herds, so the logical solution was to train the animals to stay put, too. Of course, some animals are more easily domesticated than others. The dog was probably the first domesticated animal, as hunters discovered the animal's helpfulness in tracking game. More directly related to the development of agriculture was the domestication of sheep and goats in Southwest Asia; cows in Eurasia and northern Africa; water buffalo and chickens in China; camels in Arabia and central Asia; and horses and pigs in Eurasia. Some areas of the world appear to have had few good animal candidates for domestication, such as Mesoamerica, Sub-Saharan Africa, New Guinea, and the Andes area, although the llama was domesticated in the Andes.

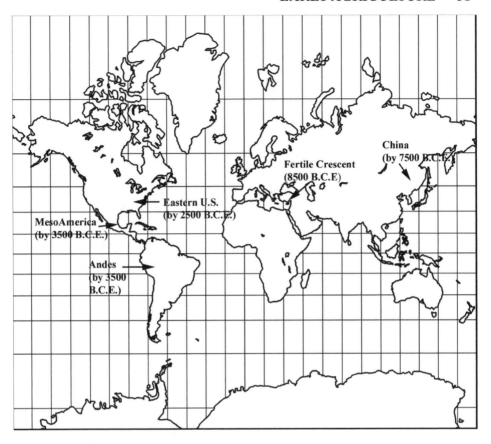

Centers of origin of food production. The map above shows some of the earliest areas where the Neolithic Revolution took place. The scattered land space and the big differences in time of production indicate that the transition from hunting and gathering to agriculture was independently invented by a number of people.

Reference: Jared Diamond, *Guns, Germs, and Steel.* New York: W.W. Norton, 1999, pp. 99-100.

The Neolithic Revolution as a "Marker Event"

Even though the changes were gradual, it is still appropriate to call the transition to agriculture a "revolution" or "marker event" because it profoundly affected the way that human beings lived. Some important changes include:

1) **People settled down** – To be near their crops, people settled into villages instead of constantly moving about as hunters and gatherers did. Because they didn't have to worry about carrying their possessions with them, people began to accumulate goods and claim pieces of land as their own. The concept of **private property** began to define human society.

2) **Division of labor** – In hunting and gathering groups, the basic division of labor was between men (the hunters) and women (the gatherers). In early agricultural settlements, people began to see the advantages of "specialization." For example, those most talented at crafting agricultural tools could do that for all the villagers, and those that best tended animals that pulled plows could do that. As a result, all work could be done more efficiently.

3) **Social inequality** – Whereas hunting and gathering groups were characterized by relative social equality, agricultural groups began to display social distinctions, and eventually social classes. Some people accumulated more land than others and passed that land down to their children, making some families "distinguished" and others not. With specialized occupations, some were awarded more respect and/or material rewards, and social inequality increased even more.

4) **Gender inequality** – The Neolithic Revolution is almost certainly responsible for the beginnings of status distinctions between men and women. Scholars offer many explanations, but most are based on the loss of women's economic power. In hunting and gathering societies, a woman's gathering skills were essential for the survival of the group. With agriculture, men took over both the care of animals and plants, and women were sidelined to domestic chores that enhanced, but were not central to, the survival of the village. One explanation for this change is that the male's superior physical strength meant that he was better able to manage when animal and plant care were merged in agricultural production.

5) **The importance of surplus** - With increasing specialization, not everyone was a farmer. For every craftsman that did not spend his days tending to crops, the farmers had to produce a surplus to support him and his family. The only way to do this was to raise a **surplus**, or more crops than the farmer needed to feed his own family. Surplus also meant that foodstuffs could be put away for later so that food supplies became more reliable. Once food supplies became more reliable, people ate more regularly, health improved, and population increased. With larger populations, more specialization could occur, and so villages grew into towns and eventually into cities that needed to be coordinated and controlled, giving way to specialized jobs in government.

6) **Religious changes** – Religious beliefs are evident in hunting and gathering societies, but most agricultural societies developed **polytheism,** or the belief in multiple gods. Whereas earlier beliefs probably centered on spirits, now "gods" with many human characteristics presided

over areas and objects important to farmers – sun gods, rain gods, gods of the harvest, and female fertility gods. Neolithic people made the connection between fertility of the soil and fertility of human beings, and many voluptuous female goddesses were celebrated in the form of clay figurines, decorations on pots, vases, and tools, and ritual objects. Infant deities represented the regeneration of human, animal, and plant life.

PERSPECTIVES: *ISHMAEL* ON THE AGRICULTURAL REVOLUTION

In his book *Ishmael,* Daniel Quinn questioned the general assumption that the Neolithic (or Agricultural) Revolution changed the course of world history for the better. He also contrasted the points of view of the "Leavers" (hunters and gatherers, who did not leave large footprints on the earth's environment) and "Takers" (agriculturalists, who transformed the landscape).

The Takers' view of the Leavers: "He's running and running and running... hunger and desperation driving him. He's terrified as well. Behind him on the ridge, just out of sight, his enemies are in pursuit to tear him to pieces – the lions, the wolves, the tigers...forever one step behind his prey and one step ahead of his enemies."

From the Leavers' point of view: "Far from scrabbling endlessly and desperately for food, hunter-gatherers are among the best-fed people on earth, and they manage this with only two or three hours a day of what you would call work – which makes them among the most leisured people on earth."

Reference: Daniel Quinn, *Ishmael.* New York: A Bantam Book, 1992, pp. 219-220.

Three Craft Industries

Three Neolithic craft industries emerged as agriculture developed: pottery, metallurgy, and textiles. Making use of natural products around them, early craftsmen fashioned goods that were useful to agricultural communities. Pottery served as containers for storing food, and was made by fire-hardening clay into waterproof pots. Copper was probably the first metal that humans shaped into useful items and jewelry because it is easily malleable. By 6000 B.C.E. people had discovered that it was even more versatile when heated to high tempera- tures, and they fashioned copper knives, axes, farm tools, and weapons. Textile production is hard to trace because fibers don't easily survive the ages, but some fragments indicated that fibers were woven together as early as 6000 B.C.E., and eventually fibers were spun into thread that was woven into cloth.

The Growth of Towns and Cities

By 4000 B.C.E. a number of villages had grown into towns, and towns into a few small cities, such as **Jericho** on the Jordan River and **Catal Huyuk** in southern Turkey. Both settlements were founded by 7000 B.C.E., and both were heavily fortified for protection. Jericho's round houses of mud and brick on stone foundations were surrounded by a ditch and a wall almost 12 feet high. Catal Huyuk's houses were joined together so that once outside entrances were barricaded, the houses could not be invaded. Both places relied upon trade to supplement their agricultural base. Jericho traded its salt, sulfur, and pitch for semiprecious stones from Anatolia, turquoise from the Sinai, and obsidian and cowrie shells from other areas. Catal Huyuk traded flint, obsidian, and jewelry with towns and villages nearby. Although it is not accurate to call Jericho and Catal Huyuk cities, their organizations and the life styles of their inhabitants foreshadowed the development of great cities and civilizations during the wa- tershed 4th Millennium B.C.E.

IDENTIFICATIONS AND CONCEPTS

agriculture
bipedalism
Catal Hayuk
cultural diffusion
division of labor
horticulture
independent invention
Jericho
Lucy
"marker events" of pre-history
Neolithic craft industries
Neolithic (or Agricultural) Revolution
Paleolithic Age
pastoralism
polytheism
primary sources

specialization
surplus

CHAPTER TWO: THE EARLIEST CIVILIZATIONS

By 3500 B.C.E. humans were organized in many ways across the globe. Many were still hunters and gatherers, making their livings in much the same ways that their ancestor did. Others had settled into small villages as horticulturists or were following domesticated herds of animals to pasture. In a few places, generally those areas where agriculture had started early, large towns were forming. In southwest Asia, in a place that the ancient Greeks called Mesopotamia, more complex organizations were beginning to grow into the first of the ancient civilizations.

Farming encouraged new forms of social organization partly because owning property was an incentive to make improvements, particularly in getting access to water. Building and maintaining irrigation ditches depended on cooperation among farmers, and irrigation needs led people to settle in villages rather than on isolated farms. These activities called for supervision and regulation, so the need for some type of formalized government arose. Once the number of people in a settlement grew so that more division of labor occurred, the village could be called a town. Even more growth and specialization led to the formation of the first cities where interconnected citizens lived in close proximity. It is no wonder, then, that the first civilizations grew up in river valleys where access to fresh water meant that crops could be irrigated and economic activities could be organized through interactions among cities, towns, and the countryside.

THE MEANING OF CIVILIZATION

What developments must occur in order for a society to be called a "**civilization**"? Some important characteristics of civilizations are:

1) **Generation of reliable surpluses** – Agricultural technology allows farmers to produce more than their families need. In the earliest civilizations, farmers supported many city dwellers and filled food storage houses to provide a reliable food source in lean times.

2) **Highly specialized occupations** – Whereas village and town life are characterized by division of labor, occupational specializations in the early civilizations were far more complex, including jobs in government, trade, merchandise, and religion.

3) **Clear social class distinctions** – With the growing complexity of occupations, the early civilizations set status distinctions among them, so that big differences appeared in prestige levels and wealth.

4) **Growth of cities** – Population centers in the ancient civilizations varied in size, but many were far larger than any that had been seen before. As economic, political, social, and cultural life grew more interrelated, towns grew into cities.

5) **Complex, formal governments** – The early needs for government to coordinate agricultural activities became even greater as more economic activities developed and cities grew larger.

6) **Long-distance trade** – The early civilizations first developed internal trade networks, and eventually developed long distance trade networks among different civilizations. This trade stimulated economic development, encouraged cultural development, and accentuated social class distinctions.

7) **Organized writing systems** – Most early civilizations developed forms of writing that enabled traders, religious leaders, and political leaders to communicate. An exception was the early development in the Andes region in South America, where even by the 16th century C.E., the highly organized Inca civilization did not have a writing system.

Using "civilization" as an organizing principle is controversial, partly because it may imply that "civilized people" are superior to "uncivilized" people. One criticism is that the very use of the word "uncivilized" implies that hunters and gatherers were inferior people. Indeed, a great deal of evidence points to the fact that early urban dwellers viewed nomadic people with disdain. After all, civilization often brings with it a "dark side" of increased crime, conflict over personal interests, a growing discrepancy between rich and poor, and devastation of the natural environment. On the other hand, the idea of civilization is useful in developing an understanding of the changing nature of early human social organization. Civilizations have allowed humans to reshape their environments and control other living species. Civilizations have built the foundation for great literature, scientific discoveries, works of art and architecture, and the efficient organization of work. Whatever its problem and merits, civilizations

ORIGINAL DOCUMENTS:
ATTITUDES OF THE "CIVILIZED"

The attitudes of people in early civilizations toward the nomadic people around them is reflected in the connotations associated with "barbarians," a term originated with the ancient Greeks. Do you see a point of view in the following quotes from ancient Romans?

"We must awaken again the ancient Roman spirit, fight our own battles, carry on nothing in common with the barbarians, drive them from every official position as well as from the senate...These barbarians, previous useful servants of our house, now intend to rule our nation!"
Synesius, 4th century Roman

"The people of the Huns...are quite abnormally savage...when they join battle they advance in packs, uttering their various war cries... None of them ploughs or even touches a plow-handle. They have no fixed abode, no home or law or settled manner of life..."
Ammianus Marcellus, 4th century
Roman historian

have shaped human development since its advent sometime in the 4th Millennium B.C.E.

CULTURAL HEARTHS

Historians specialize in the identification of **cultural hearths**, the areas where civilizations first began that radiated the ideas, innovations, and ideologies that culturally transformed the world. Early cultural hearths developed in southwest Asia and north Africa, south Asia, and east Asia in the valleys and basin of great river systems. Cultural hearths evolved much later in Central and South America, and their geography shaped cultural development not around river valleys, but around mountain ranges and central highlands. Another cultural hearth developed centuries later in west Africa, very much influenced by earlier hearths along the Nile River in northeast Africa. Another unique cultural hearth developed in the islands of the Aegean Sea, where the inhabitants were joined by easy water access among islands and mainland. From their centers, the hearths grew until they came into contact with one another, although their ability to travel to and contact other cultural hearths was limited by their levels of technology and distance.

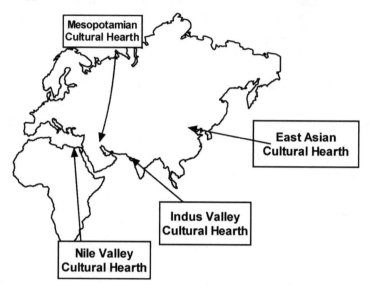

Earliest Cultural Hearths. The earliest cultural hearths were almost completely determined by their geographical locations. All were in river valleys where the soil was the most fertile and water most available for growing crops and transportation.

Cultural Hearths in the Americas. The origins of the earliest civilizations in the Americas – the Olmec and Chavin – are probably somewhat more recent than those of the cultural hearths in the Eastern Hemisphere, although recent discoveries give evidence that civilization may have existed in the Americas as early as 2000 B.C.E. Neither the Mesoamerican nor South American hearths were centered on river valleys, with the Olmec expanding out from the coastline, and the Chavin settling between the coastline and the Andes Mountain valleys.

CIVILIZATION IN MESOPOTAMIA

The earliest civilization is generally believed to have developed in **Mesopotamia**, or "land between the rivers," in southwest Asia sometime during the 4th Millennium B.C.E. By 3500 B.C.E. writing had developed, and by 3000 B.C.E. governments were entrenched. The two rivers – the Tigris and the Euphrates – rise in modern day Turkey, parallel one another for about 400 miles, and finally join just before they empty into the Persian Gulf. Because the area is geographically accessible from many directions, it became a "crossroads" for diverse groups of people that sometimes settled and sometimes moved on. Many early settlers were members of the **Semitic** language family that was the precursor to both modern Hebrew and Arabic languages. A non-Semitic group called **Sumerians**, who came into lower Mesopotamia about 5000 B.C.E., is generally credited with building the earliest civilization with many of the characteristics listed on pp. 35-36. Gradually they created small competing **city-states**, each centered on a large town that governed the countryside around it. By about 3000 B.C.E. the Sumerians had subjugated many of the Semites in the area, either by coercion or consent, and the area of their control grew larger. Sumerian power was cemented by the brisk trade resulting from their conquests that brought food produced in villages to the towns and created economic ties among the towns. Despite the growing economic interdependence, the towns remained quarrelsome, and the Sumerians' early history was characterized by unceasing warfare, often provoked by competition for control of precious irrigated lands.

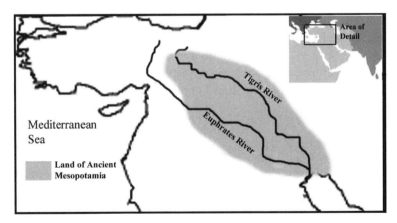

Ancient Mesopotamia. The Mesopotamian city-states grew up along the Tigris and Euphrates Rivers, where river silt provided rich soil for their crops.

Economic Development

As in all ancient civilizations, the majority of people were farmers, herders, or workers directly associated with agriculture, such as wine pressers, millers, or carters. Probably about 5% of the population lived in cities and did not grow their own food. Even those involved in trade were most likely to be involved in trading food, especially grain. However, the towns and cities were the birthplaces of literacy, and the numbers involved in occupations that required the ability to read and write - such as scribes, bookkeepers, and priests - grew as the populations grew. Craftsmen did not have to be literate, but metalworking, leather work, pottery and jewelry making, carpentry, and masonry all required special training. Many people were involved in the central task of early civilizations: creating and maintaining a reliable water source. **Labor systems** (coordinated efforts to get work done) were generally small, with craft shops usually family owned and perhaps two or three paid or slave laborers. Slaves made up a significant portion of the working population, and were often assigned unpleasant or dangerous work, such as mining or handling the dead.

Political Development

The Sumerian city-states were not politically unified until about 2300 B.C.E., when an invading Semitic group led by Sargon the Great conquered the entire area. He founded the **Akkadian Empire** that was dominated by the newly created town of Akkad. As a result of the political conquest, **cultural diffusion** of Sumerian ways spread throughout much of the area, influencing a wide swath of land from Mesopotamia to Egypt that came to be known as the **Fertile Crescent.**

Before Sargon's conquest most of the city states were **theocracies,** governed by gods or their priests. Sargon changed that tradition so that the cities were ruled by kings, but priests were so revered that the kings often obeyed their wishes. The location of the temple in the city's heart and the king's palace on the outskirts provides archaeologists with evidence for early control by priests. However, the constant warfare almost certainly increased the power of the warrior king, so that kings after Sargon assumed responsibility for the temples, city defenses, irrigation channels, and the system of justice. Sargon and his descendents secured loyalty from their soldiers by giving them land. The Akkadian Empire only lasted for a little over a century, and the city-state of Ur rose to replace Akkad in power. The government bureaucracy grew during this time, and a system of messengers and road stations speeded up communication in the area. During the 1700s B.C.E. **Hammurabi** led the **Babylonians** to conquer Mesopotamia, only to be followed by a series of other people that came through the crossroads over the centuries, including the **Hittites** in the 1500s B.C.E., the **Assyrians** in the 900s B.C.E., and finally the **New Babylonians** in the 500s B.C.E.

A significant "marker event" occurred under the Babylonians with the advent of the first known written **law code** (a systematic set of rules administered by a government). **Hammurabi's Code,** inscribed on a black stone pillar, gave

PRIMARY SOURCES: HAMMURABI'S CODE 18TH CENTURY B.C.E.

What do the following excerpts from Hammurabi's Code tell us about Mesopotamian society under the Babylonians?

117. If a man has contracted a debt, and has given his wife, his son, his daughter for silver or for labor, three years they shall serve in the house of their purchaser or bondsmaster; in the fourth year they shall regain their original condition...
195. If a son has struck his father, his hands shall be cut off.
196. If a man has destroyed the eye of another free man, his own eye shall be destroyed.
197. If he has broken the bone of a free man, his bone shall be broken.
198. If he has destroyed the eye of a peasant, or broken a bone of a peasant, he shall pay one mina of silver.
199. If he has destroyed the eye of a man's slave, or broken a bone of a man's slave, he shall pay half his value.
218. If a physician has treated a man with a metal knife for a severe wound, and has caused the man to die...his hand shall be cut off.

Source: Andrea, Alfred, and James H. Overfield, *The Human Record, Vol. 1.* Boston, Houghton Mifflin, 2001.

judges many examples of punishments for crimes meant to be used as standards for justice. These codes provide insight into much more than just laws, but also illuminate a rich assortment of beliefs and customs of the Mesopotamian people.

Social Distinctions

The Code of Hammurabi identified three distinct classes in Mesopotamia in the eighteenth century B.C.E.:

1) The free land owning class, which consisted of the royal family, priests, warriors, high government officials, merchants, and some craftsmen and shopkeepers

2) A class of dependent farmers and craftsmen, who worked for the free land owning class

3) Slaves, who often did domestic work and less desirable jobs outside the home

Slaves were often prisoners of war, and others were debtors. However, slave labor was not as important as it was later to become in ancient Greece and Rome. They were identified by a particular hairstyle, not by permanent marks or chains, so those that won their freedom could easily rid themselves of their previous status. It was not uncommon for a debtor to become a slave for a few years and then be freed when the debt was paid.

Women lost social standing and freedom with the spread of agriculture, and in the ancient civilizations – including Mesopotamia – a food surplus made larger families possible, so women were tied to their responsibilities at home. Women could own property, control their dowries, and participate in trade, but men controlled political and religious life. The status of women appears to have declined significantly during the 2nd millennium B.C.E. as urbanization and private wealth increased. In later Mesopotamian history men could take a second wife if the first did not bear children, and kings and other rich men often had several wives. Daughters of nobility were married to noblemen of their family's choosing in order to enhance the family's wealth and status. It is possible that the wearing of veils dates back to this Mesopotamian era.

Cultural Characteristics

An important "marker event" in world history occurred in Mesopotamia about 3500 B.C.E. with the Sumerian invention of writing, which had its origin in little pictures of objects on clay cylinder seals. The earliest writing evolved from their pictures that turned into symbols and eventually into phonetic elements baked on clay tablets. Writers used a wedge-shaped stick to mark the symbols on the tablets, resulting in **cuneiform** - meaning "wedge shaped" – that was used for several thousand years in the Middle East. Cuneiform writing was difficult to learn because it involved several hundred signs, so specialized scribes were generally the only ones who knew it, giving them power and status that others did not have. By about 2000 B.C.E. compilers wrote down a famous story that had been passed down orally since at least the 7th millennium B.C.E. called *The Epic of Gilgamesh*, a ruler of an early Sumerian city-state, probably Uruk. It explored human friendship, relations between humans and the gods, and particularly the meaning of life and death. Gilgamesh went on an epic journey in pursuit of eternal life, which he ultimately did not find. The story was somber, and emphasized the control that the gods had over human destiny.

CONTINUITY OVER TIME: THE GREAT FLOOD

The Epic of Gilgamesh , a story that dates back to the 7th millennium, describes an ancient flood, according to Utnapishtim, a former mortal whom the gods had placed in an eternal paradise:

"...the world bellowed like a wild bull...Enlil [a god] heard the clamor and said to the gods in council, 'The uproar of mankind is intolerable and sleep is no longer possible,' so the gods agreed to exterminate mankind...[Enlil] whispered...'tear down your house and build a boat, abandon possessions and look for life...Then take up into the boat the seed of all living creatures' ...I [Utnapishtm] loaded...all that I had of gold and of living things, my family, my kin, the beast of the field both wild and tame, and all the craftsmen...For six days and six nights the winds blew...and flood overwhelmed the world...When the seventh day dawned the storm from the south subsided, the sea grew calm, the flood was stilled...I loosed a dove and let her go. She flew away, but finding no resting-place she returned. I loosed a raven, she saw that the waters had retreated...and she did not come back....Then Enlil went up into the boat, he took me by the hand and my wife and...he touched our foreheads to bless us..."

In about the 10th century B.C.E. the Hebrew Bible recorded the story, with a main character called Noah, who did the bidding of the monotheistic religion's one god. During the 7th century C.E. the story was compiled by Islamic scholars for the Qur'an, with Noah communicating with only one God. The details of the story vary in other ways, but it is basically the same story that has been preserved over the eons, surviving the transition from polytheism to monotheism.

Source: Andrea, Alfred, and James H. Overfield, *The Human Record, Vol. 1.* Boston, Houghton Mifflin, 2001.

Religious Beliefs

Mesopotamians, like most other people in ancient civilizations, believed that deities intervened regularly in human affairs, and that their very survival depended on their ability to please the gods. Each city had its own god who it held in higher esteem than all others, and a host of supporting priests devoted their lives to that deity. A temple dedicated to the special god was usually at the center of each urban area. The most distinctive were the **ziggurats** – large multistory pyramids constructed by bricks and approached by ramps and stairs.

Priests passed their positions and their knowledge to their sons, and they enjoyed very high status in most of the city-states. The high priest performed great rituals, and others provided music, exorcised evil spirits, and interpreted dreams. Some divined the future by examining the remains of sacrificed animals. Archaeologists have also found **amulets** that were probably worn by individuals to protect them from evil spirits. Evidence also supports the regular occurrence of religious festivals in which priests read pleasing stories to the god's image in front of both nobility and ordinary people.

Gods were associated with various forces of nature, and they often displayed disagreeable human characteristics, such as quarreling and using their powers in selfish ways. Gods caused flooding (as reflected in *The Epic of Gilgamesh)*, and the afterlife was seen as full of suffering, an early version of the concept of hell.

CIVILIZATION IN EGYPT

While Mesopotamian civilization was developing on one end of the Fertile Crescent, another was growing on the other end along the Nile River in northeastern Africa. The great Egyptian civilization is arguably the longest lived in world history, stretching from its inception around 3100 B.C.E. until its conquest by the Persians in 525 B.C.E. After that conquest Egyptian rulers had to bow to more powerful civilizations, but they still participated in the interactions among civilizations for hundreds of years more. For example, the Ptolemy queen, Cleopatra, was a major player in the struggle for power in Ancient Rome after the assassination of Julius Caesar in 44 B.C.E.

The Natural Environment

The natural environments of Mesopotamia and Egypt had many common characteristics. Both were in river valleys and were not a long distance apart, so they shared similar latitudes. The weather was generally hot and dry with mild winters and a rainy season. Neither could rely on consistent rainfall for their

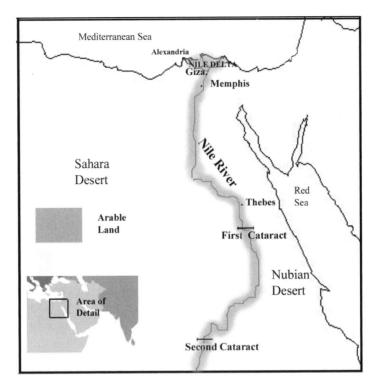

Ancient Egypt: the Gift of the Nile. Unlike Mesopotamia, Egypt was protected from invaders by deserts to the east and west, and by cataracts on the Nile. As a result, the civilization developed in relative safety for many years.

crops, so irrigation was vital to their agricultural success. However, one important contrast in their geographical locations shaped very different political, economic, and cultural beliefs and practices: Egypt was isolated for much of its existence, while Mesopotamia was at a crossroads of population movements. As a result Mesopotamia was open to assault from several directions and was repeatedly conquered by invaders, whereas Egypt was surrounded by desert with few groups of people nearby. Additionally, it was protected from invasion along the Nile River from the south by a series of **cataracts**, or areas where the water was too swift and rocky to allow boats to pass. Another environmental difference was the seasonal flooding. Both areas were subject to heavy downpours that temporarily flooded the land. However, flooding in Egypt was regular and predictable, so that farmers and political leaders could take preventive and containing measures. In contrast, flooding in Mesopotamia was irregular and unpredictable, so that people had no choice but to react to, rather than prevent and contain, the damage that was done. Not only did this difference impact economic and political life, it may have led to differences in the way that people approached life, with Mesopotamians apparently gloomy and resigned to their fate in life, and Egyptians generally more optimistic about their ability to control their destinies.

Economic Development: Mesopotamia and Egypt Compared

Like the Mesopotamians, most Egyptians were farmers, and both economies became increasingly diverse as time passed. As cities grew, craftsmen refined techniques for making pottery and textiles, and others specialized in woodworking, leather production, brick-making, stone cutting, and masonry. About 3000 B.C.E. Mesopotamian metalworkers invented bronze by alloying copper and tin to make a harder, stronger metal. Bronze was used to fashion military weapons as well as farming tools and plows, giving both warriors and farmers important advantages in their respective occupations. Egyptians did not make use of this new invention until after the 17th century B.C.E. when they were attacked and defeated by the **Hyksos** (a people from modern day Turkey) who had superior military power because of their bronze weapons. Egypt's delayed adoption of bronze was partly because their natural environment provided neither tin nor copper, and partly because their physical isolation did not encourage them to experiment with different weapons. After about 1000 B.C.E. Mesopotamians began to develop tools and weapons made of iron with carbon added to control brittleness. By this time, societies were interrelated enough that the technology spread rapidly, including to Egypt.

Another important invention that increased job specialization and economic efficiency was the wheel. No one knows exactly when the wheel was invented, but the Sumerians probably used wheeled carts long before they began to organize into city-states in the mid-4th millennium B.C.E. Wheeled carts and wagons allowed heavy loads of bulk goods to be hauled over long distances, and the technology spread to nearby areas, including Egypt. Both Mesopotamia and Egypt experimented with maritime travel, with Sumerians learning to navigate in the Persian Gulf and the Arabian Sea, and the Egyptians sailing boats down the Nile and in the Red Sea. Specialized occupations in ship and boat building appeared in both civilizations.

Increasing job specialization and transportation improvements encouraged long-distance trade. Mesopotamians and Egyptians were already trading by 3500 B.C.E., and by 2300 B.C.E., the Sumerians were trading with Harappans in the Indus River valley (in modern day Pakistan). By the time of the Babylonians (about 1900 to 1600 B.C.E.), Mesopotamians were importing silver from Anatolia in the northwest, cedar from Lebanon in the southwest, copper from Arabia in the south, gold from Egypt, and tin from Persia in the southeast. After 3000 B.C.E. Egyptians traded actively in the Mediterranean, and a few centuries later, they established regular trade across the Red Sea and eventually to an east

African land they called Punt. Egyptians offered gold, linens, leather goods, dried lentils, and silver, and traded for ebony, ivory, cattle, slaves, cosmetics and myrrh (an aromatic).

Political Characteristics

Like those of all other ancient civilizations, Egypt's political system reflected the importance of religious beliefs. At the heart of the government was the **pharaoh,** who was not considered to be just a king, but instead was a god. Although Mesopotamians often believed that their kings had special access to the gods, they saw them as purely human, not gods themselves. According to Egyptian legend, the first pharaoh was **Menes**, who supposedly lived about 3100 B.C.E., although scholars are not at all sure than he actually existed. What is clear is that the middle and lower areas of the Nile were united under one ruler who was followed by an unbroken line of god-kings until about 2500 B.C.E. The pharaohs were believed to be reincarnations of **Horus**, the sky god, so pharaohs were often represented with a hawk, the symbol of Horus. In this role he maintained **ma'at,** the divinely controlled order of the universe. The pharaoh's will was law, since he was all-knowing and forever correct as the representation of the almighty gods. His regulations were carried out without question, and as a result, pharaohs enjoyed more power and prestige than almost any other rulers in world history.

The pharaoh was represented throughout the countryside by a group of officials who were responsible only to him. They were usually landed nobility that were trained in writing and law. Governors were appointed for key regions and were responsible for supervising irrigation and great public works. Although the pharaoh usually granted his top bureaucrats a great deal of local authority, the pharaoh's power was ultimate, and the state remained highly centralized. In contrast, Mesopotamia's political system was composed of city-states, whose constantly clashing leaders made centralized government very tenuous.

The pharaohs were most powerful during Egypt's early history, probably because few outsiders challenged their power and economic prosperity was the general rule. Ancient Egypt's long political history is often divided into three eras:

- **The Old Kingdom** (3100 - 2500 B.C.E.) – These were the years when pharaohs were most powerful and the economy was the strongest. The success of this era was capped by the construction of the first of the great pyramids constructed as tombs for the pharaohs between about 2600 and 2100 B.C.E., stretching into the years of the Middle Kingdom.

- **The Middle Kingdom** (2100-1650 B.C.E.) – After a period of instability with unknown causes, pharaohs regained their power during this long, relatively peaceful period. During this era, trade with neighbors became more extensive, and a small middle class of officials and merchants developed. The peace and prosperity was ended with the invasion of the **Hyksos**, a people who came from the north to conquer the Nile Delta.

- **The New Kingdom** (1550 – 700 B.C.E.) – The Hyksos ruled the native Egyptians for almost a century, but they were defeated by princes from Thebes, and the New Kingdom was inaugurated. Even though the Hyksos intermarried with Egyptians and assimilated Egyptian culture, they were still seen as foreigners, and the new rulers were determined to reassert Egyptian power. Realizing that they no longer had the luxury of ignoring the outside world, the pharaohs aggressively expanded their control, extending their territory north into Syria and Palestine and south into Nubia. These new territories provided a buffer zone from attackers, and the formerly isolationist Egyptians actively sought to convert their new subjects to Egyptian beliefs and practices. For the first 300 years of this era, Egypt's armies were generally successful, but military reversals began during the 1300s B.C.E., and by 1100, the pharaoh again ruled only the Nile Valley. After that, the kingdom gradually weakened to foreign invasion, and lost its independence.

Social Distinctions

The modern stereotype of an Ancient Egyptian is generally that of a person with dark, straight hair and clay colored skin. In reality, even before the New Kingdom Egyptians ranged from dark-skinned people related to the populations of Sub-Saharan Africa to lighter-skinned people related to inhabitants of southwest Asia. Egyptians tended to think of themselves as superior to other people, so foreigners were generally seen with some suspicion. However, Egypt had less pronounced social divisions than Mesopotamia, where more formal classes emerged. Clearly, though, the pharaoh and his high-ranking officials had superior social status, and lower-level officials – along with priests and other professionals, and artisans – appear to have had higher status than peasants at the bottom that made up the vast majority of the population. **Social mobility** (the ability of individuals to change their social status) appears to have been possible, since Egypt relied on professional military forces and an elaborate bureaucracy of administrators to serve the pharaoh. As in Mesopotamia, slavery existed on a limited scale, and slaves were often prisoners of war or debtors that were usually freed when their debts were paid off.

Like Mesopotamia, Egypt was a **patriarchy** dominated by men. However, it is probable that the status of women was higher in Egypt than in Mesopotamia, where women's position seems to have deteriorated in its later days. Egyptian women in the upper classes were respected because marriage alliances were important for preserving the continuity of the pharaoh's line and those of his high officials. Also, Egyptian religion deified its goddesses as sources of great creativity.

HISTORICAL EVIDENCE: ANCIENT PATRIARCHIES

Even though all ancient civilizations were patriarchies, Egypt had at least one female pharaoh, Hatshepsut, who ruled from 1473 to 1458 B.C.E. during the New Kingdom. She served first as regent (a stand-in ruler) for her son, but eventually ruled on her own. She is famous for sponsoring a great naval expedition south on the Red Sea to Punt (probably in eastern Sudan or Yemen) that returned with fine luxury goods, such as myrrh, rare woods, ivory, and exotic African animals. Even so, this female ruler reflected the values of male-dominated patriarchies in two of her behaviors: she often used the male pronoun in inscriptions in referring to herself, and she also wore a fake beard. After her death, her image was defaced and her name blotted out of records, perhaps an act of patriarchal defiance.

Cultural Characteristics

Egypt is of course famous for its pyramids, some of the most impressive monuments ever built. They held religious significance, and they contained impressive art and artifacts in the burial chambers. Egyptians also built large temples and great statues, illustrating that their mastery of stonework was unrivaled among the earliest civilizations. They excelled in other art forms, including fresco painting, pottery making, fine jewelry, and miniature sculpture.

COMPARATIVE WRITING SYSTEMS: CUNEIFORM AND HIEROGLYPHICS

Both Mesopotamian cuneiform and Egyptian hieroglyphics made use of **pictographs,** or pictures representing animals, people, and objects. A writing system that depends on pictures was convenient for keeping trade records, but was very cumbersome for communicating abstract ideas. Beginning about 2900 B.C.E. the Sumerians began using graphic symbols to represent ideas, sounds, and syllables, and Egyptians, too, supplemented their hieroglyphics with symbols representing abstract ideas. The Egyptian writing remained more picteographic than cuneiform, but in both societies, the writing systems were complex, and their use was largely restricted to priests. Egyptians developed a new material to write on, **papyrus**, made from strips of a plant pressed together. Despite their sophisticated writing system, the Egyptians created no epic literary works, such as the Mesopotamian *Epic of Gilgamesh.*

Mesopotamian achievements in mathematics and astronomy were far more advanced than those of Egypt. The Sumerian system of numbers, based on units of 12, 60, and 360, are used for modern day geometry and for calculating time. Sumerians charted major constellations, and followed the movement of the sun and stars carefully, setting the foundation for the science of astronomy. The Egyptians had fewer mathematical and scientific achievements, but they did establish the length of the solar year, which they divided into 12 months, each with three 10-day weeks. The calendar was crucial to their ability to predict the Nile floods. They also had knowledge of a variety of drugs, and elements of their medical knowledge were passed down to the Greeks.

Religious Beliefs

Like Mesopotamia, Egyptian religion was polytheistic, and its chief deities were associated strongly with agriculture. Gods included **Amon-Re**, the god of the sun; **Isis**, goddess of the Nile and of fertility; **Osiris**, ruler of the afterlife; and **Horus,** son of Osiris and Isis, represented in the pharaohs. The Egyptians were very concerned with death and preparation for life in another world where supreme happiness could be achieved. They carefully mummified bodies and held elaborate funeral rituals, especially for the rulers and bureaucrats. In the earlier days, these rituals were inscribed on the coffins and pyramids of the elite, but they became much more commonplace in later times. During the New Kingdom, many incantations of these rituals were collected into papyrus texts known today as ***The Book of the Dead.*** Divided into more than 150 chapters, it was mass-produced for a prosperous clientele who each purchased a scroll, filled in the name of the deceased, and buried it with the person's body.

PRIMARY DOCUMENTS: THE NEGATIVE CONFESSION

The Negative Confession is part of *The Book of the Dead,* a compilation of incantations for use in burial ceremonies in Ancient Egypt. The scene is the Hall of the Two Truths, or the Double Ma'at, where Osiris, king of the Underworld, presides over an assembly of minor deities. All together the deities judge the suitability of the deceased to become an eternally blessed spirit. The deceased makes the following statements:

"I have not done crimes against people,
I have not mistreated cattle,
I have not sinned in the Place of Truth [any holy place],
I have not known what should not be known [secrets of the gods],
I have not done any harm.
I did not begin a day by exacting more than my due,
My name did not reach the bark of the mighty ruler [Re].
I have not blasphemed a god,
I have not robbed the poor.
I have not done what the god abhors,
I have not maligned a servant to his master.
I have not caused pain,
I have not caused tears..."

Source: Andrea, Alfred, and James H. Overfield, *The Human Record, Vol. 1.* Boston, Houghton Mifflin, 2001.

INDUS VALLEY CIVILIZATION

A third "cradle of civilization" developed in the Indus River valley in what is now Pakistan. By 5000 B.C.E. agriculture had developed, and by 3000 B.C.E. the villages and towns had evolved into cities. Much about the people remains mysterious today, partly because archaeologists were generally unaware of the civilization until the 1850s, when the British construction of a railroad across the Indus led to discovery of the remains of one of the major cities, **Mohenjo-Daro.** Some controversy surrounds the origins of the civilization. Until recently, most scholars believed that the Indus Valley people spoke a **Dravidian** language similar to languages spoken in southern India. It was thought that they were conquered around 1500 B.C.E. by **Aryans**, invaders from the northwest who spoke Indo-European languages, and that some of them moved southeast into India to escape. More recent evidence, however, does not support a sudden change in body types or civilization patterns during that time, so there is still much to learn about these early people and what changes they may have experienced.

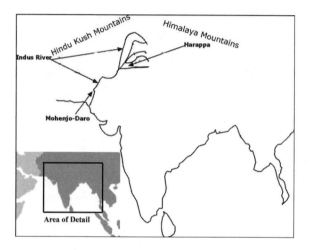

Indus Valley civilization. Mohenjo-Daro is the largest city that has been discovered, housing more than 100,000 people at its peak, probably between 2500 and 2000 B.C.E. Harappa was probably about 1/3 as big.

Geographical Features

Today the area around the Indus River is desert, with many of the ancient river-beds now dried up. However, in ancient times it was forested, green, and lush, with plenty of game animals and good pasture for domesticated animals. The river system was formed by water running from melting snow in the world's highest mountain range, the Himalayas to the northeast, and the Hindu Kush Mountains to the northwest. The river and its tributaries have been fed by **monsoon rains** that are created by seasonal winds that blow from the seas toward the Indian subcontinent. Like the Nile, Tigris, and Euphrates Rivers, the Indus River carried rich soil to the plains around it, allowing extensive agriculture to flourish.

The mountains provided some protection from invasion, but very early on, people discovered passes through them that allowed them to cross, particularly through the Hindu Kush. The **Aryans** probably used these passes as they travelled to the southeast, and eventually made their way into many parts of the Indian sub-continent, including the Indus River valley.

Economic Characteristics

The cities and towns in the Indus River valley were supported by an advanced agricultural system based on wheat, rye, peas, and perhaps rice. Cotton was cultivated, and many animals were domesticated, including chickens, cattle, goats, and sheep. As in Mesopotamia and Egypt, abundant crops allowed job specialization in the cities to develop. Beginning in the 1850s, archaeologists have discovered the remains of the largest city, Mohenjo-Daro; a second city, **Harappa;** and a huge complex of towns and villages connected to them. Because the cities were not constructed in the same way that cities in Mesopotamia and Egypt were, they almost certainly were not colonies but were part of an independent civilization.

The cities were major trading centers, with contacts in China, Southeast Asia, southern India, Afghanistan, and Mesopotamia. Jade from China and precious jewels from Southeast Asia have been excavated in the Indus River valley, and Indus stone seals have been found in Mesopotamia. Small clay wheeled carts pulled by oxen have been found at various Indus sites, suggesting that they were used as land transportation among cities, towns, and villages in the valley. Judging by the size of the cities, job specialization had to be extensive, yet their craftsmen appear to have been inferior to those in Egypt and Mesopotamia. They did cast tools and weapons in bronze, but they lacked swords, used stone for arrowheads, and bronzed the tips of their spears so thinly that they could not have been very effective.

Political Development

Very little is known about political systems in the Indus River valley, but the construction of the cities suggests a well-organized government planned them. The main thoroughfares in Mohenjo-Daro were 34 feet wide, and a sophisticated sewage system with canals running from each house to a connecting canal in the street to carry off household wastes. Some scholars speculate that Harappa and Mohenjo-Daro were twin capitals, or that there may be other unexcavated cities that each ruled the countryside around it. The two cities both had fortifications and large granaries that were probably controlled by governments, but the pieces of evidence do not yet support a good knowledge of who governed and to what ends.

HISTORICAL EVIDENCE: ANCIENT SEALS

The most important clues for unlocking the mystery of the ancient Harappan script are the many seals from the Indus Valley culture that have been found all over the area, as well as in other trading centers from Mesopotamia to China. Seals were fixed to many different objects in ancient civilizations, including pottery, boxes, doors, baskets, and leather bags. In Mesopotamia, seals were cylindrical in shape, and in the Indus Valley they were square, soft stones, with impressions of animals and a written script. They were used by traders as a way to insure that containers weren't opened during transit, or perhaps to identify the merchants.

These seals are the best clues that archaeologists have for understanding the language of the Indus River valley people, but because the inscriptions are very brief, it is difficult to find consistencies that would allow them to decipher it. However, the fact that the distinct seals have been found in Mesopotamia, China, Southeast Asia, and Afghanistan tells us that trade was a significant part of the Indus Valley economy.

Society and Culture

Although less is known about social distinctions in the Indus River valley than is known about Egypt and Mesopotamia, the evidence points to the existence of clear social classes. For example, house sizes in Mohenjo-Daro and Harappa varied considerably, with most people living in single-room dwellings in larger barracks-like structures. The wealthy had individual houses of two and three stories, with several rooms and an interior courtyard. Most of the larger houses had their own wells and brick ovens. Indus River valley society was dominated by a powerful priestly class, which ruled from the cities. The priests mediated between the people and a number of gods and goddesses, although very little is known about the religion. One popular god depicted on the seals is a naked male with a horned head, sometimes pictured in a posture of meditation, leading some to speculate that the lotus position and/or yoga originated here. Mother-goddesses appear to have been worshipped by ordinary people, whereas the horned god was favored by the priests. There is little evidence to support an interest in artistic endeavors, other than a few carved figurines of people and animals that reflect a strong interest in fertility.

If the Indus Valley writing system could be deciphered with any consistency, scholars would know much more about the civilization. Egyptian hieroglyphics were decoded with the very fortunate discovery of the **Rosetta Stone**, a tablet with a relatively long script in three languages: formal hieroglyphics, an informal Egyptian writing, and Greek. Since Greek was known, the tablet was used to find many parallel symbols in hieroglyphics. With that head start, scholars were able to decode most of the hieroglyphic writing samples that have been discovered. Archaeologists have had no such luck in the Indus Valley, but new discoveries may unearth some comparable clue in the future.

Decline of the Indus River Valley Civilization

The Indus valley cities were abandoned sometime after 1900 B.C.E., although the reasons for their decline are uncertain. No evidence of an invasion has been found, so one theory is that the civilization suffered **systems failure,** a breakdown of the political, social, and economic systems that supported it. There might have been a precipitating event, such as an earthquake or a flood, but gradual ecological changes appear to have occurred as well. The cities may have grown too fast, so that the large population put stress on the environment, burning trees to bake mud bricks for construction and farming land too intensely. Some argue that a radical change to a much drier climate occurred, or that the courses of the rivers shifted significantly, or that the population may have fallen victim to malaria. The decline was relatively gradual, with Mohenjo-Daro being abandoned in about 1200 B.C.E., and Harappa somewhat later. Almost certainly, the civilization was under stress by the time the Aryans came into the valley across the Hindu Kush Mountains sometime around 1500 B.C.E.

ANCIENT CHINA

Neolithic people of east Asia probably domesticated rice sometime about 7000 B.C.E., and by 5000 B.C.E. rice had become the staple of the diet in the Yangzi River valley. In later centuries, the people farther north around the Yellow (Huang He) River domesticated wheat, barley, and eventually millet that had probably arrived from Mesopotamia. After about 3000 B.C.E. villages along both rivers communicated and traded with others throughout the region, and by about 1700 B.C.E. they had established cities and complex political, cultural, and social systems that served as the foundation for civilization in China and other parts of east Asia.

Geographical Influences

Ancient China rose in a part of the world that was a long way away from the other centers of civilization. Although trade did exist between China and the others, distance and geographic barriers separated the areas so that in many ways east Asia developed independently from the others. Both agriculture and metalworking apparently were independently invented in China. The Huang He and Yangzi River valleys were rich with river silt, and were quite conducive to agriculture, whereas much of the land space that eventually became China was far less habitable. The Gobi Desert stretched to the north and west of the rivers; the Himalaya Mountains lay to the southwest; and the vast Tarim Basin – high, dry, and cold – occupied the west. These geographical features have shaped the development of Chinese civilization, and even today, the vast majority of China's population lives in the east along the rivers or the coastline.

The rivers absorbed a yellowish-brown dust (giving the Yellow River its name) from Central Asia so that it formed **loess**, a thick mantle of fertile and soft soil easy enough to be worked with wooden digging sticks. Like the Tigris and Euphrates Rivers, the East Asia rivers were prone to irregular flooding, and people responded by building dikes, channels, and basins to store river water and rainfall.

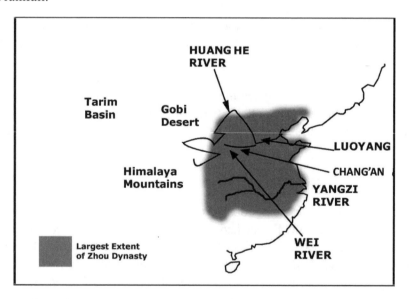

Ancient China. Geography shaped the development of Chinese civilization, with most people living along the river valleys in the east. The first known dynasty, the Shang, ruled an area around the Wei River, and the later Zhou Dynasty extended its control over a much larger area.

Economic Development

Because the Huang He (Yellow) River was so prone to unpredictable flooding, early Chinese farmers and leaders had to come up with methods to control it. Increasingly elaborate irrigation systems kept up with the expanding agriculture, and great earthen dikes were constructed to manage the flow of the river. An important early innovation was the hoe, a vast improvement over the digging stick since it had a wide, flat base. A later improvement was the four-pronged hoe that was used to turn over the soil for cultivation. Its use made Chinese agriculture much more productive so that it could support a larger urban population.

Ancient China's growth was also spurred by mastery of metallurgy, particularly in their production of bronze weapons and tools. Ruling elites controlled access to copper and tin ores, and employed craftsmen to produce bronze axes, spears, knives, and arrowheads. Bronze was also used for fittings for horse-drawn chariots, a technology probably first invented in Mesopotamia that diffused across Central Asia to the river valleys. A high level of craftsmanship is evident in bronze vessels created for religious rituals and household use for the rich. An important development that was to be of immense importance in the development of China was the pioneering of the key processes of silk manufacturing, raising silkworms on mulberry trees and carefully unraveling their cocoons to produce silk thread.

Cities were centers of political control and religion, and were surrounded by great walls of hardened earth. Large public buildings were constructed, such as palaces, political centers, storehouses, royal tombs, shrines of gods and ancestors, and houses of the nobility. Ordinary people lived in villages outside the city walls. The cities were laid out on a grid plan aligned with the north polar star, the gates opened to the cardinal directions, and all major buildings faced south, reflecting a concern with order.

Political Development

By the 18th century B.C.E. the areas north and west of the Huang He River were home to many nomadic groups who followed their domesticated animals from pasture to pasture. As would continue to happen for thousands of years, these nomadic groups often came into conflict with people that had settled into agricultural villages along the river valley. According to legend, an ancient **dynasty** (family-based kingdom) called the **Xia** came to control much of the area, but no archeological sites connected to it have been found, so their existence is still not proven. The history of China may be traced to the first written records that describe a distinctive culture with its own cuisine, beliefs, and practices in the area that emerged between 1750 and 1500 B.C.E. The culture is known as the **Shang Dynasty**, who conquered most of the other tribes, founded a kingdom that stretched north and south from the Huang He River valley, and lasted about 700 years.

The political system probably emerged from the need to control the great floods of the river, but the Shang tribe was still nomadic, and the leaders were warrior kings who fought on horseback with very effective bronze weapons. Their armies were made up of subject people, and the other warrior leaders swore fealty to the Shang monarch. The king was seen as the intermediary between a Supreme Being, Shangdi, and ordinary mortals, so the power he had was significant. Most of the people were governed by **vassals**, lords that served the king and were bound to him by personal ties. These warrior aristocrats collected **tribute** (payment usually in the form of produce) which supported the monarch and his court.

In the 12th century B.C.E., the Shang rulers were overthrown by the **Zhou Dynasty**, a group from farther west that became the longest-lived of all the Chinese dynasties. We know much more about the Zhou than we do about the Shang because they kept written records, including tax rolls, lists of imports and exports, and historical accounts of successes of the monarchs. The dynasty falls into two distinct phases: the Western Zhou (11th-8th centuries B.C.E.) with capital cities in the west, and the Eastern Zhou (8th-5th centuries B.C.E.) when the capital was moved east to Luoyang. The Zhou extended their territory far beyond the earlier borders of the Shang, but they also ruled through a system of decentralized loyalties, so that local rulers had a good deal of autonomy.

An important political development under the Zhou was the growing size and responsibility of professional bureaucrats, or **shi** (men of service). These administrators were the best-educated men in the empire, and they served as scribes, clerks, advisors, and overseers, both in the king's court and in the subordinate governments of the king's vassals. They came to specialize in keeping records, running public works or wars, or organizing rituals and ceremonies. The shi were the forerunners of a scholarly governing class that would gain great power and status in later dynasties.

Social Characteristics

During both the Shang and Zhou Dynasties, clear social distinctions characterized Chinese society. Social classes included:

"MARKER EVENT": THE MANDATE OF HEAVEN

An important "marker event" in Chinese history occurred when the Zhou overthrew the Shang in the 12th century B.C.E. Probably to justify their forcible removal of the Shang dynasty, the early Zhou rulers claimed that they had been given the right (or mandate) to rule by "heaven," or the supernatural deities who oversaw earthly life. As long as the rulers were just and fair, they retained the confidence of heaven, but if they were not, the mandate would be lost. Prosperity was a "sign from heaven" that the rulers still had the mandate, but misfortunes were usually interpreted as a communication from the deities that the ruler was not living up to their high expectations. If a ruler lost the mandate, his subjects not only had the right, but the responsibility to replace him.

The mandate of heaven is a central belief that guided China through **dynastic cycles** that lasted until the early 20th century. A dynasty rose, became strong, and then weakened, inviting takeover by a new dynasty. In between dynasties there was often a time of chaos, sometimes lasting for a few short years, but other times for several hundred years, in which other families challenged and eventually toppled the weakened dynasty.

1) **The elite** - The royal family and allied noble families enjoyed great prestige, as well as economic benefits. Their houses were palatial, and they monopolized the use of bronze weapons, tools, and decorative objects. Less privileged classes used clay pots, and had much simpler diets than the elites, who consumed most of the meat. During Zhou times, a great deal of emphasis was placed on proper behavior, including strict requirements for table manners that precluded gulping food and making unpleasant noises.

2) **Free artisans and craftsmen** - These people worked almost exclusively for the elite, providing them with bronze objects, jewelry, embroidery, and silk textiles. They lived primarily in cities in relatively comfortable houses made of pounded earth, an expensive type of construction.

3) **Merchants and traders** – Long distance trade appeared in China even during the Shang era, despite the geographic barriers that stood between China and other major civilizations of the time. The tin for bronze work came from Southeast Asia, jade came from Central Asia, and military technology, such as horse-drawn chariots, came from Mesopotamia. Merchants and traders did exist, although little was written about them until the late Zhou era.

4) **Peasants** – Peasants owned no land, but worked the land that belonged to the nobility. They lived in small houses dug deep into the earth, protected by thatched walls and roofs. Their work became easier in the late Zhou Dynasty, when iron production increased in China, and iron farm utensils became available. However, peasants were burdened by their lords' demands for labor on roads, buildings, and irrigation projects.

5) **Slaves** – As in most other early civilizations, a sizeable class of slaves existed in Chinese society, most of whom were captives of war. They performed hard labor, such as clearing new fields and laying foundations of buildings and walls of cities.

Like other ancient civilizations, women lost status as civilization progressed. Military prowess was highly valued, and males dominated the political scene. The rituals honoring the ancestors especially venerated males as the important guiding forces in the lives of family members. During Neolithic times, the female line of descent was important in determining family power, but this **matrilineal** characteristic disappeared during the Shang era. During the Zhou era, women appeared to lose even more status, since no temples were erected to honor queens, as they had been during the Shang era.

Cultural Developments

Organized religion did not play as important a role in the development of early China as it did in most other ancient civilizations. There was an emphasis on the will of "heaven" (such as the "mandate of heaven"), but the Chinese did not recognize personal deities who controlled human affairs, nor did they support a large priestly class. A few priests assisted royalty in their rituals, but connections between family members on earth and their ancestors that had passed on were a very important element of "heaven." Rulers and family patriarchs were interested in consulting the ancestors for guidance, and made use of **oracle bones,** specially prepared broad bones or turtle shells, each inscribed with a question. When properly heated, the bones would crack, and **shamans**, individuals who claimed the ability to contact the ancestors, would interpret the communication by the patterns formed. Many of these oracle bones have survived, and they tell us a great deal about early Chinese society and beliefs.

COMPARISONS: UNIQUENESS OF ANCIENT CHINA

Like other ancient civilizations, China under the Shang and Zhou was a patriarchy based on agriculture, and was characterized by large cities, specialized labor, advanced political coordination, a complex writing system, and massive public buildings. However, Chinese society differed from those in other parts of the world in several important ways:

1) The supreme importance of the family - All societies are organized into families, but the Chinese emphasized it more than most. One reason was the veneration of ancestors, based in the belief that spirits of dead ancestors continued to guide the prospects of the living.

2) The emphasis on this world - The main connections to the spiritual world were the continuing influence of the ancestors and the emperor's status as "Son of Heaven" through the mandate of heaven. Otherwise, the Chinese did not put emphasis on an array of agricultural gods, nor was there a priestly caste, such as existed in other ancient civilizations

3) Emphasis on learning and literacy - Perhaps because writing on oracle bones was a primary way to communicate with ancestors, literacy was highly valued, and eventually became an important basis for social status.

Oracle bones are also a great source of early Chinese writing, which by Zhou times was also commonly inscribed on bronze ceremonial dishes. As in Mesopotamia and Egypt, the earliest form of Chinese writing was the **pictograph,** a standardized picture of an object. Written Chinese did not include an alphabet, but pictographs were often combined to represent abstract ideas. The characters used in modern China are direct descendants of those from Shang times, and scholars have identified more than two thousand characters inscribed on oracle bones. As in Mesopotamia and Egypt, the complexity of the early language meant that only specially trained people could read and write, but in China writing was often associated with the king's court, not with merchants and long-distance trade.

Another early use of writing in China was the development of philosophy and religion, with **Confucianism** being the most famous one. Values and beliefs are reflected in the works that have survived, including *The Analects,* a collection of Confucianism; the *Book of Changes,* with instructions for shamans for divination; the *Book of History,* a collection of the deeds of Zhou rulers; and the *Book of Etiquette*, that taught the elite proper manners and behavior. Perhaps most notable is the development of early Chinese poetry, collected in the ***Book of Songs.***

COMPARISONS: DIVINATION IN MESOPOTAMIA AND ANCIENT CHINA

Most people in ancient times believed that the gods controlled human destinies and shaped earthly affairs. As a result, most ancient civilizations practiced some form of **divination**, or method for communicating with the gods to determine their intentions, and to anticipate the future.

In China, divination was controlled by special shamans who used oracle bones (either animal bones or shells) to read messages from the spirit world, especially from the ancestors who had passed on. The questions varied, from the proper performance of a ritual, to the prospect for rain, to the likely outcome of war.

In Mesopotamia, priests inspected the organs of sacrificed animals to interpret the wishes of the gods. They also "read" the trail of smoke from burning incense, as well as patterns formed when oil was thrown on water. Mesopotamians saw their destiny in the stars and planets, and their belief that movements of objects in the heavens were communications from the gods led to their early accomplishments in astronomy.

EARLY CIVILIZATION IN THE AMERICAS

Until the late 15th century C.E., developing civilizations in the Americas were almost completely cut off from those in the Eastern Hemisphere, so agriculture was independently invented and cultural diffusion took place within the geographical boundaries of North and South America. In prehistoric days humans reached the Western Hemisphere from Asia, although scholars disagree about when and how those migrations took place. The crossing of the land bridge (now the Aleutian Islands) from northern Asia to Alaska is widely accepted, although estimates of when the first migrations took place range from 35,000 years ago to about 15,000 years ago. Some contact with Polynesians may well have taken place, but the interactions did not continue on a regular basis.

Geographical Influences

The most basic impact of physical geography was the separation of the Western and Eastern Hemispheres by vast oceans and great distances. However, the tremendous distance north to south was important as well. The environments included frozen regions in the extreme north and south, tropical rain forests, vast plains, heavily forested areas, and high mountain ranges. These characteristics made farming impossible in many areas and quite possible in others, but long distances between arable areas made contact among groups difficult. The two areas where farming provided the basis for the development of early civilizations were Mesoamerica (now Mexico and northern Central America) and the Andean Mountains along the coast of northwestern South America.

The Olmec (1200-400 B.C.E.) of Mesoamerica

In Mesoamerica agricultural villages appeared by about 3000 B.C.E., and spread throughout the region over the next thousand years. They cultivated beans, peppers, avocados, squash, maize, and tomatoes – all completely different crops than those domesticated in the Eastern Hemisphere. In contrast to civilizations in the Eastern Hemisphere, they domesticated a limited number of animals. They raised turkeys and dogs, but had access to no large animals (such as horses, cattle, goats, and sheep) that were domesticable. Human labor, then, did all the work of agriculture, and without the animals to pull them, wheeled vehicles were not used to facilitate the process. Civilization appeared with the development of religious centers along the coast of the Gulf of Mexico, which grew into cities with specialized labor and sharp class distinctions. By 1200 B.C.E. (or perhaps earlier) a complex society had emerged that archaeologists called the **Olmec**, or "rubber people."

Economic Development and Social Distinctions

The Olmec civilization was based on agriculture, but they had no need for extensive irrigation because the area received abundant rainfall for cultivating crops. They built elaborate drainage systems to control water, as well as raised fields that allowed crops to grow in wetlands. The cities grew as religious and trade centers, exchanging products like salt, cacao (chocolate beans), clay for ceramics, and limestone. There is no evidence of competitive city states, such as those that developed in Mesopotamia.

Like many other early civilizations, Olmec society was probably authoritarian and hierarchical. An elite group of priests dominated the early Olmec cities who conducted elaborate religious rituals at the temples in the center of the cities. They also provided practical advice about rainfall and other important crop conditions, and directed the planning of urban centers so that they aligned with the paths of certain stars. Clearly, astronomical events were considered to be significant influences on human affairs. Another elite group included the ruler and his family, who were able to require and direct labor for city building projects from the general population, who mostly lived in areas outside the relatively small cities. Skilled artisans did carvings and sculptures for the buildings, and also produced high-quality jade figurines, jewelry and ceremonial objects. A class of merchants probably did some long distance trading in jade, obsidian, and pottery.

Political and Cultural Characteristics

Little is known about the nature of political power, but some form of kingship that combined religious and secular responsibilities appeared in the major cities. These political elite had large, elaborately decorated houses and lived very different lifestyles than those of commoners who lived in simple small structures constructed of sticks and mud. The mysterious giant heads sculpted from basalt that the Olmecs are most famous for may well have symbolized the power of the ruling families. These heads range up to 11 feet high, and have clear, distinct facial characteristics that may have been carved to honor specific rulers. However, much about these carvings remains mysterious, including some with Negroid features that have led some to speculate that these early Americans were kin to Africans. No such connection has ever been made. The Olmecs were great carvers of jade, and they traded or conquered to get it. They developed a numerical system based on 30 and a 365-day calendar (combined with a 260-day ritual cycle) that became the basis of all later Mesoamerican calendars. What language they spoke is unknown, but some scholars believe that they were the ancestors of the great Maya civilization that followed.

The decline and fall of the Olmec civilization is still a puzzle, but it appears as if they destroyed their main ceremonial centers and then deserted the sites somewhere between 900 and 600 B.C.E. No clear evidence has been found of attack from outsiders, so most scholars speculate that some sort of internal conflict occurred that caused the cities to be abandoned. By 400 B.C.E. societies in other parts of Mesoamerica had risen, and the Olmec civilization had disappeared completely by about 100 B.C.E.

The Chavin of South America (900-250 B.C.E.)

At roughly the same time that the Olmec civilization was flourishing in Mesoamerica, the Chavin dominated a heavily populated region that included both the Peruvian coastal plain and foothills of the Andes. Both civilizations differed from those of the Eastern Hemisphere in that they did not develop in river valleys, but the geographic challenge for the Chavin was particularly strong. The coast of Peru has little rainfall, and in some places is quite narrow, but the abundance of fish and other sea life provided a dependable supply of food. The Andes Mountains rise dramatically from this coast plain, with many peaks rising above 20,000 feet before they drop on their eastern slopes, and the terrain changes to thick jungle that surrounds the massive Amazon River Basin. The Chavin civilization rose in this unlikely environment that combined dry coast and high mountain valley.

ARCHAEOLOGICAL EVIDENCE: HOW OLD IS ANDEAN CULTURE?

Historians have generally agreed that agriculture started later in the Americas than it did in southwest Asia, with many estimating its occurrence about 3500 B.C.E. However, some recent excavations have challenged this assumption with the discovery of squash seeds that archaeologists believe to be about 10,000 years old. The seeds were discovered in the Nanchoc Valley on the western slopes of the Andes Mountains in northern Peru, and were dated through some new techniques of radiocarbon dating and analysis of the actual plant remains. The excavations also yielded peanut hulls that were about 8500 years old and cotton fibers that were about 6000 years old.

These results were published in 2007, and if they are accepted by the scientific community, it is possible that agricultural communities and the later civilizations actually started much earlier than presumed, perhaps not long after those in the Eastern Hemisphere developed.

Economic Development and Social Distinctions

The Chavin capital, Chavin de Huantar, was located in a high mountain valley of about 10,300 feet altitude at an intersection of trade routes connecting the west coast with mountain valleys, and mountain valleys to tropical lowlands to the east. This location helped them to control trade and gain important economic advantages over surrounding peoples. Agriculture was based on maize (probably from Mesoamerica), which could be grown in the coastal areas. Potatoes and fruits were raised in the mountain valleys, and cotton and coca leaves (a mild narcotic) in the tropical areas. Exactly how labor was organized for public works is unknown, but in later times, people were organized by communities to share the responsibility. In contrast to the Olmec, the Chavin had a domesticated beast of burden – the llama – to help with their chores. They were first domesticated in the mountains, where they carried large bundles of goods up and down mountain paths in organized trading caravans.

The Chavin independently invented metallurgical techniques that probably diffused to Mesoamerica. Craftsmen worked in silver and gold, creating decorative and ceremonial items for buildings and religious objects. Advanced techniques of production were used for pottery and textiles that were first produced along the coast, but eventually in the mountains as well. Superior-quality textile and gold crowns distinguished rulers from commoners, and the skilled artisans were probably a social class that served the elite.

Political and Cultural Development

Since the area encompassed three ecological zones that abruptly began and ended, one motivation for empire was to control all of them, as well as the connecting trade routes. Since arable land was limited, some kind of political organization was needed for irrigation and protection of land. There is evidence of early warfare, so political rulers probably directed wars, but we don't really know the nature of their rule. The fact that Chavin culture diffused over a large area is some proof that the civilization was politically well organized.

Part of the Chavin's influence appears to be based on its religion, which spread through most of the territory, and perhaps to Mesoamerica. Although the beliefs of the religion are unknown, a jaguar god with combined human and animal features was a very important symbol for the religion. Jaguars were inscribed on buildings, pottery, and textiles over a huge expanse of territory, including Mesoamerica. Other intricate stone carvings depicted snakes, hawks, eagles, and humans with feline characteristics.

EARLY CIVILIZATIONS IN THE MIDDLE EAST, 1700-1100 B.C.E.

By the 2nd millennium B.C.E., agricultural communities had developed into civilizations in the Middle East, the Americas, and east Asia. All had developed trade routes that enriched their economies and put them into contact with other groups of people. However, the Middle East had developed a broader, more intense web of interactions among various groups of people than the other areas had. The era between 1700 and 1100 B.C.E. is often called the **Late Bronze**

Age, and it is characterized by an early version of **cosmopolitanism**, or the shared cultures and lifestyles that result when different groups are in regular contact. The cultural diffusion among groups included not just trade goods, but also ideas, values, and standards of living. The web of commerce and cultures included:

- **Egypt** – The New Kingdom of Egypt began in 2532 B.C.E. after the defeat of the Hyksos. Egypt was no longer the isolated civilization of its earlier days, and it developed extensive diplomatic and commercial ties with the states of western Asia, and it maintained a large army to promote its strength in the network.

- **Mesopotamia** – The area around the Tigris and Euphrates Rivers continued to be subject to political fragmentation as cities and kingdoms waxed and waned in their military might. By 1500 B.C.E. Mesopotamia was divided into two political zones: Babylonia in the south and Assyria in the north. Although another group – the Kassites – came to power in Babylon, trade continued, and urban centers prospered.

- **Hittites** – This group originated in Anatolia (modern Turkey) and formed a large empire to the northwest of Mesopotamia. Anatolia's rich natural resources of copper, silver, and iron helped the Hittites to play a vital role in international commerce. They developed new techniques for iron working, providing them with military advantages that allowed them to conquer the area.

- **Nubians** – To the south of Egypt a great civilization rose along the Nile that connected Sub-Saharan Africa with north Africa. Nubia was richly endowed with gold, copper, and semiprecious stones, so it also played an important part in the international commercial web of the Late Bronze Age. For most of this era it was dominated by Egypt, although in the 1st millennium B.C.E. it gained power as Egypt weakened, and eventually came to control Egypt.

- **Mycenaeans** – By the late 3rd millennium B.C.E. an advanced civilization had begun to develop on the island of Crete, just south of the Aegean Sea. These people were named **Minoans** after their legendary King Minos, and excavations have unearthed a large palace complex, massive walls, and shaft graves (burial places at the base of deep, rectangular pits). They were followed by the **Mycenaeans**, an early group on the Greek mainland, who came to dominate the area by the Late Bronze Era. They were warlike and aggressive, and controlled trade across the Aegean Sea and with the other civilizations of the Middle East.

Early Aegean Cultural Hearth. This cultural hearth differed from earlier hearths in that it centered on the Aegean Sea, not on a river valley. The sea is calm and the islands numerous, allowing for easy transportation for Ancient Greeks to trade for goods that their natural environment did not provide.

Around 1200 B.C.E. many of the old cultural and economic centers of the Middle East and Mediterranean were destroyed. Many people were moving around (for reasons that are not completely clear), and one by one the civilizations began having problems. The Hittite kingdom fell to invaders, who made their way to the eastern end of the Mediterranean where they destroyed trading cities there. Egypt also experienced a major invasion by the "Sea Peoples" that they survived, but they lost many of their territories to the northeast. The Mycenaean centers also collapsed in the first half of the 12th century B.C.E., initiating an era know as the "Dark Age" of Greek history. The cosmopolitan world of the Late Bronze Age was gone by the 12th century, and the collapse of the network may well be an early illustration of a negative consequence of interdependence. The economic and cultural exchanges had contributed to their wealth and vitality, but once one fell, a piece of the network was gone, weakening other pieces that appear to have fallen away one by one, sounding a death knell for this earliest phase of civilization in the Middle East.

CONCEPTS AND IDENTIFICATIONS

Akkadian Empire
Amon-Re
amulets
The Analects
Aryans

Assyrians
Babylonians
Book of the Dead
Book of Songs
cataracts
Chavin
city-state
civilization
Confucianism
cosmopolitanism
cultural diffusion
cultural hearths
cuneiform
Dravidian
dynasty, dynastic cycles
Epic of Gilgamesh
Fertile Crescent
Hammurabi
Hammurabi's Code
Harappa
Hittites
Horus
Hyksos
Isis
labor systems
Late Bronze Age
law code
loess
ma'at
Mandate of Heaven
matrilineal
Menes
Mesopotamia
Minoans
Mohenjo-Daro
monsoon rains
Mycenaeans
Olmec
oracle bones
papyrus
patriarchy
pharaoh
pictographs

Rosetta Stone
Semitic
shaman
Shang Dynasty
shi
social mobility
Sumerians
systems failure
theocracy
tribute
vassals
Xia Dynasty
Zhao Dynasty
ziggurats

**CHAPTER THREE:
CLASSICAL CIVILIZATIONS
(1000 B.C.E. - 600 C.E.)**

By 1000 B.C.E. the old river valley centers of civilization in the Middle East had been eclipsed by many factors, including the devastating collapse of trade and cultural connections around 1200 B.C.E. No such event had occurred in eastern Asia, where the Zhou Dynasty remained strong, and civilizations continued to develop in Mesoamerica and the Andes Mountains region. Most significantly, some major changes began to usher in a new era in the world's story: the age of classical civilizations that lasted until the middle of the 1st millennium C.E.

No single "marker event" started the new era, so it is easy to argue that the era actually began or ended a little earlier or later. However, by 1000 B.C.E. some clear changes were occurring, including the shift of civilization centers away from the older centers in the Eastern Hemisphere. For example, on the Indian subcontinent, human activities were focused on the Ganges River valley to the east of the Indus River valley. In China, the Huang He (Yellow) River remained active, but farming became more intense and cities began to grow along the Yangze River valley to the south. By the mid-1st millennium B.C.E. Persia, a new empire in the Middle East, was stirring. In the area around the Mediterranean Sea a new civilization was emerging from the ashes of Mycenae in Greece by about 800 B.C.E.

These new civilizations differed from earlier ones in several ways:

- **Size and political strength** – Empire developed as a political form as rulers strengthened governmental and military organizations to allow them to rule larger land areas. For example, Rome controlled areas that stretched from northern Europe to western Asia to northern Africa. The Mauryan Empire on the Indian subcontinent was far larger than the area controlled earlier by the Harappans. Whereas the classical civilization of Han China was not larger in land space than the old Zhou Dynasty, the emperors generally had more centralized control of the area.

- **More complex cultures** – During this era several of the world's great religions emerged as forces determining the course of world history, including Hinduism, Buddhism, Judaism, and Christianity. In China the important philosophy of Confucianism emerged as a powerful cultural influence. Even though Hinduism and Judaism have roots in the earlier era, all these belief systems diffused to lands outside their areas of origin so that their overall impact on world history became enormous. Many civilization areas produced art and literature that remain "classics" today.

- **More numerous and better written records** – We know more about classical civilizations than we know about the river valley civilizations partly because they were more recent, but also because their written records were more numerous and systematic. All had developed sophisticated forms of writing, and some began to use a simplified system of symbols (alphabets) that allowed literacy to become more widespread, though not universal.

- **More complex long-distance trade** – During this era great trade routes connected the civilizations by land (The Silk Road) and by sea (the Indian Ocean trade). Although trade was still confined by hemisphere (west was not trading with east), the trade contacts and distance travelled grew tremendously. These trade routes increased the prosperity of the empires and spread ideas, including belief systems, as well as material goods.

- **More contacts between nomads and sedentary people** - Partly because of the extended trade routes, the boundaries of the empires expanded, and people from urban centers came in contact with those living on the periphery. In central Asia nomadic groups took over the transport of goods across vast plains, and in some cases settled into communities that grew into great trade cities along the Silk Road. Attacks of nomadic groups on civilization centers also grew, although a great deal of the contact was peaceful as all benefitted from growing trade routes.

- **More direct influence on modern civilizations** – Many modern beliefs and practices may be traced much more directly to the classical era than to the earliest civilization era. This is true partly because we have more knowledge of the later era, but also because classical beliefs and practices are more similar to those of the modern era. For example, modern law codes are much more similar to Roman law codes than they are to Hammurabi's Code of early Mesopotamia. Religious beliefs that developed during the classical era are still intact today, whereas the religions of Ancient Egypt and Sumeria have not survived the years.

The classical civilizations emerged in three areas:

1) **The Mediterranean** – The Greeks emerged as the first classical civilization of the Mediterranean area, followed by the Romans.

2) **The Indian subcontinent** – Two empires rose on the Indian subcontinent: the Mauryan Empire and the Gupta Empire.

3) **East Asia** – China emerged from the Warring States Period that followed the Zhou Dynasty to form the Qin Dynasty, followed by the much longer lasting Han Dynasty.

MEDITERRANEAN CIVILIZATIONS: GREECE

Settled agricultural communities had developed along the Aegean Sea in the eastern Mediterranean area by about 2000 B.C.E., probably first on the island of Crete. Although they were not far away from Mesopotamia and Egypt, their environmental conditions were quite different. Greece is mountainous with little suitable land for farming and no broad river valleys or level plains. The sea is ever-present, since much of the main land is surrounded by water inlets, and the sea itself is full of small islands. One geographical advantage the early Greeks had was good access to water through natural harbors and navigable bays, and the sea itself is calm with islands serving as multiple docking places for ships. Land travel was difficult because of the mountains and the deep water inlets, so the early Greeks became some of the most skilled sailors of their day.

The **Minoan** civilization on the island of Crete controlled most of the area by about 1600 B.C.E., and was replaced by the **Mycenaeans**, who almost certainly were part of the great trade network of the Late Bronze Age that fell apart by about 1200 B.C.E. The Mycenaeans were often at war with others around them, and by 1200 B.C.E. they were at war with the city of Troy on the other side of the Aegean Sea (in Anatolia). Their cities were also invaded about this time by people from the north, so the times were chaotic, eventually ending in the destruction of their cities, with inhabitants abandoning them. After the fall of the Mycenaean civilization, the Aegean area entered into a "Dark Age" that lasted till about 800 B.C.E., when Greek cities began to reemerge as important urban centers.

From the fall of Mycenae until about 800 B.C.E. the Greeks were isolated from others around them. This isolation ended when another seafaring group from the eastern Mediterranean, the **Phoenicians,** visited the Aegean, reestablishing

PERSPECTIVES: ALTERNATIVES TO SEDENTARY LIFE

Whereas the focus of historical study of the classical era is on the great civilizations, most of the earth's landspace was occupied by nomadic or migratory people. Two alternatives to sedentary agriculture were:

Shifting cultivation - Sometimes called "slash and burn" agriculture, this practice predominated in the rainforests of Central and South America, west Africa, east and central India, and much of south China and Southeast Asia. Shifting cultivators burned off the rain forest undergrowth, but left the large trees to protect the soil. They used the ash from the burned undergrowth to fertilize the crops before depleting the nutrients from the soil and moving on to another area to begin the process again.

Pastoral Nomadism - This practice continued from earlier days across the vast plains of central Eurasia, the central Arabian Peninsula, and areas south of the Sahara Desert in Africa. The animals the pastoralists herded were domesticated but they followed them seeking good pastures. Animals included horses, cattle, sheep, goats, camels, and reindeer. During the classical era, trade routes across central Asia were controlled by pastoral nomads, although many settled into sedentary lives in the trade cities along the Silk Road.

contact between Greece and the Middle East. Soon Greek ships were travelling across the Mediterranean, and the trade that they established brought new prosperity to the Aegean.

Political Development

The geographic features of the Greek homeland encouraged the development of the **polis**, or the city-state. Each city was separated from others by mountains, inlets, or the sea itself, so each came to dominate the countryside around it. At its peak, Greek civilization was made up of about 200 poleis, each thinking of itself as a political and cultural unit, independent of every other. Some were stronger and more influential than others, and at key times they cooperated with

MARKER EVENT:
THE PHOENICIANS' ALPHABET

The Phoenicians originated along the eastern shore of the Mediterranean Sea, and since they were unable to expand because of surrounding mountains and desert, they took to the sea to widen their horizons. They were the most significant Mediterranean traders and seafarers until they roused the Greeks in the 600s B.C.E. Phoenicia was eventually absorbed by the Assyrian Empire, but their legacy lived on in a whole series of colonies that they established in the western Mediterranean.

The Phoenicians are best known for their use of a **phonetic alphabet**, a system of 22 written marks ("letters") that each corresponded to a sound in the spoken language. Their alphabet was much simpler than any other written language of its day, and was much easier to learn and use for their trading. The Greeks built on the Phoenician alphabet by adding signs for vowels, which the original system did not have. This alphabet - with a change in letter formats - became the basis for the development of many modern languages, so the Phoenicians certainly made their "mark" on history.

one another in inter-city organizations called leagues, but they were never united under one government. Often when we refer to Ancient Greece, we are thinking about one city-state: Athens. Although its politics and culture dominated other city-states for much of the time period, Athens was always its own city-state, and its main rival was Sparta, a city-state south of Athens with very different values and practices. Each city-state had its own patron god or goddess, and held regular rituals to celebrate and maintain the patron's protection.

The poleis took different political forms, including **monarchies** (hereditary rule by one), **oligarchies** (rule by a few), **aristocracies** (rule by leading families), and **democracies** (a new form of popular government). One outcome of these conflicting governing styles was the emergence of **tyrants** by the 6th century B.C.E. These tyrants were often military leaders who won popular support against the aristocracy, and though they were not necessarily oppressive (as the modern term implies), the idea of one-man rule contradicted traditions of community governance.

**HISTORICAL EVIDENCE:
HOMER'S *ILIAD* AND *ODYSSEY***

Epic poetry may be an important source of information about societies
from the distant pass, as is illustrated by Mesopotamia's *Epic of
Gilgamesh.* Epic poetry, in the form of Homer's *Iliad* and *Odyssey,*
also provides us with much of our knowledge of the early Greek period.
No one knows whether or not Homer was an actual person, but both
poems were probably written down during the 8th century B.C.E.,
more than 400 years after the events actually occurred.

The *Iliad* tells the story of the Greek war against Troy (about 1200
B.C.E.) from the Greek point of view. The *Odyssey* recounts the
adventures of a Greek hero, Odysseus, as he returned home after the
Trojan war was over. Both stories illuminate Greek attitudes toward
their "wine dark sea," and depict their heroes as the great mariners that
they were.

Early Athens

Athens went through all of these forms of government in the period between 800
and 400 B.C.E. with democracy emerging during the 5th century. The original
monarchy was gradually forced aside by the aristocrats, who in turn gave way to
oligarchs in the 500s. The most important oligarch was Solon, a reformer early
in the 6th century, who set up laws that could be written and revised, rather than
just passed down through tradition. A rebellion in 510 B.C.E. put **Cleisthenes,**
an aristocrat, in control, but the instability of the times encouraged him to experiment with democracy.

At the heart of Athenian democracy was the "town meeting" of all free males,
who were called together to make decisions affecting the future of the polis.
All could speak freely, and they often tried to sway others to their opinions, and
their collective vote determined political actions. Also present was the Council
of 500, citizens chosen by lot for one-year terms who were responsible for making and implementing policy under the supervision of the town meeting. Since
Athens was at its height of political power during the 5th century B.C.E., it is

probable that other city-states also practiced democracy as well. It is notable that these democracies consisted of only free males, so women and slaves had no political power.

Early Sparta

Before the 7th century B.C.E. the two city-states of Sparta and Athens probably were similar in many ways, but major rebellions in and around Sparta apparently influenced a highly militaristic society to develop there. In the 700s the Spartans had defeated a neighboring city-state, Messenia, and had taken their people as servants, called **helots.** Although they were not slaves, they could not leave the land, and their role in society was to provide agricultural labor. During the 600s the Messenians rebelled over and over again, encouraging the Spartans to emphasize military control. The rebellions were put down, and the helots met the society's economic needs, while Spartan men were warriors. The Spartans were self-disciplined and rigidly obedient, and put a great deal of emphasis on physical fitness.

Economic Characteristics

In their settlements on the western edge of Anatolia, an area the Greeks called Ionia, rivers formed broad and fertile plains near the coast, but no other areas had large rivers. As a result, Greek farmers on the mainland depended entirely on sparse rainfall to water their crops. The soil was poor, and so they could only raise a limited number of crops. They usually planted barley, which was hardier than wheat, on the flat plains, olive trees at the edge of the plain, and grapevines on the lower slopes of the foothills. Sheep and goats were raised in most areas, and cattle and horses in northern Greece. Natural resources included building stones such as marble, and clay for pottery, but very few metal deposits. They traded across the Aegean for timber, gold, iron, copper, tin, and grain to allow them access to basic needs for building a civilization. The significant invention of coins (probably in western Anatolia) facilitated trade because it replaced an inefficient system of weighing gold, silver, or bronze in exchange for goods. Coins were much smaller and easier to store, and also made bookkeeping and storage of wealth more efficient.

In early Greek history, farmers also were part-time soldiers who were called up by the government of their city-state for brief periods to meet military needs. Campaigns took place when farmers were available, which meant that military actions were generally not planned during planting and harvesting seasons. These Greek farmer soldiers served as **hoplites**, heavily armored infantrymen who fought in very close contact and cooperation together. Each soldier was protected by a helmet, breastplate, and leg guards, and held a shield that protected half of his body and half of the soldier next to him. The shields were arranged in continuous formation in front of the men, who moved together so no gaps appeared between shields. When two hoplite lines met, the fighting was brutal and short with a clear victor, a convenient fighting style that allowed the survivors to get back to their crops quickly.

Colonies, such as Ionia and those areas settled along the northern Aegean, formed partly because the Greek mainland's limited land space could not support a growing population. Eventually, Greeks formed colonies far away, including Marsalia, now called Marseille, in southern France. This colonization served to spread Greek culture far and wide, as well as create new trading partners across the seas.

Social Distinctions

An important social distinction in most city-states was between citizens and non-citizens. In Sparta, the helots were a large subject-people that outnumbered citizens by perhaps ten to one. Beyond that basic distinction, all Spartan citizens were theoretically equal in status. To maintain this equality, Spartans wore simple clothing and no jewelry, nor did they accumulate possessions. Their houses were equally unadorned, and their lifestyle overall was frugal and austere. Distinctions among citizens were based on athletic prowess and military talent, and the Spartan educational system prepared boys, starting at age seven, to be soldiers. They were removed from their families, placed in military barracks, and trained until they were ready at age twenty to join the military. Sparta also maintained self-sufficiency, believing that trade and the luxuries it brought were harmful to their purity. Although the Spartans lost some of their zest for equality over time, with their aristocracy succumbing to luxuries by the 4th century B.C.E., they still maintained a society based on military values.

In Athens, the basic distinction between citizens and non-citizens was also important, but Athenians had no disdain for luxuries, and developed a clear urban-based aristocracy. Most Athenians were simple farmers that lived outside the urban area, but aristocrats also made differences between themselves and common folk within the city. These distinctions led to discontent and, in response, reforms (such as those of Solon) were enacted that gave commoners more rights, including membership in the town meeting and Council of 500. As a result, democracy spread to all free male citizens, making them more equal, but ironically deepening the division between free men and slaves. Perhaps 30 percent of the total population was enslaved, although by most accounts they were generally well treated. Only in the silver mines near Athens were slaves abused on a regular basis. Most others were personal servants, and some were craftsmen who worked for pay but were not free to seek employment from anyone other than their owners. Slaveholders usually did not own more than one or

Ancient Greece. Geographically, the Greeks settled all around the Aegean Sea, establishing colonies in Ionia, a region in Anatolia. Travel by land was difficult because of mountainous terrain and long distances to get around bodies of water, so the fastest and cheapest way to travel was by water.

two slaves, and friendships often formed between slaves and non-slaves. However, slaves had no political rights, nor could they serve in the military.

In regard to gender relations, Sparta and Athens provide an interesting contrast. Spartan women were free and equal with men, and they were encouraged to be as physically fit as the men, especially so they could have strong, healthy babies. Wives did not live with their husbands (who were away at war), so Sparta in many ways was run by women, who were left at home to take care of everything else except fighting. In Athens, gender inequality was much more clearly defined. Respectable Athenian women were confined to the home and only ventured outside under the guardianship of slaves and servants. One or two rooms of a home were reserved for women's use, always away from the street.

Rural women probably had more freedom of movement because of their many farm chores. However, no Athenian women had political rights, nor could they own property or businesses. Women were citizens, since it was important that citizenship be passed down to their children, particularly the males. Besides the respectable women, others were prostitutes who did not follow the same rules, but had even lower status than other women.

Cultural Characteristics

Like most other ancient people, Greeks were polytheistic. The main gods were Zeus and his wife Hera; Poseidon, god of the seas; Athena, goddess of wisdom and war; and Apollo, god of the sun. Greek gods, however, were not omnipotent, and they were quite capable of deceit, playfulness, jealousy, and anger. Neither did the Greeks have a priestly class, although priests served as informal leaders of religious services. Most educated Athenians did not take their gods very seriously, nor did they believe that the gods controlled human destiny. The Greek emphasis on **secularism**, or affairs of this world, led them to seek answers to the dilemmas of human existence in philosophy, in much the same way that the ancient Chinese embraced Confucianism.

The Greek word *philosophy* means "love of wisdom." The early philosophers were mainly interested in investigating the physical world. They did not believe that the gods caused natural phenomena. Instead, they invented **natural law**, or forces in nature that cause phenomena to occur. **Socrates** (470-399 B.C.E.) was the first philosopher to focus on ethical questions and truth-seeking regarding human nature, understandings, and relationships. He particularly emphasized the rational in human nature, or the ability of individuals to reason for themselves. We know about Socrates through the writings of his student, **Plato,** who wrote about his arrest, conviction, and forced suicide for "poisoning" the minds of Athens' youth. In many ways, the trial of Socrates represents the clash between traditional religious values and the new emphasis on human capabilities, particularly the ability to think for themselves. **Aristotle** was Plato's student who was interested in practically every field of human endeavor, including the natural and social sciences.

The classical Greeks also developed at least three major art forms:

1) Drama – This Greek invention arose in the 600s, probably in Athens, as a presentation of myths about the gods and their interventions in human affairs.

2) Lyric poetry – This style of poetry has the form and musical quality of a song that often expresses personal feelings. Aristotle contrasted lyric poetry with drama and epic poetry, whose intentions are to tell a story.

3) "Classical" architecture –Greek temples, including the Parthenon atop the **Acropolis** (hill) in Athens, were widely copied by the Romans, and still provide basic building principles for modern architecture.

Greek sculpture reflects how much they valued the worth of the individual, reveling in human capabilities, both physically and intellectually. The bodies depicted in the sculpture influenced later concepts of beauty and perfection, and their expressions were individualized. Greek ceramics were in great demand throughout the Mediterranean world, and craftsmen also worked in metal, leather, and wood. The overall achievement of the Greeks during their **"Classical Age"** (c. 500-300 B.C.E.) is termed **Hellenic culture,** based on the Greek name for their homeland , *Hellas.*

EVIDENCE: PLATO ON THE DEATH OF SOCRATES

Almost everything that we know about Socrates comes from his student, Plato, who could hardly have been objective about the conviction and death of his teacher. However, Socrates' ruminations about the philosophical nature of death reinforces our knowlege of the Greeks' strong belief in human rationality. Notice, though, that Socrates makes a bow to religion in the end.

"And if we reflect in another way we shall see that we may well hope that death is a good thing. For the state of death is one of two things: either the dead man wholly ceases to be and loses all sensation; or, according to the common belief, it is a change and a migration of the soul unto another place. And if death is the absence of all sensation, like the sleep of one whose slumbers are unbroken by any dreams, it will be a wonderful gain... But if death is a journey to another place...that all who have died dwell there, what good could be greater than this, my judges?

...But now the time has come, and we must go hence: I to die, and you to live. Whether life or death is better is known to God, and to God only."

SOURCEL F.J. Church, trans. *The Trial and Death of Socrates,* 2nd ed. London: Machmillan, 1886, pp 76- 77. (slightly modified)

THE RISE OF PERSIA

Ancient Persia rose in the area that is now Iran, mostly a high, dry plateau surrounded by mountains to the north, east, and west, and by the Indian Ocean to the south. Its location was in between the population centers of the Indian subcontinent and southwest Asia, so traders had crossed the area for many years before its people were organized under the first Persian warrior-king, **Cyrus the Great.** He overcame other rulers, such as the king of Medes, to extend his territory from the edge of India to the Mediterranean Sea. The empire continued to expand under his successors, and reached its maximum extent under Darius I, extending into Egypt, and an area north of Greece called Macedonia.

The success of the empire was due partly to superior military leadership and organization, but Cyrus also should be credited with the political system that he left in place after he conquered various territories. He allowed his subjects to retain their own customs and laws, under the supervision of his Persian representatives, the **satraps.** These governors were responsible for collecting tribute, such as precious metals, providing soldiers, and keeping order. The satraps had miniature courts that mimicked that of the Persian king ("The Great King, King of Kings, King in Persia, King of countries") in Persepolis, and their positions tended to become hereditary. As a result, Persians intermarried with locals, and strong ties between Persepolis and the provincial courts were possible. Darius I also established a law code based on earlier Mesopotamian codes that governed the empire.

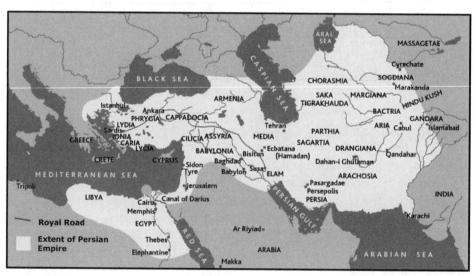

Ancient Persia. This empire was larger than any other that preceded it, reaching its maximum extent during the rule of Darius I (522-486 B.C.E.). The king kept in touch with his subjects and moved his armies along the **Royal Road** that stretched from the heart of the empire to its outlying provinces. Notice how much larger it is than its arch rival, Ancient Greece.

The Greeks v. the Persians

Most of what we know about the Persians comes to us from the Greeks, who faced them in battle throughout the early 5th century B.C.E., so their accounts are hardly objective. The wars occurred because both civilizations were expanding in Anatolia, and their clash was probably inevitable. The wars were sparked by rebellions in Ionia, an area governed by the Persians but inhabited by people with Greek backgrounds and sympathies. When Darius I sent his troops to put down the rebellion, Athens went to aid its fellow Greeks in Ionia. In order to punish their impudence, Darius then sent an army to mainland Greece, where the Greeks defeated the Persians at the legendary battle of **Marathon** in 490 B.C.E. A second series of battles began under Darius' successor, **Xerxes**, who was defeated even more decisively at the battle of Thermopylae in 480 and again at Platea in 479. Some historians see this clash between Athens and the Persians as the trigger event that set "West" (Greece) V. "East" (Persia) as a defining concept for modern day international politics. Following this line of thinking, today's clashes in the Middle East are framed in the mind set that "West" and "East" have been natural enemies since these ancient days.

The Persian Wars were significant not only for sparking the decline of Persian power, but for the boost they gave to Athens as the premier city-state in Greece. They formed an alliance with other city-states called the **Delian League**, and under their leader **Pericles,** their assertiveness offended the Spartans when they attacked Sparta's ally, Corinth. What followed was the highly destructive **Peloponnesian War** (431-404 B.C.E.) between Athens and Sparta. Although Sparta eventually won, the war set off a series of quarrels among the city-states, fueled by their long-established independence and individuality. All were weakened in the end, leaving them vulnerable to conquest by a new power to the north, Macedonia.

The Hellenistic Synthesis

Until the 4th century B.C.E., the kingdom of Macedon was a sleepy frontier state in the northern part of the Greek mainland. Some Macedonians were farmers, others were pastoral nomads who migrated seasonally between the mountains and valleys, and others made a living trading with Greek city-states. King Philip II (359-336 B.C.E.) transformed Macedonia by building a powerful military of farmer infantrymen and aristocratic cavalry. After he consolidated his power by subduing local Macedonian clan-based leaders, he turned his attention to the quarreling Greek city-states to the south. Philip was able to conquer the poleis one by one, since they were unable to agree with one another enough to form an alliance against him. In a little more than ten years, he brought all of Greece under his control. He was poised to invade Persia when he was assassinated in 336 B.C.E., so that task fell to his 20-year-old son, known in history as **Alexander the Great.**

In his short career (13 years), Alexander conquered most of the world known to the Greeks, and his feats became legendary. He inherited a well-equipped, disciplined army from his father, and his ambition drove them to conquer one area after the other, starting with Anatolia, and then Egypt, now a mere regional state, where he was greeted as pharaoh. Persia was weaker than it had been, and he dared to press his troops on till they had defeated the mighty old empire. Alexander's army made their way all the way to the Indus River valley, where the troops refused to go any farther. He planned to merge Greek and Asian institutions under his control, naming many cities *Alexandria* in his honor, and forcing his men to marry Asian women to forge the new, blended civilization. Alexander himself married multiple daughters of conquered princes. His dream of consolidating his empire was cut short by his untimely death at the age of 33 of a fever in Babylon. Without his leadership, his empire fell apart. Although his political ambitions failed, his conquests had a huge cultural impact on the course of world history.

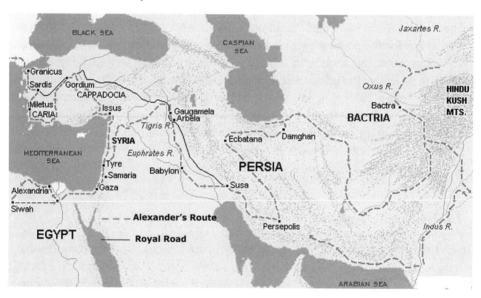

Alexander's Path of Conquest. After his father's death, Alexander marched his army into Anatolia, then south through the lands on the eastern end of the Mediterranean Sea, to Egypt, across the great Persian Empire all the way to the Indus River, and back to Babylon where he died in 323 B.C.E. His route reflects some geographic curiosity as well as a desire to conquer. For example, he was curious to know whether the Caspian Sea was connected to a great northern sea, as the Greeks had speculated. Alexander decided that it was not, since he found no salt-water marine life on the southern end of the sea.

Historians call the epoch following the conquests of Alexander the **Hellenistic Age** (323-30 B.C.E.) because of the spreading of Greek culture to northeastern Africa and western Asia. After Alexander's death, his empire was divided among his generals into three large states: Antigonus took Greece and Macedonia; Ptolemy took Egypt; and Seleucus took the bulk of the old Persian Empire. Many Greeks left their overcrowded homeland to settle in the new lands, and they took their culture with them, where it blended in a **Hellenistic synthesis** with many other cultures, creating cosmopolitan societies connected by trade and Greek culture.   Recent archaeological expeditions have unearthed Greek shrines and inscriptions in far away Bactria and India.   In the urban centers many individuals spoke Greek, dressed in Greek fashions, and adopted Greek customs. Without Alexander's conquests, little Greece probably would have remained just that. Instead, its beliefs, values, and material culture spread, so that its influence has reverberated through the ages to be one of the most influential civilizations in all of world history.

MEDITERRANEAN CIVILIZATIONS: ROME

While Greece and then Alexander held the focus of civilization around the Mediterranean Sea, a new city-state was rising to the west on the Italian peninsula. Rome was heavily influenced by the Greeks but developed its own unique characteristics, including the Latin language. Roman influence spread gradually, first on the peninsula, and eventually to an area that stretched from northern Europe to southwest Asia to northern Africa. Roman history went through many phases, encompassing more than 2000 years from start to finish, and dominating the area for more than 700 years. Rome brought many diverse people together under its rule, and came into contact with nomadic peoples who eventually contributed to its downfall.

Political Development

The **Etruscans** came into Italy about 800, where they established a series of small city-states that ruled over the native people. Exactly where they came from isn't known because they left only a small amount of writing that has never been deciphered. A federation (central government with smaller subunits) headed by Etruscan kings that managed local leaders existed from about 750 to 509 B.C.E. One of its subject communities was Rome, founded according to legend by twin brothers Romulus and Remus. In 509 B.C.E. Rome gained its independence from Etruscan rule, and established itself as a **republic**, or a state without a monarch (*res publica*). The republic lasted until the rule of the first emperor, Augustus (31 B.C.E. -14 C.E.), when it became an empire that fell in 476 C.E., although the eastern part of the empire existed until 1453 C.E.

Under the republican form of government, Rome was not a democracy, even though it was not ruled by a monarch. Instead the most important ruling body was a **Senate** composed of **patricians**, or aristocrats who passed their positions down to their sons. The **plebeians**, commoners who were about 90 %

of the population, were represented by an elective General Assembly. Even though this political structure looks democratic on the face of it, the General

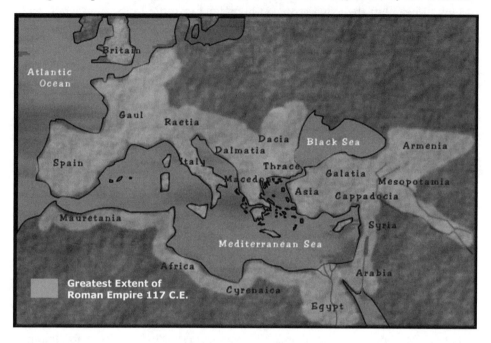

The Roman Empire. Rome began as a small city-state on the Italian peninsula during the 8th century B.C.E., and reached its greatest extent during the 2nd century C.E., when it stretched from Britain to Armenia to Egypt, and completely dominated the Mediterranean Sea.

Assembly had little power, and the patricians of the Senate controlled political decisions. The executive was headed by two **consuls,** elected from among the members of the Senate for one-year terms that were not to be repeated. Each consul had veto power over the other, and because they were usually military generals, they were often fiercely competitive and keen to challenge each other's power. These generals came to have great sway over the republic, especially after the Senate discontinued the practice of replacing the consuls every year. The plebeians protested their lack of political power, and managed to get the government to allow them representatives called **tribunes**, who at first were elected by the people, but eventually came to be controlled by the Senate by the mid 1st century B.C.E.

The Senate's power was challenged by **Julius Caesar**, a charismatic patrician general with great sway over his soldiers, and a **Triumvirate** (rule of three) was formed: Caesar, Crassus (for his wealth), and Pompey, a rival general to Caesar. Caesar eventually declared himself dictator, only to be assassinated by senators on the Ides of March (March 15), 44 B.C.E. His nephew Octavian battled a general, Mark Antony, for control of Rome. Octavian defeated Antony in the

Battle of Actium in 31 B.C.E. and the Senate declared him **Augustus** ("revered one") **Caesar,** establishing the Roman Empire.

PERSPECTIVES: WHO WAS CLEOPATRA?

How does Queen Cleopatra fit into the story of the world? Cleopatra VII was the last queen of Egypt, a direct descendant of Alexander the Great's general Ptolemy, who took control of Egypt after Alexander's death. Cleopatra was a Greek by descent, language, and culture, and she was supposedly the first member of her family in their 300-year reign to have learned the Egyptian language.

Cleopatra played a role in the history of Ancient Rome through her manueverings to form alliances with powerful Romans. She bore Julius Caesar's child, whom she wished to have named as his father's heir. After Julius Caesar's assassination in 44 B.C.E., she sided with Mark Antony in his struggle against Octavian for control of Rome. She married Mark Antony and had several children with him, but of course, Octavian defeated Antony, and Cleopatra ended up on the wrong side of history. Quite famously, she committed suicide by convincing an asp (a snake) to bite her, ending her ambitions forever. Our main source for the details of her death is the Roman scholar Plutarch, who wrote them down about 130 years after the event occurred.

Augustus Caesar did not change the old political structures of the Roman Republic. He retained the title of "consul," but in effect became consul for life. The Senate remained intact, and for the remainder of the empire's history, the Senate technically named the new emperor. In reality, though, the Senate had no real power because they gratefully gave it to Augustus for saving Rome from destruction. Augustus Caesar was a clever politician and an effective ruler, always catering to the Senate, while he made all real policy decisions. He preferred to be called **princeps** ("first citizen"), but in his forty-year rule, he overhauled the military, the economy, and the government, putting in place a system that would last for another 250 years without substantial changes.

One of the many accomplishments of Augustus was a new civil service that managed the large empire with considerable efficiency and honesty. The officials were **equites**, a class of Italian merchants and landowners who helped run the Roman Empire. The provinces were ruled by governors appointed in Rome but allowed a great deal of freedom in local affairs. Augustus studied and codified Roman Law, adding onto the code from the days of the republic - the **Law of the Twelve Tables.** He also set up a network of officials to hear cases and administer the law. A new class of legal experts rose, whose opinions and interpretations often were given the force of law. His reforms to the military included reducing its unwieldy size, so that all that remained were professional soldiers. The army also became an engineering force to build roads and public works all over the provinces. The army was made up of twenty-eight legions, each with about 6000 infantrymen supported by cavalry. The navy was reorganized effectively to combat pirates, who had been disruptive to shipping on the Mediterranean Sea and the rivers.

These reforms ushered in the **Pax Romana**, or the "Roman peace," that lasted until the late 2nd century C.E. The empire reached its largest extent during that era, and settled into a long period of peace and prosperity in which Roman strength was generally unchallenged. After that, Rome settled into a decline that eventually ended in its conquest in 476 C.E. One continuing problem was the uncertainty concerning the emperor's successor. Although heredity was important, the emperor had the right to name a non-relative to replace him, a situation that often led to intrigue, competition, and conflict.

Economic Development and Social Distinctions

The early Roman economy resembled that of Greece about three centuries before. Aristocrats controlled large plots of land that were worked by tenant farmers, but there were many independent farmers who also served in the military. The elite were called **patricians,** and the commoners were known as **plebeians.** The basic unit of Roman society was a multi-generational family with domestic slaves. The oldest living male, the "paterfamilias," had complete authority over his family, and he was tied to other family heads through **patron-client** relationships. Patrons were men of wealth who clients turned to for help and protection. A senator had many clients who depended on his political power, and in return they gave him military service, labor, and political support. The Roman Forum was the center of business for these networks, and senators with large throngs around them held high prestige. Some of the senator's more prosperous clients might in turn be patrons of poorer men, so Rome's citizenry were tied to one another in a web of inequality. Tensions existed between the classes as long as the republic lasted, as evidenced by the patricians' concession to allow plebeians political representation through tribunes.

Women in the upper classes were generally treated like children under the strict scrutiny of the men of their family. During a woman's life cycle, first her father supervised her, then her husband, and finally her son. However, compared to women in Ancient Greece, Roman women probably had more freedom, with some economic rights. By the first century B.C.E., many women supervised family businesses and the financial affairs of wealthy estates. Roman literature describes women who appeared to be well educated and vocal.

As the Roman Republic expanded on the Italian peninsula, Romans began to play a large role in the Mediterranean Sea trade. Their economy and political power were increased tremendously by their victory in the **Punic Wars** fought with Carthage between 264 and 146 B.C.E. Carthage, a former Phoenician colony, located on the southern shore of the Mediterranean, controlled the western Mediterranean before its defeat. The Romans burned the city of Carthage to the ground, salted the earth to keep anything from growing there again, and took control of the lands, rich in grain, oil, wine, and precious metals. These resources fed the continuing expansion that continued after the founding of the empire by Augustus Caesar.

With expansion came the issue of how to incorporate conquered people into the republic. Some gained Roman citizenship, wealth, and respect through military accomplishments, but others were taken as slaves. Although slaves were found in most ancient societies, Rome was one of the few in which slave labor was indispensable. Some worked in households or craft production, but gangs of slaves were used in mining and on the great agricultural estates. Slaves worked longer and harder than hired laborers, and their numbers grew to probably about two million people by the 2nd and 1st centuries B.C.E.

During the **Pax Romana** from 31 B.C.E. until 180 C.E., the empire prospered. Its borders stabilized, giving economic relief to the strains of constant expansion. Trade thrived, with transport across land and sea protected by the Roman political and military structures. Economic problems returned in the **3rd century crisis** (C.E.), after a series of problematic emperors, and under pressure from a growing number of raids by nomadic people across Roman borders.

Roman Culture

Although the Romans borrowed heavily from the Greeks in philosophy, science, and the arts, they had their share of independent invention as well. Most of their contributions were in law, bureaucratic administration, finance, and engineering. The size and diversity of the Roman civilization called for a flexible system of laws that combined effective central control with local autonomy. Their Roman legal system developed pragmatically as the republic grew, and continued to change during the years of the empire. Some of their legal inventions include:

CHANGE OVER TIME: ROMAN REPUBLIC TO EMPIRE

Why did the Roman Republic fail, and why was it replaced with an empire? The Republic first emerged in an ethnically homogeneous city-state controlled by an agricultural aristocracy who came to dominate the Senate. As Rome expanded, many diverse people came under its control, largely through conquests by a military force that relied on citizen-farmers to fight its battles. Military service required men to be away from their farms for long periods of time, and when they returned, often their land had been seized by large landowners or given as a reward to military officers. With no place to go, poor farmers poured into urban areas, and without enough work, demanded reform. Conservative aristocrats refused to change traditions, others pushed for change, and charismatic military leaders attracted the support of the poor.

Julius Caesar appeared in the midst of this social and economic crisis to claim the power to restore law and order, and even though he did not succeed, his nephew Octavian did, and as Augustus Caesar, he eased Rome through the transition from troubled republic to a stabilized empire.

1) The concept of precedent, or court decisions that help to determine how courts rule in subsequent cases

2) The belief that equity among all citizens should be the goal of the legal system

3) Interpretation of the law, or the responsibility of judges to decide what a law means and how it should be applied

4) Natural law, an idea that would be a foundation block for later European and North American societies, or the belief that all human beings have basic rights in nature that cannot be abridged

Roman Arts, Literature, and Religion

Greek art and literature shaped the everyday lives of the Roman elite so deeply that their influence sparked a debate in the early days of the empire about what Roman values actually were. Cultural diffusion from Greece was facilitated by the large number of Greek servants who worked for wealthy Romans. Most were well educated and often served as tutors for Roman children. Imitation of Greek culture also was promoted by the similarity between the religions of the two civilizations, since both had essentially the same gods and goddesses with different names.

Roman Architecture. This magnificent arch is among the ruins left by the Romans in Vaison-la-Romaines in southern France. The Romans were unsurpassed in their ability to construct elaborate arches, which allowed buildings to carry great structural weight. In this example, the arch rests on columns clearly influenced by Greek architecture.

Rome's literary contributions are not as numerous as those of Greece, partly because the Greeks were generally better read. However, the Roman poet **Virgil** linked great epic poetry like the *Iliad* and the *Odyssey* to Roman history in his *Aeneid*, which became the official version of the founding of Rome. Roman literary works also spread its language – Latin – far and wide, so that poetry written by Ovid and history written by Livy could be read in many areas of the world long after the Roman Empire was gone. Romans valued oratory skills and ethical philosophy, although they tended to value the practical more than the philosophical. This preference is reflected in the fact that they did little beyond copying Greek sculpture, and yet they made significant advances in architecture that served a particular purpose. Roman roads were built for marching armies and facilitating trade, and great aqueducts were built to carry water to the urban areas. Roman genius was unmatched when the task was to solve a practical problem.

COMPARISONS: GREEK AND ROMAN RELIGION

Like the Ancient Greeks, Romans did not look to their gods for ethical guidance. Neither civilization believed (like Gilgamesh in early Mesopotamia) that the gods could grant humans immortality. Both Greeks and Romans thought of an afterlife as an open question, as reflected in Socrates' ruminations as he contemplated his own death. Most Greeks and Romans believed that even if there was an afterlife, the gods would have nothing to do with what happened to humans after they died. The Romans, more thanthe Greeks, believed in stoicism, or the idea that service to the state and community was the highest calling.

Greek and Roman gods did have different names, although they were essentially the same:

Greek Name	Roman Name
Zeus	Jupiter
Poseidon	Neptune
Aphrodite	Venus
Athena	Minerva
Ares	Mars

The Decline of Rome

Reasons for the decline of Rome are numerous, and in most ways it was a slow process. A common problem of all the large empires was defense of a very long border, far from the capital city. This difficulty was sensed by Germanic tribes in the north, and their constant attacks meant that defense costs went up significantly. Unfortunately these attacks increased during the 3rd century C.E.

during a time when Rome had a string of incompetent, often corrupt emperors. Although the strong emperor **Diocletian** stopped the slide temporarily, the problems continued. As in the waning days of the republic, the empire by the 3rd century C.E. was rife with class struggles over land, since large estates that used slave labor had taken up most free land. Contact through easy trade and transportation had its downside as well, in the form of devastating epidemics that followed the trade routes, killing large numbers of people as they spread.

In the 4th century C.E. the Roman Emperor **Constantine** established a second capital city in the east that he named "Constantinople" in order to have better connections in that part of the empire and to escape the threatening attacks of Rome by nomads. This move had the effect of gradually sacrificing the western provinces to the Germanic groups, including the Franks, Saxons, Angles, Vandals, Visigoths, and Ostrogoths. By the early 5th century, Rome itself was sacked by the Visigoths, and the last Roman emperor was deposed in 476 C.E.

CHINA DURING THE CLASSICAL ERA

At the same time that Rome was increasing its influence around the Mediterranean Sea, China was recovering from its **Warring States Period** at the end of the Zhou Dynasty. The Warring States Period was a time of political turmoil, with regional warlords constantly challenging the authority of the Zhou. However, it was also a period that prompted much debate over how to solve China's many problems, resulting in the origins of three influential belief systems:

1) **Legalism** – Legalist thinkers believed that humans were naturally evil and would only obey authority through force. They advocated strict laws, harsh punishments, and sacrifice of personal freedom for the good of the state.

2) **Daoism** – A philosopher named **Laozi**, who reputedly lived during the 6th century B.C.E., reacted to the constant warfare by encouraging people to avoid useless struggles by following the **Dao**, or the "path." He shunned political and military ambitions as lacking morality and meaning, and guided his followers toward nature for comfort and understanding. Daoism emphasizes acceptance and individual retreat from society.

3) **Confucianism** – The philosopher Confucius emphasized the importance of hierarchical, harmonious relationships in the creation of an orderly society. Everyone has a place in society, from the ruler to his lowliest subject, and all have responsibilities in their relationships with others. Confucianism saw the family as the foundation of society that serves as a model for benevolence, duty, and courtesy.

The Qin Dynasty

Legalism met an enthusiastic response from the leaders of the state of Qin in western China, who used the philosophy of harsh, strict rule to dominate their neighbors. The Qin army was well organized and equipped with the best available iron weapons, and it defeated one state after the other, until finally the Qin had brought China under their rule. Since the Qin government had much stronger centralized authority than the previous dynasties had, the king declared himself "The First Emperor," or **Shi Huangdi**, who ruled from 221-210 B.C.E. The dynasty only survived for a few years after his death, but its brevity does not reduce its significance in the development of the Chinese state.

Shi Huangdi ruled his empire through a centralized bureaucracy from his capital near the modern city of Xi'an. The tenets of legalism served him well as he stripped the nobility of power and divided China into administrative provinces governed by administrators that served at his pleasure. He built roads to facilitate communications and move his armies. He also forced his subjects to contribute their labor to building public works, including the first fortifications of the **Great Wall** of China. Confucians widely criticized the harsh rule of the emperor, who responded by sentencing them to death. Quite famously, he demanded the burning of all books of philosophy, ethics, history, and literature, and only allowed books of practical use (such as medicine and agriculture) to be spared.

Despite his harshness, Shi Huangdi strengthened China in many ways. He standardized laws and currencies, so that they were the same across all regional states. An important step in his unification of China was his mandate that the Shang version of Chinese script be used all over the empire. The regions continued to speak their own languages, but the common script enabled people across China to communicate with one another through writing.

Although Shi Huangdi today is seen as one of the greatest figures in Chinese history, his strict rule made him quite unpopular. Shortly after his death, revolts began, resulting in the overthrow of the dynasty in 207 B.C.E., when state buildings were destroyed and government officials killed, paving the way for the Han Dynasty.

The Han Dynasty (206 B.C.E. – 220 C.E.)

Instead of falling into years of chaos, as had happened during the Warring States Period at the end of the Zhou Dynasty, China was brought under control quickly by Liu Bang, who was not a particularly talented military commander, but was a strong ruler, partly because he picked able bureaucrats who organized the new dynasty efficiently.

The Terra Cotta Army. Shi Huangdi was buried in a magnificent underground palace, surrounded by thousands of terra cotta soldiers, crafted specifically to guard the ruler after his death. These soldiers each had individual features, poses, and dress, and they were accompanied by horses and weapons. The site of the tomb and the soldiers has only been excavated since 1974, when a Chinese farmer digging for water accidentally discovered a piece of a soldier. New discoveries continue to be made, so no one yet knows just how many soldiers were created for Shi Huangdi.

Political Development

Like their contemporaries, the Romans, the Han organized and controlled their realm through a strong, nonhereditary bureaucracy. Although they kept many of the structures created by Shi Huangdi, the Han de-emphasized legalism in favor of a government based on Confucian values. The family hierarchy became the basis for government structure, with subjects owing the emperor the same obedience that children gave to their fathers. The old Zhou belief in the "mandate of heaven" was incorporated into Confucian values; the emperor had the support of the heavens as long as he was a good ruler, and people owed him their fealty. The Han brought forward the Confucian value of benevolence to substitute for the Qin strictness and reliance on force.

Liu Bang was followed by several able rulers, most notably **Han Wudi** (140-87 B.C.E., who issued a royal decree that required the nobility to divide their land between all their sons so that large estates would be broken up, checking the lords' power. The emperor's appointees expanded their authority at the expense of local lords and centralized power in the central government, sometimes going so far as to confiscate land in the name of the emperor.

Even more than Shi Huangdi, the Han rulers expanded the Chinese frontiers west, north, and south. These conquests brought the Chinese into contact with other civilizations, including the Romans, although probably only through intermediaries. Other trade contacts included India, northeast Asia, and Southeast Asia. The nomadic groups to the north were a big threat to Han stability, as they had been for the Qin. The beginning structures of the Great Wall were built to keep them out, but these skilled horsemen constantly got around it to attack settlements to their south. Han Wudi's forces defeated the nomads and annexed their pasture lands to the Han domain, although the annexation only brought temporary relief. In the east, the northern parts of Korea were conquered, and many of the various groups in Southeast Asia also came under Han control.

Economic Developments and Social Distinctions

Like Rome, Han China was an urban empire that ruled a rural and peasant population. Urban areas of China grew rapidly during this era, with the population of Xi'an (also called Chang'an) reaching to about 100,000 within the city walls, with thousands of others outside the walls and in neighboring communities. The emperor lived in the **forbidden city**, so called because only his family, servants, and closest advisors were permitted within its boundaries. Administrative buildings and houses of aristocrats and the scholar-gentry surrounded the forbidden city, and the streets bustled with commerce. Other urban areas grew as well, so that as much as 30 percent of the population lived in towns and cities. Canals were built, and the road system expanded to improve communication and commerce. The most important export was silk, and its production from cocoons on the leaves of mulberry trees was a closely guarded secret that gave the Chinese a silk monopoly.

Despite the importance of trade to the empire's prosperity, merchants did not have a high social status. Instead, the highest regard was for the **shi**, or the scholar bureaucrats (sometimes called mandarins). The shi generally fared much better under the Han than they did under the Qin, largely because their affinity for Confucianism had brought them disfavor by Shi Huangdi. The Han rulers after Liu Bang increasingly promoted Confucianism, and thorough knowledge of Confucian teachings became essential for promotion in the Han government. A university was founded in Xi'an to educate young scholars to prepare them for jobs in the bureaucracy, and an examination system was set up in the last century B.C.E. to help the government to identify the best candidates for the bureaucracy. The examinations were based almost exclusively on knowledge of the Confucian texts. Theoretically, any Chinese man could take the exams, but only the sons of the wealthy had the leisure to study for them, so the bureaucracy was generally filled from aristocratic and scholar-gentry families. The importance of social class was reinforced by the fact that many government positions were still hereditary, and automatically passed from father to son.

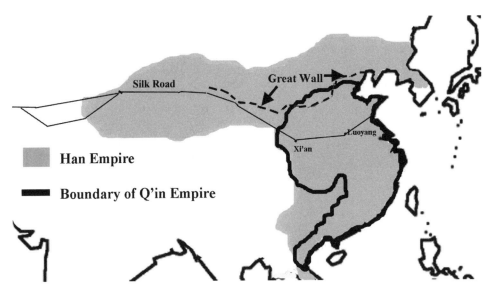

Qin and Han China. Both dynasties were expansionist, with the Han extending to the north to try to placate invading nomads, south to take over various people of Southeast Asia, and west to protect and control trade along the Silk Road.

Three main social classes characterized Han China:

1) **The scholar-gentry** – This class was linked to the shi, and eventually superseded it. Their status was based on their control of large amounts of land and bureaucratic positions in the government. Wealth from landholding supported their brightest sons to study for and win important administrative positions. These families tended to maintain homes in both the city and the countryside, and they passed their wealth and status down to their children, sometimes for many centuries.

2) **Ordinary, but free, citizens** – The common people included a broad range, with the majority being peasants. Some peasants had significant amounts of land, and occasionally might support a son to study for government examinations. Most peasants who had a decent-sized plot of land lived well. However, others were forced to work for landlords, and still others did not have enough to eat. All peasants were required to work a designated number of days each year on public works, and they also could be forced to join the army.

3) **The Underclass** – This broad category included many different groups, including non-Han Chinese on the fringes of the empire. Some were shifting cultivators driven out of their areas by the growing Han population. They were described in various accounts as bandits, beggars, and vagabonds. Slavery did exist, but it was far less prominent than it was in Ancient Rome. During the Warring States Period, dependent peasants as well as slaves worked the large estates. The Qin government tried to abolish slavery, but it persisted into the Han era. However, only a small fraction of the population was enslaved, and most people that were slaves served as domestic servants.

MARKER EVENT: THE EXAMINATION SYSTEM IN CHINA

Even though most government jobs in the Han Dynasty were filled according to heredity, the Chinese first experimented with the idea that administrative offices should be filled on the basis of merit and effort. They set up an examination system that measured a young person's knowledge of Confucian texts, and only those that passed the exams could work in certain positions in the emperor's government. This idea may seem commonplace today, but it was revolutionary in ancient times.

Although they were not given high status by the scholar-gentry, the artisan, manufacturing classes grew during the Han period as a result of numerous inventions and technological innovations. The introduction of the brush pen and paper greatly facilitated the work of the scholar-gentry, and the demand for their manufacture increased. The Han Chinese also developed water mills for agriculture, rudders and compasses for ships, and new mining techniques for iron and copper. Skilled artisans were in high demand, and most probably lived more comfortable lives than the peasants.

Like all other ancient civilizations, China was a patriarchy, but most historians believe that women's status during the Han period was higher than it was in later periods of Chinese history. Marriages were arranged according to family ties, but neither young men nor women had much say about who their partners would be. Powerful relatives usually protected their daughters from abuse by the husband's family, and women of upper-class families were often educated in writing, the arts, and music. Still, women at all social levels remained subordinated to men. Families were run by the older men, and male children were favored over their sisters. Political positions were reserved for men, and only boys could sit for the examinations. Women from peasant families played traditional roles as cooks, house cleaners, and support for men in the fields. All were legally subordinated to their fathers and husbands.

SEEING SIMILARITIES: ROME AND HAN

Often it is easier to see the differences between two societies than it is to see their similarities. However, the great classical empires of Rome and China had more in common than you might think.

Both Rome and China were huge empires with long borders to defend. Each built walls and maintained a chain of forts and garrisons. Both spent a great deal of time, effort, and money trying to defend their borders from nomadic attack, and both ultimately failed.

The economies of both societies were based on agriculture, but both grew into wealthy urban empires. Their free peasantry came into conflict with wealthy aristocrats over land ownership, and peasants in both societies rebelled when they were reduced to dependent tenant farmers.

Both Rome and Han Empires spread from a homogeneous core to encompass many diverse people. Each brought a cultural unity that conquered people came to value, and each had to delegate ruling authority to local officials. Both developed a competent bureaucracy that allowed the empires to thrive for a number of years.

Han Culture and Science

The Han were interested in decorative arts, and their bronze and ceramic figures, bowls, vases, jade and ivory carvings, and woven silk screens were of very high quality. One of the highest art forms was **calligraphy,** or the artistic rendering of the written word, a skill that is still highly prized in Chinese society. Historical record-keeping was important for the Han, with some scripts surviving until today. Mathematics, geography, and astronomy were also valued, especially for the practical inventions that were based on these sciences. An interest in the sciences led to more intensive knowledge of the parts of the body and their functions, including the circulation of blood. Acupuncture was first mentioned in the historical records of the Han Period. All and all, the Chinese were more drawn to practical scientific experimentation than theory.

Decline of the Han Empire

Although the Han Dynasty lasted for more than four hundred years, its last two hundred years were a time of gradual decline. Defending the long borders from nomadic invasions remained a problem, and the expense became burdensome. The early emperors were successful in reducing the wealth and landholdings of the aristocracy, but by the late Han era, many had regained huge tracts of land and local nobility again controlled peasants in their areas. Official corruption and inefficiency marred the government's ability to effectively rule, and peasant uprisings destabilized many parts of the empire. Like the Zhou before, the Han Dynasty suffered the ill effects of the dynastic cycle, and a period of chaos followed its downfall in 220 C.E. that lasted for 135 years.

CLASSICAL INDIA

Before the fall of Mohenjo-Daro and Harappa in the Indus River valley, the **Aryans** had migrated into the Indian sub-continent from their home north of the Black Sea. After 1000 B.C.E., they began to settle in the area between the Himalayan foothills and the Ganges River, and by 500 B.C.E., they had migrated as far south as the Deccan plateau in the south central part of the sub-continent. At first, they probably had a fairly simple society consisting of herders and farmers led by warrior chiefs and priests. As they settled, however, their social complexity grew, especially as they interacted with the native Dravidians.

The Development of the Caste System

The term **caste** – a social class of hereditary and usually unchangeable status – was first used in India by Portuguese merchants and mariners during the 16th century C.E. when they noticed the sharp social distinctions on the Indian sub-continent. The Aryans used the term **varna,** a Sanskrit word meaning "color," to refer to their social classes. By about 1000 B.C.E., four major varnas were recognized, as explained in a creation myth in which a primordial creature named Purusha was sacrificed:

- **Brahmins** – The highest social classes were the priests and scholars, who sprang from Purusha's mouth, and represented intellect and knowledge.

- **Kshatriya** – Warriors and government officials sprang from the arms of the creature.

- **Vaishya** – From Purusha's thighs came the third layer of people – landowners, merchants, and artisans.

- **Shudra** – The creature's feet were represented by common peasants and laborers.

During the classical era the caste system became much more complex, with each caste further subdivided into **jati**, or birth groups, each with its own occupation, duties, and rituals. Each jati had very little contact with others, and its members intermarried and followed the same occupations of the ancestors.

ORIGINAL DOCUMENTS: THE *LAWBOOK OF MANU*

Original documents often reflect the values and beliefs of their authors and offer us insight into the societies they belonged to. A good example is the *Lawbook of Manu*, written by an anonymous scribe in the 1st century B.C.E., who attributed it to Manu, founder of the human race according to Indian beliefs. What do these excerpts tell us about early Indian society and culture?

"It is the nature of women to seduce men in this world; for that reason the wise are never unguarded in the company of females...
When women are honored, there the gods are pleased; but where they are not honored, no sacred rite yields rewards...
In childhood a female must be subject to her father, in youth to her husband, when her lord is dead to her sons; a woman must never be independent.
She must not seek to separate herself from her father, husband, or sons; by leaving them she would make both her own and her husband's families contemptible..."

Source: Andrea, Alfred, and James H. Overfield, *The Human Record, Vol. 1.* Boston, Houghton Mifflin, 2001.

Early Religion and Culture

The period from 1500 to 500 B.C.E. is called the "Vedic Age," after the **Vedas,** religious texts that were passed down from generation to generation of Aryans in the form of hymns, songs, prayers and rituals honoring the Aryan gods. The most important is called the **Rig Veda**, compiled between about 1400 and 900 B.C.E., but was not written down until about 600 B.C.E. The Vedas reflect the conflicts between the Aryans and the Dravidians, and they identify Indra as the Aryan war god and military hero, as well as gods of the sun, sky, moon, fire, and the underworld. Over the years the Aryan religion blended with beliefs of the Dravidians, as reflected in a body of works called the **Upanishads**, which appeared in the late Vedic Age, about 800 to 400 B.C.E. The Upanishads spoke about a universal spirit, known as Brahman, who is eternal and unchanging. A central belief was that through **reincarnation**, the rebirth of a soul after the body dies, the human spirit (**atman**) could eventually join the universal spirit, as long as the human being behaved ethically. Eventually these beliefs came to be called **Hinduism,** the religion of most people that live today in the Indian sub-continent.

A second major world religion, **Buddhism**, began in India during the early classical period. Its founder was **Siddhartha Gautama** (563-483 B.C.E.), born to a kshatrya family in the north of India. Although his life as a prince was comfortable and satisfying, he left his family to seek the meaning of life, and eventually experienced an enlightenment that became the foundation of the faith. Siddhartha was called the Buddha ("Enlightened One"), and spent the rest of his life in the area around the Ganges River valley spreading his knowledge to others. He never claimed to be a god, but after his death, some of his followers elevated him to that status. Although the religion spread, most Indians remained faithful to the old beliefs, and by the 3rd century B.C.E., it looked as if Buddhism was destined to be a small regional religion.

Political Development

Political developments in India greatly impacted the growth of Buddhism, particularly after **Ashoka,** the third and greatest ruler of the **Mauryan Dynasty** converted to it. Before the 4th century B.C.E. India was politically fragmented into separate kinship groups and independent groups. Different terrains – mountains, river valleys, plains, forests, steppes, and deserts – made transportation and communication difficult, and various languages and cultural practices developed. The caste system was in place across the sub-continent, and although religious beliefs were shared, the hundreds of jati separated people into groups of identification, so political authority was of only secondary importance. Despite these divisions, the Mauryan Dynasty came to rule a good part of the area for almost 300 years, beginning in the kingdom of Magadha, in eastern India. The kingdom was wealthy and strategically located along the trade routes of the Ganges River valley, and its leader, Chandragupta Maurya expanded it into India's first centralized empire. His grandson, Ashoka, ruled over the entire subcontinent except for the southern tip of the peninsula. A large imperial army helped the dynasty to maintain control of the area.

Ashoka's early life was spent conquering different regions of India until, according to his own account, he was shocked by the bloodshed at the battle of Kalinga at the midpoint of his reign. He turned to Buddhism because of its emphasis on peace, tolerance, and nonviolence, and he spent the remainder of his years promoting these values. Ashoka's dominant image in Indian history is of a young warrior turned responsible monarch who saw himself as the father of his people. The Mauryan Empire lasted for a time after Ashoka's death in 232 B.C.E., but eventually it collapsed from the pressure of attacks in the northwest. In 184 B.C. E. India returned to its usual political arrangement – fragmented, regional kingdoms for more than 500 years.

In the early 4th century C.E., a new empire rose to centralize power once again, although it never was as large as the Mauryan Empire had been. The **Gupta Empire** began in the same powerful area, Magadha, with its founder, Chandra Gupta, modeling himself after the Mauryan founder by borrowing his name. The Gupta Empire was not only smaller, but it also never had as much control over regional lords as the Maurya had, particularly under Ashoka. The Gupta did not build a genuine bureaucracy to rule their subjects, but instead were content to draw tribute from them, allowing regional warrior elites a great deal of autonomy to rule their areas.

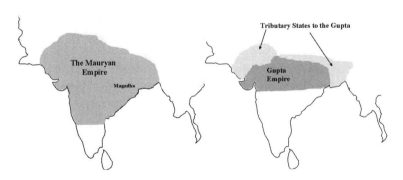

Classical India. Two great empires rose on the Indian subcontinent during the classical era: the Mauryan Empire (324-184 B.C.E.) and the Gupta Empire (320-550 C.E.). During the 500+ years between empires, India reverted to the fragmented regional rule that it knew before. The map shows that the earlier empire was quite a bit larger than the later one, which is depicted as it was about 400 C.E.

COMPARISONS: THEATRE STATE IN THE PERSIAN AND GUPTA EMPIRES

A technique used by both the Persians and the Gupta is "theatre state," or the art of awing subjects into remaining loyal to the ruling family. In both empires the ruler took the title "King of Kings," and both required tribute to be brought to their capitals, where a splendid palace, magnificent buildings, beautiful grounds, spectacular entertainment, and ornate court costumes were designed to impress the visitors.

At the Persian capital of Persepolis, visitors first entered the Gate of All Nations, a grand hall where a pair of Lamassus (bulls with the head of a bearded man) stand on the western threshold, and another pair with wings and a Persian head on the eastern entrance, to reflect the Empire's power. The palace at the Gupta capital of Pataliputra was described by a Buddhist monk, Faxian, as too beautiful to have been built by human hands, but instead was "all made by spirits which [King Ashoka] employed."

Reference: Legge, James, *The Travels of Fa-hien: Fa-hien's Record of Buddhistic Kingdoms.* Delhi: Oriental Publishers, 1971.

CLASSICAL CIVILIZATIONS: TRADE PATTERNS AND CONTACTS

One important change in world history during the classical era is the intensification and expansion of trade networks and communication patterns among the major civilizations. These trade networks were often controlled by nomads that lived in the vast expanses between civilizations and on their outskirts. As a result of these growing networks, many more areas of the world were interacting and becoming increasingly dependent on one another. Three large trade networks that developed in the Eastern Hemisphere between 300 B.C.E. and 600 C.E. were the Silk Road, the Indian Ocean trade, and the Saharan trade.

The Silk Road

This fabled trade route that extended overland from Xi'an in China to the eastern Mediterranean had its beginnings in the late 2nd century B.C.E. when a Chinese general named Zhang Jian made his way to the Tarim Basin in central Asia on an exploratory journey. There he discovered "heavenly horses" that were far better than any that had been bred in China. The Chinese had many goods to trade, including their highly prized silk, and with the discovery of the horses, they now had something that they wanted in return. The Tarim Basin was connected by trade routes to civilizations to the west, and by 100 B.C.E. Greeks

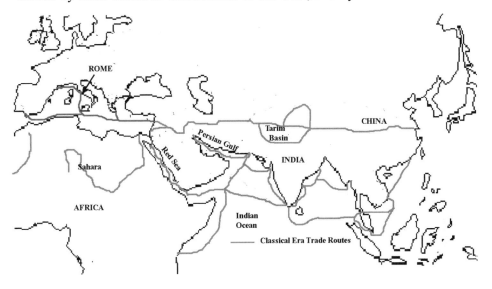

Classical Era Trade Routes. Extensive interconnecting trade routes developed in the Eastern Hemisphere during the Classical Era between 300 B.C.E. and 600 C.E.

could buy Chinese silk from traders in Mesopotamia, who in turn had traded for the silk with nomads that came from the Tarim Basin. Although the Romans and Chinese probably never actually met, goods made it from one end of the Silk Road to the other, making all people along the route aware of the presence of others. Traders going west from China carried peaches, apricots, cinnamon, ginger, and other spices, as well as the precious silk. Traders going east carried alfalfa (for the horses), grapes, pistachios, sesame, and spinach. Many other goods travelled along parts of the route, so that inventions in any place within access could make their way to other people. For example, the **stirrup** was probably invented in what is now northern Afghanistan, and warriors in many places realized what an advantage the stirrup gave them in battle, so its use spread to faraway China and Europe.

The Silk Road was essentially held together by pastoral nomads of Central Asia who supplied animals to transport goods and food and drink needed by the caravan parties. For periodic payments by merchants and bureaucrats, they provided protection from bandits and raiding parties. They insured the smooth operation of the trade routes, allowing not only goods to travel, but also ideas, customs, and religions, such as Christianity and Buddhism.

The Indian Ocean Maritime System

Water travel from the northern tip of the Red Sea southward goes back to the days of the river valley civilization, with the Ancient Egyptians probably trading with areas along the southern coast of the Arabian Peninsula. Likewise, other shorter water routes had developed in coastal areas around the Indian Ocean. During the classical era, however, these routes connected to one another to form a vast trade network that extended from southeastern China to Africa. Like the traders along the Silk Road, most Indian Ocean traders only traveled back and forth on one of its three legs: 1) southeastern China to Southeast Asia; 2) Southeast Asia to the eastern coast of India; and 3) the western coast of India to the Red Sea and the eastern coast of Africa.

COMPARISON: TRAVEL ON THE MEDITERRANEAN SEA AND THE INDIAN OCEAN

Differences in the physical geography of the Indian Ocean and the Mediterranean Sea shaped different techniques and technologies for water travel in ancient times. The Mediterranean's calm waters meant that sails had to be designed to pick up what little wind they could, so large, square sails were developed. The most famous of the ships, the Greek trireme, also had three tiers of oars operated by 170 rowers. In contrast, sailing on the Indian Ocean had to take into account the strong seasonal monsoon winds that blew in one direction during the spring and the opposite direction during the fall. Indian Ocean vessels did without oars, and used the **lateen sail** (roughly triangular with squared off points) for manueverability through the strong winds. The boats were small, with planks tied together by palm fiber, whereas Mediterranean sailors nailed their ships together. Mediterranean sailors usually stayed close to shore because they could not rely on winds to carry them over the open water. In contrast, the monsoon winds allowed Indian Ocean sailors to go for long distances across water.

Countless products traveled along the Indian Ocean routes, including ivory from Africa, India, and Mesopotamia; frankincense and myrrh (fragrances) from southern Arabia; pearls from the Persian Gulf; spices from India and Southeast Asia; and manufactured goods and pottery from China.

Trade Routes across the Sahara

Before the classical era, the vast Sahara Desert of northern Africa had long formed a geographic barrier between the people of Sub-Saharan Africa and those that lived to its north and east. The introduction of the camel to the area (probably in the 1ˢᵗ century B.C.E.) made it possible to establish trade caravans across the desert. Camels probably reached the Sahara from Arabia by way of Egypt, and in both areas effective camel saddles were developed to allow trade goods to be carried. One incentive for Saharan trade was the demand for desert salt, and traders from Sub-Saharan Africa brought forest products from the south, such as kola nuts and palm oil, to be exchanged for the salt. Extensive trade routes connected different areas of Sub-Saharan Africa, so that the connection of Eastern Africa to the Indian Ocean trade meant that goods from much of Sub-Saharan Africa could make their way to Asia and the Mediterranean. These desert routes were to extend substantially in later years, but the connections of these early years were an important beginning.

SIGNIFICANT MIGRATIONS

During the late classical era (200-600 C.E.) for reasons that are not all clear, a number of major migrations occurred, with some directly impacting the major civilizations. Some of these migrations are:

- **The Huns** – During the late 4th century C.E. the nomadic Huns began an aggressive westward migration from their homeland in central Asia. They had invaded China centuries earlier, and their motivation for movement in this later era was probably related to drought and competition over grazing lands. During the mid-5th century, **Attila** organized the Huns into a great attacking army, invading Hungary, crossing Roman frontiers in the Balkans, and venturing into Gaul and northern Italy. By the later 5th century the Huns were pouring into the Indian subcontinent. Defense of the frontier exhausted the Gupta's treasury, and the empire collapsed by 550.

- **Germanic People** – As the Huns moved westward, they competed for pasture land with various Germanic people who they displaced. The Ostrogoths, Visigoths, Franks, Angles, Saxons, and Vandals began to move as well. Even though the Huns dispersed after Attila's death, they showed the vulnerability of the Romans, and the Germanic groups took full advantage. They spent much of their time fighting one another, and the Romans encouraged this behavior to keep them weak. However, by the 4th and 5th centuries the Germanic tribes roamed through the western provinces without much resistance from the Romans, and the tribal war chiefs began creating their own kingdoms that eventually evolved into European countries. For example, the Franks settled in what would become France, and the Angles and Saxons invaded and conquered England in the 5th century.

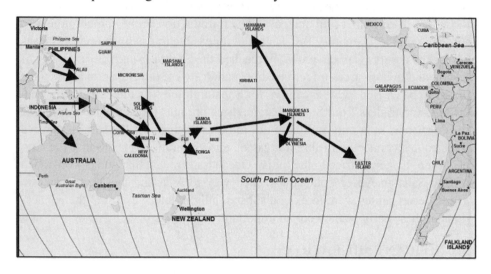

The Migration of Polynesian People. The migration began on the mainland of Asia thousands of years ago, and the spread of Polynesian people was quite gradual. It is estimated that they reached New Guinea by about 28,000 B.C.E., Vanuatu by 1500 B.C.E., the Marquesa Islands by 200 B.C.E., and Hawaii by 400 C.E.

- **Bantu** – The Bantu most likely originated in an area south of the Sahara Desert in the region around modern Nigeria. They may have begun leaving their homeland as early as 2000 B.C.E., possibly because of **desertification,** or the expansion of the Sahara Desert that dried out their agricultural lands. They traveled for centuries all over sub-Saharan Africa, but retained many of their customs, including their Bantu language. As their language spread, it combined with others, but still retained enough similarity to the original that the family of Bantu languages can still be recognized over a huge expanse of territory. Unlike the surges by the Huns and Germanic people, the Bantu migrations were quite gradual, so that by the end of the classical era, the Bantu migrations had introduced agriculture, iron metallurgy, and the Bantu language to most regions of sub-Saharan Africa.

- **Polynesians** – Although their efforts did not immediately impact civilizations on mainland Eurasia, the peopling of the islands of the Pacific Ocean was quite a remarkable feat. Like the Bantu, the migration was gradual, but between 1500 B.C.E. and 1000 C.E., almost all the major islands west of New Guinea were visited, and many were settled. The people, now called Polynesians, came from mainland Asia, and expanded eastward to Fiji, Tonga, and Samoa. They left no written records, so our knowledge of them relies on archaeological evidence, accounts by early European sailors, and oral traditions. Their ships were great double canoes that carried a platform between two hulls and large triangular sails that helped them catch ocean winds. The distances they travelled were remarkably long, and by the time the Europeans arrived in the 18th century, the Polynesians had explored and colonized almost every habitable island in the vast Pacific Ocean.

THE LATE CLASSICAL PERIOD: THE FALL OF GREAT EMPIRES

In the centuries between 200 and 600 C.E. all three of the great classical civilizations collapsed, at least in part. The western part of the Roman Empire fell, the Han Dynasty ended in disarray, and the Gupta Empire in Indian fragmented into regions. Some common reasons include:

- **Attacks by nomadic groups** - The migration of the Huns from their homeland in Central Asia impacted all three civilizations as they moved east, south, and west. Their movement caused other groups to move out of their way, causing a domino effect that put pressure on Rome, India, and China.

- **Serious internal problems** – All the empires had trouble maintaining political control over their vast lands, and were ultimately unable to keep their empires together. No governments had ever spread their authority over so much land space, and perhaps it was inevitable that their sheer sizes could not be maintained. In Rome and Han China, disputes between large landowners and peasants created instability and unrest.

- **The problems of interdependence** – Just as the earlier civilizations collapsed or suffered severe strain in the time period around 1200 B.C.E., the civilizations of the late classical age all ended before 600 C.E. When one weakened it impacted all, as trade routes became vulnerable when imperial armies could no longer protect them or when the economic resources necessary for trade were no longer available. Disease spread along the trade routes, killing people that would not have died had they not been in contact with others. Some estimates are that each civilization lost as many as half its citizens during the late classical era.

Despite their similarities, decline and fall had very different consequences for the three civilizations. Only one – Rome - did not retain its identity after it fell. India and China lost their political unity, but they did not permanently lose their identity as civilizations, and both eventually reorganized into major world powers. The Roman Empire was destined to never regain its former identity, but instead fell into many pieces that retained separate orientations. Why? What were the differences? Part of the answer lies in what happened next in the story of the world – political power is not the only "glue" that holds a civilization together. In the period before and after 600 C.E. the most important sources of identity were religious, with older religions and philosophies, such as Christianity, Buddhism, and Confucianism growing in influence that transcended political boundaries. An important new religion was on the horizon as well. Islam was destined to become the force behind one of the most remarkable land expansions in world history, a path made easier because it appeared at a time when the old political empires of Rome, China, and India had fallen.

In this new era of religious unity, Rome fell short. Christianity had become its official religion during the 4th century C.E., too late to be a unifying force for the failing empire. When political and military power failed, nothing was left except crumbling material architecture, symbols of a past era. However, the Indian subcontinent was bound together by Hinduism, and the intricate caste loyalties that supported it, so that the fall of the Gupta had only a limited impact on the civilization's development. Likewise, Confucianism had become such a part of the identity of the Han Chinese that the fall of the dynasty was not a fatal blow to the civilization. Chaos did characterize the period, but the Chinese civilization lived on to reassert its true character when political stability returned.

CONCEPTS AND IDENTIFICATIONS

"3rd century crisis"
Actium
Alexander the Great
Aristotle
Ashoka
atman
Attila
Augustus Caesar (Octavian)
Buddhism
calligraphy
castes, varna, jati
classical civilizations
Cleisthenes
Cleopatra
Confucianism
Constantine
consuls (Rome)
Cyrus the Great

Daoism
Delian League
desertification
Diocletian
equites
Etruscans
forbidden city
Great Wall
Greek "Classical Age"
Gupta Empire
Han Wudi
Hellenic culture
Hellenistic synthesis
helots
Hinduism
hoplites
Julius Caesar
Laozi
lateen sail
Law of the Twelve Tables
Legalism
Marathon
Mark Antony
Mauryan Dynasty
Minoans
monarchies, aristocracies, democracies
Mycenaeans
natural law
patricians, plebeians
patron-client relationships
Pax Romana
Peloponnesian War
Pericles
Phoenicians
phonetic alphabet
Plato
polis
princeps
Qin Dynasty
Punic Wars
reincarnation
Roman Republic, Roman Empire

satraps
scholar-gentry
secularism
Senate (Rome)
Shi Huangdi
Siddhartha Gautama
Socrates
stirrup (importance of)
Terra Cotta Army
tribunes (Rome)
Triumvirate (Rome)
tyrants (Greece)
Upanishads
Vedas, Rig Veda
Virgil
Warring States Period (China)
Xerxes

CHAPTER FOUR:
MAJOR BELIEF SYSTEMS
BEFORE 600 C.E.

Belief systems were basic building blocks for most ancient civilizations, and it is impossible to develop an understanding of them without delving into the religious and philosophical beliefs that people of these times held. Some belief systems disappeared when the civilizations ended, but others have endured to this day, including Hinduism, Judaism, Confucianism, Daoism, Buddhism and Christianity. In this chapter we will focus on these major belief systems, as well as polytheism, the religion that most ancient civilizations identified with. In this early era, as in all periods that followed, belief systems and all the values, customs, and practices associated with them have shaped the story of the world.

PERSPECTIVES: THE SACRED AND THE PROFANE, ACCORDING TO EMILE DURKHEIM

Emile Durkheim, an early 20th century French sociologist, stated that religion involves "things that surpass the limits of our knowledge." He defined religion as a social institution that focuses on a conception of the sacred. He contrasted the sacred to the profane, with the sacred being the extraordinary that inspires a sense of awe and reverence, and the profane being the ordinary, unexceptional facets of everyday life. According to Durkheim, all societies make these distinctions, understanding profane things in terms of their usefulness, and setting apart the sacred from everyday life, denoting it as forbidden.

How might we define belief systems? They include both religions and philosophies, and they form comprehensive guidelines for human behavior, both for individuals and collectivities. They often answer "big questions," such as "What is the meaning of life?"; "What things in life are most worthwhile?"; "Where did we come from?"; and "What happens after we die?" Although we may give any number of explanations as to how religions and philosophies are different, a basic distinction is that religions are more concerned with events and forces outside the natural world. Philosophies, on the other hand, are focused on human behavior in interactions with others, finding answers to the big questions in this world, not in another, less directly comprehensible one. Of course, religious and philosophical beliefs overlap significantly so that any one belief system may actually qualify as both.

EARLIEST BELIEF SYSTEMS

The earliest belief systems appear to have centered on spirits whose presence could be sensed in certain objects or in special places. For example, hunters and gatherers often believed that particular groves, springs, or wild animals were sacred. The idea of spirits lived on in later religions that came to be focused on gods as people settled into communities. **Polytheism** is the belief in many gods, with each god having a specialty, usually related to nature. The rituals of early farmers often centered on the Earth Mother, a deity believed to be the source of new life, an all-powerful male Sky God, and divinities representing fire, wind, and rain. Most of the early civilizations – including Egypt, Mesopotamia, the Indus River valley people, the Olmec, the Chavin, Greece, and Rome – were all polytheistic. Their religions were particular to the civilizations, although there were striking similarities among many of them. Ancient China was probably originally polytheistic, but it was unique in its emphasis on the will of the ancestors, and by the Han period, Confucianism had become the most important belief system binding the Chinese civilization together.

During the classical era, an important change occurred in two of the religions – Christianity and Buddhism – that allowed them both to spread to many new areas from their places of origin. The two religions followed the Silk Road and the Indian Ocean circuit, and their numbers grew greatly. Both were transformed into **universalizing religions**, with cores of beliefs that transcend cultures and actively recruit new adherents. As a result, both religions grew tremendously in the years before 600 C.E., putting them in the position of becoming new sources of societal "glue" that would hold broad areas with varying political allegiances together. Meanwhile, some important **ethnic religions**, such as Judaism, the Chinese religions (Daoism and Confucianism), and Hinduism created strong bonds among people, but had little emphasis on converting outsiders to their faiths.

JUDAISM

Judaism originated with a small Middle Eastern group called the Hebrews, a Semitic people influenced by Babylonian civilization. Information about the Hebrews comes partly from archaeological excavations and references in contemporary documents from Egypt and Assyria, but mainly from the **Hebrew Bible**, a compilation of beliefs, events, and people from their early history. These stories were transmitted orally for many years, and were written down probably in the 10th century B.C.E. The text that we have today dates from the 5th century B.C.E., with a few later additions. The founder of the religion was **Abraham,** a man born in Ur in Mesopotamia who rejected the polytheism of his homeland and migrated with his family to the land of Israel, on the eastern shore of the Mediterranean Sea. The Hebrew Bible tells about a move to Egypt, where the people were enslaved, and their return to Israel to found a kingdom. The kingdom reached its height under kings Saul, David, and Solomon during the 11th and 10th centuries B.C.E. To commemorate the faith, Solomon built a Jewish temple, but it was destroyed by the neo-Babylonians in the 6th century B.C.E. The temple was rebuilt, but was destroyed by the Romans in the 2nd century C.E. In both cases, the Hebrews suffered a **diaspora,** or a scattering of their people by the conquerors, which spread its members to many parts of the earth. The religion survived, though, to influence other major religions, including Christianity and Islam, to make monotheism a powerful religious concept.

The Jewish concept of God represents an important change in human views toward the sacred. The gods in most early religions were whimsical, capricious, and quite human, despite their supernatural powers. The Hebrews saw God as more abstract, less human, all knowing, all powerful, and always just. They also viewed their relationship to God as a covenant (agreement) that assured them divine care in exchange for their devotion to one God. The belief that God sets high standards for ethical conduct and moral behavior was also powerful, one that set Hebrews apart from other early religions and has endured through the ages.

CHRISTIANITY

Christianity emerged as a new religion in the early years of the Roman Empire in Judea, the old Jewish kingdom that had become a Roman province. Its founder was **Jesus of Nazareth,** a Jewish prophet and teacher that Christians regard as the son of God. His supporters believed that he fulfilled a long-standing belief in the coming of a Messiah. He lived during the time of Augustus, and he advocated a purification of the Jewish religion that would establish the kingdom of God on earth. He appealed especially to the poor because his message was universal: all people were welcome in the kingdom of God, no matter what their social status or ethnicity. Jesus also promised a better life, not only after death, but on earth as well, since the just would be rewarded and the evil punished with a "Second Coming" of God. His message of a moral code based on love, charity, and humility, and not on possessions and money, also made the new religion appealing. However, his talk about a kingdom of God on earth alarmed the Romans, who saw his message as insubordinate to their rule. Some Jewish officials also believed him to be a dangerous agitator that threatened their religious authority. As a result, Jesus was put to death about 30 C.E., but his followers believed that he, as the son of God, was resurrected from the dead, a belief that became central to the new faith.

MARKER EVENT: THE DEVELOPMENT OF MONOTHEISM

Monotheism, or the belief in one god, is an important marker event in world history for many reasons, including the influence it has had on many major world religions. Some scholars identify Akhenaten, an Egyptian ruler of the New Kingdom, as the originator of the idea, with his attempt to promote his god, Aten, as the supreme deity. However, the idea did not catch on outside the royal family, and the religion died with Akhenaten.

The first monotheistic religion to last was probably Judaism, originating in the Middle East about 4000 years ago. The Jewish belief in one god distinguished the Hebrews from all other people around them, and it remains basic to the faith today. Christianity and Islam have very strong roots in Jewish traditions, including the belief in one god. Another early religion with close ties to Judaism was Zoroastrianism, which recognized Ahura Mazda as a supreme deity engaged in a cosmic conflict with a destructive spirit, Angra Mainyu. Zoroastrianism was the religion of the Ancient Persians and several of the states that rose from its remains.

The new religion was spread by Jesus' disciples, twelve men who followed him, but the man most responsible for the rapid growth of Christianity was **Paul**, a missionary who appealed to Greeks and Romans. Paul was Jewish, but he had been born in a Greek city and was familiar with the Greco-Roman culture, so he put basic Christian beliefs in terms that Greeks and Romans could understand. He preached in Greece, Italy, Anatolia, and other areas around the eastern Mediterranean shores. Paul's emphasis on Christianity as a universal religion was largely responsible for the fact that by the 4th century C.E., about 10 percent of the residents of the Roman Empire were Christian. Although early Christians were persecuted, the Emperor Constantine issued the Edict of Milan in 313, which announced the official toleration of Christianity as a faith. Constantine became a Christian himself (probably on his deathbed), and thereafter all emperors in the East and West (except one) were Christians. In 381, the emperor Theodosius made Christianity the official religion of Rome, too late to serve as a new "glue" for the crumbling empire, but in time to preserve Christianity as a faith that would help to organize the chaos when political power failed.

HINDUISM

Although Hinduism is the world's third largest religion today, most of its 800 million adherents live in India. Its historical roots are grounded in the caste system and reflect the cultural development of the Indian subcontinent, making it today's largest ethnic religion. Hinduism evolved over thousands of years, blending the early religions of the Aryans and Dravidians. After Buddhism challenged the inequality endorsed by the earlier religions, Hinduism emerged during the classical era with revisions that increased its appeal to ordinary Indians, but still very much tied to Indian society and culture.

Most eastern religions, including Hinduism, emphasize a universal spirit that is responsible for what occurs in the universe that encompasses humankind. The spirit is disembodied but all pervasive, and all human souls, each called an **atman,** are actually pieces of the spirit that are trapped in physical bodies.

The soul's greatest desire is to reunite with the universal spirit, an opportunity that it has whenever a person dies. Each person has a **karma**, or a destiny that has been shaped by years of cause and effect, that is outwardly revealed by an individual's caste, or station in life. Attached to that karma is **dharma,** or a set of duties that the individual must fulfill. If a person has fulfilled his or her dharma, the atman will be reincarnated in the next life as a person of a higher caste. Members of the Brahmin caste, then, in the original Aryan religion, had attained their status through many reincarnations. Ultimately, the higher castes have the opportunity to attain **moksha**, or reunion with the universal spirit, a rare, but highly prized goal. In modern India, castes are now illegal, so the religion has been modified over time, but it is this basic entanglement between spiritual attainment and social status that Buddhism was most critical of in its early days.

Hindu beliefs allow for many different forms that the universal spirit (Brahman) may take, including almost any of the pantheon of Hindu gods. It is simplistic to say that Hinduism is polytheistic because all the gods are actually part of the universal spirit. Historically, the religion almost certainly incorporated local gods into the mainstream beliefs. The two supreme deities are **Vishnu**, the preserver, and **Shiva**, the destroyer. They are opposites, and yet each is too complex to be summed up in those basic descriptions. Different aspects of Indian gods are usually represented in sculpture or painting by the presence of multiple arms and **mudras**, or hand signals, that communicate with Hindu believers.

The doctrines of Hinduism stem from the *Vedas*, the epic poems sung by ancient priests that were eventually written down. The most significant is the *Rig Veda* that deals with deities (Indra and Varuna) and their relationships with humans. Central Hindu beliefs may also be found in the *Mahabharata*, the world's longest poem, and the *Ramayana*, a poem that demonstrates the fulfillment of dharma, particularly as it relates to husband and wife relationships. Probably the single best known story is the *Bhagavad-Gita,* a segment of the *Mahabharata* about the warrior Arjuna, who strove to treat other human beings well, while fulfilling his dharma. All of the poems provide moral guidelines for Hindus.

BUDDHISM

As discussed in Chapter Three, Buddhism started in the Ganges River valley area with Siddhartha Gautama, a member of the kshatrya caste who abandoned his privileged life to seek the meaning of life. The enlightenment that he experienced while meditating under a bodhi tree in a deer field became the heart of the religion, although it took many forms as it diffused to other parts of Asia. The Buddha ("Enlightened One") taught that everyone, regardless of caste, could attain **nirvana**, or union with the universal spirit, which offers release from human suffering. Nirvana is the rough equivalent to moksha in Hinduism, but moksha could only be achieved by the upper classes, not the people of ordinary castes. The Buddha also taught that nirvana can be reached through an understanding of the **Four Noble Truths** and the **Eightfold Path**, not through reincarnations from one caste to another. The Four Noble Truths are:

1) All of life is suffering.

2) All suffering is caused by desire for things that ultimately won't fulfill us.

3) Desire can only be overcome by ending all desire.

4) Desire can only be ended by following the Eightfold Path.

ORIGINAL DOCUMENTS; THE *BHAGAVAD-GITA*

The *Bhagavad-Gita* is a segment from the longest epic poem in the world, the *Mahabharata*. Just before the warrior Arjuna must go to battle against his cousins, his charioteer, the god Krishna in disguise, reveals to him the nature of the human soul (atman) and the cycle of rebirth:

"Our bodies are known to end,
but the embodied Self is enduring,
indestructible, and immeasurable;
therefore, Arjuna, fight the battle!
He who thinks this Self a killer
and he who thinks it killed,
both fail to understand;
it does not kill, nor is it killed.
It is not born,
it does not die...
it is enduring, all pervasive,
fixed, immobile, and timeless...
The self embodied in the
body of every being is indestructible;
you have no cause to grieve for all these creatures, Arjuna!"

Reference: Barbara Stoler Miller, *The Bhagavad Gita: Krishna's Counsel in Time of War.* New York: Bantam, 1986.

The Eightfold Path is composed of eight steps that must be mastered one at a time, and they all involve "right" thinking and acting: right knowledge, right purpose, right speech, right action, right living, right effort, right mindfulness, and right meditation. By following the Eightfold Path, anyone can attain nirvana. Buddhism has a broad appeal since its message is that through self-discipline, anyone can achieve satisfaction in life.

Buddhism survived through the sponsorship of the great king Ashoka, and it spread rapidly along the trade routes that became so active during the classical era. As it spread it intermingled with native religions along the way and developed many variations, including these major divisions:

- **Theravada** (Hinayana) – This division is the stricter version of the faith, with "Theravada" literally meaning "the narrower vehicle." Theravada Buddhism emphasizes the monastic life for both men and women, and strictly adheres to the steps that must be taken on the Eightfold Path. It claims to be the pure form of the Buddha's teaching, and does not believe that the Enlightened One was anything other than a mortal man. This branch spread mainly to Southeast Asia, although it always has remained relatively small.

- **Mahayana** – This "great vehicle" division grew to encompass most Buddhists, and took many variations. Mahayana Buddhists believe that Siddhartha Gautama took the initial steps toward defining the religion, and that other Buddhas appeared after him. A concept that came to be accepted was a **boddhisatva,** a person who had taken the Eightfold Path and reached perfection, but had delayed entering nirvana in order to help others along the way. Boddhisatvas serve as examples of inspiration that often appear in Buddhist temples beside the image of the Buddha. Mahayana Buddhists began to worship Buddha as a god, and erected stupas (mounds that symbolize the universe) over relics of Siddhartha in temple courtyards. This version of Buddhism is much more accepting of different life styles and paths to nirvana, and as it traveled to other lands, it often absorbed concepts from native religions.

CONFUCIANISM

Confucius (Kung Fu-tzu) lived in the late Zhou Era during the Warring States period. He was a middle-level bureaucrat in the Chinese government whose wisdoms became more celebrated after his death than they were while he was still alive. He did not leave any writings, but his followers compiled his teachings into *The Analects* after his death. Confucius built on earlier Chinese traditions, including the mandate of heaven and the **yin-yang** principle of opposite forces in harmony. Most importantly, Confucius based his philosophy on the model of the Chinese family. He was most concerned with the chaos of the times he lived in (551-479 B.C.E.), and his philosophy envisions an ideal society of harmony and order that contrasted greatly with the reality around him.

Confucianism rests on the principle of **reciprocity**, or the notion that people give and take equally within the context of five basic relationships of society:

- parent and child

- sovereign and minister

- husband and wife

- older and younger brother

- friend and friend

The first four relationships are hierarchical or unequal, but a natural part of society, according to Confucius. Superior rank (parent, sovereign, husband, older brother) does not mean that behavior is unchecked. Just as the mandate of heaven required the emperor to be responsible to his people, Confucius reminded those in superior positions of their duties regarding their inferiors. For those in subordinate positions, their duty is to obey and support their superiors. If everyone within these five relationships behaves as he should, society would be ideally harmonious, and such political and social turmoil as occurred during the Warring States Period, could never happen again. Confucian teachings rest on three essential values:

- **Xiao** – Filial piety is the devotion of the individual to family and the strong ties that hold families together. Xiao obliges children to respect their parents and obey family elders, look after their welfare, support them in old age, and remember them as revered ancestors after their deaths.

- **Ren** – Confucius believed that the five basic relations should be characterized by ren, or kindness and benevolence. Outward behavior that reflects ren includes courtesy, respect, diligence and loyalty. Confucius believed that the Chinese government desperately needed ren in its relationships with its subjects and other states.

- **Li** – A sense of propriety requires people to treat one another according to convention, and li puts emphasis on orderly rituals that demonstrate respect and reciprocity in relationships.

Confucian principles were reinforced after his death by his disciples, and many important poets expanded the philosophy, including Mencius and Xunzi, who established different interpretations of it in the 3rd and 2nd centuries B.C.E.

Because Confucianism lays the foundation for an orderly society, it is a "belief system" in that it touches on a broad range of human behaviors, serving as an overall guide that integrates many interrelated values and customs. It is usually seen as a philosophy because it emphasizes human societal relationships, and although it does not refute the existence of gods or "the heavens," Confucianism clearly puts people in control of their own behavior.

ORIGINAL DOCUMENTS: *THE ANALECTS* ON THE "GENTLEMAN"

Confucius idealized the "gentleman" (or noble man) as the model for all human behavior. The gentleman's behavior reflects the values of xiao, ren, and li, and he operates comfortably within the context of the five reciprocal relationships of humankind.

The following excerpts from *The Analects,* the classic compilation of Confucian beliefs and sayings, describe the gentleman:

"The gentleman first practices what he preaches and then preaches what he practices." (Vol II:13)

"The gentleman understands what is right; the inferior man understands what is profitable." (Vol IV:16)

"The gentleman makes demands on himself; the inferior man makes demands on others." (Vol XV:20)

Reference: Sources of Chinese Tradition, W. Theodore de Bary, ed. New York: Columbia University Press, 1960.

DAOISM

Unlike Confucianism that encourages people to become active citizens, **Daoism** encourages them to retreat from society and develop a reflective and introspective consciousness. Dao is the "way" of nature, or a force that is not necessarily good or bad, but is inevitable. Some works describe it as the original force of the cosmos, and others see it as a passive force that does nothing, yet accomplishes everything. Dao has often been compared to water, which even though it appears to be soft and compliant, still has the power to erode mountains. Since the Dao is inevitable, human beings must learn to live in harmony with it, which means the path of least resistance. Governments under the control of ambitious men try to defy nature, and as a result, they end in ruin. Human striving has brought about the chaos in the world because people have not accepted the Dao. A chief value of Daoism is "wuwei" – disengagement from the affairs of the world, and the ability to live simply, and in harmony with nature.

According to Chinese tradition, the founder of Daoism was **Laozi**, who lived during the 6th century. Although he wrote mainly about withdrawal from the world, he did give some advice to Chinese rulers. He warned them not to enjoy war and its spoils or to overindulge when the people were hungry. He believed that happy kingdoms resulted from wise rule, but he disagreed with Confucius on the need for a strong, centralized state. Instead, he emphasized the wise man's individual search for the meanings of life through following the Dao.

As the classical era ended, Confucianism and Daoism were well entrenched in Chinese society and had spread to Southeast Asia and the Korean Peninsula, but they were beginning to collide with the steady diffusion of the universal religions along the trade routes. Christianity spread into the western areas of China, but established a firmer foothold in the remote areas north of the Mediterranean Sea. Buddhism, however, slowly but surely picked up followers in east and central Asia, and soon challenged the foothold that Confucian scholars had established during the Han Dynasty. Only one of the world's great religions – Islam – had not made an appearance yet, but all of that changed during the 7th century as the new faith rapidly grew.

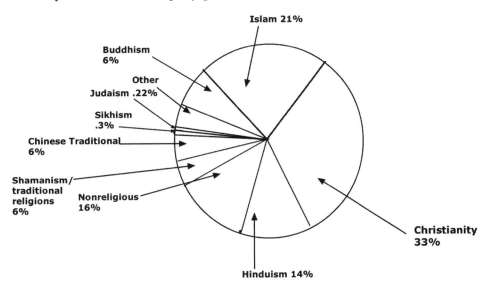

Major Religions of Today's World as a Percentage of World Population. Although there are many different religions in the world, most people that identify themselves as religious adhere to the few religions identified on the chart. 60% of the world's population identifies with one of the three universalizing religions: Christianity, Islam, or Buddhism. The largest single ethnic religion is Hinduism, with 14% of the world's population, mostly located on the Indian subcontinent.

Note: Percentages do not add up to 100% due to rounding up for all categories.

CONCEPTS AND IDENTIFICATIONS

Abraham
The Analects
atman
Bhagavad-Gita
boddhisatva
Dao, Daoism
dharma
diaspora
Eightfold Path
ethnic religions
Four Noble Truths
Hebrew Bible
Hinduism
Jesus of Nazareth
Judaism
karma
Laozi
*Mahabharat*a
moksha
monotheism
mudras
nirvana
Paul
polytheism
Ramayana
reciprocity (principle of)
Rig Veda
Shiva
universalizing religions
Vedas
Vishnu
xiao, ren, li
yin-yang

UNIT ONE QUESTIONS

Multiple-Choice Questions:

1. Most of the earliest civilizations developed in

   a) areas around the Mediterranean Sea
   b) inland areas in moderate climates
   c) areas with abundant rainfall
   d) the Western Hemisphere
   e) river valleys in warm, dry climates

2. Most experts believe that agriculture first originated in

   a) the Middle East and then spread by cultural diffusion to many
      other areas of the world
   b) the Andes Mountain area and China about the same time
   c) China and then spread by cultural diffusion to many other areas
      around the world
   d) the Middle East but also began later as independent invention in
      many other areas of the world
   e) several areas in both the Western and Eastern Hemispheres about
      the same time

3. Which of the following economic activities is most likely to produce a
   surplus?

   a) hunting and gathering
   b) shifting cultivation
   c) sedentary agriculture
   d) pastoral nomadism
   e) horticulture

4. One of the earliest cultural hearths in the Americas was developed by
   the

   a) Harappans
   b) Olmec
   c) Akkadians
   d) Maya
   e) Hittites

5. One common effect of the process of agricultural settlements developing into civilizations was

    a) the rulers came to be seen as gods
    b) the religions became more centered on spirits and nature
    c) a growing nostalgia for the nomadic lifestyle
    d) the people generally didn't have to work as hard as nomads did
    e) the status of women fell

6. Which of the following is true of both Ancient Egypt and Ancient Mesopotamia?

    a) Both were politically organized into city-states.
    b) Both had polytheistic religions.
    c) Neither had a written language.
    d) Both had to cope with very rainy climates.
    e) Neither had written law codes.

"I have not blasphemed a god,
  I have not robbed the poor.
  I have not done what the god abhors,
  I have not maligned a servant to his master.
  I have not caused pain,
  I have not caused tears…"

7. The above is an excerpt from a confession that Egyptians gave to

    a) the pharaoh before being sentenced to death
    b) the priest before being sacrificed to the gods
    c) the king of the underworld after death
    d) spouses during wedding ceremonies
    e) the river gods before the flooding season

8. The best single explanation for why so little is known about the Indus River Valley people is that

a) they had no written language
b) their civilization was less developed than that of the Egyptians and Mesopotamians.
c) most of their artifacts were destroyed by invaders
d) inscriptions on artifacts are too brief to allow the interpretation of their language
e) their sites are more difficult to excavate than those of most other ancient peoples

9. One of the most important political legacies of the Zhou Dynasty in Ancient China is

a) a written law code
b) the establishment of a theocracy
c) the tradition of having two rulers instead of one
d) participation by citizens in the decision-making process
e) the mandate of heaven

10. Which of the earliest civilizations generally differed from the others in its emphasis on the supreme importance of the family, life on earth rather than life after death, and learning and literacy?

a) China
b) Egypt
c) Mesopotamia
d) Mycenae
e) Indus Valley

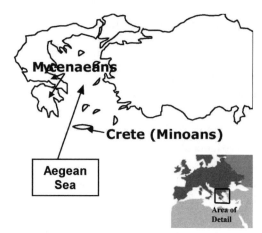

11. The cultural hearth pictured above is geographically different from most others in the Eastern Hemisphere because it is NOT

    a) next to an ocean
    b) centralized in one place
    c) in a river valley
    d) in a warm climate
    e) in an area with a great deal of rainfall

12. Which of the following classical civilizations was composed of city-states?

    a) Greece
    b) Rome
    c) Mauryan India
    d) Gupta India
    e) Han China

13. Which of the following civilizations is mismatched with an accomplishment?

    a) Phoenicia/alphabet based on sounds
    b) Greece/democratic government
    c) Rome/building of aqueducts
    d) Gupta India/Hellenistic synthesis
    e) Han China/bureaucracy based on merit

14. Which of the following is true of both Athens and Rome?

  a) Neither valued philosophy or art.
  b) Neither were patriarchies.
  c) Neither made use of slave labor.
  d) Both were monotheistic.
  e) Both had strong military organizations.

15. "The Great King, King of Kings, King in _____, King of countries" were ways of addressing the ruler of

  a) Greece
  b) the Roman Republic
  c) the Roman Empire
  d) Persia
  e) Mauryan India

16. One difference between Rome and Han China is that

  a) high government positions were more likely to be based on scholarly accomplishments in China
  b) engineering accomplishments were more significant in China
  c) religious leaders were more likely to have political power in Rome
  d) Rome had more trouble guarding its borders than China did
  e) Rome experienced more problems with free peasants clashing with wealthy aristocrats

17. Which of the following is often seen as an important accomplishment of Ashoka?

  a) He unified India into a long-lasting political dynasty.
  b) He probably kept Buddhism from dying out.
  c) He promoted the spread of Hinduism to Southeast and East Asia.
  d) He built a great Indian navy.
  e) He forged an important alliance with the Roman Emperor.

18. In comparison to the Mauryan Dynasty, the Gupta Dynasty

    a) controlled much more territory on the Indian subcontinent
    b) built a more complex government bureaucracy
    c) rose from the same powerful area in northern India
    d) did not practice as much "theatre state"
    e) did not practice Hinduism

19. The most significant common reason for both the collapse of early civilizations around 1200 B.C.E. and the classical civilizations in the years before 600 C.E. was probably

    a) a problem of interdependence
    b) attack by nomadic groups
    c) overuse of natural resources
    d) a serious climate change
    e) the growing incidence of crime and corruption

20. A technological invention used to maneuver the waters of the Indian Ocean was the

    a) square sail
    b) trireme
    c) large-hulled boat
    d) sextant
    e) lateen sail

21. Although much about them is mysterious, the clay soldiers pictured above were probably created to

    a) demonstrate Chinese artistic abilities
    b) frighten simple nomadic groups from entering Chinese borders
    c) symbolize the power of Shi Huangdi
    d) symbolically protect commerce on the Silk Road
    e) protect the tombs of early Confucian scholars

22. The most important reason that the Chinese civilization did not lose its identity after the fall of the Han Dynasty was

    a) the rapid rise of another equally powerful dynasty
    b) a shared belief in Confucianism
    c) the relative weakness of nomadic groups that surrounded Chinese borders
    d) the leadership of Shi Huangdi
    e) its relatively small geographical size

23. Which of the following is NOT a concept central to Buddhism?

   a) the Four Noble Truths
   b) atman
   c) the Eightfold Path
   d) nirvana
   e) the importance of meditation

24. Which of the following belief systems originated on the Indian subcontinent?

      I. Buddhism
      II. Hinduism
      III. Confucianism
      IV. Daoism

   a) I and II only
   b) II only
   c) II and III only
   d) II, III, and IV only
   e) IV only

25. Which of the following was a universalizing religion of the era before 600 C.E.?

   a) Hinduism
   b) Judaism
   c) Daoism
   d) Christianity
   e) Confucianism

Free-Response Questions:

For all essays, be sure that you have a relevant thesis that is supported by historical evidence.

Document-Based Question: (suggested reading time – 10 minutes; writing time – 40 minutes)

For the DBQ, be sure that you

- **Use all of the documents**

- **Use evidence from the documents to support your thesis**

- **Analyze the documents by grouping them in at least two or three appropriate ways**

- **Consider the source of the document and analyze the author's point of view**

- **Explain the need for at least one additional document**

1. Using the documents, analyze the tensions between nomadic and sedentary people during the period before 600 C.E. Identify one additional type of document and explain briefly how it would help your analysis.

Document 1

"His body was rough; he had long hair like a woman's; it waved like the hair of Nisaba, the goddess of corn. His body was covered with matted hair like Samuqan's, the god of cattle. He was innocent of mankind; he knew nothing of cultivated land….

With awe in his heart he spoke to his father: 'Father, there is a man, unlike any other, who comes down from the hills. He is the strongest in the world, he is like an immortal from heaven. He ranges over the hills with wild beasts and eats grass; he ranges through your land and comes down to the wells. I am afraid and dare not go near him. He fills in the pits which I dig and tears up my traps set for the game; he helps the beasts to escape and now they slip through my fingers.'"

> A view of Enkidu,
> in *The Epic of Gilgamesh*,
> early Mesopotamia

Document 2

"And we have not forgotten to provide for our weary spirits many relaxations from toil; we have regular games and sacrifices throughout the year; our homes are beautiful and elegant; and the delight which we daily feel in all these things helps to banish melancholy. Because of the greatness of our city the fruits of the whole earth flow in upon us; so that we enjoy the goods of other countries as freely as of our own."

> Thucydides, The Funeral Oration of
> Pericles, 431 B.C.E.

Document 3

"As early as the time of Emperors Yao and Shun and before, we hear of these people, known as Mountain Barbarians...living in the region of the northern barbarians and wandering from place to place pasturing their animals...They have no writing, and even promises and agreements are only verbal. The little boys start out by learning to ride sheep and shoot birds and rats with a bow and arrow, and when they get a little older they shoot foxes and hares, which are used for food. Thus all the young men are able to use a bow and act as armed cavalry in time of war...in periods of crisis they take up arms and go off on plundering and marauding expeditions. This seems to be their inborn nature."

Chinese historian Sima Qian
(ca. 145-90 C.E.)

Document 4

"Certain of the Han border officials...imposed upon and insulted the Wise King of the Right, and as a result he...engaged in a skirmish with the Han officials, thus violating the pact between the rulers of our two nations and rupturing the bonds of brotherhood that joined us...I have punished the Wise King of the Right by sending him west [where] he has succeeded in wiping out the Yuezhi, slaughtering or forcing to submission every member of the tribe...All the people who live by drawing the bow are now united into one family and the entire region of the north is at peace...Thus I wish now to lay down my weapons, rest my soldiers, and turn my horses to pasture; to...restore our old pact, that the peoples of the border may have peace such as they enjoyed in former times..."

Shanyu, chieftain of the Xiongnu
people of Central Asia, 2nd Century

Document 5

"We must awaken again the ancient Roman spirit, fight our own battles, carry on nothing in common with the barbarians, drive them from every official position as well as from the senate...These barbarians, previous useful servants of our house, now intend to rule our nation!"

Synesius, 4th century Roman

Document 6

"The people of the Huns...are quite abnormally savage...when they join battle they advance in packs, uttering their various war cries... None of them ploughs or even touches a plow-handle. They have no fixed abode, no home or law or settled manner of life..."

Ammianus Marcellus, 4th century
Roman historian

Document 7

"if you want to accomplish something and make a name for yourself, destroy everything that others have built and massacre everyone that you have conquered; for you are not better able to rebuild monuments than those constructed by your predecessors and there is no more noble accomplishment for you to make your name.

Advice from the mother of a
"barbarian king," 7th century

Change Over Time Essay (suggested writing time - 40 minutes)

2. Analyze the cultural and political changes and continuities in ONE of these civilizations during the early classical era from 1000 to 1 B.C.E.

- Rome

- China

Comparative Essay (suggested writing time - 40 minutes)

3. Compare and contrast the reasons for and the outcomes of the fall of TWO of the following classical civilizations:

- The Roman Empire

- Han China

- Gupta India

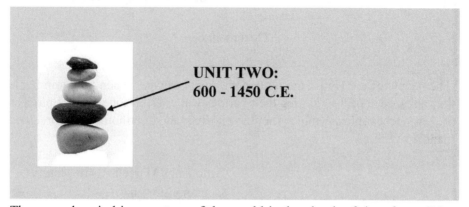

UNIT TWO:
600 - 1450 C.E.

The second period in our story of the world is the chunk of time from 600 to 1450 C.E., the **"post-classical" era.** The map of the world in 600 had changed greatly since the height of the classical era, with all the large empires split into smaller, often quarrelsome political units. Various Germanic tribes had settled into the area of the Western Roman Empire, and generally had little contact with one another except for conflicts with near neighbors. The Indian sub-continent had returned to its regional political factionalism, but Hinduism and the intricate web of jati gave continuing structure to Indian society. In 600 C.E. China had been through almost 400 years of political chaos after the fall of the Han Dynasty in the early 3rd century C.E., but was on the verge of political centralization made possible by the unifying influences of Confucianism and Daoism. This post classical era saw the emergence of important new civilizations, the revival and expansion of some old civilizations, the peak of influence of nomadic groups, the importance of belief systems as unifying forces for societies, and increasing interconnections among the world's people through an intricate network of trade.

Unit Two is divided into four chapters based on region:

- Chapter 5 focuses on the Islamic world, a vast region shaped by religious conquest that illustrates the importance of belief systems as unifying forces during this period.

- Chapter 6 follows the changes in Europe after the fall of the Western Roman Empire, including the rise of important branches of Christianity in the area.

- Chapter 7 revisits the Americas where two great empires emerged late in the era to unify Mesoamerica and the Andes Mountains area.

- Chapter 8 traces important developments in central and east Asia, including the rise of the Mongols, who formed the largest empire in all of world history.

- Chapter 9 investigates the tropical areas of the Eastern Hemisphere, including Sub-Saharan Africa, India, and Southeast Asia.

Chunking historical analysis by regions is necessary in order to keep the changes in the world's story manageable, but it is important to see important themes that run through the time period, especially as they build on the Foundations Period and create a bridge to the period that follows. Before we get to the unifying themes, let's think about what did NOT happen during the era:

1) **Eastern and Western Hemispheres were not joined.** Trade networks intensified during this era, but no sustained contact between the hemispheres occurred. The Americas were developing in isolation from the connected realms of Asia, Europe, and Africa. Other areas of the world were also developing on their own, including Australia and Polynesia.

2) **Innovations were not numerous, although technology expanded.** Expansion of technology was more characteristic than innovation, although print technology was invented in east Asia, as well as explosive powder. Previous technologies, such as camel saddles, stirrups, silk-making techniques, and steel plows, diffused far beyond the origins of innovation.

3) **No political form became dominant.** During the classical era, empire was the dominant political form. Empires in this era were smaller, and many other organizations emerged, such as kingdoms, caliphates, and khanates, so that no single form is associated with overall political organizations of the era.

4) **Environmental changes were not as great as in other eras.** More areas became agricultural, but there was no massive transformation of areas from their natural environment such as those that occurred during the classical era. For example, in earlier times, soil had been depleted of its nutrients in most areas of the Roman Empire, a factor that contributed to the decline of the civilization.

5) **Most societies remained patriarchies with clear social distinctions.** During this era we see few changes in gender relations, although in some areas, inequality between the sexes actually grew. Slavery remained characteristic of most social systems, although it did decline in some areas. Status and wealth were still based primarily on land ownership, and disputes over land distribution among classes remained problematic.

THE BIG PICTURE:
600-1450 C.E.

Three themes run through the era from 600 to 1450 C.E. that make it distinct from other eras:

1) **Belief systems were unifying forces for societies .** This period saw the rise of another great universalizing religion – Islam. Like Christianity and Buddhism, Islam spread from its origins to many different lands to be embraced by people with very different backgrounds. Like Christianity and Buddhism, Islam was a missionary religion, deliberately spread by its adherents. Buddhism became a very important force in China during this era, and made its way to Korea, Japan, and Southeast Asia. Christianity became an important organizing force in most parts of Europe.

2) **Civilization spread to many parts of the globe.** Civilization spread to Sub-Saharan Africa, northern and western Europe, and Japan. The zones of civilization spread in the Americas as well, and some important civilizations appeared in Southeast Asia. More nomads came into contact with civilization centers, and the influence of nomadic groups peaked.

3) **Trade and communications networks increased the interdependence of numerous societies**. Technologies spread from their origins, and many more cultural exchanges took place. Virtually all water and land trade routes grew more complex, bringing more goods to more people, but the spread of disease accelerated as well, with the appearance of the bubonic plague as an international epidemic in the 14th century.

Despite the spread of civilization to new areas, the influence of the classical civilizations lived on during this period. Even though political lines were re-configured and governing styles changed, the Middle East, China, India, and the Eastern Roman Empire remained quite powerful. The greatest cities of the world were in these areas, and the people of the new areas imitated the culture and social structures established in the older civilizations during the classical era. However, by the time the era ended in 1450, the world was already beginning to change as Europeans prepared to set sail on the Atlantic Ocean, largely because they were emboldened by the accomplishments of their ancestors that lived between 600 and 1450.

CHAPTER FIVE:
THE ISLAMIC WORLD

Islam is the most rapidly growing religion in the world today, and second only to Christianity in the number of people that identify with the faith. Like Christianity, its beginnings may be traced to the teachings of one man, but unlike Christianity's founder, Jesus of Nazareth, Islam's founder, Muhammad, has never been seen by Muslims as anything other than human. Islam originated in the Middle East, as did Judaism and Christianity, but in a much more remote area, the Arabian Peninsula. It was destined to become a universalizing religion, partly because its early adherents deliberately spread the new faith, but also because its principles appealed broadly to people from many different cultural backgrounds. Another important factor in the amazing early growth of the religion is its appearance on the world stage at a time when religion was beginning to play an important role as a unifying cultural and economic force in Eurasia. The post-classical era was characterized by political fragmentation, and by 600 C.E. many people had much stronger feelings about religion or philosophy than they did toward their governments. Within 150 years after its founding in 622 B.C.E., Islam had spread throughout southwest Asia into Europe and northern Africa, and its beliefs drove a remarkable political, military, and economic organization that greatly altered the map of the world and made the era 600-1450 C.E. quite different from the preceding Foundations period.

THE ORIGINS OF ISLAM

The name given to a large part of the Arabian Peninsula, the "Empty Quarter", tells us a great deal about the physical geography of the place where Islam originated. Most of the area is uninhabitable desert that stretches mile after mile with no respite. Around the fringes of the desert are scrub zones, where nomadic people had eked out a living herding camels and goats over the centuries. Although the people of this area are collectively called **Bedouins**, they were organized into kinship-based tribes and clans that often sparred with one another over scarce natural resources. Several trading towns, such as Medina and Mecca, rose in the regions close to the Red Sea, which served as organizational points for camel caravans making the long trek both ways across the desert, with destination points that served as links for the great trade networks of the day.

The struggle for existence in Arabia's harsh climate meant that survival often depended on strong ties among family members. To be cut off from family through expulsion literally resulted in death. The use of watering places and grazing lands was regulated by clan councils, and they often came to blows with other clans over these rights. Wars frequently broke out because a member of a rival clan led his animals to a restricted well or pasture, and the actions of a single person usually called clan members on each side to face one another in battle. The death of a warrior of one clan required that revenge be taken on his killer's clans, and as a result, constant infighting characterized the groups, making it almost impossible to unite under any one political leader.

Mecca had been founded by the Umayyad clan of the Quraysh Bedouin tribe, and members of the clan dominated its politics and commercial economy. The town was the largest of the trade centers along the Red Sea, partly because it was also a well established religious center, with shrines to various spirits and gods visited by many pilgrims each year. The most revered of its shrines was the **Ka'ba**, which held a sacred rock called the **Black Stone.** Stones often represented to desert people spirits called **jinns** that were believed to reside in natural objects of the desert. The Ka'ba also contained idols representing many gods, including one deity called Allah. Overall, Bedouin religion was a blend of **animism** (spirits residing in ordinary objects) and polytheism, with the Quraysh recognizing Allah to be a supreme deity. Mecca's history changed significantly around 570 C.E. with the birth of **Muhammad**, who was destined to be the founder of Islam.

Muhammad's Visions

Muhammad was born into a minor branch of a powerful Meccan family, but he was orphaned at the age of six, raised by a grandfather, and received very little formal education. He became a trader and business manager for Khadijah, a wealthy merchant's widow, whom he eventually married. Because Muhammad often traveled with his job, he came in contact with other clans, as well as with groups of monotheists, including Jews and Christians. He took a great interest in religion, and when he was about 40 years old, he had a religious experience that he described as a vision from Allah. Muhammad often spent time alone in prayer and meditation in a cave outside Mecca, and in his vision he was visited by the Angel Gabriel as a messenger of Allah. Other visions followed, in

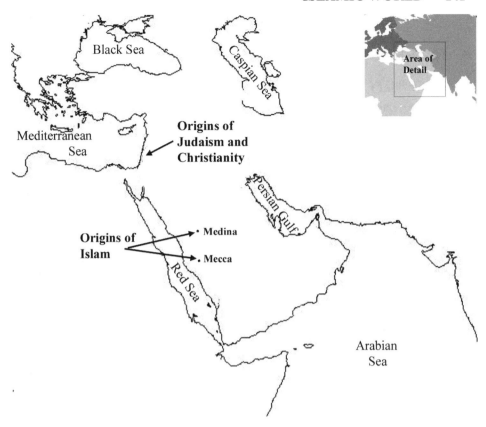

The Origins of Three Faiths. Judaism, Christianity, and Islam all originated in the Middle East, with Judaism and Christianity first rising in an area that was a crossroads of civilization. Judaism originated about 2000 B.C.E. and Christianity developed some 2000 years later. In contrast, Islam first rose in relatively remote trading cities on the Arabian Peninsula in 622 C.E. However, the historical ties among the religions are strong, with a common view of Abraham as a prophet and a belief in the existence of only one God. By the time that Islam began, Judaism and Christianity were well known monotheistic faiths, although many people on the Arabian Peninsula were polytheistic.

which Muhammad received revelations that eventually became the basic tenets of the Islamic faith, a clearly monotheistic religion that recognized Allah as the one God.

Muhammad began sharing his revelations with relatives and friends, and soon the circle of his followers grew so that prominent Umayyad political leaders and merchants felt threatened by them. They saw the new faith as dangerous to Mecca's status as a pilgrimage destination of those who came to worship the myriad of gods and spirits of the Ka'ba. Muhammad's actions set off rivalries first within the clan, and eventually with clans in other cities, so that the area was on the verge of civil war by 622. Muhammad managed to escape with his followers to Medina, where he had relatives on his mother's side, and he established himself as a leader there when he mediated quarrels between the Bedouin clans of the town. This fateful flight to Medina is known as the **hijrah,** and it serves as the founding date of the new religion. On the Muslim calendar, the year of the hijrah became the year 1, the first year of the Islamic era.

The Growth of Islam during Muhammad's Life

In Medina Muhammad proved not only to be an adept religious leader, but a political and military organizer as well. His wisdom and skill won followers who accompanied him on raids on Meccan caravans. The Quraysh responded with a series of attacks on Muhammad, who proved to be effective at defense and counter-attack, winning him even more esteem in Medina. Finally, in 628 the Quraysh signed a peace treaty with Muhammad that allowed him to visit the shrine at Ka'ba in Mecca. In 629 he triumphantly returned to Mecca with 10,000 supporters, who smashed all of the idols of the shrine, leaving the Black Stone alone to symbolize the acceptance of Allah as the one god. Muhammad gradually won over the citizens of Mecca before his death in 632. His founding of the **umma,** or Muslim community that began in Medina, now encompassed many clans that had feuded for many years, and promised to unite them under the banner of Islam.

Islamic Beliefs

After Muhammad's death, his successor, **Abu Bakr,** ordered those who had acted as secretaries for Muhammad to organize the Prophet's revelations into a book, the **Qur'an,** which achieved its final form about 650. The Qur'an, or Recitation, is believed by Muslims to be the sacred word of Allah, not just the collected sayings of Muhammad. Because of this belief, the Qur'an is different from other holy books, such as the Hebrew Bible and the Christian Bible, which were written by numerous hands over many centuries. Second in importance to the Qur'an is the **hadith,** a collection of stories about and sayings of Muhammad. Whereas the Qur'an is one, relatively compact book, the hadith exists in many documents that Muslim scholars have pored over for years, sorting out those that are authentic from those that are not. In time, Muslim societies developed **shari'a** law based on beliefs in the Qur'an and hadith. Through shari'a, Muslim beliefs developed into a way of life, complete with customs and law derived from Islamic religious principles.

From the beginning, Islam contained beliefs and practices that strongly appealed to people of many different backgrounds, and eventually led it to become a universalizing religion, along with Christianity and Buddhism. Of course, in its early years only Arabs embraced the religion, but Muhammad accepted many monotheistic beliefs of Jews and Christians, and after his death, he was hailed as the **Seal of the Prophets,** or the last of the prophets sent by God to communicate with human beings. Other prophets, including Abraham and Moses, are accepted by all three religions, and Muslims accept Jesus not as the Son of God, but as one of the prophets. Even the angel Gabriel, who is believed to have shared Allah's revelations with Muhammad, is mentioned in the holy books of all three religions.

The **Five Pillars of Faith**, the basic principles of Islam, also reflect its status as a universalizing religion that appeals to people of diverse backgrounds:

1) **The confession of faith** – To become a Muslim, a person must make this statement: "There is no God but Allah, and Muhammad is his Prophet."

2) **Prayer** – Muslims must pray five times daily, turned to face Mecca.

3) **Fasting** – For one month of the Muslim year (Ramadan), Muslims must fast from sunup to sundown, demonstrating to the umma their commitment to the religion.

4) **Alms** – The faithful must give a portion of their wealth as alms to help the needy, a requirement that also helped to build cohesion in the umma.

5) **Hajj** – Once in a lifetime, any Muslim who could possibly do it is expected to make a pilgrimage (called the hajj) to Mecca to worship Allah at the Ka'ba. Every year this gathering in Mecca is still a highly visible testament to the universal character of the religion.

Along with the Five Pillars the Qur'an and hadith established other customs, beliefs, and laws for Islamic society. Muslims were not to eat pork nor drink alcoholic beverages. A man could marry as many as four wives (as Muhammad had done), but only as long as he could provide for them. Marriage with non-Muslims was forbidden. No priesthood developed for the Muslim community, but prayer leaders directed people as they prayed in unison in the local **mosque**, or temple. Islam stressed the equality of all believers in the eyes of Allah, and encouraged the well-to-do to take care of the poor, as evidence in the Five Pillars of Faith.

MUHAMMAD'S SUCCESSORS

Muhammad died in 632 without naming a successor or establishing a procedure for choosing a new leader. On the afternoon of his death the umma leaders met to select a **caliph**, or a political and religious successor to Muhammad. One of the main candidates, Ali, the cousin and son-in-law to Muhammad, was passed over in favor of **Abu Bakr**, one of Muhammad's earliest followers and closest friends.   Under Abu Bakr, Muslim military commanders raided into areas north of Arabia as far as present-day Iraq and Syria and eastward into Egypt. These raids revealed the vulnerabilities of the post-classical Byzantine and Sassanid Empires, remnants of the greater Roman and Persian empires from earlier days.

EXAMINING THE EVIDENCE: THE QUR'AN ON MUHAMMAD'S NIGHT JOURNEY

The 17th Sura [Chapter] of the Muslim Qur'an begins with the following deceptively simple verse: "Glory to Him who took His votary [servant] to a wide and open land from the Sacred Mosque (at Mecca) to the distant Mosque whose precincts We have blessed, that We may show him some of our signs." This verse is the basis for one of the most colorful and controversial stories of Muhammad's life. Devout Muslims believe that the phrase "farthest mosque" referred to a place in Jerusalem, and that Muhammad was miraculously transported to Jerusalem where a creature, Al Burak, flew him to heaven and back again. According to Muslim belief, it was on this trip that Muhammad saw the face of Allah, making him the only human being that ever has had that experience.

To commemorate the event after Muhammad's death, the Dome of the Rock was built in 691 to enclose the sacred rock where Muhammad began his ascension to heaven. The Dome has caused controversy because the rock that Muslims believe to be the entrance to Paradise is also sacred to Jews, who believe that the rock is the spot where Abraham offered to sacrifice his son Isaac. The Dome is not far from the street that Jesus travelled on his way to his crucifixion, so Jerusalem is claimed as a special city to all three monotheistic religions, and has served as a source of contention over the years.

Source: Al-Quran, trans. by Ahmed Ali. Princeton: Princeton University Press, 1994, p. 240.

With no political powers to stop them, Arab soldiers poured into the old centers of civilization and took over their governments under the three successor caliphs to Abu Bakr. One hundred years after Muhammad's death, Islamic lands stretched from northwest Africa and Spain in the west to the Indus River to the east.

The remarkable success of the Arab conquests certainly was made easier by the weakness of the post-classical empires that the early Muslims attacked, but it may also be attributed to their religious fervor. The Arabs were passionate about their new faith, as reflected in the term **jihad** that is sometimes used to describe their warfare. Jihad loosely translates as "struggle," and originally referred to an internal effort of an individual Muslim to understand the faith and be a submissive follower. For many, that struggle applied to defeating non-Muslim areas, especially in hopes that their efforts would secure berths in "paradise," the Muslim equivalent of "heaven."

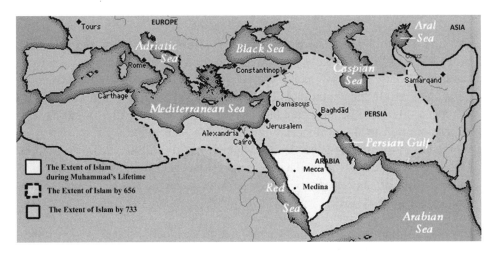

The Spread of Islam in the Hundred Years after Muhammad's Death. Under Muhammad's successors, the size of Islamic lands increased rapidly as neighboring territories were conquered by Muslim soldiers. By 733 C.E. the caliphate's control extended from Spain and northwest Africa in the west to the Indus River in the east.

Despite the success of the Muslim armies, tensions existed within the umma regarding the succession of caliphs, with the first four being negotiated among powerful Arab clans. Of these early caliphs, all but Abu Bakr were assassinated by rival clans. The fourth caliph was Ali, Muhammad's son-in-law, whose assassination in 661 set off a furious factional war. Ali's supporters argued that legitimate caliphs could only be members of Muhammad's family, and they resisted the authority of the caliph put in place by Ali's enemies. They came to be called **Shi'ites**, and they formed a significant minority within Islam that continues to the present. Shi'ites disclaimed the authority of the first three caliphs and also Ali's successor, Muawiya, who founded the **Umayyad Dynasty,** with political authority passed down through hereditary lines. The supporters of Muawiya and his successors were known as **Sunni**, the large majority of Muslims at the time, as well as in present day. Sunnis believed all of the early caliphs to be legitimate, and agreed that the Umayyads also had the right to rule. The split has never healed, and the dreams of the early caliphs that Islam would remain a united empire were undermined by feuds reminiscent of those of the early Bedouin tribes and clans.

The Umayyad Dynasty (661-750)

The first four caliphs after Muhammad's death were elected, but after the political turmoil surrounding Ali's death in 661, the **caliphates** (Islamic empires) became hereditary, although new caliphs were still formally elected. There were two Islamic dynasties: the Umayyad Dynasty (661-750) and the Abbasid Dynasty (750-1258). The caliphs were both religious and political leaders who ruled over an increasing number of non-Arab people, many of whom eventually converted to Islam.

The first of the Umayyads was Muawiya, whose election led to the split between Shi'ite and Sunni sects. He moved the capital from Medina to his native Damascus, a city in Syria much more centrally located in the growing Islamic state. As a result, the center of rule moved from the relatively remote Arabian Peninsula to an area heavily populated by non-Arabs. The office of caliph became more powerful and imperial, with a lavish palace and court that greatly contrasted to the simple lifestyles of Muhammad and his successors. Before Muawiya died, he made sure that the umma leaders accepted his son as his heir, and from then on, the hereditary succession was not seriously questioned for the remainder of the dynasty.

Under the Umayyads, the military continued to conquer east and west, but the rate of growth slowed considerably. In the east, Afghanistan came under their control, and to the west they conquered northern Africa and Christian Spain. At least part of Spain would remain Muslim until the 15th century when the combined rule of Ferdinand and Isabelle finally recaptured all of Spain for Christendom. The Muslim advance was finally halted in 733 at the battle of Tours in central France by the Frankish leader Charles Martel.

From Damascus the Umayyad caliphs built a bureaucracy to govern their vast lands. The core of the caliph's government and the army officers were Muslim Arabs who generally lived in urban centers and shared in the rewards gained from new conquests. Rural areas were populated almost exclusively by non-Arab subject people who paid taxes to support the government, unlike Arab Muslims who only were taxed for charity. The Umayyads attempted to keep interactions between Arab Muslims and subject people to a minimum, but to little avail, as the groups intermarried, and subject people converted to Islam. Non-Arab Muslim converts received few financial or social benefits, so conversions were not as common as they were to become later. They still had to pay property taxes, and often special head taxes, as well, and they were not considered to be a part of the umma. The **"People of the Book"** – Jews and Christians – were considerably better treated, although they had to pay the same taxes as other subject people. However, adherents to the two monotheistic religions were allowed to worship as they pleased, and their communities and legal systems remained intact. The name they were given ("People of the Book" or dhimmis) explains why; Muslims perceived Christianity and Judaism to be governed by Holy Books with shared beliefs and common roots with Islam.

The Umayyad exclusion of non-Arab subjects (mawali) proved to be problematic as Arab administration centers became more far flung. In the 740s rebel mawali joined forces to demand social and religious equality with Arab Muslims, and eventually overthrew the Umayyad Dynasty. All fell into chaos until the Abbasid clan took control of the caliphate in 750, when they moved the capital from troubled Damascus east to their newly built city of Baghdad, which was destined to rule over the golden age of Islamic civilization for 500 years.

The Abbasid Dynasty, 750-1258

The Abbasids claimed to be descendants of Muhammad's uncle, so at first they were more acceptable to Shi'ites than the Umayyads had been. The Abbasids also learned from the mawali rebellion that a change in policy toward non-Arabs was due. Their actions of opening the religion to all on an equal basis did a great deal toward establishing Islam as a universalizing religion that would eventually expand far beyond the Islamic domain of the 8th century. Gradually, others found their way into powerful positions in the caliphate, and gained wealth that had once only been allowed to Arabs. As a result, a cosmopolitan mix of cultures combined to create a dynamic, heterogeneous civilization. However, the Abbasids could not solve the intractable problem that the classical civilizations before them had faced: how to centrally govern a vast, multi-ethnic domain. Within a century from its founding, the Abbasid government began to lose control, first on the fringes, but eventually in lands closer to Baghdad. The After years of decay, Abbasids were finally defeated by the Mongols, but not before Islam came to serve as the cultural "glue" that held their lands together, just as Confucianism in China and Hinduism in India had provided cohesion as political power failed in the late classical age. With the exception of Spain, virtually all other areas conquered by the Muslims during the era of the caliphates have remained Muslim, even though their populations have been governed by a variety of political organizations.

Under the Abbasids the Muslim **shari'a** took shape, with religious scholars called the **ulama** interpreting the Qur'an and the hadith to create Islamic law codes. Because religion and law were intertwined, the decisions of the ulama impacted most areas of people's lives. The Abbasid government in Baghdad operated under the **vizier**, a head of government directed by the caliph, and a state council. Each of the provinces was governed by an emir, who was responsible for collecting taxes and keeping the peace. The Muslim army traditionally had been headed by the caliph (originally by Muhammad), but under the Abbasids, the commanders gained not only military power, but independent political clout as well. The army was international in composition, including slaves as soldiers, and was huge in numbers. The larger it grew, the more difficult it was for the caliph to control the commanders, further eroding his power. The caliph's authority was further undermined by the ulama, who exercised almost complete control of shari'a that defined acceptable religious, social, and political behavior of Muslims.

COMPARISONS: WANDERING HOLY MEN IN BUDDHISM, ISLAM, AND CHRISTIANITY

Wandering holy men, or mystics, have played significant roles in the development of all three universalizing religions: Buddhism, Islam, and Christianity. Despite their broad appeal, the three religions also have had adherents who believe in a direct, personal path to the true meaning of their faith. Buddhism's founder, Siddhartha Gautami, became a wandering holy man (or aesthetic) in order to reach enlightenment. Buddhist monks, particularly of the Theraveda branch, believe that a simple life devoted to meditation is the best path to nirvana. Christianity also has a place for those who wish to live monastic lives. During the Middle Ages in Europe, many religious orders, including the Dominicans and Franciscans, went from place to place doing the work of the church, devoting their lives to religious endeavors. The **Sufis,** a branch of Islam that grew quite rapidly during the Abbasid Dynasty, believed in a life devoted to seeking individual connections to divine truth. Some famous examples of Sufism were groups in Turkey called the Whirling Dirvishes. In order to reach an ecstatic connection with God, they whirled as they danced to lift their minds from everyday consciousness. Sufis organized into religious associations that helped spread Islam far into Asia and Africa.

THE GOLDEN AGE OF ISLAM

Historians like to refer to "**golden ages**" in the lives of many civilizations. If you look at the characteristics of civilizations on pages 35 and 36 (reliable surpluses, specialized occupations, distinct social classes, large cities, complex governments, long distance trade, and organized writing systems), all of these would be present during a golden age, but the term usually implies more. During a golden age, a civilization is usually quite prosperous, and they also tend to be innovative in arts, science, and literature. These characteristics are based on the principles of civilization. For example, surpluses and specialized occupations often lead to prosperity because economic activities are specialized and efficient with food supplies to support them. Innovations in arts, science, and literature require the time to focus on these endeavors, so prosperous societies with surpluses can generally afford to support scholars, artists, and technologists. During the Abbasid Dynasty, Islamic civilization experienced a "golden age" that stretched from about 800 to 1200 C.E.

Economic Activities and Social Distinctions

As with all early civilizations, the economy of Islamic domains was based on agriculture. As they conquered areas very different from their homeland, Arabs certainly encountered crops they had never seen before. As authority over their lands centralized, a well organized system of trade, exchange, and communication encouraged the sharing of new crops and farming techniques. For example, the western regions began to grow sugar cane, rice, spinach, and artichokes for the first time. The overall result was a significant increase in food supply and in turn a surplus of crops that could support the growth of cities. Cities such as Baghdad, Damascus, Jerusalem, Cairo, and Toledo had busy marketplaces where thousands of merchants and artisans sold their wares. The cities were also government and religious centers.

The Abbasid Dynasty at its height displayed imperial majesty, with caliphs living lavish life styles much more similar to a Persian "King of Kings" than to the earliest caliphs in Medina. The Abbasid age was one of great urban expansion with the magnificent city of Baghdad at its heart. The dynasty peaked at a time when world trade networks were reviving after the fall of the great classical empires, and Arabs controlled much of the trade. Their **dhows**, or sailing vessels with lateen sails, carried the goods on the Indian Ocean routes, and Muslim merchants of the Abbasid Dynasty grew wealthy. The profits from trade were used to stimulate new businesses, and the cities were filled with people who benefitted from the thriving interconnections across the Eastern Hemisphere. In the center of most Muslim cities were elaborate mosques, public baths, government buildings, and religious schools. Craftsmen were an important part of urban life as well, with many catering to the tastes of the wealthy in furniture, carpets, glassware, jewelry, and tapestries. Some formed organizations for their particular craft meant to enforce production standards and promote wages and working conditions for their members.

Much of the unskilled work of the dynasty fell to slaves, with many working as domestic servants, but others did hard labor on rural estates and government projects. Some of the most destitute were the Zanj slaves, non-Muslim east

PERSPECTIVES: GENDER ROLES IN EARLY ISLAMIC SOCIETIES

It may surprise modern day westerners that women in early Islamic societies generally had more rights than women in the areas the Muslims conquered, such as the Byzantine and Sassinid Empires. The Qur'an and Muhammad's teachings stressed the moral and ethical responsibilities of marriage and urged men to respect women. Muhammad's first wife, Khadijah, was a business owner who was one of his most devout followers. Women went to battle with men as they fought to establish the new faith in the Arabian Peninsula. Muhammad's fourth wife (and widow) actively stood up for the rights of the Umayyads, and Ali's daughter, Zainab, fought on the other side. However, in a similar pattern to that in the classical civilizations, the more refined and urbane the caliphates became, the more the status of women suffered. Restrictions on the movements of upper-class women in particular were severe by the age of the Abbasids, eventually resulting in the development of the harem, or forbidden area where an elite male's wives and concubines lived in isolation from the rest of the world. Although most followed Muhammad's example of only having four wives, elite men collected as many concubines (unofficial wives) as they could afford. The harem was guarded by eunuchs (castrated males) who offered the master no competition for his women's affections.

Africans, who did the most onerous jobs, such as draining marshlands. From the mid-9th century they were an ever-present source of social unrest.

Literary, Artistic, and Scientific Accomplishments

One unifying force within the Islamic caliphates was the widespread use of the language. It was promoted partly because by sacred belief the Qur'an could only be written in Arabic, so educated Muslims in every part of the caliphate had to be literate in Arabic. Arabs also borrowed an invention from China – paper – to share writing cheaply and easily, making the production of books possible. Probably their greatest literary art was poetry, with thousands of poems created during Islam's golden age. The poems were meant to be sung and recited aloud in Arabic. One famous poet was Jalal al-Din al-Rumi, whose mystic poetry gives us insight into the beliefs of Sufis. Arabic literature also reflects a love of storytelling, such as the compilation of folk tales into *The Thousand and One Nights.* Based on the stories told by Scheherazade, a clever young bride trying to save her own life, they tell us a great deal about elite society during the Abbasid's golden age. The tales not only describe the elaborate lifestyles of the rich in Baghdad; they also exhibit a sense of humor and a fondness for exaggeration.

The caliphs also established urban universities called **madrasas** that actively preserved and translated the writings of the ancient Greeks and Indians. Muslims recognized the importance of scientific and philosophical works from these earlier civilizations, and became particularly intrigued with the works of Aristotle. After the fall of the Western Roman Empire, knowledge of Plato, Aristotle, Ptolemy, Hippocrates, and other Greek scholars had been lost, so the concerted effort by Islamic universities to gather them together saved their works to be passed on to later civilizations, including those that rose in Europe.

Muslim art is distinct from most others because of its intricate, geometrically based format. The Qur'an strictly forbade the lifelike representation of the human figure, based on the belief that only Allah could create human life. Particularly blasphemous was any attempt to reproduce the figures of Allah or Muhammad. Some Persian art depicted Muhammad, but always with a veil over his face to represent the belief that he was the only human to ever see the face of Allah (on the Night Journey, p.144). Stricter Arabic interpretations disapproved of such Persian art. As a result the motifs of their painting, ceramics, mosaics, and inlay work were based on garlands, plants and geometric figures such as triangles, diamonds, and parallelograms. Like the Chinese, the Arabs also excelled in calligraphy in several different styles, all equally beautiful. Public buildings were often elaborately decorated with brightly colored ceramic tiles, semiprecious stone, and gold and silver filigree, particularly palaces and mosques. In the larger cities, the courtyards of the mosques were surrounded by columns and arches and were eventually enclosed by great domes. A key feature of the mosque was the **minaret,** or prayer tower, where a specially trained muezzin would call the faithful to prayer five times a day.

Arabs also built on the mathematical knowledge of ancient Hindu scholars, who had invented the concept of zero and a number system based on 10. Their "Arabic numerals" are still the ones that we use today, and these numbers allowed the development of al-jabr, or algebra. Muslim contributions to the sciences tended to be more practical than those of the classical civilizations, especially the Greeks and Indians. Arabs made advances in optical science, pharmacology, and anatomy. Arabic and Persian writers and travelers also put together an extensive collection of geographical information, including maps of Islamic domains.

MARKER EVENT: THE DEVELOPMENT OF ARABIC NUMERALS

Despite the implication of the name, Arabic numerals were an invention first devised in classical India. During Abbasid times, Arabs saw their usefulness and spread knowledge of them throughout their realm. Even though it is difficult to come up with an exact date of invention, the development of arabic numerals represents a very important marker event in world history. The Indian method is a 10-based system, with separate columns for ones, tens, hundreds, and so forth, as well as a zero sign to indicate no units in particular columns. This system is a vast improvement on older numerical systems, such as Roman numerals, because it allows for calculations not possible before, particularly of large sums in the millions and billions.

The first numerals from 1 to 9 appear on copper plates as early as 595 C.E., and a sign for zero has been found on plates as early as the 8th century. Muslims during the Abbasid age built on the Indian system to develop algebra, and to calculate distances of far away objects in the heavens, including those that form the Milky Way. Today the system of Arabic numerals is the only truly global language, readily understood across many cultures.

THE DECLINE AND FALL OF THE ABBASID CALIPHATE

Even while Islamic civilization was reaching the height of its golden age, the political power of the Abbasids was declining. As early as the mid-9th century, many parts of the vast caliphate were beginning to slip away. The caliphates were always weakened by the religious splits within their ranks, particularly those between Sunnis and Shi'ites. Shi'ites continued to deny the authority of the Umayyad caliphs and helped the Abbasids win power. Yet the Abbasids generally were no more tolerant of the Shi'ites than the Umayyads had been, and so over the years, hostility increased between Sunnis and Shi'ites. Another problem was the difficulty of holding together a highly diversified empire from one central location in Baghdad. When local administrators failed to obey orders, the caliph could not effectively respond, and when rebellions broke out, it was difficult to move armies across the great distances of the domain. Slave revolts and peasant uprisings plagued the regime, and to make matters worse, many of the later Abbasid caliphs were incompetent.

Gradually, during the 800s, most areas in Africa and Arabia broke away and proclaimed their independence, leaving the Abbasids in control of only the Middle East. Increasingly the Abbasids depended on **Seljuk Turks**, a nomadic people originally from central Asia who lived primarily on the borders of the Abbasid lands. As highly skilled horsemen, they were hired as soldiers in the Abbasid armies, and by the mid-11th century, their leaders had more political power than the caliphs. In 1055 the caliph recognized the Seljuk leader Tughril Beg as **sultan** ("chieftain"), and soon afterwards, Tughril took over Baghdad and the caliph became a figurehead, a ruler in name only. Other Turkish groups invaded Anatolia and northern India, and soon Turkish groups were quarreling with one another, leaving themselves prey to an invasion by the Mongols, who seized the Baghdad throne in 1258, destroying the last of the great Islamic caliphates and replacing it with the Mongol Il-Khan Empire. Despite the political conquest, by the 13th century Islam was so well-entrenched in such a wide variety of lands that the Mongols could only destroy the political structure, but could not weaken the faith. Instead the Il-Khan leaders themselves converted to Islam, so that we can observe "the fall and rise" of Islam, undaunted by political and military defeat.

IDENTIFICATIONS AND CONCEPTS

Abu Bakr
animism
Bedouins
Black Stone
caliph, caliphate
Five Pillars of Faith
"golden age"
hadith
hajj
harem
hijrah
jihad
jinns
Ka'ba
madrasas
minaret
mosque
Muhammad
The Night Journey

People of the Book
Qur'an
Seal of the Prophets
Seljuk Turks
shari'a
Shi'ites, Sunni
Sufis
sultan
The Thousand and One Nights
ulama
Umayyad Dynasty
umma
vizier

CHAPTER SIX:
CHRISTIAN SOCIETIES IN
EUROPE AND THE MIDDLE EAST

While Islam was spreading rapidly in regions from Spain to India, the older religion of Christianity was growing as well, with footholds in areas that overlapped with Islam. Just as Islam became the dominant religion in the lands controlled by the caliphates, Christianity came to dominate many of the areas formerly controlled by the Roman Empire. Whereas Islam successfully united its lands politically until the 9th century, no such political unification characterized the Christian lands. Instead, a patchwork of tribal kingdoms emerged in western Europe, and the Byzantine Empire rose in the lands around the eastern Mediterranean Sea. However, in this age when societies were unified by belief systems, Christianity, like Islam, provided order and organization that political leaders did not offer. By the end of the era (1450), the Byzantine Empire was on the verge of collapse under pressure from Turkish invasions, and Western Europe, though still politically divided, had laid the foundation for the central place it would occupy on the world stage for the next 500 years.

WESTERN EUROPE: AFTER THE FALL OF ROME

Historians refer to the period of western European history from 500 to 1500 C.E. as the **"Middle Ages"**, or **medieval times**. The term "middle" means that the period falls in between two others, preceded by the Roman Empire and followed by the European Renaissance. Another way of referring to the time is "The Dark Ages," which implies that the periods on either end are "light." Indeed, the metaphor is not inappropriate if you take the view that civilization is superior to simpler forms of life, such as hunting and gathering, pastoral nomadism, or simple subsistence farming (see discussion on pages 36-37). The characteristics of civilization (generation of reliable surpluses, specialized occupations, clear social class distinctions, cities, complex governments, long distance trade, and organized writing systems) were securely in place for the area during Roman times and the Renaissance. During the Middle Ages civilization was clearly suspended. However, the period is more complex than that. It is helpful to divide the era in two:

1) **The Early Middle Ages** (500-1000 C.E.) – During this era the Germanic tribes that had invaded the Roman Empire settled into various parts of Europe. Most of the inhabitants of their kingdoms were pastoral nomads or subsistence farmers, and their political leaders were tribal chieftains. Very few people could read and write, little long-distance trade took place, and settlements were mainly villages and small towns.

2) **The High Middle Ages** (1000-1500 C.E.) – About midway through the Middle Ages, signs of recovery began, accelerating especially after about 1200. Towns grew, small cities emerged, trade with other areas of the Eastern Hemisphere was established, and the social class system grew more complex with the emergence of a middle class. By the end of the era, the European Renaissance was well entrenched in Italy and was spreading into northern Europe.

The Early Middle Ages

When the Western Roman Empire fell, western Europe was left in the chaos that resulted from the collapse of the political, social, and military order formerly imposed by Rome. Continuing invasions and conflicts among the invaders left the successor states in jeopardy, and in this uncertain environment they sought and gradually built a new political and economic order. New infrastructures were built within the framework of the Christian church based in Rome, which provided a cultural unity throughout western Europe despite the lack of political centralization. Although Christianity had come too late to provide the necessary cultural glue to hold the Roman Empire together, it served that purpose during the Early Middle Ages in Europe, enabling the area to regain economic, political, social, and military organization that had been lost when Rome fell.

Political Development

In the last years of the Western Roman Empire, the Roman provinces were dismantled by the Germanic tribes, and the borders of their kingdoms changed constantly with the fortunes of war. The Roman governors were replaced by tribal chieftains, but more importantly, the Roman concept of rule by law was replaced by informal governments based on family ties and personal loyalty. The Germanic people did not identify with a state, or even a kingdom, but with an extended family that followed a particular leader. Warriors were bound to their chief through oaths of loyalty, and in return the chief gave them food, shelter, and weapons. The kingdoms were loose configurations of many such loyalty patterns that allowed little opportunity for centralized government to form.

Economically, people settled on manors, or large estates operated by leaders who provided protection for others, in exchange for free labor. Eventually, the peasants lost land claims to the "lords," so that the groundwork was laid for the development of **feudalism**, a complex system of political and military loyalties that linked lords together, and **manorialism**, an economic system in which peasants were tied to the land to supply labor to their lords.

Early Medieval Europe. After the fall of the Western Roman Empire, the Germanic tribes that had invaded the empire settled into different parts of western Europe and formed their own kingdoms. The map above shows the major kingdoms that were in place by the beginning of this period (600 C.E.) The borders of the kingdoms changed frequently as the groups invaded one another's territory, and many other smaller groups were involved in the fighting.

For a brief time in the late 8th and early 9th centuries, it looked as if one group – the **Franks** – would unite all of western Europe under one king. Even though they eventually failed, their imprint for political and economic organization was left on the entire area. The Franks managed to organize a series of Germanic kingdoms under their kings mainly through military conquest, starting with

Clovis, who was their ruler from 481 until 511. Clovis and his supporters first destroyed the last vestiges of Roman power, then imposed control over other Franks, and finally organized campaigns against neighboring Germanic peoples. By the time of his death, the Franks clearly had formed the most powerful kingdom in western Europe. Significantly, Clovis converted to Christianity, which won support for him from other Christians as well as the pope in Rome.

PERSPECTIVES: WILLIAM MANCHESTER ON THE DARK AGES

Many explanations have been given for why historians have dubbed the era from about 500 to 1000 in Europe as the "Dark Ages." Most of them center on the notion of lost civilization that was eventually regained at the end of the period. One controversial interpretation may be found in *A World Lit Only by Fire,* by historian William Manchester, who describes a time that was indeed dark:

"The Dark Ages were stark in every dimension. Famines and plague, culminating in the Black Death and its recurring pandemics, repeatedly thinned the population...It says much about the Middle Ages that in the year 1500, after a thousand years of neglect, the roads built by the Romans were still the best on the continent...Among the lost arts was bricklaying; in all of Germany, England, Holland, and Scandinavia, virtually no stone buildings, except cathedrals, were raised for ten centuries...
Surrounding them was the vast, menacing, and at places, impassable Hercynian Forest, infested by boars; by bears; by the hulking medieval wolves who lurk so fearsomely in fairy tales handed down from that time; by imaginary demons; and by very real outlaws, who flourished because they were seldom pursued..Although homicides were twice as frequent as deaths by accident...only one of every hundred murderers was ever brought to justice..."

Reference: A World Lit Only by Fire, by William Manchester. Boston: Little, Brown, 1993, pp. 5-6.

Clovis' descendants lost control of the Frankish realm to Charles Martel ("Charles the Hammer") of the **Carolingian family**, whose grandson, **Charlemagne** ("Charles the Great"), conquered most of mainland western Europe, temporarily unifying it. He ruled for half a century, and as long as he was alive, his growing kingdom paid him allegiance. One important factor in explaining the rising power of the Carolingians was the need for protection from the wave of attacks on Europe from the **Vikings,** raiders from Scandinavia, that began in 793 and continued for the next two centuries. Charlemagne kept control through military prowess, but he also insured the loyalty of those conquered by setting up an administrative system divided into counties. Each county was governed in the king's name by a powerful landholder called a count. The counts administered justice and raised armies, and Charlemagne wisely placed checks on their power by sending out royal agents called **missi dominici** (the sovereign's envoys) as the "eyes and ears" of the king to report back on any abuses of power. Charlemagne himself constantly moved around his kingdom in order to make his presence felt. In 800 the pope crowned Charlemagne "emperor," implying that he was heir to the Roman throne. Of equal importance is that the act symbolized the superior authority of the church over political leaders, even though in reality Charlemagne needed no such endorsement to maintain his empire. This distinction between religious and political leaders would lead to clashes between popes and kings throughout the Middle Ages in Europe.

After Charlemagne's death, his empire fell apart under his less talented heirs. His son, Louis the Pious, divided the empire among his three sons, who fought among themselves for supremacy. Their disputes were settled by the Treaty of Verdun, which divided western Europe along general linguistic and cultural borders which still exist today. Had Charlemagne's successors kept his empire together, the course of European history would almost certainly be quite different. Instead, Europe fragmented into smaller political units that would compete and quarrel with one another for centuries.

The model for political organization set in place by the Franks is a version of **feudalism** based on loyalties among the elite: lords, vassals, and overlords. Partly because the origins of the system were local and informal, the web of connections was incredibly complex. For example, a lord may have controlled his vassals (those that owe loyalty to him), but he in turn was a vassal to an overlord, who in turn was a vassal to a king. The authority of the king was based on these ties, which could come to cross-purposes with loyalties owed to a rival. These often contradictory loyalty ties led to conflict characterized by heavily armed knights in combat to fulfill their loyalty obligations. The European version of feudalism allowed knights (vassals) to own land usually granted to them by their lords, so they were not just a fighting force, but were also a part of the overlapping hierarchies among elites.

Economic Development

The economic system that evolved in western Europe during early medieval times was **manorialism,** which defined both economic and political obligations between lords and peasant laborers. Most people were **serfs** who lived on and were tied to self-sufficient agricultural estates (manors). Serfs received protection, administrative justice, and the right to graze their animals from the lord

ORIGINAL DOCUMENTS:
CAPITULARY ON THE MISSI

One way that Charlemagne kept order in his kingdom was by sending *missi dominici* (the sovereign's officials) to oversee the work done by the counts, or the regional administrators. In 802 Charlemagne issued the *Capitulary on the Missi,* a document that established regulations for the *missi* to enforce. The *Capitulary* was written by Charlemagne's secretaries in his name, since he was unable to read or write. The following excerpts reflect some of Charlemagne's concerns about his empire as well as an attempt to reestablish the rule of law:

"5. That no one shall presume to rob…the churches of God, or widows, or orphans, or pilgrims, for the lord emperor himself…has constituted himself their protector and defender…

7. That no one shall presume to neglect a summons to war from the lord emperor; and that no one of the Counts shall be so presumptuous as to dare to excuse any one of those who owe military service…

8. …no one shall dare to neglect to pay his dues or tax.

28. …That the counts…shall provide most carefully, as they desire the good-will of the emperor, for the *missi* who are sent out…

32. Murders, by which a multitude of the Christian people perish, we command in every way to be shunned and to be forbidden…"

Source: University of Pennsylvania Translations and Reprints. D. C. Munro, trans. Philadelphia: University of Pennsylvania, 1900, vol. 6 no.5, pp. 16-27.

of the manor, and in return they were obliged to give a portion of their products to the lord and to stay on the land. The manorial system originated in the later Roman Empire, but it strengthened during early medieval days once trade declined and Roman political protection disappeared. As a result of these developments, the manors became self-sufficient. In the early Middle Ages, trade was based on **barter**, or the exchange of goods directly. Because manors were self sustaining, trade with outsiders was limited, and money wasn't necessary. At first, the serfs' labor was difficult as they tried to use wooden plows for the heavy soils of France and Germany, but during the 9th century a better plow with an iron plate, the moldboard, made the work a little easier. Another

9th-century development was a new three-fields system, which improved productivity through a rotation of crops that involved leaving one third of the fields unplanted each year. Serfs were not slaves. They were not bought and sold, and they had ownership rights to their houses and lands as long as they honored their obligations to the lord.

The Political and Religious Power of the Roman Catholic Church

In the early 4th century the Roman emperor Constantine moved his capital from Rome to Constantinople, far to the east on the Bosporus between the Black Sea and the Mediterranean Sea. After his conversion to Christianity, church officials were recognized all over the empire, with the most important settling in Rome and Constantinople. The split in political authority between the two cities also led to a split in religious authority, with the bishops in Rome eventually called "popes" who headed the Roman Catholic Church. "Patriarchs" in Constantinople were associated with the Eastern Orthodox Church that allowed the emperor a good bit of authority in religious matters. Over the years the two branches of Christianity developed different practices, and even though the formal split did not come until the 11th century, in reality they operated independently from one another long before that. The Frankish king Clovis converted to Roman Catholicism, an event that hastened the emergence of the church as an important political and religious power in Western Europe.

Beginning in the 300's and 400's, many Roman Catholic missionaries traveled across Western Europe, converting the Germanic and Celtic people to the religion. One of the most famous was St. Patrick, who established Christian churches throughout Ireland. The conversion of Clovis was particularly important because many Germanic groups had chosen a branch of Christianity called Arianism. Catholic Christians considers the Arians heretics, so Clovis's conversion marked a partnership between Frankish kings and the Catholic Church. The church developed a hierarchical organization that gave structure to the politically fragmented groups across Western Europe, and church officials soon gained political as well as religious power.

Bishops generally directed churches in urban areas, but since Roman cities dwindled in size, the church supported monasteries in rural areas. Here Christian men and women gave up their private possessions to live simply and devote their lives to the church. Like the local priests, monks and nuns were expected to be poor, chaste, and obedient. Rules for their behavior were written by Benedict around 540, and included daily rituals of prayer, manual labor, and simple eating. **The Benedictine Rule** came to be followed by almost all Italian, English, and Frankish monks and nuns. The monasteries played an important role in providing stability during the Dark Ages. They protected refugees, operated schools, maintained libraries, and copied books. Many books had been destroyed as Rome was attacked by the Germanic tribes, but some of those that survived did so because monk-scholars carefully copied the manuscripts, saving at least a portion of the intellectual heritage of the classical civilizations.

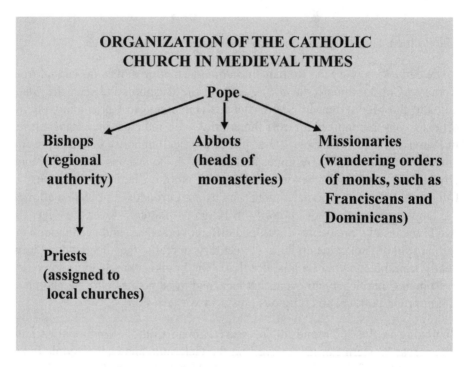

ORGANIZATION OF THE CATHOLIC CHURCH IN MEDIEVAL TIMES

Pope

Bishops (regional authority)

Abbots (heads of monasteries)

Missionaries (wandering orders of monks, such as Franciscans and Dominicans)

Priests (assigned to local churches)

The Catholic Church provided organizational "glue" for western Europe during medieval times by ensuring that its presence was felt in many ways. The pope gained authority as the head of a hierarchy that included regional and local churches, monasteries, and missionary orders. Other high officials included cardinals who appointed popes from their ranks and archbishops who supervised the bishops.

The Revival of Civilization: The High Middle Ages

By 1000 C.E. Western Europe was showing some signs of waking from its years of self-sufficiency and isolation. Gradually, agricultural techniques and technologies from eastern Europe and Asia were making some difference, particularly the moldboard plow, the three-field system, and a new horse collar that allowed horses to pull plows without choking. The use of the stirrup in warfare spread from central Asia, and better agricultural methods were promoted by the monasteries. During the 10th century, Viking raids became less serious as regional governments grew stronger and Vikings settled into European communities to intermarry with the natives. As agricultural production increased, so did the population, creating a demand for more trade, which in turn caused towns to grow. As local economies grew, political and cultural changes occurred as well.

Political Developments

By its very nature, feudalism discouraged the growth of strong central governments. The political power of the Catholic Church also countered the power of the kings. The church not only established moral boundaries for its members, but it also set **canon law,** or rules for behavior that first filled the void of political authority in the early days, but eventually meant that political authority could not develop. For example, the church had the power to **excommunicate** its members, or separate them from the church and its sacraments. Even more powerful was the **interdict,** which excommunicated all people within a ruler's realm. In this Age of Faith, that meant that all babies born could not be baptized, no marriages would be valid in the eyes of the church, and no last rites could be read to those on their deathbeds. If a ruler misbehaved, the church could put his region under an interdict in order to pressure the ruler to submit to the will of the church. As political leaders grew stronger, friction grew between kings and popes – a dynamic that worked against the development of centralized political power. Another limitation to the growth of strong central government was resistance by the nobility, who enjoyed the independence that feudalism and manorialism afforded them.

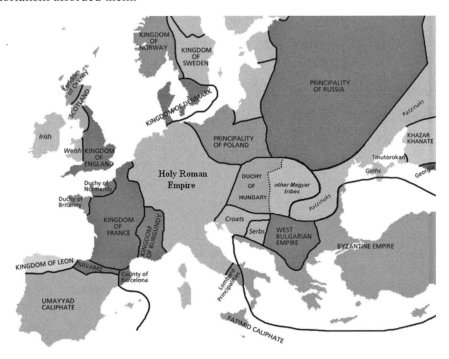

Europe about 1000 C.E. By 1000 the map of Europe shows kingdoms, principalities, duchies, and empires that form the basis for modern European countries. However, feudalism decentralized power, so that local aristocrats and church leaders also had a great deal of political power.

Because of these limitations, many areas of Europe remained feudalistic long past 1450, including the **Holy Roman Empire,** established in spirit with Charlemagne's crowning in 800, but not officially until 962, when a loose confederation of German princes named one of their own as emperor. The emperor was crowned by the pope, implying that power rested in the hands of the pope, and the princes always asserted their independence and never paid too much attention to the emperor. In most areas of eastern Europe feudalism also remained in place for many years, partly because trade and commerce grew more rapidly in the west. In England, France, Spain, and other kingdoms in the west, the power of monarchs grew into centralized governments by 1450, although not without many challenges along the way. For example, our modern concept of **limited government** (limits on the power of the ruler) is based partly on the **Magna Carta**, a document that nobles forced King John of England to sign that guaranteed rights to the nobility. Late in the 13th century, **parliaments** were created to give nobility and the clergy a voice in policymaking. Although competition for political control remained a contest among the elite (clergy, nobles, and political leaders), these struggles created the cradle that fostered the eventual growth of modern democracies.

Stronger monarchs were able to gather larger armies, so one result was some large-scale warfare during the late Middle Ages. For example, William of Normandy (the "Conqueror") was able to command a large army to invade and conquer England in 1066, when English forces clashed with Normans at the Battle of Hastings. The **Hundred Years War** during the 14th and 15th centuries between the kings of France and England was fought over territories the English king controlled in France – a great conflict between the old governing rules under feudalism and the newly emerging claims of national states.

The Impact of the Crusades

By the 11th century, Western European states were expanding in many directions: south into Spain to push back the Muslims, eastward into sparsely populated areas of Poland; and at the end of the century, into the Middle Eastern lands controlled by Muslims. Population increases fueled the expansion, as did the missionary zeal of Christians. The most dramatic moves were those made into the Middle East in a series of attacks called the **Crusades,** prompted by a request from the Byzantine emperor, Alexius I, for help in raising troops to resist Turkish incursions into his territory. In 1095 Pope Urban II called upon Christian knights to save the holy city of Jerusalem from "an accursed race" [the Turks] by undertaking a journey "for the remission of your sins, and be assured of the reward of imperishable glory in the Kingdom of Heaven." The response was immediately overwhelming, with the crowds responding, "God wills it! God wills it!" In 1096 between 50,000 and 60,000 knights from western Europe joined the Crusades, beginning a series of attacks that lasted for two centuries.

The First Crusade managed to win Jerusalem from the Turkish armies and establish a number of forts in the area around it. Although the Crusaders held Jerusalem for close to a century, the Turks reorganized under the great Muslim

PERSPECTIVES: MOTIVATIONS FOR THE CRUSADES

The Christian Crusades were phenomenal events in which thousands of European knights left their homes - with full knowledge that they probably would never return - in order to fight for a cause. This mass movement of people from one area to another is unusual enough that a good historian should ask, "How did it happen?" and "Why did they go?"

From the pope's perspective: By the late 11th century, Byzantine and Roman Christians had gone their separate ways for some time, with the pope claiming to be the supreme head of the Church, and the Byzantine emperor denying the claim. Pope Urban II almost certainly hoped that a successful Crusade would convince the Byzantine emperor to change his mind. Besides, from the pope's point of view, it was better to have the knights fighting the Turks than one another.

From the knights' perspectives: The First Crusade was undoubtedly fueled by religious fervor, especially since the pope promised forgiveness of sins for any man that died in the Crusades. For other knights, the Crusades were a chance to win glory in battle. Especially in the later Crusades, plunder was a motivation, because the lands of the Middle East were far richer than those in western Europe.

general, **Saladin**, who took it back during the 12th century. The Crusaders never succeeded in recapturing Jerusalem, and Venice turned the Fourth Crusade during the early 13th century into an attack on its commercial rivals in Constantinople. Ultimately, the Crusaders failed to accomplish their goals.

The failure of the Crusades does not alter their importance in shaping the course of history during the era from 600 to 1450. More than any other single factor, the Crusades laid the foundation for the emergence of European countries in the next era as powerful forces on their way to eventually controlling most other areas of the world. Why? Most importantly, it put them in direct contact with the oldest areas of world civilizations and made them aware of worlds they never knew existed. Those that returned brought back with them material evidence of civilization: fine silks, beautiful porcelains, exquisite carpets, perfumes, spices, and preservatives. No longer would Europeans be content to remain in their isolated, drafty castles; they had tasted the pleasures of civilization, and change was inevitable.

Economic Developments

Two cities that directly benefitted from the Crusades were Venice and Genoa in Italy. Because they were so close to the heart of the old Roman Empire, the cities of Italy never quite succumbed to the feudalistic patterns in the rest of Europe. Instead each city maintained control over the countryside around it and continued to serve as a trade center. When the Crusades began, Venice and Genoa promoted a sea route for the knights to travel to the Holy Lands, disembarking from one of the cities and arriving on the eastern end of the Mediterranean Sea. Since most European knights had little money, they often offered their services to protect the ships from pirates and internal disputes in exchange for their passage. The ships carried goods both ways across the sea, bringing woolen and cotton textiles and French wines from Europe, and delivering luxury goods from the Middle East to Europe. By the time of the Fourth Crusade in the early 13th century, both cities were wealthy enough to rival older trade cities such as Constantinople.

With the growth of Genoa and Venice, Italian business people introduced banking to the West to facilitate the long-distance exchange of money and goods. Towns in France, the Holy Roman Empire, and England grew in response to the trade, and the use of money spread steadily. Wealthy merchants invested in trading ships and the goods they carried, hoping to make a profit. Internal trade grew as well, with towns exchanging timber and grain from the north for cloth and metal products in the south. Cities in northern Germany and southern Scandinavia formed the **Hanseatic League** to facilitate trade as more towns purchased charters from kings and severed their feudal ties to lords on the rural manors. The towns became a strong source of revenue for kings, who were able to use the money to build armies and gain power over the aristocrats. The craftsmen in the towns formed merchant **guilds**, associations of people who worked in the same occupation. These groups grew powerful enough to control trade, but they also were responsible for training apprentices and setting standards for membership that encouraged the quality of their products to increase.

The growing towns and cities were home to the rising merchant class, who often allied with kings as a counterbalance to the landed aristocracy. Although the manorial system still existed in rural areas, more people were living in towns, and the social class structure grew complex as former serfs became craftsmen, traders, and merchants. The new urban classes often clashed with the landed no-bility, sometimes in open warfare, and by the early 1300s, traders had achieved an independent political status, protected by their own warriors as well as their

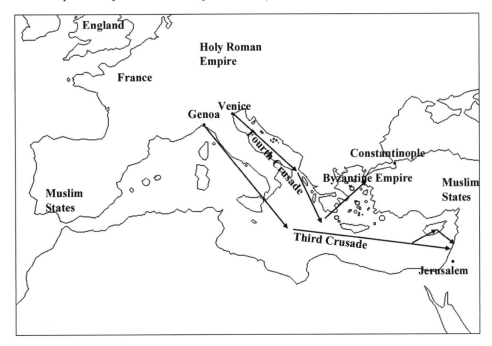

Venice and Genoa. Two Italian trading cities became wealthy through new contacts established by the Cru-sades. During the Third Crusade, knights disembarked from Genoa and headed toward Jerusalem. By the time of the Fourth Crusade, Venice influenced Crusaders to attack Constantinople, even though the Crusades originally began as an effort to help Constantinople. With the sacking of the city, Venice profited by securing trade routes to the Middle East.

wealth. The growth of trade and banking in the late Middle Ages formed the ba-sic building blocks for western capitalism, especially as merchants invested in trading ventures hoping to make a profit, but taking the risk of losing everything if the ship sank or was looted by pirates. Because the Catholic Church took an official stand against **usury** (the charging of interest for the use of money), bankers were often Jews, the descendants of those who had fled Israel during the earlier diasporas (see p.115). The Church eventually eased its policies and allowed Christians to participate more fully in the new capitalism. The Church had promoted the commercial and naval growth of Venice, and church officials sought the patronage of the rising merchant classes. By the 13th century, the Church itself had become a great property holder, as well as a lender of money.

European Christians demonstrated their religious fervor not just by driving back the "infidels" (Muslims) from Jerusalem, but also through their treatment of Jews, who often lived completely segregated from the Christian majority in small urban areas called **ghettos.** Other forms of discrimination against Jews included restrictions on owning land or entering craft guilds, so banking and trading were some of the only occupations open to them. Until the 13th century, Jews were seldom attacked, but in that century, English and French kings denounced and expelled them and seized their property. About the same time, **pogroms,** or anti-Semitic mob actions, drove Jews from western to eastern Europe, where they experienced less discrimination.

As medieval social and economic life grew more complex, a familiar pattern became apparent: more restrictions on the lives of women. Germanic customs in early medieval times allowed women considerable freedom, and women were thought to have the gift of prophecy and a special holiness. As in most other agricultural societies, they carried out all household duties with the help of slaves, and their advice was often sought and respected. Strong matrilineal ties existed, and the relationship between a man and his sisters' sons was particularly strong. The Christian emphasis on the equality of all souls, as well as the reverence for Mary, the mother of Jesus, almost certainly gained women more respect than they had in many other societies. They were not as segregated in religious services as were Islamic women, although they could not lead them. Women also had an alternative to married domestic life; monastic life was open to them as well as to men. However, with the growth of cities, women were often excluded from guilds, and their roles in local commerce seem to have decreased during the High Middle Ages. The literature of the day stressed women's roles as subservient to men and praised docile and obedient women as the ideal.

Culture and Arts

Once trade and new businesses created some wealth in western Europe, more specialized occupations grew, allowing cultural developments to follow. As early as the 700s Charlemagne had brought learned men to his court to teach and train others. He opened a school for clergy and government officials headed by Alcuin, an Anglo-Saxon monk of great ability and skills. Although the era is sometimes referred to as the "Carolingian Renaissance," it did not last, and the court collapsed after Charlemagne's death. Shortly after the Crusades began, the first universities were established in Italy, not surprisingly, since Italy was the first area of Europe to directly benefit from the trade sparked by the Crusades. Other universities were founded later in France, England, and Germany. Most of them were created for the clergy, but as early as the 1200s they were combining Christian learning with books of the Greek and Roman Classical age. Since the Muslims in the Middle East had preserved and copied many of these books, once western Europeans came in contact with these areas during the Crusades, Greek and Roman learning made its way back into Europe. Christian teachers, such as Thomas Aquinas, Albertus Magnus, and Peter Abelard used arguments of Aristotle and Socratic methods to teach the truths of Christian faith. A notable intellectual development was **scholasticism,** or the attempt to reconcile the beliefs and values of Christianity with the logical reasoning of Greek philosophy.

ORIGINAL DOCUMENTS: THOMAS AQUINAS ON BUSINESS AND TRADE

By the 13th century, the Catholic Church was modifying its earlier denunciations of business practices, particularly of usury, or the charging of interest. The change in policy is reflected in these passages from *Summa Theologica,* written between 1265 and 1274 by **Thomas Aquinas,** the great medieval theologian:

"Buying and selling seem to be established for the common advantage of both parties...The just price of things is not fixed with mathematical precision, but depends on a kind of estimate, so that a slight addition or subtraction would not seem to destroy the equality of justice...Nothing prevents gain from being directed to some necessary or even virtuous end, and thus trading becomes lawful."

Reference: The Summa Theologica, Thomas Aquinas, in *Basic Writing of Saint Thomas Aquinas,* edited by Anton C. Pegis. New York: Random House, 1945.

For example, St. Thomas Aquinas believed that is was possible to prove rationally that God exists by seizing on Aristotle's argument that a conscious agent had set the world in motion.

An important development in medieval literature was the use of **vernacular languages**, beginning in the 13th century. Before that, all serious literature was generally written in Latin, but starting with Dante Alighieri's *Divine Comedy*, written in Italian, the common people's oral languages (the vernacular) began to replace the old Roman language. Somewhat later came the first important work in English: Geoffrey Chaucer's *Canterbury Tales*, which provided a great deal of insight into medieval life in England. Other works following in German, French, and Spanish vernaculars, so that by the end of the 14th century, Latin was no longer the preferred written language.

Gothic cathedrals are the most impressive of late medieval art forms, combining architecture, painting, sculpture, inlay, carving, stained glass, music, and literature. A cathedral took many years to construct, and was almost always the most impressive building in town. Particularly after the 13th century, European painting became more sophisticated, demonstrating experimentation with perspective (making a painting look three-dimensional) and portrayal of individual faces.

Romanesque and Gothic Architecture. Before the end of the 11th century, Europeans had recovered enough from the fall of Rome to begin to build some impressive churches. The photo on the left is the interior of a Romanesque church in Comps, France. Its simple design and small windows reflect the architectural style of early medieval Europe, borrowed from Roman designs. In contrast, the photo on the right shows the towering Gothic style of the Salisbury Cathedral in England – a later design with large stained glass windows, very high ceilings, and complex vaulting.

Most formal art was produced for the church as an institution or for wealthy clergymen. By the 1300s art and culture were beginning to take shape in Italy as the **Renaissance**, or rebirth, which would spread over Europe and come to full flower during the 15th and 16th centuries.

THE BYZANTINE EMPIRE

After the Western Roman Empire fell, the Eastern Empire lived on for almost a thousand years, known during most of that time as the **Byzantine Empire**, after "Byzantium," the town that Constantine renamed "Constantinople" as the capital city. The empire controlled the eastern Mediterranean until the 12th century, the only classical civilization to survive into this era. The Byzantines inherited the Roman line of authority, complete with Roman roads, communications, and functioning imperial institutions. The Empire also became an economic powerhouse, and its manufactured goods were highly desirable, especially its silks, which matched the quality of Chinese products. Its cultural impact was also significant since the Slavic peoples of eastern Europe and Russia were very much influenced by the Byzantines, and many adopted the Eastern Orthodox religion. By the 12th century, the Empire had weakened, with the Islamic states crowding them to the east, Slavic people dominating the lands to the north, and western Europeans gaining strength to their west. However, the empire survived until 1453 when Constantinople fell to the Ottoman Turks who renamed the city Istanbul.

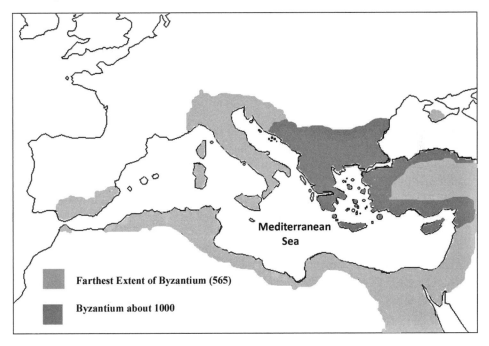

The Byzantine Empire. At its largest, the Byzantine Empire spread from Italy to Anatolia, and included the southern Mediterranean coastline and the southern coast of Spain. Much land was lost, however, and by 1000 the empire only controlled lands in Greece and Anatolia.

Political Developments

Although Germanic invasions threatened the eastern empire as well as the western empire, the east was better fortified because it was wealthier than the west. The major political threat of the early Byzantine Empire was the **Sassanid Empire** to the east. The Sassanids had sought to rebuild the old Persian Empire, but their hopes were dashed when they were attacked and defeated by the Arab Muslims in the 7th century. The precedent for leadership style was set by Constantine, who claimed divine favor and sanction for his rule. In contrast to separation of political and religious powers developing in the west, the emperor often intervened in theological disputes, and used his political position to define "orthodox" (accepted, true) beliefs and condemn others as **heretical** (false, often considered to be dangerous). This policy of political and religious power concentrated in the emperor's hands was called **caesaropapism** (caesar and pope). Emperors stood above the law, and their power was enhanced by a bureaucracy so large and complex that today we use the adjective "byzantine" to describe unnecessarily complicated or outdated structures.

The most important of the early Byzantine emperors was **Justinian**, who ruled from 527 to 565 C.E. Like Constantine, Justinian put a great deal of time, money, and effort into public buildings in Constantinople, most notably the **Hagia Sophia**, or Church of Holy Wisdom, that still stands today as one of the most important examples of Christian architecture in the world. Justinian also embarked on a major military campaign to win back the lost lands of the Roman Empire, and he made significant progress toward that goal, reclaiming lands in northern Africa and Spain. His efforts were ultimately a failure, since within two generations almost all of the reconquered areas had fallen to new invaders. Justinian's most important contribution was his codification of Roman law. Over the centuries, Roman law had been revised and systemized, first under the republic and then during imperial times, but Justinian's work is usually seen as the definitive codification of Roman law. It is preserved in his *corpus iuris civilis (Body of the Civil Law),* and it served as the basis for civil law codes that developed throughout much of western Europe.

From the early 600s the empire was under almost constant attack for two centuries. The Muslims almost took Constantinople in 717, when the Byzantines famously used "Greek fire" (a combustible liquid) to drive them back to sea. The Arab threat continued, and the Turks seriously pressured the empire during the 11th century, resulting in the call for help to the Catholic pope in the west in 1095. Meanwhile, Slavic kingdoms, especially Bulgaria to the north, had to be held back from their incursions into Byzantine territory. In the 19th century a Bulgarian king took the title of "tsar", Slavic for Caesar, reflecting his ambitions. The Bulgarian army was defeated soundly in 1014, and Bulgaria became part of the empire. All in all, the Byzantines showed a remarkable ability to survive despite the continuing threats to their power.

Economic Development and Social Distinctions

The Byzantine economy was centrally controlled by the bureaucracy in Constantinople, with a large peasant class that supplied food to people in the cities. The bureaucracy kept food prices artificially low to placate the urban lower classes, but this policy put great hardship on the peasants. Constantinople was by far the largest city, not just because it was the capital, but also because of its geographic position at the Bosporus that connected the Black Sea to the Mediterranean Sea. This location not only was ideal for defending the city, but also for controlling long-distance trade routes that connected to East Asia, India, and Russia to the growing market in western Europe. Once the Byzantines learned the Chinese secrets for silk production, they developed a brisk silk production business, and also began manufacturing cloth, carpets, and other luxury products. Like the Chinese, the Byzantines did not grant merchants political power, primarily because the government bureaucrats did not want to share their power. In contrast to both China and Byzantium, merchants in western Europe had gained a greater political voice.

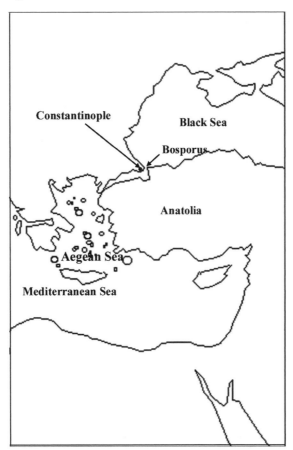

Constantinople's Geographic Advantage. Constantinople became one of the great cities of the world during the period from 600 to 1450 C.E. partly because of its geographic location on the Bosporus, a narrow connection between the Black Sea and the Aegean Sea. From that position the city was central to long distance trade that connected east Asia, India, and Russia to western Europe. The position was also easily defensible since three sides of the city were surrounded by water, and ships could easily be seen from a long distance. On the one vulnerable side of the city to the west, strong walls were built, just as the Romans had done for centuries.

The situation for women deteriorated from the earlier freedom that Roman women had to venture outside their homes. Of course, the "paterfamilias" (oldest male authority) had controlled family and public life, but during Byzantine times, women increasingly found themselves confined to the home. Some sources say that when they left their homes, they concealed their faces with veils. The only men they socialized with were members of their families. Despite these restrictions, it is interesting to note that from 1028 to 1056 women ruled the Byzantine Empire jointly with their husbands. Much earlier, Empress **Theodora** had exerted a great deal of influence over her husband, **Justinian**, who listened to and often followed her advice.

Cultural Achievements

In the early days of the Byzantine Empire, the official language was Latin, but most of the inhabitants spoke Greek. Eventually, Greek replaced Latin in government documents as well. The philosophy and literature of classical Greece had a much deeper influence in Byzantium than in western Europe, especially notable in Byzantine education. Byzantine aristocrats often hired tutors to provide private instruction for their children, girls as well as boys. Additionally a state-organized school system offered a primary education in basic reading, writing, and grammar, and those that entered the bureaucracy additionally studied classical Greek literature, philosophy, and science. Most peasants and many urban workers had no formal education, but basic literacy was widespread. The most ambitious and accomplished citizens attended a school of higher learning in Constantinople to study law, medicine, and philosophy. Byzantine scholars studied and wrote about the works of Homer, Plato, and Aristotle, and they copied many classical Greek works between the 10th and 12th centuries, preserving and transmitting the classical legacy.

One of the biggest accomplishments of the Eastern Orthodox Church was the conversion of many eastern Europeans to their branch of Christianity. Beginning in the 9th century, a competition emerged between the Eastern Orthodox and the Roman Catholics for the allegiance of the Slavs. Both religions gained converts, with the Eastern Orthodox being most successful in Russia, Romania, Serbia, Bulgaria, and Greece. In those areas, Constantinople served not only as a religious model, but also as a legal, literary, and artistic influence as well. In contrast, the Poles, Czechs, and Croats turned more toward the Roman Catholic Church, as demonstrated in their adoption of the Roman alphabet for their languages. The **Cyrillic** writing system was adopted in the Eastern Orthodox countries, as invented by two Byzantine missionaries in order to communicate. with their followers in their native languages. The expansion of both religions into eastern Europe deepened the rift between them that had been developing since the 4th century. After many years of friction and uneasy truces, the division came out into the open in 1054 when the Roman Catholic pope clashed with the Eastern Orthodox patriarch over a number of issues, with each attacking the other's practices. It ended with the two leaders excommunicating each other, resulting in a division that still exists to this day.

COMPARISON: ROMAN CATHOLICISM AND EASTERN ORTHODOXY

The two major branches of Christianity split gradually over time, partly because they had very different geographic centers. They shared many common beliefs, but the chart below defines some of their differences.

ROMAN CATHOLICISM	EASTERN ORTHODOXY
Separation between political and religious leaders; competition between popes and kings for political power	Union between political and religious leaders (caesaro-papism)
Religious art conveyed Jesus as suffering for the sins of mankind.	Religious art conveyed Jesus as majestic and divine.
Priests could not marry.	Priests could marry.
Gothic architecture was used for churches.	Church architecture was inspired by ancient Rome (arches, domes).
Theology was less influenced by Greek philosophy.	Theology was more influenced by Greek philosophy.

Byzantium and Russia

To the north of Byzantium, a Slavic people known as the Russians began to organize a large state from several principalities. The most important early city was Kiev, a thriving trading center on the Dnieper River along the main trade route between Scandinavia and Byzantium. Kiev came to dominate many of the other principalities, and their princes sought alliances with Byzantine rulers. Many Russian merchants visited Constantinople, became acquainted with Byzantine culture, and sparked the interest of their rulers in Orthodox Christianity. After the conversion of Prince Vladimir of Kiev in about 989, Byzantine influences flowed rapidly into Russia, including art, the Cyrillic alphabet, architecture, law codes, and missions. By the early 12th century Kiev's population approached 30,000, and the city controlled trade all over the region, with eight thriving marketplaces within its borders. Long after Constantinople fell to the Turks in 1453, Byzantine influences lived on in Russia, with the Orthodox faith and Byzantine customs spreading rapidly as the Kievan principality transformed over time into the great Russian Empire that stretched from the Baltic Sea to Alaska.

MARKER EVENT IN RUSSIA: ACCEPTANCE OF BYZANTINE CULTURE

As Russia began to develop from the early Kievan state, Vladimir I made some important decisions that oriented Russia toward Byzantium and away from western Europe. When he first came to rule, he built a temple to the six gods his Slavic subjects worshipped, but soon became interested in the monotheistic religions developing in regions around him. The earliest Russian chronicle reports that Vladimir decided against Islam became of its ban on alcohol, and rejected Judaism because he could not understand how a powerful god would allow his people's temple to be destroyed. Although it is unclear why he did not choose Roman Catholicism, he almost certainly was swayed by the magnificent wealth of 10th century Constantinople and the beauty of Orthodox churches.

Once Orthodox Christianity was accepted, the Cyrillic alphabet began to be used and trade was oriented toward Byzantium. Once the Byzantine Empire fell, Russia became the incubator for Byzantine ways, and despite later attempts by Russian tsars to "westernize" and form alliances with western European nations, a different path was set for Russia. The cultural divide set the stage for many tensions between eastern and western Europe that developed in later times, including the "Cold War" of the 20th century.

As the era 600-1450 came to an end, western Europe was very much on the rise, and Byzantium was headed for its final fall in 1453 when a Turkish sultan captured Constantinople with a powerful army, equipped with artillery purchased from western Europe. Despite its demise, the Byzantine Empire left a lasting imprint on the world's history through its law codes, distinctive architecture, religion, and organizational structure long after the other classical civilizations had crumbled.

IDENTIFICATIONS AND CONCEPTS

barter
Benedictine Rule
Byzantine Empire
caesaropapism
canon law
Carolingian family
Charlemagne
Clovis
Crusades
excommunication, interdict
feudalism
Franks
ghettos
guilds
Hagia Sophia
Hanseatic League
heresy
Holy Roman Empire
Hundred Years War
Justinian, Justinian Code
limited government, parliaments
Magna Carta
manorialism
"Middle Ages"
missi dominici
pogroms
Renaissance
Saladin
Sassanid Empire
scholasticism
serfs
Theodora
usury
vernacular languages
Vikings

CHAPTER SEVEN:
THE AMERICAS

While civilizations in the Eastern Hemisphere were changing during the era from 600 to 1450 C.E., civilizations in the Western Hemisphere were continuing to evolve along their separate paths. Nomadic groups and subsistence farmers populated North America, and more complex civilizations developed in Mesoamerica and the area around the Andes Mountains in South America. The earlier Olmec society of Mesoamerica had collapsed by 300 C.E. and was replaced by the Maya, the people of Teotihuacan, the Toltecs, and eventually the Aztecs. In South America, the Chavin society was also in decline by 300 C.E., and was replaced by several regional cultures, including the Mochica state and the Chimu state. By the end of the era, the people of the Americas were in their last days of isolation from the east, and most were enjoying halcyon days before the devastation that the 16th century would bring to their civilizations.

SOCIETIES IN MESOAMERICA

Scholars usually divide the era from 600 to 1450 C.E. in Mesoamerica into two sub-periods: classical (ending about 900) and post-classical (900 to 1450). Notice that the classical era in Mesoamerica occured several hundred years after the classical era in the Eastern Hemisphere, reflecting the independent development of the two hemispheres until 1450. Classical civilizations include the Maya and the people of Teotihuacan, and examples of post-classical civilizations are the Toltecs and the Aztecs.

Classical Mesoamerica

The Olmec civilization disappeared completely by about 100 B.C.E., but many of their practices and beliefs appear to have been carried on in later civilizations. The earliest heirs of the Olmec were the **Maya**, who centered their society to the east and south of the Olmec settlements in what is now southern Mexico, Guatemala, Belize, Honduras, and El Salvador. The first permanent Maya villages appeared during the 3rd century B.C.E. in the highlands of Guatemala, with its fertile soil for agriculture. There they built a ceremonial center, Kaminaljuyu, that dominated other communities around it. By the 4th century C.E., Kami-naljuyu fell under the control of Teotihuacan, and the Maya moved the center of their civilization to the poorly drained Mesoamerican lowlands. From about 300 to 900 C.E., the Maya built more than eighty large ceremonial centers in the lowlands, all with pyramids, palaces, and temples. These large centers were real cities with tens of thousands of people, but most of the populations were peasant villagers who lived in settlements on the periphery of the cities.

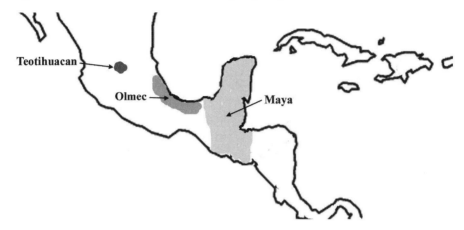

Early Mesoamericans. The Olmec civilization was the oldest, and disappeared by 100 B.C.E. Its heirs in the classical era that followed (to 900 C.E.) were Teotihuacan and the Maya.

In these heavily jungled areas, the thin soil quickly lost its fertility, and in the early days the Maya, like many other people who lived in rain forests, practiced **slash and burn (or shifting) agriculture.** This type of subsistence agriculture would not have been enough to support cities, such as Tikal, Quirigua, and Panlenque, so the Maya built terraces that trapped silt carried by the rivers, supported by irrigation and swamp drainage systems. These techniques boosted their agricultural productivity, with Maya cultivators raising maize, cotton, and cacao (for chocolate) in abundance to support their urban populations of 30,000 to 80,000 people. The cities were primarily religious and administrative centers, and trade seems to have been a relatively minor part of Maya life. They varied in size and layout, but almost all included large pyramids with temples on top, complexes of administrative buildings, houses for the elite, a ritual ball court, and often a series of altars and memorial pillars, called **stelae.** Stelae were built to commemorate great actions of Maya leaders or to mark ceremonial occasions, and they were inscribed with hieroglyphic script.

Maya society had clearly delineated social classes, with rulers and other members of the elite serving both priestly and political functions. They decorated their bodies with paint and tattoos and wore elaborate costumes of textiles, animal skins, and feathers. Although kings were not believed to be divine, they communicated directly with supernatural beings and deceased ancestors through rituals in which they drew blood from different parts of their bodies and fell into hallucinogenic trances. Vast numbers of commoners were needed to build the elaborate altars and temples, since everything was constructed without the aid of wheels or metal tools.

CHANGE OVER TIME; CLASSICAL AND POST-CLASSICAL MESOAMERICA

How did Mesoamerica change from the classical era (to 900 C.E.) to the post-classical era (900- 1450 C.E.)? All civilizations had similar religious beliefs and practices, architecture, urban planning, and social organization, but some important changes occurred over time.

CLASSICAL (Maya, Teotihuacan)	POST-CLASSICAL (Toltec, Aztec)
Overall population was lower.	Population density increased, with larger cities, and overall population.
Land was less intensively farmed.	Agriculture intensified, partly because of increased population.
Warfare among groups happened frequently.	Warfare intensified, becoming more frequent and involving more people as competition for land increased.
Small armies, relatively simple forms of government were characteristic.	Centralized, strong governments maintained large armies.

Religion was central to Maya life, with a pantheon of gods important to sustain agriculture, and many of the rituals included human sacrifice. Many victims were prisoners of war, especially defeated elite. Captured commoners were more likely to be used as part of the labor force to construct public buildings and irrigation and drainage systems. Priests had magical powers that gave them access to the underworld, which consisted of nine levels of hell. The gods, like those of Sumeria, were believed to interfere in human affairs, and they possessed both human and animal traits, most frequently those of the jaguar. The Maya believed that it was important to please the gods, who expected honor and reverence from their human subjects. Bloodletting pleased the gods, so sacrifice victims were often lacerated before being decapitated in order to produce more blood.

One task of Maya priests was the construction of elaborate calendars, which wove two kinds of years: a solar year of 365 days based on the agricultural cycle, and a ritual year of 260 days. By combining the calendars, each day had specific characteristics that distinguished it from others, and the priests divined what activities could take place and when. Priests also wrote the inscriptions on temples and monuments and produced books on paper made from beaten tree bark or on vellum made from deerskin.

By about 800 C.E., most Maya populations had begun to leave the cities, and within 100 years most of the cities had disappeared. No one knows for sure why the civilization declined, although many theories have been proposed. Some historians have proposed foreign invasion; others say civil war occurred; still others think that epidemic diseases decimated the cities. Gradually, the jungles grew over the cities, temples, and monuments, only to be uncovered by modern archaeologists, although many more are yet to be discovered.

About the time the Maya were reaching their peak, another civilization began to develop in the highlands to the north. The area was the site of several large lakes fed by water from the surrounding mountains, and the earliest settlers channeled the water into their fields to produce an abundance of crops. Their central city was **Teotihuacan**, which began to grow rapidly after about 200 B.C.E. Like the cities of the Olmecs and the Maya, Teotihuacan was a center of religious rituals and government administration. Their monuments were in the pyramidal form found all over Central America, but the Pyramids of the Sun and the Moon are among the largest masonry structures ever built. Some scholars believe that Teotihuacan might have been the first real city of the Western Hemisphere, with a population estimated between 125,000 and 200,000. Just as with the Maya, most of what we know about Teotihuacan must be interpreted from the architecture and art, and the city is unusual in that it laid out barrios, or quarters, for the ordinary people who farmed the fields surrounding the city. It had scores of temples, several palatial residences, busy markets, and hundreds of workshops for craftsmen.

Unfortunately, most of the written records perished when the city itself declined, so the remaining architecture is an important source of our knowledge of the people of Teotihuacan. Paintings and murals suggest that priests were an important part of the elite, just as they were in Maya society. Also similarly to the Maya, priests kept the calendar to ensure that crops were planted at the right time. In contrast to Maya cities, Teotihuacan was a center of extensive trade and exchange, with professional merchants trading their products throughout

Mesoamerica. The city reached its peak during the 7th century C.E., although the political leadership is still a mystery. No public art displays or honors individual rulers, as was found in Maya society, but the city was so well-planned that some kind of centralized planning must have taken place. Some have theorized that powerful families ruled cooperatively. The city collapsed around 750 C.E. for unknown reasons, but city walls had been built only about 150 years earlier, suggesting that the early days were more peaceful than the later days were. Some of the murals uncovered by archaeologists suggest that the city's final decades were violent, with most of the important temples in the city center, as well as the houses of the elite, burned down and religious images defaced.

The Pyramid of the Sun. This colossal pyramid in Teotihuacan is not as tall as the Great Pyramid of Egypt (constructed much earlier), but it occupies nearly as much space. The main street of the city ran between the Pyramid of the Sun and the Pyramid of the Moon, with shops and residences lining the street. The stairs to the top of the pyramid probably led to a sacrificial alter.

Post-Classical Mesoamerica

After the decline of Teotihuacan and the Maya cities, several regional states rose in Mesoamerica, who fought constantly among themselves. These groups illustrate one of the changes from classical to post-classical societies: more emphasis on military organization. Their capital cities stood on well-defended hills, and their art often illustrated warriors. The **Toltecs,** a group that migrated from northwestern Mexico, were the first to unify central Mexico again after the people of Teotihuacan. Their capital was Tula, northwest of modern Mexico

City, which probably reached a population of about 60,000 between 950 and 1150 C.E. Like the people of Teotihuacan, the Toltecs tapped the waters coming down from the mountains to irrigate crops of maize, beans, peppers, tomatoes, chiles, and cotton.

The Toltecs created their centralized state based on military power, and they conquered lands from Tula south to Central America, including many of the areas formerly controlled by the Maya. Their military orientation appeared in public buildings and temples, which were decorated with representations of warriors or with scenes of human sacrifice. Apparently, the Toltecs had two rulers rather than one, a fact that may have eventually weakened their power. Their most famous ruler was **Topiltzin,** a priest associated with the god **Quetzalcoatl**, who was forced into exile in the east, "the land of the rising sun." After his exile, the Toltec state began to decline, to be replaced by the Mexica, more commonly known as the **Aztecs.**

EXAMINING THE EVIDENCE: MESOAMERICAN LEGENDS

Mesoamerican cultures were rich in legends passed down from one group to the next, often by stories told orally, but many were written down in the Aztec pictographic records, or *codices*. The Spanish preserved some of these records, and a Franciscan monk, Bernardino de Sahagun, compiled many others from years of individual interviews with Aztecs. One of the most famous legends is that of Topiltzin, a Toltec priest affiliated with the god Quetzalcoatl ("feathered serpent") who lost a struggle for power with another faction and was forced into exile. When he left, he promised to return, an event so much anticipated that the Aztecs, who followed the Toltecs to power in central Mexico, at first were hospitable to the Spaniards because they believed the Spanish leader to be the exiled hero. The following is one account of Topiltzin's departure:

"Thereupon he [Topiltzin] looked toward Tula, and then wept...And when he had done these things...he went to reach the seacoast. Then he fashioned a raft of serpents. When he had arranged the raft, he placed himself as if it were his boat. Then he set off across the sea."

Source: Quoted in Nigel Davies, *The Toltec Heritage: From the Fall of Tula to the Rise of Tenochtitlan.* (Norman: University of Oklahoma, press, 1980), 3.

According to Aztec legend, they built their main city, **Tenochtitlan**, in a place identified by an eagle perched on a cactus with a snake in its mouth. The city grew to be one of the largest cities on earth, with as many as 300,000 people at its height, positioned on a number of small islands in Lake Texcoco. Several causeways connected them to the mainland, and the city's central marketplace was described by the Spanish as far grander than anything they had ever seen. The area was part of a chain of lakes connected by marshes, and the Aztecs adopted their lifestyles to an aquatic environment. Like the people of Teotihuacan before them, they drained swamps, constructed irrigation works and terraces, and used **chinampas**, or floating gardens. This unique adaptation consisted of narrow artificial islands constructed by heaping muck from the lakes on beds of reeds anchored to the shores. Chinampas made it possible to sustain urban life by boosting agricultural production. The Aztecs imposed a **tribute system** on conquered peoples, who had to contribute maize, beans, and other foods to support Tenochtitlan.

Like the Toltecs before them, the Aztecs rose to power through military might, with tough fighting skills and a tendency toward aggressive expansion. By the early 15th century, they emerged as an independent power that dominated their allies. The ruling group among the Aztecs was made up of militaristic aristocrats, whose lives centered on conquest. At the top of the social hierarchy was a semi-divine king, who was selected by election from among the male members of the ruling family. Below him were his officials, who had earned their positions through heroic military leadership and ruled conquered people in the provinces like feudal lords. Next was a class of warriors who were recruited from ordinary freemen, and proved themselves in battle by taking at least four prisoners for sacrifice. Most Aztecs were ordinary free people who tilled the fields, built the buildings and roads, and carried burdens for others. At the bottom were serfs, whose rights and duties were similar to those of medieval European serfs, and the slaves, who were war captives or debtors. Aztec society was patriarchal, but women received high honor for bearing warrior sons, and the spirits of women who died in childbirth were believed to help the sun god in his journey through the sky each day.

The Aztecs also had a large and powerful group of priests. They served as advisers to the king and his officials, and they conducted the elaborate religious rituals that were central to Aztec society. The chief god, Huitzilopochtli, ruled from the position of the sun at noon, and in order to keep him in his proper place in the sky, the Aztecs believed they must feed him human blood. This blood came from frequent human sacrifices on altars that lined the main streets of Tenochtitlan. Although other Mesoamerican groups practiced human sacrifice, the Aztec rituals were particularly bloody, with thousands of victims taken as war captives or tribute for just that purpose. A special part of the ritual was cutting the heart from a live victim's chest, and the heart was then eaten by the Aztec nobility. Priests conducted these sacrifices with large obsidian knives. The fact that the sacrifices were carried out in front of large crowds that included the masses, as well as leaders from enemy and subject states, was a message that almost certainly impressed the viewers with the power of the Aztec elite.

COMPARISONS: THE CONTINUITY OF THE MESOAMERICAN BALL GAME

Archaeologists have found consistent evidence that all the Mesoamerican groups – from the Olmec to the Aztecs – enjoyed ball games, with most of the civilizations building large courts in their cities. The game was played with a solid rubber ball on slope-sided courts. These ball courts varied considerably in size, but they all featured long narrow alleys, with side-walls for bouncing the balls. The rules of the ball game are not known, but based on its descendent, the modern game of ulama, it was probably similar to racquetball or volleyball, where the object is to keep the ball in play. In the most widespread version of the game, the players would strike the ball with their hips, although sometimes they allowed the use of forearms, rackets, bats, or handstones. The ball was made of solid rubber, with sizes that differed greatly over time or according to the version played. While the game was played casually for simple recreation, including by children and perhaps even women, the game also had important ritual aspects, often featuring human sacrifice. Some representations show balls that closely resemble the human head.

ANDEAN CIVILIZATIONS

The Chavin, the earliest civilization of the Andes region in South America, declined sometime after about 100 B.C.E., but on its foundations a new group of people, the **Moche,** built a society that thrived from about 100 to 700 C.E. The Moche built an extensive irrigation system from rivers coming out of the mountains, and cultivated maize, beans, manioc, and sweet potatoes in the lower coastal areas, and coca in the higher elevations. Moche society was highly stratified, with wealth and power concentrated in the hands of priests and military leaders. The wealthy adorned themselves with rich clothing, jewelry, and tall headdresses. Because the Moche had no written records, all that we know about them comes from archaeological evidence, especially from a recently excavated tomb that revealed masterfully crafted ceramics, gold ornaments, jewels, and textiles. Like so many other ancient people of the Americas, the Moche's decline is not well understood, although it appears to have coincided with a succession of natural disasters, including an earthquake and flood followed by thirty years of drought.

COMPARISONS: THE UNIQUENESS OF ANDEAN CIVILIZATIONS

The Andean civilizations shared many characteristics with other civilizations of the 600 to 1450 era, but in some ways they were unique, partly because they developed in relative isolation from others. Another factor was their special natural environment that combined dry sea coast, high mountain valleys, and dense jungle. Their only beasts of burdens were llamas and alpacas, animals not found in other areas of the world until they were later exported from the Andes area. Two ways that the Andean civilizations were unique are as follows:

1) No written language – None of the Andean civilizations had written languages, a fact that has led some observers to the conclusion that these civilizations were not very advanced. However, in most other areas, they were highly skilled and organized. They kept records with a system of knotted colored cords, **khipus,** that helped government administrators to count population and determine tribute obligations.
1) The **mit'a** labor system – Communities were organized into **ayllus,** who were obligated to aid each other in tasks that required more labor than one household could provide. Once kingdoms organized, this mutual obligation system extended to responsibilities to the kings, and a mit'a labor system developed for public works. Each ayllu contributed a set number of workers for specific tasks each year, including road building and maintenance, and irrigation and drainage projects. Members of ayllus also worked the fields and cared for the animals that belonged to the aristocracy.

Other people, including the Tiwanaku and Wari, occupied the Andes region after the Moche, but the most powerful and well-organized civilization was the **Inca,** who formed a vast imperial state during the 15th century. The Inca began in about 1100 in Cuzco, a town set on a plateau 11,000 feet above sea level. Strong and ambitious leaders consolidated political power during the 1430s and began an aggressive expansion that eventually led them to control a long stretch of land that extended about 2500 miles north to south along the Andes range.

The expansion of the Inca Empire was made possible by agricultural advances that led to an increased food supply. Andean Indians had long understood that different crops grew at different altitudes, and with the help of metal tools, fertilizer, irrigation systems, dams, and canals, they began to store large surpluses to support both a large army and a leisure class. The Inca also built terraces on the steep hillsides so crops could be planted, and the use of llamas and alpacas as beasts of burden gave them an advantage over their contemporaries in Mesoamerica. The cultivators were mostly peasants who worked the lands and gave portions of the products to the aristocrats. Surpluses went into state storehouses to save for times of famine and for those unable to cultivate land for themselves. Under the **mit'a system,** each person owed compulsory labor services to the Inca state, with men doing heavy labor and women making textiles, pottery, and jewelry. With the aid of the **khipu,** a system of cords and beads for counting, Inca bureaucrats kept track of the labor service and tribute owed by local communities, called **ayllus.**

The chief ruler, called the **Inca,** was considered to be a deity descended from the sun, and his senior wife was seen as a link to the moon. In theory, the Inca owned everything, and he governed as an absolute, all-knowing ruler. Through the bureaucracy, which consisted mainly of aristocrats, the Inca allocated land to his subjects, who farmed it on his behalf. The Inca's status as a god-king was reflected in his elaborate dress, with fine textiles woven just for him. A special group of women made clothing and jewelry for the Inca and his family in ceaseless industry, since each day required new outfits, with those from the previous day discarded, never to be worn again. Inca aristocrats and priests led privileged lives consuming fine foods and dressing in embroidered clothes made by peasant women. The aristocrats wore large ear spools that enlarged the ears so much that the Spaniards later called them *orejones,* or "big ears." Priests were highly educated, and major temples supported hundreds of priests who conducted the many religious rituals. Noticeably absent was a distinct merchant class, since long-distance trade was less important than it was in Mesoamerica, with the Inca emphasizing self-sufficiency and state regulation of production and surplus.

Inca religion was polytheistic, and the most important deity was the god of the sun, with the Inca (the leader) as the sun's representative on earth. Deceased rulers were mummified and then treated as intermediaries with the gods, given food and gifts, and displayed during public festivals. Part of the expansion of the Inca state was encouraged by the belief that each new Inca needed to secure his own land and wealth, so that the dead Inca's mummy could be supported by his cult for eternity. The magnificent Temple of the Sun in Cuzco was the center of the state religion, and the mummies of the past Incas were kept within its walls. The temple is an example of the fine stone buildings of royal Cuzco that were constructed without mortar, held together by perfectly constructed stones and still standing today. The cult of the sun spread throughout the empire, but local gods were often worshipped as well.

The Inca Empire extended some 2500 miles from north to south and was connected by an estimated 10,000 miles of roads, paved with stone and connected by suspension bridges over mountain gorges and rivers.

The expansion of the Inca state was accomplished by a large and well-organized military, and the empire was held together by a remarkable system of roads running north and south both along the coast and in the mountains. A corps of official runners carried messages along the roads so that the ruler and his bureaucracy could keep in touch with their subjects. The roads also facilitated the spread of the **Quechua** language and the religious cult of Cuzco. Generally local administrators were left in place when a group was conquered, and they were overseen by Inca administrators drawn from the Inca nobility in Cuzco. Reciprocity based on the mit'a system extended to new subjects, who often benefited from incorporation into the Inca Empire with its roads and sophisticated irrigation and drainage systems.

THE PEOPLE OF NORTH AMERICA

In contrast to Mesoamerica and the Andes region in South America, no major civilization controlled large amounts of land in North America. Instead a variety of people lived there with many different languages and lifestyles. Many were nomadic, hunting bison or deer, or in the arctic area whale, seals, and walruses. Others gathered nuts, berries, roots, and grasses to supplement fish or meat. In several regions of North America, agriculture allowed settlements in growth. For example, in what is now the southwestern United States, the **Anasazi** people used river water to irrigate crops of maize, beans, squash, and sunflowers. The hot, dry climate brought periodic drought and famine, but by 700 C.E., they were constructing permanent stone and adobe buildings called pueblos. These multistory stone-and-timber villages were connected by roads to one another, with most pueblos containing ritual enclosures called kivas. The nature of the ceremonies is still not known, but ritual items, including feathers and skeletal remains of macaws from Mexico have been found in the kivas. The Anasazi deserted their dwellings during long droughts and moved to greener pastures, but eventually abandoned the area by about 1300.

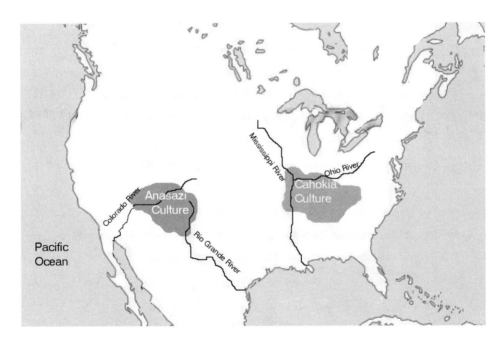

Agricultural People of North America. Most people of North America during the period from 600 to 1450 C.E. were nomadic, but in two areas, agricultural people built permanent settlements. The Anasazi Culture developed in the southwest in the areas around the Colorado River and the Rio Grande River. The Cahokia Culture used the waters of the Mississippi River and Ohio River to grow their crops.

COMPARISONS: AZTECS AND INCA

The two great North American empires that were in place at the end of the era from 600 to 1450 C.E. were the Aztecs in Mesoamerica and the Inca in the Andes region of South America. The chart below summarizes some similarities and differences between these two groups.

	Aztecs	**Inca**
Social	Distinctive social classes with priests important elites; Large middle class of merchants and traders	Distinctive social classes with priests important elites No real merchant middle class; trade controlled by government
Cultural	Religion central to society Practiced much human sacrifice Elaborate calendar, writing system	Religion central to society Human sacrifice practiced, but less central to rituals Quechua native language; no written language
Economic	Tenochtitlan - large city and suburbs Economy based on agriculture Trade important to economy Built chinampas ("floating gardens")	Cuzco - small city and suburbs Economy based on agriculture Trade not as important to economy Built elaborate terraces for crops; extensive road system
Political	Powerful elite families who chose the ruler; bureaucracy less elaborate; powerful military	The "Inca" god-king ruled with absolute power and help of large bureaucracy; powerful military

Large-scale agricultural societies also emerged in the woodlands east of the Mississippi River. Like the Anasazi, they cultivated maize and beans, but their natural environment was quite different, with abundant trees and rain. A number of different groups lived in this area, and the most distinctive feature of their culture was the construction of enormous earthen mounds built as stages for ceremonies, platforms for dwellings, and burial sites. The largest and most important mound-builder settlement of this period was at **Cahokia,** located near modern-day East St. Louis, Illinois. It appears as if the people who built Cahokia built other settlements around the Mississippi River valley, but Cahokia is the most impressive, with about eighty mounds of different sizes there. The site was abandoned about 1300 for reasons still not understood. Since peoples north of Mexico had no writing, information about their societies comes almost exclusively from archaeological discoveries, and we know little about their political and social organization and religious beliefs. By 1450, most people in the Western Hemisphere lived in small kinship-based groups that spoke a variety of languages and practiced different customs. From Alaska to South America, nomadism was common, as was subsistence agriculture. Two large empires controlled areas that were a considerable distance apart: the Aztecs in Mesoamerica, and the Inca in the Andes region of South America. These two empires were all that stood in the way of Spanish conquerors when they arrived in the early 16th century.

IDENTIFICATIONS AND CONCEPTS

ayllus
Aztecs
Cahokia
chinampas
classical, post-classical Mesoamerica
Inca
khipus
Maya
mit'a
Moche
Quechua
Quetzlcoatl
slash and burn (shifting) agriculture
stelae
Tenochtitlan
Teotihuacan
Toltecs
Topiltzin
tribute system

CHAPTER EIGHT:
CENTRAL AND EAST ASIA:
THE REVIVAL OF CHINA AND THE
IMPACT OF THE MONGOLS

Like the Western Roman Empire, the Han Empire was beset by nomadic invasions during its latter years. When the dynasty fell in the early 3rd century C.E., China fragmented into regional kingdoms that fought constantly with one another for almost 400 years. This Era of Division saw the Chinese bureaucracy collapse, and the position of the scholar-gentry declined sharply as families with large landholdings vied for power. Non-Chinese nomadic warlords ruled much of China, and Buddhism gained popularity, challenging Confucianism as the prime cultural force in East Asia. Without a central political force to maintain it, the Great Wall was poorly defended and did little to keep nomadic people from crossing it to raid the kingdoms. Trade and city life declined throughout the bickering kingdoms, reminiscent of the Warring States Period that had occurred between the Zhou and Qin Dynasties. Just as Shi Huangdi emerged to unite China at the end of the Warring States Period, a member of a prominent north Chinese noble family rose to reunite China at the end of the 6th century to establish the **Sui Dynasty**. Although the Han and Roman Empires suffered many of the same setbacks that led to their downfall, Chinese civilization eventually rose again, whereas Roman civilization disappeared forever.

THE SUI-TANG ERA

China was reunited in 589 C.E., when Wendi, a Chinese nobleman, first forged a marriage alliance with a neighboring kingdom in the north, and then gained the support of nearby nomadic military commanders. Reunification of China came with the defeat of the Chen kingdom, which had long ruled much of the south, so that most areas that the Han had ruled centuries before were now united as the Sui Dynasty under Wendi. The turmoil, however, did not end with Wendi's victories. Just as Shi Huangdi's short-lived Qin Dynasty paved the way for the long-lasting Han Dynasty, the Sui Dynasty paved the way for the **Tang Dynasty** that ruled China for almost three hundred years. Wendi was murdered by his son, Yangdi, whose extravagant and demanding personality inspired his ministers to assassinate him in 618. Instead of falling back into chaos, the tenuous

Chinese empire was held together by one of Yangdi's officials, Li Yuan, the Duke of Tang, who became the first of the Tang emperors.

The Tang emperors and nobility descended from the Turks who had built small states in northern China after the Han era, as well as from Chinese officials who had lived in the area. They upheld Confucian values, but they also were very much influenced by the cultures of central Asia, including Buddhism and a strong military organization. The Tang established a capital at Chang'an near the old Qin capital, where the emperors presided over one of the most brilliant epochs of China's long history.

Political Organization

Li Huang, together with his son, Tang Taizong, built the foundation for the great dynasty by extending the empire's borders and placating the nomadic people who had long threatened Chinese stability. The emperors played one nomadic group off another to gain control, and they completed repairs to the Great Wall that the Sui had begun. The Tang military forces were formidable, and succeeded in getting leaders of Turkic tribes to submit as vassals to the Tang rulers, who took the title "heavenly khan." Daughters of the Turk leaders often married into the Tang family, and sons were sent to Chang'an as hostages, where they learned Chinese ways and loyalties. The Tang armies also defeated kingdoms on the Korean peninsula, and received tribute from the Silla Kingdom that long remained a loyal vassal to the Chinese.

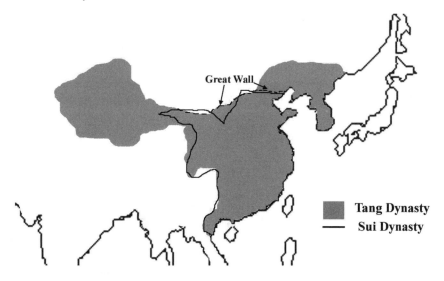

The Sui and Tang Dynasties. The short-lived Sui Dynasty united regional kingdoms in 589 C.E., but fell to the Tang Dynasty in 618. The Tang united much the same land space that the Han had ruled during the Classical Era.

The early Tang emperors also rebuilt the elaborate bureaucracy that had developed during the Han era. Even though the Tang were heavily influenced by their central Asian roots, they identified with Chinese culture, and very much valued the scholar-gentry tradition based on knowledge and appreciation of Confucianism. The bureaucracy was much needed, especially with the expansion of the empire, and the scholar-gentry also helped to offset the power of the land-holding aristocrats whom the Tang recognized as threats to their rule. In the Tang era, the numbers of educated scholar-gentry rose far above those in the Han era, and the examination system was greatly expanded. The scholar-gentry class filled most of the high government positions and oversaw a vast bureaucracy in an arrangement that was to continue in later dynasties.

The Tang managed to establish regional **hegemony** (control) over much of east Asia through military prowess and the reestablishment of a tributary (payment by subjects) system. The Chinese called their empire **"The Middle Kingdom"** because they saw themselves as central to the world around them, and their demands for gifts from neighboring lands and peoples were part of the natural order of Chinese domination. Envoys from tributary states delivered their goods to the Tang Court with a **kowtow**, a deep bow before the emperor in which the forehead touched the ground. The Chinese returned the favors with gifts of their own, and even though subordinate lands often did as they pleased otherwise, the ceremonies established diplomatic contacts and encouraged trade and cultural exchanges.

Economic Changes and Social Distinctions

An important accomplishment of the early Tang emperors was their check on the power of aristocratic land-owning families by establishing the **equal field system** that restricted the inheritance of land. When a farmer died, his land went to the government and was allotted to individuals and their families according to the fertility of the land and the needs of the people. About one-fifth of the land remained under hereditary control, but the rest was available for redistribution. In this way, the equal field system not only checked the power of the aristocrats, but very much improved the lot of the average peasant, making them much happier with their benevolent rulers.

The Tang's reemphasis on the scholar-gentry also impacted the social class system in China, elevating the status of the bureaucrats and relegating the landed aristocracy to marginal government positions. The imperial university first established by the Han was expanded to allow about 30,000 students to train each year for the examinations, and it was possible for bright commoners to enter the university (usually with the sponsorship of their villages), pass the examinations, and successfully land a high position in government. Birth and family connections continued to be important, however, and often established bureaucrats used their influence to see that family members received government positions.

During the Tang period, Chang'an became one of the largest cities in the world as the hub of a vast trade network at the eastern end of the revived Silk Road. Though the 1100-mile **Grand Canal** built by the Sui did not reach Chang'an, it linked the Yellow River with the Yangzi as a key component to internal trade within the empire. Other urban areas grew along the trade routes, and urban life was quite diverse, with perhaps as many as 100,000 west Asians living in Chang'an by the end of the Tang period.

MARKER EVENT: CONSTRUCTION OF THE GRAND CANAL

Although China's Grand Canal is not as internationally renowned as the Great Wall, its construction is every bit as impressive a technological accomplishment. By connecting two large east/west river systems - the Yangzi and Huang He (Yellow) Rivers - it facilitated trade between northern and southern China. The Canal was one of the world's largest waterworks projects before modern times, extending for more than 1100 miles and measuring about forty paces across. Roads ran parallel to the waterway on either side. Sui Emperor Yangdi used canals dug as early as the Zhou dynasty, but he linked them into a network that allowed food crops to be transported easily across the empire, particularly the abundant rice crops of the Yangzi River valley.

More than just a technological achievement, the Grand Canal not only integrated the economies of northern and southern China; it served as a basis for political and cultural unity as well, making it possible for China to maintain hegemony over east Asia for many years. The Canal was the major conduit for internal trade in China until railroads were built in the 19th century, and even today it still serves vital trade functions.

Cultural Developments

The cosmopolitan Tang Dynasty was shaped by both Chinese and Turkic culture. The leaders continued the Confucian examination system for candidates for the bureaucracy, but they also valued central Asian expertise in horseman-ship and the use of iron stirrups. Massive statues of the Buddha were carved out of rocky cliffsides, and the style was strongly influenced by that of central and even west Asia. The statues are better known for their sheer size than for artistic refinement, but stone cutting and metalworking sills were clearly well devel-oped. Tang artists and sculptors often focused on the horses and two-humped camels used along the Silk Road, and their human images were of foreigners from all over central Asia, including camel drivers and grooms for the horses. Tang literature described foreign foods, music, and customs, and one of the fa-vorite pastimes of aristocrats – both men and women – was polo, a game which originated in Persia.

During the Tang era an accomplished gentleman was expected to be able to write poetry, a skill necessary for passing the civil service examinations. Over 48,000 Tang poems by some 2,200 writers have been preserved, with two of China's most beloved and admired poets – **Li Bo** and **Du Fu** – living during the Tang era. Li Bo is known for his freedom of spirit and a love of nature so strong that it is said that he died by drowning while trying to fish out the reflection of the moon on the waters of a lake. In contrast, Du Fu's poetry was more formal and more concerned with social injustice and the suffering of ordinary people.

Although the government relied on Confucian knowledge, Buddhism was very influential, especially during the early Tang era. The most famous traveler of the time was a Buddhist monk, Xuanzang, who traveled to India and returned in 645 C.E. with hundreds of Buddhist texts that he used to advance the un-derstanding of Buddhism in China. Xuanzang's efforts helped to popularize Buddhism, and monasteries were established all over the empire. A number of sects flourished, including Chan (Zen), which emphasized the importance of meditation in reaching nirvana. Buddhist monasteries and temples often per-formed important economic functions, such as operating mills and oil presses and performing banking services. The temples also held much land, and they profited from their connections with wealthy patrons who sought to avoid taxes by registering land under a temple name. Much temple wealth was channeled into building and the arts.

By the mid-9th century, Confucian and Daoist rivals began to attack Buddhism as an impure influence on Chinese society. The Confucian scholar-administra-tors eventually convinced the Tang rulers that the wealthy monasteries posed an economic challenge to the government, particularly since they could not be taxed. Under Emperor Wuzong (842-847), thousands of monasteries and Bud-dhist shrines were destroyed, and hundreds of thousands of monks and nuns were forced to return to civilian lives. Monastery lands were divided among landlords and peasants and became fully taxable. These actions had disastrous effects on Buddhism, and even though the religion survived, Buddhists never again had as much political influence and wealth as they did during the early Tang Dynasty. Instead, Confucianism emerged as the central ideology of Chinese civilization from the 9th to the early 20th century, but Buddhism remained central in Southeast Asia, Tibet, and parts of central Asia.

ORIGINAL DOCUMENTS: HAN YU'S MEMORIAL ON BUDDHISM

One of the leaders of the Confucian counterattack on Buddhism during the early 9th century was Han Yu, a classical prose stylist and poet. His "memorial" so enraged Emperor Tang Xianzong that he banished Han Yu from the court, but his witty essay stands as a famous example of the tensions that existed between Buddhism and Confucianism. In the excerpt below, Han Yu makes fun of the custom of gathering artifacts from the Buddha, including a bone from Buddha's finger.

"Now I hear that by Your Majesty's command a troupe of monks went to Fengxiang [a western city] to get the Buddha-bone, and that you viewed it from a tower as it was carried into the Imperial Palace; also that you have ordered that it be received and honored in all the temples in turn...How could a sublime intelligence like yours consent to believe in this sort of thing? ...Now the Buddha was of barbarian origin. His language differed from Chinese speech; his clothes were of a different cut...He did not recognize the relationship between prince and subject, nor the sentiments of father and son...How much the less, now that he has long been dead, is it fitting that his decayed and rotten bone, his ill-omened and filthy remains, should be allowed to enter in the forbidden precincts of the Palace? Confucius said, 'Respect ghosts and spirits, but keep away from them.'...Your servant is truly alarmed, truly afraid."

Reference: Han Yu's *Memorial,* from *Ennin's Travels in Tang China,* Edwin O. Reischauer, pp. 221-224.

The Decline of the Tang Empire

As early as the mid-700s the Tang Dynasty was weakened by a neglectful emperor who inspired a rebellion that grew into a devastating war that encompassed the empire. The dynasty never recovered, although it did put down the rebels. As so often occurred during Chinese history troubles began along the northern borders. This time a nomadic Turkish people, the **Uighurs,** sacked Chang'an and Luoyang as payment for their aid in defeating the rebels. During the 9th century a series of rebellions spread through the Chinese countryside and fueled popular discontent. The Tang emperors granted more and more power to regional military commanders, and the great empire gradually lost control over them, with the last Tang emperor abdicating his throne in 907.

THE SONG DYNASTY

With the collapse of the Tang Dynasty, China again fell into a time of chaos that followed each of the strong dynasties. Warlords competed for regional power, and by 960 three major states competed to replace the Tang:

1) **The Liao Empire** – The Khitan people, pastoral nomads related to the Mongols, established this empire on the northeastern frontier of China. They governed from several cities, but the emperors spent time going from one nomadic encampment to another.

2) **The Xi Xia (Tanggut) Empire** – The Minyak people established the Xi Xia Empire in western China, named to reflect their connections to the former Tang Empire.

3) **The Song Empire** – In 960 a military commander, who would come to be called Emperor Taizu, reunited much of China under central imperial control, although the empire never had as much military strength as the Tang Empire had.

Although the Song Empire unified China, its leaders were under constant pressure from the northern and western empires. Beginning in 1004 the Song leaders were forced by military defeats to pay tribute to the Liao Empire to keep it from raiding Song domains. Only a few years later, a northern people called the Jurchens destroyed the Liao capital in Mongolia and proclaimed their own empire – the Jin. The Jurchens exacted tribute from Song China, took a significant part of their land, and forced the Song to relocate their capital from Kaifeng to Hangzhou. This invasion of the Jurchens marks the division between the two eras of the Song Dynasty: the years from 960 to 1127, often called the "Northern Song," and the era from 1127 to 1279, referred to as the "Southern Song."

Political Development of the Song Empire

Even during their early years the Song never matched the Tang in political or military strength, partly because the empire was designed to address the weaknesses of its predecessor. The Tang had fallen when regional military commanders became independent rulers who raised their own armies and collected their own taxes. To remedy this, the Song subordinated the military to the civilian administrators of the scholar-gentry class, allowing only civil officials to be governors. They further weakened the military by rotating military command-ers from region to region, subjecting them to the authority of the Confucian scholar-gentry. The result was a reinvigoration of Confucian thought as well as a military organization that could not consistently resist the advances of the Xi Xia, Liao, and Jin Empires.

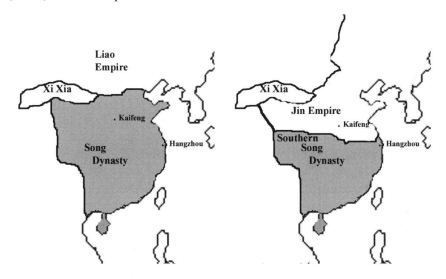

China during the Song and Southern Song Dynasties. The map on the left shows the Song Dynasty as it existed about 1100 C.E., and the map on the right shows the extent of the dynasty by 1140, after military defeats to the Jin Empire that captured the Song capital at Kaifeng. The Southern Song paid tribute to the Jin until the Mongols conquered them in 1234. The Southern Song fell to the Mongols in 1279.

The scholar-gentry class filled the bureaucracy through a broadening of the civil service examinations at three levels: district, provincial, and imperial. Standards were adjusted so that more candidates passed the exams and filled the growing number of government positions, and political power flowed from the aristo-crats and Buddhist rivals to the Confucian scholar-gentry. The growing bureau-cracy put pressure on the imperial treasury, and when the emperors tried to raise taxes, the peasants rebelled, increasing the need for military action and increas-ing the imperial debt. Scholar bureaucrats led Song armies in the field and made military decisions, even though they had little military education, making them vulnerable to defeat by the strong armies of the northern empires.

Economic Development of the Song Empire

Despite its military and political limitations, the Song Dynasty is known for the revolutionary economic changes that occurred in industry, agriculture, and com-merce. Industrial growth peaked during the earlier era, whereas agricultural and commercial growth continued even after the loss of the north in 1127.

- **Industry and production** – Paper making and all the processes involved in book production advanced during the Song Dynasty, as did salt and tea processing and the production of ceramics. In north China, as later in Europe, deforestation provided the incentive for coal production, with much of the coal used to smelt iron, making China's coal and iron industry the most advanced in the world. The Chinese developed the technology for smelting iron and carbonizing it to produce steel. Much of the iron and steel went into the production of military equipment, such as swords, armor, and arrow tips. Other products were tools for farmers and craftsmen, stoves, nails, needles, bits for drilling wells, and chains used to support suspension bridges. Two other important technologies were gunpowder and printing. Daoist alchemists had discovered how to make gunpowder during the Tang Dynasty, and by the Song era, gunpowder was used in bamboo "fire lances" and primitive bombs. The earliest gunpowder had limited military effectiveness, but knowledge of gunpowder chemistry diffused through Eurasia, and gained military importance with the development of metal-barreled cannons in the late 13th century. Before the Song era, printers used wooden blocks to print entire pages with ink. By the mid-11th century printers were experimenting with reusable, movable type, so that individual characters could be rearranged for new printings. As a result, the printing process became much more flexible and less expensive, so that texts could be produced quickly in large quantities.

- **Commerce** – Song commerce built on the earlier trade developed during the Sui and Tang Dynasties. The Song capital, Kaifeng, was located near the junction of the Yellow River and the canal system leading to the prosperous southeast, where it served as a government and commercial center. Kaifeng was a center for textiles, drug and chemical shops, shipyards, building material suppliers, and a thriving restaurant and hotel industry. Professional guilds, similar to those developing in Medieval Europe, were located there. When Kaifeng was conquered by the Jin Empire, the political loss was greater than the economic loss, since by this time a good two-thirds of China's population and wealth were in the South and remained under Song control. Commercial transactions were facilitated by the use of paper money, a Chinese innovation. In the 11th century, paper money was issued for the first time by the government, although it eventually suffered from severe inflation when the government printed too much of it. China's oceangoing ships were large, capable of carrying several hundred men, and were navigated with the aid of the compass, also produced by the Chinese. The greatest of the trading cities of the south was Hangzhou, which also became the capital of the Southern Song and home to merchants, craftsmen, and government officials. Its primary exports included silks, copper coins, and ceramics. Shards of the highly desirable ceramic objects have been found throughout south and Southeast Asia, in the Middle East, and along the east coast of Africa.

- **Agriculture** – Industry and commerce could not have been supported without a remarkable increase in agricultural yields, since the Chinese population surpassed 100 million during the Song era. The size of harvests was increased by the use of improved farm tools, advances in water control, wider application of fertilizers, and the introduction of new varieties of rice. Different strains of rice were cultivated to suit particular locations, and in the southeast many rice paddies produced two crops a year. Because most of this agricultural growth occurred in the south, it was not disturbed by the Jurchen invasion of the north, and in contrast to the coal and iron industries in the north, agricultural production continued to grow during the era of the Southern Song.

Cultural Change in Song China

After the closure of Buddhist monasteries during the late Tang era, persecution of Buddhists eased, but the Song emperors actively supported Confucianism, sponsoring Confucian scholars and subsidizing the printing and distribution of Confucian writings. The appeal of Buddhism forced Confucians to rethink their philosophy, creating **neo-Confucianism**, a new version of the older ideology. Neo-Confucianism emphasized the interpretations of **Mencius** (370-290 B.C.E.) of the old master's thought, and was most famously expressed by Zhu Xi, in his commentaries on the four books, or the classical Confucian works. Neo-Confucianism continued to emphasize complementary opposites, such as the ancient yin and yang, but more central to their thought was the pairing of "li" and "qi". This li is not to be confused with the earlier term meaning ritual, and is usually translated as "principle." Li is the underlying pattern of reality that defines the essence of life, and qi is its material form that is presented in all forms of nature, including earth, rocks, and air. In many ways, these thoughts borrow from the Buddhist tradition of logical thought about the nature of the soul and the individual's relationship with the cosmos. However, neo-Confucianism differed from Buddhism in its emphasis on the importance of social life and its rejection of withdrawal through individual meditation. Neo-Confucians thought that formal education in morals and the arts and sciences was an absolute necessity for a decent life, and that it could not be left to the "enlightenment" of the individual seeker to determine the welfare of the community.   Neo-Confucians emphasized traditions that reinforced class, age, and gender distinctions, particularly as they were expressed in occupational roles.   Because the Confucians were reacting to Buddhism for their revised philosophy, the Song era was very rich in philo-sophical thinking that encouraged consideration of both belief systems, as well as Daoism.

The re-emphasis on Confucian male-dominated hierarchy had an impact on family life and the status of women. During the Tang and early Song era, wom-en enjoyed access to a broad range of activities, as is indicated by a surviving pottery figure from the early Tang period of a young woman playing polo. One of the early Tang emperors, **Wu Zhao,** was the only woman in Chinese history to rule in her own name. She turned to Buddhism for legitimacy, claiming that she was an incarnation of Maitreya (Buddha of the Future), and she favored Buddhists and Daoists over Confucians in her court and government. Under Empress Wu, Tang power reached its furthest geographic extent, but later Con-fucian writers expressed contempt for Wu and other powerful women. Empress Wu was accused of grotesque tortures and murders, and powerful concubine Yang Guifei was blamed for the outbreak of a major rebellion in 755. The neo-Confucians attacked the Buddhists for promoting careers for women, such as scholarship and the monastic life, at the expense of marriage and raising a family. They created laws that favored men in inheritance, divorce, and fam-ily interactions, and they excluded women from an education that might allow them to enter the civil service.

Perhaps no better example of female subordination during the late Song era is the practice of **foot binding**. The origins of the practice are obscure, but by this era upper-class men had developed a preference for small feet for women. Foot binding involved tightly wrapping a young girl's foot so that it could not grow normally, but instead the toes broke and usually curled under the feet. Women with bound feet could not walk normally, and they needed canes to walk by themselves. Their condition assured that they would not venture far from home and that their lives would be managed by their husbands or other male guard-ians.

OTHER EAST ASIAN SOCIETIES: KOREA, VIETNAM, AND JAPAN

By the era from 600 to 1450, other societies in east Asia had developed dis-tinctive identities and cultural traditions, including Korea, Vietnam, and Japan. All three societies were involved in world trade patterns, and all were deeply influenced by Chinese political, economic, and cultural developments. Chi-nese armies occasionally invaded Korea and Vietnam, and Chinese merchants traded with merchants from Korea, Vietnam, and Japan. Buddhism spread to these societies after it had been filtered from India through Chinese society and culture, bringing much diversity to the religion as it gradually diffused. These east Asian societies emphasized their links to China more than links to the wider world, a fact that tended to isolate Korea and Japan even though they struggled to keep their autonomy. Vietnam was not as isolated because it had a strategic location in the Indian Ocean trade basin, and its interactions with India and other cultures in Southeast Asia kept the Vietnamese highly involved with non-Chinese regions.

ORIGINAL DOCUMENTS: SONG POETRY

As in the Tang era, poetry-writing was highly valued during the Song Dynasty, and despite the general decline in the status of women, one of the most celebrated Song poets was a woman, Li Qingzhao. Both of her parents were well educated, and she was raised in the family of a scholar-official. She became well known for her talent in writing poetry when she was still a teenager. In the lyric below, Li Qingzhao describes bringing out an old dress in autumn:

"Up in heaven the star-river turns,
 in man's world below curtains are drawn.
A chill comes to pallet and pillow, damp with tracks of tears.
I rise to take off my gossamer dress
 and just happen to ask, "how late is it now?"
The tiny lotus pods, kingfisher feathers sewn on;
as the gilt flecks away the lotus leaves grow few.
 The same weather as in times before, the same old dress -
only the feelings in the heart are not as they were before."

Reference: An Anthology of Chinese Literature, Stephen Own, translator and editor (New York: W.W. Norton, 1996), pp. 581-2.

Korea

Sometime before the 2nd century B.C.E. people on the Korean peninsula had organized a state called Jeoson, but the northern part of the peninsula was conquered by Han China in 108 B.C.E. Korean tribes managed to win some of the territory back, and during the 2nd century C.E., several Korean tribes united to form the state of Koguryo. Two other states – Paekche and Silla – formed a little later, joining Koguryo to be called "The Three Kingdoms." Buddhism, which the Koreans learned from the Chinese, became the chief religion. By the

600s Silla had conquered the other two kingdoms and taken control of the entire peninsula. Confucianism, like Buddhism, had diffused from China, and became a strong influence on Koreans of the Silla Kingdom.

The **Silla Dynasty** ruled Korea from 668 until the late 9th century, when they were replaced by the **Koryo Dynasty** that ruled until 1892. It was during this period that Chinese influences peaked and Korean culture achieved its first full flowering. During the 7th century Tang armies conquered much of the Korean peninsula, but the Silla armies prevented them from taking over their capital. A compromise was reached when Chinese forces withdrew from Korea in exchange for the Silla king's recognition of the Tang emperor as his overlord. In theory, Korea was a tributary state to Tang China, but in reality the Silla Kingdom operated with a great deal of independence. The arrangement benefitted both sides, with envoys of the Silla kings regularly delivering gifts to Chinese emperors in exchange for gifts from China to Korea. Most importantly for the Koreans, the tributary relationship opened the doors for Korean merchants to trade in China. The Silla capital at Kumsong was rebuilt to look like the Tang capital at Chang'an.

Although Confucianism and Buddhism became a part of Korean traditions during this era, Chinese and Korean societies differed in many ways. Some Korean elites studied the Confucian texts and took the exams, but Korea never established a bureaucracy based on the examination system, and political control remained very much in the hands of the royal family and the aristocracy. No strong conflicts emerged between Confucianism and Buddhism as happened in China during the late Tang era. Instead the Korean elite tended to favor Buddhism over Confucianism, and the Korean royal family lavishly endowed monasteries. Buddhist monks attended the ruler and the royal family, and both Buddhist and Confucian schools were founded. More than in China, a small aristocratic elite controlled Korea, with their members filling most of the posts in the bureaucracy and dominating the social and economic life of the entire kingdom. Artisans were seen as their servants, and no distinct social class developed for merchants or traders.

Koreans often rivaled the Chinese in artistic and technological endeavors. Although the Koreans first learned techniques for manufacturing porcelain from the Chinese, the Koreans created pale green-glazed bowls and vases called "celadon" that the Chinese admired and collected and that remain today highly prized items for both individuals and museums. Korean woodblocks were also superb, and the oldest surviving woodblock prints in Chinese characters were produced in Korea in the middle 700s. Like the Song Chinese, Koreans experimented by the early 13th century with movable type, although the demand for books was less than in China because fewer of the Korean elite were literate.

Still, many Koreans today believe that movable type was first discovered in the Koryo Kingdom, not in Song China.

Vietnam

Vietnam had been invaded and occupied in earlier years by Han Chinese forces, and when the Tang attacked them, they put up a fierce resistance, and even after they were defeated, rebellions broke out sporadically against the Chinese conquerors. The Viet people, who had settled in the region around the Red River, nevertheless absorbed Chinese culture and technology rather readily. The Viets adopted Chinese agricultural methods and irrigation systems, they studied the Confucian texts, and they traded merchandise with the Chinese. However, even though some Vietnamese authorities formed tributary relationships with the Chinese court, the Viets resented Chinese efforts to dominate their land, and when the Tang Empire fell, they won their independence. Still, Chinese traditions impacted Vietnam substantially. Vietnamese authorities modeled the Chinese administrative system and bureaucracy, and Buddhism came to Vietnam from China as well as India.

PERSPECTIVES: CHINESE AND VIETNAMESE POINTS OF VIEW

The Chinese first referred to the Viets as a group of "southern barbarians," and thought of them as inhabitants of just another rice-growing area to be annexed to their ever-expanding civilization. However, the Viets had a separate identity based on a sophisticated, embedded culture of their own. The Viet language was not related to Chinese, and they valued village autonomy and the nuclear family in contrast to Chinese political centralization and emphasis on the extended family. They traded regularly and shared cultural traits with India and other Southeast Asian cultures. Vietnamese women also had greater influence and freedom than their Chinese counterparts, and they preferred long skirts to the black pants that nonelite women wore in China. The Viets also tended to be much more devout in their Buddhist beliefs, and their literature was distinct from Chinese literature. Chinese officials found it hard to conceal their disdain for these "barbaric" differences, and as a result, the strong-willed Vietnamese resisted their overlords to win an independence that lasted from 939 until the 19th century, when they were conquered by the French.

Japan

For most of its early history Japan developed in relative isolation without much contact with people on mainland Asia. Its earliest inhabitants were probably nomadic peoples from northeast Asia, although some scholars have theorized that some early settlers came from islands to the south. As the population grew, groups that were separated by the mountainous terrain developed into small states dominated by aristocratic clans. Japan's geographical isolation from the mainland meant that the language that developed was unrelated to Chinese, as was its native religion, **Shintoism.** Shintoism is an animistic religion that emphasizes nature and spirits, or kami, that inhabit objects in nature. Japan's early clans, or uji, worshipped their own special kami, with some becoming more powerful than others by the 7th century C.E. By that time, the Japanese clans were well aware of the Tang Empire, and even though the Tang never conquered them, some trade existed, and Japanese emissaries visited China. When the Yamato clan began to centralize power, they established a court modeled on the Tang court in Chang'an.

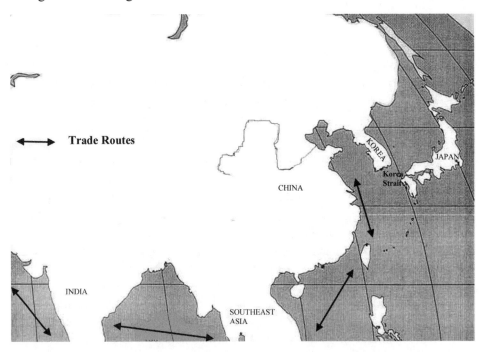

Geographical Relationships in East Asia. Like all other places on earth, Japan's geographical location has greatly impacted its development. Its location northeast of major trade routes that connected China, Southeast Asia, and India often kept it out of the line of attack and invasion. Unlike Korea, Japan is an island, and could only be reached by sea. To further insulate the islands, the waters of the Korea Strait are treacherous and very difficult for an invading navy to cross. As a result, Japan was one of the few areas in east Asia that China never successfully attacked.

Fujiwara Rule

By the mid-8th century Confucianism and Buddhism were established in Japan, although the native Shintoism remained influential. The Japanese mastered Chinese building techniques and established massive Buddhist temples that rivaled and perhaps surpassed the grandeur of Chinese structures. The earliest capitals were at Nara and Kyoto, where legally centralized government lasted until 1185. Members of the **Fujiwara family** controlled power and protected an emperor, who belonged to a family that was believed to have ruled Japan since the beginning of history. Unlike the changing Chinese dynasties, the ruling Japanese dynasty never changed, enduring largely because it never wielded true political power. During times of turmoil, the ruling families, parties, or factions have been thrown out, but the imperial house has survived. In the era between 794 and 1185, known as the **Heian Era,** the Fujiwara family was the power behind the throne, and they very much appreciated Confucian learning and Chinese classics, painting, poetry, and interior decoration.

Todaiji Temple. This enormous Buddhist temple was built in the 8th century near Nara, and provides a splendid example of the fine wooden architecture of early Japan. In 752 dignitaries from all over Asia gathered at Todaiji to celebrate the "eye-opening" ceremony of the Great Buddha statue. Todaiji is reputedly the largest wooden building ever constructed in world history.

The refined court of the Fujiwara family was captured in a remarkable novel, *The Tale of Genji,* written by the noblewoman Murasaki Shikibu. The book was the first to be written in Japanese, and it described the life of a fictitious prince named Genji, who lived a life of refinement, writing poetry in his fine calligraphic hand to woo the ladies of the court. The detail of the novel provided a fine view of the lives of the nobility, as told by a lady-in-waiting in the Heian court. Because the elite families of Fujiwara Japan did not encourage education for women, it is notable that the most important piece of literature in a court that prided itself on its sophistication was written by a woman.

ORIGINAL DOCUMENTS: *THE TALE OF GENJI*

Mirasaki Shikibu's acclaimed novel, *The Tale of Genji,* was written about 1000 C.E., and provides a vivid description of life in the Heian court of Japan during the time that the Fujiwara family ruled. One skill that was important for both men and women of the court was spontaneous poetry writing. The passage below describes a scene when Prince Genji walked past the house of a lady he had been visiting in strict secrecy. When no one answered his knock at the door, he wrote a poem for an attendant to read to the lady:

> Even when I wander
> lost under mist-shrouded skies
> at break of day,
> I cannot pass beyond
> the gate of my beloved.

The lady promptly answered:

> If you have halted,
> loath to pass the rustic fence
> enshrouded in mist,
> the closed door of a grass-thatched hut
> should prove no obstacle.

Reference: Genji &Heike, translated by Helen Craig McCulough (Stanford: Stanford University Press, 1994), p. 106.

Since the noble Fujiwara family spent most of their time pursuing their elegant lifestyles, they tended to entrust responsibility for local government, policing, and tax collection to their warriors. By the mid-1100s the nobility lost control of the government, and the warriors fought one another for power. Two power-ful warrior families – the Taira and the Minamoto – struggled for years, and the Minamoto emerged victorious in 1185. Like the Fujiwara before them, the Minamoto ruled in the name of the emperor, who maintained a separate court. The clan leader was installed as **shogun** – a military governor who ruled in place of the emperor – who lived in Kamakura, near modern Tokyo, while the imperial court remained at Kyoto. The Minamoto clan dominated political life in Japan for the next four centuries.

Japanese Feudalism

After they defeated the Taira family in 1185, the Minamoto clan established the **bakufu** ("tent"), or military government, beginning the medieval period of Japanese history that lasted until the 16th century. As in Europe, a feudal political order developed in which regional lords wielded power and authority in areas where they controlled land and economic affairs. These lords competed for power, which they gained through military prowess. In contrast to the Fujiwara family, these warrior clans valued military talent and discipline rather than etiquette and courtesy. The lords were supported by devoted professional warriors called **samurai,** who provided police and military services in exchange for food, clothing, and housing. They lived by the code, bushido, ("the way of the warrior") that emphasized absolute loyalty to one's lord. If a samurai were to fail his master, he ended his life by seppuku, (also called hari-kiri or "belly slicing") a ritual suicide by disembowelment. The entire era is characterized by much in-fighting, even within the ruling families. Farmlands were ravaged as the samurai of rival lords clashed and the power of the shogun was challenged. The danger was so great that the shogun's palace had devices installed beneath the floors that reproduced bird singing to warn the master of the presence of tiptoeing intruders.

Despite the original inspiration from the Tang Empire, Japanese society had taken a very different form from that in China. Japan borrowed from China Confucian values, Buddhism, and the ideal of centralized imperial rule, but the feudalistic system they developed had more in common with western European societies of the day. They had no use for elaborate bureaucracies, and loyalty ties between lords and warrior-vassals were emphasized, with peasants providing the necessary agricultural labor. Both feudalistic systems developed rituals to demonstrate relationships among the elite. Both Japanese and European political systems were less sophisticated than those of empires such as the Tang, partly because neither area had the resources or experience to create a well-developed bureaucracy. However, despite their similarities, some important differences remained between western European and Japanese feudalism:

1) Western feudalism placed more emphasis on written contracts. In the west, feudal loyalties were sealed by negotiated contracts that spelled out exactly what benefits all parties would receive. Japanese feudalism relied more on group and individual loyalties that were cemented by ideals of honor, not written contracts. This difference had important consequences for each area, with the West developing parliaments to defend their contracts, and Japan relying on collective decision-making teams that connected to the state. Even in today's world, with the globalizing effect of international business, western businesses still rely more on written contracts, while Japanese companies have more awareness of "honor codes" that govern business relationships.

2) Samurai were granted land rights from their lords, but they did not own land; European knights often received land ownership for their services. As a result, the social division between lord and samurai remained clear, whereas knights often became lords themselves. Both systems had intricate loyalty relationships, but the system of lords and overlords in European kingdoms was endlessly baffling.

THE RISE AND FALL OF THE MONGOLS

During the Foundations period of world history (before 600 C.E.), nomadic people occupied many parts of the world and were in contact with people who lived more sedentary lives. Nomadic people often connected one civilization to another, such as the traders that travelled the Silk Road, or the camel herders that traversed the Sahara and Arabian Deserts. Nomadic migrations, such as those of the Huns and the Germanic peoples, greatly impacted the civilizations of the day and played a major role in the decline of the classical civilizations. In this era (600 to 1450 C.E.) we have already seen how the nomadic people of the Arabian Peninsula united under Muslim leaders to conquer territories from Spain to the Middle East and eventually became sedentary themselves. Of the many nomadic groups that have played roles in the unfolding of the world's history, perhaps the most impressive was the Great Mongol Empire that began in the steppes of central Asia and eventually formed the largest, if not the longest lasting, empire of all times.

Genghis Khan and the Rise of the Mongols

Before their rise to power, the Mongols were a relatively small group of steppe (dry grassland at high elevation) nomads whose sources of food included herds of livestock and the bounty of their hunting. Their strong Mongol ponies could survive the brutal weather of the northern steppes, and the Mongols were excellent horsemen, fighting with bows and arrows from the backs of the ponies. They lived in portable houses called yurts, and they were politically organized into kinship-based clans and tribes.   It was in this setting that **Temujin** was born, later known to the world as **Genghis Khan,** one of the most famous warriors in history. As a young man he sought vengeance by decimating the rival clan who had poisoned his father. Very early on he gained a reputation for ferocity and brutality, killing survivors rather than taking captives, and boiling defeated enemies alive. Beyond these frightful characteristics, however, he was also a shrewd diplomat who understood loyalty to allies and demonstrated an ability to convince unaffiliated tribes to side with him. Genghis Khan also was quite capable of turning on troublesome allies, and gradually strengthened his position to rule all of the Mongol tribes by the end of the 12th century. In 1206 at a meeting of clan elders at the capital of Karakorum, he accepted the title of "universal ruler," or "Genghis Khan."

THE BIG PICTURE: THE IMPORTANCE OF NOMADIC MOVEMENTS

In the era 600 - 1450 C.E., the impact of nomadic movements reached its greatest extent in world history. In the 7th century the Bedouins of the Arabian Desert carried their Islamic faith to their many conquered territories, only to have the last major caliphate destroyed by the Mongols in the 13th century. The Mongols also conquered the Russian principalities, central Asian kingdoms and empires, and the Southern Song of China. A third group of people whose movements affected a great many Eurasians were the Turks. Turkish people never formed a single, homogeneous group, but were organized into clans and tribes that often fought bitterly with one another. They spoke related languages and believed that shamans interceded between humans and nature spirits. Turkish peoples entered Persia, Anatolia, and India at different times and for different purposes. Many converted to Islam, like the Seljuk Turks that the Christian Crusaders from Europe fought. The Turks moved far beyond their original homes in central Asia, and their conquests served as a prelude to the massive onslaught staged by the Mongols during the 13th century.

Genghis Khan combined traditional Mongol fighting strengths with new methods of organization. He organized his armies under a pyramid of officers leading units of 100, 1000, and 10,000 mounted warriors. These units not only improved the accountability of his officers, but they also served to break up old alliances based on tribes or clans, leaving all to be loyal ultimately to him. His highest officials were family members, and his four top military commanders were his sons, and after his death, the great Mongol organization passed to grandsons and other relatives. The armies were further divided into light and heavy cavalry, with the light cavalry able to move more swiftly, and the heavy cavalry able to wear Chinese-style armor for greater durability. Despite his tendency to favor family members for military leadership, promotion within the army was usually based on merit, and intertribal quarrels declined significantly.

Once he unified the Mongols, Genghis Khan turned east toward China, pierced the Great Wall of China in 1211, and took the Jin capital (later Beijing) in 1215. By the time of his death in 1227, he had also conquered Xi Xia, the great Tang-gut empire that had long fought against the Southern Song. There he mastered their weapons of siege warfare: the mangonel and trebuchet that could catapult huge rocks, giant crossbows mounted on stands, and gunpowder launched in bamboo tubes from longbows. The Mongol bow was short enough to maneu-ver from horseback, and Mongol arrows found their marks from long distances away. Mongol leaders were also fond of conducting fake retreats that caught their enemies off guard before they abruptly turned back to resume the battle. The Mongol armies turned west as well, conquering the central Asian empire of Kara-Khitai and the Turkish empire, Khwarizm. Genghis Khan went as far as Tabriz and Tbilisi in the Caucasus area between the Black and Caspian Seas before he turned back toward China in the years before he died in 1227.

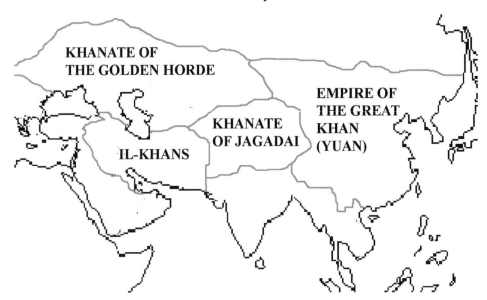

The Mongol Empire in the Mid-13th Century. After Genghis Khan's death, the empire was divided into four khanates, each ruled by one of Genghis' sons or grandsons. The empire was the largest political state to ever exist in world history.

The Mongols After Genghis Khan

As reflected in his title ("universal ruler"), Genghis Khan had large ambitions for conquest, and his sons and grandsons that followed him continued the quest for territory. They returned to Russia to add to the previous conquests, and drove the army of the legendary Teutonic Knights of Germany almost back to the walls of Vienna. Only the sudden death of the Great Khan Ogodei (Genghis Khan's son) saved western Europe from Mongol attack, since all leaders were called back to Karakorum to choose another leader. Persia and Iraq, however, were not spared, as Genghis' grandson, Hulegu, returned to the tottering Abbasid Caliphate to defeat and kill the last Baghdad caliph and his son. Some of the caliph's relatives fled to Egypt where a much-reduced caliphate continued to exist under the protection of the Mamluk Sultanate. The conquest of China was completed in 1279 by **Kubilai Khan**, another of Genghis' grandsons. The empire at its greatest extent in the late 13th century stretched from eastern Europe to the Pacific Ocean, encompassing most of Asia north of India, much of the Middle East, and eastern Europe.

After Genghis Khan's death, his heirs divided the vast realm into four regional empires that grew as new conquests were made:

1) **Khanate of the Great Khan** – This empire was first ruled from the old capital at Karakorum in Mongolia, but was moved to Khanbalik, the Mongol name for the old Jin capital at Beijing. This Khan was seen as the successor to Genghis Khan, and the position was first held by Ogodei and eventually by Kubilai Khan. In China, this khanate was called the Yuan Dynasty.

2) **Khanate of Jagadai** – This khanate in central Asia was ruled by the descendents of Genghis' son, Jagadai. The leader **Timur** (Tamerlane) later rose from this khanate, although he never assumed the title *khan* because he was a Turk with only an in-law relationship to Genghis' extended family.

3) **Khanate of the Golden Horde** – The origins of the name is not clear, but one story is that it is based on the sun catching the shields and weapons of the great Mongol army as it marched toward its victims. This khanate conquered southern Russia and established their capital at Sarai on the Volga River, where they ruled over a Muslim Turkic population. The most famous leader of the Golden Horde was Batu, another of Genghis' grandsons.

4) **Il-Khan** – Established by Hulegu, yet another grandson, this state controlled parts of Armenia, all of Azerbaijan, Mesopotamia, and Iran.

Hulegu's forces captured the Abbasid's capital in Baghdad in 1258, but were defeated decisively at Ain Jalut by the Mamluk forces from Egypt. As a result, all Islamic lands did not go to the Mongols, but Hulegu and his successors ruled the Islamic heartlands from Azerbaijan for almost a hundred years.

The Mongol expansion was made possible by the superior Mongol bow that could shoot arrows about one-third farther than those of the enemy. The Mongols also enlisted men from conquered territories, so that in their later years their armies were composed of truly international forces.

PERSPECTIVES: VIEWS OF THE MONGOLS

Historians must always be alert to the fact that descriptions of nomadic people are usually written by more literate urbanites, who tend to view their subjects as inferior people. Many accounts written about the Mongols reflect such biases, but a very valuable source of information was actually written by a Mongol, perhaps even a member of Genghis Khan's household. *The Secret History of the Mongols* is clearly an insider's account, written just after Genghis Khan's death. The Mongols were illiterate before the time of Genghis Khan, who adopted the script of the Uighurs of central Asia that was used in this book. The passage below describes the importance of *anda,* a bonding between Mongol males, in this case Temujin and Jamugha, a young noble.

So Temujin and Jamugha said to each other:
"We've heard the elders say,
'When two men become *anda* their lives become one.
One will never desert the other and will always defend him.'
This is the way we'll act from now on.
We'll renew our old pledge and love each other forever."
...They held a feast on the spot
and there was great celebration.

Reference: The Secret History of the Mongols: The Origin of Chingis Khan: An Adaptation of the Yuan Ch'ao Pi Shih, based primarily on the English Translation by Francis Woodman Cleaves. Expanded edition (Boston: Cheng and Tsui, 1998).

The Fragmentation of the Empire

The Mongols dominated the 13th century, but by the time that Kubilai Khan died in 1294, the parts of the huge empire had split along ethnic lines. Just as other large empires before it, the sheer distance between its capital and its borders made it impossible to maintain unity for long. First China, then Russia and the Middle Eastern lands separated, weakened and divided not only by distance but by serious feuds between khans of the Golden Horde and Il-Khan. Another

ORIGINAL DOCUMENTS: WILLIAM OF RUBRUCK ON MONGOL WOMEN

Once the Mongols invaded eastern Europe, the Pope initiated a series of embassies to various Mongol khans to discover their designs regarding western Europe and to convert them to Catholic Christianity. One of the earliest missionary-ambassadors to the Great Khan was William of Rubruck, a Franciscan priest who kept detailed accounts of his journey. He was usually very objective, and his description of Mongol roles for men and women generally confirm the tendency for women to have higher status in nomadic societies than in the early civilizations. He describes social gatherings where the wife of the headman sits side by side with her husband, and men and women enjoy music and drinking together. However, his opinions of Mongol customs come through in the following description:

"...they believe that [a widow] will always return after death to her first husband. This gives rise to a shameful custom among them whereby a son sometimes takes to wife all his father's wives, except his own mother... When anyone has made an agreement with another to take his daughter, the father of the girl arranges a feast and she takes flight to relations where she lies hid. Then the father declares: 'Now my daughter is yours; take her wherever you find her.' Then he searches for her with his friends until he finds her; then he has to take her by force and bring her, as though by violence, to his house."

Reference: The Mongol Mission, Christopher Dawson, ed. (New York: Sheed and War, 1955), pp. 103-104.

reason for the empire's fragmentation was the tendency for Mongol rulers to adopt the cultural preferences of the people that they conquered. For example, Kubilai Khan favored Buddhism, and the rulers of Il Khan and the Golden Horde adopted Islam, although the Russian people remained Eastern Orthodox

Christians. By the late 14th century, the Mongol-ruled khanates had disappeared from Eurasian maps, and the largest empire in world history was no more.

Impact of the Mongols

One important overall impact of the Mongol conquests was at first the disruption, and then the encouragement of the long-distance trade routes of Eurasia. After the initial shock of Mongol attacks, a **Pax Mongolica** (Mongol Peace) was established that created a similar order that the Romans had created in their heyday (Pax Romana). Lines of direct communication opened between east Asia and western Europe. For about a century, people, goods, ideas, and even diseases traveled faster than ever before from one end of the Eurasian landmass to the other. When the empire broke up, so did the Pax Mongolica, and the trade along the Silk Road disappeared forever, although many turned to the Indian Ocean trade instead.

Another important impact of Mongol unification was the creation of one of the worst pandemics in world history, known in Europe as the "**Black Death.**" As occurred with the interactions of the earliest civilizations, one cost of increased contacts among distant peoples is the spread of disease along trade routes. In southwestern China the bubonic plague had festered in Yunnan province since the early Tang period. Mongol troops established a garrison in the area, and the military and supply traffic allowed flea-infested rats to carry the plague into many parts of China and central Asia. The terrible plague spread out of Asia and struck Mongol armies attacking the city of Kaffa on the Black Sea in 1346. A year later traders from Genoa in Italy carried the disease from Kaffa to Italy and southern France. During the next two years the Black Death spread across Europe, sparing some places and killing two-thirds of the population in others. In many ways the plague brought more devastation than the Mongol attacks themselves, and the disruption it caused to Eurasian societies was a factor in the breakup of the Mongol Empire.

The Mongols and Islam in the Middle East

The conflict between Mongol and Muslim beliefs is illustrated by the fate of the last Abbasid caliph when Hulegu's troops stormed Baghdad in 1258. In accordance with Mongol customs for the execution of high-born persons, the caliph had been rolled in a rug and trampled to death by horses to prevent his blood from spilling on the ground. Muslims were shocked and outraged by this behavior, and over time remained repelled by the Mongols' worship of idols in their shamanistic religion. The tension was not relieved until the Il-Khan ruler, Ghazan, converted to Islam in 1295. Eventually the Il-Khans declared themselves the protectors and advocates of Islam, and all Mongols in the Il-Khan

Empire were ordered to convert to Islam. The Il-Khan legal code was altered to include the principles of Islam, and the rulers supported scholars, historians, astronomers, and mathematicians in their studies that contributed to the reputation of the era as the "Golden Age of Islam." In these ways, the mighty Mongols were "civilized" by Islamic culture, illustrating the superior holding power of religion as the "glue" that held societies together during this period of world history.

The peace of the Il-Khan was broken by the ambitions of **Timur**, or Tamerlane, who came from the Khanate of Jagadai to attack the entire area between northern India and Moscow during the late 14th and early 15th centuries. Timur was also a Muslim, but that did not prevent him from destroying virtually everything in his war path. He ruled from his capital in Samarkand, and like Genghis Khan, conquered huge amounts of territory. However, he ruled through tribal leaders who were his allies, and did not create an imperial administration, so after his death, his empire fell apart, although his successors held on to control of the region from Persia to Afghanistan for more than a century. Timur was Turkish, and in many ways, his conquests opened the door to more Turkish migrations into the Middle East. Among those that came was **Osman**, who settled in Anatolia and gathered a following of supporters. In 1299 he declared independence from the Seljuk Turks and established himself as the founder of the **Ottoman Turks,** named in his honor. By the 1440s the Ottomans began to expand into the Byzantine Empire and eventually capture Constantinople in 1453, renaming the great city "Istanbul."

The Mongol Impact on Russia

When the Mongols invaded Russia, they found an area divided into many petty kingdoms, each ruled by local princes. The great trading city of Kiev was in decline by the 13th century, and another major center had developed to the northeast in Novgorod. Because the kingdoms refused to cooperate, they were roundly defeated by the Mongols, with Kiev, which had reached a population of more than 100,000, falling in 1240. Novgorod survived, largely because its prince, **Alexander Nevskii**, agreed to Mongol demands for tribute. For two and a half centuries, the Mongols dominated Russia, and Russian princes served as vassals of the khan of the Golden Horde. Fear of Mongol raids almost certainly forced peasants to seek protection from the nobility, and they bound themselves to the land as serfs, a condition that lasted in Russia until the 19th century. However, many Russians benefitted from the Pax Mongolica through increased trade, including the princes of Moscow, who along with the Novgorod princes, almost completely eclipsed the power of Kiev. Moscow became a tribute collector for the Mongol khans, spread their control over towns as punishment for failing to pay their dues, and grew much wealthier and influential as a result, eventually becoming more powerful than Novgorod. Once Mongol power declined, the Moscow princes were strong enough to step forward to claim independent power and set Russia on the road to eventually become a unique world power.

Historians don't always agree on the importance of Mongol rule in shaping Russian development. Since Kiev was already declining by the time of the invasion, perhaps it was inevitable that some other city, such as Moscow or Novgorod, would come to power. Russia was already shaped by Orthodox Christianity and other influences of the Byzantines, setting the Slavic people of the area on a very different path than western Europe. However, Mongol rule arguably cemented Russia's isolation from Christian lands farther west, cutting them off from the changes brought about by the Renaissance in the west, while at the same time protecting them from attack by Christian knights from more powerful kingdoms to the west. For example, the Teutonic Knights, a militant crusading Christian order of Germany, were determined to free the area of Orthodox Christianity, which they considered to be a heresy to Catholicism. Because of Mongol protection, the Russian princes escaped the knights' fervent efforts to control them, and were left to rule their feudal kingdoms in relative isolation.

China under Mongol Control

The Mongols rose to power during the era of the Southern Song, a time when China was militarily and politically weaker than it had been during the Tang era. The Song emperors were paying tribute to the Jin Empire of the Jurchen people who controlled all of northern China. By 1215 the Mongols had captured the Jurchen capital near modern Beijing and renamed it Khanbalik ("city of the khan"). The Jurchens continued to fight the Mongols for many years, and thwarted Genghis Khan's desire to conquer China is his lifetime. The Southern Song managed to hold them off until the Khanate of the Great Khan fell to Genghis' talented grandson, **Kubilai Khan.** From his base in Khanbalik, he attacked the Song dynasty in southern China, and the Song Empire lasted only three years after Kubilai captured their capital at Hangzhou in 1276. In 1279 he proclaimed himself to be the Chinese emperor and founded the **Yuan Dynasty** that lasted until 1368. Despite his success in China, Kubilai never conquered Vietnam or the other kingdoms of Southeast Asia, and he famously failed twice in his attempt to attack Japan across the treacherous waters of the Korean Strait. On both occasions, typhoon winds deflected his vessels, and the Japanese retained their independence, aided by what they came to call the kamikaze ("divine winds").

The China that Kubilai Khan organized included many ethnicities other than the Han Chinese that formed the basis for the identity and unity of the Song Empire. Not only were Mongols included, but also the Jurchens, the Tanggut, Tibetans, and many other people of central and northern Asia. Confucian scholars and other Han Chinese still thought of themselves as inhabitants of the great "Middle Kingdom," and saw the Mongol intruders as foreigners and barbarians. Yet they had to submit to Kubilai Khan and his successors. The Mongol rulers were certainly aware of the biases against them that of course also existed in other "civilized" parts of their empire, including Islamic lands. With this knowledge, Kubilai organized his government with Mongols as the top officials who replaced the authority of the Confucian scholars, and he dismantled the old Confucian examination system. The scholar-gentry often retained positions with the government, but they were reduced to middle-level administrators with statuses lower than even the central Asians and northern Chinese who outranked them because they had come under Mongol control almost two generations earlier. The resentments of the Confucians boiled below the surface until they were able to reassert themselves as Mongol power waned in the mid-14th century. One reason for their hostility is an old one that had played a role in the breakup of the Tang Dynasty – many subjects of the Yuan Dynasty were Buddhists and represented a threat to the deep Confucian roots of China.

Another important difference in the orientation of Yuan leaders was their favoring of merchants, who were often Middle Easterners or central Asians. To the Confucians, merchants were quite inferior to scholars since they contributed little to society by just trading items that already existed. The Yuan also elevated the status of physicians, who were regarded by the Confucians as mere technicians. Instead, Yuan leaders encouraged the sharing of Chinese medical and herbal knowledge with westerners from Christian and Muslim lands. To keep the Confucian scholars from challenging Mongol authority, Kubilai passed many laws intended to keep Mongol and Chinese identities separate. Chinese scholars were forbidden to learn the Mongol script, and Mongols were not allowed to marry ethnic Chinese. As an example, Kubilai included no ethnic Chinese women in his large harem. Mongols also retained their religious beliefs and showed a keen interest in Buddhism, especially the versions favored in Tibet.

Despite these differences, Kubilai Khan was fascinated by Chinese civilization. His capital in the north was built on the site occupied by earlier dynasties, and he retained Chinese rituals and music in his court proceedings. He also used the Chinese calendar and made sacrifices to his ancestors. Khanbalik was surrounded by Chinese-style walls, and the complex – the forbidden city – was retained and expanded. Confucianism, while not encouraged, was at least tolerated, reflecting the Mongols' open attitude toward other ways of life. Kubilai was very curious about other ways of life, and his cosmopolitan court reflected his tastes with a welcoming attitude toward travelers and emissaries from many foreign lands, including the famous Marco Polo from Italy.

The Decline of the Yuan and Rise of the Ming

Even before the end of Kubilai Khan's long reign, the dynasty showed signs of weakening. Not only were relations tense between Mongols and Han Chinese, but Kubilai's failure to defeat Japan and Vietnam undermined his strength. The last years of his rule were not his strongest, as he sank into an apathy probably brought on by the deaths of his favorite wife Chabi as well as the son he hoped would succeed him. The rulers that followed Kubilai were weak, and their bureaucracies were characterized by greed and corruption. The scholar-gentry encouraged others to rebel again their "barbarian" oppressors, and banditry was widespread in the countryside, as was piracy on the open seas. China fell into a familiar chaos as the dynasty dissolved, but this time, rather than a regional warlord, power was claimed by a poor peasant named Ju Yuanzhang, who founded

COMPARISON: CUSTOMS AND ATTITUDES OF MONGOL AND CHINESE WOMEN

Both Mongol and Chinese societies were patriarchies, but true to their nomadic roots, Mongol women had more freedoms and independence during the Yuan Dynasty than their Chinese counterparts. They refused to bind their feet, and they kept their rights to own property and move about outside their homes. Many accounts of the day, including that of William of Rubruck, described Mongol women participating in activities that were reserved for men only in China. For example, Mongol women formed their own hunting parties, and one of Kubilai's female relatives married the only one of her suitors that could throw her in a wrestling match.

Kubilai's favorite wife, Chabi, reflected the spirit of Mongol women as the influential adviser to her husband. Like other Mongol women, she was politically savvy, encouraging her husband to respect Chinese culture while retaining Mongol control. Like her husband, Chabi had cosmopolitan tastes, and was equally curious about other ways of life than her own. However, the Mongol era was too brief in Chinese history to bring about any permanent change in male and female gender roles, and even before the overthrow of the Yuan Dynasty, the pattern of old inequalities had clearly settled in again.

the **Ming** ("brilliant") **Dynasty** that was to rule China for the next three centuries.

In 1368, Ju Yuanzhang was renamed Hongwu, the first Ming emperor, and his most important goal was to remove all traces of Mongol rule. Once the Mongols retreated to the steppes, he established a government on the model of traditional Chinese dynasties. He revived the Confucian educational and civil service systems and restaffed the bureaucracy, and he centralized authority in the new capital, Nanjing, far south of the Mongol capital at Beijing. The Ming emperors insisted on absolute obedience to their directives and were highly suspicious of any non-Chinese subjects. They relied on emissaries called mandarins, who visited local officials to be sure that the emperor's directives were followed. Even more than earlier emperors, the Ming relied on eunuchs (castrated males) for governmental services, since they could not have families that might challenge the dynasty's power.

The Ming emperors believed that China had been weakened by its contact with other people, and so they were much more cautious in their trade with outsiders, and much more likely to believe that it was best for China to remold itself in the greatness of the past. China still had many desirable products to trade, especially once Ming craftsmen began creating distinctive and beautiful blue-and-white porcelain. The dynasty understood that the empire's wealth rested on trade, but its leaders were always wary of outsiders, afraid to lose China again to rule by non-Chinese. So they set about to rebuild the empire as independently as possible, repairing irrigation systems, factories, internal trade connections, and even the Great Wall. Ming emperors actively promoted Chinese cultural traditions, particularly the Confucian and neo-Confucian schools. During its early years the Ming Empire lived up to its name ("brilliant"), and built a strong China that clearly reflected its age old conflict between opening its doors to others and swinging them tightly shut to keep the intruders out.

IDENTIFICATIONS AND CONCEPTS

bakufu
Black Death, bubonic plague
Du Fu
equal fields system
foot binding
Fujiwara family
Genghis Khan
hegemony
Heian Era
Il-Khan
Jagadai

Khanate of the Golden Horde
Khanate of the Great Khan
Koryo Dynasty
kowtow
Kubilai Khan
Li Bo
Liao Empire
Mencius
"The Middle Kingdom"
Ming Dynasty
neo-Confucianism
Nevskii, Alexander
Osman, Ottoman Turks
Pax Mongolica
samurai
Shintoism
shogun
Silla Dynasty
Song Dynasty
Sui Dynasty
The Tale of Genji
Tang Dynasty
Temujin
Uighurs
Wu Zhao
Xi Xia Empire
Yuan Dynasty

CHAPTER NINE:
TROPICAL AFRICA
AND ASIA

We have seen that the influence of Islam did not decline as a result of the fall of the Abbasid Caliphate to the Mongols in the 13th century. Instead, the Mongols that captured Baghdad generally allowed the practice of the religion to continue, and in many cases even converted to Islam themselves. Islam also continued to grow in the lands south of the areas that the Mongols controlled, sometimes spreading quietly and other times suddenly and violently. These tropical lands that extended from Sub-Saharan Africa to south Asia to Southeast Asia were linked not only by this common religion, but also by increasingly complex long-distance trade networks.

THE TROPICAL ENVIRONMENT

Geographically, the "tropics" are the lands that lie between the Tropic of Cancer and the Tropic of Capricorn on the world map. In the Eastern Hemisphere, the tropics include most of Africa, southern Arabia, most of India, and all of Southeast Asia. Instead of the hot and cold seasons of temperate climates, the tropical areas around the Indian Ocean have wet and dry seasons that are influenced heavily by alternating winds called **monsoons.** A high-pressure that hovers over the Himalaya Mountains from December to March produces dry winds that blow southward to the Indian Ocean, creating the dry season in south Asia. Between April and August a low-pressure zone over India allows a northward movement of air from the Indian Ocean, bringing winds laden with moisture, creating the rainy season. In Africa, the complex wind patterns create some areas that rarely see rain at all (the Sahara and Kalahari Deserts), and others that have persistent heavy rains (the rain forests around the Congo River). Not surprisingly, most of the people of Africa live between the deserts and rain forests where moderate rain falls during the rainy seasons. Dry areas also extend through much of the Arabian Peninsula and parts of India. The monsoons, as well as different land elevations and topography, create diverse geographic lands, despite the fact that they all have warm temperatures.

SUB-SAHARAN AFRICA

Until about 1450, Islam provided the major external contact between Sub-Saharan Africa and the rest of the world. New centers of civilization and political power rose in several areas, building on the effects of the earlier Bantu migrations that had slowly spread throughout the continent. Despite their commonalities, the civilizations that developed in this era were quite diverse – from the Sudanic empires of Mali, Ghana, and Songhay to the city-states along the Swahili coast in east Africa – with many that were very connected to the rest of the world. In contrast, other areas of Sub-Saharan Africa remained remote and unconnected to the growing world network.

A common form of social organization in Africa during and after the Bantu migrations is sometimes called a **stateless society**, with no hierarchy of government officials but instead relying on kinship relationships or other forms of personal obligations for order. In stateless societies, people often live in villages of extended families and tend to live fairly self-sufficient lives. During this era (600-1450) many stateless societies continued to thrive, but large states developed as well, with rulers, bureaucrats, armies, and nobility. Through economic, political, and social specialization many of these states developed the ability and the desire to connect to other parts of the world.

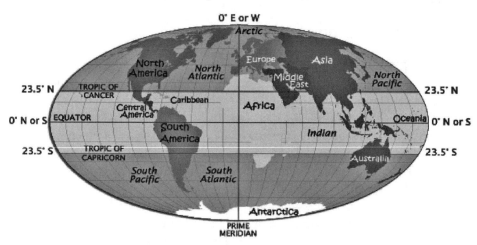

Tropical Areas of the World. The "tropics" lie between the Tropic of Cancer at 23.5° north latitude and the Tropic of Capricorn at 23.5° south latitude. In the Eastern Hemisphere, tropical lands include most of Africa, southern Arabia, much of India, and all of Southeast Asia.

Empires of the Western Sudan

The long-distance trade patterns that formed during the classical era across the Eastern Hemisphere stretched to Sub-Saharan Africa as caravan routes developed across the Sahara Desert. The camels that crossed the Sahara could not

SEEING SIMILARITIES: "AFRICANITY"

Despite their varied nature, African societies in the era 600-1450 shared many common characteristics. The spread of the Bantu-speaking peoples meant that even though languages differed, common vocabulary and word structures allowed some understanding between neighboring Bantu speakers. Most Africans also shared similar animistc religions that remained in place even after the spread of Islam and Christianity. The rituals of drumming, dancing, and divination were similar, as well as the rhythm of and instruments for music. Another commonality was the penchant for wearing masks, often of intricate and creative design. The masks of different groups were very differently constructed and decorated, but they were of central importance in rituals and beliefs to most groups. The isolation of kings was also common, whether they led complex states or simple villages. The Belgian anthropologist, Jacques Maquet, called these common qualities "Africanity," a clear but puzzling cultural unity that existed despite the large size of the African continent.

survive in the forest areas of Africa's mid-belt, so the Sahel, the extensive grassland belt between the desert and the forest became a point of exchange between south and north Africa. In this area, several African trading states rose between 600 and 1450. By the 8th century, the state of **Ghana**, south of the Sahara in the Western Sudan, was exchanging gold from west Africa for salt or dates from the Sahara or for goods from the Mediterranean coastal areas. Founded probably in the 3rd century as a kingdom that rose to power from among the Soninke people by taxing the salt and gold exchanged, its rulers had converted to Islam by the 10th century, about the time that the state was at the height of its power. The kings' conversion to Islam improved relations with Muslim merchants from north Africa as well as Muslim nomads from the desert who transported goods across the Sahara. Ghana's power was based partly on the king's ability to field a large army, and its defeat by the Almoravids (a desert Berber people) in 1076 contributed to its decline. In its place the state of **Mali** grew to dominate the area between the 13th and 15th century, which in turn was followed by the state of **Songhay** in the 15th and 16th centuries. Further to the east the **Hausa** states and Kanem Bornu came to be powerful during the 15th century.

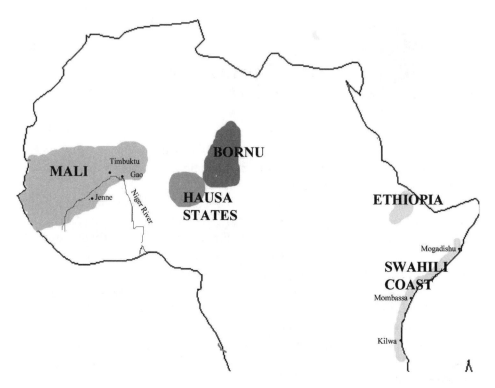

African States, 1200-1500. Many African states – including Mali, Hausa, Bornu, Ethiopia, and the Swahili Coast – had strong links to the trade that crossed the Sahara and the Indian Ocean.

Most people of the Sudanic states were farmers or fishers that lived in small villages. Farming was not easy because the soil was sandy and shallow, but they grew rice in the river valleys, as well as millet, sorghums, and some wheat, fruits, and vegetables. Most farms were small, land was cleared communally, and most families were large. Polygamy was common in the region since large families could farm larger areas of land than small ones. Despite the importance of farming, during this era trading cities grew and occupations became more specialized.

The Kingdom of Mali

Ghana fell into decline by the early 13th century, partly because it was weakened by the Berber defeat of its army but also because their sources of gold were drying up. Regional leaders warred with one another until the emergence of **Sundiata,** the legendary "lion-king" who conquered all others in the mid 13th century to found the kingdom of Mali, which survived until about 1450. Stories of Sundiata formed the foundation of the great oral traditions of western Africa, as told by **griots** (master storytellers), who advised kings and used their tales to pass down important traditions from generation to generation. Many of these stories were written down much later, and Sundiata emerges as a great hero described as having the stateliness of a lion and the strength of a buffalo. He

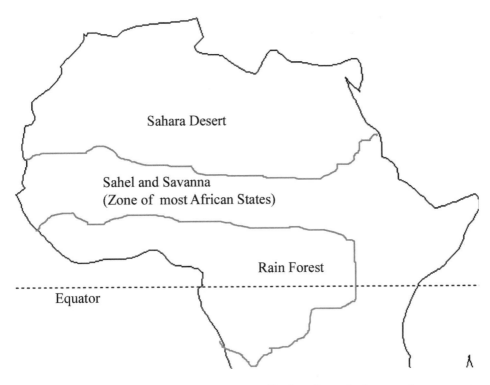

The Sahel and Savanna of Africa. The geography of Africa is so diverse that human settlements cannot easily form in many areas, including the vast Sahara Desert of the north and the impenetrable rain forests of central Africa. Most early settlements (and nomadic groups before them) formed in the areas in between: the Sahel (dry, mainly treeless steppes, or semiarid grass-covered plains) and the savanna (grasslands with some rain that the Sahel). The Sudanic states of the west generally grew up in the Sahel, and Ethiopia developed in the east.

made wise alliances with local rulers, gained a reputation for courage in battle, and built a large army. Mali grew to be much larger than Ghana, encompassing lands that include the modern state of Mali, Mauritania, Senegal, Gambia, Guinea-Bissau, Guinea, and Sierra Leone.

Mali built a trading state that was larger and more successful than Ghana had been, controlling and taxing almost all trade that passed through west Africa. Great caravans linked Mali to north Africa, and their capital city of Niani attracted merchants who traded gold along the routes through prosperous market cities like Timbuktu, Gao, and Jenne. By the 14th century, Timbuktu probably had a population of about 50,000, with a great mosque that contained an impressive library and sponsored a university where scholars, jurists, and theologians studied. Like the kings of Ghana, Mali kings were Muslims who provided protection, lodging, and services for Muslim merchants from the north. Islam was not forced on the population, and though its spread was encouraged, many people continued to practice native religions. Mali reached its peak of importance in long-distance trade networks during the reign of Sundiata's grand-nephew **Mansa Musa,** who ruled from 1312 to 1337. Most famously, on his pilgrimage to Mecca, Mansa Musa formed a huge caravan of soldiers, servants, and slaves, with camels carrying satchels of gold. Along the way, he passed out lavish gifts to those he met, and distributed so much gold in the trade center of Cairo that he caused a rapid and widespread decline in the metal's value on the trade circuits. After his return from Mecca, Mansa Musa built mosques and established madrasas (religious schools) in Mali's cities, encouraging Islam to spread to more people in the area. He brought back poets, architects, and teachers from areas that he had visited, further connecting Mali to other areas of the world. A cosmopolitan court life developed as merchants and scholars were attracted by the power and protection of Mali.

Songhay

The people of **Songhay**, who lived in the middle areas of the Niger River valley, had formed an identity by the 7th century and established a capital at Gao that was controlled by Mali during its heyday. By the 15th century, the power of Mali was waning, and a successor state, Songhay, began to emerge from within the old kingdom's borders. Like people in the earlier states, most were farmers, herders, and fishers, and the kings gained power as coordinators of trade. Songhay began to prosper by the late 14th century as new sources of gold from the west African forests were discovered, and Gao became a large city with a foreign merchant community. The best known Songhay leader was Sunni Ali, who was a talented military commander who headed a large cavalry that seized Timbuktu and Jenne, consolidating trade under Songhay control. By the mid-16th century Songhay dominated the central Sudan. All of Sunni Ali's successors were Muslim, and they, like the Mali leaders, continued to build mosques, support Muslim scholars, and support book production for mosques and libraries. As powerful as the Songhay state grew, it did not anticipate the technology that led to its defeat. In 1591, a small Muslim army from Morocco marched into Songhay lands equipped with muskets, and since the Songhay army knew nothing of gunpowder technology, it had no chance to win.

The Swahili States of East Africa

The Sudanic states in west Africa were important centers of Islamization for Sub-Saharan Africa, and they played an important role in connecting the area with long-distance trade networks of the Eastern Hemisphere. Another center of trade and Islamization was developing at the same time long the east coast

SEEING SIMILARITIES:
SUDANIC STATES OF AFRICA

During the era 600-1450 several empires rose in the Sudan, an area in western Africa between the Sahara Desert and the rainforests of central Africa. These "Sudanic States" had different strengths and weaknesses, as well as different periods of greatness, with Ghana rising first, Mali next, and eventually Songhay, Hausa, and Kanem-Bornu. However, they shared some important similarities.

All the states were led by the patriarch or council of elders of a leading family or group of related families. Usually these states centered on people who spoke the same language and shared other cultural traits, but all the states extended their authority over nearby groups of people. The rulers were considered sacred, and their legitimacy was reinforced by rituals and traditions that separated them from their subjects. In all the states the rulers and other elite converted to Islam, but the bulk of the population remained faithful to native, usually animistic, religions. Culturally, all the states had well developed oral traditions in which they shared stories of a family or people that were passed down from generation to generation by word of mouth. Griots, or master storytellers, were highly valued in most west African kingdoms, and many of the stories they told are still well known today.

of Africa in several trade centers, giving the area the name **"the Swahili Coast"** after the common language that was spoken. The connections of cities along the east coast of Africa to the Indian Ocean trade go back to at least the 1st century C.E., but no one knows whether these early traders were Africans or immigrants from the Arabian Peninsula. However, by the beginning of the era 600-1450, Bantu-speaking people had reached the coastal areas from interior Africa. Over the centuries, people from areas across the Indian Ocean had settled there as well, and the language that they came to speak – Swahili – was Bantu-based but Arabic-influenced.

By the 13th century, Chinese porcelains and silks, Indian cotton fabrics, and glass beads were brought across the ocean to be traded for African products, such as iron, timber, ivory, and animal hides and shells. Most importantly, gold from Africa's interior – Great Zimbabwe – was traded, making cities such as

Kilwa quite wealthy. A string of trade cities stretched up and down the coast, such as Mogadishu, Mombasa, Malindi, Kilwa, and Zanzibar, that flourished from the 13th to the 15th century.

Muslim foreigners and local Bantu-speakers intermarried, and often their children were raised as Muslims. Many Africans along the Swahili Coast converted to Islam for the same reasons that people in the Sudanic states did; it made trading with Arab Muslims easier. The cities were cosmopolitan, and boasted handsome stone mosques and multi-story public buildings. They had efficient plumbing systems, and their ruling elites and wealthy merchants wore silk and fine cotton clothing, and used porcelain dishes imported from China. Muslim scholars from Arabia and Persia lived in the cities that were ruled individually as city-states. The cities were economically connected, but no central government had power over them.

Great Zimbabwe

Inland from the coastal cities was a powerful state on the plateau south of the Zambezi River, whose capital city was known as **Great Zimbabwe.** The earth surrounding the city yielded great quantities of gold that was mined there and traded through Great Zimbabwe overland to one of the Swahili coastal cities – Sofala – and then shipped across the Indian Ocean to join the long-distance trade network. With this wealth, a magnificent stone complex rose within Great Zimbabwe's walls. The largest structure, a walled enclosure about the size and shape of a large football stadium, contained many buildings, including a large cone-shaped stone tower. Zimbabwe's kings controlled and taxed the trade between the interior and coastal regions, but its inhabitants were not Islamic, as were few other people in southern Africa's interior. Many aspects of this state are still mysterious today, but historians estimate that the city of Great Zimbabwe probably had about 18,000 inhabitants at its height.

Ethiopia

Many inhabitants in one area in eastern Sub-Saharan Africa – Ethiopia – were Christian, not Muslim. Christianity had been founded there by the middle of the 4th century, when the ruling elites of the kingdom of Axum declared their faith, possibly to enhance their relations with Christian Egypt, which had been reached by Christian missionaries during the 1st century C.E. After the decline of Axum, Islam expanded to most areas around the Ethiopian highlands until a new ruling dynasty began a campaign to promote Christianity. Starting in the 12th century, Christianity became the preferred religion of the Ethiopian elite. However, because Egypt and the rest of northern Africa were conquered by Muslims during the 7th and 8th centuries, Ethiopian Christians were cut off from Christians in other lands. As a result, its beliefs reflect those of native African religions that recognize the existence of evil spirits and the need to carry amulets for protection from their spells. African Islam reflected similar interests, and accepted rituals and practices from native religions, including the use of amulets. During the 16th century, the Portuguese reached Ethiopia and reestablished contact with other Christians. Meanwhile, the Portuguese also introduced Roman Catholicism to the kingdom of Kongo, but Christianity did not grow much beyond these areas until the 19th century. In other parts of Africa, Islam continued to grow, especially among ruling elites and merchants. Muslim converts built mosques, founded madrasas, and set up Islamic law codes (shari'a) all over Africa as the faith gradually spread to more and more areas.

THE SPREAD OF ISLAM TO INDIA AND SOUTHEAST ASIA

By 600 the Gupta Empire had disintegrated, and India had once again fragmented into regional kingdoms that had characterized most of its earlier history. Even though it was not politically united, its powerful social and cultural traditions formed the "glue" that held Indian society together. The caste system and the Hindu religion were strong influences throughout the subcontinent, giving the region its own distinct identity. However, during the era 600-1450, Islam was also introduced to India, although its arrival was much more violent than in west Africa or the Swahili Coast.

The Delhi Sultanate

Beginning in the early 11th century, Afghan warlords invaded the Indian subcontinent, inspired by both their desire to spread their Islamic faith and their awareness of India's political weakness. Led by Mahmud of Ghazni, they looted Hindu and Buddhist temples of their gold and jewels, and frequently established mosques or Islamic shrines on the sites of the temples that they destroyed. During the late 12th century, Mahmud's successors attacked India again, and within a few years they had conquered most of the Hindu kingdoms in northern India, establishing an Islamic state known as the **Delhi Sultanate.** The sultans established their capital at Delhi and ruled northern India at least in name from 1206 to 1526. For the first time, a Muslim Empire was established on the Indian subcontinent itself, and was not merely an extension of a Middle Eastern or central Asian empire. The sultans were of Persian, Afghan, Turkic, or mixed descent, and they fought the Hindu princes for control of the Indus and Ganges River valleys. The sultans depended on large armies to expand their rule, and they maintained extravagant courts and large bureaucracies. In general, the southern part of the subcontinent largely escaped the invasions, and Hindu rulers in the south continued to preside over small states. One state, the kingdom of Vijayanagar, located in the northern Deccan Plateau, was established by two Muslim converts, but they renounced Islam, returned to their native Hinduism, and established an independent empire. As in the north, political division and conflict between states continued to characterize the south.

Once the Muslim sultanate was established, Indians were generally allowed to keep their native religions, although Buddhists dwindled significantly in numbers during this time period. Sizeable Muslim communities developed in different parts of India, especially in Bengal to the east and in the northwestern Indus valley, and most of the conversions were voluntary. Merchants were the main carriers of the faith, and Sufi mystics were especially active in recruiting adherents. They established mosques and schools and organized their supporters into militias for protection against bandits or ambitious princes. Sufism grew partly because it welcomed Indians of the lower castes to the faith, and they often impressed people with their magic and healing powers. Some conversions resulted from the desire to avoid the head tax the Muslim rulers placed on unbelievers, and others occurred when Muslim migrants married local people.

Despite the fact that Muslims ruled India and many people converted to Islam, most Indians remained faithful to Hinduism. Especially to high-caste Indians, the new rulers practiced an upstart faith that they had little respect for. Many Hindus took positions as administrators in the bureaucracies of Muslim overlords, others served in the sultan's army, and most traded with Muslim merchants. However, they maintained socially separate lives, and they often lived in separate communities or sections of cities. Almost certainly, Hindus only tolerated Muslims, believing that they would soon be overwhelmed by the superior Hindu culture of the subcontinent. Some Muslim princes adopted Hindu practices in their courts, and decorated their palaces and engraved their coins with the likenesses of Hindu gods, such as Vishnu and Shiva. They adopted Indian foods and styles of dress, and they organized their states along caste lines, with recently arrived Muslim leaders on top, but with high-caste Hindu converts next.

The differences in the two religions – Islam and Hinduism – were so profound that it was nearly impossible to reconcile them. Islam emphasized equality, and Hinduism was squarely based on the hierarchical caste system. Islam expected believers to be completely submissive to one god, Allah; Hinduism's concept of a universal spirit easily encompassed many gods. Some mystics tried to minimize the differences, but they won only small numbers of followers. Neither religion wished to bend to the other. Once it was clear that the Muslim leaders meant to stay, the Brahmans denounced the Muslim as destroyers of Hindu temples and criticized their meat-eating habits. On the other hand, Muslim ulamas, or religious experts, warned against the pollution of Islam by Hindu practices, and they worked to promote unity within the Indian Muslim community in opposition to the majority Hindu population.

In contrast to the hierarchical diffusion of Islam in Africa, where many kings and other elites converted to Islam while their subjects practiced native religions, Islam in India met some stiff resistance from Hindu elites. In Africa, the religion gradually spread, displaying its historical tendency to tolerate the existence of other religions. India was ruled by Muslims and others converted to the religion, but many Hindus believed that their religion was superior to Islam, and that their rich culture would eventually prevail to cast out the intruders. Muslims resented this attitude, and so tensions built between the two religions, a condition that generally did not develop in Africa.

Southeast Asia

The expansion of Islam to India set the stage for its spread to Southeast Asia, since Arab traders and sailors of the Indian Ocean trade routes regularly visited ports in both places. In many ways, Southeast Asia's central location on the trading routes made it a crossroads of travel and a haven for diverse peoples. Geographically, people from China came there regularly, as well as those from India and the Arabian Peninsula. They brought their religions and customs with them, and people from all over the Indian Ocean basin came to settle there. In earlier years Buddhism and Hinduism had taken root in Southeast Asia, but by the 8th century onward, Muslim traders had taken over coastal trade in India, and by the 13th century, Islam was widely spread to Southeast Asia. Islam's foothold was strengthened considerably by the downfall of the powerful Shrivijaya trading empire, whose leaders were Buddhists. Once the Shrivijaya were gone, Muslim trading centers were founded, and missionaries arrived to convert Southeast Asians to the newer religion.

Most contacts between Muslims and others were peaceful, and conversions generally were voluntary. From the powerful trading city of Malacca, where merchants and traders shared their religious convictions, Islam spread from the mainland to Sumatra and other islands. Once key trading cities became Islamic, it was often in the best interest of others to follow suit to strengthen personal ties and provide a common basis in Muslim law. As in other areas, Sufis allowed natives to keep many of their rituals and local beliefs, as long as they paid homage to Allah and followed Islamic doctrines.

TWO TRAVELLERS

By 1000 long-distance travel had been increasing in importance for many centuries. During the classical era, the Silk Road linked people from the Mediterranean to China. After the fall of the classical civilizations, Silk Road traffic suffered but revived again after 600 C.E. with unification provided by the Tang Empire and the Muslim caliphates. Between about 1000 and 1400 long-distance interchanges were encouraged by the migrations of Vikings, Turks, and

Mongols. Even though these contacts often involved wholesale destruction, they also brought knowledge of other parts of the world with them, and in all cases, the migrating people often settled into areas that they conquered.

Two important unifying forces made long-distance travel more appealing during the era between 1000 and 1450 C.E. – the Pax Mongolica (the Mongol peace) and Dar al-Islam (the house of Islam). As we have seen, the Mongol Empire politically unified and pacified a huge part of the northern Eastern Hemisphere under the extended family of Genghis Khan. Kubilai Khan, Genghis' grandson and the ruler of the Yuan Dynasty in China, was a cosmopolitan leader, who was always interested in cultures far away from his capital at Khanbalik. One of his most famous visitors was a young Italian named **Marco Polo,** who visited China in the late 13th century and returned to Europe to write a journal of his travels. Dar al-Islam united the tropical lands south of the Mongol Empire, even after the demise of the last major caliphate, the Abbasids, in the mid-13th century. Religious motives and ties were important driving factors in this unification, and educated Muslims, no matter what their ethnic origins, shared knowledge of the sacred language of Arabic. As a result, they could communicate with one another. Muslims also shared the obligation of hajj, the pilgrimage to Mecca that they must make during their lifetimes if at all possible. Africans, Spanish, Iranians, Indians, and east Asians travelled to Arabia's holy sites by established pilgrimage routes, and this movement of people encouraged cultural and material exchanges. The most famous traveler to Muslim lands was **Ibn Battuta,** who visited many areas of the tropics and beyond in his journeys between 1325 and 1354. Like Marco Polo, he created an account of his travels that was widely distributed and read, and the accounts of the two men have provided historians over the years with vivid descriptions of life in diverse parts of the Eastern Hemisphere in the years preceding 1450.

Marco Polo

Around 1260 Marco's father and uncle, both merchants from Venice, sailed across the Mediterranean and Black Seas, and from there made an overland trek to the court of Kubilai Khan. In a display of his broad interests, the Great Khan requested that they visit the pope and ask him to send one hundred missionary-scholars to northern China. Although Pope Gregory X issued the two men a commission to return to China with two Dominican friars, the expedition fell apart when the friars fearfully refused to continue the journey they started, but the merchants continued on, this time with Niccolo Polo's seventeen-year-old son, Marco. They arrived at the court of Kubilai Khan in 1274 or 1275, when Marco entered the service of the Great Khan, although it is impossible to say what offices he actually held. Whatever his position, he spent close to two decades travelling over Kubilai's vast empire.

After Marco Polo's return to Venice, he was captured by soldiers from the rival trade city Genoa, where he spent time in prison. He enthralled the other prisoners with stories of his adventures, and together with a fellow prisoner, he produced a written account of the sites, people, and events Marco had experienced in Asia. The book became a best-seller of its day, and was widely translated and distributed throughout Europe, where readers found his stories and descriptions fascinating. Partly because Marco Polo enjoyed exaggeration, some came to question the truth of his stories, a skepticism that continues among scholars to this day. No matter how much his account may have blended truth with fiction, Marco Polo sparked great interest among Europeans in a world beyond theirs, and contributed to the growing connectedness of Europe to the rest of the world. This sense of adventure that he encouraged set the stage for Europeans to embark on major explorations to parts of the world unknown to them – the Americas and Africa - during the era that followed.

Ibn Battuta

Ibn Battuta was born in 1304 into an upper class family in Tangier, Morocco, where he studied Islamic law and Arabic literature. As a young man he left home to make the first of his several pilgrimages to Mecca. Over the next three decades he visited Constantinople, Mesopotamia, Persia, India, Burma, Sumatra, Spain, Mali, and probably southern China. Most of his stops along his 73,000 mile journey were within the cultural areas of Dar al-Islam, so despite the varied cultures, they were unified by the religion. During the last few years before his death in 1369, Ibn Battuta narrated his many travel experiences and observations to a professional scribe who wrote a book of travel that was widely popular, especially among hajj travelers. His detailed account gives us invaluable information about life in Islamic lands, and conveys a sense of the ties that Islam created across diverse cultures.

LONG DISTANCE TRADE AND TRAVEL: PATTERNS, MOTIVATIONS, AND CONSEQUENCES

During the era 600-1450 long-distance trade in the Eastern Hemisphere still relied primarily on the Silk Road for overland travel and the Indian Ocean routes for travel by water. Also significant was the growing amount of trade across the Sahara Desert to link Sub-Saharan kingdoms to cities on the Mediterranean where goods joined the other major world circuits. Luxury goods that were light in relation to their weight – such as silk and precious stones - usually travelled the Silk Road where they could easily be carried by camels. Bulkier goods - such as steel, stone, coral, and building materials – were more practically carried by ships crossing the Indian Ocean.

ORIGINAL DOCUMENT: ACCOUNT OF IBN BATTUTA'S VISIT TO THE SWAHILI COAST

Ibn Battuta's acounts of his journeys through Muslim lands in the 14th century are valuable documents for historians partly because of the large numbers of places that he visited and compared, but also because he described the places he visited in such detail. He was in East Africa around 1331-1332, and in the excerpts below he described the Swahili coastal areas.

"We arrived at Mombasa, a large island...The people [of the island] do not engage in agriculture, but import grain...The greater part of their diet is bananas and fish. They follow the Shafi'i [sect of Islam], and are devout, chaste, and virtuous....We spent a night on the island and then set sail for Kilwa...Kilwa is one of the most beautiful and well-constructed towns in the world. The whole of it is elegantly built. The roofs are built with mangrove pole. There is very much rain. Their [the people's] chief qualities are devotion and piety..."

Although in this excerpt he was complimentary of the people he visited, he did not hesitate to criticize his hosts. For example, in another account he describes himself as laughing at a "trivial" gift offered to him by the Sultan of Mali. He also had little tolerance for people who were not (in his opinion) devout enough in their practice of Islam.

Reference: *The East African Coast, Select Documents* G.S.P.. Freeman-Grenville (London: Oxford University Press, 1962), pp. 31-32.

Motivations for Long Distance Travel

Trade was certainly an important motivation for travel, but other motives were diplomacy and missionary activity. Events of the time, including the growing trade network and migrations of people, called for political and diplomatic contacts among political and religious leaders. For example, the movement of Seljuk Turks into the Middle East motivated the Byzantine Emperor to call on the Roman Catholic Pope to help defend the Christian Holy Lands from Muslim attack. As a result, many European knights traveled to the Middle East, and although they did not achieve their goals, they changed Europe forever with the contacts and trade connections they encouraged. Another example of political diplomacy occurred after the Mongols destroyed the Muslim Abbasid Dynasty.

Pope Innocent IV sent diplomats to invite the Mongols to become Christians and join them in their struggle against the Muslims. The Khans declined the invitation and suggested that western Europe would be better off under Mongol control, an event that never occurred. On his travels, Ibn Battuta often took governmental positions because his knowledge of shari'a law qualified him to serve as an advisor to sultans and a judge in Islamic courts.

Missionaries for Islam and Christianity also were motivated to travel. Sufi mystics ventured to newly conquered or converted areas to encourage the growth of Islam in India, Southeast Asia, and Sub-Saharan Africa. Sufis often tolerated the worship of traditional deities, as long as new converts were pious and devoted to Allah. Roman Catholic missionaries also traveled long distances to spread their religion, seeking to convert Mongols and other people in China. For example, John of Montecorvino, an Italian Franciscan, spent most of his life in China during the late 13th and early 14th centuries. He translated parts of the Bible into Turkish, a language used at the Mongol court, and he built several churches in China. Roman Catholic and Eastern Orthodox missionaries competed for converts in Russia, with the Eastern Orthodox envoys having the most success. Christianity made few inroads into east Asia during this era, partly because distances were still too far and resources for sustaining the effort were lacking. Roman Catholics were most successful in spreading Christianity to Scandinavia, eastern Europe, Spain, and islands in the Mediterranean that western European kingdoms had seized from Islamic control.

Consequences of Interregional Networks and Contacts

The increased amount of trade, travel, and communications among regions of the Eastern Hemisphere had many important consequences, including agricultural and technological diffusion, the spread of disease, and demographic changes.

- **Technological and agricultural diffusion** – Some technological diffusion actually facilitated long-distance travel itself. For example, the magnetic compass was developed in China and spread throughout the Indian Ocean basin, allowing mariners to sail long stretches of deep water without getting lost. Another Chinese invention, gunpowder, was used by Mongols as bombs to catapult into cities under siege. Muslim armies soon responded with similar techniques. By the early 14th century, armies from China to Europe were using primitive cannons, with the Mongols mainly responsible for the quick spread of the technology. Contact with others also meant that a larger variety of food was enjoyed by people in many parts of the Eastern Hemisphere. For example, west Africans were introduced to citrus fruits and Asian varieties of rice. Muslims learned how to crystallize sugar refined from cane by the 12th century, and introduced Europeans to the delight of sugar cubes in their tea and coffee.

- **Spread of disease** – The spread of the bubonic plague ("Black Death") from the Yunnan region of southwestern China to areas in other parts of Asia and Europe during the 14th century had devastating consequences. The disease was spread by fleas that infected rodents, who in turn infected humans. The disease spread through the Mongol military campaigns and along the trade routes. About 60 to 70 percent of all humans infected died, so the demographic changes in population patterns were dramatic. China's population under Mongol control dropped by millions, as did numbers in southwest Asia, Egypt, and north Africa. Europe lost about 25 percent of its people as a result of the plague. Societies were disrupted by these losses, with no group being spared. Artisans, merchants, bankers, priests, nuns, government officials, peasants, and city workers all died, often leaving cities and towns with little infrastructure for those that survived. In western Europe, workers demanded higher wages since labor was so short, and when their wages were frozen, rebellions resulted.

- **Demographic changes** – The plague was contained by the late 14th century, and it did not take long for urban population levels to recover in Europe, the Middle East, and east Asia. The tremendous growth of cities along trade routes continued as traders, merchants, brokers and bankers crowded to places like Khanbalik, Hangzhou, Samarkand, Baghdad, Cairo, Constantinople, Venice, Kilwa, and Timbuktu. Unlike trade patterns in earlier times, many merchants traveled the whole distance from Europe to China in pursuit of profit, and they found comfortable resting places in the cities. A more long-lasting impact of the plague was felt by nomadic groups, not the people in urban areas. Because there were fewer of them, nomadic people could not as easily replace those that died, and townspeople took advantage of their weakness by reestablishing their age-old pattern of dominance. The Mongols and Turks greatly impacted the course of world history during this era, but nomadic groups never again had that kind of power. Instead sedentary peoples first resisted and then dominated them, a condition that continues to this day.

Growth in long-distance travel during the era 600-1450 was a part of the larger trend toward more communications, travel, and contacts among peoples of the world that has progressed throughout world history. During the time when the earliest civilizations were forming, trade networks were generally local, with some contacts stretching to other nearby groups. By 1200

B.C.E. a trade and contact network had built up throughout much of the Middle East, but it fell apart soon afterward. During the classical era contacts became interregional as the Silk Road and Indian Ocean trade connected Asia, Europe, and northern Africa. Between 600 and 1450 those trade networks grew tremendously, and contacts among diverse people were much greater than they had been at any other time before. However, by 1450 Europeans, Asians, and Africans had yet to establish any sustained contacts with the people of the Western Hemisphere. In the next era, that too would change.

COMPARISONS: COMMUNAL VS. CONVERGENT CITIES

Cities grew in number and size during the period 600-1450 in many areas of the world, with all having unique characteristics but also sharing commonalities. Historians and geographers use two alternate theses to explain the history of cities. The first one is communal; it emphasizes the uniqueness of cities as they represent the culture of the territories around them. During this era, cities in Europe illustrate this thesis, largely because strong central governments did not exist, and cities operated with independence and tended to dominate the area around them. For example, the city of Paris came to be uniquely "French," and London came to be uniquely "English." Islamic and Chinese cities of the era better illustrate the thesis of convergent cities – places where many people of different ethnicities come together to trade goods, sell arts and crafts, and visit government centers. The view that cities are convergent emphasizes the commonalities that they all have – busy centers connected to other busy centers that in many ways look and function alike. Neither theory describes any one city of the era with complete accuracy, but the contrasting theories do focus on the fact that European cities were less connected to world trade circuits than Islamic and Chinese cities, and that cities like London and Paris were not yet the cosmopolitan centers that they would later become.

IDENTIFICATIONS AND CONCEPTS

Africanity
communal vs. convergent cities
Delhi Sultanate
Ghana

Great Zimbabwe
griots
Hausa
Ibn Battuta
Mali
Mansa Musa
Marco Polo
monsoons
Songhay
stateless society
Sundiata
Swahili Coast

UNIT TWO QUESTIONS

Multiple-Choice Questions

1. Which of the following factors was MOST supportive of the rapid spread of Islam in the years after its founding in the early 7th century?

   a) strong communications and travel networks on the Arabian Peninsula
   b) its appearance in the post-classical era, with weaker organized states to oppose it
   c) the support of elite rulers in the areas that the religion spread
   d) the lack of other strong religions in the areas where the religion spread
   e) the high literacy rates in the Middle East and northern Africa

2. One reason that Pope Urban II called for the Crusades in 1095 was to

   a) support the Seljuk Turks in their efforts to capture Constantinople
   b) defend Europe from attack by the Seljuk Turks
   c) promote Eastern Orthodoxy
   d) improve trade relations between Europe and the Middle East
   e) unite the knights in a common cause for Roman Catholicism

3. Which of the following is an inaccurate statement regarding "big picture" characteristics of the period 600 to 1450?

   a) No one political format dominated the era.
   b) Trade and communications networks were weaker than they had been before 600.
   c) Belief systems were unifying forces for societies.
   d) Eastern and Western Hemispheres were not joined.
   e) Most societies remained patriarchies with clear social distinctions.

4. Which of the following is true of both South America and west Africa during the period 600-1450?

   a) Large, organized political states rose in both areas.
   b) The economy in both areas was based mainly on trade.
   c) Both areas traded regularly with Europe and the Middle East.
   d) Civilizations in both areas centered on river valleys.
   e) The main crops in both areas were potatoes, maize, and beans.

5. The religious split between Sunni and Shi'ite Muslims originated in a disagreement about

   a) strategies for expansion of the faith
   b) whether or not Muhammad was a divine being
   c) the basis for succession of the caliph
   d) the location of the capital city of the caliphate
   e) the treatment of conquered peoples

6. Which of the following is an accurate comparison of the political systems of western Europe and Japan during the era 600-1450?

   a) Both areas were ruled by a highly centralized government.
   b) Japan's political system was highly centralized; western Europe developed multiple monarchies.
   c) Political systems in both areas were based on feudalistic ties among elites.
   d) The western European political system was highly centralized; Japan's political system was headed by two rulers in two different places.
   e) In both systems, political legitimacy was based on the belief that rulers were gods on earth.

7. Which of the following was the most important commodity controlled by west African states in the long-distance trade networks between 600 and 1450?

   a) slaves
   b) exotic animals
   c) rice
   d) gold
   e) guns

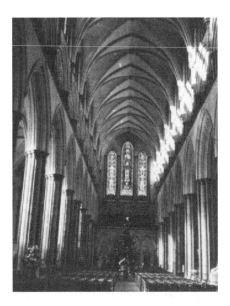

8. The architecture of the church interior in the photograph above is an example of

    a) Gothic architecture
    b) the influence of the Romans
    c) the revival of interest in Greek architecture
    d) the triumph of the Eastern Orthodox Church
    e) Renaissance architecture

9. Among Muslims, the "People of the Book" were

    a) Jews and Christians
    b) devout Sunni Muslims
    c) devout Shi'ite Muslims
    d) scholars who interpreted Islamic principles to common people
    e) those who lived in urban areas of the Middle East

10. Islamic law codes that became well developed during Abbasid times are called

    a) the Qur'an
    b) hadith
    c) shari'a
    d) qanun
    e) the Five Pillars of Faith

11. The photograph above of Todai-ji Temple in Japan is an example of

    a) Shinto architecture
    b) the influence of Confucianism in Japan
    c) the power of the shogun
    d) respect for the emperor
    e) the influence of Buddhism in Japan

12. Which of the following was NOT one of the Germanic tribes that settled in Europe after the fall of the Roman Empire?

   a) Visigoths
   b) Franks
   c) Huns
   d) Vandals
   e) Angles

"That no one shall presume to rob…the churches of God, or widows, or orphans, or pilgrims, for the lord emperor himself…has constituted himself their protector and defender…

That no one shall presume to neglect a summons to war from the lord emperor; and that no one of the Counts shall be so presumptuous as to dare to excuse any one of those who owe military service…

…no one shall dare to neglect to pay his dues or tax.

…That the counts…shall provide most carefully, as they desire the goodwill of the emperor, for the *missi* who are sent out…

Murders, by which a multitude of the Christian people perish, we command in every way to be shunned and to be forbidden…"

13. The quote above from the *Capitulary on the Missi* issued in 802 was meant to solidify the power of

   a) the pope
   b) the lords
   c) King John of England
   d) Charlemagne
   e) local priests

14. Franciscans and Dominicans are examples of

   a) patriarchs in the Eastern Orthodox Church
   b) bishops in the Roman Catholic Church
   c) abbots in the Roman Catholic Church
   d) Jewish religious orders in medieval Europe
   e) wandering religious orders in the Roman Catholic Church

15. The reorganization of Roman law codes in a format still used in the west was the work of

    a) Charlemagne
    b) Constantine
    c) Justinian
    d) Urban II
    e) Clovis

16. The mit'a labor system was used by the

    a) Maya
    b) people of Teotihuacan
    c) Toltecs
    d) Aztecs
    e) Inca

17. Which of the following was NOT characteristic of all Mesoamerican civilizations between 600 and 1450?

    a) Ball games were an important part of life.
    b) All used chinampas to raise agricultural produce.
    c) All were polytheistic.
    d) All practiced human sacrifice.
    e) None relied heavily on animals to get their work done.

18. One difference between Roman Catholicism and Eastern Orthodoxy during the period 1450 to 1750 is that in Eastern Orthodoxy

    a) priests could not marry
    b) a separation exists between political and religious leaders
    c) Gothic architecture was used for churches
    d) theology was more influenced by Greek philosophy
    e) religious art conveyed Jesus as suffering for the sins of mankind

19. In all Mesoamerican civilizations the highest social status was given to

a) merchants
b) artisans
c) priests
d) land owners
e) bureaucrats

20. A difference between the Tang and Song Dynasties of China is that during the Tang Dynasty

a) China was militarily weaker
b) culture was more refined
c) China had less land space
d) women had more freedom to move about
e) the ruling family was Han Chinese

21. An important religious clash occurred during the late Tang era between

a) Buddhism and Confucianism
b) Islam and Buddhism
c) Daoism and Confucianism
d) Shintoism and Daoism
e) Hinduism and Confucianism

22. During the era of the Tang Dynasty, a tributary state that cooperated with the Chinese but operated with a great deal of independence was

a) Vietnam
b) Minamoto Japan
c) Silla on the Korean Peninsula
d) the Jurchens
e) the Uighurs

23. *The Tale of Genji* was the first book to be written in

    a) Chinese
    b) Japanese
    c) Korean
    d) Vietnamese
    e) Mongolian

24. The nomadic group that formed the largest empire in world history was the

    a) Huns
    b) Turks
    c) Uighurs
    d) Jurchens
    e) Mongols

25. During the period from 600 to 1450 the Indian subcontinent experienced

    a) competition between Buddhism and Hinduism
    b) the introduction of Hinduism
    c) Islamic rule
    d) sustained political fragmentation
    e) economic prosperity based on trade

Free-Response Questions:

For all essays, be sure that you have a relevant thesis that is supported by historical evidence.

Document-Based Question: suggested reading time - 10 minutes; suggested writing time - 40 minutes

For the DBQ, be sure that you

- **Use all of the documents**

- **Use evidence from the documents to support your thesis**

- **Analyze the documents by grouping them in at least two or three appropriate ways**

- **Consider the source of the document and analyze the author's point of view**

- **Explain the need for at least one additional document**

1. Using the documents analyze the impact that the Mongol invasions had on Eurasia. Identify one additional type of document and explain briefly how it would help your analysis.

Document 1

"Emperor Taizu [Genghis Khan] received the mandate of Heaven and subjugated all regions. When Emperor Taizong [Ogodei Khan] succeeded, he revitalized the bureaucratic system and made it more efficient and organized... one Mongol, called the governor, was selected to supervise the prefects and magistrates [who] all had to obey his orders...As soon as Menggu arrived [as the governor], he took charge. Knowing the people's grievances, he issued an order, 'Those who oppress the people will be dealt with according to the law. Craftsmen, merchants, and shopkeepers, you must each go about your work with your doors open, peaceably attending to your business without fear. Farmers, you must be content with your lands and exert yourselves diligently according to the seasons. I will instruct or punish those who mistreat you.' After this order was issued, the violent became obedient and no one nay longer dared violate the laws. Farmers in the fields and travelers on the roads felt safe, and people began to enjoy life."

An epitaph for the gravestone of a
Mongol governor by a Chinese literati

Document 2

"You now, Pope: If you want to have peace and friendship with us, come with all the kings and potentates who serve you to our court. You should listen to this response of ours: Subject your will to us and bring us tribute, for if you do not obey our instructions and do not journey to us we are certain that you will have war with us. After that, to be sure, we do not know what the future holds. Only God knows that."

A letter from Kuyuk Khan, ruler of
the Mongols, to Pope Innocent IV

Document 3

"It happened in 1237. That winter, the godless Tatars [Mongols], under the leadership of Batu, came to the Riazan principality from the East through the forests. Upon arriving they encamped at Onuza, which they took and burned. From here they dispatched their emissaries – a woman witch and two men – to the princes of Riazan demanding a tithe…The princes of Riazan…did not allow the emissaries to enter the city…and moved against the godless and engaged them in a battle…Thus angered, the Tatars now began the conquest of the Riazan land with great fury. They destroyed cities, killed people, burned, and took [people] into slavery…On December 21, the Tatars took the city of Riazan, burned it completely, killed Prince Iurii Igorevich, his wife, slaughtered other princes, and of the captured men, women, and children, some they killed with their swords, others with arrows and [then] threw them into the fire; while some of the captured they bound, cut, and disemboweled their bodies."

A Russian chronicle, 1237

Document 4

"In just one year they seized the most populous, the most beautiful, and the best cultivated part of the earth whose inhabitants excelled in character and urbanity. In the countries that have not yet been overrun by them, everyone spent the night afraid that they may yet appear there, too…Thus, Islam and the Muslims were struck, at that time by a disaster such as no people had experienced before."

Ibn al-Athir, a Muslim chronicler

Document 5

"Previously, during the final years of the Yuan dynasty, there were many ambitious men competing for power who did not treasure their sons and daughters but prized jade and silk, coveted fine horses and beautiful clothes, relished drunken singing and unrestrained pleasure, and enjoyed separating people from their parents, wives, and children. I also lived in that chaotic period. How did I avoid such snares? I was able to do so because I valued my reputation and wanted to preserve my life. Therefore I did not dare to do these evil things."

Hongwu, first Ming emperor

Document 6

"What army can equal the Mongol army? In time of action when attacking and assaulting, they are like trained wild beasts out after game, and in the days of peace and security they are like sheep, yielding milk, and wool and many other useful things. In misfortune and adversity they are free of dissension and opposition. It is an army after the fashion of a peasantry, being liable to all manner of contributions, and rendering without complaint what is enjoined upon it…It is also a peasantry in the guise of an army, all of them, great and small, noble and base, in time of battle becoming swordsmen, archers and lancers in whatever manner the occasion requires…"

Ala-ad-Din-Juvaini, a high-ranking
Persian Muslim

Change Over Time Essay: suggested writing time - 40 minutes

2. Analyze major political and economic changes and continuities in Sub-Saharan Africa between 600 and 1450. Be sure to include evidence from specific kingdoms or other groups of people.

Comparative Essay: suggested writing time - 40 minutes

3. Compare and contrast the political and cultural characteristics of the Aztecs and the Inca during the time period 600 to 1450.

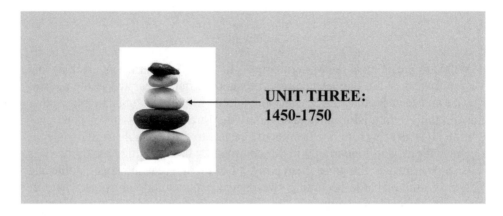

UNIT THREE:
1450-1750

The third period in our story of the world is the chunk of time from 1450-1750 C.E., a considerably shorter era than the previous two, but one in which momentous changes took place. It is often called the **"early modern" period** because events that occurred then have directly shaped important regional political units of today's world and influenced interrelationships among modern cultures. This period is distinct from the 600-1450 era for many reasons, but a very important difference is that power centers shifted away from the Middle East and Asia toward western Europe. Beginning in 1450, western Europe was transformed from decentralized, quarreling kingdoms to powerful, centralized states that dominated large parts of the world trade network by 1750. The world became smaller as international trade grew, and technological developments made transportation faster and easier. Despite the ascendancy of western Europe, power centers continued to exist in other parts of the world, as the Middle East and Asia still played host to large, wealthy empires that held regional hegemony in much the same way that their predecessors had. However, the balance of power was clearly shifting westward, as Europeans set their sights across the Atlantic, and joined the two hemispheres in sustained interactions that greatly altered the ever-shrinking world.

Unit Three is divided into five chapters based on region and theme:

- Chapter 10 analyzes the transformational developments in Europe that fueled its rise to world prominence.

- Chapter 11 focuses on the relationships formed between the New World and the Old and the consequences of joining the hemispheres.

- Chapter 12 investigates the impact of the new world economy on Africa.

- Chapter 13 visits the new Islamic Empires that developed in the Middle East and India.

- Chapter 14 analyzes change and continuity in Asia and traces the development of the Russian Empire.

An important shift took place during the era 1450-1750 between land-based and sea-based powers. **Land-based powers** followed the patterns that political organizations had used in most places since the classical era. Governments controlled land by building armies, bureaucracies, roads, canals, and walls that unified people and protected them from outsiders. The focus was on land. During this era **sea-based powers**, such as those in western Europe, built their power by controlling water routes, developing technologies to cross the seas, and gaining wealth from trade and land claims across the oceans. Although Europeans were not the first to discover the importance of sea-based trade, communications, and travel, they took the lead in the new world economy that was developing, and took advantage of the opportunity to capture the world stage by 1750.

THE BIG PICTURE:
1450-1750

Themes that run through the period 1450-1750 that make it distinct from other periods include:

1) The two hemispheres of the world were at last joined in sustained contact, and as a result, world trade networks greatly enlarged and many fewer people remained outside its influence.

2) The balance of power in the world changed as kingdoms of western Europe claimed the lands of the Western Hemisphere and gained control of many older trade routes.

3) Land-based empires remained important as they expanded their borders and conquered many nomadic groups with the power that gunpowder gave them.

4) Labor systems were transformed, as slavery expanded into the new world and became much more central to economic activities than it had ever been before.

5) The natural environment changed drastically, as imported domestic animals trampled grasslands and altered native farming habits. New crop exchanges meant that soil conditions changed in many areas, and much land was cleared for farming, including some of the world's great rain forests. Population compositions changed as disease spread to previously isolated people.

CHAPTER TEN:
THE TRANSFORMATION
OF EUROPE

In 1450 Europe was connected by trade, communication, and travel to other parts of the Eastern Hemisphere, but the region was still on the periphery of interactions among regions. The old centers of civilization in the Middle East, south Asia, and west Asia still were the most important axes of commerce and culture, while Europeans had only recently recovered from the Dark Ages that followed the fall of the Western Roman Empire. By 1750 Europe had moved to front and center stage, although the older centers continued to be important players in world interactions. How did this transformation occur? Three inter-related changes help to explain the rise of Europe:

1) **Important cultural changes** – including the Renaissance, the Reformation, and the Enlightenment – oriented European minds toward invention and allowed them to escape the social and intellectual boundaries of the Middle Ages.

2) **Political consolidation of strong centralized states** meant that kings had enough power and money to control regional lands and people and to sponsor trade expeditions and diplomatic envoys to other civilizations.

3) **Technological advances and the development of capitalism** allowed European states to increase their riches through trade and territorial claims in the Western Hemisphere. Although they often built on inventions from previous eras and by other people, Europeans made good use of their innovations.

In the period between 1450 and 1750 these three changes evolved together, and changes in one area brought about reactions in the others, which in turn brought further alterations in the first area. By 1750, these changes interacted to bring about the transformation of the continent, so that the Europe of 1750 was almost totally different – politically, culturally, socially, and economically – from the Europe of 1450.

IMPORTANT CULTURAL CHANGES

Cultural changes in Europe during the era 1450-1750 began with economic changes late in the previous era. The Crusades of the 12th and 13th centuries started a movement of European knights to the Middle East, which stimulated trade and contact between the Middle East and Europe. Two Italian city states – Genoa and Venice – grew wealthy from the new interactions, so it is not surprising that cultural changes began in Italy and worked their way to the north.

The Italian Renaissance

By 1450 the Renaissance was already well launched in Italy. The intellectual and artistic creativity of northern Italy was more than a "rebirth," although it was characterized by a renewed interest in the ancient classical civilizations of the Mediterranean – Greece and Rome. **Humanism**, or the interest in the capabilities and accomplishments of individuals, grew from Greek culture, but during the Italian Renaissance, it was reflected through portrait painting, autobiography, and philosophies that challenged the authority of the Roman Catholic Church. Writers such as Petrarch and Boccaccio had revived interest in classical writing and secular subjects (such as love and pride) in opposition to the emphasis on theology and spiritual topics of the Middle Ages. Many new works were written in the vernacular (Italian) rather than the Latin that medieval monks and scholars had used for their works. Religion declined as a central focus of interest in almost all areas of life.

By the 14th century, northern Italy had many urban areas, while the rest of Europe was still mostly rural. Urbanization was a function of the region's growing trade and the resulting wealth of merchants, who came to dominate politics and society as well as business. Genoa and Venice, as well as Florence and Milan, were powerful, independent city-states that ran their own affairs, each collecting taxes and supporting an army. Wealthy merchants competed with one another for economic and political power, and by the 15th century, they also were **patrons,** or supporters of the arts. Patrons found talented artists, often when they were young, and bankrolled their work, allowing them the time to spend on artistic endeavors. Three famous examples of patron-supported artists were **Leonardo da Vinci, Michelangelo,** and **Raphael,** all born in the mid-to-late 1400s. They, and countless other artists and writers, were sponsored by rich merchant families, including the powerful **Medici** family of Florence. The Catholic Church also sponsored Renaissance endeavors, and some of the most famous patrons were the popes in Rome. Many artists were interested in science, philosophy, and politics, giving rise to the concept of the **"Renaissance Man,"** or the person – often genius – who knows a great deal about many things. For example, Leonardo painted and sculpted, but he also made numerous drawings of inventions that demonstrate an extensive knowledge of mathematics and science, as well as a vivid imagination.

These cultural developments were made possible by the wealth created by commerce, but they in turn changed the nature of business and politics because humanistic values that emphasized individual capabilities and accomplishments supported an entrepreneurial spirit. Partly because of the emphasis on individual endeavors, Renaissance merchants improved their banking techniques and became more openly competitive and profit-seeking. City-state leaders, who were also the patrons of the arts, experimented with new ways to govern. Since their political positions were not hereditary or determined by claims to divinity, political power came to be based on individual efforts to promote their city's well being and cultural accomplishments. Despite the increasing emphasis on the secular, they also competed to see who could build the most glorious churches. The construction of religious buildings inspired experimentation with architecture that strayed from the medieval Gothic model to focus on grand and architecturally challenging domes. The churches were filled with sculpture and paintings of the best artists, further stimulating cultural creativity. The original interest in classical models remained, but the innovations of the Renaissance era resonated in culture, religion, politics, science, literature, and the economy.

Renaissance Architecture in Florence. In this view of modern-day Florence, Italy, Renaissance architecture still dominates the skyline. The large dome near the center is the Duomo, or the Dome of the Cathedral, Santa Maria del Fiore, that was completed in the mid-15th century.

Italian city-states began to decline politically by about 1500, but Renaissance creativity remained alive by spreading northward. Northern humanists were more religious than the Italians, and as a result, tended to blend secular and religious interests. For example, Erasmus of Rotterdam, a humanist Dutch priest, published the first edition of the New Testament in Greek in 1516, and also produced a revised Latin translation that corrected mistakes made over centuries of copying manuscripts. Two famous writers of the northern Renaissance were **William Shakespeare** and **Miguel de Cervantes** (author of *Don Quixote)*, who were both quite interested in secular life.

ORIGINAL DOCUMENT: *THE PRINCE* BY NICCOLO MACHIAVELLI

During the early 16th century, a time when Leonardo, Raphael, and Michelangelo were at their peak of creativity, the Italian city-states were attacked repeatedly by the French, Spanish, and German armies, and their very existence as independent states was threatened. In response to these threats, **Niccolo Machiavelli** wrote *The Prince,* a famous philosophical view of the ideal political leader, based on his view of ancient Roman rulers:

"Here the question arises; whether it is better to be loved than feared or feared than loved. The answer is that it would be desirable to be both but, since that is difficult, it is much safer to be feared than to be loved, if one must choose. For on men in general this observation may be made: they are ungrateful, fickle, and deceitful, eager to avoid dangers, and avid for gain, and while you are useful to them they are all with you, offering you their blood, their property, their lives, and their sons so long as danger is remote...but when it approaches they turn on you. Any prince, trusting only in their words and having no other preparations made, will fall to his ruin... Men have less hesitation in offending a man who is loved than one who is feared, for love is held by a bond of obligation which, as men are wicked, is broken whenever personal advantage suggests it, but fear is accompanied by the dread of punishment which never relaxes."

Reference: *The Prince* (1513) Niccolo Machiavelli, trans. and ed. by Thomas G. Bergin (New York: Appleton-Century-Crofts, 1947), p. 48.

The influence of the humanists was enhanced after 1450 with the printing advances made by a German goldsmith and printer, **Johann Gutenberg** of Mainz. The Gutenberg Bible was first printed in 1454, and the craftsmanship that created it was widely admired and imitated across Europe. Although movable type had been invented earlier in China and Korea, Gutenberg's printing press made it practical for European humanists to work closely with printers to make their writings available to wider audiences. By 1500 at least 10 million printed copies of books were circulating around Europe, greatly increasing the number of people that had access not only to Bibles, but also to Renaissance ideas.

The Protestant Reformation

The increased access to printed materials also played an important role in the religious upheaval of the 16th and 17th centuries, a series of events that resulted in the weakening of the religious and political control that the Roman Catholic Church had held during medieval times. These rebellions against the church are known collectively as the **Protestant Reformation,** and they resulted in a permanent new division in Western Christendom: Catholics vs. Protestants. The Reformation began in 1517 when a German monk named **Martin Luther** made his *95 Theses* public. This document consisted of 95 propositions that criticized the Catholic Church, particularly in their sale of **indulgences,** or grants of salvation in return for money. Luther's protests struck a cord with other Christians who were concerned about the growing wealth and corruption of a church that had become quite involved with erecting beautiful buildings and buying great works of art. Luther was very interested in the idea of salvation, or the reward of going to heaven after death, and he came to believe that only faith expressed between a believer and God could gain salvation. To his way of thinking, the church had put itself between the individual and God, breaking the bond that was the essence of religious beliefs. Luther was a prolific and convincing writer, and he soon began publishing criticisms of many practices of the church, an endeavor much assisted by the improved print technology.

Although Luther was eventually excommunicated from the church, his works inspired Protestant movements all over Europe that split religious unity, not just between Catholic and Protestant, but also between Protestant and Protestant, as different versions of protest appeared. One Protestant variation was established in Switzerland by **John Calvin**, whose religion centered on the belief in a stern and vengeful god, whereas Luther's followers believed in a merciful god. Calvinism spread to the British Isles, but Britain soon embraced yet another version of Protestantism when Henry VIII established the **Anglican Church.** Henry's actions were not based on religious beliefs, but instead on the pope's refusal to allow him to divorce his wife, who had not borne a male heir to the throne.

The Catholic Reformation

The Catholic Church responded forcefully to the Protestant rebellions and managed to retain control of most of southern Europe, Austria, Poland, and much of Hungary. The church initiated reforms, including the banning of indulgences, and Roman Catholic authorities sought to persuade Protestants to return to the Roman church. The church's actions are collectively known as the **Catholic Reformation,** a movement to revive the church's reputation and membership roles. An assembly called the Council of Trent gathered bishops, cardinals, and other high church officials together periodically between 1545 and 1563 to discuss religious doctrines. The council acknowledged many abuses that Protestants criticized, and the resulting reforms included the establishment of schools and seminaries to prepare priests properly for their roles. A new religious order called the **Jesuits** was founded whose members went all over Europe convincing many to return to the church. As we will see, Jesuits eventually became international missionaries with numerous converts in Asia and the Americas.

The most obvious consequence of the Protestant and Catholic Reformations was the breakup of the Catholic Church's powerful hold on the political, religious, economic, and social life of Europeans. The successful questioning of the basic doctrines of the church fed the humanistic influences from the Renaissance that put faith in the ability and accomplishments of individuals. Luther encouraged people to read the Bible to find the meaning of Christianity, an individual act that led to an individual's decisions about religious faith. In doing so, Luther not only encouraged humanism, but also literacy, since one had to be able to read to find meaning in the Bible. More literate Europeans not only gained a different perspective on religion, but they also could take jobs that required literacy, and they could learn about innovations of fellow Europeans.

Religious tensions also led to religious wars between Protestants and Catholics. Religious wars spread through France for thirty-six years, pitting Calvinists against Catholics, ending with the granting of tolerance to Protestants through the **Edict of Nantes** in 1598, although the edict was later revoked by King Louis XIV. In Germany, the **Thirty Years War** broke out in 1618, involving almost all regions of the Holy Roman Empire. It ended in 1648 with the **Treaty of Westphalia**, which allowed principalities and cities to choose their own religion, creating a patchwork of religious affiliations throughout the Empire. Religious divisions in Britain played out through Henry VIII's daughters: Queen Mary was a Catholic who tried to turn the kingdom back to Rome, and Queen Elizabeth I was a Protestant who ensured the continuation of the Anglican Church. During the early 17th century, the **English Civil War** was partially provoked by the Catholic leanings of the Stuart kings. Religious issues dominated European politics for almost a century, but eventually settled into an acceptance of religious pluralism, although the tensions led many to leave Europe. Some headed to the Americas.

The Scientific Revolution

Just as it impacted art, literature, and religion, the growing humanistic emphasis of the era 1450-1750 shaped attitudes toward scientific thought. Scientists loosened their research from the theories devised during the classical era, and based their knowledge of the natural world on direct observation and mathematics. The new vision of science developed during the 17th and 18th centuries is known as the **Scientific Revolution,** and its reliance on human reason for understanding scientific phenomena reinforced changes brought about by the Renaissance and the Reformation, including a further weakening of the influence of the Roman Catholic Church.

The methods devised by scientists of these early modern times form the basis for science today: mathematical formulation, **empirical evidence** (information verifiable by observations), and freedom of inquiry. The new science contrasted to the **scholasticism** of the Middle Ages, in which scholars based their inquiry on the principles established by the church. This new emphasis on the freedom of inquiry sometimes resulted in clashes between scientists and religious and political authorities, and so the researchers didn't always make their findings public. One of the first European scientists to experience this conflict was **Nicholas Copernicus,** a Polish monk and mathematician who based his early mathematical tables and models on those developed by **Nasir al-Din**, an Islamic scholar of the 13th century. Copernicus was commissioned by Pope Paul III to revise the Julian calendar – devised during the time of Julius Caesar – to correct for slight inaccuracies that caused the calendar year to continuously lose time. Copernicus analyzed the astronomy underlying the calendar, which the Romans had based on the work of the Greek Astronomer Ptolemy. Ptolemy believed that the earth was at the center of the universe, and that all heavenly bodies revolved around it, including the sun and the moon. Ptolemy's theory had been adopted by the church as official doctrine, so to question Ptolemy was also to question the church. Based on his own empirical observations, Copernicus discovered that the earth was revolving around the sun. His formulations also revealed that the earth turned on its axis every 24 hours, so that differences in night and day were not caused by the universe revolving around the earth. Since his free inquiry led him in a direction contrary to church doctrine, he tested his developing theory over and over again, and only revealed his outcomes just before his death. Even then, the findings were released only to a handful of scientists and mathematicians.

Two astronomers that followed – **Tycho Brahe** and **Johannes Kepler** – used the Copernicus model to develop a more comprehensive theory that showed the earth and other planets revolving around the sun in elliptical orbits. Unlike Copernicus, Kepler published his results as a relatively young man, fueling a controversy between religious officials and scientists. Protestant leaders criticized the new scientific models, too, with Martin Luther attacking the Copernican model as early as 1539. The Catholic Church was slower to condemn it, but in 1610, it declared Copernicus' work a heresy, and by 1616 all writings that claimed that the earth moved on its axis were forbidden to be taught or read. This course of events entangled an Italian astronomer, **Galileo Galilei,** as he turned the newly invented telescope toward the sky in 1609. The telescope had been created for optical purposes in the Netherlands, but Galileo was the first to use it to study the heavens, where he discovered that the Milky Way was a huge collection of stars, the moon's light is reflected from the sun, and the earth is not the only planet with moons. These discoveries and many more were disconcerting to people of early modern Europe because they indicated that the earth is nothing special, and is only one of many heavenly bodies in the universe. For the religious, these discoveries implied that the earth was not central to God's creation, and they called in question the belief that God's throne is in a fixed place in heaven. Galileo – like Copernicus, Brahe, and Kepler – stressed his

ORIGINAL DOCUMENTS: GALILEO ON SCIENCE AND THE BIBLE

Galileo's boldness in discussing the relationship between science and the Bible eventually got him into trouble with the church. In the following excerpts from his *Letter to the Grand Duchess Christiana* in 1615, he argued that the Bible and science don't necessarily contradict one another. His words also illustrate two basic precepts of the Scientific Revolution: empirical observation and reliance on human reasoning.

"The reason produced for condemning the opinion that the earth moves and the sun stands still is that in many places in the Bible one may read that the sun moves and the earth stands still...I think that in discussions of physical problems we ought to begin not from the authority of scriptural passages, but from sense-experiences and necessary demonstrations; for the holy Bible and the phenomena of nature proceed alike from the divine World, the former as the dictate of the Holy Ghost and the latter as the observant executrix of God's commands...I do not mean to infer that we need not have an extraordinary esteem for the passages of holy Scripture...but I do not feel obliged to believe that the same god who has endowed us with senses, reason, and intellect has intended to forgo their use and by some other means to give us knowledge which we can attain by them."

Reference: Discoveries and Opinions of Galileo by Galileo Galilei. Trans. and ed. by Stillman Drake (Garden City, N.Y.: Doubleday Anchor Books, 1957), pp. 181-183.

own empirical observations, but more than the earlier scientists, he wrote for a general audience, not for just scientists. His writings were in the vernacular (Italian) as well, so the impact of his bold questioning of church doctrine was greater. In 1633 Galileo was tried by the Church and found guilty of teaching his theories against the orders of the church. He was forced to recant his beliefs and spent the rest of his life under house arrest. His book, *The Starry Messenger*, was put on the "Index of Forbidden Books," and he was prohibited from publishing anything else on the subject of heavenly bodies and their movements.

The most famous European scientist of the era was **Isaac Newton,** whose late 17th century work built on the work of his predecessors. In 1687 he published his *Principia Mathematica,* which built the framework of natural laws that have guided scientists through the 20th century. His book described the basic principles of motion, and most famously the universal law of gravity. Newton explained how his laws governed the universe, including the planetary orbits that Kepler had identified. He worked out mathematical formulas for the pull of gravity, and so doing, greatly advanced the mathematical underpinnings of theoretical research. As complex as his formulas could be, he captured the vision of a natural universe in simple laws that helped to organize scientific thought for subsequent research.

The Scientific Revolution combined with the Renaissance and the Reformation to transition Europe from medieval to modern times. Science had the biggest impact among educated westerners first, while most people continued to believe traditional explanations of the natural world. For example, many people continued to believe that witches had supernatural powers to affect nature, and accusations of witchcraft were still taken seriously in courts of law during much of the 17th century. However, people eventually came to believe that their environment could be controlled by humans. Doctors promoted a more scientific approach to illness and publicly denounced popular healers. Writers began to question religious miracles, and some intellectuals rethought conceptions of God through the explanation that a divinity set natural laws in motion, a system of thought called **Deism.** Science had certainly been important in other eras in different parts of the world. For example, China had long been a source of innovative thought about the nature of the universe. However, the Chinese approach was generally a practical one, and their interest in science was based on its perceived usefulness. The thinkers of the European Scientific Revolution were enthralled with the idea of general laws of nature that could explain broad patterns that the Ancient Greeks and Romans and Islamic scholars before them had also been interested in. More than anything, these new scientists were absolutely convinced that it was fully within the reasoning power of human beings to understand, and by implication to control, the vast workings of the universe.

The Enlightenment

The new emphasis on human abilities and accomplishments and the importance of independent, rational thought was displayed in another movement of the era called the **Enlightenment.** The Enlightenment thinkers were inspired by scientists to understand the natural laws of the universe, but their interest lay in how they affect human society and government. One of the first Enlightenment thinkers was **John Locke**, a 17th century Englishman who sought to understand the impact of the "laws of nature" on human liberties and equality and the implications for government. He questioned the gloomy prediction of the earlier English philosopher, **Thomas Hobbes,** that human beings by nature would inevitably be controlled by absolute rulers. In his *Second Treatise of Government,* Locke suggested instead a "social contract" between ruler and subject that required a governor to get the "consent of the governed" to establish a legitimate government. Another Englishman, **Adam Smith,** analyzed the natural law of supply and demand that governed economics in his classic book *The Wealth of Nations.*

By the 18th century, the center of Enlightenment thought was France, where "philosophes", or intellectual philosophers, debated questions such as, "What is true human nature?" and "Can liberty exist in a society without compromising equality?" and "What is the best form of government to preserve human freedoms?" They wrote histories, novels, and philosophical treatises on political and social issues, and they often gathered in salons, usually hosted by socially prominent women in their homes, for the purpose of discussing the leading ideas of the day. One influential French thinker was Charles Louis de Secondat, known as the **Baron de Montesquieu,** who much admired the British Parliament that had successfully gained power at the expense of the king. He admired parliament's power in the British government, and he advocated something more radical – a government with three independent branches that share political power. Another French philosophe, Francois-Mari Arouet, who used the pen name **Voltaire,** wrote witty criticisms of the French monarchy and the Roman Catholic Church. He believed both institutions to be despotic and intolerant, characteristics that limited the freedoms that individuals deserved by the laws of nature. The most radical of the philosophers was **Jean Jacques Rousseau**, who famously proclaimed in his *Social Contract* that "Man is born free; and everywhere he is in chains." Since society had corrupted human nature, Rousseau advocated a return to nature in which people live in small, cooperative community with no ownership of property.

As was also true for the natural scientists, most Enlightenment thinkers wrote for one another and a relatively small number of well-educated Europeans. However, their works were to have broad consequences that impacted people at all levels of society. Two great revolutions based on Enlightenment thought were fought at the end of the 18th century that not only transformed their societies but also ushered in a modern age of democracy. Enlightenment voices were to reverberate throughout the ages.

POLITICAL CONSOLIDATION

The many cultural changes in Europe during early modern times were accompanied by political changes, most notably the consolidation of weak medieval kingdoms into strong, centralized states. These states claimed relatively small land spaces, but the constant competition among them inspired each to seek power through land exploration and trade claims in other parts of the world. European kings generally benefitted from the Reformation because the Catholic Church lost its political power as many Christians joined the ranks of the Protestants. Kings and popes had long clashed over political power, and the 16th-century religious crisis gave kings and princes the opportunity to assert themselves. Religion remained very important, and religious issues continued to fragment the Holy Roman Empire, but strong kings emerged in England, France, and Spain by the late 16th century.

For a time – the early 16th century – it looked as if Europe would fall under the control of one family, the path to empire that so many regions of the world had followed before. The powerful **Habsburg Family,** whose ancestral home was Austria, had land claims all over Europe from Spain to Italy to the Netherlands to Hungary. All Holy Roman emperors had been Habsburgs since 1273, and Emperor Charles V dreamed of unifying all of these areas under his centralized control. Holy Roman emperors had never had much political power before, and Charles' efforts were doomed to failure, partly because of religious conflict between Protestants and Catholics. The Habsburgs were Catholic, and Protestants did not want to see them gain political power, and Charles experienced strong opposition from the French king and the Ottoman sultan. In the end he abdicated his throne to join a monastery in Spain, and his land holdings fragmented, with his son Philip II inheriting the Habsburg lands in Spain.

After Charles V's unsuccessful attempt to unify Europe, his son, Philip II, ruled Spain at the height of its power. The kingdom had only been unified in the late 15th century by the marriage of Ferdinand and Isabelle, which combined the two smaller kingdoms of Castile and Aragon. This powerful couple not only sponsored the voyages of Christopher Columbus, but they drove the last of the Muslim rulers from southern Spain with the conquest of Granada in 1492. Spanish rulers remained devoutly Catholic, and they presided over a state that grew rich from New World wealth. The Spanish and French kings gained enough power to become **absolute monarchs**, who held complete control over their kingdoms. French kings steadily built their power during the 17th century as their armies grew and nobles became less rebellious, especially with the threat of cannon fire on their castles. French kings built a strong bureaucracy that helped them collect taxes and keep their eyes on dissidents, and they cultivated a belief in the **divine right** of kings. With God's blessing of the king's authority, the legitimacy of royalty across Europe was enhanced. The apex of absolutism in France occurred under the long reign of **Louis XIV** during the 17th and 18th centuries. Louis understood the importance of the "theatre state," by building a magnificent palace at Versailles, far grander than any castles of the nobility. There he entertained regularly and extravagantly, helping the nobility to forget

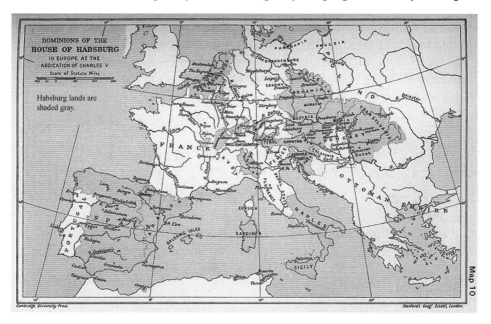

Habsburg Land Claims in 1556. The above map from *The Cambridge Modern History Atlas* (1912) shows the widespread holding of the Habsburg Family at the time of Charles V's abdication of the Holy Roman Empire's throne. The Habsburg lands included Spain, the Netherlands, much of the Holy Roman Empire, and southern Italy. The attempt to consolidate Europe into one empire was resisted by Protestants, the French royal house, and the Ottoman sultan.

their complaints against the king. Known as the "Sun King," his likeness surrounded by sun beams was placed all around the palace – on medallions above doors, on furniture, and woven into carpets. His famous statement, "L'etat c'est moi*"* ("I am the state") succinctly summed up his absolute rule. The monarchies of Prussia in eastern Germany and the Habsburg kings in Austria-Hungary also practiced absolutism, with the Prussian rulers particularly emphasizing a strong military.

Meanwhile, Britain and the Netherlands developed a different style of government, **constitutionalism.** In these states rulers shared power with a parliament, a body of representatives selected by the nobility and leading urban citizens. In Britain, parliamentary power had been growing gradually since the days of William the Conqueror, and had been reinforced by Henry VIII's need for parliamentary support in forming and heading the Anglican Church. Queen Elizabeth I relied on parliament to fund the navy, finance exploratory voyages, and fight wars. The English Civil War of the early 17th century pitted the king against parliament, and though the forces of parliament won and King Charles I was beheaded, Britain eventually settled on a strongly Protestant pair from the Netherlands – William and Mary – to rule together with parliament, with parliament retaining the power of the purse. Both Britain and the Netherlands were growing commercial and colonial powers, and wealthy merchants were involved in political affairs and often members of parliament. Government in the Netherlands was decentralized, but the House of Orange was highly influential. The term "constitutionalism" implies not a written constitution as such, but an agreement that the ruler, like everyone else, is subject to the **rule of law,** with laws of course passed by parliament.

COMPARISON: ABSOLUTISM VS. CONSTITUTIONALISM IN EARLY MODERN EUROPE

CONSTITUTIONALISM	ABSOLUTISM
Degree of centralization varied	Highly centralized state
Rule of law	Rule by divine right of kings
Rule over relatively homogeneous populations	Degree of homogeneity varied
Practiced mercantilism	Practiced mercantilism
Power of king shared with parliament	No sharing of power with parliament
Recognition of some individual rights	No recognition of individual rights

THE DEVELOPMENT OF CAPITALISM AND TECHNOLOGICAL ADVANCES

The cultural and political changes of early modern Europe were accompanied by equally important economic developments that supported the growing emphasis on individual abilities and accomplishments. A unique European development was **capitalism,** an economic system based on private ownership of property and businesses that produce goods to be bought and sold in a free market. Private individuals pursue their own economic interests, hire their own workers, and decide which goods to produce. Capitalism was explained by Adam Smith in his *Wealth of Nations* as an economic system controlled by an "invisible hand" – the natural law that defines the relationship between supply and demand. Fair prices are set because supply and demand naturally vary together, and no government intervention is necessary. European governments (especially Britain and the Netherlands) also believed in **mercantilism,** or the responsibility of government to promote the state's economy to improve tax revenues and limit imports to prevent profits from going to outsiders. Whereas mercantilism implies more government control than capitalism, both emphasize the advantages of allowing individuals to develop their own business initiatives. Capitalism does require merchants and businessmen to take risks with their money, and so some support from government and other organizations could minimize the damage if enterprises went awry.

Early capitalism in Europe came to be supported by institutions organized to promote the accumulation of wealth and the ease of buying and selling products. Some of these institutions – such as banks, investment organizations, and insurance underwriters – had been in existence for many years in the older civilizations, who had experimented with various credit and trade mechanisms, some more successfully than others. Banks began appearing in all major European cities, where businessmen and merchants could keep their money and secure loans for their business ventures. Insurance companies formed to share the risk of these ventures, as did **joint-stock companies,** which organized commercial ventures on a large scale by allowing investors to buy and sell shares. Companies such as the East India Company were able to put together the largest businesses in history to that point, and often made a great deal of money for stockholders. If the business failed, all were damaged, but it was less likely that anyone would be completely ruined. Most joint-stock companies formed in Britain and the Netherlands, states that were supportive of rule by law and the use of contracts, whereas in Spain, where absolutism held sway, the government was more likely to control business ventures directly. In Britain and the Netherlands, governments chartered joint-stock companies, enforced contracts, and settled disputes among businessmen and merchants.

The new capitalist system largely replaced the old guild system of the Middle Ages. The craft guilds had monopolized the production of goods by fixing prices and wages and regulating standards of quality. Because guilds represented collective – not individual – efforts and did not emphasize profit-making, entrepreneurs sought to find ways to operate without them. One tactic was to produce goods in the countryside outside the guilds' control through the "**putting-out system,**" in which entrepreneurs delivered raw materials to workers in their homes, where they transformed them into finished products to be picked up later by the entrepreneur or his representative. For example, a rural family received raw wool that they spun into yarn, and then weaved the yarn into cloth to be sold in town by the entrepreneur for a profit. Only later would factories organize, where workers came to a central place to produce goods. By 1750 most workers were still operating under the putting-out system.

Technological advances also greatly contributed to the transformation of Europe between 1450 and 1750. Mostly, Europeans altered inventions made elsewhere to suit their needs. For example, they designed the hulls of their sailing ships to sail the deep waters of the Atlantic and to carry heavy arms. They used the compass for navigation, an earlier invention of the Chinese, but Europeans improved it by making it less likely to inaccurately respond to the magnetic pull of iron in the ship's structure. A new mapmaking technique produced the **Mercator Projection,** which was particularly well suited for travel on the Atlantic. The Chinese had invented gunpowder many centuries before, but Europeans made advances in metalwork that allowed them to make cannon – and eventually guns – that were more accurate and less dangerous to use than those used by the Mongols. These last innovations were particularly important in the buildup of European military might. Their ships mounted with cannons and soldiers armed with guns had a tremendous advantage over much larger armies without them, including those of the Aztecs and Inca half a world away.

DEMOGRAPHIC AND SOCIAL CHANGES

Underlying the economic, political, and cultural changes in Europe during the period 1450-1750 was an important demographic change: rapid population growth. Birth rates did not rise dramatically, but healthier diets were made possible by an increase in food available from the expanding trade networks, and old diseases proved to be less deadly than before. These two factors increased the average life span and led to population increases during the 16th century. The Thirty Years War of the early 17th century caused a temporary decline in population, but after the war ended, population levels continued to grow throughout the era, with overall increases from about 80 million in 1500 to 120 million in 1700. Largely as a result of increasing levels of commerce, rapid urbanization also took place, and both London and Paris had populations of about 500,000 by 1650. Other cities grew rapidly, including Madrid, Amsterdam, Berlin, Copenhagen, and Stockholm. Population growth allowed the rapid economic expansion of the era, and it also provided the fuel for European settlements in the New World.

The economic expansion had some important implications for social life. Many people in urban areas profited from the brisk increase in commerce, and the

MARKER EVENT: THE MERCATOR MAP PROJECTION

Mapmaking is a skill that became well-developed during classical times, but the Mercator Projection was a new one, developed during the 16th century by Gerhard Kremer, known as "Mercator" (the merchant) because his maps were tailored to aid European ocean traders. Although the interiors of North and South America and Africa were still unexplored, he still was able to outline their coastlines, even though his methods exaggerated the size of any land that was a long distance from the equator. In order to represent the globe on a flat surface, Mercator drew the lines of longitude – which actually meet at the poles – as parallel lines, a process that made areas like Greenland and Antarctica look much larger than they really are. The advantage for sailors on the Atlantic was that they could draw a straight line between their point of departure and their destination, making their travel more reliable. As a result, Atlantic trade was stimulated, and the Mercator projection is still a common one. Europeans also may have liked it, though, because in proportion to other landmasses, it made Europe look bigger than it really is!

putting-out system brought wealth to the countryside as well. New wealth encouraged people to buy more goods, stimulating the economy further. The possibility for financial independence had implications for families since it allowed young people more flexibility in establishing their own homes at an earlier age. The nuclear (small, two-generation) family was already more common in Europe than in other parts of the world, but the development of capitalism certainly reinforced this pattern. Marriages were no longer as tied to the interests of the extended family, since people tended to have economic and emotional independence, making it much more possible to marry for love. Since nuclear families are small, they tend to intensify the emotional bonds among family members, making them more independent from outsiders but more dependent on one another.

The transformation of Europe between 1450 and 1750 had many mutually reinforcing cultural, political, and economic components that changed the power balance in the world. While older civilizations were either in decline or holding their own, small European states were flexing their muscles in ways that would not only impact this era, but those that followed. These changes encouraged Europeans to venture across the seas to join the hemispheres for the first time in world history, and to contact people in almost every corner of the world as well.

IDENTIFICATIONS AND CONCEPTS

95 Theses
absolutism, absolute monarch
Anglican Church
Brahe, Tycho
Calvin, John
capitalism
Catholic Reformation
Cervantes, Miguel de
Copernicus, Nicholas
Deism
divine right
"early modern" period
Edict of Nantes
empirical evidence
English Civil War
Enlightenment
Galileo
Gunpowder Empires
Gutenberg, Johann
Habsburg Family
humanism
indulgences
Jesuits
joint-stock companies
Kepler, Johannes
land-based powers, sea-based powers
Leonardo da Vinci
limited (constitutional) monarchy
Locke, John
Louis XIV
Luther, Martin
Machiavelli, Niccolo

CHAPTER ELEVEN: HEMISPHERES UNITED

By 1450 people had been traveling across the world's seas and oceans since ancient times. The earliest water travel was generally by river, particularly in the areas of the river valley civilizations. Phoenician, Greek, and Roman ships crossed the Mediterranean Sea on a regular basis by the classical era, and dhows and Chinese junks traversed the wide expanses of the Indian Ocean. By the era from 600 to 1450, these trade patterns had intensified, canals connected rivers in China, and Polynesians had explored and settled on islands from the East Indies to Easter Island to Hawaii. Scandinavians had also made their way across the northern Atlantic to North America, but no sustained contact resulted from their travels. In the Americas, the Arawak were travelling around the Caribbean by 1000 C.E., and the Carib settled in many of the same areas by 1500, and had traveled to the North American mainland. All of these ventures throughout the world laid the basis for the extensive sea travel and trade that developed between 1450 and 1750 and made it possible for sea-based states to gain preeminent power in the world.

ZHENG HE'S VOYAGES

No solid historical proof exists that anyone crossed the Pacific Ocean before the early 16th century, and even though some islands in the Atlantic were settled, the Atlantic Ocean provided a great barrier between Europe, Africa, and the Americas. However, some incredible voyages were undertaken by China in the early 15th century. Chinese junks were the largest, most seaworthy ships of the day, and Chinese sailors were well trained. The expeditions were led by a Chinese Muslim, **Zheng He,** who was commissioned by the Ming Emperor **Yongle.** Although most of the Ming emperors emphasized self-reliance for China and discouraged extensive contacts with other civilizations, Yongle was something of a renegade who supported a series of seven maritime expeditions between 1405 and 1433, all commanded by Zheng He. The fleets were huge, with as many as 317 vessels and 28,000 men. The voyages stretched from China to Southeast Asia, India, the Red Sea, and east Africa. One purpose of the voyages was to reassert China's power after the demise of the Yuan Dynasty, and the ships carried expensive gifts for people along the way. In the time-honored tradition, Chinese vessels exacted tribute from those they encountered, who were influenced to co-operate by the size of the expeditions and the impressive ships. Zheng He also brought back exotic animals and plants to his emperor, most famously transporting a giraffe from Africa to China, where this wondrous creature was publicly displayed to people who had never seen such a sight.

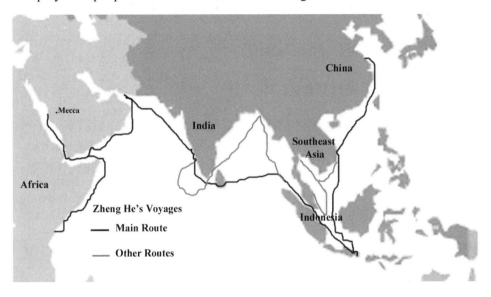

Zheng He's Voyages. Zheng He took seven voyages from Nanjing to different destinations in the South China Sea and the Indian Ocean basin. He visited many ports in Southeast Asia and India, stopped by Mecca to fulfill his hajj, and docked in major cities along the Swahili Coast of Africa. He rid the Malacca Strait and surrounding waters of pirates, settled disputes among locals in several locations, and collected tribute and distributed gifts along the way.

After Yongle's death, the Ming made the decision to stop the voyages, leading many people in later times to speculate about how the course of world history might have been altered had they continued them. The voyages ended only a few decades before Europeans began venturing across the Atlantic and around the tip of Africa. If the Ming had not stopped the voyages, might the Chinese have "discovered" the Americas first? Indeed, a recent best-selling book concluded that it is probable that Zheng He made his way to the California coast. Most historians disagree with that conclusion; however, in many ways, the Chinese ships were more seaworthy (though not as agile) than the small European ships that later landed in the Americas. The fact remains that the Ming did stop the voyages, a perfectly understandable occurrence within the context of the dynasty's overall orientation to the world. Yongle was in many ways an exception to other Ming Emperors, whose general orientation was to be very skeptical about contact with foreigners. After all, the Mongols had taken over China not too many years before. The overall behavior – to sponsor gigantic voyages and then abruptly stop them – reflects China's on-again-off-again attitude toward the Middle Kingdom's relationship with the world: trade was vital to China's greatness but it also could bring great harm and destruction. Besides, money was needed yet again to contain attacks from nomadic groups on the northern and western borders, so the voyages were deemed too expensive.

PORTUGUESE AND SPANISH VOYAGES AND COLONIES

The first Europeans to take long voyages away from home during this era were the Portuguese and Spanish. Both had just consolidated their governments and built strong militaries, and they were well situated on the Atlantic Ocean, close to the Strait of Gibraltar that led to the Mediterranean Sea. However, the two kingdoms had little hope of competing for trade on the Mediterranean because it was dominated by Venice and Genoa. These two city-states had forged trade alliances with Muslim states to continue the lucrative trade with the East that had begun during the era of the Crusades, and they had little interest in exploring possible trade routes across the Atlantic. Spain and Portugal were inspired by the new cultural and economic forces that were transforming Europe, and they also were interested in finding new converts to Christianity. Spain was newly united under Ferdinand and Isabelle, who, as devout Catholics, in 1492 finally defeated Granada, the last Muslim kingdom on the Iberian Peninsula, and ordered all Jews to be expelled only three months later. Their religious devotion, coupled with newly centralized political power, provided incentive to spread Christianity to new regions.

The Portuguese began their explorations in the early 15th century after they attacked the rich Muslim Moroccan city of Ceuta, which was only across the Strait of Gibraltar from the newly conquered Muslim state of Granada. There the Portuguese observed the caravans that brought gold and slaves across the Sahara from the African states to the south, which encouraged them to sail down the African coast in hopes of establishing some trade contacts. These first ventures were led by the third son of the Portuguese king, Prince Henry, who devoted his life to navigation, and is known in history as **"Henry the Navigator."** His most important contribution was the creation of a navigation school, which became a magnet for the Genoese, Jewish cartographers who were familiar with Arab maps, and a number of young Portuguese men, some of whom became far more famous than he. Henry and his staff studied and improved navigation technology, including the magnetic compass and the astrolabe, which helped mariners determine their locations on the oceans. The Portuguese also made some important advancements in the design for ships, since the square-sailed vessels propelled by oarsmen in the Mediterranean would not work in the more turbulent Atlantic Ocean. The new ship developed by the Portuguese was called the **caravel,** which was much smaller than a Chinese junk, but its size allowed the exploration of shallow coastal areas and rivers, yet it was strong enough to withstand storms on the ocean. The caravel had two sets of sails: one set had square sails to catch ocean breezes for speed, and the other set were the triangular lateen sails that had been used for maneuverability for many years on the Indian Ocean. The newly perfected European cannon made the caravel a fighting ship as well.

Henry had to convince others to strike out along the coast of Africa because of common concepts that southern waters were boiling hot and full of monsters, and so it took the Portuguese many years to venture beyond southern Morocco. They were further discouraged by the long stretch of desert that extended for hundreds of miles south of Morocco. Although it was not originally Henry's goal, some of the students from his school, most notably **Bartholomew Dias** and **Vasco da Gama**, set out to find the tip of Africa and connect beyond it to the Indian Ocean. These feats were accomplished by the end of the 15th century, after years of experimenting with wind and ocean currents and discovering the fastest and safest ways to return home to Portugal. These experiments also encouraged both the Portuguese and the Spanish to venture away from the coast and take to the high seas. In 1500 Pedro Cabral sailed too far west and reached the South American coast by mistake, but it allowed him to claim Brazil for Portugal, its one possession in the New World.

Spanish exploration developed much less gradually, with the rulers only becoming interested in overseas explorations during the last decade of the 15th century. A Genoese mariner named **Christopher Columbus** convinced Ferdinand and Isabella to sponsor a voyage across the Atlantic after he was turned down by the Genoese and Portuguese governments. Columbus believed that he could reach east Asia by sailing west, and he used the calculations of the Ancient Greek geographer Ptolemy when he estimated the distance. Ptolemy believed that the circumference of the earth was about 16,000 miles, 9,000 miles short of reality. As a result, it is not surprising that Columbus thought he had reached the East Indies when he arrived in the Americas in 1492. He made three voyages between 1492 and 1498, and continued to insist that he had reached Asia even after he sighted the coast of South America on the third voyage. Of course, he had encountered the New World instead, which would be named "America" after Amerigo Vespucci, a later explorer sponsored by Spain and Portugal.

The Treaty of Tordesillas

Despite the fact that the two kingdoms of Portugal and Spain sent explorations in different directions, they began to argue shortly after Columbus' first voyage about who controlled the newly discovered lands. Both looked to the Catholic Church for guidance. First, in 1493, the Spanish-born Pope Alexander VI endorsed an imaginary line drawn through the Atlantic from the North to South Pole as the boundary for Spanish land claims, allowing Spain all land west of the line. Portuguese King John II protested the line that ran 100 leagues west of the Cape Verde islands and the Azores, so both countries agreed in the **Treaty of Tordesillas** in 1494 on a line moved to 370 leagues west of the islands. As Portugal pushed its explorations to India and beyond, and the Spanish began to explore the Pacific Ocean, they eventually began to argue about lands on the opposite side of the earth, resulting in a treaty in 1529 that set the line in the Pacific. A Spanish adventured named Vasco Nunez de Balboa crossed the Isthmus of Panama from the east and "discovered" the Pacific Ocean on the other side in 1513, and **Ferdinand Magellan** was commissioned by Spain in 1519 to sail westward from Spain, cross the Atlantic, find a way through the Americas, cross the Pacific, and come back home to Spain. Though Magellan himself died in the Philippines, one of his ships made it all the way back to Spain, a significant accomplishment because it was the first to circumnavigate the globe.

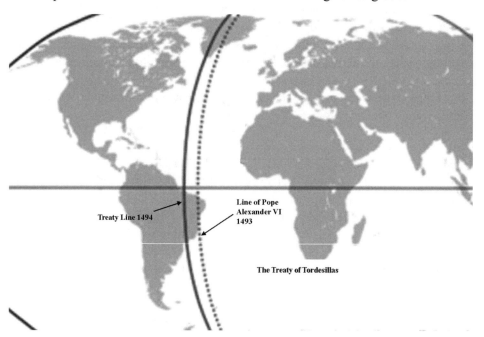

The Treaty of Tordesillas. The first line drawn by Pope Alexander VI gave Spain all the land west of the dotted line. Portugal protested, resulting in the treaty line of 1494, the Treaty of Tordesillas, that moved the line west, allowing Portugal to claim lands east. Notice that the move allowed Portugal to claim Brazil, a area given to the Spanish by the first line.

The Treaty of Tordesillas was a fateful agreement for both Spain and Portugal, since it oriented Spain toward the Americas (except for Brazil) and Portugal toward Africa and the Indian Ocean. As the Portuguese entered the Indian Ocean basin, they encountered well-established trade routes and ports frequented, shared, or controlled by many different people. With their sea-worthy cara-vels equipped with very effective cannon, the Portuguese were able to dominate trade from Africa to China during the 15th century. As their ships rounded the Cape of Good Hope at the tip of Africa, they first turned their attention to the Swahili city-states, many of which they burned to the ground. However, be-cause different ports along the basin were pieces of the loosely connected Indian Ocean community, the "enemy" could not be defeated clearly through a blow to a non-existent head of state. The Portuguese, then, had to be content with quick profits from trade, and they seldom settled in ports they controlled. Muslims, Buddhists, and Hindus had very little interest in converting to the Christianity that they tried to impose, and despite the violence that the Portuguese dealt, in many ways life along the Indian Ocean trade circuit went on as it always had. On the other hand, the Spanish turned toward the New World, a place where they discovered that after the conquest of two clear enemies – the Aztecs and the Inca – all would be theirs. Thus began the transformation of the Americas.

The Spanish Empire in the Americas

The Spanish set about their conquest of the Americas in the same manner that they drove the Muslims out of the Iberian Peninsula. Through a combination of religious fervor to spread their faith and a desire for riches, individual **conquis-tadors** (conquerors) ventured out from Hispaniola (the place where Columbus landed in the Caribbean), to search for gold and convert the natives to Chris-tianity. **Hernan Cortes** left Cuba in 1519 with 600 soldiers to march toward the interior of Mexico, where they sought to find the Aztec capital. They were aided in their search by Amerindian people along the way who were controlled by but not loyal to their Aztec overlords. Particularly important was Malintzin (Malinche), a native woman who became a translator and guide for Cortes after she had been given to him as a mistress. Meanwhile, the Aztec emperor, **Mocte-zuma,** decided to welcome the Spaniards to Tenochtitlan, an action that, at least according to legend, may have been inspired by the belief that Cortes was Quet-zalcoatl returning home at last. The natives had never seen men with beards before, and descriptions that were relayed to Moctezuma may have sounded like the "feathered serpent." Whatever his real reason, it was clearly a mistake, and the Spanish took over the city and imprisoned Moctezuma, who was soon killed in a counterattack. How did 600 men take over the great city protected by thousands of Aztec warriors? One secret was the disloyalty of other Am-erindian groups that sided with the Spanish against the Aztecs. Another was the outbreak of smallpox that hit Tenochtitlan after the Spanish arrived. The natives had never been exposed to the disease that they carried, even though the Spanish themselves were immune to it. It has been said that more Aztecs died from smallpox than from battle wounds. However, the battle wounds were also important because the Spanish had a weapon that the Aztecs did not have: guns.

Spanish swords were also the fine results of years of technological diffusion and perfection all across the Eastern Hemisphere. As Jared Diamond said, "guns, germs, and steel" made all the difference.

COMPARISONS: ETHNOCENTRISM IN EARLY EUROPE AND CHINA

Ethnocentrism is a term that describes the tendency of human beings to view other cultures through the eyes of their own, and usually conclude that their own culture is superior. Ethnocentrism is not necessarily malicious, but it almost always involves the belief that one's culture is the "center" of the world, and all others revolve around it.

Very early, ethnocentrism was reflected in China, whose people referred to their land as "The Middle Kingdom," or the culture at the center of all others. During the early part of the era 1450-1750, the Ming Dynasty ruled China, and one of their greatest fears was the threat that outside influence would harm Chinese purity. During the same time period, the Spanish and Portuguese were quarreling over land claims, generally oblivious to the presence of other powers on the earth. For example, Portugal hoped to capture India, a feat that was virtually impossible since a strong, established civilization was already in place there. Like most other societies in history, the Spanish and Portuguese saw land as theirs to conquer, with one another as the only real threat, an attitude that spurred great accomplishments, but also reflected a great deal of ethnocentrism.

A few years after Cortes conquered the Aztecs, another conquistador, **Francisco Pizarro,** led a group of soldiers to the Andes to find the Inca, a great empire that he had heard about while living in Panama. The Inca had just been through a bitter civil war between two rival brothers for the throne, and though one – **Atahualpa** – had won, the empire was much weakened. Pizarro met Atahualpa near the city of Cajamarca in 1532, where his small group of soldiers seized Atahualpa from a litter carried by Inca nobles. The Spaniards were surrounded by 40,000 Inca soldiers, but their guns and swords carried the day. Atahualpa was imprisoned, and agreed to fill rooms with gold in exchange for his release. Atahualpa kept his promise, but the Spaniards did not. Atahualpa was first baptized as a Christian and then strangled. A massive native rebellion followed that made the Inca victory take longer than the Aztec conquest, but by 1540 the Spanish had the former Inca Empire under control.

With these two conquests, the Spanish conquistadors marched into other parts of Mesoamerica, South America, and the southern part of North America, claiming land as they went, converting natives to Christianity, and searching for gold. By the end of the 16th century, they had built a massive colonial empire in the New World.

PERSPECTIVES: BARTHOLOMÉ DE LAS CASAS ON THE SPANISH IN THE NEW WORLD

The view that most people have of the Spanish conquest of the New World has been shaped by the writings of Bartholomé de Las Casas, a conquistador turned priest who dedicated himself to protecting Amerindian rights. Sometimes called the "Black Legend," the vicious reputation of the Spanish was forged in *A Short Account of the Destruction of the Indies*, a book that Las Casas dedicated to the Spanish king Philip II to inform him of the abuses in the New World, as described in these passages:

"They [the Spanish] forced their way into native settlements, slaughtering everyone they found there, including small children, old men, pregnant women, and even women who had just given birth. They hacked them to pieces, slicing open their bellies with their swords as though they were so many sheep herded into a pen. They even laid wagers on whether they could manage to slice a man in two at a stroke, or cut an indivudal's head from his body, or disembowel him with a single blow of their axes...They spared no one, erecting especially wide gibbets [gallows] on which they could string their victims up with their feet just off the ground and then burn them alive thirteen at a time, in honor of our Savior and the twelve Apostles..."

Reference: A Short Account of the Destruction of the Indies by Bartholomé de Las Casas, translated by Nigel Griffin (Penguin Classics, 1992), pp. 14,15.

Iberian Colonial Organization

Once the Inca and Aztecs were conquered, The Spanish and Portuguese governments took control of the land the conquistadors had claimed, although the Portuguese were preoccupied with their interests in Africa and Asia until the early 18th century. The Portuguese kings first allowed court favorites to administer Brazil, then appointed a governor general, and finally a viceroy in 1720. The Spanish established two centers of authority in the Americas – Mexico and

Peru – but later divided their possessions into four **viceroyalties** and the Audiencia of Chile. In the old Aztec capital of Tenochtitlan they built a Spanish city called Mexico City, and they also built their own administrative buildings on the foundations of old Inca centers in Cuzco. However, Cuzco was in the interior mountains, so the Spanish moved their capital to Lima in 1535, a city along the coast much more accessible for trade.

Colonial Latin America in the 18ᵗʰ Century. At first the Spanish had only two viceroyalties: New Spain in Mexico, and Peru in the Andes area. During the 18ᵗʰ century, they created new viceroyalties that separated from Peru: La Plata and New Granada.

The **viceroys** were the king's representatives in the New World, and they wielded a great deal of power over their lands. Spain was far away, and despite the fact that the king set up "audiencias", or special courts, to review the viceroys' decisions, communication was so difficult that the viceroys operated fairly in-dependently. Each viceroy set up his government in an urban area, so the members of the large bureaucracy lived nearby, and army headquarters were also in the cities. Until the 17th century almost all colonial officials were born in Spain, but eventually, with new generations, Spaniards born in the New World took some of the posts. Settlement patterns in Portuguese Brazil were similar. Almost everyone that lived outside urban areas was Amerindian, with one important exception. True to the goal to convert as many natives to Christianity as possible, most ships that arrived in the New World from the Iberian Peninsula carried Catholic priests, particularly Jesuits, who were actively promoting the Catholic Reformation, and Franciscans, who had traditionally taken care of the poor. Priests went out into the countryside in order to contact the natives, and individually or in pairs they often set up residences and churches in areas far from other Europeans in the cities. Priests also saw to the spiritual needs of Europeans and established schools, universities, and printing services. However, their willingness to spread out throughout the countryside and live among the Amerindians was primarily responsible for the tremendous number of conversions they had. This pattern almost certainly made many priests quite sympathetic to the Amerindians, with some speaking up and eventually protesting Spanish exploitation.

The Colonial Economy in Latin America

The epidemic diseases that the immune Europeans carried with them to the New World may have helped the Spanish to defeat the Aztecs in Tenochtitlan, but the large number of natives that died from smallpox, measles, diphtheria, whooping cough and influenza certainly inhibited the economic development of the colonies. The Spanish set up silver mines in Peru and Mexico, where huge silver deposits were found, as well as agricultural plantations in the Caribbean, and the Portuguese organized sugar plantations in Brazil, since there were few precious metals there. Both mines and plantations required large work forces that the Europeans planned to fill with native workers. Even before the colonial administrative systems developed, individual conquistadors had forced natives to work for them under the **encomienda** system, which gave Spanish settlers – known as **encomenderos** – the right to force natives to work in their mines or fields. In return, they were responsible for their workers' well-being, including conversion to Christianity. In Peru this system of forced labor was modeled after the old Inca **mit'a** system that required one-seventh of adult male Amerindians to work at any give time for two to four months each year for their Spanish masters. In both arrangements, work was greatly hampered by the death of so many Amerindians. Often the plantations and mines had too few workers to function, and the mit'a system broke down as the Spanish first increased the time commitments, but eventually could not make it work as it had under the

Inca rulers. As a result, the Spanish and Portuguese turned more and more to importing slaves from Africa.

The Portuguese sugar plantations had always relied on slave labor, and even after disease killed so many natives, slave raiders forged inland to find new workers in more remote areas. Importing slaves was more expensive, but the Africans proved to be more resistant to disease, so in the long run, were better investments. In Mexican and Peruvian mines, the mit'a eventually gave way to a system of wage workers, who were paid good wages to take on the dangerous work. The amount of silver produced rose dramatically in the late 16th century as the population stabilized, and for several decades, silver from Spanish mines dramatically affected the world economy, and made Spain one of the richest states in the world. Mining stimulated the Spanish American economy, and rural estates (called haciendas) produced abundant food for the workers, and small textile shops made their clothing.

The silver mines were a mixed blessing for the Spanish. Since Spanish galleons crossing through the Caribbean and the Atlantic toward Spain were almost always carrying silver, pirates often attacked them, as did ships from rival European countries. Silver that did arrive in Spain flowed out of the country to pay for its many wars with England, France, and the Ottoman Empire, and to buy manufactured goods through the long-distance trade networks. So much silver went into circulation that prices rose sharply, setting off an inflation that greatly wounded the Spanish economy.

Society in Colonial Latin America

The political and economic structures put in place by Spain and Portugal greatly impacted social classes and practices. Since Amerindians were seen by the Iberians as their subjects, the greatest societal division was that between European and Amerindian. The political administrators, military leaders and soldiers, and plantation and mine owners were European; the workers were Amerindian. The old Aztec and Inca class distinctions were wiped away, as all were treated the same by Europeans. Once Spanish and Portuguese children were born in the New World, a distinction arose between those born in the Old World (**peninsulares**) and those born in the new (**creoles***). Over time, the peninsulares faded, and creoles came to dominate politics and the economy. However, few women came over from Spain and Portugal, so Spanish soldiers and officials took native wives and mistresses, and their children – part European and part Amerindian – were called **mestizos.** Once African slaves arrived in the new world, another dimension for social distinctions was added. People who were of both European and African descent were called **mulattoes,** and together with the mestizos they composed the **castas,** a middle-level status between Europeans at the top, and Amerindians and blacks at the bottom.

The Spanish and Portuguese carried their traditional patriarchal societies across the ocean, and fathers had a great deal of authority over their children. Women were subordinate to men, and could not hold political positions or run plantations or mines. However, a woman with a dowry (payment made to her husband at marriage) maintained control of it throughout the marriage. Widows often carried on family businesses after husbands died, and women also had full rights to inheritance.

THE EXPLORATION AND SETTLEMENT OF NORTH AMERICA

Three other European powers set their sights on land in the Americas: the Netherlands, Britain, and France. The Netherlands developed as a center of trade during the High Middle Ages, and unlike the Iberian Catholics, the Dutch Protestants were not particularly interested in spreading their religion to new lands. Instead, their religious zeal was channeled by the **Protestant work ethic** that encouraged individual endeavors toward gaining wealth. Newly empowered by independence of the Netherlands from Spain in the late 16th century, shrewd Dutch businessmen noticed that Portugal was losing control of the Indian Ocean trade by the early 17th century. Dutch ships headed toward eastern destinations, where they bought luxury goods from east and Southeast Asia and sold them for a profit in Europe. They prospered partly because many Muslims preferred to trade with them since the Protestants did not try to convert them to Christianity as the Portuguese Catholics attempted to do. However, the Dutch, like the Portuguese, were not averse to using their cannon to back up business deals. The Dutch, like the British and French, organized **joint-stock companies** to share the risk of their business ventures, with the largest and most famous one being the Dutch East India Company that specialized in the spice and luxury trade of the East Indies. The company quickly gained control of Dutch trading in the Pacific during the early 17th century, and by the late 17th century they shifted their attention to the trans-Atlantic African slave trade. Meanwhile the Dutch also crossed the Atlantic, and in 1624 the Dutch West India Company established the colony of New Netherland with its capital located on Manhattan Island in North America.

The British got a rather late start in their colonization efforts, partly as a result of an internal power struggle – The War of the Roses – that took their attention and drained their resources during the 15th century. Struggles between Catholics and Anglicans resulted from Henry VIII's establishment of the Anglican Church in the early 16th century, but by the reign of his daughter, Elizabeth I, England demonstrated its superior naval power when its fleet defeated the Spanish Armada in 1588. Their first venture to North America was a disappointment – Sir Walter Raleigh's "Lost Colony" on the Carolina coast failed – but by the early 1600s, they had founded several joint-stock companies to begin English settlement of the eastern coast of North America.   Beginning with Jamestown (Virginia) in 1607, the British established diverse colonies up and down the coast. Puritans, who had broken with Anglican England, settled in Massachusetts; Quakers under the guidance of William Penn sought refuge in New Jersey and Pennsylvania; and Catholics found respite in Maryland. The joint-stock companies intended to make profits, and many that came to North America under their sponsorship had economic rather than religious goals. In 1664 the English solidified their control of the Atlantic coast from Massachusetts south when they seized New Netherlands from the Dutch to rename it "New York." This victory came on the heels of two successful wars against the Dutch that secured England's status as the world's leading naval power by the late 17th century.

Like England, France entered the race for colonies in the Americas rather late. They explored the waterways of the Gulf of St. Lawrence and the St. Lawrence River to establish colonies at Port Royal (Nova Scotia) in 1604 and Quebec in 1608. French explorers eventually set up forts along the Ohio and Mississippi Rivers, and French colonies were founded in the Caribbean as well. As in all other European colonies in the New World, control of the French colonies ultimately rested with the king. The French, like the Spanish and Portuguese, were also interested in converting natives to Catholicism, so some of the early inhabitants were Jesuit priests. The French were particularly interested in the strong European fur market. French fur traders set up traps along the waterways and involved natives in the trade as well. They exchanged guns, textiles, and alcohol for furs, a practice that not only led to over hunting, but also put firearms into the hands of Amerindians that they later used in confrontations with European settlers, making warfare more deadly. Even though the fur trade flourished, population in French colonies grew more slowly than in English colonies. The cold Canadian colonies held little appeal for French settlers, and France did not allow Protestant Huguenots to settle in their North American colonies. Also, the lifestyle of fur traders, constantly on the move to follow traps and trade deals with natives, was not conducive to family life. In contrast, the English colonies were often settled by families, who came to farm and to provide work for the joint-stock companies.

The English and Dutch governments tried to control the economies of their colonies in the Americas through **mercantilism,** a system in which they intervened in the market constantly, with the understanding that the goal of economic gain was to benefit the mother country. The official policy was that goods and services that originated in the home country could be exported to colonies only and all colonial exports had to go to the home country. Whether the government controlled the economy directly, as it did in France, Spain, and Portugal, or through government-endorsed joint-stock companies, as happened in England and the Netherlands, New World endeavors expanded the mother country's economy far beyond its borders, helping to tilt the balance of power in the world toward Europe.

Governments in North America

Because Dutch and English colonies were often privately financed by joint-stock companies, their governments were more likely to have more independence from the mother country than Latin American colonies, which were financed directly by the kings. In North America a company charter spelled out the responsibilities and rights of the colonists, so the governments weren't all organized exactly the same. Alternately, Maryland was a proprietary colony, granted to Lord Baltimore himself and not to a stock company. When the Virginia Company (a joint-stock company) failed, the king assumed control of its lands, making Virginia a royal colony directly under his control. In English colonies, the governments had assemblies, often with two houses that mimicked the House of Lords and the House of Commons in the mother country, and just as the lords and commoners in England had asserted in earlier centuries, the colonists came to think that they should share with the king to right to determine their own rules and regulations. No powerful, authoritarian viceroys were set up, and no large urban areas comparable to Mexico City or Lima developed till much later.

Relations with Amerindians

In contrast to the densely populated Aztec and Inca Empires, the Amerindian populations in North America were generally small in the areas that the Dutch, British, and French explored and settled. Most practiced slash-and-burn agriculture or other semi-nomadic life styles, so European colonists could displace them rather easily, usually forcing them further inland. North American natives were just as susceptible to the diseases brought by Europeans, so their populations were further reduced as more settlers arrived. As Amerindians were pushed westward, some adapted to their new environments by hunting rather than agriculture, a lifestyle made possible by the earlier introduction of horses by the Spanish in Mexico during the 16th century. As some Amerindian groups migrated away from the Europeans, they intruded into lands claimed by other natives, setting off numerous territorial wars. Although Europeans interacted with North American natives, sometimes cooperating with them and sometimes mistreating them, they did not have to conquer any powerful empires as the Spanish had to do in order to control Latin America.

Less rigid social classes developed in the English colonies based on ethnicity, such as the mestizos of Latin America, partly because the European and Amerindian groups led separate lives in the early days. With Amerindians out of the way, the colonies were composed of all English people, and so there were fewer differences among them to form the basis for social class distinctions. Intermingling of blood did take place, but was more common as settlers pressed westward. The southern English colonies developed strict social classes between blacks and whites, and anyone of mixed race was considered to be black, even though the term "mulatto" was used as it was in Latin America. The English believed that blacks and native people were inferior people, but because they maintained strict geographical boundaries between natives and Europeans, the social classes that developed within the middle and northern colonies were mainly among Europeans (except in the south), and were more fluid than in Latin America, where the races were in closer everyday proximity. French trappers, on the other hand, often took native wives, and the French relationship

PERSPECTIVES: HOW NATIVES AND NEWCOMERS SAW ONE ANOTHER

As Europeans came to the Americas during the period 1450-1750, conflicts arose between natives and the newcomers, with Amerindian rebellions continuing through the 19th century. From the beginning, each side saw the other through the lens of their respective cultures, as reflected in the quotes below.

"We consider ourselves...much happier than thou, in this that we are very content with the little that we have...[We] find all our riches and all our conveniences among ourselves, without trouble, without exposing our lives to the dangers in which you find yourselves constantly through your long voyages."
                    An anonymous Quebec Indian leader to French settlers

"In respect to us, they are a people poor, and for want of skill and judgement in the knowledge and use of our things, do esteem our trifles before things of great value...[It] may be hoped, if means of good government be used, that they may in short time be brought to civility, and the embracing of true religion."
                    Captain Arthur Barlowe, describing natives in Virginia

References: *New Relation of Gaspesia,* Father C. Leclercq, trans. and ed. by William F. Ganong. (Toronto: The Champlain Society, 1910.) *Voyages and Travels by John Pikerton,* Arthur Barlowe (London: Longman, 1812, Vol. 12) p. 604.

COMPARATIVE COLONIES IN THE AMERICAS

LATIN AMERICA	NORTH AMERICA
Encomienda, mit'a, and slave labor systems developed.	Labor systems that developed were slavery and indentured servitude.
Many single men came as soldiers from Europe and married native women.	More families came, and so less intermarriage took place until settlers began moving west.
Governments were authoritarian viceroyalties with no assemblies and elaborate bureaucracies.	Governments operated more independently from the kings, with assemblies and less elaborate bureaucracies.
Amerindians were forced into labor by Europeans.	Amerindians were usually pushed aside and not used as a labor force.
Social structures were hierarchical, with several classes strictly based on ethnicity.	Social classes were hierarchical in the southern colonies (based on black vs. white), but generally less hierarchical and rigid than in Latin America.

with natives was generally more cooperative, especially since they shared fur-trapping responsibilities and rights.

Because most of the English colonists came to settle in North America, whether as a result of religious persecution or the desire to make economic gains, most of them farmed or went into trade, so forced labor systems developed differently than those in Latin America, where encomienda and mit'a systems predominated. Slaves were brought to North America, just as they were to the Caribbean and to Brazil, but were not practical in areas with small farms, such as New England. In the English middle colonies, another type of compulsory labor appeared: **indentured servitude.** An indentured servant was usually ethnically the same as a free settler, but he or she was bound by an "indenture" (contract) to work for a person for four to seven years in exchange for payment of the voyage to the New World. At the end of the contract, the indentured servant would often get a small piece of land, tools, and clothing.

GLOBAL EXCHANGES

Once European ships were regularly crossing the Atlantic and venturing into the Pacific Ocean as well, the sustained contact between hemispheres had profound implications for almost all areas of the world, not just for Europe and the Americas. Some of the new exchanges were biological – plants, food, animals, human beings, and disease – and others were commercial, involving manufactured goods, non-biological raw materials, and money. Both types of exchanges combined to establish global networks of trade and communications such as had not been seen before in world history.

The Columbian Exchange

The **Columbian Exchange** was the global diffusion of crops, other plants, human beings, animals, and disease that took place after the European exploratory voyages to the New World of the late 15th and 16th centuries. More than previous diffusions, the Columbian Exchange put people of the world in touch with biological species that were radically different from what they had known before. In previous times, species had developed separately, resulting in an almost completely different set of flora and fauna in the Western and Eastern Hemisphere, as well as in Oceania. When these worlds were brought together, people had access to all three, bringing about vast changes in natural environment, health, and demographic patterns.

A dramatic demographic change occurred in the New World with astoundingly high death rates among Amerindians as a result of contact with Europeans. Because of their long isolation, they had no immunities to smallpox, influenza, typhus, measles, and diphtheria, and once diseases were communicated, they spread rapidly, killing the majority of the people. Smallpox was the deadliest of the early epidemics, but often it combined with other diseases to increase mortality rates even more. Death rates were highest in densely populated areas, such as the Aztec and Inca empires, but they spread to other areas as well. Persistent accusations were made that Europeans spread their diseases on purpose, but only limited historical proof has been found to support them. However, the exchange worked both ways, and by the mid-17th century, European immigrants to the Caribbean were dying of malaria, a disease found in the tropical country along the Gulf of Mexico. As Europeans made their way into Oceania, contagious diseases spread to many previously unexposed people, resulting in high death tolls, although on a smaller scale than in the Americas.

As devastating as the disease pathogens were, the Columbian Exchange also had some very positive consequences, and over time, it probably increased rather than decreased world population overall. Supplies of food increased so that people were less likely to go hungry in times of drought or local food shortages. The variety of available food increased with the exchange, giving people wider access to an assortment of nutrients necessary for good health. Even though it took some time to adjust to new types of food, caloric intake increased in many areas, a trend especially important for growing children.

NEW EXCHANGES IN THE COLUMBIAN EXCHANGE

The Americas	The Eastern Hemisphere
beans, squash, tomatoes, sweet potatoes, peanuts, chilis, chocolate, maize (corn), potatoes, avocados, pineapple, manioc	wheat, rice, olives, grapes, bananas, rice, citrus fruits, melons, figs, sugar, coconuts horses, cattle, pigs, sheep, goats, chickens, rabbits, rats

The introduction of European livestock greatly altered the environment and life styles of people in many parts of the Americas. Because they had no natural predators (except people) in their new environment, cattle, pigs, horses, and sheep multiplied rapidly so that herds of wild animals roamed the plains of Argentina and northern New Spain. They destroyed natural vegetation, but they also supplied meat, milk, hides, and wool. Probably the single most important new animal was the horse, which allowed natives to travel much further than before, pursue buffalo herds, hunt more efficiently, and wage a different type of warfare.

The Great Circuit and the Atlantic Economy

The voyages of discovery not only revolutionized biological exchanges, but they allowed the economic innovations developing in Europe to magnify, as capitalism, especially in the form of mercantilism, was applied to exchanges across the Atlantic and Pacific Oceans. The joint-stock companies began the process in North America, as did the government-sponsored expeditions in Latin America. Investors sought profits in the production and export of colonial products, some native and some introduced from the Old World. For example, Europeans learned about the uses of tobacco from natives and found that Virginia and North Carolina were good places for tobacco to grow and then shipped to Europe. Sugar, on the other hand, originated in the Eastern Hemisphere, but Brazil and the Caribbean Islands became the world's principal sources of sugar by 1700. Sugar, by the nature of its production, had to be raised on large plantations because raw sugar cane could not survive the voyage from the New World to the Old. The cane had to be processed before it was shipped, so the producer had to not only maintain the growing fields but a processing plant as well. This investment was quite large, and only a few could afford it, so small farmers could not survive, and only large plantations with many workers could be successful. After some early attempts to use indentured servants in the Caribbean, most plantation owners settled on slave labor, since indentured servants had few opportunities to establish their own farms on islands where land was already claimed by plantations.

New products, experimentation with labor systems, new methods of transportation, new lands, and capitalistic enterprise all combined to create a clockwise network of sea routes known as the **Atlantic Circuit.** Ships first went from Europe to Africa, where they carried guns, cotton textiles, and other manufactured goods to sell at ports along the western coast of Africa. Some ships returned to Europe with gold, ivory, and other traditional African products, but many loaded slaves to be taken on the next leg of the circuit – known as the **Middle Passage** – across the Atlantic to the New World. Most were destined for the Caribbean and Brazil, but some came to the southern English colonies and other parts of Latin America. On the third part of the circuit, ships laden with goods produced in the New World were taken to Europe, where they began the circuit all over again. New world products included sugar, tobacco, gold, silver, and food crops. Ships also crossed the Pacific, most notably the **Manila galleons,** which crossed between Manila in the Philippines, where they picked up Asian luxury goods, and Acapulco on the west coast of Mexico, where they loaded their large cargo areas with silver.

By the late 16th century European mariners had connected many ports of the world. By 1750 they had stimulated world trade networks that linked almost all parts of the world, with the notable exception of Australia. The trade patterns established during this time period continued in later times, so that those that profited most – generally the Europeans – gained not only economic power, but political and social control as well.

The period 1450-1750 brought tremendous change to the Americas. In previous eras the Western Hemisphere had developed in relative isolation from the rest of the world, but by 1750 its people were brought into sustained contact with others, and the Americas became an integral part of the world trade network. As a result, the first truly global economy developed in which changes in one part

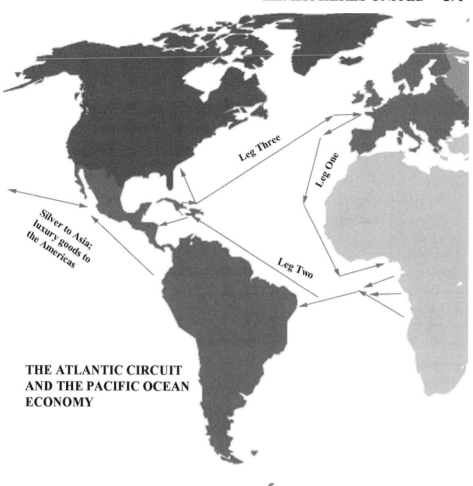

New Trade Routes – 1450-1750. European ships loaded with manufactured goods (Leg One) stopped first in Africa, sold goods and reloaded with slaves on the Middle Passage headed for the New World (Leg Two), and finally headed home again (Leg Three) loaded with colonial products. Spanish galleons (ships designed with large hulls to hold the silver) also headed from the New World to Manila in the Philippines, where they traded silver for Asian luxury goods.

of the world potentially impacted many other areas. The old Aztec and Inca empires were toppled, and were replaced by Spanish and Portuguese viceroyalties in Latin America, and natives of more sparsely populated North America were pushed inland and westward by English settlers. Natives along interior waterways came in contact with French trappers, who cooperated with them in a thriving fur trade that served international markets.   Environmental and demographic changes occurred as well. Newly introduced plants and animals changed diets and lifestyles, and in turn altered the natural environment. Population increases in Europe spurred interest in the New World, since opportunities in Europe became more competitive, and new business and transportation innovations allowed migrations from Europe to the Americas. Dramatic population decreases in the native population occurred during the 16th century as a result of exposure to European diseases, but populations later rebounded as the nutritional and economic benefits of the Columbian Exchange began to take effect.

IDENTIFICATIONS AND CONCEPTS

Atahualpa
caravel
castas
Columbian Exchange
Columbus, Christopher
conquistadors
Cortes, Hernan
creoles
Da Gama, Vasco
Dias, Barthomew
encomienda, encomenderos
Great Circuit, Atlantic Circuit
Henry the Navigator
indentured servitude
joint-stock companies
Las Casas, Bartholomé de
Magellan, Ferdinand
Manila galleons
mercantilism
mestizos
Middle Passage
mit'a
Moctezuma
mulattos
peninsulares
Pizarro, Francisco
Protestant work ethic
Treaty of Tordesillas
viceroyalties, viceroys
Yongle
Zheng He

CHAPTER TWELVE:
AFRICA AND THE NEW
WORLD ECONOMY

During the period from 600 to 1450 several great trading empires had risen in Sub-Saharan Africa, although a large number of Africans remained organized by kinship-based tribes and small communities as they had for centuries. Sudanic kingdoms such as Ghana, Mali, and Songhay, as well as the Swahili states in east Africa, had grown rich from the trade of gold, ivory, and other traditional African products, and many of Africa's elite had converted to Islam, uniting them with Islamic leaders throughout the Middle East and the tropics. These connections led Africa directly into the new world economy that developed between 1450 and 1750, and Africans played a vital role in the new patterns that developed. However, during this later era, their most valuable contributions were human beings, who entered the second leg of the Atlantic Circuit as slaves headed toward the New World, making the world's reliance on slave labor systems reach its peak during the era 1450-1750. The slave trade transformed the parts of Africa that it touched, although in many parts of the continent, life went on as it always had, without being much affected by the changes swirling around them.

EARLY CONTACT WITH EUROPEANS

The slave trade of the era from 1450 to 1750 was not new to Africa. Camel caravans had carried slaves across the Sahara for many years, with most destined for the Middle East where they became servants, soldiers, or concubines to wealthy men. Internal slave trade also was common, with slaves generally captured as prisoners of war. Africans enslaved by other Africans before 1450 were not seen as private property, but those that controlled them were able to amass wealth through their labor. These slaves sometimes obtained their freedom or became members of the controlling group's clan. However, the first contact of Africans with the Portuguese during the 15th century opened the new slave market that eventually crossed the Atlantic. According to Philip Curtain in *The Atlantic Slave Trade: A Census*, about 10 million Africa slaves arrived in the Americas before the slave trade was outlawed, making the voyages probably the largest forced major migration in world history. The first contacts with the Portuguese occurred in the early 15th century with the exploratory voyages along Africa's western coast sponsored by Prince Henry the Navigator. At first their progress was slow, but by 1487 they had reached the Cape of Good Hope in 1487. Along the way they established forts and trading posts called **factories,** where local African merchants brought goods to be traded. The Portuguese were not militarily strong enough to venture inland, and they traded by the African merchants' terms. At first they were more interested in gold and ivory than slaves, but some slaves were brought to Portugal as early as 1441.

Christian missionaries accompanied sailors on the voyages, and one of their earliest successes was in **Kongo,** a kingdom just south of the Congo River. There they converted members of the royal family, and the whole kingdom was brought to Christianity in the early 16th century. At first, interactions between the Portuguese and Kongo kings were relatively equal, but soon the attempt to "Europeanize" the natives reflected the general Portuguese view that Africans were inferior. Unfortunately for the people of Kongo, the growing slave trade to the Americas that began about the same time encouraged the Portuguese to look to the Kongo to supply slaves for the Atlantic Circuit trade. They sometimes went on slave raids themselves, but more often made deals with native traders and local leaders who captured and delivered slaves in exchange for manufactured goods, especially guns. By 1665 the king of Kongo was so distressed by slave raiding that he went to war with the Portuguese, but superior arms (including guns) helped the Portuguese to win. Further south, the Europeans colonized Angola, which became another source of slaves for the Atlantic trade. Eventually other European nations set up competing trading posts, especially along the "Slave Coast" north of the Kongo. Once the Portuguese rounded Cape Good Hope at the southern tip of Africa, they captured and took over Swahili trading cities, where they intensified the slave trade already taking place across the Indian Ocean.

THE ATLANTIC SLAVE TRADE

From these early beginnings, a massive slave trade took place from the 15th to the 19th century, masterminded by Europeans whose ships carried Africans to plantations in the Western Hemisphere. Generally, the endeavor involved the cooperation of African elites, who traded war captives, criminals, and individuals expelled from their groups to Europeans. The trade grew steadily during the 17th century, but the high point came during the 18th century, with probably about 55,000 slaves arriving every year. The majority were young men, who were valued for the physical strength necessary for hard work in plantation fields. For 150 years the Portuguese controlled the trade

PERSPECTIVES: SLAVE TRADE STATISTICS AND THE IMPORTANCE OF SUGAR

Historian Philip Curtain revised common conceptions about the Atlantic slave trade in his 1969 study, *The Atlantic Slave Trade: A Census.* He carefully studied how many slaves came, as well as where they arrived in the Americas. Below are some of the estimates he compiled by studying records of the slave trade between 1521 and 1773. Notice that the vast majority of slaves were destined for areas where sugar plantations dominated the economy.

DESTINATION	NUMBERS OF SLAVES
Brazil	3,646,800
British West Indies	1,665,000
French West Indies	1,600,200
Spanish America	1,552,000 (702,000 to Cuba alone)
Dutch West Indies	500,000
United States and pre-1776 North America	399,000
Danish West Indies (now the Virgin Islands)	28,000

Reference: *The Atlantic Slave Trade: A Census.* Philip D. Curtin (Madison: University of Wisconsin Press, 1969).

and took most of the slaves to Brazil and the Spanish colonies. As the demand for slaves grew in the Caribbean, other Europeans joined, including the Dutch, English, and French, although France did not become a major carrier until the 18th century. Each country established trade forts along the African coastline, where its agents contacted local rulers, paying a tax or offering gifts. Slaves were brought to the coast as military captives or as victims of kidnappers who searched for them to trade for profit. Many of the African states were small and fragmented, and their quarreling produced many war captives who provided labor for the victors. European merchants were able to benefit from existing trade routes and markets, but the new demand for slaves in the New World stimulated and transformed the nature of slavery as a forced labor system in which slaves were bought and sold as property.

COMPARISONS: AFRICA'S ISLAMIC AND EUROPEAN CONTACTS

Since the 7th century, the African continent had been affected by contact with the Islamic world. First, most of northern Africa was conquered by Islamic armies. Then with trans-Saharan trade, the religion diffused to Sub-Saharan areas, first to elites, and eventually to the general population, although native religions remained strong among most ordinary people. These kingdoms remained independent and greatly involved in trade, although the Moroccan defeat of the Songhai army in the late 16th century shifted control of trade routes eastward to the Hausa trading cities. The slave trade to the Islamic north from the Sudan and the Swahili states in eastern Africa was sizeable, probably about 2 million combined, but significantly smaller than the 10 million from Africa to the New World. Both men and women were in demand in Islamic countries, whereas most slaves that went to the Americas were young men who were destined for field work.

In contrast to the slow diffusion of Islamic contacts through Africa, Europeans had few contacts in Africa before the 15th century. For the next three and a half centuries, Africans gave up little territory to Europeans, and Europeans almost never ventured farther inland than the factories (forts and trading posts) set up along coastal areas. They established only two beachheads – one in Portuguese Angola, and the other in the Netherland's Cape Colony in South Africa. As a result, European cultural influence was quite limited, with few conversions to Christianity outside Angola and (much earlier) in Ethiopia.

The Middle Passage

Slaves usually were carried from Africa to the Americas in ships with specially built holds where they were packed together, although girls, boys, and women were in separate compartments from the men. The voyage lasted from four to ten weeks, depending on the weather, and some cargoes arrived more safely than others. The traders wanted to keep as many slaves alive as possible, but they usually packed the ships to maximize their profits. Voyages before 1700 usually lost larger percentages of their slaves than later ships did, so the traders appear to have improved their ability to figure the most practical number of bodies they could keep in cargo. Male slaves were chained together to keep them from jumping overboard while still close to land, but the ships had special nets around their outsides to catch any that decided to jump together. Once the voyage was underway, African men were kept below the deck and were only brought up in small groups under close guard. Deaths aboard ship were caused by contagious disease, bad food, dysentery, and refusal to eat. Others died from whippings or on occasion execution. Crew members also died from disease, and were particularly vulnerable to malaria, a disease that Africans were immune to but Europeans were not.

EXAMINING THE EVIDENCE: THE ACCOUNTS OF OLAUDAH EQUIANO

Much of our knowledge about the experience of Africans captured by slave traders comes from Olaudah Equiano, who was born east of the Niger Delta, kidnapped as a slave in Africa, and crossed the Atlantic on the Middle Passage to be sold in the New World. Because New World slaves were not taught to read and write, very few first-person written accounts exist, and so we rely on Equiano, who learned English and later became active in the abolitionist movement. His feelings when he first boarded the slave ship are described below.

"I was immediately handled and tossed up to see if I were sound by some of the crew, and I was persuaded that I had gotten into a world of bad spirits and that they were going to kill me. Their complexions too differing so much from ours, their long hair and the language they spoke (which was very different from any I had every heard) united to confirm me in this belief... When I looked round the ship too and saw a large furnace or copper boiling and a multitude of black people of every description chained together, every one of their countenances expressing dejection and sorrow, I no longer doubted of my fate; and quite overpowered with horror and anguish, I fell motionless on the deck and fainted. When I recovered a little I found some black people about me...they talked to me in order to cheer me, but all in vain..."

Reference: Equiano's Travels. Paul Edwards, ed. and trans. (Oxford Heinemann Educational Books, 1967) pp. 25-42.

The Africa Diaspora

One of the most important demographic changes during the era 1450-1750 was the **African Diaspora,** or the spreading of Africans to many other parts of the world, especially to the Americas. Once their journey on the Middle Passage ended, most were destined for sugar plantations in Brazil and the Caribbean, but later they worked producing rice, cotton, and tobacco. Some worked in Spanish mines or became urban household servants, and some eventually got their freedom, but most did forced agricultural work. Always slaves were at the bottom of the social hierarchy, whites were at the top, and in between were mulattoes who often worked as house servants or skilled laborers rather than in the fields.

In most areas of the Caribbean where large sugar plantations dominated the economy, slaves formed the vast majority of the population. Some whites owned small farms, and others served as colonial officials and retail merchants, but their numbers were relatively small. Brazil's population was more diverse, and manumission (freeing a slave) was much more common than elsewhere, so slaves made up only about 35% of the population. An equal number of free "people of color," who were descendants of slaves, also lived in Portuguese Brazil, so people of African origins or descent formed 2/3 of the population. In both the Caribbean and Brazil, death rates were much higher than those in the healthier climate of the southern British colonies, so slaves newly arrived from Africa were numerous. In the southern British colonies more slave children survived, so natural increase filled most of the demand for labor there. As a result, North American slaves gradually became more removed from African culture than their counterparts in the Caribbean and Brazil.

The diaspora had a tremendous impact on family life, with women outnumbered by men almost everywhere. Family members often went to different plantations, so family structures were seriously challenged. Despite the separations from one another as well as their native lands, aspects of African culture came with them and influenced the developing American cultures. For example, most Africans converted to Christianity, but many of their native religious practices continued, with some religions surviving almost intact, such as Vodun in Haiti.

The Impact of the Atlantic Slave Trade in Africa

The slave trade impacted some parts of Africa more than others. Many interior groups, such as the kingdoms of Rwanda and Bugunda and the Masai and Turkana of east Africa were not affected much, partly because they were geographically far away from the slave trading activity. Many Africans benefited from the trade, such as the Asante, Dahomey, and Oyo people, whose leaders were enticed by the promise of gun sales to organize slave routes and sponsor raids. However, the empires of Asante and Dahomey represent two different responses to the European presence in Africa.

The empire of **Asante** rose in western Africa in the area called the Gold Coast. The region lay between the coast and the Hausa and Mande trading centers to the north, and it also produced significant amounts of gold and kola nuts.

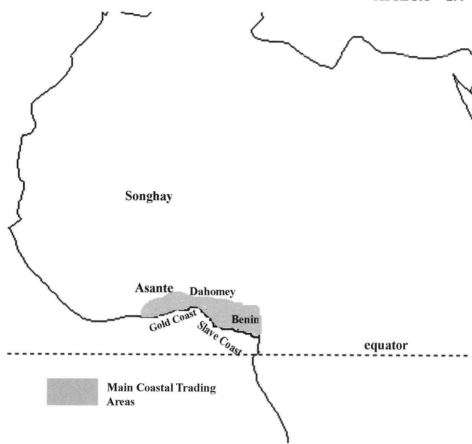

West African States and Trade. Between 1450 and 1750 powerful states rose in west Africa, including Songhay, Asante, Dahomey, and Benin. All based much of their power on the Atlantic and trans-Saharan trade, with Asante and Dahomey the most active states in the slave trade across the Atlantic.

Many different clans had coexisted before, but the Oyoko clan subjugated the others by using guns obtained from Europeans. In the late 17th century the Asante leader, Osei Tutu, united the many clans under his authority, and his officials controlled the gold, as well as the slave trade, with slaves making up most of their commerce. The Asante leaders allowed subgroups to keep some of their autonomy, and they were advised by a council of clan leaders that generally stressed unity. Asante remained the most powerful state in the Sudan until the early 19th century. Farther to the east, the kingdom of **Benin** had developed by the time that the Portuguese arrived in the 15th century, but Benin never was a significant player in the slave trade, relying instead on traditional products, such as ivory, textiles, and their unique bronze castings. In between Asante and Benin was the kingdom of **Dahomey,** which united the Fon people, and, like Asante, used firearms to create its power base. However, in contrast to Asante, the Dahomey leaders were authoritarian, and often brutal in forcing compliance to the royal court. Dahomey aggressively conquered areas around it, killed the royal families, and imposed its own traditions on the conquered. The Dahomey kingdom lasted into the 19th century, but its government was based mainly on force, whereas the Asante leadership was more cooperative.

Many areas of Africa suffered greatly from the trade. Besides the loss of millions of young men, which created a severe sex ratio imbalance, the slave trade brought political unrest to African societies. Although warfare was already commonplace, the slave trade stimulated arguments that increased tensions among many groups. Violence escalated with access to effective firearms sold by Europeans, and some states – such as Dahomey – used guns to expand control over their neighbors. On the east coast of Africa, the Swahili cities continued to trade on the Indian Ocean circuit, once they adjusted to the military presence of the Portuguese. Links to the interior brought ivory, gold, and slaves to the coast, as they always had. Some New World-style plantations were set up on Zanzibar and other nearby islands, and the slave markets of the Red Sea continued until the end of the 19th century. The Dutch set up **Cape Colony** at the Cape of Good Hope to serve as a stopping point for ships on their long trip from Europe to Asia and back again. Unlike most other European contacts, the Dutch moved inland to develop farms, and they depended on slave labor – sometimes from Indonesia and Asia, but also from locals – to do agricultural work. Most other interior areas of Africa remained relatively isolated from outside contacts.

Perhaps surprisingly, overall African populations probably did not shrink as a result of the slave trade. Just as the native population in the Americas recovered from exposure to European diseases, the nutritional benefits of the Columbian Exchange meant that people who remained in Africa had diets enriched by American food crops, especially maize (corn) and cassava, a Brazilian plant with edible roots. Cassava had the highest yield of calories per acre of any staple food, did well in poor soils, and could be made into bread that would keep for several months. These, as well as peanuts, probably were responsible for population stability despite losses from the slave trade.

CONCEPTS AND IDENTIFICATIONS

African Diaspora
Asante
Benin
Cape Colony
Dahomey
Equiano, Olaudah
factories
Kongo
Middle Passage

**CHAPTER THIRTEEN:
ISLAMIC LAND-BASED
EMPIRES**

The rise of sea-based powers in Europe is a major theme of the 1450-1750 era, but it is not the only one. Traditional land-based powers continued to dominate the Middle East and Asia, and a new land-based empire – Russia – grew in eastern Europe. In contrast to the new sea-based powers, these empires continued to rely on armies, roads, and inland urban areas to secure their political authority and economic influence. Both sea-based and land-based powers made use of guns, cannon, and muskets to defeat foes without those technologies, making the old nomadic empires – such as the Mongols – a thing of the past. The era after 1450 is often called the age of **Gunpowder Empires** because virtually every powerful state used guns effectively to subjugate their enemies and build their control. Important land-based Gunpowder Empires of the era included Russia, Ming and Qing China, Japan, the Ottoman Empire, the Safavid Empire, and the Mughal Empire. The three latter empires were all Islamic, and together they represent the height of Muslim political and military power in world history. Together with other land-based empires, they countered the growing European global influence, but all three – the Ottomans, Safavids, and Mughals – were on the decline by 1750, whereas sea-based powers were still on the rise.

THE OTTOMAN EMPIRE

Like all three Muslim empires of this era, the Ottoman Empire began as a small warrior state in a frontier inland area. It was named for its founder **Osman,** a leader of a band of semi-nomadic Turks who migrated to northwestern Anatolia in the 13th century. The empire lasted until 1922, but its peak of power came during the 16th century, when it expanded to control land all around the eastern Mediterranean, the Red Sea, and eastward deep into the Middle East. During the 16th century, the Ottomans had designs on much of Europe, and successfully conquered territory in eastern Europe, until they were finally stopped just outside of Vienna.

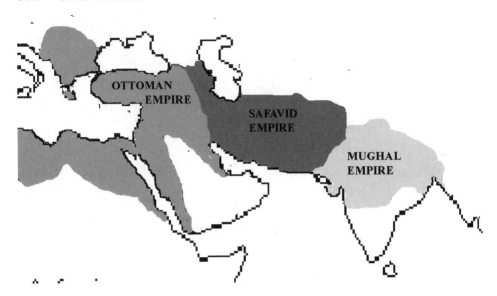

The Muslim Empires. The Ottoman, Safavid, and Mughal Empires were all traditional land-based powers, although the Ottomans dominated the Mediterranean Sea for a time with their strong navy. The Safavid and Mughal Empires had strong armies, but no navies to speak of and both had inland capital cities.

The Rise of the Ottomans

Before the Ottomans came to control it, Anatolia had long been a stage for conflict among civilizations. During the earliest days, the Hittites had risen from Anatolia to successfully attack the people of Mesopotamia. In the 4th century B.C.E., Alexander the Great had crossed and conquered Anatolia as part of the Persian Empire, and during the classical era the Romans had conquered it, and renamed Byzantium, the city that straddled the Bosporus, after the emperor Constantine. Constantinople, at the point where Anatolia meets the European mainland, became the capital of the Byzantine Empire, which controlled much of Anatolia until the Seljuk Turks from central Asia came through, only to be challenged by Christian Crusaders from Europe. Although they survived the Crusaders, the Seljuk kingdom fell to the Mongols, who were more interested in areas other than Anatolia, which they raided but did not directly rule. In the chaos, Osman's group came to dominate others, and by the 1350s had advanced across the Bosporus into Europe. The Ottomans were conquered by Timur, the leader of Jagadai Khanate, but they reunited their areas after Timur's empire fell apart.

As the Ottomans moved into Europe, they bypassed Constantinople, but in 1453 they put the city under a successful siege, and upon its capture, renamed it Istanbul. The city that had been the most important center of Orthodox Christianity became an important Muslim center, and its great church, the Hagia Sophia, constructed by Justinian in the 6th century, became an important mosque, a center for Islamic worship. The Ottomans continued to expand their empire, which reached its height of power under **Suleiman the Magnificent,** who ruled from 1520 to 1566. Suleiman commanded the greatest Ottoman assault against Europe, conquering Belgrade in 1521, laying siege to Vienna in 1529, and retreating only when the onset of winter made it impractical to stay. Had Vienna fallen, some historians speculate that the Ottomans may well have overrun the weak Holy Roman Empire and threatened the budding western states, just as they were beginning their voyages of discovery across the Atlantic. Was the siege of Vienna a turning point in history? Perhaps – it is one of those "what if" events that could have changed the course of history had the outcome been different. As it is, Suleiman was stopped, but the Ottomans remained an important world power that controlled much of the water traffic between the Black and Mediterranean Seas. They reduced Venice to a tributary state, and their huge army continued to expand and defend their frontiers.

Political Characteristics

Clearly military might was the key to Ottoman success, so the sultans not only were political leaders, but military commanders as well. In the empire's early years, its army elites were cavalry leaders who were given land grants as rewards for military service, and by the 16th century, they had developed into a warrior aristocracy. As the empire expanded the sultan and his bureaucracy had practical issues of controlling new lands, so the warrior aristocrats were granted a great deal of control over land and food production in their areas. Eventually some came to challenge the sultan, but their power came to be checked by the appearance of a new elite military group called **Janissaries.** When the Ottomans conquered the Balkans, they instituted a system known as "**devshirme**" in which they required Christians of the area to contribute young boys to become slaves of the sultan. The boys were specially trained, learned Turkish, and converted to Islam, and then either sent to serve the sultan as bureaucrats or as infantrymen in the army. This group almost certainly never would have been more than a footnote in history except for a fact that the cavalry elite probably took little notice of: they were given guns and heavy artillery. These early firearms were too heavy to be carried by men on horseback, and artillery was best managed by men on foot. The Janissaries were the recipients of the blessings of technology: they came to control the weapons that ensured the Ottomans' continuing military success, and with it came political and economy power. By the time the cavalry recognized the important shift that had taken place, it was too late, and the old aristocrats found themselves out of military power just as economic weaknesses in the empire greatly reduced their incomes from land. By the mid-16th century the Janissaries were so sure of their importance that they expected to have a say in the sultan's decisions, as indeed they did.

PERSPECTIVES: SULEIMAN "THE MAGNIFICENT"

Europeans added the description "Magnificent" to Suleiman's name, and the man who was sultan during the Ottoman heyday hardly disagreed with their assessment. The following is an inscription by Suleiman from a citadel built by the Turks in the northern Balkans, an area of Ottoman conquest.

"I am God's slave and sultan of this world. By the grace of God I am head of Muhammad's community. God's might and Muhammad's miracles are my companions. I am Suleiman, in whose name the *hutbe* [sermon] is read in Mecca and Medina. In Baghdad I am the shah, in Byzantine realms the Caesar, and in Egypt the sultan; who sends his fleets to the seas of Europe, the Maghrib and India. I am the sultan who took the crown and throne of Hungary and granted them to a humble slave. The voivoda Petru raised his head in revolt, but my horse's hoofs ground him into the dust, and I conquered the land of Moldavia."

Reference: The Ottoman Empire: The Classical Age, 1300-1600. Trans. by Norman Itzkowitz and Colin Imber (New Rochelle, NY.: Aristide D. Caratzas, 1989), p. 41.

The Ottoman sultans presided over large bureaucracies which, after 1453, were centered in Istanbul. The sultan was aided by a **vizier,** the head of the imperial administration that took care of the day to day work of the empire. Early sultans, including Suleiman, took an active part in directing the government and often led the armies personally. However, as time went by, the viziers gained more political power than the sultans, and the central government was increasingly challenged by the Janissaries, the fading cavalry leaders, and Islamic religious scholars who retained the same administrative functions as religious scholars had during the days of the caliphate. Like the caliphates before them, the Ottomans were plagued by problems of succession when a sultan died. Steppe traditions from their central Asian nomadic roots also involved family disputes over leadership roles. Since the principles of hereditary rule were vague, the death of a sultan often led to arguments and court intrigue regarding his successor, and it was quite common for his numerous sons to go to war with one another.

Economic Challenges

With its many conquered lands and control of the Black and Mediterranean Seas, the Ottoman Empire of the 16th century was one of the wealthiest in the world. Istanbul, like Constantinople before it, was one of the most cosmopolitan cities in the world, with many trade route circuits passing through it and people of many different backgrounds and occupations inhabiting it. It was the primary Ottoman seaport, and its famous harbor teemed with trading vessels from ports both distant and near. The city and its suburbs stretched along both sides of the Bosporus, and its great bazaars were filled with merchandise from around the world. However, an economic decline set in gradually, beginning in the mid-17th century. One important reason for the decline is that the empire had probably reached the limits of expansion by then. As had happened with many other large empires in world history, the Ottoman Empire was too large to be maintained, especially with the slow pace of overland transportation and communications available to land-based powers. One indication that the central government could not control local governments was increasing corruption among local government officials, who were taxing peasants heavily but pocketing much of the tax revenue. Peasant revolts resulted from dissatisfaction with these officials, deepening the political and economic problems. Succession issues also led to holding the sultan's sons as hostages in the palace to prevent coups, leading to sheltered, pleasure-loving, generally less competent rulers. Another issue was created by the increasing demands of the Janissaries, not only for political power, but for higher salaries as well. To pay the Janissaries, the sultan started reducing the number of landholding cavalrymen, causing unrest among displaced cavalrymen.

A negative global impact on the Ottoman economy was inflation caused by the increasing amount of New World silver being pumped into the world economy. European traders who controlled the silver could buy more goods with the same quantity of silver than the Ottomans could because the sultan's government collected taxes according to legally fixed rates, so as the value of the silver declined, tax revenues stayed the same. As a result, the Ottomans were at a disadvantage when trading in the world market because religious law limited the government's ability to reform tax laws, and when bureaucrats came up with special surtaxes, they were often met with resistance from many who were already suffering from the spiraling economic problems.

Cultural and Social Characteristics

The majority of people in the Ottoman Empire were Sunni Muslim, but expansion into Europe, the Caucasus, and Egypt meant that large numbers of Christians and Jews were also subject to the sultan's rule. The most cosmopolitan place was Istanbul, where the crossroads of trade led many people from other parts of the world to settle. The sultans supported public works projects, particularly in Istanbul, and they invited religious scholars, artists, poets, and architects to the royal palace. A goal of early sultans was to restore the city to its former glories, and many beautiful palaces, religious schools, hospitals, and mosques were built. The Hagia Sophia was restored as a mosque, aqueducts were built, and the city's walls were repaired. The most spectacular building was the Suleymaniye Mosque constructed under the supervision of Suleiman the Magnificent, with impressive domes that make it one of the great engineering feats of Islamic civilization.

The Ottoman social structure included a large number of merchants and artisans who lived in the empire's urban areas. Artisans were organized into guilds, just as their counterparts in Europe had been, and craft standards were generally high, especially since guild activities were much more closely supervised by the government than they were in Europe.

The influence of Islamic clerics is apparent in the success they had in insulating the empire from new cultural and technological developments in Europe. Europeans who visited Istanbul or other Ottoman cities often wrote journals about their travel experiences, but no comparable journals have been found for Ottomans visiting Europe. Generally, they still saw European societies as backward and marginal, and their own civilization as infinitely superior. This attitude kept them from understanding the tremendous changes that Europe was bringing to the world. For example, the European printing press was brought to Istanbul by Jews who had been expelled from Spain, but they were not allowed to print anything in Turkish or Arabic, the languages of the majority of Ottomans. As a result, the empire was virtually untouched by the impact of the print revolution on literacy and innovation in Europe and other areas of the world.

The changing in the balance of power between Europe and the Middle East during this era is illustrated by the loss of Ottoman control of the Mediterranean Sea, once known as the "Ottoman Lake." The empire lost a famous sea battle at Lepanto to Philip II of Spain in 1571, and although the Ottoman fleet was rebuilt within a year, control of the Mediterranean was never regained. The Ottomans and their Muslim allies also lost control of many ports along the Indian Ocean basin as the Portuguese gained much of the lucrative trade once reserved for them.

THE SAFAVID EMPIRE

Like the Ottomans, the Safavid Empire grew from a Turkish nomadic group from a frontier area. However, unlike the Ottomans, the Safavids were Shi'ite, not Sunni Muslim. The division originated after the religion's founder, Muhammad, died without a designated heir, a significant problem since his armies had conquered many lands. The Sunnis favored choosing the caliph (leader) from the accepted leadership (the Sunni), but the Shi'ites argued that the mantle should be hereditary, and should pass to Muhammad's son-in-law, Ali. When Ali was killed in the dispute, the Shi'ite opinion became a minority one, but they kept their separate identity, and carried the belief that the true heirs of Islam were the descendants of Ali. These heirs, called **imams**, continued until the 9th century, when the 12th descendant disappeared as a child, only to become known as the **"Hidden Imam."** Until the Safavids, these Shi'ite beliefs did not have a united political base, but in the early 16th century, an army emerged under **Ismail,** who united a large area south of the Caspian Sea and west of the Ottoman Empire. Ismail declared the official religion of his new Safavid realm – named after a Sufi mystic called Safi al-Din – to be **Twelver Shi'ism,** based on the legacy of the Hidden Imam.

As the Safavid Empire expanded during the early 16th century, it began to challenge the borders of the neighboring Ottomans. Hostility between the groups was strong, intensified by the Shi'ite/Sunni split, with the Ottomans very wary of this new Shi'ite empire. In 1514 the two armies met at Chaldiran in Northwest Persia, and there is little doubt that religious conflict was at the heart of the struggle. The battle was also important because it illustrated the importance of the new gunpowder technology. Ismail sent his best cavalry, the **qizilbash** ("redheads," for their distinctive turbans), armed with swords and knives, to fight the Ottoman Janissaries, with their cannon and muskets. The Safavid cavalry was slaughtered, and the Ottomans won a decisive victory, one that they were unable to follow up because of the approaching winter. The Safavids recovered, built up their artillery, and continued to fight the Ottomans for another two centuries without either side winning decisively. The battle at Chaldiran was a significant "marker event" in the development of the Islamic world because it set the limits for Shi'ite expansion, with consequences still apparent today. The modern inheritors of the Safavid Empire are Iran and parts of Iraq, Shi'ite nations in the midst of predominantly Sunni countries around them. Modern conflicts between Shi'ites and Sunnis in Iraq trace their way back to Chaldiran, and to the ancient 7th-century split between Ali and his foes.

The Safavids reached the peak of their power under **Shah Abbas I,** who ruled from 1588 to 1629. In a similar move to the Ottoman seizure of Christian boys in the Baltic States to become Janissaries, under Abbas' direction, boys in Russia were captured, educated, and converted to Islam to become soldiers. These so-called "slave infantrymen" were trained to use firearms, and their control of this new technology gave them increasing power at the expense of the traditional qizilbash. Abbas understood the importance of European technological knowledge, and he brought in European advisors to assist him in his wars with the Ottomans. He learned from them how to cast better cannon and make good military use of muskets, but his emphasis remained on building land-based power. His army swelled in size and efficiency, but no Safavid navy was built, and the capital city at Isfahan was far inland, away from the sea-based trade that was transforming the world.

ORIGINAL DOCUMENTS: DESCRIPTION OF SHAH ABBAS THE GREAT

When Shah Abbas I took the Safavid throne in 1588, the empire was on the brink of disintegration, with special pressure coming from Ottoman invaders from the west. Abbas withstood this threat and later defeated the Mughals of India and the Uighurs to the north. This remarkable shah was also much more open to influences from the outside world than most Muslim rulers, as reflected in this excerpt from his biography, written by his secretary, Eskander Bey Monshi.

"As regards his knowledge of the outside world, he possesses information about the rulers (both Muslim and non-Muslim) of other countries, about the size and composition of their armies, about their religious faith and the organization of their kingdoms, about their highway systems, and about the prosperity or otherwise of their realms. He has cultivated diplomatic relations with most of the princes of the world, and the rulers of the most distant parts of Europe, Russia, and India are on friendly terms with him. Foreign ambassadors bearing gifts are never absent from his court, and the Shah's achievements in the field of foreign relations exceed those of his predecessors."

Reference: Eskander Bey Monshi: History of Shah Abbas the Great, Vol. 1 (Boulder, CO: Westview Press, 1978), p. 533.

Politics and Religion

As in the Ottoman Empire, Safavid rulers based their authority on military prowess and religious piety. The Safavids traced their origins to a Sufi religious order that rulers promoted throughout the 16th and 17th centuries. The expansion of the empire was seen as an extension of Islam to new lands, and as the shahs faced the Ottomans, they saw themselves as the champions of Shi'ism. The Safavids, like the Ottomans, saw the Europeans as infidels, but they also believed that defeating the Sunnis was an important act of faith.

Ancient Persian traditions shaped the Safavid political system, with the shahs taking grand titles, such as "king of kings," "the great king," and "king of countries." Their palaces were sumptuous, and court life was highly ritualized. Ismail allowed suggestions that he himself was the Hidden Imam, and even that he was an incarnation of Allah. Although later leaders did not make such claims, they still saw themselves as exalted far above the status of the local Turkish chiefs, and a great deal of the legitimacy of the regime lay in the belief that the shahs were the keepers of Shi'ism. Mullahs, or local mosque officials and prayer leaders, were supervised and supported by the state, which gave the government the upper hand.

Economic and Social Organization

Tension between Persian and Turkish culture shaped the Safavid social structure. Turkish chiefs challenged the early shahs, who were often vulnerable because of family infighting over succession rights. The chiefs were gradually transformed into a warrior nobility very similar to the cavalry elite in the Ottoman Empire. They supervised local farm work in the regions where they lived and asserted political power as well, with some capturing powerful positions in the imperial bureaucracy. To counter their power the shahs appointed Persians to fill other bureaucratic positions, and they also gave authority to the "slave infantrymen."

The shahs generally promoted trade, with Abbas I setting up his capital at Isfahan as a major center of international trade, complete with a network of roads and workshops to manufacture textiles and the Persian rugs that the Safavids were famous for. However, Isfahan was far inland, and so visitors and merchants from other areas were much less numerous than they were in Istanbul, although Abbas brought in Jews, Hindus, and Armenian Christians to handle outside trade. Guilds organized the merchants as they did in Istanbul, and silk production and trade was a major industry. However, the manufacture of deep-pile carpets became their signature business, and the knotted rugs were highly valued within the empire as well as elsewhere. Despite the economic activity, Isfahan was far from cosmopolitan, the Armenians were kept in a suburb across the river from the city's center, and most people that lived in Isfahan were Shi'ites. Most of the empire's people lived in rural areas, doing the same kind of farm work that their ancestors had engaged in. In these areas, many nomadic groups continued to live as well, with chiefs that had little interest in building the agricultural economy. Like the Ottomans, the Safavids were negatively impacted by the inflation caused by the flood of silver into the world trade networks, making it difficult for the government to pay the army and bureaucracy.

Cultural Characteristics

Cultural influences in the Safavid Empire were a complex mixture of Turkish and Persian traditions, but even before Shah Ismail imposed Shi'ism on his subjects, the area had a distinctive culture based on that of ancient Persia. Islamic scholars often knew both the Arabic and Persian languages, but Iranian scholars were more likely to use Persian, and their counterparts in other Islamic lands were more likely to read and write in Arabic. Persian had been written in the Arabic script from the 10th century onward, but a wealth of cultural traditions – including poetry, history, drama, and fiction – kept Persian identity strong. Gradually the area around Baghdad (modern day Iraq) became a separating area between Arabic and Persian culture, so that clear differences in culture could be seen by the time the Mongols invaded. When Ismail recreated Iran as a Shi'ite state, the religion reinforced cultural differences that were already in place. For example, the architecture of mosques in Isfahan stood in clear contrast to those in Istanbul. Whereas both styles relied heavily on domes with tall prayer towers surrounding the main structures, the domes in Isfahan were decorated in brightly colored floral patterns that greatly resembled Persian carpets. In contrast the domes in Istanbul were noted for their massive simplicity. Calligraphy styles in the two areas were almost completely different as well.

Another important characteristic of Safavid culture was the blending of Sufi mysticism with militant political objectives. Sufism had long been a branch of Islam, and Sufi mystics could be found in most Islamic cultures. However, the Safavids traced their ancestry back to Safi al-Din, the leader of a Sufi religious order in northwestern Persia, so the empire was literally founded on Sufi beliefs. Ismail deployed his armies to spread Shi'ism with an emphasis on mystic union with God in the style of the Sufis. However, once Shi'ism was established, later Safavid shahs banned all Sufi orders from the empire, although Sufism continued to thrive anyway.

Like the Ottoman Empire, the Safavid Empire gradually lost its vigor, but unlike the Ottomans, it collapsed entirely in the 1720s under Turkish and Afghani attack, a victim of Islamic infighting, as well as the ever-growing dominance of sea-based powers that left the great Islamic land-based empires greatly weakened by the mid-18th century.

THE MUGHAL EMPIRE

In 1450 much of the Indian subcontinent was tenuously controlled by the Delhi Sultanate that had begun in the early 13th century when an Afghan Turkish leader conquered Delhi and declared himself to be the Sultan of Delhi. By 1450 the old tendency for political units to fragment regionally was clearly present, compounded by the difficulty of integrating the Turkish warlords into a single, stable state. The Muslim leaders presided over a population that remained primarily Hindu, creating religious frictions that have continued to the present day. In 1523 India was attacked again, this time by **Babur** – a descendant of Timur and Genghis Khan – who founded the **Mughal Empire** in 1526, a mixture of Mongol and Turkish peoples from central Asia. The empire dominated India until the early 1700s, although it continued to rule in name until 1858.

PERSPECTIVES: BABUR'S REFLECTIONS ON INDIA

Babur's fame is based on his role as the founder of the Mughal Empire, one of the greatest empires of the world during the 16th and 17th centuries. Although he came to live in Delhi and his name is forever associated with the Indian subcontinent, his reflections excerpted below show that he had no real fondness for India and that his heart remained in central Asia.

"Most of the people of India are infidels, called Hindus, believing mainly in the transmigration of souls...India is a country of few charms. The people lack good looks and good manners. They have no social life or exchange of visits. They have no genius or intelligence, no polite learning, no generosity or magnanimity, no harmony or proportion in their arts and crafts...They have no baths and no advanced educational institutions...Their residences have no pleasant and salubrious breezes, and in their construction [there is] no form or symmetry...
It was the hot season when we came to Agra. All the inhabitants had run away in terror. We could find no grain for ourselves nor corn for our horses... The year was a very hot one, pestilential simooms [sandstorms] were striking people down in heaps, and masses were beginning to die off.
For all these reasons, most of the best warriors were unwilling to stay in India; in fact, they determined to leave..."

Reference: The Babur-nama in English (Memoirs of Babur). Trans. by Annette Susannah Beveridge. (London: Luzac, 1922).

Babur's invasion of India was motivated by the loss of his ancestral homeland in central Asia through intertribal warfare and probably by his dreams of living up to the reputations of his illustrious ancestors. His military strategies, including one that caused his opponent's elephants to stampede, were responsible for his success in capturing Delhi. His family's control was challenged after his death, and despite losing control of Delhi for several years, his son Humayan eventually recaptured northern India, and the empire expanded to control much of the subcontinent under his remarkable grandson, **Akbar,** who ruled from 1556 to 1605. It was under Akbar that the empire reached its height in power and influence, although its borders continued to grow until the early 18th century.

Political Characteristics

Like the Ottomans and Safavids, the Mughals were autocratic rulers who based a great deal of their power on military might and religious authority. Like the Safavids, the Mughals had no navy, so all of their military power was based on their army. Religious ideals required the spreading of Islam by fighting infidels, who to Mughal leaders were the Hindus. Some Mughal leaders, such as Akbar, were more tolerant of Hinduism than others, but the responsibility of Mughal rulers to Islam was always clear. Like the Ottomans and Safavids, Mughal princes fought with one another to become heir to the throne, so political instability caused by family controversies always threatened the empire.

An important move taken by Akbar to alleviate tensions between Muslims and Hindus was the incorporation of many Hindu rajas, or regional leaders, into the highest positions of the military and the bureaucracy. He pursued a policy of cooperation with the rajas and encouraged intermarriage between the Mughal aristocracy of the families of the Hindu rajput, and he abolished the jizra, or head tax, that all non-Muslims paid. He ended a ban on the building of new Hindu temples, and ordered Muslims to respect cows, which Hindus considered to be sacred. He built a strong bureaucracy modeled on a military hierarchy for collecting taxes. Each region of India was surveyed and evaluated by government officials, and tax rates were based on the region's potential for wealth. In most areas local officials, most of whom were Hindu, were allowed to keep their positions as long as they swore allegiance to the Mughal rulers and paid their taxes, so a great deal of power was left in the hands of local rulers. Akbar's reforms that encouraged cooperation between Muslims and Hindus lasted through the reigns of his successors until his great-grandson Aurangzeb, a devout Muslim, reinstituted many restrictions on Hindus in the late 17th century.

Economic and Social Characteristics

As in the Ottoman and Safavid Empires, the government granted land revenue to military officers and government officials in return for their service. Many grew wealthy through revenue from various economic activities on their land grants, such as farming and trade, and the taxes they collected filled the coffers of the central government as well. As the Mughals conquered more and more territory, they came to control commercial networks based on cotton, indigo, and silk. By the late 17th century, trade with Europeans was brisk, with much of it taking place overland through trade cities such as Surat in the northwest. Since the Mughals had no navy, Indian merchant ships were privately owned, and many Indian goods that went into the Indian Ocean trade circuit were transported on English and Dutch vessels. Europeans brought trade goods from throughout Asia to exchange for Indian cotton cloth and clothing. India's cotton products had been highly valued since classical times, and demand for them grew in Europe, first among the lower and middle classes because they washed so easily, and eventually to the courts of royalty.

The Mughal Empire, like the Ottoman and Safavid empires, was a patriarchy, with unequal societal and economic roles for men and women. However, the wives of rulers often played key political roles in all three empires. For example, Suleiman the Magnificent's favorite wife, Hurrem, had a great deal of influence over her husband's political decisions. Harem intrigue was a common theme, but Hurrem's power was evident in her ability to convince Suleiman to execute his eldest son so that her own son could succeed to the throne. The political influence of one Safavid ruler's wife so enraged the qizilbash that they murdered her. In the Mughal Empire the classic example is Mumtaz Mahal, the wife of Shah Jahan, who amassed a great deal of power behind the throne, as well as her husband's devotion. When she died the shah immortalized their love by building the **Taj Mahal,** a building of breathtaking beauty built of white marble inlaid with precious stones. The Shah planned to build his own monument of black marble nearby to complement it, but he was imprisoned by his sons in a family struggle for succession to the throne, and his plans could not be completed. Instead, he is buried beside his wife in the Taj Mahal, and his tomb is much less impressive than that of his wife.

Despite the power of rulers' wives and concubines, the status of women in the rest of Indian society remained low. Child marriage was common, with brides as young as nine, and the Hindu practice of **sati,** or the suicide of widows by jumping into their husband's funerals pyres, spread, even though Akbar and Shah Jahan outlawed it. As in many other patriarchal societies, seclusion – called **purdah** – was more strictly enforced for upper class women, who did not venture outside their homes unescorted. Muslim women were always veiled when they left their homes.

Cultural Characteristics

As in the earlier Delhi Sultanate, the conflicts between Muslim and Hindu religious beliefs permeated Indian life during the Mughal Dynasty. Akbar's many attempts to reconcile the two were capped by his invention of a new **"Divine Faith"** that combined Muslim, Hindu, Zoroastrian, Christian, and Sikh beliefs. His hope was that it would not only unite the many religious groups in his realm, but would also cement loyalty to the emperor. The religion did not outlive him, and it was clear by the time of his death that this effort would fail.

Akbar's "Divine Faith" was not the first attempt to blend Islamic and Hindu beliefs. Even before Babur invaded India, **Nanuk** (1469-1539) stressed meditation as a means of seeking enlightenment and drew upon both religions in his teachings. He became the first **guru** (religious leader) of a new religion called **Sikhism.** Nanuk developed a following of people who formed a community free of caste distinctions, and he at first tried to reconcile Hinduism and Islam. However, the religious fervor of the Mughal Shah Aurangzeb, a devout Muslim, changed the nature of Sikhism when he ordered the ninth guru beheaded in 1675 because he refused to convert to Islam. The tenth guru vowed to avenge his father's death, and he led an **"army of the pure"** to challenge the Mughal army and to assert Sikh beliefs aggressively. Sikhs reflected their devotion to their beliefs through outward signs, such as leaving their hair uncut beneath their turbans, and carrying symbols of their faith: a comb, a steel bracelet, and a sword or dagger. Sikh rebellions combined with other upheaval of the 18th century to seriously weaken the Mughal regime.

The two shahs that followed Akbar – Jahangir and Shah Jahan – kept most reforms in place, but they had less interest in military conquests and politics than their predecessor. However, they both followed Akbar's example as patrons of fine arts. A particular art form of the day that they promoted was the painting of exquisite miniatures, most depicting scenes of life at court, important battles and events, and animals and plants. All the Mughal leaders built many public buildings, including mosques, tombs, schools, palaces, and government buildings. The architecture was a distinctive blend of Persian and Hindu influences, with the domes, arches, and minarets characteristic of Islamic tradition, and the detail and lavish ornamentation that Hindus like. Whereas the Persians used ceramic tiles to finish their buildings, the Indian style was to ornament them with white marble and inset with semiprecious stones in lavish patterns. The most famous example is the Taj Mahal, and the reflecting pools that surround it. The Mughal love for magnificent architecture is no better illustrated than by **Fatehpur Sikri**, Akbar's entirely new capital city. Although it was abandoned after his death, its beauty was famous throughout the Muslim world. The court library contained the largest collection of books in the world, and Akbar invited scholars of all religions from throughout Asia to come to his city as teachers and students. Although he was illiterate, Akbar loved to have books read to him, and he cultivated the use of the official Persian language in Indian literature. Akbar's reputation as an important Indian leader is based partly on his ability to revive the sense of political and cultural unity that the subcontinent had not had since the Gupta era.

CHANGE OVER TIME:
INDIA – FOUNDATIONS
TO 1750

In your study of world history, it is important to understand how different societies interact during a particular period, but you must also keep up with how societies change over time. Below are summarized some major characteristics of the Indian subcontinent as it changed over time up to 1750.

Foundations – The first civilization on the Indian subcontinent probably began in the Indus River Valley, where two great cities – Mohenjo Daro and Harappa – formed the centers of a prosperous civilization that fell apart around 1200 B.C.E. The Aryans invaded the subcontinent beginning about 2000 B.C.E., bringing their religion and customs that became the foundation of Hindu society. Buddhism began in India during the 6th century, but was more successful in east and Southeast Asia, where it diffused from India. During the classical era, the Mauryan and Gupta Empire temporarily united India politically. (See pages 51-55 and 100-104 for more).

600-1450 – Fragmented political rule continued until the 13th century, but Hindu religion and culture were the "glue" that kept Indian identity intact. Beginning in the 13th century, Turkish invasions from the northwest periodically disrupted the regional kingdoms, with one group of Afghan Turks capturing Delhi and forming the Delhi Sultanate. The Turks brought their religion of Islam with them, introducing friction between Muslims and Hindus. (See pages 231-233 for more)

1450-1750 – At the beginning of the 15th century, Babur, a Turk from Central Asia led an army into India that toppled the Delhi Sultanate. This new Mughal Dynasty was stronger than the Delhi Sultanate, and their most astute leader, Akbar, tried to reconcile differences between Muslims and Hindus. He did not solve the problem long term, but religious tolerance increased during the 16th and 17th centuries. Like other land-based Islamic empires, the Mughals were less powerful in the 18th century than they had been in the previous centuries. (See pages 310-316 for more)

Despite their support for artistic endeavors, Jahangir and Shah Jahan were not faithful administrators of government. Their love of pleasure meant that important political, economic, and military issues were neglected, and the man that succeeded them, Aurangzeb, made an effort to restore the empire. However, he also tried to rid the Indian subcontinent of Hinduism and other non-Muslim religions, and as a result, stirred up a great deal of resentment toward him. Aurangzeb did manage to conquer much more land, but the expenses of the endless warfare left his treasury empty. While he was preoccupied with war, local leaders began to plot against him and gain more authority over their areas. His rollback of most of Akbar's reforms undermined the legitimacy of his government. When he died, the empire was larger than it had ever been, but it was also quite unstable. Political power again began to fragment, as it had almost always done before, but this time, some European observers stood ready to take advantage of the disunity, as British, French, and Dutch joint-stock companies eagerly sought to expand their profitable trade in India.

CONCEPTS AND IDENTIFICATIONS

Akbar
"army of the pure"
Babur
devshirme
"Divine Faith"
Fatehpur Sikri
Gunpowder Empires
guru
Hidden Imam
imam
Ismail
Janissaries
Mughal Empire
Nanuk
Osman
Ottoman Empire
purdah
qizilbash
Safavid Empire
sati
Shah Abbas I
Shi'ism
Sikhism
Suleiman the Magnificent
Taj Mahal
Twelver Shi'ism
vizier

COMPARISONS:
ISLAMIC EMPIRES
1450-1750

The Islamic Empires – the Ottomans, Safavids, and Mughals – had many important characteristics in common, but some significant differences existed among them.

Political – In all three empires, the sultan/shah was an autocratic ruler who based his authority on both military prowess and religious piety. They all built large bureaucracies to administer the government, and they all gave land grants to the aristocracy, usually in reward for military service. All empires relied on gunpowder to withstand nomadic invaders and to enlarge their landspace, but the Ottomans had a powerful army AND navy, whereas the Safavids and Mughals had no navy. By 1750 all three were in political decline.

Economic and Social – All three economies were based on agriculture, although trade was important for all. Of the three, the Ottomans were most favorably located for trade, with Istanbul situated on the Bosporus. The Safavids and Mughals had inland capitals and any sea vessels were privately owned, leaving a great deal of control of sea ports to Europeans. All three economies were at a disadvantage in the world economy because of inflation caused by New World silver, which Europeans controlled. By 1750, all three were in economic decline. All three societies were patriarchies, but wives of rulers and other elite often had a great deal of influence.

Cultural – Although all were primarily Islamic, the Safavids were Shi'ites, and the other two empires were primarily Sunni. These cultural differences contributed to frequent warfare between the Ottomans and the Safavids. All three were influenced by Sufi mysticism. The Mughals were distinct from the other two because a Muslim minority ruled over a Hindu majority. All three empires encouraged the arts, and some unique artistic styles developed in art and architecture. All styles placed value on domed buildings and calligraphy, with Persian calligraphy emphasized in the Safavid Empire. The Indian styles were influenced by the Hindu preference for intricate design.

CHAPTER FOURTEEN: LAND-BASED POWERS ON THE RISE – RUSSIA AND EAST ASIA

The rise of sea-based states in Europe between 1450 and 1750 is a major "marker event" in world history because it represents an important shift in the balance of world power from those that controlled the land to those that controlled the sea. This tilting away from the land-based powers may be seen in the gradual weakening of the Muslim Empires, which all were more powerful in the 16th century than they were in 1750. However, three important land-based empires of the era did not lose ground to the European upstarts, but were either on the rise or at their peak at the end of the era. Russia, Qing China, and Tokugawa Japan reached their greatness through traditional land-based methods, and they all addressed challenges from the West in different, yet equally successful ways.

THE RUSSIAN EMPIRE

By 1450 the Russian princes had escaped Mongol control, and the power of Muscovy (later Moscow) was on the rise, but Russia was still a backwater area in the eyes of other organized states. They had aligned themselves much earlier to Byzantine culture and politics, a decision that seemed to doom them when the last of the Byzantine Empire slipped away with the Muslim capture of Constantinople in 1453. The princes' lands were located far inland and to the north of most other civilizations, and logically the ascendancy of sea-based powers between 1450 and 1750 should have ensured their continuing obscurity. However, the gradual concentration of political power, supported by actions and policies of its tsars, defied the odds and propelled Russia to the ranks of the great empires by 1750.

The Expansion and Centralization of Russia Before 1650

Even before the Mongols were ousted in 1480, Moscow princes began to expand their control of nearby lands. As Mongol presence weakened, the princes continued to pay tribute, but acted virtually independently in the years leading up to 1480. The leader who ultimately refused to pay tribute to the Mongols was **Ivan III,** also known as Ivan the Great, who declared himself "tsar" – a derivative of "Caesar" with the claim that he was establishing the "Third Rome." Ivan acquired new lands by war, marriage, and purchase, and he consolidated his hold by recruiting peasants, called **cossacks,** to settle in new territories in exchange for their freedom from serfdom. After the demise of the Byzantines, Ivan saw Russia as the carrier of Roman tradition, although with the distinct cultural characteristics of the Eastern Empire, including the Russian Orthodox Church. Like the Byzantine emperors, Ivan III ruled not only as head of the government but as head of the church as well, and as a result, the influence of the church increased as Ivan's power grew.

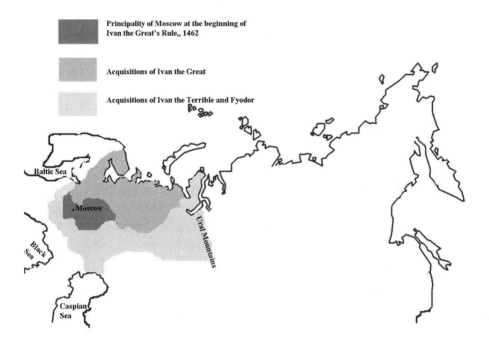

Principality of Moscow at the beginning of Ivan the Great's Rule,, 1462

Acquisitions of Ivan the Great

Acquisitions of Ivan the Terrible and Fyodor

The Expansion of Russia before the Romanovs. When Ivan the Great became tsar in 1462, the principality of Moscow was a totally landlocked territory that grew from the old city of Muscovy. Ivan expanded Russia north and east, greatly increasing the size of the Empire. Russia continued to grow under Ivan the Terrible and his successor, Fyodor, so that it stretched from the Baltic Sea to the Caspian Sea and eastward to the Ural Mountains.

Centralization of power continued under Ivan's grandson, **Ivan IV,** but his nickname – Ivan the Terrible – reflects the problems that tsars faced as their power increased. Russia's economic system was based on feudalism, with the nobility, called **boyars,** holding land worked by serfs. The boyars also had military responsibilities to overlords, including the tsar, that were similar to those of western European knights and Japanese samurai. As the tsar centralized his power, the boyars resisted, and Ivan responded by redistributing their lands to a new aristocracy, the oprichniki, and by killing the rebels, often in very cruel ways, such as cooking them and skinning them alive. Ivan insured that the time that followed his rule would be called "The Time of Trouble" when he executed his oldest son, touching off competition among boyar families for control of the throne and encouraging nearby kingdoms to invade Russian territory. Amidst the chaos, the boyars cooperated to select Mikhail Romanov from the distinguished **Romanov family,** as the heir to the throne. The Romanovs ruled Russia until the early 20th century, when the last tsar was executed by a new regime of communist leaders.

Peter the Great

Although Ivan III, Ivan IV, and the early Romanov tsars expanded the Russian Empire greatly, the tsar most responsible for transforming Russia into a great world power was **Peter the Great,** who ruled from 1682 to 1724. Peter understood, perhaps better than anyone else of his era, the ongoing changes that were occurring in the global balance of power, and he realized that Russia was far from the cutting edge of innovation. He looked to the West, saw the importance of controlling the oceans and seas, studied European methods of shipbuilding and engineering, applied all that his brilliant mind could put together, and pulled Russia by the bootstraps into its new role as an important player in global history.

As a young man Peter was caught up in the intrigues of boyar competition for political influence. Although the Romanovs were clearly in control, boyar families still strove for power, a situation that was exacerbated by the fact that his father had two wives, one after the first one's death. When Tsar Alexis died, infighting between the two wives' families eventually led to Peter succeeding his father, but not till after he had his half-sister removed as regent and placed in a monastery. Tsars were absolute rulers, and Peter never hesitated to use his power, including the order he gave much later in his life to execute his son for conspiring against him. Despite this absolute power, the threat from boyar uprisings was always present, and many of Peter's goals for the empire were met with resistance from the nobility, making his accomplishments even more remarkable.

Peter did not reject his predecessors' efforts to centralize power and to expand the empire, but his appreciation for the importance of sea power led him to direct the expansion toward access to warm water ports. He was successful in gaining access to the Baltic Sea, and built a new capital on its shores, St. Petersburg, often called his **"Window on the West."** The city served as a port for the navy he built, and it also allowed closer access to western countries. He tried to capture lands adjacent to the Black Sea, but the Ottomans held it, and Peter's efforts were ultimately unsuccessful.

MARKER EVENT:
PETER THE GREAT AND
THE SEXTANT

Peter the Great grew up in a Russia that was quite isolated from the many changes going on in western Europe during the 17th century. However, when Peter was sixteen, a Russian prince brought him a present from France: a sextant . Peter was amazed by the instrument "by which distance and space could be measured without moving from the spot," and he quickly learned the arithmetic and geometry necessary to learn how to use it. With instruction from a Dutchman living in the "German suburb" outside of Moscow, Peter went on to learn about the western countries that used the sextants, and he developed an interest in shipmaking after he and his tutor came across a ruined English ship in a building filled with junk. The Dutchman explained to him that the ship would have had sails, which Peter had never seen before. The young tsar eventually went to western Europe to see these wonders for himself, and he brought back a host of ideas about how to apply the new technology in Russia. No doubt, Peter would still have been a remarkable tsar if the sextant had not been presented to him when he was a boy, but his drive to modernize Russia may well be traced to that event.

Reference: *Peter the Great,* Robert K. Massie (New York: Alfred A. Knopf, 1980), pp. 71, 72.

Peter's program for westernization included these reforms:

- **Military reform** – Peter built the size of his army by drafting peasants to serve as professional soldiers and increasing pay. He encouraged the use of western technology, including the training of troops in the use of cannon and firearms. He ordered the building of roads and bridges to more easily transport troops and equipment across the countryside. He built a navy from scratch, and brought in European experts on shipbuilding, sailing, and navigation. Ports, including St. Petersburg, were built to accommodate the new ships.

- **Social reform** – Peter ordered the boyars to dress like Europeans, which meant they had to abandon their bearskin capes and beards. By tradition, boyars grew their beards without shaving, giving them a very un-western appearance, so Peter ordered them to shave. If they refused, Peter himself was known to hack their beards off with scissors, although eventually the beards could stay if their owners paid fines to the government. Until Peter's rule, Russian women followed the Byzantine custom of secluding themselves at home and wearing veils in public. Previous tsars' courts were all-male, but Peter insisted that women appear unveiled in his court, dressed as European ladies of fashion. He extended rights in less superficial ways as well, such as a decree that young people, rather than their parents, should determine for themselves who they would marry.

- **Bureaucratic reform** – In order to pay for and promote his expanded army, new navy, and improved infrastructure, Peter reorganized the bureaucracy to more efficiently gather taxes and to encourage industrial production. He replaced boyars with government officials selected according to his newly established **Table of Ranks,** which allowed officials to attain government positions based on merit, not on aristocratic status. He eliminated many titles of nobility, and he ensured that the new bureaucrats were loyal to him as the person responsible for their newly acquired positions.

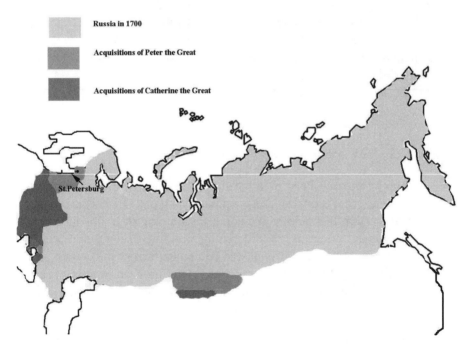

Russia in 1700

Acquisitions of Peter the Great

Acquisitions of Catherine the Great

St.Petersburg

The Expansion of Russia. By 1700 Russia had grown from its origins in the east to encompass land in northern Eurasia all the way to the Pacific Ocean. Both Peter and Catherine sought access to the Baltic and Black Seas that would connect them to the world waterways that were replacing overland trade in importance.

At the end of his reign, Peter had brought many changes to Russia, including a basic conflict that had not existed in Russia before: the Slavic, traditional ways vs. the new impetus to westernize. Peter only selectively imitated western ways; he took little interest in Enlightenment ideas about government, although in truth those influences were far greater in the years that followed his death in 1725. He also did not aim to build an international export-oriented economy, as was characteristic of the West, and he saw economic development mainly as a way to support his military efforts. He continued to rule autocratically as tsars always had, but he sent a very strong message to his subjects that European ways were to be emulated. A successor tsar, Catherine the Great, understood both sides of the cultural conflict that Peter had created, and she too continued the autocratic traditions of the tsars, although she was fully aware of Enlightenment ideas of her contemporaries of the late 18th century. Russians continued to value their Slavic ways, including their Russian Orthodox religion, but after Peter, they began to turn one ear toward the West.

EAST ASIA: 1450-1750

Like the Muslim Empires, most of the civilizations of east Asia generally continued to think of Europe as a backward area of the world, and yet the global effects of European expansion were beginning to be felt by the 17th and 18th centuries. Southeast Asia was probably most affected by the Europeans, since Portuguese and Dutch ships began to claim ports and control trade through this crucial linking area between the Indian Ocean and the South China Sea. Europeans took over the governments of two island regions of Southeast Asia – the Philippines and Indonesia – and established regimes that favored the interests of European merchants. In the Philippines, Manila became the center of Spanish commercial activity in Asia. The Dutch had a more tenuous hold on Indonesia, but from their hub in Batavia on the island of Java, they exercised control over much Southeast Asian trade. China, Japan, and Korea were much more resistant to European efforts to control trade.

Despite the fact that European traders and missionaries began to appear in China, the empire generally went about business as usual, and Japan actively tried to keep Europeans out of their lands. Nomadic invasions continued to preoccupy the Ming Dynasty, just as they had distracted previous dynasties, and European excursions to the New World were only of marginal interest to them. Although both China and Japan ventured into the seas around them and conducted a vigorous trade with one another, most of their concerns were land-based and remained focused on their own internal affairs.

The Late Ming Dynasty

The Ming Dynasty began with the overthrow of the Mongols in 1368, and it lasted for almost 300 years.   During its early years the government was effective, population and food supply grew, and commercial activity continued, even though the Ming emperors were generally wary of outsiders. The experience with Mongol rule had emphasized the old Chinese tendency to protect their culture from outside influences, and so the Confucians regained much influence that they had lost during the Yuan Dynasty. Yet, China's precious goods, including silk and porcelain, were still highly prized in international trade, so the Ming did not turn their backs completely on the highly profitable commerce that had enriched them in the past.

Political Characteristics

China's ancient concept of the all-powerful but not divine emperor continued with the Ming, and the real power of the emperor probably reached its height during their early years. A corps of palace eunuchs served as the emperor's eyes and ears, and they had almost exclusive direct access to the emperor. After the first Ming emperor's rule from Nanjing, the government returned to Beijing, where the emperor's **forbidden city** expanded to house more than 20,000 people to serve the emperor and his family. The examination system for the bureaucracy was revived, and essentially stayed in place until the 20th century. The exams were largely unchanged, requiring extensive knowledge of Confucian thought, and positions in the civil service bureaucracy were filled with those that did well on them. The Ming armies were vast in numbers, with good leadership and organization, although their firearms were not as advanced as those of the West.

Economic Progress and Technological Resistance

Arguably, commercial activity in China during the 16th century was stronger than in any other empire or kingdom in the world. A large percentage of people were engaged in trade and manufacture, despite the fact that merchants had a low status in Chinese society. When the Portuguese made their way to Chinese ports, they traded New World silver for Chinese luxury goods, but their behavior was so offensive that the Chinese government confined their activity to one port – Macao. Urban areas in China grew rapidly under Ming control, inland cities as well as port cities, such as Macao, Guangzhou, Hangzhou, and Shanghai.   Unlike their modern counterparts, people in these cities appear to have been decently housed and well fed.

Despite the economic prosperity based on both external and internal trade, the Ming Chinese were not known for their technological innovation, as the Song

Chinese had been. Chinese science and technology led the world until at least the 1200s, but during the Ming era, many inventions from earlier Chinese times were adapted and improved by the Europeans. Examples include gunpowder and movable type printing. In their quest to preserve their identity, the Chinese took little notice of technological advances that would eventually prove to be their undoing. But for this era, the brilliance and prosperity of the Ming were not overshadowed by their lack of technological progress.

The Great Wall of China. This modern photograph shows the Great Wall as it was rebuilt during the Ming Empire. Extensive repairs fortified and expanded the wall that had first been constructed during the Qin era, 3rd century B.C.E.

Trade and Cultural Contacts with Outsiders

The attitude toward the outside world was that the Middle Kingdom needed little from anyone else. The voyages of Zheng He were a notable exception to the overall Ming policy. The Ming period was a high point in cultural and commercial interactions between China and Japan, with the shoguns often embracing Chinese culture and buying decorative artifacts from China. Japanese and Chinese pirates, who often cooperated to raid coastal ports, plagued both countries, and were never eliminated. Trade contacts with westerners were limited to a few trading enterprises with the Dutch and Portuguese, but an important opening for Europeans was the Ming tolerance of Christian missionaries who shared with them some of the mysteries of western technology. Like Kubilai Khan's reaction to Marco Polo, the Ming found their European visitors interesting and amusing, but almost certainly a distraction to the real business of the court – keeping the ancient land-based empire safe and secure from much more traditional threats than the Europeans.

Christian missionaries had ventured into China much earlier, but the outbreak of the plague and the collapse of the Yuan Dynasty had caused Christianity to be almost eliminated in China by the end of the 15th century. The efforts to convert the Chinese to Roman Catholicism were revived in the 16th century, and the **Jesuits** – the order stimulated during the Catholic Reformation in Europe – led the way. The most famous of the Jesuit missionaries was **Matteo Ricci,** an ambitious Italian who hoped to convert Emperor Wanli to his faith. Ricci understood that the Chinese revered learning and refinement, and that they were repulsed by the crude European sailors that had landed on their shores. Ricci used his own erudition and curiosity about all things Chinese to impress the emperor, and to accomplish his underlying motive of establishing China as a Christian nation. Ricci was able to master reading and writing in Chinese, no small accomplishment considering the thousands of characters in the language. He also discovered that the emperor's court was curious about European science, technology, and practical mechanical inventions. The Jesuits knew math and astronomy, so they used their calculations to correct Chinese calendars that had been slightly inaccurate and to prepare beautiful world maps with China placed strategically in the middle. To spark Chinese interest, the Jesuits intrigued them by displays of bronze cannons, cuckoo clocks, and most famously, a giant mechanical clock that chimed the hours.

The Jesuits brought these European innovations to the Chinese court as gifts, and then took advantage of the good will that they created by devising ways to convince the emperor of the similarities that they saw between Confucianism and Christianity. They held religious services in Chinese, and they allowed converts to continue to keep their shrines to their ancestors. Despite these clever, concerted efforts to promote Christianity, the number of converts was disappointing, so that by 1750 only about 200,000 Chinese (out of a population of 225 million) had adopted the faith. The Jesuit mission ended after the pope became alarmed by the comparisons between Confucianism and Christianity and ordered the priests to ban ancestral veneration and conduct services according to accepted European practice. The Chinese emperor responded by ordering a ban on Christian proselytizing. Although the priests did not cease their efforts, the mission was weakened, since it had neither papal nor imperial support. Although the Jesuits failed in their primary goal of creating a Christian China, they did open the country to European influence, primarily through their gadgets and technology. Their writings also stimulated an interest in China among Europeans, which resulted in both increasing demand for Chinese products in Europe and an admiration for Chinese values, decorum, and customs.

PERSPECTIVES: MATTEO RICCI ON CHINESE CULTURE

Matteo Ricci, a Jesuit priest who lived in China between 1582 and 1610, faithfully kept a journal during those years with some keen observations of Chinese values and customs, as seen through the eyes of a Christian European. Some excerpts from his remarkable journal appear below.

"...the entire kingdom is administered by the Order of the Learned, commonly known as the Philosophers. The responsibility for orderly management of the entire realm is wholly and completely committed to their charge and care. The army, both officers and soldiers, hold them in high respect and show them the promptest obedience and deference, and not infrequently the military are disciplined by them as a schoolboy might be punished by his master....Philosophers far excel military leaders in the good will and the respect of the people and in opportunities of acquiring wealth...
The order and harmony that prevails among magistrates, both high and low, in the provinces and in the regal Curia is also worthy of admiration. Their attitude toward the King, in exact obedience and in external ceremony, is a cause of wonderment to a foreigner. The literati would never think of omitting gifts. In the courts and elsewhere, inferiors always bend the knee when speaking to a superior, and address him in the most dignified language..."

Reference: *China in the Sixteenth Century: The Journals of Matthew Ricci, 1583-1610,.* Matthew Ricci, trans. by Louis J. Gallagher, S.J. (New York: Random House, 1953), pp. 54-59.

The Decline of the Ming

In many ways the decline of the Ming Dynasty followed the old model of dynastic cycles very closely. Large land-based empires always had problems defending their borders and maintaining control over their far-flung holdings. Again, central Asian nomadic groups that had long threatened China made successful forays across the Great Wall, despite the Ming's valiant attempts to make it impregnable. A series of weak emperors tolerated corruption among their imperial administrators, particularly the long-resented eunuchs, and court factions bickered for the emperor's favor. Peasant rebellions, a threat to most previous dynasties, multiplied as the central government lost its grip on local landlords. Just as had occurred during the 13th century, a group living north of the Great Wall was ready to seize China from emperors who had lost the mandate of heaven. This time, instead of the Mongols, the Manchurians won the prize, after they realized that their overlord – the Chinese emperor – could no longer defend his lands. In a move that is reminiscent of the Zhou, who many centuries earlier had devised the mandate of heaven to justify their overthrow of the Shang Dynasty, the Manchurians named their new empire the **Qing** [pure] **Dynasty** as an indication that they were throwing the rogues out to restore the purity of Chinese culture and society. The biggest flaw in their presentation was the fact that they were not Han Chinese, but instead were "barbarians" from the north, a fact that nevertheless did not impede their ability to found and maintain a brilliant new era for China.

The Qing Dynasty

Once the Manchu gained control of Beijing in 1644 they began a campaign to conquer the rest of the Ming territories, and by the end of the 17th century they had gained control of south China and captured the island of Taiwan, putting it under Chinese control for the first time. By the late 18th century China reached its largest size in history and was also the largest country in the world. The transition from Ming to Qing dynasties was not nearly as difficult as the period that followed the Mongol invasion in the 13th century. The Manchu had been close to Chinese civilization for a long time and had already adapted many Chinese customs and attitudes by the time the dynasty began. Because many Ming officials were disillusioned with the weakness of the most recent emperors, some gave their support to the Manchu in taking over the government.

Political Organization

Even though the Qing rulers admired Chinese culture, they still encouraged a separation between Manchus and Chinese. Like the Mongols, all highest political posts were filled by Manchu, although they left the Confucian scholar-gentry in most of the positions of the bureaucracy, and the scholars continued to do the day to day work of the empire. The Manchu showed a desire to preserve their identity by forbidding intermarriage between Manchu and Chinese, and they forced Chinese men to shave the front of their heads and grow a **queue** – a Manchu style patch of hair gathered long and uncut in the back – as a sign of submission to the dynasty. The civil service examinations continued to determine who entered the ranks of the scholar-gentry, and they became more competitive than ever, with tests given on the district, provincial, and metropolitan levels. Few could pass the metropolitans, and most students took the exams several times before they passed.

As in the Ming Dynasty, the state was tightly controlled at the center, and the traditional view of the emperor as the "son of heaven" was clearly in place. The emperor led a secluded but highly privileged life inside the forbidden city, with all of his needs met and his activities highly ritualized through official duties and ceremonies. "Theatre state" was apparent in the sumptuous palace surroundings and in customs that emphasized the glory of the ruler. For example, certain designs could only be displayed on the emperor's clothing, and everyone who came to see him had to perform a special **kowtow** that consisted of three separate kneelings.

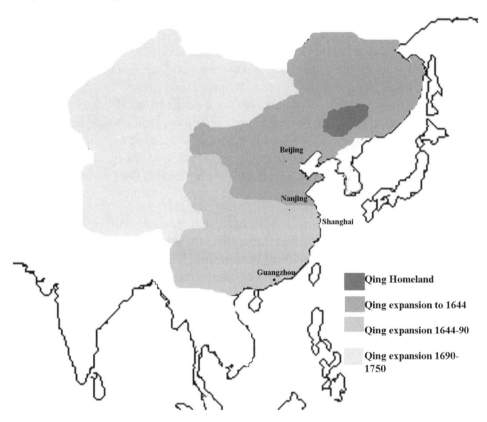

The Qing Empire. By 1750 China had reached its largest extent of land ever under the Qing Dynasty, founded by the Manchu of northeastern Asia. By 1644 they captured Beijing and much other territory around their homeland, and by the end of the 17th century they had conquered southern China.

The Manchu dynasty was strengthened by the long rules of two very strong emperors: **Kangxi,** who ruled from 1661 to 1722, and **Qianlong,** who ruled from 1736 to 1795. Together their rule spanned more than 130 years, enough to cement a prosperous, powerful, and culturally rich empire. Both emperors were sophisticated Confucian scholars, who managed the Chinese economy effectively as well. Under Kangxi, the empire grew dramatically, partly because he was a talented military leader. Qianlong's reign brought so much prosperity that he cancelled tax collections on four occasions because the royal coffers were full and the government did not need money. By the late 18th century, China was a well-organized empire, with its influence firmly established in most parts of east Asia.

Economic and Social Characteristics

The prosperity of China under the Qing rulers was based on agriculture, maximized by intensive agricultural methods that produced high yields of food crops, especially rice, wheat, and millet. Food production was enhanced further by the arrival of American food crops across the Pacific Ocean by way of the Philippines. Maize, sweet potatoes, and peanuts could be raised on soils that had not been appropriate for previous crops, and the new food supplies helped to sustain a rapid increase in population. Eventually population growth began to outpace food production, but the imbalance was not evident before 1750. Population growth supported trade that needed a large labor force, and commerce was also boosted by the influx of American silver, which was traded for Chinese luxury goods. Chinese workers produced silk, porcelain, and tea for consumers all over Eurasia, so in contrast to the effect that they had on the Muslim Empires, the new silver supplies generally helped the Chinese economy.

Chinese society remained highly patriarchal, and the control that men had over women's lives probably increased during the late Ming and Qing dynasties, as it usually did when Confucian ideals were strong. The preference for male children was clear, since only boys were allowed to take the examinations, which in turn could boost a family's status if a male son became a scholar-bureaucrat. Widows were encouraged to commit suicide after their husbands died, and foot binding became very popular during this time. Women could not divorce their husbands, but men could put their wives aside for disobedience or adultery.

The high status of scholar bureaucrats grew even stronger during this era. They wore distinctive clothing, and commoners treated them with extreme deference. Their principal source of income came from government service, and they usually lived in urban areas, although most of them owned land that usually brought additional income. Below the gentry were peasants, artisans, and merchants, with merchants having the lowest status of the three groups. Artisans included craftsmen, physicians, tailors, and workers in manufacturing establishments, who all generally made more money than peasants. However, Confucian principles considered the honest work of peasants more worthy of respect than the profit-based trade of merchants, who were viewed as less worthy because they did not actually create any tangible products. However, many gentry families had ties to commerce, with at least some family members acting as merchants, a practice that often created enough wealth to support talented sons while they studied for examinations. As in earlier days, the lower classes were often called "mean people," which included slaves, indentured servants, and beggars.

CHANGE OVER TIME: CHINA – FOUNDATIONS THROUGH 1750

China's long history is a challenge for anyone to understand, so it is important to recollect its story as it changed between the Foundations Era and 1750.

Foundations – China's earliest known dynasty emerged sometime before 1500 B.C.E. in the Yangzi and Huang He river valleys of east Asia. Early developments include the veneration of family and departed ancestors, as well as an emphasis on the importance on writing and learning. The Shang Dynasty was overthrown by the Zhou Dynasty in the 12th century B.C.E., which instituted the belief in the mandate of heaven. Confucianism, Daoism, and Legalism were philosophies that developed during the late Zhou Dynasty. During the 3rd century C.E. (the classical era) Shi Huangdi unified China as the short-lived Qin Dynasty under legalism, to be followed by the Han Dynasty, based on Confucianism, which lasted until the 3rd century C.E. Dynastic cycle patterns were well established by the end of the Foundations period. (see pp. 55-64, 93-100)

600-1450 – A long era of chaos ended in the 7th century with the short Sui Dynasty, followed by the much longer Tang Dynasty. Buddhist influences were strong, but during the dynasty's later years, Confucians regained control, beginning neo-Confucianism. The Song Dynasty was founded in the 10th century based on neo-Confucianism. The Tang and Song were culturally rich, although military and political strength was greater during the Tang. The Song were defeated by the Mongols, who established the Yuan Dynasty, which was very much in touch with other areas of Eurasia. The Yuan were overthrown in the 14th century by the Ming Dynasty, which rebuilt Chinese institutions including Confucianism and protection of Han Chinese identity. The Ming had very mixed feelings about contacts with the outside world. (see pp. 192-202, 218-221)

1450-1750 – The Ming were at their strongest in the early part of this era, but they lost control of China to the Manchus, a semi-nomadic people from northeastern Asia in the mid-17th century, when the Qing Dynasty was established. The Manchus strengthened China through their large, efficient army and the competent, long rules of Kangxi and Qianlong. In 1750 China was the largest country in the world and still one of the strongest. (see pp. 323-332)

Cultural Influences

Beyond the strong neo-Confucian influences during Qing times, a rich cultural life emerged in philosophy, literature, and history, partly because the emperors supported printing and distribution of materials at their expense. The Ming emperor Yongle had sponsored a huge project that compiled much Chinese knowledge into the *Yongle Encyclopedia,* but only three manuscript copies were made. In contrast, Kangxi's *Collection of Books* was much more influential because he had it printed and widely distributed. In literature, popular novels circulated among the literate middle classes, with books written about the lives of both gentry and commoners. Most of the authors are unknown, and no one knows just how many novels were written, but two of the best known to survive are the *Book of the Golden Lotus* and *The Dream of the Red Chamber.*

Porcelain had long been a distinctive product of China, but it became a major art form during both the Ming and Qing eras. Wealthy Europeans sought to buy Chinese porcelain for their dinner tables, and the Ming and Qing vases, decorative bowls, and painted scrolls and screens were in such great demand that their prices rose even as production increased. Many of these items did not go into international trade because the large number of prosperous Chinese filled their urban homes with the luxury goods. By the 1700s China had many educated people who read the books produced and sent their children to schools and academies of higher learning. As always, beautiful calligraphy, painting, and poetry was more prized than math and science, as the members of the scholar-gentry class generally led highly refined, comfortable lives.

JAPAN

From the 12th century through the 16th century, Japan was organized politically and economically into feudalistic hierarchies with an emperor who ruled in name only. The symbolism of the emperor was important, but the shogun, or the top military authority, wielded the most real power. However, the powerful territorial lords, called **daimyos,** still had a great deal of local control, and political power was fragmented as a result. Some daimyos had more influence than others, but each maintained his own governments and had his own samurai loyal to him. All daimyos pledged an allegiance to the shogun as an overlord, but they acted quite independently, and they also quarreled frequently among themselves. In the late 1500s civil war broke out, and several warlords emerged that dominated separate Japanese islands. The most famous was **Toyotomi Hideyoshi,** a competent general who broke the power of the warring daimyos and eventually unified Japan under his authority by 1590. Hideyoshi's ambitions stretched far, however, and he dreamed of ruling Korea, China, and even India with his newfound power base in Japan. His attacks on Korea eventually stalled, and he died before he could fulfill his ambitions, but his actions sparked the unification of Japan for the first time in history, a step that would be crucial in the country's rise to world power three centuries later.

MARKER EVENT:
KOREAN "TURTLE BOATS"

Many people believe that the first ironclad ships appeared during the American Civil War of the 1860s, but the Koreans had ironclad "turtle boats" almost 300 years earlier. When the Japanese warlord Hideyoshi attacked Korea first in 1592 and again in 1597, Korean Admiral Yi Sun-shin invented a 70-foot boat with a curved iron covering to defend his peninsula. The iron covering, which made the boat look like a giant turtle, was spiked to discourage enemies from boarding, and each boat had holes for oars and cannon. A dragon head with steam pouring from its nostrils was carved on its prow to frighten the enemy in a more traditional way. The turtle boats sank hundreds of Japanese vessels, even though the Japanese carried new weapons – called muskets – that they had bought from Portuguese traders. Although the Japanese overran the peninsula and invaded Manchuria as well, they ultimately had to withdraw and make peace after losing a tremendous portion of their navy. Hideyoshi planned to attack China once he got a foothold in Korea, and although we'll never know whether or not he could have conquered the powerful Ming, the turtle boats may well have altered the course of Asian history significantly. Admiral Yi was killed in one of the Japanese attacks, and his curious boats were never used again, but Japan did not attempt another attack of the Korean peninsula until the 20th century.

The Tokugawa Shogunate

After Hideyoshi's death, the daimyos met together under the leadership of **Tokugawa Ieyasu** to establish a centralized government in 1603 called the **Tokugawa Shogunate**, with its capital at Edo, now Tokyo. Kyoto remained an important trading center, and roads were built to connect the two cities. The government was also called the Tokugawa **bakufu,** or "tent government," implying that it was only a temporary replacement for the real power of the emperor. Ieyasu and his descendants controlled Japan until 1867, more than 250 years.

Despite the fact that Japan was more unified than it had ever been, daimyos still had a great deal of power and autonomy, and the shogun's authority was clearly based on military might. To keep the daimyos in check, the shoguns carried out a policy of **"alternate attendance"** that required them to spend every other year at the Tokugawa court. This weakened the daimyos in two ways: first, their wealth was affected because they had to maintain two households, one at home and one at Edo; and secondly, the daimyos' absence from their lands meant that their ability to establish separate power bases at home was impaired.

Economic and Social Change

Political unification encouraged economic growth, partly because it put an end to much of the fighting that had consumed Japan during the preceding years. Like many other Asian economies, including China, the growth was rooted in increased agricultural production as the result of water control, irrigation, and the use of fertilizer. As in China, the increased yields of rice and other food products brought about a rapid growth in population, which was curbed by birth control, late marriage, abortion, and infanticide. These measures – especially the extreme one of infanticide – were taken largely because Japan had only limited land space available. Not only did the islands constrain geographical perimeters, but much of the land was mountainous, and soil was often poor.

The Japanese social hierarchy was influenced by Confucianism, with its emphasis on obedience and responsibilities among people of unequal ranks. The ruling elites included the shogun, daimyos, and samurai warriors; the middle class consisted of peasants and artisans; and at the bottom, as in China, were the merchants. However, as peace settled in, and trade flourished, the land-owning daimyos came to be less prosperous than the merchants. With their riches based on rice production, the price of rice did not rise as quickly as that of luxury goods in the growing cities, and so despite their low status in the social hierarchy, by 1700 merchants – including rice dealers, producers of sake and silk, and pawnbrokers – were among the wealthiest people in Japan. Meanwhile, the samurai were literally left with nothing to do, since times were peaceful. The strict social hierarchy kept them from entering into any other profession, and many fell into debt at the hands of those who had money – the merchants.

Arts and Learning

During the Tokugawa era, Japanese culture continued to be shaped by a combination of Confucianism, Buddhism, and Shintoism. The elite were most influenced by neo-Confucianism, with many Japanese scholars writing in Chinese. Buddhism and Shintoism were more influential among common people. However, many scholars emphasized the importance of Shintoism – the native Japanese religion – as an important source of Japanese identity. Even though the Tokugawa court promoted neo-Confucianism, some scholars scorned it as a Chinese influence that diluted Japanese culture that they considered to be superior to all others.

Since the Japanese language is based on far fewer characters than Chinese, literacy rates were quite high in Japan and continued to increase during the 18th century. Wood-block printing presses, and eventually movable type, made mass production of reading materials possible, and as a result, literature aimed at the urban middle class became popular. Poetry, novels, social satires, and **kabuki** plays were the most common forms of urban literature. Kabuki theater was a new form of drama that consisted of several acts – separate skits with singing, dancing, and elaborate staging. The format allowed actors to improvise, and in so doing, endear themselves to the audience. Since kabuki was enormously popular in 17th and 18th century Japan, some actors became well-known stars who everyone wanted to meet. The settings for the plays were often the "**floating world**," an urban jumble of teahouses, public baths, and brothels that allowed people to escape from the rigid public decorum required in outside society. Another form of entertainment that emerged was bunraku, or puppet theater in which a team of three people told a story acted out by puppets accompanied by music. Both kabuki and bunraku attracted large audiences, and the art forms are still alive and well in modern day Japan.

Japan and the Europeans

At the same time that Japanese leaders were attempting to unify Japan under one central government, European ships were beginning to make their way to the islands. Beginning with the Portuguese in the mid-16th century, European traders and missionaries arrived, with traders bringing goods mainly from the Asian mainland to exchange for pottery, lacquerware, and copper. Westerners also brought firearms and technological devices, with European firearms playing an important role in Hideyoshi's invasion of Korea. Missionaries began arriving soon after the traders, and just as in China, their main goal was to convert the natives to Roman Catholicism. At first, the priests had some success with their strategy of converting the daimyos first, who in turn would influence their vassals to accept the faith. The first daimyos were those nearest the ports in the southwest, and they eventually set their sites on Nobunaga, a powerful daimyo who appeared to be on his way to ruling Japan. When Nobunaga was murdered, his successor, Hideyoshi, was much less enthusiastic about Christianity, and eventually grew concerned about converts who refused to obey their overlords' commands if they conflicted with their Christian beliefs. Hideyoshi ordered Christian missionaries to leave the islands in the late 1580s, and within a few years he was actively persecuting both the Catholic priests and native converts to the religion. Ieyasu – the first Tokugawa shogun – banned the practice of Christianity in 1614, and his forces drove the missionaries from the islands and killed any who refused to go. Japanese converts were forced to renounce Christianity, and those that did not were tortured, imprisoned, or executed. At the same time, the Tokugawa regime began to seriously restrict foreign traders as well as Japanese ships traveling to other lands. By the 1640s only a limited number of Dutch and Chinese ships were allowed to trade with the Japanese on the small island of Deshima.

EXAMINING THE EVIDENCE: JAPANESE ISOLATIONISM

Before the era from 1450 to 1750 the Japanese were isolated from other civilizations primarily by geography. The choppy waters of the Korean Strait made contact with or invasion from the mainland very difficult, as Kubilai Khan discovered when his attempted conquest of Japan failed in the late 13th century. By the 16th century, however, European adventurers had made their way to Japan, just as the shoguns were beginning to centralize political power.

When geography could no longer be counted on to maintain Japanese independence, the shoguns used their power to enforce restrictions on contact with all outsiders, including westerners. They expelled Catholic missionaries, forbid the practice of Christianity, limited the number of Dutch and Chinese ships, banned all Western books, and allowed foreigners to live and travel in very small restricted areas. These measures allowed the shoguns to concentrate on strengthening the internal control they had, although many daimyos were quite interested in and knowledgeable about European innovations. Partly as a result of these tactics of protecting themselves from the outside while building power within, Japan was poised to become a world power by the early 20th century.

Once outside influences were controlled, the Tokugawa set about consolidating their control over the daimyos. By 1750 the struggle for power between shogun and daimyos was still very central to the Japanese political system, but the shogun's court at Edo held more sway over its vassal lords than any court in previous eras. The Japanese also kept a close eye on European innovations through the small window of Dutch arrivals to Deshima. In contrast to the Chinese scholar-gentry of the mid-18th century, who dismissed European technology as the work of barbarians, the Japanese better understood the threat that these new visitors would pose to Asian lands in the 19ᵗʰ century.

CONCEPTS AND IDENTIFICATIONS

"alternate attendance"
bakufu
boyars
cossacks
daimyos
"floating worlds"
forbidden city
Hideyoshi, Toyotomi
Ieyasu, Tokugawa
Ivan III
Ivan IV
Jesuits
kabuki
Kangxi
kowtow
Ming Dynasty
Peter the Great
Qianlong
Qing Dynasty
queue
Ricci, Matteo
Romanov family
Table of Ranks
Tokugawa Shogunate
"Window on the West"

UNIT THREE QUESTIONS

Multiple-Choice Questions:

1. Which of the following political states was (were) MORE powerful in 1750 than in 1450?

   I. Britain
   II. Ottoman Empire
   III. Mughal Empire
   IV. Russia
   V. Japan

   a) I only
   b) I, II, and IV only
   c) II and III only
   d) I, IV, and V only
   e) IV and V only

2. All of the following were important events that affected the development of Christianity between 1450 and 1750 EXCEPT:

   a) the Protestant Reformation
   b) the initial split between Roman Catholicism and Eastern Orthodoxy
   c) missionary efforts by Jesuits in the Americas, China, and Japan
   d) the Catholic Reformation
   e) the promotion of Russian Orthodoxy by Russian tsars

3. Which of the following is true of both Spain and France in the period between 1450 and 1750?

   a) Both had strong parliaments.
   b) Both were stronger in 1750 than in 1550.
   c) Both practiced absolutism.
   d) Both preferred to finance exploratory voyages through joint-stock companies.
   e) Neither had significant land claims in the Americas.

4. Which of the following did NOT live during the period 1450 to 1750?

    a) Shi Huangdi
    b) Michelangelo
    c) Martin Luther
    d) Akbar
    e) Suleiman the Magnificent

5. Which of the following was MOST negatively affected by the infusion of New World silver into the world economy?

    a) Portugal
    b) Britain
    c) China
    d) Russia
    e) Ottoman Empire

6. Sati, the practice of a widow throwing herself onto her husband's funeral pyre, was most commonly practiced in

    a) the Ottoman Empire
    b) the Ming China
    c) Tokugawa Japan
    d) the Russian Empire
    e) the Mughal Empire

7. Which of the following was the LEAST politically unified during the 16th century?

    a) Renaissance Italy
    b) Ming China
    c) Spain
    d) the Mughal Empire
    e) the Ottoman Empire

(Questions 8 and 9 are based on the following map):

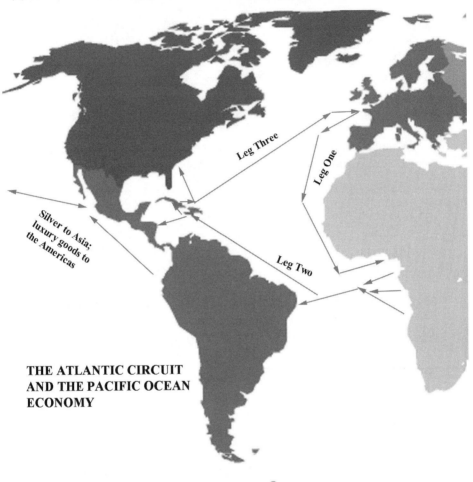

**THE ATLANTIC CIRCUIT
AND THE PACIFIC OCEAN
ECONOMY**

8. Which of the following was most commonly carried on "Leg Two" of the Atlantic Circuit?

   a) guns
   b) sugar
   c) tobacco
   d) slaves
   e) gold

9. Which of the following profited the MOST from the Atlantic Circuit during the 16ᵗʰ century?

   a) Kongo
   b) France
   c) Spain
   d) the English colonies in North America
   e) the Swahili states

10. In Russia, the position that most closely matched the position of "daimyo" in Japan was

   a) tsar
   b) boyar
   c) vizier
   d) *opricniki*
   e) patron

11. Which of the following correctly described Britain during the early 18ᵗʰ century?

   a) It had established colonies in South America.
   b) It had established a constitutional monarchy.
   c) It controlled trade on the Indian Ocean.
   d) It was politically and economically weaker than Spain.
   e) It had established a stable and growing trade with Japan.

12. Most sugar plantations in the New World were located in

   a) the southern British colonies and Mexico
   b) the Caribbean and Peru
   c) the French colonies in North America and Brazil
   d) New Granada and La Plata
   e) the Caribbean and Brazil

13. Which of the following had the LEAST real political power during the era 1450-1750?

   a) the Spanish king
   b) the Ottoman sultan
   c) the Safavid shah
   d) the Japanese emperor
   e) the Russian tsar

14. Most people that lived in the Safavid Empire during the 16th century were

    a) Sunni Muslim
    b) Shi'ite Muslim
    c) Sikhs
    d) Hindu
    e) Buddhist

15. The architecture depicted in the photo above is best described as

    a) Medieval Gothic
    b) Arab Islamic
    c) Persian Islamic
    d) Hindu
    e) Renaissance

16. Which of the following is an accurate comparison of the African slave trade to the Middle East and the African slave trade to the Americas?

    a) The overall number of slaves that went to the Middle East was much larger.
    b) Women made up a larger percentage of the total slave trade to the Americas.
    c) Women made up a larger percentage of the total slave trade to the Middle East.
    d) A larger percentage of the slaves that went to the Middle East were destined for work in plantation fields.
    e) The Africans controlled the slave trade to the Americas; Middle Easterners controlled the slave trade to the Middle East.

17. Which of the following rulers most directly applied sea-based technology to his land-based empire?

a) Kangxi
b) Suleiman the Magnificent
c) Abbas the Great
d) Peter the Great
e) Babur

"I do not feel obliged to believe that the same god who has endowed us with senses, reason, and intellect has intended to forgo their use and by some other means to give us knowledge which we can attain by them."

18. The quote above from Galileo's *Letter to the Grand Duchess Christiana* in 1615 most directly reflects a belief in

a) scholasticism
b) humanism
c) Roman Catholicism
d) Orthodox Christianity
e) mercantilism

19. Which of the following had the highest social status in Latin American colonies?

a) peninsulares
b) creoles
c) Amerindians
d) mestizos
e) mulattos

20. Which of the following most accurately compares the relationship that English and Spanish colonists had with Amerindians?

a) Both English and Spanish colonists rejected Amerindian crops and planting techniques.
b) The English colonists dominated Amerindians; Spanish colonists pushed Amerindians out of the way.
c) The English colonists pushed Amerindians out of the way; the Spanish colonists put Amerindians to work for them.
d) English colonists were more likely to marry Amerindians than the Spanish colonists were.
e) The English colonists were more interested in converting Amerindians to Christianity than Spanish colonists were.

21. Which of the following areas was probably the destination for the MOST slaves during the period 1450 to 1750?

a) Brazil
b) British West Indies
c) French West Indies
d) Spanish America
e) Southern British colonies

22. The most vigorous protests to European slave raiding in Africa came from

a) Benin
b) Dahomey
c) Songhay
d) Asante
e) Kongo

23. The status of which of the following was in jeopardy in Japan by 1750?

a) the shogun
b) the emperor
c) samurai
d) merchants
e) daimyos

"…the entire kingdom is administered by the Order of the Learned, commonly known as the Philosophers. The responsibility for orderly management of the entire realm is wholly and completely committed to their charge and care…Their attitude toward the King, in exact obedience and in external ceremony, is a cause of wonderment to a foreigner."

24. In the passage above from his journal, Matteo Ricci is describing

a) Japan
b) China
c) Russia
d) the Inca
e) Renaissance Italy

25. Which of the following is the clearest example of Portuguese and Spanish ethnocentrism during the late 15th century?

a) the Treaty of Westphalia
b) the Edict of Nantes
c) the Protestant work ethic
d) the Treaty of Tordesillas
e) the Columbian Exchange

Free-Response Questions:

For all essays, be sure that you have a relevant thesis that is supported by historical evidence.

Document-Based Question: suggested reading time 10 minutes; suggested writing time 40 minutes

For the DBQ, be sure that you

- **Use all of the documents**

- **Use evidence from the documents to support your thesis**

- **Analyze the documents by grouping them in at least two or three appropriate ways**

- **Consider the source of the document and analyze the author's point of view**

- **Explain the need for at least one additional document**

1. Using the documents, analyze the concepts that rulers had of themselves, as well as expectations that subjects had of their rulers, during the period from 1450 to 1750. Identify one additional type of document and explain briefly how it would help your analysis.

Document 1

"As regards his knowledge of the outside world, he possesses information about the rulers (both Muslim and non-Muslim) of other countries, about the size and composition of their armies, about their religious faith and the organization of their kingdoms, about their highway systems, and about the prosperity or otherwise of their realms. He has cultivated diplomatic relations with most of the princes of the world, and the rulers of the most distant parts of Europe, Russia, and India are on friendly terms with him. Foreign ambassadors bearing gifts are never absent from his court, and the Shah's achievements in the field of foreign relations exceed those of his predecessors."

A description of Abbas the Great
by his secretary,
Eskander Bey Monshi

Document 2

"Let tyrants fear; I have always so behaved myself, that under God I have placed my chiefest strength and safeguard in the loyal hearts and good will of my subjects; and, therefore, I am come amongst you as you see at this time, not for my recreation and disport, but being resolved, in the midst and heat of the battle, to live or die amongst you all – to lay down for my God, and for my kingdoms, and for my people, my honour and my blood even in the dust. I know I have the body of a weak, feeble woman; but I have the heart and stomach of a king – and of a King of England too, and think foul scorn that Parma or Spain, or any prince of Europe, should dare to invade the borders of my realm; to which, rather than any dishonor should grow by me, I myself will take up arms – I myself will be your general, judge, and rewarder of everyone of your virtues in the field…"

Elizabeth I of England
An address to her army before
the attack by the Spanish Armada

Document 3

"I am God's slave and sultan of this world. By the grace of God I am head of Muhammad's community. God's might and Muhammad's miracles are my companions. I am Suleiman, in whose name the hutbe [sermon] is read in Mecca and Medina. In Baghdad I am the shah, in Byzantine realms the Caesar, and in Egypt the sultan; who sends his fleets to the seas of Europe, the Maghrib and India. I am the sultan who took the crown and throne of Hungary and granted them to a humble slave. The voivoda Petru raised his head in revolt, but my horse's hoofs ground him into the dust, and I conquered the land of Molda-via.

> An inscription by Suleiman the
> Magnificent on a Turkish citadel

Document 4

"God is infinite, God is all. The prince, as prince, is not re-garded as a private person; he is a public personage, all the state is in him; the will of all the people is included in his. As all perfection and all strength are united in God, so all the power of individuals is united in the person of the prince. What grandeur that a single man should embody so much!

Behold an immense people united in a single person; behold this power, paternal and absolute; behold the secret cause which governs the whole body of the state, contained a single head: you see the image of God in the king, and you have the idea of royal majesty. God is holiness itself, goodness itself, and power itself. In these things lies the majesty of God. In the image of these things lies the majesty of the prince."

> French bishop Jacques-Benigne
> Bossuet
> Court preacher to Louis XIV and
> tutor to Louis' son

Document 5

"Since our accession to the throne all our efforts and intentions have tended to govern this realm in such a way that all of our subjects should, through our care for the general good, become more and more prosperous. For this end we have always tried to maintain internal order, to defend the state against invasion, and in every possible way to improve and to extend trade. With this purpose we have been compelled to make some necessary and salutary changes in the administration, in order that our subjects might more easily gain a knowledge of matters of which they were before ignorant, and become more skillful in their commercial relations."

Peter the Great
Decree on the Invitation of
Foreigners

Document 6

"The extent of their kingdom is so vast. its borders so distant, and their utter lack of knowledge of a transmaritime world is so complete that the Chinese imagine the whole world as included in their kingdom. Even now, as from time beyond recording, they call their Emperor, Thiencu, the Son of Heaven, and because they worship Heaven as the Supreme Being, the Son of Heaven and the Son of God are one and the same. In ordinary speech, he is referred to as Hoamsi, meaning supreme ruler or monarch, while other and subordinate rulers are called by the much inferior title of Guam...Though we have already stated that the Chinese form of government. is monarchical, it must be evident from what has been said, and it will be made clearer by what is to come, that it is to some extent an aristocracy. Although all legal statutes inaugurated by magistrates must be confirmed by the King in writing on the written petition presented to him, the King himself makes no final decision in important matters of state without consulting the magistrates or considering their advice...."

Matteo Ricci, Italian Jesuit Priest
Description of China

Change-Over-Time Question: suggested writing time 40 minutes

2. Analyze the demographic changes that occurred in Europe, the Americas, and Africa between 1450 and 1750. Be sure to include causes for the changes that you analyze.

Comparison Question: suggested writing time 40 minutes

3. Compare the impact of technological developments of the period 1450-1750 on TWO of the regions below. Be sure to analyze both similarities and differences.

- Russia

- Ottoman Empire

- Sub-Saharan Africa

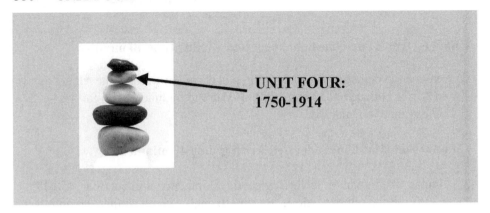

UNIT FOUR:
1750-1914

Whereas the era from 1450 to 1750 witnessed the rise of European powers, the era from 1750 to 1914 saw the hegemony of the West, which not only controlled the sea, but also much of the land space in the world. The meaning of "the West" also expanded during this period to include the United States and Canada, as well as Australia, and New Zealand. Other states grew in political stature from their first unifications in the previous era, particularly Japan and Russia. On the other hand, some of the oldest civilization areas, such as the Middle East and China, declined significantly between 1750 and 1914. Revolutionary change in political and economic organization and technological innovation also characterize the era, so that overall, the rate of change accelerated over that of previous eras, so that the world of 1914 was a very different place from the world of 1750.

Unit Four is divided into five chapters based on region and theme:

- Chapter 15 examines major political changes in the Atlantic world, including revolutions that transformed governments.

- Chapter 16 turns our attention to the Industrial Revolution, an important economic change that was one of the greatest "marker events" in world history.

- Chapter 17 looks at how both the economic and political transformations of the era impacted the Americas.

- Chapter 18 focuses on the decline of land-based empires in the Middle East and Asia and the rise of Russia and Japan.

- Chapter 19 analyzes the rise of imperialism, especially as manifested in the new British Empire.

The era from 1750 to 1914 has often been called "The Age of Revolutions," and for most people, the phrase brings to mind a vision of wars among competing militaries. However, other types of revolutions occurred during this era, most notably the Industrial Revolution that was not characterized directly by military conflict. In its broadest sense, a revolution, in contrast to reform, implies change at a basic level, and involves either a major revision or an overthrow of existing institutions. A revolution usually impacts more than one area of life. For example, the Industrial Revolution first altered the economies of Europe from manorialism to capitalism, but eventually changed their political systems, transportation, communications, literature, and social classes. Likewise, the French and American Revolutions were directed at the political systems, but they significantly changed the economies and societal practices of both countries, and spread their influence throughout the globe.

During the period 1750 to 1914 the long trend toward increasing interdependence among various regions of the world continued. By 1750 the two hemispheres had united through trade and cultural exchanges, but the frequency and intensity of international contact grew immensely by 1914. The era was characterized by many technological innovations that now spread rapidly to more areas of the world than had been possible before. As a result, even though this era is much shorter than the previous one – only 164 years – much change took place, and by 1914 the world was on the brink of even more changes as the old European habit of internal squabbling threatened to tear the new world order apart.

THE BIG PICTURE:
1750-1914

Important themes of the era from 1750 to 1914 that make it distinct from other eras include:

1. The world was dominated by western civilizations, which based their power on technological innovations of the Industrial Revolution. The new ability of western states to make international commercial contacts through the use of steamships, railroads, and telegraphs allowed them to not only increase wealth but also control other areas of the world.

2. Industrialization altered many areas of life other than the economy, including changes in population structures and movements. Industrialized countries experienced falling birth rates that have continued to the present day. Population movements included those from rural to urban areas and from less to more industrialized countries. Cities grew and family size began shrinking in industrialized countries. The environment, too, was significantly altered, as populations grew, factories were built, and air and water pollution became problematic.

3. Politically, the British parliamentary model spread widely as the empire grew, and democratic government forms were spawned by major revolutions in North America and France. Absolutism remained a viable form of government, but democracy based on Enlightenment ideals took root and began to spread.

3. Inequality, among both individuals and states, became a major source of interest, and reform movements attempted to address it. Slave systems were successfully dismantled by abolitionist movements, and other movements for equality began in industrialized states. Meanwhile, inequality among states grew as western countries gained power and economic resources at the expense of most other areas of the world, including Africa, the Middle East, and China.

CHAPTER FIFTEEN: POLITICAL REVOLUTIONS AND INDEPENDENCE MOVEMENTS IN THE ATLANTIC WORLD

By 1750 Europe had been economically, politically, culturally, and socially transformed, setting the stage for its ability to dominate the world in the era from 1750 to 1914. An important force at work was Enlightenment thought, which challenged traditional political regimes that rested on aristocratic privilege and the inherited power of monarchs. Throughout history settled agricultural societies had been ruled by kings, emperors, caliphs, khans, or sultans who did not claim to share power with anyone else. Their authority usually rested on military power, hereditary lines, and/or divine sanction, and even though their will was sometimes backed by law codes, rulers often had an extraordinary amount of power. Their authority was challenged when armies failed, or abilities to rule slipped, and their replacements were generally those who could restore the respect for authority that had been lost. Almost always, the ruler was expected to act in the best interest of his subjects, but he was held accountable only if his military and political skills did not withstand a direct challenger to the throne. The Enlightenment required people to rethink these basic premises about political power, and accept the notion that "subjects" are also citizens with individual rights of life, liberty, and property, as explained by European philosophers of the 17th and 18th century.

These radical thoughts came from people on both sides of the Atlantic, and they inspired political revolutions first in North America, then in France, and eventually in many other parts of the network that had formed around the Atlantic Ocean in the previous era. These revolutions influenced the development of strong national identities based on the abstract concept of the nation-state instead of the authority of a king.

THE AMERICAN REVOLUTION

The first major Enlightenment-inspired revolution occurred among the British colonies in North America, far from the Enlightenment's philosophical centers in Europe. The forces that led to the American Revolution were part of a wider mid-18th-century struggle for power between England and France that caused the two countries to fight the Seven Years' War on fronts not only in North America, but also in Europe and India. In North America the conflict was known as the **French and Indian War**, and even though the British won, their efforts had been extraordinarily expensive. To help pay for the war and the administration of their newly enlarged empire, the British Parliament levied new taxes on the colonies, an action that was quite unpopular in North America. The colonists were not only incensed by new laws, such as the Stamp Act of 1765, the Townshend Act of 1767, and the Tea Act of 1773, but by a strict enforcement of old navigation laws that had been widely ignored before. Their argument of "no taxation without representation" was testament to the power of Enlightenment thought: as British subjects, they should have a say in the creation of policies that affected their welfare. Tensions escalated as colonists boycotted British products, dumped British tea into Boston Harbor, and skirmished with British troops charged with keeping order in the area around Boston, where resistance was most evident.

On July 4, 1776 a representative delegation signed the **Declaration of Independence** that, from their point of view, severed ties to Britain and created an independent country. Since Britain did not agree, a war followed, fought entirely in North America, that eventually resulted in victory for the colonists and a humiliating defeat for one of the most powerful empires in the world. The last battle was fought at Yorktown, Virginia in 1781, where British forces surrendered to General **George Washington**. The peace treaty was finally signed in Paris in 1783.

Many factors shaped the success of the American Revolution, including the ability of the colonies to enlist the help of France in their struggle for independence. The revolutionaries were persistent, the British made some serious blunders, and French participation threatened to escalate the conflict, so in the peace treaty of 1783, the British government formally recognized American independence. In 1789 the new country, the United States, created a constitution based on Enlightenment principles, with separation of powers and checks and balances among the branches of government and written guarantees of individual liberties. Some limited voting rights gave the government a basis in popular sovereignty (rule of the people), and a **federalist system** was created in which political powers were divided between national and state levels in an effort to avoid concentrating control in the hands of one person.

Despite the revolutionary nature of the political changes in late 18th century North America, social changes were not as radical. Although a number of representatives at the Constitutional Convention in 1787 supported the abolition of the slave trade, the decision was to extend it for 20 years, and the institu-

ORIGINAL DOCUMENTS: THE AMERICAN DECLARATION OF INDEPENDENCE

The first paragraphs of the American Declaration of Independence provide an enduring example of the influence of Enlightenment thought on the political revolutions of the late 18th and early 19th centuries. Penned by Thomas Jefferson, John Locke's ideas are evident in his references to "the laws of nature," "natural rights," and the "consent of the governed." Below are some excerpts:

"We hold these truths to be self-evident; that all men are created equal, that they are endowed by their Creator with certain unalienable rights, that among these are life, liberty, and the pursuit of happiness.
That, to secure these rights, governments are instituted among men, deriving their just powers from the consent of the governed.
That whenever any form of government becomes destructive of these ends, it is the right of the people to alter or to abolish it, and to instutute new government, laying its foundation on such principles, and organizing its powers in such form, as to them shall seem most likely to effect their safety and happiness...when a long train of abuses and usurpations, pursuing invariably the same object, evinces a design to reduce them under absolute despotism, it is their right, it is their duty, to throw off such government, and to provide new guards for their future security."

tion of slavery was left intact. Voting rights were established by the states, but generally only property-owning free males could vote, leaving a large number of people without the franchise. Even so, the framework of the new political system, based on Enlightenment values of freedom and equality, provided the basis for extending individual rights in later years.

THE FRENCH REVOLUTION

A few years after the American Revolution, the Enlightenment spawned an important revolution in France. Whereas the American Revolution was fought in North America, with colonists challenging their mother country, the French Revolution was a civil war. No doubt, the French Revolution was inspired by the success of the American Revolution, particularly since French military personnel had fought in North America on the Americans' side. However, the roots of the French Revolution began to develop much earlier. Whereas the major goal of the American Revolution was independence (or liberty) from the mother country, the French Revolution directly challenged the country's basic political and social structure, demanding an end to absolutism and aristocratic privilege in France. The French slogan, "liberty, equality, fraternity [brotherhood]," reflects the multiple goals of their revolution that literally shook French society to its core.

ORIGINAL DOCUMENTS: THE DECLARATION OF THE RIGHTS OF MAN AND CITIZEN

Like the American Declaration of Independence, the French Declaration in 1789 was based on the ideology of John Locke. Thomas Jefferson, who by 1789 was the U.S. ambassador to France, advised the French as they constructed their document, as is evident from the following excerpts from the Declaration of the Rights of Man and Citizen.

"First Article: Men are born and remain free and equal in rights. Social distinctions may be based only on common utility.
Article 2. The goal of every political association is the preservation of the natural and inalienable rights of man. These rights are liberty, property, security, and resistence to oppression.
Article 3. The principle of all sovereignty resides essentially in the nation. No body and no individual can exercise authority that does not flow directly from the nation.
Article 4. Liberty consists in the freedom to do anything that does not harm another. The exercise of natural rights of each man thus has no limits except those that assure other members of society their enjoyment of the same rights. These limits may be determined only by law..."

Financially, the American Revolution directly contributed to the events that led to the French Revolution. The French government was already in serious debt when they decided to help the Americans, and the military expense involved may well have pushed the financial situation into crisis. For many years the French kings had resisted calling the Estates General – a medieval assembly of nobility, church officials, and **bourgeoisie** (middle class business and professional people) – because doing so would question the absolute rule of the king. However, the need for tax reform was so great that King **Louis XVI** called the assembly to meet in the spring of 1789. He hoped to convince the assembly to support new and increased taxes to pay the bills for multiple wars and an extravagant royal life style, but the middle-class representatives drew strength from gathering in one place, and decided to demand that the Estates General become a real parliament that shared power with the king. The bourgeoisie gained support from some of the nobles and clergymen and succeeded in out-maneuvering Louis in their demands for political power. A series of events over the summer of 1789, including a mob attack on a royal prison (the Bastille), involved ordinary Parisians, and the rebellion spread to the countryside. By October, a large group of women marched from Paris to the King's palace at Versailles, demanding that Louis and his wife, Marie Antoinette, pay attention to the fact that their children were starving. The king and queen remained prisoners in Paris until the new parliament, the **National Assembly**, called for their executions in 1793.

Like the Americans, the French wrote an Enlightenment inspired declaration, but unlike the American Declaration of Independence, the **Declaration of the Rights of Man and Citizen** was not intended to declare political independence, but rather to proclaim freedom of thought. Both documents affirmed the "natural rights" of citizens. The French also began writing a constitution for their new republic with the intention of providing a blueprint for a new political system that limited the power of the king and gave new authority to the National Assembly. However, the conflict did not end there for the French, but instead spawned internal disagreements about the type of government they wished to establish. On one side, the radical Jacobins stressed the Enlightenment value of equality, and on the other, the king's supporters were more interested in controlling the king's restrictions on personal liberties. When the radicals won the debate, a government was formed by Maximilien Robespierre that eventually decided that there was no place in the new republic for a king. After the king's execution, many others who were suspected of disloyalty to the new regime went to the guillotine, a device meant to provide more humane executions. This time of mass executions in 1793 and 1794 was known as the **Reign of Terror**, and it ended only with the guillotining of Robespierre himself.

Despite the contrasting early outcomes of the two revolutions, both played a role in the creation of a new type of political organization based on the concept of a **nation,** a group of people bound together by a common political identity. Common identities may be seen in earlier civilizations, such as the Chinese identity as "Han" or religious identities based on Islam, Christianity, or Hinduism. What was newly created by the revolutions of the late 18th century was the separation of political identity from loyalty to a king or ruler, replacing it with constitutions and laws that provided the necessary political unity. Ideally, political boundaries were drawn around cultural identities, so that "Americans" and "French" would each be united under their own government that presided over people with a common language and similar customs. One result was **nationalism,** or the sense of belonging and identity that distinguishes one nation from another. Nationalism has often been translated as patriotism, or the resulting pride and loyalty that individuals feel toward their nations. This transition from "Long Live the King!" to America's "My Country 'Tis of Thee!" and the rousing French anthem, "La Marseillaise," was an important "marker event" that eventually produced a world organized into competing nation-states, each with its own sense of righteousness and destiny.

EXAMINING THE EVIDENCE: "LA MARSEILLAISE"

Amour sacré de la Patrie,	Sacred patriotic love,
Conduis, soutiens nos bras vengeurs	Lead and support our avenging arms
Liberté, Liberté chérie,	Liberty, cherished liberty,
Combats avec tes défenseurs ! (bis)	Fight back with your defenders! (repeat)
Sous nos drapeaux que la victoire	Under our flags, let victory
Accoure à tes mâles accents,	Hurry to your manly tone,
Que nos ennemis expirants	So that our enemies, in their last breath,
Voient ton triomphe et notre gloire !	See your triumph and our glory!
Aux armes, citoyens !	To arms, citizens!
Formez vos bataillons !	Form your battalions!
Marchons, marchons !	March, march!
Qu'un sang impur	May tainted blood
Abreuve nos sillons !	Water our fields!
Aux armes, citoyens !	To arms, citizens!
Formons nos bataillons !	Let us form our battalions!
Marchons, marchons !	Let us march, let us march!
Qu'un sang impur	May tainted blood
Abreuve nos sillons !	Water our fields!

The French National Anthem. Above are the last verse and the chorus of the official French National Anthem, "La Marseillaise," written during the French Revolution. It reflects the spirit of nationalism that existed by the late 18th century and still thrives in France today. The complete song has many verses that have changed over time, but have shared one continuity – the necessity of bloodshed in support of one's country. A less gory version of the anthem is taught to young children.

THE IMPORTANCE OF NAPOLEON

As the Reign of Terror came to an end with Robespierre's death in mid-1794, France was in chaos. Thousands had been executed, and even more people had fled the country to seek refuge in Britain, other areas of Europe, or the Americas. To make matters worse, the French were at war with Austria, where Queen Marie Antoinette's brother ruled, and other monarchs in Europe were beginning to ally against the upstart republic. From the anarchy, a young army officer saw an opportunity he never would have had under the old regime, and he took it upon himself to save France, and in promoting himself, he played a pivotal role in the creation of the new political order, the world of nation-states. This man, **Napoleon Bonaparte,** was destined to be one of the most famous men in world history, partly because of the charisma of his leadership, but also because he inspired French nationalism that lived on long after he was gone.

The Rise of Napoleon

Napoleon, who grew up in Corsica (an island off the southern coast of France), would never have been more than a middle-rank officer had the revolution not come along because only French nobility could hold high military positions. Under the new egalitarian regime, he made a name for himself by successfully leading the army against Austria, invading Egypt to gain access to the Red Sea, and threatening British control of the sea route to India. He was invited to join the five-person Directory that governed France after Robespierre's death, but when Austria, Britain, and Russia formed an alliance in 1799 to attack France, he took the opportunity to stage a coup d'etat, name himself "consul" (as in Ancient Rome), and eventually crown himself emperor in 1804.

Napoleon's Rule

Once Napoleon gained control of France, military victories made him a popular leader, and he stabilized the country by rolling back some of the most radical measures passed during the Reign of Terror. For example, Robespierre had seized property from the Catholic Church and had even tried to eliminate it as an anti-egalitarian force in the republic. Napoleon retained church property for the state, but he recognized Roman Catholicism as the preferred religion of France, and he agreed to pay the clergy as employees of the state. He reduced the National Assembly to a rubber stamp, but he confirmed religious freedom, and guaranteed equal rights for men, though not for women, in new laws organized as the **Napoleonic Code.** Meanwhile, he began aggressively attacking countries around him, and by 1810 he was at war with every other major power on the continent. At its height, this new French Empire directly held or controlled as dependent states most of western Europe. One testament to his power was the elimination of the Holy Roman Empire, a configuration that was never to appear again on a map of Europe. His drive to power was halted in 1812 when he unsuccessfully attacked Russia, where most of his men died from the cold, not from Russian bullets. The tactical blunder of marching an army toward Moscow so far from his supply lines resulted in tremendous loss of military personnel, and he also met stiff resistance from Spanish rebels on the opposite side of Europe. The British led the alliance against Napoleon that captured Paris in 1814, and finally defeated him in 1815 at the Battle of **Waterloo** (present day Belgium). He was banished first to Elba in the Mediterranean Sea, and then to St. Helena, a small island in the Atlantic, where he died several years later.

Napoleon's Empire at its Height. By 1812 France controlled Europe to the borders of Russia, either through conquest, agreement, or alliance. Napoleon's decision to attack Russia was a tactical error that stopped the expansion of France and proved to be the turning point for his decline.

The Aftermath

Diplomats from major European powers met at the **Congress of Vienna** to decide what to do with France once Napoleon was exiled. The decisions made there put in place a **balance of power** in Europe that stabilized the continent for more than fifty years. France lost most of its new territories, and the countries around it were made stronger with a tactic called "the encirclement of France":

the Austrian Netherlands was united with the Dutch Republic to form a single Kingdom of the Netherlands, the German Confederation united previously disparate German states, and Switzerland was recognized as an independent and neutral nation. The French monarchy was also restored, with Louis XVI's brother crowned as Louis XVIII. In an effort to balance power, Britain gained new colonial territories and Russia gained substantial holdings in Poland.

PERSPECTIVES: ALEXIS DE TOCQUEVILLE ON AMERICAN DEMOCRACY

In the 1830s a young Frenchman named Alexis de Tocqueville became quite interested in the question of why a democratic republic took root in America much more readily than it did in France. In his classic book, *Democracy in America,* which reflected a great deal of respect for the young United States and its people, Tocqueville identified several reasons:

1) Abundant and fertile soil – America's vast, open lands created many opportunities for people to acquire property and make a living. Success was possible by just moving west.
2) No feudal aristocracy – In contrast to France, no feudal aristocracy monopolized the land, or imposed taxes or legal restraints on commoners.
3) Independent agriculture – The nation was populated with small, independent farmers, unlike the traditional European arrangement of landless peasants with no control over their land.
4) Individualism – Tocqueville identified "moral and intellectual characteristics" of Americans that supported a democratic republic. He saw the value of individualism as a central characteristic – the belief that individuals are responsible for their own actions and well-being.

If we compare the results of the two revolutions – American and French – as of 1815, the contrast appears to be stark. By 1815 America again had defended itself successfully against Britain in 1812, and had settled in with its new form of government to concentrate on a major expansion west. France had slipped into chaos, turned to a military general who became emperor, and finally returned to a monarchy. Indeed, it seemed as if the experiment had failed in France. However, the new nationalism sparked by the revolution and then by Napoleon did not die, but instead lived on as a strong movement in France to restore the republic. The republicans battled the supporters of the king, and the country teetered back and forth between republican government and monarchy, with the last king forced to flee the country in 1848. The republic that followed was taken over by Napoleon's nephew, Napoleon III, who restored the empire for about 20 years, until France suffered a humiliating military defeat by Prussia. A shaky republic emerged in 1871, but even by the end of this era – 1914 – the French were still suffering the effects of radical shifts back and forth between very different styles of government.

Despite the problematic effects of revolution on French political stability, the impacts of the two revolutions reverberated far beyond the United States and France. In Latin America independence movements against Spain and Portugal succeeded, and in Europe new political ideologies clashed with old to inspire revolutions in Greece and the Balkans. The importance of the revolutions was summed up by Ralph Waldo Emerson when he described the first fighting at Lexington that started the American Revolution in 1775 as the "shot heard round the world."

19TH-CENTURY IDEOLOGICAL INFLUENCES

In Europe, three conflicting ideologies shaped the 19th century after the fall of Napoleon:

- **Conservatives** wanted to roll back the clock to the days before the French Revolution to restore the monarchies in all countries, including France. These voices prevailed at the Congress of Vienna and remained strong, especially in Russia, Prussia, and Austria.

- **Liberals** were interested in checking the power of monarchs and increasing parliamentary authority. They supported the original goals of the French Revolution, including a government defined by constitutional law and the guarantee of personal freedoms of religion, press, and assembly. Most liberals were **bourgeoisie** – middle class professionals or businessmen – who wanted their views to be represented in government and their economic goals to be unhampered by government interference.

- **Radicals** emphasized equality more than liberty, with most advocating wider voting rights and more direct government participation for ordinary people. Many promoted social reforms to help the poor gain some measure of economic security. A small branch of radicals attacked private property as the source of inequality and urged the government to actively work to increase equality. This branch of radicalism gave inspiration to Karl Marx, sometimes known as the father of communism, by the mid-19th century.

Nationalism was often a theme that both liberals and radicals supported, and political protests against the traditional monarchies were common, even in the more conservative states. A revolution broke out in Greece in 1820, as nationalists successfully gained independence from the Ottoman Empire, inspiring a gradual dismantling of the Ottoman Empire in the Balkans. Another French Revolution broke out in 1830 that ousted Louis XVIII and replaced him with a king who was more willing to share power with the National Assembly. Also in 1830, the Belgian Revolution resulted in the creation of the independent country of Belgium.

An important result of nationalism was the unification of two areas of Europe into centralized political states: Germany and Italy. After gaining liberal support, **Count Camillo di Cavour** of the Italian state of Piedmont formed an alliance with France that allowed him to challenge Austrian control of northern Italian states in 1858. The war inspired other Italian leaders, including Giuseppe Garibaldi in the south, to join him in uniting most of Italy under King Victor Emmanuel II in 1861. About the same time, **Otto von Bismarck**, the prime minister of Prussia, instigated a series of wars that expanded Prussian power in Germany. Like Cavour, Bismarck used growing nationalist trends to consolidate people who had not been politically united before. For example, he attacked Denmark to take two heavily German provinces from Danish political control in the name of German nationalism. His consolidation of large parts of what had once been the Holy Roman Empire reinforced German pride, especially after he attacked and soundly defeated France in the Franco-Prussian War 1871. The Prussian military had been powerful for many years, and Bismarck added support from liberals by seeing that the new German Empire had a national parliament with a lower house directly elected by the people. His nod toward the conservatives was an upper house that favored state governments. Remarkably, Bismarck pulled many of the ideological strands running through 19th century Europe together by "blood and iron," the latter a reference to one of Germany's natural resources that fueled German prosperity. Under Bismarck's leadership, Germany began to change the balance of power in Europe in a way that challenged the traditional strength of France of Britain.

The three ideologies – conservatism, liberalism, and radicalism - would interact throughout the 19th century all over Europe, even in areas that did not have official revolutions, and would eventually create by the early 20th century the environment that would again lead European states to quarrel as they had done for centuries, but this time with more far-reaching consequences.

REVOLUTIONS IN THE CARIBBEAN AND LATIN AMERICA

Enlightenment values appealed to many people throughout Europe and the Americas, especially after the successes of the American and French Revolutions. The earliest response was in Haiti when slaves in the French colony of Saint-Domingue rebelled against their masters, and later revolutions broke out all across Latin America, so that by 1830, most Spanish and Portuguese colonies had gained their independence.

The Haitian Revolution, 1789-1804

In 1789 the French colony of Saint-Domingue was one of the wealthiest in the Americas, with its large plantations producing sugar, cotton, indigo, and coffee. However, the turmoil in France destabilized the established order as French colonists interpreted Enlightenment values in different ways. For the large plantation owners, revolutionary trends were an opportunity to gain home rule and greater economic freedom, or perhaps even independence, as the United States had achieved. However, another group called **gens de couleur** – mixed-race small planters and urban merchants – sought political equality with whites. They did not seek freedom for slaves because many owned slaves themselves, but they wanted to end the discrimination that they believed kept them from the prosperity that the large plantation owners enjoyed. The tension between the aristocratic planters and the gens de couleur was heightened by the message from France that all slavery was illegitimate. When a leader of the gens de couleur returned from a mission to France, he was murdered by the planters, setting off open warfare between the two groups.

As slave owners fought among themselves, slaves saw their opportunity to rebel, and under the leadership of **François Dominique Toussaint L'Ouverture,** a former domestic slave, the rebellion spread throughout the colony. Plantations were destroyed, crops were burned, and slave owners were killed. Toussaint was a talented leader who organized the rebellion and built a strong, disciplined army. By 1797 his forces controlled most of Saint-Domingue, and in 1801 he produced a constitution that granted citizenship and equality to all residents of the colony, although he did not declare independence from France. These events were occurring at the same time that Napoleon was reaching the height of his power, and Napoleon responded by sending French troops to restore order in Saint-Domingue. Toussaint was arrested and sent to France where he died in prison. Despite the loss of their leader, the slave forces gained the upper hand in their struggles against the French soldiers, who died in large numbers when yellow fever swept through their ranks. In 1804 Toussaint's successors declared independence, making Haiti the first independent black republic in the Western Hemisphere. Unfortunately, independence did not restore stability: the economy had been destroyed, public administrators had been corrupted by years of disorder, and violence and economic problems continued in Haiti throughout the 19th and 20th centuries.

Wars of Independence in Latin America

By 1800 the creoles (Europeans born in Latin America) far outnumbered the peninsulares (Europeans born on the Iberian Peninsula), who still ruled the Spanish and Portuguese colonies. Many creoles were wealthy and powerful owners of plantations and ranches, and others were well-to-do urbanites involved in trade or business. Like their counterparts in the British North American colonies, the creoles resented control by representatives from their mother countries. Many were well read in Enlightenment philosophy, and like the bourgeoisie in France, wanted political rights that were equivalent to their economic accomplishments. As a result, creoles were attracted to the idea of political independence as the British colonies in North America had achieved, but they were not particularly interested in social egalitarian reform, such as the revolution in Haiti had aimed for. Between 1810 and 1825 creoles led revolutionary movements all over Latin America that resulted in their taking political control of the newly independent countries.

The precipitating event for most of the revolutions was Napoleon's invasion of Spain and Portugal in 1807, and the rebel groups that resisted his control created instability on the Iberian Peninsula, especially since Napoleon named his brother Joseph as the king of Spain. In Latin America **juntas,** or organizations of military leaders, were set up to rule in the name of the deposed King Ferdinand of Spain, but soon the juntas – which were mainly staffed with creoles – had their own agendas to follow.

Spanish South America

Independence movements in Spanish South America started in two places: northern South America near Caracas and southern South America near Buenos Aires. The first one began in 1810 under the leadership of **Simón Bolívar,** a wealthy Creole military officer who raised enough support between 1817 and 1822 to win a series of victories against the Spanish in Venezuela, Colombia, and Ecuador. His junta spurred large numbers of loyalists to rally freed blacks and slaves to defend the Spanish Empire. Bolívar was able to eventually defeat the Spanish, partly through military skill, and partly through the force of his personal ability to hold the loyalty of his troops, attract new allies, and build coalitions. Until 1830, the area that he controlled was called Gran Colombia, and Bolívar dreamed of someday uniting all South Americans under one government. However, political and regional interests led to the breakup of Gran Colombia, and to the south, another junta leader, **José de San Martín** was rising in Argentina. Buenos Aires was a growing trade city whose residents resented

Spanish restrictions, and Martín, like Bolívar, hoped to unite many people under him. His army united Chileans and Argentines who crossed the Andes Mountains to attack Spanish strongholds in Chile and Peru. Just as Bolívar could not keep regional factions from forming, San Martín was not able to stop splits among Argentina, Uruguay, Paraguay, and Bolivia. By 1825, all of Spanish South America had gained its political independence, and all the new states founded republics with representative governments.

Independent Nations of the Americas. By 1830 most of the American colonies were independent nations. Exceptions were British North America (now Canada); British Guiana, Dutch Guiana, and French Guiana in northern South America; Cuba, the Bahamas, Jamaica, Puerto Rico and Trinidad in the Caribbean; and Patagonia in southern South America, which was disputed by Argentina and Chile.

Brazil

The movement for independence took a different path in Brazil, partly because of the large number of slaves that worked the sugar, cotton, and cacao plantations. Although the planters sometimes resented Portuguese control of trade and political decisions, they were more afraid of a general slave uprising such as had occurred in Haiti. As a result, potential movements inspired by Enlightenment ideas were unsuccessful until Napoleon's troops invaded Portugal in 1807, causing the entire Portuguese royal family to flee the country to find a haven in Brazil. The family ruled in exile from Rio de Janeiro, and all government business was conducted from this new capital city for the Portuguese Empire. Seeing the rising tide of independence movements in Spanish America, King Pedro I took the initiative in declaring Brazil an independent empire in 1822. Of course, the empire was a monarchy, but Pedro was willing to concede many liberal principles, including a written constitution in 1824 which provided for an elected parliament. He granted personal liberties, but he made some enemies when he openly opposed slavery. After he ratified a treaty with Britain in 1831 to end Brazilian participation in the slave trade, slave owners cried out against him, and military losses to control neighboring Uruguay made his rule more difficult still. He was forced to abdicate to his five-year old son, Pedro II, who became emperor after a nine-year regency and ruled until he was overthrown by republicans in 1889.

Mexico

Napoleon's invasion of Spain also caused unrest in Mexico, the largest and richest of the Spanish colonies in the Americas. The Mexican Revolution began in 1810 when a priest, **Miguel Hidalgo y Costilla,** called upon his parishioners to rise against Spanish officials. In the tradition of priests as champions for the rights of natives, Father Hidalgo was particularly charismatic, and tens of thousands of Amerindians joined his movement. Their targets were not only Spanish officials but also many wealthy creoles who owned mines and ranches that exploited workers. As a result, the creoles supported Spanish authorities and turned on Hidalgo's masses, capturing and executing Hidalgo in 1811. Despite the death of its leader, the popular rebellion continued for another few years under the guidance of another priest, José María Morelos, who was caught and executed in 1815. At that point, events from Europe again intervened when a military revolt in Spain weakened the king and the central government. Not wanting to be cast with Spanish officials, a creole military officer, **Augustín de Iturbide,** struck an agreement with the rebellious peasants, and with combined forces declared Mexico's independence in 1821. However, Iturbide was proclaimed emperor of Mexico, a conservative solution that greatly offended liberals, and he was overthrown by the military and executed. This rapid turnover of leadership In the first few years of Mexico's independence created an atmosphere of instability and military coup d'etats that have characterized Mexico's political system ever since.

COMPARISONS: MOTIVES FOR REVOLUTION

Almost all the revolutions of the late 1700s and early 1800s in the Atlantic world were rooted in Enlightenment philosophy. However, each revolution emphasized different aspects of the ideology, resulting in some complex, contrasting motivations to both lead and support the insurgencies. For example, the main motivation of colonists in the American Revolution was independence from Britain, and its leaders emphasized the Enlightenment value of liberty. French leaders valued liberty, but the radicals that took over the French government during the Reign of Terror pushed for equality among male citizens and sought to rid the country of all vestiges of the old unequal social order, including the nobility and the Catholic Church. In Latin America, the creole leaders generally were attracted to the same goals that appealed to the colonists in North America - freedom to conduct their own affairs, free of Spanish or Portuguese control. In contrast, Toussaint L'Overture led a slave rebellion in Haiti, emphasizing the inequality of that social system and reflecting another aspect of Enlightenment thought. Mexico's complex sequence of events that led to its independence in 1821 weaves several Enlightenment themes: oppression of Amerindian people, creole desires for independence, and the motivation to establish a republican government. In contrast to France, where the Catholic Church was seen as a cause for unequal stations in life, in Mexico the cry for equality first came from a Catholic priest, Father Hidalgo.

REVOLUTIONARY IDEALS: SLAVERY AND WOMEN'S RIGHTS

Enlightenment-inspired revolutions generally resulted in some measure of liberty and/or equality for middle class and elite males, but applying the concept of "natural rights" to women and slaves was another challenge that called for even more serious breaks with past traditions. In both cases, solutions did not come immediately during or after the revolutions, but as a result of reform movements that achieved their goals gradually over time.

The Abolitionist Movement

The movement to end slavery began in the late 1780s, as **abolitionists** who blended Enlightenment thought with principles of Christianity sought to end the slave trade. The earliest push came from members of the British Parliament who succeeded in passing legislation in 1807 to end the slave trade. Other countries soon followed with anti-slave trade legislation: the United States in 1808, France in 1814, the Netherlands in 1817, and eventually Spain in 1845. The British even sent their navy to patrol African ports to enforce their law, although the illegal slave trade continued for a number of years until governments took action to outlaw the practice of slavery as well. In Haiti slavery ended with the success of the slave rebellion in 1804, and many newly independent countries in Latin America passed laws forbidding slavery. Eventually slavery was ended by all the Atlantic states by the end of the 19th century, with Britain banning slavery throughout its empire in 1833. The United States ended slavery in 1865, and Brazil was the last major American state to ban slavery in 1888.

Once slavery was abolished, political equality did not follow immediately. Property requirements kept most former slaves from voting, and even though constitutions were changed – as in the United States – economic, political, and social inequality continued to be issues for minorities of African background for years to come. Although the slave trade and the slave system were banned, they were not totally abolished and are still practiced today. However, the abolitionist movements of the 19th century did put an end to the extreme reliance on slave labor that characterized the era from 1450 to 1750 and set the stage for later equality movements of the 20th century.

Women's Rights

The Enlightenment philosophes generally focused on natural rights for men, and did not question traditional role for women in family and society. Even early advocates of women's rights, such as British writer **Mary Wollstonecraft,** emphasized the importance of educating women to make them better mothers and wives. During the revolutions of the late 18th and early 19th centuries, women generally played supportive roles to men by sewing uniforms or flags – like Betsy Ross in the American Revolution – and by managing affairs at home while men were fighting or organizing governments. In France, the fabled Parisian women's march to Versailles to protest their families' hunger was an important step in achieving the goals of the revolution. Under radical rule, the French republican government opened public education to girls, granted women property rights, and legalized divorce. However, under Napoleon's rule, women lost these new rights, and women in the Americas were not granted them until much later.

Although the immediate responses to revolutions were disappointing to women's rights reformers, the movement persistently continued throughout the 19th century. Many women who supported the abolitionists' cause also worked for women's equality, especially focusing on gaining suffrage, or the right to vote. Even though the movement received support in Europe and North America, very few of its goals were achieved until the 20th century. Some inroads were made in providing more formal education for women, but very few women were allowed to work as professionals, and in no countries were they allowed to vote.

EXAMINING THE EVIDENCE: ABOLITIONISTS AND FEMINISTS

Elizabeth Cady Stanton and Lucretia Mott were two Americans who took Enlightenment ideals seriously in their support for the international abolitionist movement of the early 19th century. Both women attended the International Anti-Slavery Convention in London, England in 1840, Stanton with her delegate husband and Mott selected as a delegate in her own right. However, the convention refused to allow them to participate in the meetings, and instead, required them to sit in a roped-off section away from the men's view. One prominent male abolitionist, William Lloyd Garrison, was so offended by the convention's decision that he refused to take his seat, and instead sat with the women.

Stanton and Mott were impressed by the irony of this situation and decided to focus their attention on the fledgling women's rights movement instead. As a result of their efforts, a conference of feminists was called in 1848 at Seneca Falls, New York (Stanton's hometown) that produced the famous Declaration of Sentiments, a document for women's rights based on the Declaration of Independence.

CONCEPTS AND IDENTIFICATIONS

abolitionists
balance of power
Bismarck, Otto von
Bolívar, Simón
bourgeoisie
Cavour, Count Camillo di
Congress of Vienna
conservatives, liberals, radicals
Declaration of the Rights of Man and the Citizen

federalist system
French and Indian War
gens de couleur
Hidalgo Y Costilla, Father Miguel
Iterbide, Augustín de
junta
Louis XVI
Napoleon Bonaparte
Napoleonic Code
nation, nationalism
National Assembly
Reign of Terror
San Martín, José de
Tocqueville, Alexis de
Toussaint L'Ouverture, François Dominique
U.S. Declaration of Independence
Washington, George
Waterloo, Battle of
Wollstonecraft, Mary

CHAPTER SIXTEEN:
THE INDUSTRIAL REVOLUTION

In the period between 1450 and 1750 Europeans used many technological in-novations to capture control of most of the world's waterways, a substantial accomplishment that tilted the balance of power among world civilizations in their favor. During the late 18th century westerners continued to build their knowledge, so that they laid the basis for a great technological revolution that brought about more economic change between 1750 and 1850 than had oc-curred in all of world history. The Industrial Revolution, along with political transformations brought about by Enlightenment ideals, eventually impacted virtually every part of the globe in almost all areas of life.

BRITISH BEGINNINGS

Simply defined, the **Industrial Revolution** was an economic change in the source of energy for work. Before the Industrial Revolution, energy was pro-vided primarily through human and animal effort. Civilizations had always organized around this basic principle, and had built economic, social, and politi-cal structures to support it. Agricultural societies had used many arrangements: serfs had toiled for lords; small farmers had labored in their own fields; govern-ments had ordered workers to construct public buildings; and plantation owners had bought and sold people to work for them. The substitution of human and animal labor by machines changed these basic building blocks of civilization forever, and although it did not eliminate old forms of work entirely, the rela-tionship of people to their work was fundamentally altered. Early inventions that changed the source of energy first used moving water and then steam to operate large machines in mills and factories, and the experimentation began first in Britain.

Industrialization consisted of two types of changes: technological innovation and organizational changes. Technological innovation made it possible to produce goods by machines rather than by hand, and organizational changes moved the place of work from homes and farms to factories where workers were brought to run the new machinery. Instead of agricultural needs determining the division of labor, work was divided according to what was necessary to make the machinery operate the most efficiently. Because the machines grew larger, more complex, and more expensive, large businesses with plenty of capital were encouraged to form. This process began in Britain because many changes in Europe during the 1450 to 1750 era paved the way for the new systems to succeed.

Why Britain?

Why did the Industrial Revolution begin in Britain? Some reasons include:

1) **A well-developed middle class and capitalist structure** – Through years of trading and entrepreneurship, Britain's middle class, or **bourgeoisie**, was large and growing. The land owning lords were no longer the wealthiest people in the realm, and urban areas were the well-established homes for entrepreneurs who often had connections in many other lands. The English colonies were spread around the world, and even with the loss of the North American colonies, trade with them did not end. The English national bank had been in existences since the early 17th century, and the English stock markets provided a flexible way to raise capital. Enlightenment ideals had inspired people to pursue individual goals, and widely available printed materials had increased literacy rates, making the achievement of their goals more likely.

2) **Agricultural improvements** – Before the Industrial Revolution occurred, an Agricultural Revolution increased food production dramatically. One important change was the acceptance of the potato that had arrived in Europe from the Andes region of South America during the 16th century. In cool, humid regions like Ireland, potatoes often yielded two or three times more food per acre than traditional European crops like wheat and oats. Another factor was the **enclosure movement,** in which landowners claimed (or enclosed) commons that had in the past been open to all. With these new lands, fenced to keep others out, they experimented with crops and livestock, and they discovered many new techniques to improve crop yields, including the use of manure fertilizer, crop rotation, and the use of hybrid seeds. Many ordinary tenant farmers or sharecroppers were left without land, and they moved to urban areas just as businessmen were looking to fill their new factories with laborers. As a result, a ready urban labor supply was at hand.

3) **Population increase** – Despite the overall tendency for industrialization to encourage smaller families, other forces led to population increase in the early days of the Industrial Revolution. Partly because food produc-

tion increased, Britain's population soared during the 18th century, probably about 15 percent per decade, creating not only a larger labor force but also a larger consumer market for goods that industry produced. More dependable food supplies and better job opportunities led people to marry at earlier ages and have more children. All the reasons for the population increase are not clear, but the death rate steadily fell and the birth rate steadily rose in Europe after 1750, with particularly large growth rates in England.

4) **Transportation** – At a time when water transportation was far cheaper and more efficient than land travel, Great Britain had the advantages of an indented coastline, navigable rivers, and a growing network of canals. Britain's relatively flat topography and relatively short distances between places made moving goods across land not as difficult as in most places.

5) **Stable government** – Britain's government had developed into a stable constitutional monarchy by the mid-1700s, in contrast to many countries – such as France – that were experiencing revolutionary upheavals in the late 18th and early 19th centuries. Parliament had developed into two bodies, with a House of Commons where merchants and businessmen were well-represented. The government was generally supportive of entrepreneurial efforts and allowed a great deal of private control over business matters.

6) **Early inventiveness** – The English were the first to experiment with new energy sources, and it was an Englishman – James Watt – that built the first steam engine. This important invention became the standard form of mechanical energy during the 19th century, and it spawned other inventions that revolutionized energy production. Once the inventions began, England had a head start in their use and improvement.

7) **Raw materials** – A key ingredient for providing the fuel for the new steam engines was coal, and England's coalfields were plentiful. As the Industrial Revolution developed, factories were built in areas with abundant coal and iron-ore deposits, and Britain's healthy supply of coal meant that much industry could develop in Britain.

Early Technological Innovations

One of the earliest technological experimentations in Britain was **mass production** – the making of many identical items by dividing the work into simple repetitive tasks – of pottery. China and Korea had produced fine porcelain for many years, but the high cost of transporting it to European countries meant that only the wealthy could buy it. Especially as the English developed a taste for tea and coffee sweetened with sugar from the Caribbean, the demand increased for dishes that wouldn't spoil these treats. The first to develop a pottery business that specialized in mass produced porcelain was **Josiah Wedgwood,** who divided the work among his employees to maximize efficiency. For example, some unloaded the clay, others mixed it, some specialized in pressing the pieces or putting handles on cups. He also used molds for creating identical dishes, a much faster process than shaping each dish by hand. The Wedgwood factory grew to employ several hundred workers, and Wedgwood "China" became popular on the European continent as well.

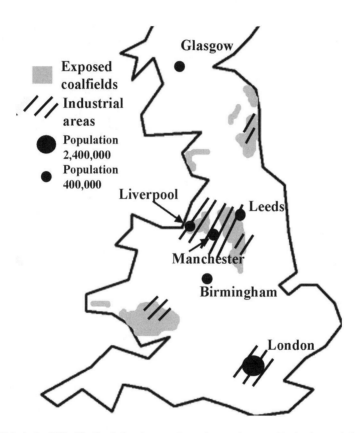

Industrial Britain by 1850. The first industries arose in northern and western England around abundant coal and iron-ore deposits. Railroads connected the major cities to one another and to the coast for shipping.

Another industry that experimented with more efficient, less expensive ways to produce goods was textiles, particularly cotton. Cotton had been produced by hand in China, India, and the Middle East for many years, but like porcelain, it was expensive for Europeans to import, although people often preferred it to wool. Beginning in the 1760s a series of inventions made it possible to produce cotton cloth in Britain, although the climate was too cool to actually grow the plant. The first was the spinning jenny that twisted cotton fibers into thread. Once thread production speeded up, inventors were inspired to come up with machines to weave the threads into cloth, and even more inventions for perfecting the quality of thread and cloth produced. By the 1830s large English textile mills were performing the entire process of transforming raw cotton into printed cloth at lower prices for the consumer because of the large quantities they were able to produce. **Eli Whitney's** American invention of the cotton gin (a device that separated the cotton fibers from the boll, or seed) in 1793 increased the amount of cotton that farms in the American South were able to produce, so America became a major supplier to the British textile mills.

The iron industry also experienced a major transformation during the 18th century after Abraham Darby discovered that coke (a purified form of coal) could be used in smelting iron, and since coal was abundant in Britain, the innovation made it possible to mass-produce iron in Europe. Although coke-produced iron was not as high quality as had earlier been crafted using charcoal, it was much less expensive, and iron became an important component for buildings, machines, firearms, and **interchangeable parts** – standardized parts that could be used in all machines produced. The ability to repair a complex machine by replacing only the defective part with an identical part produced for that reason was critical in keeping factories running efficiently.

Probably the most important invention of all was the **steam engine,** a substitute for energy produced by humans, animals, wind, and water. In 1764 **James Watt** from Glasgow devised a way to efficiently produce steam from coal for engines that had multiple uses. The steam forced a piston to turn a wheel, whose motion could be used to power machines in many industries Watt's steam engines were used in the textile industry, where they greatly increased productivity. During the early 19th century inventors produced steam engines that could power locomotives and ships that revolutionized transportation because railroads and steamships dramatically lowered transportation costs. Much larger cargoes could be carried, and the amount of time required for travel was cut significantly. Thousands of miles of railroad tracks were built, first in Britain, and eventually all over Europe, the United States, and other parts of the world. Railroads triggered industrialization in new areas because they provided efficient transportation of goods to market. Steamboats greatly facilitated travel on rivers in the United States, and in 1838 two steamers crossed the Atlantic on steam power alone. Sailing ships remained important means of water transportation throughout the 19th century, but the new steamships helped to keep pace with the rapid growth of world trade.

Communications were revolutionized by the simultaneous development of the **electric telegraph** in Britain and the United States, although the invention in Britain required five wires for transmission. The American Samuel Morse introduced a code of dots and dashes that could be sent on a single wire, and in 1843 he built a telegraph line between Washington and Baltimore. In 1851 a telegraph cable was laid across the English Channel from England to France, and eventually a network of cables connected the entire globe.

The Factory System and the Evolution of Big Business

The Industrial Revolution was fueled by technological innovations, but new ways of organizing work were equally important in the transformation of economies. Most of the new machinery was too large and expensive to be used at home according to the old putting-out system, so it made sense to centralize it close to the areas where it was produced. The workers were brought to the machines, each doing a specialized task in a highly coordinated production process. Managers now could directly supervise work and demand discipline from workers in ways that were not possible under the earlier arrangement. The factory system created a strict division between workers and managers, as well as a small group of factory owners who bought the equipment and machinery. As the wealth of the latter group increased, the pay of workers generally did not, and the gap between the rich and poor grew substantially. The managers often became a part of the urban middle class, although they might aspire to factory ownership if they could only raise the substantial amount of capital necessary. The new division of labor on the factory floor, where each worker performed the same task over and over, was often quite tedious, and workers who had been artisans before now had no place in the factory setting. The jobs were broken down into such small tasks that unskilled workers – or even children – with low wages could perform them. Managers were expected to pressure workers to speed up production, often at the expense of their safety. The new industries transformed England's landscape. Cities grew dramatically, especially in the Midlands of north-central England, where a belt of major coalfields extended from west to east.

Joint-stock companies had already promoted large capitalist enterprises during the era from 1450 to 1750, so they laid the foundations for the development of **corporations,** private businesses owned by many individual and institutional investors who provided necessary capital by buying stocks representing shares in the company. When the corporation made a profit, investors received a dividend, and if a corporation went bankrupt, shareholders lost their investment, but none of their other assets could be taken away. By the late 19th century,

ORIGINAL DOCUMENTS: ADAM SMITH ON THE IMPORTANCE OF DIVISION OF LABOR

In his classic book, *The Wealth of Nations* (1776), Adam Smith explained the transformational potential of technological innovations, especially as they are allowed to exist within a free market system of capitalism. In the excerpt below, he gives an example of the power of division of labor.

"[In pin-making] one man draws out the wire, another straightens it, a third cuts it, a fourth points it, a fifth grinds it at the top for receiving the head; to make the head requires two or three distinct operations; to put it on is a peculiar business, to whiten the pins is another; it is even a trade by itself to put them into the paper; and the important business of making a pin is, in this manner,divided into about eighteen distinct operations...ten persons, therefore, could make among them upwards of forty-eight thousand pins in a day. Each person, therefore, making a tenth part of forty-eight thousand pins might be considered as making four thousand eight hundred pins in a day... But if they had wrought separately and independently, and without any of them having been educated to this peculiar business, they certainly could not each of them have made twenty, perhaps not one pin in a day...In every other art and manufacture, the effects of the division of labour are similar to what they are in this very trifling one..."

Reference: *The Wealth of Nations,* Adam Smith (London: Everyman's Library, M. Dent & Sons, Ltd., 1910), Book I, Chapter 1.

corporations owned most businesses that were the building blocks of the Industrial Revolution, such as railroads, steel, iron, and armaments. As corporations grew, competition often became quite cutthroat, and contests began to try to drive others out of business, resulting in **monopolies,** or giant corporations that controlled a single industry or production process. Meanwhile, banks and brokerage firms grew in importance because they provided the corporations with services they needed in order to grow.

THE SPREAD OF THE INDUSTRIAL REVOLUTION

Industrialization took place primarily in Britain during the late 1700s and early 1800s, but by the mid-1800s, it had spread to France, Germany, Belgium, and

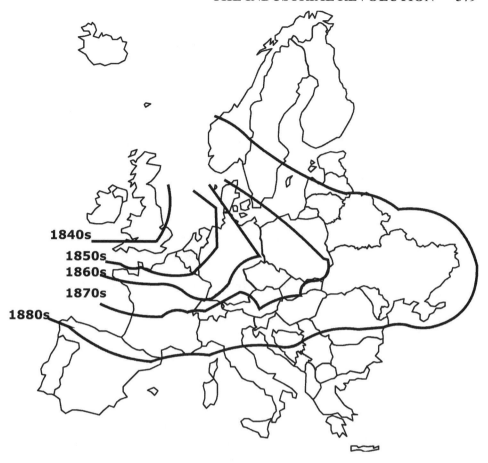

The diffusion of the Industrial Revolution across Europe. The Industrial Revolution began in England in the late 18th century, and diffused across Europe, following belts of coalfields and iron ore.

the United States. By then, the continent had settled down after the disruptions of the French Revolution and the Napoleonic wars, which had done away with many previous trade barriers between countries. Industrialization on the continent first appeared in Belgium, which had rich coal deposits to fuel machinery for new glass, iron, and textile factories. From Belgium, an industrial belt developed that followed coalfields that stretched from northern France and the Netherlands through Germany to Poland by the 1870s. By 1830 French businesses were adopting the new mechanized production methods, and industry continued to grow during the 19th century as railroads were built across the country. Germany developed industry later, partly because of political instability caused by competing German states. Once Germany united as a country in 1871, rapid industrialization followed.

Industrialization also diffused westward across the Atlantic to North America, where natural resources and available land space encouraged economic development. The first U.S. textile mill was built in Rhode Island in 1791 by Samuel Slater, a former worker in an English factory. The U.S. government protected the industry through embargoes on European trade, and the industry grew accordingly. Before 1860 industry concentrated on processing North America's abundant food and lumber resources. Iron and steel industries rapidly developed during the late 19th century. Most early industry flourished along the coast of the northeastern United States, where despite a lack of abundant natural resources, the large populations from Boston in the north to Washington D.C. in the south provided a large market for consumption of industrial products. New York City became one of the world's great ports, with a huge skilled and semiskilled labor force, and a fine natural harbor for **break-of-bulk** (transfer of cargo from one type of carrier to another) from ships to trains and trucks and vice versa.

After 1870 industrialization spread to two other important areas of the world: Russia and Japan. In Russia the tsarist government promoted industrialization by encouraging the construction of railroads to link the far-flung parts of the empire. The most ambitious was the Trans-Siberian Railroad line, which spanned the distance from Moscow east to the Pacific Ocean. The line made it possible to access the coal and iron resources in Siberia and also provided a transportation link between western Europe and east Asia. By 1900 Russia had well developed coal, iron, oil, and steel industries. In Japan, the government that followed the Tokugawa Shogunate pushed industrialization by modernizing iron foundries and dockyards. The new government also built railroads, opened mines, organized a banking system, and became much more involved in international trade. By 1900 Japan was the most industrialized area in Asia and had laid the foundation for becoming a world power in the 20th century.

SOCIAL EFFECTS OF EARLY INDUSTRIALIZATION

The reorganization of work impacted human lives far beyond the technological innovations that people learned to work with. One important change was the movement of many people in industrializing countries from rural to urban areas. Large landowners who experimented with new crops also adopted farm machinery that increased production, making small farms less viable. Families were disrupted as young people from the farms flocked to the cities, where everyday life was not always an improvement over rural living. As workers moved to be close to the factories, many neighborhoods became overcrowded, and sanitation and crime became huge problems that the city governments were not prepared to cope with. Middle-class families tried to escape the pollution and crowded living space of the cities by moving farther away, forming the basis for a new style of suburban living.

The New Urban and Rural Environments

Long before the Industrial Revolution began, very few wilderness areas were left in western Europe because almost all land was altered by agriculture. The most serious problem of the period from 1450 to 1750 was deforestation, especially as people cut timber to build ships and construct merchant areas for the growing trade that characterized the era. In this era, deforestation pressures were relieved in Europe because coal and iron ore were replacing wood as energy sources. In the United States, the environment changed rapidly as populations increased and moved west. East of the Appalachian Mountains, pioneers cut down and burned trees to build houses, and then a few years later, moved further west to start the whole process again. In the American South, forests were cut down to plant cotton, a crop that rapidly drained nutrients from the soil, and the depleted land was deserted to plant more cotton on new soil.

Industrialization caused cities and towns in western Europe and the United States to grow rapidly. In 1700 London had about 500,000; by 1850 its numbers had grown to about 2,400,000 – the largest city the world had ever known. Other large cities were Manchester and Liverpool in England, and New York City in the United States. The inequality caused by industrialization was evident as the wealthy built fine homes and patronized museums, theaters and churches. On the other hand, as people migrated to cities to labor in the factories, developers often built inexpensive, shoddy row houses for them, and these tenements became overcrowded. In these neighborhoods, sanitation and safety became big issues, and air and water pollution plagued the areas around the factories. Diseases, such as small pox, dysentery, and tuberculosis, often became epidemic.

Social Class Distinctions

In rural societies, wealth was based primarily on land, so the basic division of social classes was almost always drawn between those who owned land and those who did not. In the new industrial order, the wealthiest people were the captains of industry who headed big businesses. This new elite came to challenge the traditional aristocrats, such as Europeans who held titles of nobility. The middle class grew substantially with industrialization – the owners of small businesses, factory managers, accountants, and service professions like doctors and lawyers. Their comfortable life styles were made possible by the wealth generated from industry, although they did not have as much wealth as the big businessmen. The lower classes in urban areas were the laborers who worked in the factories, and a substantial number also worked in mines owned by the elite. Most had fewer skills than artisans of earlier periods, and they generally worked for low wages and lived in crowded urban housing or in company-towns in mining areas. Their work hours were long, and usually all able-bodied family members worked outside the home, including women and children.

Family Life

Families from all social classes faced adjusting to a major change: the separation of the work place from family life. Farm families generally worked together, all on the same land, so that work and family life blended together and everyone understood the work that all family members did. In industrialized society, people had to leave home to go to work, and were often gone all day, and then came home to another world at night. This new arrangement profoundly affected the ways that family members interacted, often causing them to lead separate lives. Reports that described children toiling long hours in British textile factories alarmed the British Parliament so that by the 1840s laws were passed to regulate child labor and eventually outlaw it.

Social class greatly affected family life styles and the roles that men and women played in society. Among the working classes, both men and women worked outside the home for wages so meager that the family could not survive without two incomes. In a sense, this situation gave men and women "equality," except that women's wages were generally lower than men's. Many lower-class women also became domestic servants for the growing middle classes and elites, so that they were still doing "women's work," but just in someone else's home. Gender roles in middle-class and elite families were quite different. Successful businessmen generally enjoyed an elevation in status, since their responsibilities gave them a great deal of economic power. One source of pride for such a man was the fact that his wife did not have to work and that his income alone was enough to keep the family comfortable. Middle-class men in particular were interested in self-improvement, and so reading books, attending lectures, and supporting churches became some of their leisure-time activities. They sometimes tried to instill these values in their workers who often did not see the point, especially if their jobs were composed of tedious chores created by the new division of labor at factories and businesses. From their perspective, leisure time was better spent in escapist activities, like attending sporting events and spending evenings in bars and pubs. These developing differences in social values tended to deepen the social class distinctions that were already clearly delineated at work.

For the middle classes the gender distinction between work and family was complete, and more than any other group, middle-class women were limited to the roles of wife and mother. They enjoyed considerable luxuries, with homes full of manufactured items and staffed with servants, and a chief goal was for women to provide private refuge at home for men from the rough and tumble world of business. Middle-class women were often responsible for handling spending accounts and family correspondence, but their positions as keepers of the hearth led to idealized concepts of women as paragons of virtue, and all that is good and pure in the world. This separation of women from the world outside the home and the creation of an insulated world of home, servants, children, and management of the family's social life is sometimes called the "**cult of domesticity.**"

The Demographic Transition

An important demographic change came about in the industrialized West as families adjusted to industrialization. Birth rates began to fall as children lost their economic value as workers on the farm, and instead became family members that had to be supported by adult workers. In the middle classes, the value of self-improvement was instilled at an early age, and mothers became most responsible for the emotional and social development of the children. Instead of working, middle-class children spent their time being educated, making them dependent on their parents for a longer period of time. The expenses of this life style encouraged husbands and wives to limit the number of children that they had, creating a **demographic transition** during the second half of the 19th century. Low birth rates combined with low death rates from improved hygiene and health to create a fairly stable population level in most western countries. By the end of the century, many people – even those in the working class – in western countries enjoyed a life style above the subsistence level. Diets and housing improved, and deaths of infants and children declined significantly, partly because of better hygiene during childbirth and better care at home. Medical advancements – such as Louis Pasteur's discovery of germs – allowed doctors and nurses to develop more sanitary health care.

REACTIONS TO INDUSTRIAL SOCIETY: REFORM AND RADICALISM

One ideological reaction to industrialization was **laissez-faire,** a policy most famously espoused by **Adam Smith** in *The Wealth of Nations,* written in 1776. Smith believed that the force behind the economy should be the "invisible hand" of competition, not the forceful hand of government. Under Smith's system, the laws of supply and demand should govern the marketplace. If demand increases, prices rise, and producers scramble to meet the demand. Once demand is met, supplies naturally dwindle, since people aren't willing to pay for the product. To Smith, any government control is "interference" with supply and demand. This theory led governments to dismantle previous regulations, and the booming population meant that the supply of labor went up, so wages were low, and the gap between the rich and poor grew.

Socialism

In opposition to laissez-faire inspired practices, a ideology called **socialism** grew, and its advocates worked to combat the economic inequalities that industrialization had brought. The term "socialism" first appeared around 1830 in the form of **utopian socialism,** which sought to set up ideal communities based on political, social, and economic equality. Early socialists, such as Charles Fourier and Robert Owen, planned model communities based on cooperation, not competition, and no one was rich or poor, but basic needs were met for all. Experimental communities grew up in many countries during the 19th century, but most ultimately failed while life in urban industrialized areas continued on, causing other reformers to turn to other means to address the problems.

The most radical of the socialists was probably **Karl Marx,** a Germany theorist who believed that revolution – not reform – was the only solution to the misery and unfairness that resulted from industrialization. Often known as the father of communism, he addressed the issues in a sweeping interpretation of history and vision for the future, *The Communist Manifesto,* written in 1848. He believed capitalism – or the free market – to be an economic system that exploited workers and increased the gap between the rich and the poor. He believed that conditions in capitalist countries would eventually become so bad that workers would join together in a revolution of the **proletariat** (workers), and overcome the **bourgeoisie**, or owners of factories and other means of production. Marx envisioned a new world after the revolution, one in which social class would disappear because ownership of private property would be banned. According to Marx, communism encourages equality and cooperation, and without property to encourage greed and strife, governments would be unnecessary, and they would wither away. He developed his views fully in a longer work called *Das Capital.*

Labor Unions

A less radical, yet controversial, reaction to industrialization was the formation of labor unions. The old guilds from medieval times had been dismantled during the era from 1450 to 1750, leaving no organizations for workers in place during the early years of industrialization. Starting in the 19th century, labor unions formed to protect the rights of workers within the new work arrangements that industrialization had brought. Through most of the 19th century, both employers and governments considered labor unions to be illegal on the grounds that they restrained trade. One of the most controversial union tactics was the strike, when union members refused to work until their demands for wages and/or working conditions were met. Employers tried to hire replacements, who often got into violent confrontations with strikers, and governments were enjoined to order union members to go back to work.

Gradually, unions gained power and respectability and were instrumental in gaining better working conditions and pay for workers by the early 20th century.

ORIGINAL DOCUMENT:
THE COMMUNIST MANIFESTO
BY KARL MARX

Karl Marx is one of the most influential theorists in modern history, and his socialist views, often referred to as "communism," have shaped the development of many nation-states and the direction of world politics. One of his basic ideas was that the private ownership of property is the root of all inequality, and to create a just society, it should be eliminated in favor of communal sharing. Below are the closing statements to his famous 1848 work, *The Communist Manifesto.*

"In short, the Communists everywhere support every revolutionary movement against the existing social and political order of things. In all these movements, they bring to the front, as the leading question in each, the property question, no matter what its degree of development at the time. Finally, they labor everywhere for the union and agreement of the democratic parties of all countries.
The Communists disdain to conceal their views and aims. They openly declare that their ends can be attained only by the forcible overthrow of all existing social conditions. Let the ruling classes tremble at a communist revolution. The proletarians have nothing to lose but their chains. They have a world to win.
Proletarians of all countries, unite! "

Reference: *The Communist Manifesto,* Karl Marx and Frederick Engles, 1848. trans. by Samuel Moore, 1888.

Like political revolutions, the Industrial Revolution brought changes that impacted Europe greatly in almost all realms of life. Because of ties to Europeans that started in the 1450 to 1750 era, the Americas were tightly bound to influences from Europe, and during the 1750 to 1914 era, events in the Americas – such as the American Revolution and technological inventions in the United States – reverberated in Europe. By 1914 industrialization had clearly transformed the western world, and the innovations to the ways that economic life was organized had far-reaching implications for virtually every corner of the globe.

PERSPECTIVES;
SAMUEL GOMPERS CALLS
FOR A STRIKE

One of the most significant leaders of the labor movements in the United States was Samuel Gompers, the president of the American Federation of Labor for all but one year between 1886 and 1924. Gompers was not a theoretical social reformer, but instead emphasized practical tactics to gain higher wages and shorter hours for workers. He saw the strike as the main weapon of workers, as reflected in the speech excerpted below.

"I have never declared a strike in all my life. I have done my share to prevent strikes, but there comes a time when not to strike is but to rivet the chains of slavery upon our wrists...Yes, Mr. Shirtwaist Manufacturer, it may be inconvenient for you if your boys and girls go out on strike, but there are things of more importance than your convenience and your profit. There are the lives of the boys and girls working in your business...If you [the workers] had an organization before this, it would have stood there as a challenge to the employers who sought to impose such conditions as you bear...This is the time and the opportunity, and I doubt if you let it pass whether it can be created again in five or ten years or a generation. I say, friends, do not enter too hastily but when you can't get the manufacturers to give you what you want, then strike. And when you strike, let the manufacturers know you are on strike!...If you strike, be cool, calm, collected, and determined. Let your watchword be: Union and progress, and until then no surrender!"

Reference: "Speech at a Cooper Union Meeting," New York City, first published in the *Call,* November 23, 1909.

CONCEPTS AND IDENTIFICATIONS

bourgeoisie
break-of-bulk
The Communist Manifesto
corporations
cult of domesticity
demographic transition
electric telegraph
enclosure movement
Gompers, Samuel
Industrial Revolution

interchangeable parts
laissez-faire
Marx, Karl
mass production
monopolies
proletariat
Smith, Adam
socialism
steam engine
utopian socialism
Watt, James
The Wealth of Nations
Wedgewood, Josiah
Whitney, Eli

CHAPTER 17:
THE AMERICAS
AFTER INDEPENDENCE

The paths of the two Americas – North America and Latin America – had diverged almost from the beginning of their colonization, with different European powers controlling each region. North America was explored by the French and English, and the English eventually drove the French out so that the British colonies had room to grow westward. Once the colonies gained their independence to become the United States, their economic and cultural ties to Britain insured that industrialization would easily diffuse to their lands during the 19th century. On the other hand, the newly independent nations of Latin America had traditions rooted in two waning European powers – Spain and Portugal – and would not take so naturally to the new world order, making it a struggle for them to prosper.

THE RISE OF THE UNITED STATES

The American Revolution was born in the midst of a great competition between England and France for world power. The two countries had been rivals for many years, but by the late 18th century the world was their stage, and the colonies' ability to gain independence came largely because their leaders understood the rivalry and acted to capitalize on it. The new nation – the United States – had much internal development at hand in the early 19th century and was preoccupied with westward expansion and political stability, and an ocean separated them from Europe. As a result, Americans tried their best to stay out of European affairs, a philosophy reflected in George Washington's farewell address to the nation in 1797. In 1823 this **isolationist policy** was written down in the **Monroe Doctrine,** which warned against European meddling in the Americas. Meanwhile the nation expanded rapidly, with the Louisiana Purchase in 1803, the annexation of Texas in 1845, and the acquisition of California and other western territories after a war with Mexico in 1848. By mid-century, the country extended coast to coast, and the new lands provided opportunities for Americans to prosper. Immigration from Europe intensified during the 1840s, especially from Ireland – suffering from the potato famine – and Germany as a result of political turmoil. These new immigrants also provided labor necessary for industrialization as technological innovations took place in the United States, as well as Britain.

ORIGINAL DOCUMENT: WASHINGTON'S FAREWELL ADDRESS

When George Washington stepped down as the first president of the United States, he allowed a Philadelphia newspaper to publish his Farewell Address. Most of it addressed domestic problems, but the part relating to foreign affairs is best known. In the excerpts below, notice how Washington lays the groundwork for isolationist foreign policy and an emphasis on the internal development of the United States.

"Against the insidious wiles of foreign influence...the jealousy of a free people ought to be *constantly* awake, since history and experience prove that foreign influence is one of the most baneful foes of republican government...

The great rule of conduct for us in regard to foreign nations is, in extending our commercial relations, to have with them as little political connection as possible...

It is our true policy to steer clear of permanent alliances with any portion of the foreign world, so far, I mean, as we are now at liberty to do it...in my opinion it is unnecessary and would be unwise to extend them..."

Reference: The America Spirit, Vol. I, Thomas A. Bailey and David M. Kennedy eds. (Lexington, Mass.: D.C. Heath, 1984), pp. 153-155.

The Civil War

The most important "marker event" for the United States during the 19th century was the Civil War, fought between 1861 and 1865. The war pitted northern states versus southern, and had complex causes based on conflicting regional interests. The northern economy was growing increasingly industrial, and most farmers worked small parcels of land that did not provide much food for export or trade. On the other hand, the South had large plantations that grew tobacco, sugar, and increasing amounts of cotton for export. Some small farmers did agricultural work as well, but the economy was dominated by export-oriented plantations that were worked by slaves. The abolitionist movement grew stronger in the North, and put pressure on government officials to end slavery. Whether or not they would have succeeded without a war is not known because it was the secession of the southern states from the union that sparked the conflict. From the South's point of view, the central government was dominated more and more by the North, undermining southern interests. From the North's point of view, the war was fought to keep the country united, although many supported it because they opposed slavery. The North's victory resulted in the emancipation of the slaves, although their civil rights were severely restricted by state laws and local ordinances passed all over the South during the late 19th century. Another important consequence was that the United States remained as one country, a fact that almost certainly laid the groundwork for its rise as a world power during the 20th century.

Economic Development

The Civil War accelerated industrialization in the United States, a process that had been well underway by the time the war began in 1861. Heavy industry developed, especially in the North, to support the war effort, including not only armaments and other supplies for the army, but also railroad building to facilitate transportation to war fronts. After the war was over, rail lines were built that connected the country coast to coast, encouraging settlement in the west. Increasing mechanization of farming meant that newly settled farmland could be more productive, and settlers experimented with new agricultural methods to adjust to different climates in the country's interior. The armaments manufacturers began to seek foreign markets once the war was over, and other industries followed them as they sought to broaden their horizons. The booming industry attracted a new wave of immigrants from southern and eastern Europe starting in the 1880s, providing the necessary labor to keep industry growing.

Diplomacy and Cultural Development

During the late 19th century, the traditional U.S. foreign policy of isolationism began to change. The defeat of Spain in the Spanish American War in 1895 brought some new territories in the Caribbean and the Pacific under U.S. control, although overseas holdings were nothing like those of Britain, France, and Germany. Theodore Roosevelt, president of the U.S. between 1901 and 1909, understood the importance of sea power, and he promoted an expansion of the navy and the building of the U.S.-controlled Panama Canal, which opened to traffic in 1908 and allowed the U.S. navy to more easily travel from coast to coast. However, despite these changes, isolationism remained a strong thread in American diplomacy, and the United States had very little influence outside the Western Hemisphere by 1914.

American culture had its own uniqueness, but it remained quite dependent on European culture throughout the 19th century. Many artists and writers, such as James McNeill Whistler and Henry James, studied in Europe, and often lived there for long periods in their lives. **Romanticism,** an important movement in arts and literature, began in Europe and spread to the United States. Romanticism was a reaction to the Enlightenment's emphasis on rational thought, and it held that emotion and impressions shape the human experience at very deep levels. Artists and novelists sought to touch human emotions by depicting beauty, passion, or tragedy, and romantics and their successors often broke the rules set during Enlightenment times. On the other hand, advances in science kept the rationalist tradition alive, and during most of the 19th century, Europeans took the lead. An important milestone came in 1859 with the evolutionary theory of **Charles Darwin,** who argued that all living species had evolved from earlier species through time as they adapted to changes in the environment. Darwin's ideas contradicted traditional Christian beliefs that humans were created by God, and the debate spread to greatly impact U.S. society. The social sciences continued to rely on the scientific method for their development, although a Viennese physician, **Sigmund Freud,** greatly altered psychology and related fields with his theories of the irrational, subconscious mind. Although the U.S. had its own technological and scientific innovators, it remained dependent on European culture and science throughout the 19th century.

THE DOMINION OF CANADA

In contrast to the United States and most of the countries of Latin America, Canada did not experience a war for independence. It officially remained a British colony until 1867, but independence came gradually through a series of agreements with Britain on general principles of autonomy. Although most Canadians were ethnically English, a significant minority were descendants of French settlers, and the divisions between the two groups remain problematic for Canadian identity today. Their ability to agree to remain as one country was due partly to the fear of takeover by the United States, and with good reason, since U.S. forces invaded Canada (without success) during the War of 1812. The British imperial governors of Canada did not want a repeat of the American Revolution, so they expanded home rule in Canada and permitted the provinces to govern their own internal affairs.

As the United States pushed westward, its rapid expansion encouraged Britain to grant independence to Canada. The British North America Act of 1867 joined Quebec, Ontario, Nova Scotia, and New Brunswick together as the **Dominion of Canada,** a self-governing political system still officially tied to Britain. Each province had its own government, with a provincial legislature and a lieutenant governor representing the British crown, and all provinces were governed by a central government headed by a governor-general who acted as the British monarch's representative. Like the United States, Canada was designed to be a **federalist system,** with powers shared by the central government and its sub-units, but unlike the United States, Canada became a **parliamentary system,** with a prime minister from parliament, rather than a **presidential system,** with a strong president with powers separated from those of Congress.

Canada in the 19th century. The Dominion of Canada was created in 1867 by uniting New Brunswick, Nova Scotia, Quebec, and Ontario under a central government in Ottawa. British Columbia and the Northwest Territories (Yukon split off in 1898) joined in 1870, followed by other provinces as the Canadian Pacific Railway encouraged the settlement of the interior. The railroad connected to existing lines in the east, and extended all the way to Vancouver in the west.

After its independence was established, Canada moved to expand its territories to the Pacific Ocean, just as the United States had done. Within a few years, all of British North America had been incorporated into the Dominion, and by 1885 the new lands were joined by a transcontinental railroad that stretched from sea to sea, encouraging settlement in the interior lands that eventually became the provinces of Saskatchewan and Alberta. As a result of a program of economic development known as the National Policy, Canada actively encouraged immigration, with millions coming from eastern Europe and Asia, and industry and agriculture grew along the Canadian Pacific Railroad that linked east to west.

LATIN AMERICA

After independence Latin American countries faced many of the same challenges that the United States and Canada faced in establishing stable political and economic systems. Simón Bolívar had dreams of uniting a large amount of territory under a strong central government. Latin American countries put written constitutions and elected assemblies in place. However, unlike the United States and Canada, which both succeeded in uniting territory from the Atlantic to Pacific Oceans, Latin American countries fragmented and had problems establishing the legitimacy of their central governments.

Political Fragmentation and Constitutional Experiments

The wars of independence at first encouraged a sense of solidarity in Latin America, but after the defeat of the colonial powers, the unity dissolved. Simón Bolívar's Gran Colombia split into three parts – Venezuela, Colombia, and Ecuador – and Central America broke away from Mexico and formed a union, which itself fragmented in 1838. Other parts of Latin America dissolved into numerous independent states. One reason for the fragmentation was **regionalism**, or identity with a particular region rather than a large area. Regionalism had threatened the United States and Canada, but they had been able to keep their citizens united. The United States had fought its bloody Civil War to establish unity, and Canadians had united in fear of what might happen if they didn't – takeover by the United States. The North American colonies also had experienced a great deal of self rule before their independence, and the mother country – Britain – had established the tradition of democratic assemblies. As a result, both countries found the necessary stability to stay together. In Latin America, it was a different story. The leaders of their independence movements were creole elites who often controlled regions, and ordinary people usually did not participate in public affairs. Even though the elites usually espoused Enlightenment values and republican principles in theory, they had little experience in putting their principles into practice. Anyone who disagreed with decisions made by the new leaders had no way to voice opposition except to rebel, and so Latin America was plagued with violence and instability.

All of the new countries in the Americas experimented with constitutions, often having to rethink their concepts of representative governments. For example, the first constitution in the United States, called the Articles of Confederation, failed to keep order in the new country, and with the threat of the country falling apart, a new constitution was put in effect in 1789. In Latin America, most countries went from one constitution to another as leaders and citizens with little experience with representative government struggled to find something that worked. The weakness of central governments invited challenges from other elites, and so the disorder continued with little relief. Men with charismatic influence often rose to power through the force of their personalities, leading to **personalist rule** that gave them authoritarian control over their followers. Regional elites gathered large armies behind them to challenge others, and became known as **caudillos,** or independent military leaders with large personal followings. One example was **Juan Manual de Rosas**, who rose from the pampas of Argentina to attempt to restore order in a country divided between the ranchers of the Pampas and the urban elite of Buenos Aires. He first subdued other caudillos in the pampas and eventually came to rule the country, but only as a despot with his own personal army. His force of personality and the use of terror kept him in charge throughout his lifetime, but republican ideals were lost in the process. The pattern of government takeovers by personalist rulers led to even more instability in the form of frequent coup d'etats, especially when the rulers died, either by natural or unnatural means.

The Catholic Church also played a role in creating political instability in Latin America, dividing conservatives – who saw a role for the church in politics – from the more secular liberals. The scenario had been a part of the French Revolution, with the wealthy church holding a great deal of land and other assets. Many revolutionists came to see the church as just as much of an obstacle to equality as the nobility had been. For example, in Mexico the church had long had a say in politics, and its properties accounted for almost half of all the productive land. President **Benito Juárez,** a personalist leader with liberal, secular leanings, started **La Reforma,** a movement that aimed to limit the power of the military and the church in the name of equality, or "land and liberty," according to its slogan. It limited the privileges of priests and military elites, and confiscated their lands to redistribute more equitably among the people. La Reforma did not end political instability, however, and Mexico fell under the dictatorship of Porfirio Díaz, another military general, who restored many privileges to the elites. As the 20th century opened, Mexico was in chaos, with a revolution touched off by the overthrow of Díaz and the rise of competing caudillos that fought one another for decades.

Economic Dependency

Just as lack of political institutions led to the instability of Latin American governments, the absence of experience with capitalist privately-based economic systems limited economic development and placed the countries at a disadvantage in trading with other areas of the world, especially where capitalist structures supported industrialization. In the early days of colonization, Spain and

Portugal could not meet the demands in their colonies for manufactured goods, so they allowed them to trade with other countries. In contrast, Britain followed the policy of mercantilism more closely, requiring its colonies to trade only with the mother country, even though the policy was not always strictly enforced. Latin American elites had no incentive to develop capitalist markets because they profited from European trade and investment, with most of the money going into their pockets.

COMPARISONS: PERSONALIST LEADERS IN NORTH AMERICA AND LATIN AMERICA

Both North America and Latin America had personalist leaders who relied on their charismatic abilities to mobilize and direct followers rather than on the authority of constitutions and laws. However, Latin America's slow development of stable political institutions made personality politics more influential than they were in North America. For example, Andrew Jackson rose in the United States to become a military general known for his ability to inspire devotion from his men and also for his impatience with civilian authorities. His popularity and charisma led to his election as president, where he challenged constitutional limits on his authority, and substantially increased the powers of the presidency. However, he bowed to firmly established precedents to step down after two terms as president, so the rule of law remained in place. Like Jackson, José Antonio Páez rose from poverty to become a military leader, but his path was quite different because his home country of Venezuela had no strong political institutions in place. Páez led the independence movement of Venezuela against the efforts of Simón Bolívar to include it as part of Gran Colombia, and Páez' success put him in control of the government as a dictator for eighteen years. Despite the fact that his programs did little to help the masses, he remained wildly popular by skillfully portraying himself as a common man. Venezuela had no political institutions in place to check his ambitions, so in contrast to Jackson, he ignored republican principles and was unrestrained by Venezuela's ineffectual constitution.

Foreign investment started rather slowly because the Latin American market was relatively small, but Britain, France, and eventually the United States began investing more heavily in the last half of the 19th century. For example, British investors helped to develop the meat industry in Argentina after the invention of refrigerated cargo ships that allowed meat to be transported safely to distant markets. Cattle and sheep raised in the pampas region were shipped for export to urban areas like Buenos Aires, where migrant laborers worked to prepare them for overseas shipment. The Argentine economy was stimulated by the business since it provided employment for many people, but the British controlled the profits and reaped most of the benefits of the trade. Another example of foreign investment occurred in Mexico during the dictatorship of **Porfirio Díaz** from 1876 to 1911. Díaz reversed the policies of his predecessor, Benito Juárez, who had seized land from the church and other elites to redistribute to commoners. Díaz promoted the interests of large landowners, wealthy merchants, and foreign investors – mainly U.S. businessmen. Under the advice of "cientificos," a group of men who believed in bringing scientific progress to Mexico, he encouraged entrepreneurship and foreign investment that resulted in the construction of railroads and telegraph lines and the production of mineral resources. However, like in Argentina, Mexico was dependent on the investments of capitalists from other countries, and much of the money went into the pockets of the U.S. businessmen and top government officials, including Díaz himself. Even as the economy grew, most Mexicans did not benefit, and without effective political channels to bring about change, the inequality of the situation led to a violent revolution in 1911.

Latin American economies grew rapidly during the 19th century, but they were controlled by foreigners, a situation that unstable governments could do little to change. Products for export included copper and silver from Mexico, beef and wheat from Argentina, tobacco and sugar from Cuba, bananas from Central America, and coffee and rubber from Brazil. The faster the economies grew, the more the countries became dependent on foreign investments, and the more unequal the trading partnerships grew.

THE ABOLITION OF THE SLAVE TRADE AND SLAVERY: IMPACT ON THE AMERICAS

The abolitionist movement had a more direct impact on the Americas than it did on Europe because slave systems were so widely employed in Brazil, the Caribbean, other parts of Spanish America, and the southern United States. In both the United States and Latin America strong antislavery sentiments were expressed while the countries were gaining their independence. The movement continued to gain strength after independence was won, and the United States and most Spanish American republics prohibited the slave trade by the 1830s. However, the growing international demand for sugar and coffee stimulated the plantation economy, and Brazil and Cuba increased their imports of slaves in response. Slavery in British colonies was abolished in 1834, and in the United States, slavery was prohibited in 1865 as a result of the northern victory in the Civil War. Slavery in the Caribbean lasted longest in Cuba and Puerto Rico, Spain's remaining colonies. The slave systems there were weakened by Britain's use of naval force and diplomatic tactics to limit the arrival of African slaves, but both colonies had large white and free colored populations that counterbalanced the threat of slave rebellion, as had occurred in French Haiti. However, Puerto Rico eventually abolished slavery in 1873, and Cuba took gradual steps toward finally abolishing slavery in 1886. Brazil was the last country in the Americas to officially end slavery in 1888 after the number of free blacks increased as slaves were awarded freedom in exchange for serving in the Brazilian army in a war with Paraguay between 1865 and 1870. As in other American countries, educated Brazilians began to push for abolition at the same time that they came to view slavery as an obstacle to economic development.

PERSPECTIVES: SLAVERY AND EMANCIPATION: ECONOMIC OR IDEOLOGICAL MOTIVES?

"Slavery was not born of racism: rather, racism was the consequence of slavery."

In the statement above, historian Eric Williams expresses the point of view that slave systems became dominant during the period from 1450 to 1750 because they made economic sense. Motives, then, were economic. Europeans wanted to make money, so they enslaved Africans in order to do it. Then, once slavery started, racism – the belief that one race is superior to another – justified it, despite the fact that enlightenment ideals of equality seemed to contradict it.

Likewise, we might explain the emancipation of slaves as based in economic motives. As countries industrialized, slavery became impractical, and because slavery was no longer economically viable, the voices of abolitionists were heard, and laws were passed forbidding slavery. On the other hand, Enlightenment ideas were powerful, and many could not help but see the inconsistency of only applying them to white men. Besides, economic motives do not account for the fact that Africans were enslaved. Why didn't Europeans enslave other Europeans? Racism is a plausible answer that leads to an opposite conclusion that belief systems (racism) create economic systems.

Reference: Capitalism and Slavery by Eric Williams (Chapel Hill: University of North Carolina Press, 1944), 7.

IMMIGRATION TO THE AMERICAS

During the 19th century the economic development of the Americas was fueled by the mass migration of Europeans and Asians to the Western Hemisphere to work in factories, railroad construction sites, and plantations. The immigrants brought their cultural beliefs and customs with them, and as a result, significantly diversified American countries.

In North America, immigrants with few skills were welcome as factory workers, since the new economy was based on division of labor that created simple tasks that could be done by almost anyone. Industrialists were able to pay them low wages, and so profits were maximized and money was freed to invest in expanding plants or opening new companies that led to more industrialization. By the 1850s about 2.3 million immigrants lived in the United States, and even more came over in a wave of immigration that began around 1880. Some moved west to farm the abundant lands in the Ohio and Mississippi River valleys, but many stayed in the eastern cities where they found work in factories and businesses. In the late 1800s many came from southern and eastern Europe, and most of them stayed in the cities along the Atlantic coast. Chinese immigration increased during the 1840s as a result of turmoil in China, and peaked between 1852 and 1875, with about 200,000 Chinese migrating to California during that time. Most came as indentured servants since the Qing government allowed foreigners to recruit them in China, and they came to work in agriculture or on the construction of the Central Pacific Railroad. Some had come in response to the discovery of gold in California in 1849, along with people from the eastern United States that came west to find their fortune. Others came from China to Canada to search for gold or to work on the Canadian Pacific Railroad.

Immigrants to Latin American countries came mainly to work on agricultural plantations. During the 1880s and 1890s about four million Italian immigrants came to Argentina, and others went to Brazil to work on coffee plantations after slavery was abolished in 1888. Chinese indentured servants also went to Latin America, where some worked on sugar plantations in Cuba. Others migrated to Peru to work in the cotton fields and to help build railroads. A large number of Japanese immigrants also came to Peru during the late 1800s. Once the U.S. expanded its sugar and pineapple industries to Hawaii, many Chinese, Japanese, Filipino, and Koreans immigrated to Hawaii to work on island plantations.

RELATIONS BETWEEN NORTH AND LATIN AMERICA

As the United States rapidly industrialized after the Civil War, commerce and investments began to expand into Latin America, particularly Mexico and Central America where populations were growing, creating new markets for U.S.

industries. An important event occurred in 1898 when the **Spanish American War** broke out, instigated by events in Cuba and Puerto Rico, Spain's last colonies in the Americas. Cuban nationalists had been fighting for some time for independence, and U.S. investors had interests, particularly in sugar, and the United States was a major market for Cuban sugar. The U.S. joined Cuba in war against Spain, and U.S. forces occupied not only Cuba, but also Puerto Rico and the Philippines, two of Spain's other colonies. Spain had only the remnants of its former power, and U.S. intervention in its dispute with Cuban nationalists resulted in the loss of Spain's last colonies.   Instead of allowing Cubans to direct their own affairs, the U.S. kept troops there and controlled the actions of the new government in accordance with U.S. interests.

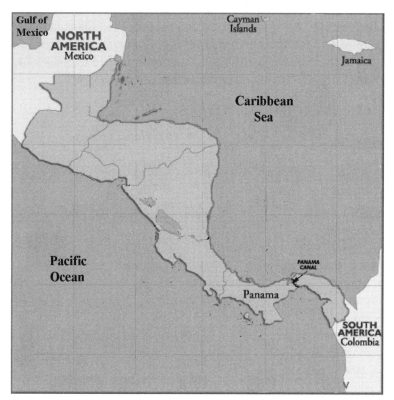

The Panama Canal. The politics surrounding the building of the Panama Canal led to a great deal of resentment among Latin American countries toward the United States, but its completion made international travel much more efficient. The U.S. Congress did pay Colombia an indemnity of $25 million for its loss of Panama, but not until 1921, 17 years after the building of the canal began.

The U.S. alienated Cubans and Puerto Ricans by controlling them as the colonial powers had done, and the resentment of others in Latin America accelerated after U.S. intervention in Panama's bid for independence from Colombia. Under President Theodore Roosevelt, the U.S. had begun to build its navy, but it had a decided disadvantage in the geographical separation between the waters of east and west coasts. In order for a ship to go from one coast to the other, it had to go around the tip of South America, a very long journey. In the 1860s, the British and French had built the Suez Canal to connect the Mediterranean and Red Seas, greatly facilitating trade between Europe and Asia. The French had tried to build a canal in Central America to connect the Atlantic and Pacific Oceans, but had experienced engineering problems and malaria had spread rampant among French crews. A cure was found for malaria, but the French wanted out of their canal commitment, and so proposed that the U.S. take over the project. The U.S. proposed to Colombia – since the Isthmus of Panama was part of that country – a plan to construct the canal, and when Colombia balked at the terms of the deal, the U.S. instead backed an independence movement in Panama. With U.S. help, the Panamanians established their own country and signed an agreement that gave the U.S. control over the canal and its operation. Needless to say, Colombia was resentful of U.S. intervention, and the aggressive actions of the growing North American power earned it a nickname – "**the Bully of the North**" – among its Latin American "neighbors."

CONCEPTS AND IDENTIFICATIONS

"the Bully of the North"
caudillos
Darwin, Charles
Díaz, Porfirio
Dominion of Canada
federalist system
Freud, Sigmund
isolationism, isolationist policy
Jackson, Andrew
Juárez, Benito
La Reforma
Monroe Doctrine
Páez, José Antonio
parliamentary v. presidential system
personalist rulers
regionalism
romanticism
Rosas, Juan Manual de
Spanish American War
Washington's Farewell Address

**CHAPTER EIGHTEEN:
LAND-BASED EMPIRES IN
THE MIDDLE EAST, ASIA,
AND RUSSIA**

As European countries consolidated their power during the era from 1750 to 1914, traditional land-based powers – such as the Ottoman Empire, Qing China, Russia, and Japan – experienced some significant problems that challenged their political authority and economic health. In 1750 the Ottomans were already in steep decline, whereas Qing China weakened during the 19th century. Russia experienced both conservatism and reform, and the Japanese government took drastic measures to consolidate its power and strengthen the economy. All the empires were greatly affected by the actions and beliefs of western countries, although they reacted to them in different ways.

One common experience that all four land-based empires had was that they had unsuccessful confrontations with western military forces. All had been military powers in the past, but they found that industrialized nations had much stronger armies and navies than they did, and they struggled to compensate for their weakness. However, European countries and the United States were often able to force concessions from them, usually in the form of rights for western businesses to set up favorable trade and investment arrangements with the land-based powers. The result was to further strengthen the industrialized West, mostly at the expense of non-industrialized areas. Another problem common to the four empires was internal vulnerability caused by population pressures and declining crop production, which in combination sometimes led to famine. These problems led to falling income for the governments, which made it difficult to maintain military strength. All faced corruption within their governments and discontented peasants who rose in rebellion, especially during the second half of the 19th century. These problems left the societies open to western intervention and put them at a disadvantage in dealing with foreigners.

The land-based countries attempted political, social, and economic reform to meet the challenges, including the adoption of written constitutions, limited government, the restructuring of education, and the attempt to industrialize. Reform was problematic in the Ottoman Empire, Qing China, and Russia, and in 1914, all were in complete crisis. In Japan, the story was different, as the Tokugawa Shogunate ended, and a new regime began that was well on its way to becoming a world power by the early years of the 20th century.

THE DECLINE OF THE OTTOMAN EMPIRE

By 1750 the Ottoman Empire was clearly in decline, although it still had extensive land holdings in the Middle East, eastern Europe, and northern Africa. It had reached its peak during the 16th century under the leadership of Suleiman the Magnificent, and the government had always been quite dependent on the energies and talents of the sultan and the grand vizier, his top administrator. Despite the fact that it had a large bureaucracy, the government operated best when the sultan and grand vizier were strong because it relied on absolutism. The 18th-century sultans had a great deal of trouble keeping the empire together, partly because of internal family squabbles, and were unable to make the Qur'an-based shari'a law code work in the changing world. The era was characterized by conservatism and reverence for tradition, characteristics that kept them from competing effectively with an increasingly technological and aggressive West. The central government lost power to provincial governors, who formed their own private armies to support the sultan in exchange for more control of their provinces. By the early 19th century the Ottoman government could no longer combat European economic intrusions or prevent massive loss of territories, with Egypt declaring its independence, France occupying Algeria, and European states capturing northern and western territories.

Military Weakness and Territorial Losses

The Ottomans had always depended on a strong military to expand and protect their lands, but by the late 17th century they had reached the limits of expansion. Because they were slow to adopt the new military technology, they were outpaced by Europeans in strategy, tactics, and weaponry. Another problem was a serious breakdown in the effectiveness of the Janissary corps, which had been so important in winning military victories during the 16th century. The Janissaries refused to adopt new technologies for fighting, and they were often more interested in maintaining special economic privileges than in changing with the times. The Janissaries that served as provincial governors in the Balkans were greatly resented for their heavy-handedness, and protests began, especially in Serbia. The Balkans were also vulnerable because of rising Russian power during the 18th century, and the expansionist Russian government took over poorly defended territories to the east, in the Caucasus and central Asia, and hovered expectantly over the Balkans. The forces of nationalism also worked against the Ottomans, as the empire's unity was disrupted by successful independence movements in Greece in 1830 and Serbia in 1867. In those areas, many people felt a nationalist identity based on Christianity, and in Greece many responded to the idea that they were fighting to revive the glories of Ancient Greece, a western tradition in opposition to the Muslim Middle Eastern orientation of the Ottomans.

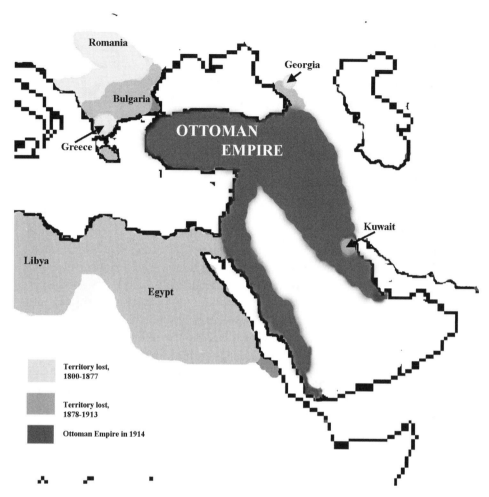

Decline of the Ottoman Empire. By 1914 the Ottoman Empire was much smaller than it had been at the beginning of the 19th century. The Ottomans also lost some territory west of Libya between 1800 and 1877 that is not shown on the map.

In northern Africa Napoleon invaded Egypt in 1798, with the hope of using it as a staging area to attack the British Empire in India. Although Napoleon eventually had to pull out when the British cut off his army's supply line, the invasion sparked competition among Egyptian elite leaders for control, and the talented and energetic **Muhammad Ali** emerged victorious. Ali built a powerful army by drafting peasants and hiring French and Italian military officers to train his troops. Ali was aware of the military superiority of European armies, and he implemented a program of military reforms by dispatching military leaders to study in France and bringing in technicians to advise him. He also began a program of industrialization, and built important industries in cotton textiles and armaments. Under Muhammad Ali, foreign investment played a key role in Egypt's modernization, including the building of railroads and laying the plans for the construction of the Suez Canal, financed and opened by the French and English in 1869 after Ali's death. While he remained nominally subordinate to the Ottoman sultan, Egypt was actually an autonomous region within the Ottoman Empire; however, Ali's forces invaded Syria and Anatolia, and he may well have toppled the empire if British forces had not intervened in an effort to shore up the Ottomans as a defense against Russia's expansion. Egypt officially remained a part of the Ottoman Empire until 1882 when British forces came to permanently occupy the area.

The Crimean War and Reform

The **Crimean War,** fought in 1853-4, revealed to all the major powers how weak the Ottoman Empire had grown. The war was sparked as Russia's armies attacked southward, threatening Ottoman lands. Fearing that the Ottomans would fall under Russian pressure, France and Britain sent troops to the area. Much of the fighting took place on the Crimean Peninsula on the north shore of the Black Sea, and it resulted in a sound, humiliating defeat of Russia, but it also cast the Ottomans in the role of a lesser power that had to be protected by others. The Crimean War was significant beyond the individual countries that fought in it because it marked a transition from traditional to modern warfare. The high casualty rate was due partly to varying levels of technology that were used by different sides at different times. For example, highly trained cavalry traditionally had been used to break through the front lines of the infantry while the infantrymen reloaded their guns. The cavalry did not carry guns because they were too heavy, a situation that made the men vulnerable to new technologies of the percussion cap and the breech-loading rifle. Both inventions made firing rapid and more accurate, and had been adopted throughout Europe in the years preceding the Crimean War, and the result was a widespread slaughter of cavalry. Warfare methods had to change, since a line of marching soldiers could be decimated by the new technology.

Even before the war began, Ottoman rulers tried to bring about reforms to stop the empire's slide. In the late 18th century Sultan Selim III tried to remodel his army based on the western model. However, the new forces, trained by European military advisors and equipped with modern weapons, threatened the Janissaries, who rose in revolt, killed the new troops, and imprisoned the sultan. Sultan Mahmud II revived the reforms in the 1820s, calling them a renewal of the old Ottoman military power, and again the Janissaries blocked the programs, but this sultan ordered his loyal troops to kill them, and cleared the way for the reforms to take place. The reforms centered on the military, with European drill masters and equipment, but they soon spread to education, with newly established schools that taught European curricula. In the 1830s an Ottoman imperial school of military sciences, later to be named Istanbul University, imported instructors from western Europe in chemistry, engineering, mathematics, and physics in addition to military history. Mahmud also transferred power from the ulama, the Islamic leadership, to European-style ministries, and even though the Ottoman Empire lost territories, the government was more efficiently organized by the time of Mahmud's death in 1839.

MARKER EVENT:
HYGIENE ON THE BATTLE FIELD

Throughout history, a soldier who escaped death on the battlefield did not always survive the war. Often people died from diseases, such as septicemia and dyssentery, or from wounds that bled excessively or became infected. An important turning point for hygiene for battlefield wounds came in the mid-1800s when a young Englishwoman named **Florence Nightingale** applied techniques she learned in France and Prussia to bring about significant improvements in British healthcare. Nightingale went to the Crimea to tend to wounded soldiers in the war there in 1853-1854, and she found the need to improve the sanitation of the hospitals. Her influence led the British government to flush out the sewer systems and improve ventilation, measures that greatly reduced death rates. When she returned to London she established institutes for nursing that were widely imitated in other countries.

One reason that Florence Nightingale became so well known is that she lived in a time when another technological marker event - the telegraph - made it possible for news from the battlefield to get back home quickly. To sell their papers, journalists looked for heroic actions, and Florence Nightingale became a "star" with the folks back home.

An intensified period of reform that followed Mahmud was known as the **Tanzimat,** meaning "reorganization," and it lasted until 1876. Again, the military was a primary target, but the Tanzimat reformers also substituted French legal codes for shari'a law, and the rulers issued decrees that guaranteed public trials, rights of privacy, and equality before the law for all Ottoman subjects, although marriage and divorce laws were still determined by shari'a. A state ministry of education was created, and a system of state-sponsored public schools was put in place.

The Tanzimat reforms drew harsh criticism from the ulama and other religious conservatives who wished to preserve shari'a law, and protests came from within the government bureaucracy from those who believed that the sultan had gained too much power. From the latter group, radical dissidents seized power in a coup in 1876 and placed on the throne Abd al-Hamid II, who was given the position of sultan with his acceptance of a constitution that limited his authority. Once in power, he suspended the constitution, dissolved parliament, executed bureaucrats, and ruled the empire autocratically until 1908. He continued the reforms of his predecessors, but his despotism inspired the formation of many liberal opposition groups, especially as bureaucrats and army officers absorbed Enlightenment values from the European curriculum they were taught. The best known and most influential of the protest organizations was the Ottoman Society for Union and Progress, nicknamed **"The Young Turks,"** which formed in Paris among a group of Turks exiled for their resistance to the sultan's rule. The Young Turks were inspired by Turkish nationalism, and they wished to restore the 1876 constitution that Abd al-Hamid II had rejected. Their activism included publication and distribution of works that denounced the regime and promoted reform, as well as assassination attempts and plots for coups. In 1908 their efforts paid off when sympathetic army officers led a successful coup that forced the sultan to restore parliament and the 1876 constitution. The following year Abd al-Hamid was dethroned, and a new but powerless sultan, Mehmed V. Rashid, was named.

The Ottoman Empire of the early 20th century was much smaller than it was before, a fact that Turkish nationalist groups – such as the Young Turks – tried to capitalize on in order to create Turkish unity since many of the diverse people formerly ruled by the empire were now outside its borders. They pushed to make Turkish the official language, although many subjects still spoke Arabic or one of the Slavic tongues. Syria and Iraq were especially opposed to the new Turkish identity, and they pushed for independence. In the early years of the 20th century, the Ottoman Empire had earned the title, "Sick Man of Europe," reflecting its failed attempts to westernize and the turmoil that continued to divide its people.

CHINA'S LAST DYNASTY

In contrast to the Ottomans, the Qing Dynasty was very strong in 1750, with China prosperous, large, and well-ruled by the Manchu that had taken over from the Ming in the 17th century. However, by the late 18th century, some signs were beginning to point toward the decline of the Qing dynasty, just as had happened with all dynasties in China before. One problem was corruption within the government. The exam system was marred by cheating and favoritism, with sons of high bureaucrats ensured a place in the government. Examiners were often

EXAMINING THE EVIDENCE: THE WESTERNIZATION OF THE OTTOMAN EMPIRE

In an attempt to stop the overall decline of their empire during the 19th century, the Ottomans restructured their military, political, and educational institutions based on western models. The modernization of the army included the introduction of modern weapons, drill, and military dress. Beards were banned as unhygienic and as downright dangerous when in contact with gunpowder. Ottoman soldiers had to give up their loose trousers and turbans, but they did not adapt well to European-style military caps, which had leather bills on the front to serve as sunshades. The problem was that the bills did not allow the heads of the Muslim soldiers to touch the ground during their daily prayers, and so they refused to wear them. A modification resulted in a brimless cap called the *fez* that was adapted from the high hats that the Janissaries had traditionally worn.

bribed, and "substitutes" sometimes took the exams for their less adept companions. Government revenues often made their way into bureaucrats' pockets so that less money was available for public projects necessary to keep the society's infrastructure in repair. This lack of funding was particularly devastating for those that lived along the great rivers where people depended on well maintained dikes to prevent flooding. By the 1860s millions of peasants near the mouth of the Yellow River had been displaced when their lands and livestock were wiped out by floods. Other problems – such as food shortages, vagabond bands roaming the countryside, and banditry – convinced many that the Qing rulers were losing the mandate of heaven and it was time for a new dynasty to take its place. However, this dynastic change would prove to be quite different than any in history because the world had become much more interconnected, and the Europeans that had seemed so far away were now at China's doorstep.

The Mccartney Expedition

An early indication that the Europeans and Chinese would clash came in 1792 with the **Mccartney mission,** a delegation headed by George Mccartney sent by the British government to open more trade between China and Britain. The government was worried about a massive trade deficit with China brought about by the huge demand for Chinese luxury goods in England that was not balanced by any Chinese demands for British goods. British silver went to China to pay for the imported tea, silk, and decorative items, but Britain was offended by the Qing restrictions on trade, called the **Canton system,** because British goods had to come into only one Chinese port – Canton. The failure of the Mccartney mission is a classic study in ethnocentrism on both sides, with each considering itself to be superior to the other, and neither willing to bend. Macartney expected the Qing bureaucracy to accept his credentials from the British government, but they refused to acknowledge them. The Qing officials insisted that Mccartney perform the kowtow, which he refused, and he in turn asked Qing officials to bow before a portrait of the king of England, and they refused. Macartney went home frustrated and empty handed, and British attitudes toward China began to change from admiration to criticism of the regime as authoritarian, self-satisfied, and out-of-date.

The Opium Wars

Following the death of Qianlong in 1795, the era of strong leadership that had begun with Kangxi in the mid-17th century ended. The late Qing emperors were conservative and their government officials were often corrupt, and the empire did not keep up with technological innovations that were changing the world around them. Although the Chinese regarded the Europeans as "barbarians" similar to those that had incurred on Chinese territory throughout history, the Scientific Revolution and industrialization had transformed the European countries into formidable foes. England was much smaller in population than China, but its technology was superior, and its government and military were well organized. However, the issue that sparked the dispute between Britain and China reflects something about the desperation the British felt over their inability to solidify beneficial trade between the two countries. The trade imbalance was so serious that the British looked carefully to find a product to sell to the Chinese, and they found it in India. By the early 19th century the East India Company had monopolized trade in India and had discovered that the Chinese would trade their porcelain, tea, and silk for Indian opium, allowing the company to avoid paying with precious gold and silver. The British had the crop grown cheaply in India, and their ships carried it from Indian ports to Canton, where the trade was so brisk by the 1820s that China was not only exporting luxury goods but was paying large amounts of silver for the drug.

Most people in China had never used opium before, but once its addictive effects became apparent, the Chinese government began to protest the trade in the name of public health. From the early 18th century, Qing emperors had forbidden the opium traffic, but little had been done to enforce them. First, Chinese

PERSPECTIVES:
LIN ZEXU ON THE OPIUM TRADE

In 1838 the Chinese official Lin Zexu was sent to Canton to enforce the government's ban on the opium trade there. His aggressive attempts to stop the trade triggered the Opium Wars between China and Britain, with Britain claiming that he abused British citizens' rights to free trade and private property. When the Chinese lost the war, Lin was exiled to a remote province of the empire. However, his reasons for the stern measures he took are revealed in a letter to Queen Victoria of England, written in 1839 to convince her to halt the flow of opium. The letter was never sent, but the excerpts below reflect his strong opinions.

"...this poison has spread far and wide in all the provinces. You, I hope, will certainly agree that people who pursue material gains to the great detriment of the welfare of others can be neither tolerated by Heaven nor endured by men.. Heaven is furious with anger, and all the gods are moaning with pain! It is hereby suggested that you destroy and plow under all of these opium plants and grow food crops instead, while issuing an order to punish severely anyone who dares to plant opium poppies again...

Since a Chinese could not peddle or smoke opium if foreigners had not brought it to China, it is clear that the true culprits of a Chinese's death as a result of an opium conviction are the opium traders from foreign countries. Being the cause of other people's death, why should they themselves be spared from capital punishment?"

Reference: China in Transition by Dun J. Li (New York: Van Nostrand, 1969), pp. 64-67.

government officials filed protests with the East India Company and then with the British government with no results. Next, the government began to enforce the ban on opium trade and drove opium dealers from Canton to nearby islands and other areas along the coast. Still the illegal trade continued, so the emperor sent a high official, Lin Zexu, to Canton to blockade European trading areas, search their warehouses, and confiscate and destroy any opium they found. The British reacted by proclaiming that Lin's actions had violated the principle of "free trade," and that the property rights of British merchants in Canton had been abused. In 1839 the British declared war on China, and the conflict that followed reflected how badly the Chinese had fallen behind western nations in war technologies. The Chinese war junks were routed by the British gunboats, and on land the Chinese fought with swords, knives, spears, and outdated muskets against well-trained British infantrymen with the latest, most accurate rifles. The Chinese government surrendered after the British sent their steam-powered gunboats up the Yangzi River and the Grand Canal, where they took over virtually all territory along the way. A second conflict broke out in the late 1850s, after which the British government was able to control trade with China with little resistance from Qing government officials.

The Unequal Treaties

After the Opium War of 1839-42, the Chinese and British signed the **Treaty of Nanking,** which dismantled the old Canton System, and increased the number of ports open to foreigners from one (Canton) to five (Canton, Xiamen, Fuzhou, Ningbo, and Shanghai), and the island of Hong Kong became a long-term British colony. British residents in China gained extraterritorial rights, which meant that they could live and conduct business under British laws rather than Chinese laws. The Qing government had to accept a low tariff of 5 percent on imports and had to pay a stiff penalty for "starting" the war. The following year a treaty forced the Chinese to guarantee **most-favored-nation status** to Britain, giving it trading advantages over all other nations. After the second set of wars of 1856-60, Beijing was occupied by British and French soldiers, and more treaty ports were opened, including inland centers along the Yangzi River, now patrolled by British gunboats. Through this series of treaties known as the **unequal treaties,** the Qing government lost control of foreign trade, and the opium trade continued to expand. The treaties applied not only to Britain, but to many other European countries, the United States, and Japan. By 1900 most Chinese ports were controlled by foreign powers as **spheres of influence,** with each port controlled by a designated foreign nation.

The Taiping Rebellion

The defeat of China by Britain in the wars of the early 1800s and the Qing government's loss of control of Chinese trade and economic policies sparked massive internal rebellions that had been brewing for some time as the regime weakened. China had weathered many rebellions in its long history, but the European encroachment magnified the problems that very nearly toppled the dynasty. The worst of the movements was known as the **Taiping Rebellion,** led by **Hong Xiuquan,** a Christian from Guangxi province in the south, an area with stubborn social problems that had been experiencing disorders since the beginning of the 19th century. Hong was a Hakka, a minority group with deep resentments toward the majority, and he led a religious movement called the "Heavenly Kingdom of Great Peace" whose mission it was to drive the Manchu

(Qing) out of China. His followers, mainly Hakkas like Hong, believed him when he claimed to be the younger brother of Jesus, and they saw their movement as the salvation of China destined to rid China of the "creatures of Satan," the Qing. As the rebellion grew, it encompassed many diverse people who were discontented with the status quo. Many of the reforms advocated by the Taiping were quite radical, including the abolition of private property, the prohibition of foot binding, free public education, and the establishment of democratic political institutions. The movement had many characteristics of a cult in the degree to which the leaders tried to control the lives of their followers, and their fervor gave the Taiping army the power it needed to sweep through southeastern China and eventually take Nanjing as their capital city in 1853.

Once the Taiping kingdom had a base in Nanjing, its army campaigned throughout China looking for converts, and if towns or villages resisted, conversion to their cause took place by force. In 1855 they threatened Beijing before being repelled by the Qing, but by 1860, they set their sights on Shanghai. Not until 1864 did government forces put down the rebellion for good, and then only with the combined forces of regional armies led by the scholar-gentry with the aid of European advisors and weapons. The 20 to 30 million people who lost their lives during the Taiping Rebellion make it the world's bloodiest civil war, and it caused such massive declines in agricultural production that people in war-torn areas starved and epidemic disease was rampant because the dead were not buried properly.

The Self-Strengthening Movement

Just as regional scholar-gentry leaders took the initiative in putting the Taiping Rebellion to an end, they organized China for the **self-strengthening movement** of the late 19th century. Its main goal was to counter the challenge from the West by modernizing China from within. They encouraged western assistance in building railroads and factories, and they borrowed western technology to update their armies. Although these regional leaders professed loyalty to the emperor, their growing military and political power clearly revealed that China was fragmenting and that the Manchu had lost control. The emperors refused to adopt the reforms that might have saved them, even after China lost a war with Japan in 1895. One of the best known rulers of these last years of the dynasty was **Cixi,** the dowager empress who dominated her emperor son to fiercely resist reform movements initiated by the regional leaders. She famously defied the assistance of western countries by spending their money on building an extravagant marble boat permanently anchored on a lake next to the Summer Palace. Members of the Qing family secretly encouraged the **Boxer Rebellion,** a popular uprising at the turn of the century which aimed to expel the "foreign devils." This rebellion was put down, but only with help from westerners, reinforcing China's loss of control of its own destiny.

Cixi's Marble Boat. Cixi built an extravagant but useless boat with money given by western powers to fund the Chinese navy, said to be Cixi's backhanded reference to the intention of the funds. The boat is "docked" by her Summer Palace, and it came to symbolize China's demise under her rule.

The End of the Dynasty

By the end of the 19th century the resistance to the Qing Dynasty was strong, with many young gentry and merchants joining secret societies whose main goal was to overthrow the regime. Their discontent was fed by the disintegration of Chinese power after defeat at the hands of Japan, cession of the ancient tributary of Vietnam to France, control of Korea surrendered to Japan, and domination of Manchuria by Russia. Many young men, especially in the port cities, had received European-style educations, and many dreamed of reshaping China into a nation-state instead of just replacing the Qing with another dynasty. They had mixed feelings about the West because even though their vision of the new China was based on a western model, these young Chinese still resented the spheres of influence, and they blamed the Manchus for losing control. In defiance of the regime, many cut off their queues (braided ponytails) to express their disgust with the dynasty's weakness. Finally, the unrest led to the **Revolution of 1911,** a spreading rebellion that deposed the last emperor of China, and **Sun Yat-sen** – the victorious leader of the revolution – attempted to establish a republican form of government in China. However, the early 20th century would hold more unrest and uncertainty for China as its power was eclipsed by the West before it settled on a very different regime type in 1949.

EXAMINING THE EVIDENCE: WHO WAS CIXI?

The last rulers of the Qing Dynasty were deeply embroiled in the conflicting attempts to salvage the dying regime, and Empress Dowager Cixi has most often been blamed for hastening its demise. Cixi is only one of three women to ever rule China, and she came to power when her son Tongzhi ascended the throne in 1861 at the age of five. She dominated him while he was alive, and was rumored to have killed her daughter-in-law and unborn grandchild so that her nephew Guangxu could be emperor. However, her nephew had a mind of his own, and defied Cixi in his support of western-style reform. He attacked the Manchu court as corrupt and inefficient, and initiated in 1898 his "Hundred Days of Reform" with decrees meant to transform China while still retaining Confucian principles. He supported western-style schools, the abolition of the civil service exams, and the dismissal of many high-ranking officials. With the help of some of those targeted officials, Cixi had Guangxu placed under house arrest, and she regained control of the government until her death in 1908. She has been epitomized as the "dragon lady" who brought China to its knees; however, she saw herself as the protector of traditional Chinese values against western interference. Although she certainly didn't intend it, she laid the foundation for the Revolution of 1911, which ended the Qing Empire, as well as the entire dynastic era of Chinese history.

CONSERVATISM AND REFORM IN RUSSIA

By 1750 Russia had experienced significant westernization under Tsar Peter the Great, who built a navy, improved the military, expanded to the shores of the Baltic Sea, and increased Russia's interactions with western Europe. His reforms were solidified and expanded by **Catherine the Great,** who ruled Russia from 1762 to 1796, the time when Enlightenment thought stimulated the American and French Revolutions. Like Peter, Catherine had a vision of a more powerful Russia supported by western technology and warm-water ports. Catherine also was an absolute ruler, but her acquaintance with Enlightenment philosophes, such as Denis Diderot, and her knowledge of western thought earned her the curious title of **"enlightened despot"** that she shared with other eastern

European rulers, such as Joseph II of Austria and Frederick II of Prussia. Catherine was not Russian, but instead was a German princess who married Peter the Great's grandson, who eventually became Tsar Peter III. Her husband was killed in a palace coup that Catherine almost certainly supported, and she ascended the throne in 1762, following a tradition set by Peter the Great, who had named his wife as his successor.

Catherine was well-read, and she followed events in western Europe carefully, but she understood the dangers that democratic institutions – such as parliaments and constitutions – posed to her autocratic rule. She supported the economic development of Russia's towns and cities, but she was not willing to allow them to have any substantial political power. She also supported the nobility, especially in regard to their rights over peasants who served as serfs on their lands. Catherine encouraged the nobles to travel in western Europe but she was always mindful of keeping her own power and authority. Her willingness to resort to despotism was illustrated by her reaction in 1773-1774 to a major rebellion led by Emelian Pugachev, a Cossack who lived in the steppes north of the Caspian Sea. Pugachev raised an army to support his goals to end taxes and the military draft and to secure the right for peasants to own land. The tsar's army crushed the rebellion, captured Pugachev, and displayed his quartered body publicly, just as previous tsars had reacted to rebellious subjects. After Pugachev's rebellion, Catherine's tendencies toward absolutism were more apparent than her need to reform Russia, especially after she saw the results of the French Revolution, which occurred late in her reign.

Under Catherine, Russia continued to expand, gaining lands that gave Russia access to the Black Sea, as well as some of the lands of Poland, a kingdom to Russia's west. Catherine coordinated plans with Frederick II of Prussia and Maria Theresa of Austria to attack Poland and "partition" the kingdom among the three great powers that surrounded it. At Catherine's death in 1796, Russia was much stronger than it had been when she took the throne, but she did little to change the tradition of the tsar's absolute rule. The cultural conflict created by Peter – westernization in order to gain power versus the Slavic tendency to protect old traditions – continued under Catherine's reign and shaped Russia's development during the 19th century.

Conservatism of the Early 19th Century

Catherine's conservatism was reinforced by the excesses of the French Revolution, and her successors of the early 19th century responded to the Napoleonic Wars with the same cautious protection of the rights of monarchs. Tsar Alexander I successfully led Russia to resist Napoleon's 1812 invasion, which quelled his early leanings toward liberal philosophy, and he responded by supporting conservative forces at the Congress of Vienna. He formed a **Holy Alliance** with Austria and Prussia as a defense of the established order, which included both monarchs and religious officials.   Despite Alexander I's efforts, he was

ORIGINAL DOCUMENT: RUSSIA'S POLICY OF "OFFICIAL NATIONALITY"

Tsar Nicholas I (r. 1825-1855) resisted all attempts to reform Russia, largely because he wanted to protect the empire from the political turmoil that had occurred in western Europe during the Napoleonic era. In the document excerpted below, Nicholas' minister of education, S.S. Uvarov, explains the basic principles behind the tsar's policy of "official nationality."

"In the midst of rapid collapse in Europe of religious and civil institutions, at the time of a general spread of destructive ideas...it was necessary to establish our fatherland on firm foundations upon which is based the well-being, strength, and life of a people; it was necessary to find the principles which form the distinctive character of Russia, and which belong only to Russia....Sincerely and deeply attached to the church of his fathers, the Russian has of old considered it the guarantee of social and family happiness...A Russian devoted to his fatherland, will agree as little to the loss of a single dogma of our Orthodoxy as to the theft of a single pearl from the tsar's crown. Autocracy constitutes the main condition of the political existence of Russia...An innumerable majority of the subjects of Your Majesty feel this truth...The saving conviction that Russia lives and is protected by the spirit of a strong, humane, and enlightened autocracy must permeate popular education...Together with these two national principles there is a third, no less important, no less powerful: nationality."

Reference: cited in *Nicholas I and Official Nationality in Russia, 1825-1855,* by Nicholas Riasanovsky (Berkeley: University of California Press, 1959). pp. 74.75.

not able to stop the filtering of liberal ideas into Russia, which inspired some intellectuals to question the status quo. Shortly after the tsar's death, his successor, Nicholas I, faced the **Decembrist Revolt,** a major uprising in 1825 led by western-oriented army officers who sought political reform. As most tsars before him had done, Nicholas responded with repression, and after crushing the rebellion, paid little attention to reform for the rest of his reign. Newspapers and schools were strictly supervised, political opponents were arrested, and the secret police was expanded – all in an effort to protect Russia from western influences that threatened Slavic roots. Russian tsars continued their efforts to maintain political authority, but at the same time, they kept their ambitions to expand Russian territories, which meant that they became embroiled in international politics. For example, Russia supported many nationalist movements in the Balkans, even though they reflected liberalism. The Russian desire to weaken the Ottoman Empire by stirring up trouble among its subjects was greater than the Russian commitment to conservatism, especially since Russia stood to gain territory at the expense of the Ottomans.

Russia's resistance to westernization during the early 19th century extended to industrialization. In response to Western demands for Russian grain, the government tightened the labor obligations of serfs rather than look to technology to increase production. In Russia, as well as most other areas of eastern Europe, the labor system remained feudalistic, although some western machinery was imported and a few factories opened to imitate western Europe. This pattern continued until Russia's territorial ambitions were stopped by their loss of the Crimean War in 1856, in which the superior technology and war tactics of France and Britain clearly showed how far behind Russia had fallen. This humiliating defeat robbed them of the opportunity to encroach on the periphery of the weakening Ottoman Empire, and served as a wake up call that Russia's power could no longer be promoted by conservatism alone.

The Reform Era

Alexander II, the tsar that followed Nicholas I, reacted to Russia's disastrous defeat in the Crimean War by focusing on the economy, particularly the need to industrialize. He saw the serf labor system as the biggest obstacle to crafting an industrial economy, and as a result, serfs were emancipated in 1861, just a few years before slaves were freed in the United States. Serfdom had been abolished in western Europe after 1789, and in Prussia and Hungary after they had experienced revolutions in 1848. Alexander did not wish to turn away from Russian traditions completely; he was trying to keep the balance between westernization and preservation of Slavic traditions. The decision to eliminate serfdom was a practical one that he hoped would pave the way for a more productive economy that would restore Russia's place in a world where balance of power among nations was increasingly important. Although serfs received a great deal of land (in contrast to slaves in the U.S.), they got no new political rights, and they were still tied to their villages until they could pay for the land they were granted. Since these payments were difficult for most peasants to make, they came to resent the nobles who collected their money. As a result, in many ways discontent worsened rather than improved after emancipation.

Another reform implemented by Alexander II was the creation of local political councils, called **zemstvoes,** to replace the nobility's traditional authority over the serfs. The zemstvoes set local policies, such as road building and educating children, and they gave a voice to some middle class professionals, such as doctors and lawyers, in the political process. However, they did not limit the tsar's power, nor did they restrict national policies set by the tsar's extensive bureaucracy. Alexander II also strengthened the army by extending recruitment and improving the education of soldiers. Improved education meant that literacy rates climbed considerably during the late 19th century, but the tsar made no moves to increase political rights for commoners.

Since the middle class was very small in Russia, initiatives for industrialization had to come from the central government, a process that was similar to the model for westernization set up by Peter the Great 200 years before. A major achievement was the building of the **Trans-Siberian Railroad**, which connected the bulk of the population in the east to the Pacific Coast by the end of the 19th century. The railroad not only stimulated the iron and coal industry, but it made the export of Russian grain to the West easier, bringing more capital for further industrial development. Siberia's many natural resources became much more accessible as a result of the railroad, and Russia was able to turn some attention toward protecting and promoting its Asian lands. By the 1880s, modern factories appeared in Moscow and St. Petersburg, attracting rural peasants to move to the cities to become urban workers. There they produced textiles and fashioned metals into saleable items. Western investment was encouraged, and by 1900 about half of Russian factories were foreign owned, especially by British, German, and French entrepreneurs.

Political Unrest and Protest

Despite – or perhaps because of – Alexander's attempts to moderate the changes by balancing westernization with traditional Slavic society, Russia became increasingly unstable during his rule. One problem was that his reforms encouraged people to make even more demands, including minority nationalities that Russia had encompassed as it expanded. The emphasis on Russian nationalism encouraged them to assert their own identities, and many educated Russians listened to their concerns through the lens of Enlightenment ideals that they had read about and discussed. A group of radical **intelligentsia** emerged – people encouraged to voice political opinions through the expansion of universities and access to the printed word. Some were so alienated from the political elite that they formed groups that endorsed terrorism as a way to bring about change. The groups had diverse goals and philosophies, but most considered westerners to be materialistic and morally inferior to Russians, and they saw the tsar and his government as stumbling blocks to achieving Russian greatness. Many became **anarchists** opposed to any formal government, and they sought to attack the existing order through assassinations and bombings. In 1881, one of the groups managed to assassinate the tsar by a terrorist bomb, and the tsar that followed,

Alexander III, saw the event as a sign that reform had gone too far. He returned to conservatism and repression, but his actions only spurred the protest groups to intensify their attempts to overthrow the regime.

ORIGINAL DOCUMENT:
WHAT IS TO BE DONE?
BY V.I. LENIN

Vladimir Ulyanov, better known as Lenin, wrote an important pamphlet called *What is to be Done?* that circulated around radical intellectual circles in early 20th century Russia. His doctrine argued that the proletariat revolution could occur in a pre-industrial society such as Russia if stimulated by a small but dedicated group of visionaries. His ideas came to be known as **Marxism-Leninism,** which altered Marxism to fit the situation in Russia. The following excerpt explains his radical concept of the "**vanguard of the revolution.**"

"Class political consciousness can be brought to the workers only from without, that is, only from outside the economic struggle, from outside the sphere of relations between workers and employers. The sphere from which alone it is possible to obtain this knowledge is the sphere of relationships of all classes and strata to the state and the government, the sphere of the interrelations between all classes…To bring political knowledge to the workers the Social Democrats [Bolsheviks] must go among all classes of the population; they must dispatch units of their army in all directions…For it is not enough to call ourselves the 'vanguard', the advanced contingent; we must act in such a way that all the other contingents recognise and are obliged to admit that we are marching in the vanguard."

Reference: Collected Works, Vol.5. V.I. Lenin (London: Lawrence and Wishart, 1973),

One current of philosophy that had begun in the West a few decades earlier was particularly powerful in promoting the crisis that occurred in Russia at the beginning of the 20th century. Marxism – with its message of proletariat revolution – appealed to some Russian intelligentsia, most notably to **Vladimir Ilyich Ulyanov,** known as **Lenin.** However, according to Marxism, socialist revolutions would take first place not in Russia, but in more developed capitalist countries like Germany, France, and England. At the turn of the century, Russia was still primarily an agricultural society in the early stages of industrial development. In his 1905 pamphlet, *What Is To Be Done?,* Lenin changed the meaning of

CHANGE OVER TIME: RUSSIA IN THREE PERIODS FROM 600 TO 1914

Russia experienced many changes between 600 and 1914, as summarized below. Continuities include absolutism, Romanov rule (from the early17th century on), and an agriculture-based economy.

600-1450 – Russia developed when a Slavic people north of Byzantium organized several principalities, with the most powerful early state being Kiev. The Kievan princes converted to Eastern Orthodox Christianity and were heavily influenced by Byzantine culture, an important element of Russian identity. The Russian states were defeated by the Mongols, and the princes of Moscow rose in power as collectors of tribute for the Mongols. When the Mongols receded, Moscow (Muscovy) emerged as the most powerful principality. (See pp. 175-176, 214-218)

1450-1750 – With the fall of Constantinople to the Ottoman Turks in 1453, Russia came to see itself as the proud carrier of Byzantine culture, particularly Christian Orthodoxy. Moscow (Muscovy) grew to dominate more land under its early tsars,but divisions within its nobility led to a "Time of Troubles" that left the state in disarray. The boyars (nobles) agreed to support the Romanov family as rulers, and Romanov tsars reigned until 1917. Russia was seen as "backward" by the states in western Europe, but Russians took great pride in their Slavic roots. In the late 17th century, Tsar Peter the Great set a great conflict in motion within the Russian political culture when he borrowed western technology to modernize Russia. His efforts to control the boyars and their Slavic ways were successful enough to create a powerful Russian military and a force to reckon with in the constellation of European nations. (See pp. 318-323)

1750-1914 – Peter's reforms were reinforced by Catherine the Great, but the tsar's absolute power remained intact. Russia continued to expand under Catherine, but she resisted Enlightenment ideas that advocated republican forms of government. The tsars of the early 19th century were conservatives who supported absolute monarchies and resisted all western influences, but their unwillingness to change threatened Russia's power, and the loss of the Crimean War sparked Tsar Alexander II to initiate reforms, including modernization of the military, emancipation of the serfs, and industrialization. However, anarchist groups led by Russian intelligensia seriously threatened political stability by the early 20th century. (see pp. 413-419)

Marxism when he argued for **democratic centralism**, or a "vanguard" leadership group that would lead the revolution in the name of the people. Lenin believed that the situation in Russia was so bad that the revolution could occur even though it was still primarily an agricultural society. His followers, known as **Bolsheviks,** grew in numbers as Russian workers – far more radical than their Western counterparts – were attracted to Lenin's political ideas.

Russia's loss of its war with Japan in 1904-05 sparked the **Revolution of 1905.** The fighting in the Russo-Japanese War took place in Manchuria, a long distance away from most Russians who lived in the western part of the Empire. The Russian army received its supplies by means of the Trans-Siberian Railroad, and even though the railroad represented Russian progress, the distances were too great to make for a smooth flow of supplies. Perhaps no one was more surprised by the Japanese victory than the Japanese themselves, but their army and navy were better trained and better equipped than the Russians. The shock of the defeat led to the popular uprising, the Revolution of 1905 that forced Tsar Nicholas II to concede a constitution and an elected parliament, called the **Duma.** However, the reforms were too little too late to meet the growing anger of the radical intellectuals, who inspired ordinary Russians to follow them as they supported Marx's vision of an egalitarian society that contrasted so starkly with the unequal lifestyles of the rich and the poor in Russia.

REGIME CHANGE IN JAPAN

In 1750 Japan was a society in transition from a military to a civil society, even though the Tokugawa Shogunate was still firmly in place. Tension between the shogun and the daimyos continued, and the decentralized nature of the government limited its effectiveness. However, commerce and manufacturing were growing, merchants were beginning to outnumber samurai, and a lively urban culture was developing. During the first half of the 19th century, the government was often strapped for funds, since taxes were based on agriculture, and not on the growing wealth of commercial sectors. Maintenance of the largely idle samurai was costly, since the government paid them stipends in return for their loyalty. As mid-century arrived, the Tokugawa Shogunate was weaker than it had ever been, with slow economic growth, agriculture constrained by lack of technology, and an increasing number of rural protests aimed at landlords.

The Importance of Perry

In 1853 the arrival of **Matthew Perry's "black ships"** (as the Japanese called them) in Edo Bay near Tokyo created a crisis that forced Japan to directly tackle its problems. Perry was an American commodore who delivered a letter from the president of the United States demanding that the Japanese open its ports to foreign trade, and he threatened to bombard Japan if the government did not agree. The confrontation fulfilled Japanese fears of outside interference that had so far been repelled by forced isolation of the islands, even as China was being carved by European powers into spheres of influence. The arrival was a surprise, since always before western ships had appeared from the south, but Perry came from the east, representing a country that was not yet a major western power. Perry returned a year later with a fleet of seven ships to receive the answer from the Japanese government, and the shogun agreed to sign an **unequal treaty,** the Treaty of Kanagawa, similar to treaties that China had to sign after their defeat in the Opium Wars. However, Japan was not to fall into decline, as China had done, but instead, the events sparked a civil war that led the country out of its feudal past into modern world power over the next few decades.

The Meiji Restoration

When the shogun capitulated to Matthew Perry's demands, many daimyos were furious with his decision, and so an underground movement calling for the overthrow of the Tokugawa regime began. Provincial leaders emerged who demanded the rejection of the Treaty of Kanagawa, and they united in their cause to attack the shogun, creating a brief but intense civil war that ended in 1868 with the overthrow of the Tokugawa Shogunate. The new regime was called the **Meiji Restoration,** using the young emperor Mutsuhito's reign name of "Meiji" ("enlightened rule") to legitimize their overthrow as a "restoration" of the power of the emperor, who had always been a figurehead only in the Japanese political system. The new rulers, or **oligarchs** (several leaders) as they came to be called, went so far as to establish what was named **"the cult of the emperor,"** or a wide campaign to glorify the emperor as a symbol of Japanese power. However, the emperor remained a ruler in name only, and Japan's transformation was masterminded by a small group of highly talented men intent on making their country a world power.

Above all, the oligarchs wanted to protect Japan from being taken over by western countries, but they also believed that the best way to accomplish their goal was to modernize from within. Unlike China, where regional lords promoted reform and Qing emperors such as Cixi resisted it, the Japanese oligarchs agreed on the path they should take. The transformation of Japan was complete, involving dramatic economic, political, social, cultural, and educational changes, and the program was imposed from the top rung of government – the oligarchs. In all areas, Japan completely abandoned the cautious, isolationist policies of the past, and embraced foreign ideas, institutions, tactics, and technologies that might strengthen the nation. The revolutionary policies of the Meiji Restoration included:

1) **Education** – Japan already had a literacy rate higher than any other Asian country in 1868, and the education system put in place increased literacy even more. The goals of the completely revamped education system were literacy, competency, and loyalty to Japan. Education be-

came universal with primary schools for all, and science and technical subjects were stressed. Elite students that went on to the university level also took science and technology courses, and many Japanese students were encouraged to study technical subjects abroad. However, western influences were mainly technological and scientific, and Japanese students received a traditional moral education that stressed loyalty to the country and Confucian values such as filial piety, reverence for ancestors, social order, and respect for superiors. The government strictly supervised the education process, and textbooks were censored for dangerous western moral content.

2) **Military organization** – The old feudal order was abolished, including the daimyos and samurai, who had to adjust to the new order. The daimyo-samurai feudal forces were replaced with a modern army based on conscription (drafting soldiers for compulsory service), an efficient organization, the latest technology in weaponry, and professional discipline. With the aid of western advisors, a modern navy was established. The samurai rose in rebellion in 1877, but the government's army defeated them in 1878, and no further military challenges occurred after that.

3) **Political policies and structures** – Government finance was completely revised, with stipends for samurai abolished. Some samurai were sent overseas to study economic and political institutions and technology, and others fell into poverty. Taxes were broadened to include all economic activities, not just agriculture, and as a result, government income increased. The bureaucracy was reorganized, and positions were filled through merit-based civil service examinations. Meiji leaders traveled abroad to study foreign governments, and they settled on a parliamentary system, with an upper house of the legislature modeled after Britain's House of Lords. The Japanese House of Peers was filled with Meiji leaders and former daimyos, and its lower house, called the **Diet**, was given the power to pass laws, approve budgets, and otherwise advise government, but not control it. The emperor was put in direct control of the military, as based on the German model, and the emperor named his ministers. However, just as before the Restoration, the real power was not in the hands of the emperor, but rested behind the scenes in the hands of the oligarchs.

4) **Industrialization** – A major goal of the oligarchs was to industrialize Japan as quickly as possible, and new government banks and railroads were put in place to support economic development. The government took the initiative in operating mines, shipyards, steel factories, and ar-

maments plants, and the government's Ministry of Industry set overall economic policy. The Japanese modeled European industrial development in their promotion of private enterprise, and opportunities opened for people in the lower classes to gain wealth and status. However, private initiatives generally were more carefully supervised by the government than they were in the West. The industrial development was truly remarkable, but by 1914 it was far from equal to the industrial levels in the West, a situation that was to change later in the 20th century.

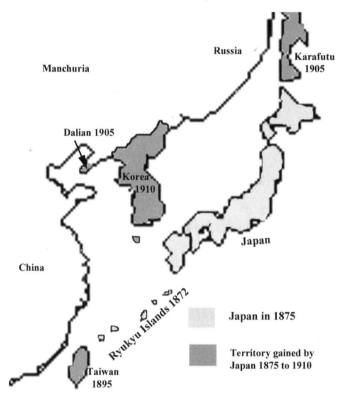

Expansion of Japan. As Japan industrialized, it sought overseas colonies, just as European nations had done. Japan took Taiwan from China in 1895, Karafutu from Russia in 1905, and finally annexed Korea in 1910.

Foreign Successes

The Meiji foreign policy became increasingly aggressive during the late 19th century, as the newly strengthened country successfully challenged the Chinese juggernaut, already reeling from the loss of economic control to European imperialists. After seizing islands claimed by China, including Taiwan, Japan went on to annex Korea, the kingdom that had successfully resisted attack by the Japanese warlord Hideyoshi during the late 16th century. In great contrast to China, Japan was able to gradually eliminate the unequal treaties signed with the western powers in the 1850s and 1860s. By the end of the 19th century, Japan traded with Europeans as equals, whereas China was economically dominated by the West.

CHANGE OVER TIME: JAPAN, 600-1914

600-1450 – Japan developed in relatively isolated groups of people on islands separated from the mainland of Asia. Very early on it developed its native religion of Shintoism, and by the mid-8th century Confucianism and Buddhism had diffused to the islands. Between 794 and 1185 the Fujiwara family ruled a feudalistic Japan and protected a ceremonial emperor. By the mid-1100s the Minamoto warrior family rose to power, and installed a shogun to rule by bakufu or military government. Feudalistic loyalty ties between daimyos and samurai held Japan loosely together with decentralized political power. (pages 205-210)

1450-1750 – The power of Japanese daimyos had risen to the point that one general, Toyotomi Hideyoshi, attacked the mainland, threatening Korea and China. The longest lasting and strongest of the shogunates - the Tokugawa - rose to power in the early 1600s, and maintained control of the daimyos by keeping them close to the Edo court. The economy was based almost exclusively on agriculture, and Shintoism, Buddhism, and Confucianism blended to form an influential religious complex. The Japanese repelled most European attempts to establish trade and find converts to Christianity, and continued to live and build political and military power in relative isolation. (pages 332-337)

1750-1914 – The Tokugawa continued to rule in the early part of this era, but they found it increasingly difficult to control the daimyos and to keep westerners out. In 1853, Matthew Perry's "black ships" came to Japan to demand open trade, and the shogun's agreement to an "unequal treaty" sparked a civil war that resulted in the overthrow in 1868 of the Tokugawa, the last shogunate. In its place, the Meiji oligarchs brought about sweeping political, military, educational, and economic changes that incorporated western technologies and organizations into Japanese society. The transformation was almost complete, with the old feudal order displaced and replaced with a modern society. Japan's transition to the modern era was unique in that it occurred without the upheaval of protracted revolution, such as those that occurred in China and Russia. (pages 420-425)

The biggest accomplishment, in terms of gaining international attention, was the Russo-Japanese War of 1904-05. This war ended in victory for the Japanese, announcing to the world that Japan had become a major power. The annexation of Korea came largely as a result of this war, and even though Japan did not get as much territory as they believed they deserved, their victory put them in position to bid for even more ground after Russia lapsed into civil war in 1917.

The Meiji Restoration was truly a "marker event" in Japanese history that paved the way for Japan to rise to world power during the 20th century. As such, it meant that Japan was to avoid the revolutions that so debilitated Russia and China during the early 20th century. Although the rapid changes caused some internal tensions between old and new, Japan's success in resisting incursion by western powers was unparalleled in the world of the late 19th and early 20th century, and constitutes a remarkable achievement.

CONCEPTS AND IDENTIFICATIONS

anarchists
Bolsheviks
Boxer Rebellion
Canton System
Catherine the Great
Cixi
Crimean War
cult of the emperor
Decembrist Revolt
democratic centralism
Diet
Duma
Holy Alliance
Hong Xiuquan
intelligentsia
Lenin, V.I.
marble boat
Marxism-Leninism
Mccartney mission
Meiji Restoration
most favored-nation status
Muhammad Ali
Nightingale, Florence
Opium Wars
Perry, Matthew; "black ships"
Revolution of 1911 (China)

Revolution of 1905 (Russia)
Russia's "official nationality"
self-strengthening movement
spheres of influence
Sun Yat-sen
Taiping Rebellion
Tanzimat
Trans-Siberian Railroad
Treaty of Nanking
vanguard of the revolution
"What is to be Done?"
the Young Turks
zemstvoes

CHAPTER NINETEEN: IMPERIALISM AND THE GROWTH OF THE BRITISH EMPIRE

Throughout world history societies have built empires by extending their power over others. Motivations for empire have been numerous, including the desire to control natural resources, defeat potential enemies, or gain wealth and glory. Generally empires were built by expanding control by land, but once sea-based powers emerged between 1450 and 1750, the nature of empire-building began to change. Lands could be controlled that were geographically a long distance away, as was the case for the European countries that established control over lands in the Americas. By the 19th century, new types of **imperialism** – or empire building – appeared that differed substantially from earlier versions practiced by land-based empires.

During the era from 1750 to 1914 the forces of nationalism and industrialization made it possible for European nations to build global empires that stretched across the continents. The famous statement that "the sun never sets on the British Empire" describes the huge network of control that Britain was able to establish during the 19th century, making it among the most powerful empires in all of world history. Nationalism enabled governments to rally their citizens' support for overseas expansion. Industrialization allowed them to produce goods to sell in foreign markets, and it encouraged them to look for raw materials not available at home. The European countries that became great imperialist powers during the 19th century – Britain, France, Germany, the Netherlands, and Russia – were mostly small countries in land space (with Russia as the exception). Claiming lands far away increased their ability to create wealth and assert power. Industrialization also made communications and transportation so much more efficient that it became possible to link lands together across the globe under one imperial banner. By the early 20th century, the United States and Japan had joined Europeans in forming overseas empires, giving the West – and increasingly Japan – hegemony over virtually every corner of the globe.

TYPES OF IMPERIALISM

The term "imperialism" was coined to describe the new type of empire-building that began in the 19th century with European nations and eventually included the United States and Japan. These countries did not always take over territories completely as in previous days, but limited their control in terms of their motivations. Several types of imperialism could be combined in different ways to gain the power that the imperialistic country wanted:

1) **Colonial imperialism** – This type of imperialism is the most complete, with a territory or colony actually occupied and ruled by a foreign nation. This "old style" imperialism was illustrated by the conquest of the Americas during the 16th and 17th centuries, where the areas were completely taken over, with European countries setting up governments, controlling the economy, and imposing their lifestyles on the people they defeated.

2) **Political imperialism** – In this form of imperialism, the dominant country uses diplomacy or military force to influence the internal affairs of a weaker nation. As we will see in this chapter, European countries tried to break down tribal affiliations and ruling councils in order to establish more "modern" governments in Africa, and the United States took over the government of the Dominican Republic to manage its affairs so that it would not be taken over by a European country.

3) **Economic imperialism** – This type of imperialism was inspired by the desire to control global trade and commerce, especially as industrialization of western countries made their production and transportation capacities greater. A good example of economic imperialism during the 19th century was the creation of spheres of influence in China. The main motivation for the British declaration of war in the Opium Wars was economic; they had no desire to occupy China and take over the government, and the spheres of influence were created to establish trade zones. Matthew Perry's demands of Japan in 1853 were economic, and even though the demands were backed by the powerful presence of his "black ships," the United States was not motivated by the desire to occupy and rule Japan.

4) **Social-cultural imperialism** – Empire-building may be based on a desire to influence a territory to adopt the cultural values and social customs of the imperialist country. For example, the controlling county might expect the people to speak its language and prefer the foods that its own citizens enjoy. Social-cultural imperialism may be seen in some actions of Christian missionaries as they tried to convert people in other

lands to western religions. Although imperialism implies force, and missionaries were not known for the use of force, in many cases their attempts were unwanted (as in Japan), and their actions reflected the point of view that their religion was superior to that of the natives.

PERSPECTIVES: RUDYARD KIPLING'S *"THE WHITE MAN'S BURDEN"*

The British writer and journalist Rudyard Kipling lived a great deal of his life in India, a place that he deeply loved, and yet his famous poem, *"The White Man's Burden"* reflects his belief that British customs and values should be instilled, a form of social-cultural imperialism. Notice it in the excerpts below.

"Take up the White Man's burden -
　Send forth the best ye breed -
Go bind your sons to exile
　To serve your captives' needs;
To wait in heavy harness,
　On fluttered folk and wild -
Your new-caught, sullen peoples,
　Half-devil and half-child...

Take up the White Man's burden -
　And reap his old reward;
The blame of those ye better,
　The hate of those ye guard -
The cry of hosts ye humor
　(Ah, slowly!) toward the light;

Why brought ye us from bondage,
　"Our loved Egyptian night?"

Take up the White Man's burden -
　Ye dare not stoop to less -
Nor call too loud on Freedom
　To cloak your weariness;
By all ye cry or whisper,
　By all ye leave or do,
The silent, sullen peoples
　Shall weigh your Gods and you."

Reference: "The White Man's Burden," by Rudyard Kipling. *McClure's Magazine* 12:4 (1899): 290-291.

In any one situation, more than one type of imperialism could be practiced. Colonial imperialism by its very nature encompasses the other three types because taking over an area completely means that political, economic, and social-cultural imperialism will take place.

FORMS OF IMPERIALISM

By the end of the 19th century, imperialist countries had set up two types of colonies: **tropical dependencies** in Africa, Asia, and the South Pacific; and **settle-**

ment colonies, such as Canada, Australia, New Zealand, South Africa, Algeria, Kenya, and Hawaii. In tropical dependencies, a small number of Europeans ruled non-western people who came under European rule during the late 19th and early 20th centuries. Settlement colonies were destinations for European settlers, so their populations had large percentages of people of European ancestry. In some – such as Canada, New Zealand, and Australia (and the United States before its independence) – the majority of the population were European, since the relatively small number of indigenous people had been pushed out of the way or had died of disease. In others – such as South Africa, Algeria, Kenya, and Hawaii – large numbers of indigenous people continued to live in the area, and as a result, European land claims were often contested, with frequent clashes over land rights, control of natural resources, and cultural and social differences.

COMPARATIVE COLONIES: TROPICAL DEPENDENCIES VS. SETTLEMENT COLONIES

During the 19th century, European countries - and eventually the U.S. and Japan - practiced many types of imperialism, but when they chose to set up colonies, they used two different models, as compared in the chart below.

Tropical Dependencies	Settlement colonies
Areas generally less appealing to European settlers	Areas generally more appealing to European settlers
Main goal usually exploitation of natural resources	Dual goals of settlement and exploitation of natural resources
Few European settlers, many natives	Many European settlers; some had few natives, other had equal numbers of natives
Problems included control of natives, potential uprisings, native elite resentment, control of governments	In colonies with few natives, fewer conflicts occurred; in those with many natives, problems were similar to those in tropical dependencies
Most colonies located in Africa, Asia, and the South Pacific	Colonies located in many areas, including Canada, New Zealand, Australia, Hawaii, and South Africa

INDUSTRIALIZATION AND IMPERIALISM

Industrialization fundamentally changed the nature of empire-building among European nations. Instead of seeking gold and silver and land for growing crops as empire builders did in the Americas before the 19th century, they looked for raw materials for the factories – cotton, hemp, metals, and dyes. As European nations became the global center for manufacturing goods, they also looked for overseas markets for machine-made goods that were so rapidly being produced. Production was spurred on by competitiveness among European nations, as each tried to capture raw materials and markets before the others could reach them. A second wave of technological advances that began around 1860 made it possible to spread the influence of industrialized nations to many more parts of the globe. One important innovation was the **Bessemer steel converter** that allowed iron ore to be converted to steel efficiently. Steel is stronger than iron, and its use greatly accelerated the effectiveness of machinery and other manufactured products, such as rails for railroads. Chemical industries grew after 1870 with the production of synthetic substances for dyes for textiles, fertilizers for agriculture, and explosives for construction. Plastics became available in the late 19th century. Inventors were also experimenting with electricity, most notably **Thomas Edison,** whose laboratory produced incandescent light bulbs, fuses, sockets, and switches.

Industrialization made it possible for Europeans to penetrate beyond the sea coasts in many lands. Whereas in the previous era sea-based powers were often confined to sea-lanes (except in the Americas), steamboats and railroads allowed them to explore internal rivers and lands far away from the coasts. Since industrialization most directly impacted the economy, it promoted economic imperialism above all other types, and if economic goals could be accomplished without controlling a territory's government, social customs, and cultural beliefs, the imperialist countries often would be content with simply controlling economic policies and actions.

An important consequence of industrialization for world commerce was the construction of the **Suez Canal** (1859-1869) and the **Panama Canal** (1904-14). These canals were incredible engineering accomplishments that were made possible by new industrial technologies. They greatly facilitated the travel of ships between the world's seas and oceans, and lowered the costs of trade between imperial powers and the territories they controlled. The canals also made communications much easier. For example, in the 1830s it often took as long as two years for someone in Britain to receive a reply to a letter sent to India by sailing ship. Once steamships came along by the 1850s the time was cut to about four months. However, after the construction of the Suez Canal, it took less than two weeks for a steamship to get from Britain to India.

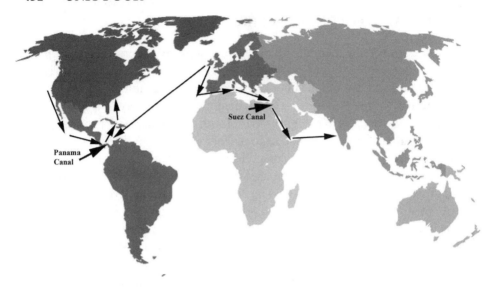

The Canals and World Transportation. The completion of the Suez Canal in 1869 and the Panama Canal in 1914 greatly decreased many travel distances from one place in the world to the next. The Suez Canal was a joint project of England and France, and it allowed both countries to more quickly reach their colonial possessions in Asia. The Panama Canal gave Europeans another route to reach east Asia, and it also allowed the new American navy to travel between the east and west coasts of the United States.

THE BRITISH EMPIRE IN INDIA

One of the first of the great land-based empires to feel the impact of European imperialism was India. As Mughal power weakened in the 18th century, Muslim princes – called **nawabs** – asserted regional control at the expense of the empire, and they often made independent agreements with British, Dutch, and French companies that were eager to establish trading posts along the long shorelines of India. By 1750 these European outposts were staffed by **company men,** whose job it was to organize trade and protect warehouses and offices. To assist in the protection, the company men often hired and trained Indian troops known as **sepoys.** An early center for Britain's East India Company was Calcutta, and after the widely publicized death of some company men arrested and imprisoned in a small cell by the local nawab, company forces overthrew the nawab to avenge the treatment of their men in this "Black Hole of Calcutta." As a result of their actions, the East India Company gained permission from the weak Mughal emperor to allow the company to rule Calcutta and the region (Bengal) around it by 1765. Other areas were secured in the south and on the western coast at Bombay, and as Britain gained the upper hand in the Seven Years' War (1756-1763) with France, the East India Company often secured trading posts at the expense of the French, who also had an early interest in trade with India.

Rule by the East India Company

By 1818, the East India Company had secured so many footholds in India that it controlled vast areas of the subcontinent, establishing the **British raj** (reign). Since the company's motives were economic, this early control is a good example of economic imperialism, even though the British government was not directly involved. However, protection of property and trading rights led to political imperialism as company officials came to rule the regions in place of the nawabs. To keep order, the company expanded the number of sepoy regiments, and they also disarmed Indian warriors that had formerly fought for the nawabs. The company also encouraged Christian missionaries to come to India to convert Indian people, and although they had limited success with conversions, this social-cultural imperialism kept pressure up for British-style social reforms. On the other hand, just as the company had to rely on Indians to fill the ranks of their armies, they also felt it necessary to allow Indian princes to rule under the supervision of their British overlords. This arrangement gave Indian princes – both Muslim and Hindu – more power than they had ever had before in India's history of political fragmentation. As a result, a dual message was sent to Indians: preserve your cultural heritage but also conform to British customs and beliefs. As the Industrial Revolution progressed, economic demands changed as well, in some cases helping the Indian economy, but in other cases hurting it. The British raj created new jobs for Indians in trade and the military, but the Indian handicraft textile industry was seriously weakened by competition from British factories. India had once been the leading exporter of cotton finished goods, but by the mid-19th century, British manufacturing centers were demanding that India export raw cotton, not finished goods, to them.

The Sepoy Rebellion

By the 1850s the East India Company was much more than a business enterprise, but still the British government was not directly involved in ruling India. That situation changed with the massive **Sepoy Rebellion** in 1857 that convinced the British government that only colonial imperialism would work in India. The rebellion was sparked by a classic conflict of cultures when new procedures for firing rifles were implemented. The bullets for the new shipment of Enfield rifles fired from cartridges that were protected by paper waxed with animal fat, and the British officers instructed the sepoys to tear the paper off with their teeth. Hindu sepoys refused because the fat might be from cows, which they considered to be sacred, and Muslim sepoys refused because the fat might be from pigs, which they believed to be unclean. Even though the British officers changed the procedures as soon as they understood the problem, the incident sparked a rebellion that almost certainly was already festering. The sepoys staged a mutiny and proclaimed their allegiance to the Mughals, and they were soon joined by elites and peasants alike, so that the rebellion became widespread enough that it threatened British rule in India. As a result, the British government sent forces to India to contain the trouble, and by 1858 order was restored and direct imperial rule was imposed.

British Imperial Rule

Queen Victoria established a cabinet position within her government that was responsible for India, and a viceroy representing British royal authority was sent to India. The viceroy's elite **Indian Civil Service** was staffed almost completely by Englishmen, although some Indians served in low-level bureaucratic positions. The British formulated and executed virtually all domestic and foreign policy in India from 1858 on, resulting in significant lasting changes for almost everyone that lived on the subcontinent. The last traces of Mughal and company rule were eliminated, but British rule continued to emphasize both Indian tradition and modern reform. Queen Victoria proclaimed that all Indians had equal protection of the law and the freedom to practice their religions and social customs. The rights of Indian princes to rule their territories were also guaranteed, as long as they served as her loyal subjects. However, their power was compromised by the large, efficient bureaucracy set up by the British to establish a strong central government for India.

To establish the legitimacy of the viceroys, the British government set them up in luxurious palaces with many servants, in order to simulate the pomp that had surrounded the Mughal rulers. Elaborate ceremonies honored the Indian princes, and great pageants called "durbars" were staged to celebrate British events, such as the proclamation of Queen Victoria as the "Empress of India" in 1877 and the coronation of King Edward VII in 1902-1903. The Indian Civil Service held the senior administrative and judicial positions, and British-style courts were set up throughout the empire. Theoretically, these highly desirable positions were open to everyone, but the examinations for entrance into service were given in England, making it almost impossible for Indians to take them, and as a result, excluding them almost entirely from the top posts.

Economic imperialism transformed India through massive British investment in the Indian infrastructure, committing money to cities, harbors, canals, and other public works. Railroad building received priority and by 1870 India had the largest railroad system in Asia and the 5th grandest in the world. The companies that owned the railroads were British, as were the top officials, although the vast majority of the employees were Indian. Steamboats travelled Indian rivers, as well as canals that the British built to connect them. Indian products, involved for centuries in long-distance trade, now became part of international trade as shaped by the needs of industrial England. Most of the exports were agricultural commodities for processing in England, including cotton, opium, tea, silk, and sugar.

Another impact of British economic reorganization in India was the growth of cities with easier access in and out of them. Disease travelled as people moved about the country, increasing deaths from cholera during the 19th century. The epidemic spread to Europe, and the deaths were mounting when officials connected the rise of cholera to the Hindu practice of bathing and drinking from sacred rivers and pools. A new sewage system was installed in Calcutta in 1865 and a filtered water supply in 1869, significantly reducing cholera deaths there. Other sanitary measures eventually lowered death rates in other areas, but by 1914, cholera was still a serious health threat in India.

EXAMINING THE EVIDENCE: BRITISH REFORM AND TRADITION IN INDIA

Even thought the main motives of the British East India Company in India were economic, the company was pressured by social reformers in Britain to actively promote changes in Indian social customs and beliefs. The reformers, many of whom were evangelical Christians, believed that the decadent Indian civilization would benefit from a western-style education, so they pushed for schools that taught the English language and customs. The reforms were supported by non-evangelicals who also believed in the superiority of British culture.

The reformers were most vocal in their opposition to the practice of sati, the Indian ritual in which widows threw themselves onto the burning funerals pyres of their dead husbands. Sati was most usually practiced by upper caste Hindus, but by the 19th century, it had spread to other castes as well. In the 1830s, the British raj outlawed sati, and those that protested what they considered to be a violation of Indian customs were punished according to British custom: hanging and confiscation of property.

Indian Nationalism

During the early 19th century the British decided to emphasize western-style schools for the children of Indian elite. Part of the reason was practical: the raj needed people to fill administrative posts who understood the English language and customs, and they also envisioned that such Indians would help keep order among their fellow citizens. These schools transmitted technical and scientific knowledge necessary to keep the new economy running, and they also taught western literature and manners and instilled western values and beliefs. By the late 19th century, a sizeable group of Indians had received such educations, and some had studied in England or in other British colonies. Since they all spoke English, a unity developed among these Indians who previously had been separated in fragmented parts of the subcontinent, and some unintended consequences followed. They soon found out that they had some common grievances: although they had developed into "Englishmen" in almost every sense of the word except for race, they were still excluded from the top jobs and they were socially segregated from the Europeans. On the other hand, western-educated Indians no longer had many things in common with traditional Indians, including their own family members.

In their studies, this new class of Indians encountered liberal values that had been spawned by the Enlightenment and honed through the revolutions that promoted them. Ideas such as "equality," "justice," and "freedom" did not escape the notice of these new western recruits, and they could not help but apply these values to their own situations. Why were they excluded? If people could fight for the right to identify as a French nation, why couldn't they fight to preserve an Indian identity? Weren't their rights being abused? Such thoughts led to discussions in their common language of English, and thus the Indian nationalist movement was born.

The earliest of the prominent Indian nationalists was **Rammohun Roy**, who promoted Pan-Indian nationalism in the early 19th century. He founded a society called Brahmo Samaj, whose goal was to reconcile western values with the ancient religious traditions of India, and he joined the British in their campaign to ban sati, or the burning of widows at their husbands' funeral pyres. By the late 19th century other leaders were emerging from the growing Indian middle class, which had prospered from India's industrialization. In 1885 a group of educated and ambitious Indians convened the first **Indian National Congress,** which aimed to create a larger role for Indians in the Civil Service. However, in the years before 1914, they were unable to develop a broad appeal among ordinary Indians, and so their movement did not bring about much change in British India until well into the 20th century.

IMPERIALISM IN SOUTHEAST ASIA

Competition among European powers led them to Southeast Asia, with its advantageous location for trade, as early as the 16th century when Spain claimed the Philippines as a foothold for controlling trade between China and Spanish America. In the 16th century many islands in Southeast Asia were captured by

PERSPECTIVES: ROMESH DUTT ON INDIAN NATIONALISM

By the turn of the 20th century, Indian nationalism was beginning to turn its focus from just getting better jobs for Indians within the British system to asserting the need to get rid of the British entirely. In the following excerpt, Indian Nationalist Romesh Dutt expresses the growing discontent with British rule.

"The British manufacturer [strangled Indian competition and] millions of Indian artisans lost their earnings; the population of India lost one great source of their wealth. It is a painful episode in the history of British rule in India; but it is a story which has to be told to explain the economic condition of Indian people...The invention of the power-loom in Europe completed the decline of the Indian industries; and when in recent years the power-loom was set up in India, England once more acted towards India with unfair jealousy. An excise duty has been imposed on the production of cotton fabrics in India which disables the Indian manufacturer from competing with the manufacturer of Japan and China, and which stifles the new steam-mills of India...

The dawn of a new century finds India deeper in distress and discontent than any preceding period of history...and every Englishman and every Indian, experienced in administration and faithful to the British empire, feel it their duty to suggest methods for the removal of the gravest danger which has ever threatened the Empire of India."

Reference: The Economic History of India under Early British Rule, Vol. I, by Romesh Dutt (London: Kegan Paul, Trench, Trubner, 1902; reprint edition, New York: Augustus M. Kelly, 1960), pp. ix-xi, xxiii-xxiv.

the Dutch, and as European rivalries intensified during the 19th century, Dutch officials tightened control and claimed most of the islands that today make up Indonesia, calling their land the Dutch East Indies. The islands were important sources of sugar, tea, coffee, tobacco, rubber, and tin, and so were important colonies for the Dutch to hold on to.

Once the British took possession of India, they turned toward Southeast Asia in order to stimulate more trade between India, Southeast Asia, and China. By the 1880s they had gained control of Burma, which was a valuable source of teak, rubies, jade, and ivory. The port of Singapore had been established by the British in the 1820s, and during the 1870s and 1880s they used it as a base to conquer Malaya (now Malaysia), which not only had many lucrative ports, but also had abundant supplies of tin and rubber. After the French lost their claims in India to the English, they too turned toward Southeast Asia, to establish French Indochina (now Vietnam, Cambodia, and Laos). In order to avoid border disputes, Britain and France agreed that neither would claim Siam as a colony, although the king of Siam could hardly act independently in a region dominated by Europeans. In 1898 after the defeat of Spain in the Spanish American War, the United States took the Philippines as a territory, so by the turn of the 20th century the only independent kingdom in Southeast Asia was Siam (now Thailand). From the imperialist point of view, Siam was left alone because it served as a buffer state between British Burma and French Indochina.

Imperialism in Southeast Asia. By the turn of the 20th century, virtually all of Southeast Asia, except for Siam, was controlled by four western countries: the Netherlands, Britain, France, and the United States. Siam was left as a buffer zone between Britain and France to ward off conflicts.

IMPERIALISM IN AFRICA

The Industrial Revolution in western nations brought dramatic change to Africa. The phrase "deepest, darkest Africa" was coined to describe the great mysteries of the continent from the European point of view. Before the 19th century, European explorers and traders were consigned to the peripheries of Africa, to establish their trading posts but never to go far into the interiors. Once the technological capacity to go inland was possible, the abundance of diamonds, gold, and copper in central and southern Africa stimulated western explorations. The "**Scramble for Africa**" – European nations competing for land claims – was further promoted by modern journalism that provided stories about the mysterious continent to its readers. Among the early adventurers were Christian missionaries such as **David Livingstone,** whose whereabouts became a subject of great interest to Europeans and Americans alike.

Northern Africa

Egypt under **Muhammad Ali** (1769-1849) was one of the first kingdoms to come under European sway. Technically subservient to the Ottoman sultan, he envisioned Egypt as a beneficiary of western technology, introducing new irrigation projects to boost the productivity of Egyptian cotton farmers. The cotton fed European textile mills, but Ali also established mills in Egypt, modernized the army, built a system of secular state schools, and increased the efficiency of the government. Unfortunately, too much money was borrowed for internal improvements, and the debt became crushing just about the time the American Civil War ended, allowing American cotton to return to the world marketplace and decrease the demand for Egyptian cotton. These hardships led European creditors to lean heavily on the Egyptian government, first insisting that European advisors be installed in the Egyptian government, and eventually leading to Britain sending its forces into Egypt to protect the Suez Canal. By the 1880s Egypt had become one of Britain's subject countries.

The French asserted control in Africa first by invading Algeria in 1830 to suppress piracy and to collect debts owed them by the Algerian government. They occupied Algiers and two other ports, and when they showed no signs of leaving, resistance to their presence erupted under Abed al-Qadir, who raised an army to defend the government that he set up to establish Algerian independence. Warfare broke out, and even though the French won, hostility toward their occupation continued to fester, and new revolts broke out. By the 1870s the French occupied even the rural areas, and had opened Algeria to French settlers.

South Africa

The Dutch established Cape Colony at the southern tip of Africa in 1652 as a stopping point for their ships going back and forth between Europe and south Asia. Other Europeans settled there as well, and it grew slowly over the years. During the early 19th century, the expansion of the colony contributed to political and social unrest among the surrounding African states. In 1816, a leader named **Shaka** seized control of his small **Zulu** kingdom, organized an army, and attacked neighboring African states in competition for grazing land. Although the fighting was traditional with spears, shields, and knives, Shaka devised a short, stabbing spear that gave his men a tremendous advantage over their adversaries. The state grew to be one of the most powerful in Africa by the time Shaka was killed by his relatives in 1828. Despite the fact that his reign only last ten years, Shaka's armies displaced other groups – such as the Soshagane, Nguni, and So-tho people – and many came within the borders of the Cape Colony. Meanwhile, the British had gained control of the Cape Colony as a result of their victories

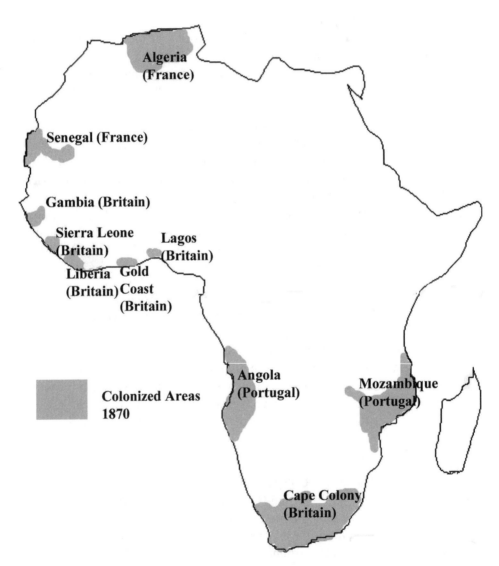

Africa in 1870. By 1870 evidence of western overseas expansion can be seen along the coastal areas where Britain, France, and Portugal set up trading posts and port cities. By 1900 only Liberia and Ethiopia were left as independent states. All other land space on the continent had been claimed by European countries.

in the Napoleonic Wars, and in reaction, many Dutch settlers moved inland away from British-controlled port cities. This "Great Trek" of people of Dutch descent (called "Boers") inland to claim land for farming added to the turmoil of Africans newly displaced by the Zulus, with the Boers fighting the natives, enslaving some of them, and restricting others to reservations while claiming the best lands for themselves. The Boers established two republics in the interior, named the Orange Free State and the Transvaal, where they sought freedom from British control, and the British paid little attention to them until diamonds were discovered in the Orange Free State in 1867.

When the Suez Canal was completed in 1869 it seemed as if the Cape Colony had lost its usefulness, but the discovery of diamonds and gold deposits in the 1870s and 80s revitalized the area, and brought a whole round of new Europeans to seek their fortunes there. British entrepreneurs, such as **Cecil Rhodes,** and prospectors moved into the Orange Free State, increasing hostilities between British and Dutch settlers, as both competed to control the diamond and gold mines. Rhodes, an aggressive imperialist, once said he would "annex the stars" if he could, and he founded De Beers Consolidated, a company that began in the Orange Free State diamond fields, and came to dominate the world's diamond trade. Rhodes was not content with economic success, but also wished to establish British political domination as well, and at his encouragement, the British South Africa Company pushed into central Africa. There two new colonies were named after Rhodes: Southern Rhodesia (now Zimbabwe) and Northern Rhodesia (now Zambia). When the British tried to annex the Boer republics, Transvaal and Orange Free State, they sparked the South African War (called the "Boer War" by the British) between the Dutch (also called Afrikaners) and the British between 1899 and 1902. Although the British won the war decisively, the British government left the settlers to govern themselves, and the Afrikaners eventually came to dominate the government of the country created in 1910 - the Union of South Africa.

Explorers and Missionaries

Before the middle of the 19th century European missionaries were heading to Africa, with the most famous one, **David Livingstone,** arriving in 1841 at his post at the edge of the Kalahari Desert in southern Africa. A Scottish Protestant, he was clearly influenced by the reform movements of his day in his desire to not only convert Africans to Christianity but also to free them from slavery. He also was one of the greatest European explorers of Africa, whose journeys inland were inspired not only by the desire to find new converts, but also to explore and map areas previously unknown to Europeans. He made several expeditions throughout southern and central Africa and made detailed maps of the areas he explored. He also sent descriptive journals home that appeared in magazines and newspapers, enough to develop a great interest in his travels in Europe and the United States. His most extensive early travels were along the great Zambezi River that flowed from the interior of Africa to the Indian Ocean. On a return trip to Britain he made a round of speaking tours and published his best-selling "Missionary Travels and Researches in South Africa" that filled huge gaps in western knowledge of central and southern Africa. When he returned to Africa, he began a search for the source of the Nile River in central Africa, and it was this journey that secured his fame throughout the western world. After nothing was heard from him for several months, an American journalist, **Henry Stanley,** set off amidst great publicity to find him. He finally met Dr. Livingstone near Lake Tanganyika in October 1871, and greeted him with the famous phrase: "Dr. Livingstone I presume?" Although he received new supplies from Stanley, Dr. Livingstone died a few months later without accomplishing his goal of locating the Nile's source. Mr. Stanley returned home by way of the Congo River, where he established trading stations for King Leopold II of Belgium. He profited personally from both the publicity of his expedition and the trading arrangement with King Leopold, and he – as well as Dr. Livingstone – stimulated the "Scramble for Africa" that followed.

The Scramble for Africa

Between 1875 and 1900 European imperial powers set off to claim lands in Africa, inspired by the information and maps compiled by adventurers and explorers such as Livingstone and Stanley. The knowledge gained about the great African rivers – the Nile, Niger, Congo, and Zambezi – allowed others to reach inland regions, following Henry Stanley's example of developing commercial ventures. King Leopold II declared the basin of the Congo River to be a free-trade zone, but he filled it with rubber plantations run by forced African labor that increased his personal wealth. Meanwhile, the British laid claims to Egypt, and other European statesmen feared that their countries would be left behind unless they too claimed territories. Using the principle of balance of power, as established by the Congress of Vienna in 1815, Otto von Bismarck, chancellor of the newly created German Empire, called a meeting of fourteen states to convene in Berlin in 1884. **The Berlin Conference** was meant to calm rivalries and avoid war, and it produced an agreement that any European state could establish colonies in unclaimed land in Africa, but must first notify the other states of its intentions. Representatives from European countries then sat down with a map of Africa and literally carved its territories up among them. Then each country sent armies to validate claims, and the Africans' spears and outdated muskets were no match for European cannon and machine guns. By 1900 all areas of Africa were colonized, except for Ethiopia, which successfully kept the Italians at bay until the 1930s, and Liberia, a small republic in west Africa of freed slaves from the United States.

**ORIGINAL DOCUMENT:
EXCERPT FROM
DR. LIVINGSTONE'S JOURNAL**

One of the most impressive "discoveries" that David Livingstone made on his journey down the Zambezi River was a huge waterfall that the natives called *Mosi-oa-Tunya*, or "smoke that thunders." He named the falls after the queen of England, Victoria, and described in his journal his reactions upon seeing them for the first time:

"After twenty minutes' sail from Kalai we came in sight, for the first time, of the columns of vapor appropriately called 'smoke'; rising at a distance of five or six miles, exactly as when large tracts of grass are burned in Africa. Five columns now arose, and, bending in the direction of the wind, they seemed placed against a low ridge covered with trees; the tops of the columns at this distance appeared to mingle with the clouds. They were white below, and higher up became dark, so as to simulate smoke very closely. The whole scene was extremely beautiful; the banks and islands dotted over the river are adorned with sylvan vegetation of great variety of color and form...no one can imagine the beauty of the view from any thing witnessed in England. It had never been seen before by European eyes; but scenes so lovely must have been gazed upon by angels in their flight. The only want felt is that of mountains in the background. The falls are bounded on three sides by ridges 300 or 400 feet in height, which are covered with forest, with the red soil appearing among the trees."

Reference: "Livingstone Discovers Victoria Falls, 1885," Eyewitness to History, http://www.eyewitnesstohistory.com/livingstone.htm

IMPERIALISM IN THE PACIFIC

In the Pacific Ocean basin, European powers established settler colonies in Australia and New Zealand, but most of the smaller Pacific islands became tropical dependencies with largely native populations left in place. In 1770 **Captain James Cook** anchored on Australia's southeast shore, close to modern day Sydney, and declared that the area would be suitable for British settlement. A few years later about 1000 settlers arrived – most of them convicted criminals – to establish the colony of New South Wales. Most became sheepherders, and soon non-convict colonists arrived, with a great increase in immigration after gold was discovered in Australia in 1851. Soon the nearby islands of New Zealand became destinations for British settlers, who settled into agriculture and trade.

In both Australia and New Zealand, the arrival of European settlers was disastrous for the native people, partly because diseases such as smallpox and measles killed large numbers of them. In Australia, the aborigines were primarily hunters and gatherers, so the British did not consider them true inhabitants of the land. Land was seized, and the more British settlers who came, the farther into the desert the aborigines were pushed. When the aborigines fought back, they were evicted by military force from most lands suitable for agriculture or herding. In New Zealand, the native people – called the Maori – signed a treaty that put them under British protection, and British settlers soon took the best lands, provoking a series of wars between settlers and natives from 1860 to 1864. Like the aborigines in Australia, the conflict resulted in most Maoris being placed on reservations.

Until the late 19th century, Europeans had little interest in colonizing the small islands of the Pacific. Most visitors to the islands were whalers, missionaries, and merchants, each with their own goals, which did not include colonization. However, as competition among European nations increased with the Scramble for Africa and the takeover of Southeast Asia, the imperialist countries began to stake their claims in the Pacific as well. France claimed Tahiti, the Marquesas, and New Caledonia; the British colonized Fiji; and Germany took over the Marshall Islands. The Berlin Conference that partitioned Africa also struck agreements regarding Oceania.

Hawaii – far away from the islands of the South Pacific – did not become a colony until the United States annexed the islands in 1898, although, like Australia, Hawaii was visited by Captain James Cook in the late 18th century. Cook found a people untouched by modern technology. On his second trip there, he was killed by warriors who tried to take his ship for its metal nails. The British soon convinced a Hawaiian prince to unify the islands under him, and with western tutelage he won a series of wars that resulted in a friendly environment for western merchants and businessmen. Protestant missionaries from New England were inspired to come to Hawaii after two powerful queens banned female subordination, and large numbers of conversions to Christianity followed. The missionaries established western-style schools, and Hawaiian customs, dress, and languages were discouraged. As in many other places of colonization, disease struck the native population, and by 1850 only about 80,000 Hawaiians remained, in contrast to the 500,000 or so who lived there when the Europeans first arrived. Western investors began buying up land for sugar plantations, and increasing numbers of settlers came to the islands, especially from the United States. Asian workers were brought in to work on the plantations, further diversifying the population. With a series of weak Hawaiian kings after 1872, disorder threatened the plantations, so the planters turned to the United States to protect them. An American naval base was established at Pearl Harbor, and eventually American troops were posted all around Honolulu, the main city. An annexation movement led by western settlers convinced the U.S., fresh from victory in its "Splendid Little War" with Spain in 1898, to officially take over Hawaii in order to protect American lives and property, as the planters successfully argued. Hawaiians were not enslaved, and soon they ceased to threaten the planters at all, and so the territory settled in as a diverse population of Americans, native Hawaiians, Chinese, and Japanese.

GLOBAL CHANGES IN THE AGE OF IMPERIALISM

Just as industrialization widened the gap between the rich and the poor within industrial nations, imperialism widened the gap between rich and poor nations. The global economy that developed consisted of countries that controlled and countries that were controlled, or the "haves" and the "have nots." Almost all areas of the world were affected by industrialization, even if they remained agricultural, because by 1914, many of those areas were under the sway of imperialism, either as direct colonies, or as subordinates fashioned by unequal treaties for trade and business. The forces of industrialization became more powerful as the 19th century progressed, so that western nations explored the ends of the earth for natural resources and markets to keep their burgeoning prosperity going. By 1914, western European nations were joined by Russia, the United States, and Japan, and the competition that resulted from their quest for expansion affected more and more people around the world.

- **Economic Changes** – The global economy was reorganized so that imperialist countries controlled natural resources in their subject societies around the world. Many of these resources served as raw materials destined for the factories of Europe, North America, and Japan. Global trade in diamonds, rubber, petroleum, and timber increased as new natural resources were discovered and means of transportation improved with larger, faster ships and rail lines built across land. As in the previous era, trade in cotton, tea, coffee, gold, silver, and cacao continued, but at a more rapid pace. Sometimes the subject lands continued to produce what they had long produced, such as cotton in India, but in this era India sent raw cotton to Europe for manufacture, instead of making textiles by hand in India. In other cases, crops that had never been produced in an area were introduced, so that much of the land space was taken up by crops for export, often at the expense of raising food necessary for the subject people. For example, rubber plantations came to dominate agriculture in Malay and Sumatra, and also along the Congo River in Africa.

- **Labor Migrations** – In order to more efficiently make use of the natural resources they found all over the globe, imperialist countries encouraged people to migrate to areas where their labor was most needed. As a result, massive worldwide migrations took place to areas where job opportunities abounded. Many of these migrants – especially those from Asia, Africa, and the Pacific islands – became **indentured servants,** who worked in return for payment of their passage.   As slave labor systems declined, the plantations made use of contract laborers recruited from lands where poverty levels were high and populations were dense. Some common patterns included Indian migrants to work on rubber plantations in Southeast Asia, South Africa, and the Pacific Islands; Chinese laborers to work on sugar plantations in the Caribbean, gold mines in South Africa and Australia, and railroad construction sites in the United States, Canada, and Peru; Japanese and Chinese to sugar plantations in Hawaii; and African laborers to sugar plantations in the Caribbean islands. A large-scale migration of Europeans also occurred during this era, but most were not indentured servants; instead they sought cheap land to cultivate as independent farmers or paid laborers in factories. Most of these migrants headed to the colonies controlled by their homeland, such as Australia and New Zealand, and to the United States, where expansion west provided cheap land and the industrializing cities offered plentiful factory jobs.

- **Social Consequences** – As people from different lands came into contact with one another, conflicts often emerged, especially between colonizers and colonized. As Europeans went to the colonies, they tended to segregate themselves from the natives, living in all-white enclaves and socializing only with one another. In most areas, mixed marriages or living arrangements were frowned upon, a taboo reinforced by the large number of missionaries who travelled to the colonies. Particularly for women and children, who did not have the work-related contacts that the men had, their European world was highly insulated from its surroundings, so that the only natives they knew were servants or nannies. Upper and middle-class natives seldom socialized with Europeans, and their exclusion from the imperialists' world bred resentments that eventually developed into support for independence movements. One important consequence of colonization for some women in traditional societies was the creation of educational opportunities they had not had before. Missionary girls' schools were first established to provide literacy skills to deprived social groups, but by the end of the 19th century women from the growing middle class were also attending schools sponsored by European colonizers. As men in these societies became increasingly westernized, some began to wish the same for their wives, so educational opportunities were opened for women. However, most schools with European curricula were male-centered, and education for women tended to focus on improvement of their domestic skills. Some European women who went to the colonies – either as settlers, missionaries, or nurses – found liberation in their new roles from social constraints back home, although others that made the journey found a recreated European social system in place in their destinations.

- **Scientific Racism** – The new imperialist world order benefitted European countries, the United States, and Japan much more than the lands that were colonized, and alongside the economic changes came an academic pursuit known as **scientific racism.** The studies were based on the assumption that the world is divided into four main racial groups, each with its own distinct traits. One early theorist, Joseph Arthur de Gobineau, characterized Africans as lazy and unintelligent, Europeans as intelligent and morally superior, Asians as smart but non-assertive, and American natives as arrogant yet dull. Other scientists who agreed with him supported the notion that Europeans were an inherently superior race, and by implication, the natural masters of the world. Scientific racists used **Charles Darwin's** theories in *The Origins of Species* **(1859)** to devise their theories of **Social Darwinism.** According to Darwin, an English biologist, all species developed over time through a process of survival of the fittest, so that species that didn't adapt to changing times died out, and those that did adapt survived. Whereas Darwin's arguments had to do strictly with biological evolution, Social Darwinists applied survival of the fittest to social situations as well. The best known Social Darwinist was **Herbert Spencer,** who argued that successful individuals and races emerged to dominate others as a result of "survival of the fittest." His ideas were used to justify both the wealth of entrepreneurs in opposition to their laborers, as well as the domination of European imperialists over subject peoples.

During the era from 1750 to 1914 massive political and economic changes in Europe first transformed societies there, but increasingly impacted other areas of the world as the 19th century progressed. Political ideas, such as liberalism and nationalism, spread throughout the world as Europeans came to dominate other areas as a result of their new industrial might, and the economic world order changed as non-European people and lands came to supply the labor and natural resources needed by industrialized countries. The United States and Japan emerged as new industrial powers, but as the era drew to a close, competition among European powers was increasing, and their conflicts would draw others into a world war that impacted virtually all areas of the world in 1914.

CONCEPTS AND IDENTIFICATIONS

Berlin Conference
Bessemer steel converter
British raj
company men
Cook, Captain James
Darwin, Charles, *The Origin of Species*
Edison, Thomas
imperialism (colonial, political, economic, social-cultural)
indentured servants
Indian Civil Service
Indian National Congress
Livingstone, David
Muhammad Ali
nawabs
Panama Canal
Rhodes, Cecil
Roy, Rammohun
scientific racism
Scramble for Africa
sepoys, Sepoy Rebellion
settlement colonies
Social Darwinism
Spencer, Herbert
Shaka
Stanley, Henry
Suez Canal
tropical dependencies

UNIT FOUR QUESTIONS

Multiple-Choice Questions:

"It is our true policy to steer clear of permanent alliances with any portion of the foreign world, so far, I mean, as we are now at liberty to do it...in my opinion it is unnecessary and would be unwise to extend them..."

1. The quote above is excerpted from

   a) Adam Smith's *The Wealth of Nations*
   b) The Declaration of the Rights of Man and Citizen
   c) Charles Darwin's *The Origin of Species*
   d) the American Declaration of Independence
   e) George Washington's Farewell Address

2. In which of the following revolutions was a slave labor force the MOST important as a force for change?

   a) the American Revolution
   b) the French Revolution
   c) the Haitian Revolution
   d) early 19th-century revolution in Venezuela
   e) early 19th-century revolution in Brazil

3. Italian and German unifications during the late 19th century were both inspired by

   a) conservatism
   b) socialism
   c) Marxism
   d) mercantilism
   e) nationalism

4. During the period from 1750 to 1914, which of the following movements for change was LEAST successful in reaching its goals?

   a) the abolitionist movement
   b) independence movements in Latin America
   c) the abolition of absolute monarchy in France
   d) the women's rights movement
   e) more political rights for the bourgeoisie

5. Which of the following changes occurred in France as a direct result of Napoleon's rule?

    a) Religious and individual freedoms were incorporated into a comprehensive law code.
    b) The Catholic Church was stripped of all of its land.
    c) Women gained the right to own property and divorce their husbands.
    d) Radicalism became the prevailing political philosophy among bourgeoisie and peasants alike.
    e) France came to dominate Europe for most of the 19th century.

6. In which of the following areas did juntas play an important role in the success of revolutions during the period from 1750 to 1850?

    I. Gran Colombia
    II. France
    III. Argentina
    IV. The United States

    a) I and II only
    b) I and III only
    c) II and IV only
    d) II, III, and IV only
    e) I, II, III, and IV

7. The enclosure movement in Britain most directly impacted the development of the Industrial Revolution by providing

    a) access to natural resources
    b) a ready labor supply for factories and businesses
    c) political and economic support for entrepreneurs
    d) railroad transportation to shipping points
    e) ready cash supplies for funding new industries

8. The marble boat pictured above was built in order to

    a) reflect the historical naval supremacy of China
    b) warn the Japanese not to attack China
    c) show the engineering skills of those that constructed it
    d) illustrate the Qing Dynasty's disdain for western money
    e) disguise the illegal opium trade going on in Canton

9. Which of the following is the MOST direct cause of the 19th century demographic transition in western countries?

    a) the Columbian Exchange
    b) political revolutions
    c) growing emphasis on values that supported large families
    d) the Industrial Revolution
    e) growing number of immigrants coming into western countries

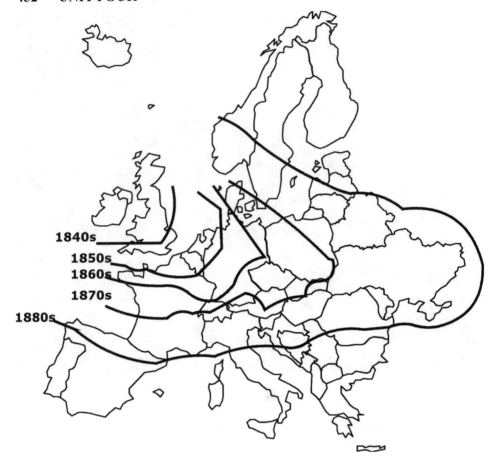

10. The map above shows the 19th century spread of

    a) the Industrial Revolution
    b) liberalism as a political ideology
    c) availability of products from the Americas
    d) political control of the British Empire
    e) communism

11. The set of cultural values called "the cult of domesticity" applied primarily to

    a) working-class men in industrial societies
    b) lower-class women in industrial societies
    c) peasant families in Southeast Asia and Sub-Saharan Africa
    d) landed nobility in east Asia
    e) middle-class women in industrialized societies

12. The Monroe Doctrine most clearly reflects the United States foreign policy of

a) laissez-faire capitalism
b) isolationism
c) internationalism
d) mercantilism
e) liberalism

13. The political system set up in Canada in 1867 is best described as a(n)

a) self-governing political system still officially tied to Britain
b) presidential system with strong economic ties to the U.S.
c) British colony with some powers of self-government
d) independent country with most official ties to Britain severed
e) constitutional monarchy with many powers given to parliament

14. Which of the following is the BEST explanation for why personality politics were more important in shaping Latin America than in North America?

a) Most Latin American countries had parliamentary systems; North American countries had presidential systems.
b) Stable political institutions were slower to develop in Latin America than in North America.
c) More charismatic men came to leadership in Latin America than in North America.
d) The rule of law was well in place in Latin America, and was not very effective in North America.
e) Latin American countries did not set up legislatures; North American countries set up strong legislatures.

15. "Slavery was not born of racism; rather, racism was the consequence of slavery.'

The statement above supports the explanation that slavery and emancipation had

a) ideological roots that led to economic consequences
b) economic roots that led to ideological consequences
c) roots in both ideology and economic interests
d) little impact on the nature of racism
e) motives that were neither economic nor ideological

16. The main reason that the country of Siam on the map above was not claimed by an imperialist power is that

   a) the king of Siam effectively resisted imperialist control
   b) the English and French agreed to leave it as a "buffer zone"
   c) it was protected by the Japanese
   d) it had established a formal alliance with India
   e) its control of trade in the region was too well established to allow for an imperialist takeover

17. Which of the following did the Young Turks in the Ottoman Empire and the Boxers in the Qing Empire have in common?

    a) Both believed that their empires would be better off if they became more dependent on western powers.
    b) Both supported their emperors in the struggle to maintain power in the face of western aggression.
    c) Both believed that conflicts among regional lords were the biggest threats that their empires faced.
    d) Both were nationalists groups that sought to keep their nation's identity in the waning days of empire.
    e) Both organized against nationalist groups who wanted to replace the emperors with republican governments.

18. Which of the following land-based empires experienced significant degrees of industrialization by the end of the 19th century?

    I. Ottoman Empire
    II. Russia
    III. Qing China
    IV. Japan

    a) I and II only
    b) I and III only
    c) II and IV only
    d) III and IV only
    e) II, III, and IV only

19. A significant social reform that took place in Russia during the 19th century was the

    a) emancipation of the serfs
    b) large-scale redistribution of land to peasants
    c) recognition of political rights of the bourgeoisie
    d) recognition of women's suffrage rights
    e) restriction of the rights of nobility to claim hereditary lands

(Questions 20 and 21 are based on the map above):

20. The map shows that colonized areas in Africa in 1870 were primarily

    a) controlled by the Portuguese
    b) controlled by the French
    c) located along coastal areas
    d) challenged by native Africans
    e) weak and ineffective

21. A map of Africa 30 years later (1900) would differ from the map
    above in that it would show

    a) many more areas of Africa controlled by European powers
    b) fewer British possession and more French possessions
    c) almost no areas of Africa controlled by European powers
    d) many areas controlled by Japan
    e) more Portuguese possessions and fewer French-controlled areas

"The transformation of the country was complete, involving dramatic economic, political, social, cultural, and educational changes, and the program was
imposed from the top rung of government – the oligarchs."

22. The statement above accurately describes late 19th century

    a) Ottoman Empire
    b) China
    c) Japan
    d) Russia
    e) Germany

23. Which of the following colonies is BEST described as a tropical
    dependency colony?

    a) Australia
    b) India
    c) New Zealand
    d) South Africa
    e) Hawaii

24. Which of the following events of the 19th century occurred FIRST?

    a) the opening of the Suez Canal
    b) the invention of the steam engine
    c) the completion of the Trans-Siberian Railroad
    d) the Meiji Restoration
    e) King Leopold's sponsorship of rubber plantations along the Congo
       River in Africa

25. The most important incentive for the "scramble" of European countries to colonize areas of central and south Africa during the late 19th century was the

   a) desire to control sea-based trade between Europe and the Indian Ocean Basin
   b) discovery of diamond and gold deposits
   c) wish to convert African natives to Christianity
   d) aggressive attempts by the Japanese to colonize Africa
   e) search for new agricultural lands for their growing populations

Free-Response Questions:

For all essays, be sure that you have a relevant thesis that is supported by historical evidence.

Document-Based Question: suggested reading time - 10 minutes; suggested writing time - 40 minutes

For the DBQ, be sure that you

- **Use all of the documents**

- **Use evidence from the documents to support your thesis**

- **Analyze the documents by grouping them in at least two or three appropriate ways**

- **Consider the source of the document and analyze the author's point of view**

- **Explain the need for at least one additional document**

1. Using the documents, analyze motives for revolution that occurred in various countries between 1750 and 1914. Identify one additional type of document and explain briefly how it would help your analysis.

Document 1

"We hold these truths to be self-evident; that all men are created equal, that they are endowed by their Creator with certain unalienable rights, that among these are life, liberty, and the pursuit of happiness. That, to secure these rights, governments are instituted among men, deriving their just powers from the consent of the governed. That whenever any form of government becomes destructive of these ends, it is the right of the people to alter or to abolish it, and to institute new government, laying its foundation on such principles, and organizing its powers in such form, as to them shall seem most likely to effect their safety and happiness...when a long train of abuses and usurpations, pursuing invariably the same object, evinces a design to reduce them under absolute despotism, it is their right, it is their duty, to throw off such government, and to provide new guards for their future security."

> The American Declaration of
> Independence, 1776

Document 2

"Article 2. The goal of every political association is the preservation of the natural and inalienable rights of man. These rights are liberty, property, security, and resistance to oppression.

Article 3. The principle of all sovereignty resides essentially in the nation. No body and no individual can exercise authority that does not flow directly from the nation."

> The Declaration of the Rights of
> Man and the Citizen, France,
> 1789

Document 3

"I was born a slave, but nature gave me a soul of a free man...In overthrowing me, you have done no more than cut down the trunk of the tree of the black liberty in St-Domingue – it will spring back from the roots, for they are numerous and deep."

> Toussaint L'Ouverture,
> Leader of Revolution in Haiti

Document 4

"...could we take off the dark covering of antiquity [pertaining to the origin of kings and of the State] and trace them to their first rise, we should find the first of them nothing better than the principle ruffian of some restless gang; whose savage manners or pre-eminence in subtlety obtained him the title of chief among plunderers; and who by increasing in power and extending his depredations, overawed the quiet and defenseless to purchase their safety by frequent contributions."

Thomas Paine,
English Colonist, author of
Common Sense

Document 5

"In short, the Communists everywhere support every revolutionary movement against the existing social and political order of things. In all these movements, they bring to the front, as the leading question in each, the property question, no matter what its degree of development at the time. Finally, they labor everywhere for the union and agreement of the democratic parties of all countries.

The Communists disdain to conceal their views and aims. They openly declare that their ends can be attained only by the forcible overthrow of all existing social conditions. Let the ruling classes tremble at a communist revolution. The proletarians have nothing to lose but their chains. They have a world to win.

Proletarians of all countries, unite!"

Karl Marx,
Communist Manifesto, 1848

Document 6

"An army of our brothers, sent by the Sovereign Congress of New Granada, has come to liberate you…Moved by your misfortunes, we have been unable to observe with indifference the afflictions you were forced to experience by the barbarous Spaniards, who have ravished you, plundered you, and brought you death and destruction. They have violated the sacred rights of nations. They have broken the most solemn agreements and treaties. In fact, they have committed every manner of crime, reducing the Republic of Venezuela to the most frightful desolation. Justice therefore demands vengeance, and necessity compels us to exact it. Let the monsters who infest Colombian soil, who have drenched it in blood, be cast out forever; may their punishment be equal to the enormity of their perfidy, so that we may eradicate the stain of our ignominy and demonstrate to the nations of the world that the sons of America cannot be offended with impunity. Despite our just resentment toward the ubiquitous Spaniards, our magnanimous heart still commands us to open to them for the last time a path to reconciliation and friendship; they are invited to live peacefully among us, if they will abjure their crimes, honestly change their ways, and cooperate with us in destroying the intruding Spanish government and the reestablishment of the Republic of Venezuela...Fear not the sword that comes to avenge you and to sever the ignoble ties with which your executioners have bound you to their own fate. You are hereby assured, with absolute impunity, of your honor, lives, and property. The single title, "Americans," shall be your safeguard and guarantee. Our arms have come to protect you, and they shall never be raised against a single one of you, our brothers...Spaniards and Canary Islanders, you will die, though you be neutral, unless you actively espouse the cause of America's liberation. Americans, you will live, even if you have trespassed."

> Simón Bolívar, Liberator of Venezuela, Brigadier of the Union, General in Chief of the Northern Army; to his fellow countrymen June 15, 1813

Document 7

"I would rather die standing than live on my knees!"

> Emiliano Zapata
> Early 20th Century Mexican Revolutionist

Change Over Time Essay: suggested writing time - 40 minutes

2. Analyze the political and social changes and continuities between 1750 and 1914 in ONE of the following areas. In your analysis be sure to discuss the causes of the changes and the reasons for the continuities.

    - Japan

    - Latin America

    - Russia

Comparative Essay: suggested writing time - 40 minutes

3. Compare and contrast how industrialization and its outcomes affected TWO of the following areas during the 19th century.

    - India

    - China

    - Sub-Saharan Africa

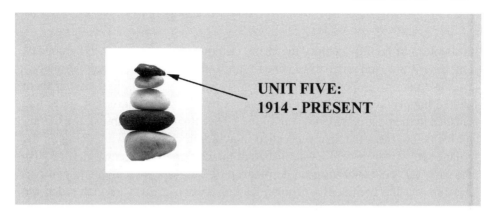

UNIT FIVE:
1914 - PRESENT

Most historians agree that analyzing the "marker events" and important patterns in recent years is more difficult than assessing the earlier periods, largely because we don't know yet what the full consequences of the present and recent past will be. It is clear that major changes did occur during the 20th century, and that the world of 1914 was very different from today's world, but the process of identifying the most important events and trends is by its very nature a tentative one. As we have seen throughout history, each era builds on the developments of the previous one, and the era of 1914 to the present began with the important "marker event" of World War I.

The world in the early days of the 20th century before 1914 was very much dominated by western powers, who exercised political, economic, and social-cultural control over lands in Africa, Latin America, Asia, and the Pacific Islands. This global power resulted from three interrelated changes that occurred during the era from 1750 to 1914:

1) **The formation of nation-states** – Political organizations were transformed from those that relied on the traditional power of kings to those based on the concept of nation-states – people bound together by a common identity and rule of law. As a result, governments were better able to mobilize popular support for their ambitious economic and political endeavors.

2) **The Industrial Revolution** – The economic power of western states was greatly enhanced by the Industrial Revolution, which increased production and technological capacity dramatically and provided a market incentive to control other areas of the world.

3) **Imperialism** – The new world order created by industrialization divided countries into "have" and "have not" categories, and increased inequalities between rich and poor nations, allowing western powers to exercise political, economic, and social-cultural control.

At the turn of the 20th century the British Empire was very much in its heyday, and other European powers – such as France, the Netherlands, and Germany – were also strong imperialists. However, tensions were building among them as had happened in Europe so many times before. The quarreling states had clashed in the post-Napoleonic era of the 19th century – for example, the Crimean War – but they had also succeeded in avoiding conflicts by agreeing on the balance of power principle established at the Congress of Vienna in 1815. By the early 20th century European dominance of the globe increased competitiveness among the continent's nations, leading to two great wars that ended the imperialist world order of the 19th century.

The pace of change quickened significantly after 1914, so even though this era has not run quite 100 years so far, dynamics of interactions among societies are radically different today than they were in the early 20th century. As a result, we can periodize this era into three phases that correspond to unit chapters:

- **Chapter Twenty** – 1914 to 1945 – Two world wars with a great depression in between led to the crisis and collapse of the imperial world order that had taken shape during the 19th century. The decline of western European power was accompanied by a major regime change in Russia, and revolutions in China and other non-western countries.

- **Chapter Twenty-One** – 1945 to 1991 – The imperial order was replaced by the Cold War hegemonies of the United States and the Soviet Union, and the division of the globe into "Three Worlds" based on the strategic positioning of the two "superpowers."

- **Chapter Twenty-Two** – 1991 to the Present – The new world order is still taking shape, but Cold War politics clearly have been replaced by new interactions and patterns, including both globalization and fragmentation based on established allegiances and divisions.

Although we cannot know the future consequences of events of this period of world history, clearly some important developing patterns are shaping the world's continuing story. The relative influences of major civilization areas are being rebalanced, contacts among civilizations are intensifying, and patterns of interactions are evolving. No matter what the eventual outcomes are, they will be heavily influenced by the people, events, and processes that preceded them, as the threads of the past are inextricably woven with those of the present and future.

THE BIG PICTURE:
1914 - PRESENT

Themes that run through the period from 1914 to the present that make it distinct from other periods include:

1. The hegemony of western Europe was broken by 1945, and was replaced by competition between two "superpowers": the United States and the Soviet Union. This Cold War world order ended in 1991 with the collapse of the Soviet Union.
2. International organizations became increasingly important during the time period, so that by the early 21st century new power arrangements may be supplanting the political division of the world into nation-states.
3. Nationalism continues to be important during this era, just as it was between 1750 and 1914. However, it has taken new patterns, as exemplified in fascism, decolonization, racism, genocide, and the breakup of the Soviet Union.
4. Like the era 1750 to 1914, political revolutions have characterized this period. Democratic values that had inspired earlier revolutions have created waves of democratization that have impacted many more parts of the world than before. Radical movements that began during the 19th century offered important political alternatives to the western liberal democracies.
5. Social reform and social revolution have continued during this era, with many consequences, including changes in gender roles, peasant protests, the spread of Marxism, and religious fundamentalism.
6. The increasing interactions of societies that had developed over the ages have resulted in economic, technological, scientific, and cultural globalization during this era.
7. Demographic changes include a decrease in proportions of populations that live in western nations. Environmental changes have continued as industrial and post-industrial development reach many parts of the world.

CHAPTER TWENTY:
CRISIS AND COLLAPSE OF
THE IMPERIAL ORDER
1914-1945

By the early 20ᵗʰ century the world order was clearly based on imperialism and the ability of western countries to dominate all others. However, the competition that imperialist possibilities provoked among European nations led to World War I in 1914, a deadly conflict that did not resolve underlying issues. The war was followed by a disastrous economic depression and then a second world war fought on a much grander scale than the first. By the end of World War II, the countries of western Europe were seriously weakened, and the foundations of European imperialism had crumbled. Although most colonies were not officially lost until after 1945, the overall impact of the two wars and the depression was so devastating to Europe that the United States and the Soviet Union emerged as the world's superpowers even before World War II ended.

WORLD WAR I (1914-1918)

The Great War, as it was called before World War II began, lasted from August 1914 to November 1918 and involved more countries than any previous war in history. It was the first **total war** in which the governments mobilized virtually every person and natural resource available to support the war effort. Nationalism bound civilians to the war much more than in the past, as winning the war became a matter of national pride. Technologies brought about by industrialization allowed the war to take place on a vast scale, and the number of human casualties – both military and civilian – was enormous. The number of military casualties alone was far greater than those of any previous war, with about nine million soldiers dying, and twenty-one million suffering injuries from combat. This total war not only killed and maimed; it seriously damaged the national economies of European nations on both the winning and losing sides, as most were left with huge public debts and rising inflation. World War I was the first step toward the loss of western European hegemony, and it opened the way for the United States and the Soviet Union to emerge as world powers later in the century.

Underlying Causes of the War

European countries have had a long history of conflict, dating back to the days when they were competing kingdoms and principalities with feudal loyalties that were often at cross-purposes. In more recent times, the continent was engulfed by the Napoleonic Wars, which were intensified by fierce feelings of nationalism. Although the Congress of Vienna in 1814-1815 struck a balance of power among nations to achieve peace, that balance was upset during the late 19th century by the creation of new empires, particularly Germany. Otto von Bismarck's armies humiliated older powers such as France, and a united Germany challenged even Britain, despite the latter's control of a vast worldwide empire. The economic and military competition extended to the world stage, as Germany joined the quest for new colonies in Africa and Asia.

Some factors that contributed to the outbreak of the war include:

1) **Rivalries intensified by nationalism** – By the late 19th century, all the industrialized nations of Europe were aggressively competing for foreign markets, but the rivalry between Britain and Germany had become the most intense by 1914. The rapid industrialization of Germany had brought its share of the world's total industrial output to about 14%, roughly equal to Britain's. In 1870 Britain's share had been about 32% and Germany 13%, a comfortably wide margin. Whereas the increase in production in the United States was largely responsible for Britain's drop, British production was beginning to slow, increasing Germany's threat. An expensive naval race heightened tensions between the two nations, and Germany was playing catch-up to Britain's lead in sea power. The intense competition led both countries to develop huge navies.

2) **Colonial disputes** – The scramble for empire was spurred by nationalist rivalries among European countries, and it spread their historic rivalries to virtually every corner of the globe. In their haste to grab land, they often came into conflict with one another. For example, Britain and Russia disputed land claims in Persia and Afghanistan, and Britain and Germany argued over east and southwest Africa. Since Germany had only been a unified country since 1871, its leaders had a late start, but they aggressively challenged the French and English in many parts of the globe. England and France argued so intensely in Southeast Asia that they allowed Siam to remain independent as a buffer zone between British-owned Burma and French Indochina. In 1905 France and Germany almost went to war over Morocco in northern Africa, and war among the Balkan states in 1912-1913 created hostilities among European states who wished to exploit the unrest.

PERSPECTIVES: KAISER WILHEIM II AND THE GERMAN NAVY

An important component of Kaiser Wilheim II's plan to build German power was his decision to construct a massive navy, and he was particularly determined to match England's development of a revolutionary battleship type, the Dreadnought. As the German navy grew, the British responded by building more ships, leading to a dangerous military buildup that eventually led to war. Wilheim's political motivations were mixed with personal ones that reflected his mixed heritage: his father was Prussian, but his mother was the daughter of the English Queen Victoria, and as a boy Wilheim spent a great deal of time in England. The kaiser explained his reasons for building the German fleet at a dinner aboard one of his proudest ships, the *Hohenzollern*, in 1904:

"When, as a little boy, I was allowed to visit Portsmouth and Plymouth hand in hand with kind aunts and friendly admirals, I admired the proud English ships in those two superb harbors. Then there awoke in me the wish to build ships of my own like these someday, and when I was grown up to possess as fine a navy as the English."

The kaiser's chancellor, Bernhard von Bulow, censored the speech for the press because he feared that the Reichstag (parliament) would not fund naval construction based on the kaiser's "personal inclinations and juvenile memories."

Reference: Quoted in *Dreadnought,* by Robert K. Massie (New York: Random House, 1991), p. 151.

3) **Self-determination** – The spirit of nationalism that spread throughout Europe and many other parts of the world during the 19th century supported the notion that people with common national identities have the right to form their own sovereign states. This belief was formalized into the doctrine of **self-determination** that inspired many people in eastern Europe to fight for their independence. Many of them were encompassed by the multinational empires of the Ottoman, Habsburg, and Russian dynasties, and they hoped to follow the examples of Greece, Romania, and Bulgaria who had gained their independence from the weakening Ottoman Empire. In Austria-Hungary, many Slavic people – such as Czechs, Slovaks, Serbs, Croats, and Slovenes – had nationalist aspirations that spawned resistance to Habsburg rule. Russia,

always hoping to gain lands that accessed the Black Sea, encouraged **Pan-Slavism,** a feeling of cultural and ethnic kinship among the Slavic people that the empire hoped would weaken Austria-Hungary's hold in the Balkans.

4) **Entangling alliances** – The Great War was sparked in 1914 by the assassination of Archduke Ferdinand of Austria-Hungary by a Serb nationalist, an incident that would never have led to widespread war had it not been for the system of alliances that had been building in Europe over the previous decades. As countries competed, they looked for backing from others in order to challenge their enemies. For example, as Germany moved to become stronger than Britain and France, it formed an alliance with Austria-Hungary and Italy in 1902 called the Triple Alliance. France and England responded with an Entente ("understanding") in 1904, with Russia joining in 1907. These alliances combined with a build-up of each country's military to divide Europe into two hostile armed camps, poised for war.

A Serbian nationalist group called "The Black Hand" claimed responsibility for the assassination of Archduke Ferdinand in Sarajevo, a city in Austria-Hungary with a large population of Serbs who believed it should become a part of Serbia. Austria-Hungary declared war on Serbia, touching off agreements made within the alliances to provide military aid for those attacked. Germany supported Austria-Hungary and Russia backed Serbia's position, and one by one, the countries of Europe took sides, and within days, most of them had declared war on one another. Ties of empire drew millions of colonists into the war to serve as soldiers and laborers, and the Great War began.

The Course of the War

The war began with France, Britain, and Russia on one side (The Triple Entente) against Germany, Austria-Hungary, and the Ottoman Empire (**The Central Powers).** Even though Italy had allied with Germany and Austria-Hungary before the war, the Triple Alliance broke up when Italy ultimately joined the Entente after a secret agreement that guaranteed its control of land in the north disputed with Austria-Hungary. Most other European countries took one side or the other, but a few – such as Spain, Switzerland, and the Scandinavian nations – remained neutral. As the Triple Entente gained allies, they came to be known as the "**Allied Powers.**" The United States and Japan joined later in the war, contributing to the worldwide nature of the conflict.

The war was fought along two major fronts: the **Western Front** where German troops faced French and British troops, and the **Eastern Front,** where Germany and Austria-Hungary fought against Russia. Once Italy joined the war in 1915, a third Italian front developed between the Italians and the Austrians. The war also took place at sea, where German submarines blockaded British ports and attacked sea lanes that brought people and supplies to Britain. These attacks on U.S. ships were largely responsible for U.S. entry into the war in 1917.

The style of fighting on the Western Front was called **trench warfare,** where soldiers dug opposing trenches for protection from the enemy, but modern technologies made it impossible to avoid high casualty rates. Both sides made use of machine guns that were responsible for a great deal of the slaughter, and the use of poison gas made warfare deadly even when the artillery was silent. The war quickly bogged down into a stalemate, with one side launching an offensive that gained a few of the other side's trenches, only to lose them again when a counteroffensive was launched. By 1916 the Germans had lost 850,000 men, and the French and English combined lost 1,100,000, all with no real progress on either side. The countryside – mostly in northeastern France – was pocked by miles of trenches divided by areas called "no man's land" strewn with shell craters and body parts.

Most of the fighting on the Eastern Front took place in western Russia, but fighting also spread to the Balkans, where Austria defeated Serbia and the other small states joined one side or the other. Because the front was much longer, fighting was more fluid than on the Western Front, but Germany had the challenge of covering both fronts, and the forces of Austria-Hungary were relatively weak, providing too little support for the strong German forces. However, the Russian army fought badly, first driven out of East Prussia and Poland in 1915, and then failed in its counterattacks in 1916 and 1917. The heavy casualties and lack of leadership increased hostilities toward Tsar Nicholas II and brought chaos and civil war to Russia, leading to the overthrow of the tsar, the takeover by V.I. Lenin and the Bolsheviks, and the eventual withdrawal of Russia from the war in 1917. When the U.S. joined the war in 1917, most of its soldiers went to the Western Front where fresh troops – called "doughboys" – helped to break the stalemate.

The War Outside Europe

The United States at first remained neutral in the conflict, with many Americans believing it to be a European war. American businesses sold goods to both sides, but on balance, the American leadership was pro-British, and German submarine warfare against U.S. ships eventually convinced the country to officially side with Britain and France. The United States was only involved in the war for eighteen months, and none of the fighting took place there, and as a result, the country did not suffer nearly as many ill effects as the European nations did from the war. British dominions of Canada, Australia, and New Zealand also sent forces to several fronts throughout most of the war.

World War I. Europe was divided into two camps: the Triple Entente Powers (and allies) and the Central Powers, with several neutral states, including Switzerland, Denmark, Norway, Sweden, and the Netherlands. Fighting on the Western Front was stalemated in trench warfare between Germany on one side and France and Britain on the other, with the United States sending troops there in 1917. Germany and Austria-Hungary fought Russia on a much more fluid Eastern Front. The British unsuccessfully tried to take the Dardanelles from the Ottomans, before turning to subvert the Empire from within.

Minor skirmishes were fought around the German colonies in Africa, involving Africans as colonial troops, and France also sent many of its African colonists to fight on the Western Front. Large numbers of troops from India fought for the British in Europe, and many Indian nationalists hoped that their support would promote India's independence once the war was over. Japan and China both entered the war on the side of Britain and France, and Japan advanced its own imperialist designs by taking over German holdings in China's Shangtung Province. In the Middle East, the British successfully weakened the Ottoman Empire by sponsoring an internal rebellion by Arab nationalists against the sultan's forces. The British also gained support from Jewish settlers in Palestine by promising to help them carve a homeland out of the Ottoman Empire. Allied actions set in motion the drive for independence among the various Ottoman subjects, bringing about the final collapse of the empire when the Central Powers lost the war.

ORIGINAL DOCUMENT: THE BALFOUR DECLARATION

After the fighting on the Western Front settled into stalemate, the British tried to defeat the Central Powers by subverting internal support for the weakest member of the alliance, the Ottoman Empire. They gained cooperation from Arab nationalists within the empire, and the British Foreign Secretary, Sir Arthur Balfour, responded positively to Jewish nationalists - called **Zionists** - who wanted to carve a Jewish homeland out of the Ottoman Empire in Palestine. Below is the statement from the Foreign Secretary, called the **Balfour Declaration:**

"His Majesty's Government view with favor the establishment in Palestine of a national home for the Jewish people and will use their best endeavors to facilitate the achievement of that object, it being clearly understood that nothing shall be done which may prejudice the civil and religious rights of existing non-Jewish communities in Palestine."

The British were concerned with the immediate need to win the war, and did not foresee that the statement would contribute later to conflicts between Palestinian and Jewish settlers.

The Home Front

World War I was a total war that involved not just military might but civilian support as well, creating a **home front** that ran parallel to the actual war fronts where the fighting took place. In most cases, the war strengthened the power of central governments, which took control of coordinating the countries' resources with the needs of the armies. This control included **conscription** – or mandatory military service – of recruits and government supervision of private businesses to turn their enterprises to war production. Laissez-faire capitalist notions could not be tolerated, and civilians had to give up personal needs and wants to the common cause. To ensure that civilian support was constant, the governments churned out war propaganda, or information campaigns that inspired nationalism as well as hostility toward the enemy. For example, Germans were depicted in cartoon-like English and French posters as primitive, war-mongering monsters, and German propaganda pictured Russians as semi-Asiatic barbarians. Governments also established wage and price controls, and sometimes determined workers' hours. Freedom of speech and the press were curtailed in the name of national security, and bad news from the war front was censored.

An important consequence of the war effort was the large-scale filling of jobs in the labor force by women. Since most able-bodied men volunteered or were drafted into the army, women worked in traditional male jobs, such as managing their husbands' farms and businesses, working in factories, and serving as postal employees and police officers. Especially crucial to the war effort were the several million women who worked in munitions plants, making shells and working with explosives. Many middle- and upper-class women, who had long been confined to their homes in Victorian polite society, reported that the experience of directly supporting the war effort was liberating. Women who had seldom ventured into the business world sometimes found themselves relying on themselves rather than their husbands or fathers, and these feelings almost certainly pressured legislatures to pass women's suffrage measures after the war was over. For working-class women, the war brought fewer changes, since most were working outside their homes before the war began. Their wages did rise, and most of the governments promised equal pay for equal work, but the wage gap between men and women never closed. When the war was over and the men returned, traditional roles resumed, but some important changes were put in motion, with voting rights extended to women in Britain in 1918, Germany in 1919, Austria in 1919, and the United States in 1920.

The End of the War

After the Russian Revolution took the tsar from power in late 1917, the new government led by V.I. Lenin had little interest in carrying on what they considered to be the "tsar's war." Instead the new country – the Union of Soviet Socialist Republics – turned its attention to restructuring Russian society and to addressing the civil war that the revolution provoked. As a result, the Soviet government signed the **Brest-Litovsk Treaty** with the Germans in March 1918, giving up substantial territories in western Russia as a concession. However, Germany had to dedicate considerable manpower to occupying the new territory, taking away from its ability to address the issues on the Western Front, where the Entente powers now had the advantage of an infusion of fresh soldiers from the United States. The French, English, and Americans launched a counterof-fensive in response to a failed German surge, and Germany simply could not provide the troops to keep the war effort going. After the failure of Habsburg forces in Italy and the Balkans and the abdication of the German Kaiser, the Central Powers surrendered in November 1918, bringing the war to an end.

POST-WAR DIPLOMACY

In 1919 diplomats of the victorious nations gathered at Versailles Palace in France to fashion a peace settlement. None of the Central Powers were rep-resented nor was Russia, so those countries had no say in the agreement that resulted from the compromises reached by the twenty-seven nations that were present. The most influential leaders at the conference were those from Britain, France, and the United States, and the three countries had very different views about what the terms of the peace settlement should be. President Woodrow Wilson of the United States approached the conference with a vision of making the world "safe for democracy," and a dream that this war would be a "war to end all wars." He expressed his point of view is a document called the **Fourteen Points** that he presented to the other Allied powers as his plan for peace. Brit-ain and France had more practical approaches shaped by the history of conflict among European nations, and they both looked to punish Germany. France par-ticularly wanted revenge, and both countries sought **reparations** (payment of war expenses) from Germany, as well as the permanent weakening of German power. Most of the fighting on the Western Front had occurred in France, and almost 1,400,000 French soldiers had died, and more than 3,000,000 wounded. In contrast, the U.S. casualty rates were 115,000 dead and 206,000 wounded. While the conference was going on, the British continued to blockade German ports, and the Allies threatened to renew the war if the Central Powers did not accept their terms. In the end a compromise was reached, but overall, the agree-ment heavily penalized Germany, creating resentments and economic hardships that erupted twenty years later in a far larger war, a second and more deadly installment of 20th century global warfare.

The Versailles Treaties

Several treaties were signed at Versailles, with the central treaty laying down the terms for Germany, including these:

- **War guilt** – Article 231 was the "war-guilt" clause that placed sole blame for World War I on German aggression. As a result, the treaty dictated that Germany had to pay reparations to the Allies to compen-sate for the enormous costs of the war. The final reparations bill came to $31 billion which Germany was to pay in installments over the next 30 years. This acceptance of war guilt was not only expensive, but also psychologically difficult for Germans because they thought it was unfair for one country to be blamed for starting the war.

- **Territorial losses** – Germany lost about 13 percent of its land where nearly 10 percent of its people lived. France, Poland, Belgium, and Denmark all received parts of this land. France regained Alsace-Lorraine, which Germany had taken in the Franco-Prussian War in 1871. Poland, which had disappeared from the map of Europe in the 1790s, once again became an independent nation, with land carved from Russia and Germany. All of Germany's territories in Africa and the Pacific were given as **mandates** to Britain, France, and Japan, which meant that they were administered on behalf of the **League of Nations**, the new international peace organization created by the treaty. The Allies were to govern these lands until they determined their readiness for independence.

- **Military restrictions** – The size of the German army was strictly limited, and could place no troops at all in the Rhineland, a strip of land in western Germany between the Rhine River and the French border. Germany was also forbidden to manufacture war materials, including airplanes and submarines. The intent of these restrictions was to keep Germany from ever again waging war against other European nations.

- **The creation of the League of Nations** – The Allies agreed to create an international peace organization charged with keeping another war from occurring. The League of Nations was one of Wilson's Fourteen Points, and he saw it as a forum where differences among nations could be worked out peaceably rather than by resorting to war. The League's Executive Council was to consist of the United States, Britain, France, Italy, and Japan (the winners of the war), and a general assembly would represent 42 Allied and neutral nations. Germany and Russia were not given representation in the new organization.

The treaty clearly reflected the revenge that France and Britain desired, and its intentions to check German power are clear. The treaty with Germany was just one of five signed in France during 1919 and 1920, and other Central Powers were penalized in the other ones. For example, Bulgaria had to give up land to countries that had supported the Allies – Romania, Greece, and the newly created Yugoslavia. Bulgaria also had to pay almost half a billion dollars in reparations. Austria-Hungary and the Ottoman Empire were totally dismantled, and their lands distributed among newly created countries and mandates. Russia, too, was severely punished in the agreements because, even though the country had fought on the Allied side, the tsar had been overthrown, and the Versailles powers did not trust the new government led by V.I. Lenin. First, Germany had to cancel the Treaty of Brest-Litovsk in which it had taken large amounts of Russia's territory in the west, but that land was not returned to Russia. In fact, Russia lost even more land space as a result of the treaties signed at Versailles than it had in the earlier treaty with Germany.

ORIGINAL DOCUMENTS: THE PRINCIPLE OF SELF-DETERMINATION IN WOODROW WILSON'S FOURTEEN POINTS

U.S. President Woodrow Wilson had thought through his aspirations for peace long before he departed for the Versailles Conference in 1919. In fact, he presented his Fourteen Points for peace to Congress on January 8, 1918, several months before the war actually ended. His speech strongly supported the principle of self-determination, or the idea that people should have the right to determine for themselves who governs them and how. Wilson explained his support for self-determination in these words:

"What we demand in this war, therefore, is nothing peculiar to ourselves. It is that the world be made fit and safe to live in; and particularly that it be made safe for every peace-loving nation, which, like our own, wishes to live its own life, determine its own institutions, be assured of justice and fair dealing by the other peoples of the world as against force and selfish aggression. All the peoples of the world are in effect partners in this interest, and for our own part we see very clearly that unless justice be done to others it will not be done to us."

Reference: "President Wilson's Fourteen Points," http://wwi.lib.byu.edu/index.php/President_Wilson%27s_Fourteen_Points.

Despite the punitive nature of these agreements, the Allies did not simply seize all of the land for themselves. Instead, the principle of national **self-determination** that rose from 19th-century liberal traditions played some role in the recreation of the map of Europe at Versailles. Austria-Hungary was carved into new countries based on ethnic identity. Poland was recreated for the Poles, since it had been seized by Prussia, Austria, and Russia more than 100 years earlier; Czechoslovakia was created for two different Slavic people – the Czechs and the Slovaks; and the borders of Yugoslavia encompassed Serbs, Croats, and Slovenes. Out of Russia came Finland, Estonia, Latvia, and Lithuania, which had all declared their independence in 1918 but were now officially recognized by the Allied Powers. Despite the application of the principle of self-determination, there were inconsistencies that stirred up problems and resentments. For example, one third of the people in Poland did not speak Polish, and Czechoslovakia also had large populations of Germans, Ruthenes, and Hungarians. Part of the problem was that drawing political boundaries was difficult because populations were often intermixed or unevenly divided among ethnic groups within a given area.

The Mandate System

One of the most controversial decisions made at Versailles had to do with the creation of the **mandate system,** which set up territories as "trusteeships" under the care of the newly created League of Nations. Whereas eastern European people were organized into independent states, however imperfectly, many of the Arab territories of the Ottoman Empire and Germany's former colonies in the Pacific and in Africa were designated as mandates. According to Article 22 of the Covenant of the League of Nations, these areas were "inhabited by peoples not yet able to stand by themselves under the strenuous conditions of the modern world…the tutelage of such peoples should be entrusted to the advanced nations who…can best undertake this responsibility." The establishment of mandates among the Arab states of the former Ottoman Empire violated promises made to Arabs by both France and Britain during the war, and Jewish nationalists in Europe saw the system as a violation of the Balfour Declaration. As soon as the war was over, Italy and Greece tried to take lands around Istanbul that were inhabited primarily by Turks. These efforts were met with fierce resistance by the Turkish leader, **Mustafa Kemal,** or **Ataturk,** who managed to negotiate a new Turkish republic in 1923. However, the rest of the Ottoman holdings were divided up as mandates of the League of Nations, with Britain controlling Palestine and Iraq, and France taking Syria and Lebanon. In response, other kingdoms – such as Iran and Saudi Arabia – organized to assert control over their own lands. The results were a fragmented Middle East and a legacy of resentment toward western nations.

Problems with the League of Nations

The acceptance of the League of Nations as an integral part of the peace treaties was in many ways a "marker event" in world history because it signaled a new type of international organization whose purposes went beyond those of nation-states. According to Woodrow Wilson's 14th point, "a general association of nations must be formed under specific covenants for the purpose of affording mutual guarantees of political independence and territorial integrity to great and small states alike." He clearly did not see the League as a substitute for the nation-state, but as a power that could help countries avoid war in the future. Unfortunately, the organization was doomed almost from the start, even though 26 of the original 42 members were non-European, signaling a truly international organization.

COMPARISONS: POST-WORLD WAR I TREATIES AND EUROPEAN BIASES

At the Versailles Conference, U.S. President Woodrow Wilson protested the idea of Allies taking lands controlled by the Central Powers as colonies, and he insisted that the principle of self-determination be applied. The other Allied powers agreed, but the differences they made among possessions reflect their belief in the superiority of people of European ancestry. Eastern Europe was divided into new ethnically-based countries, acknowledging their rights to self-determination. However, the Turks - a non-European people - had to fight and negotiate to be recognized as an independent nation, as did Iran and Saudi Arabia. Other Arab people - in Lebanon, Syria, Palestine, and Iraq - did not win independence at all; their lands were put under the protection of France and Britain, causing them to deeply resent their treatment. Germany's African and Asian colonies also did not receive their independence. Whether these actions are interpreted as kindly gestures that resulted from the "White Man's Burden," as Rudyard Kipling explained, or as simple disguises for imperialistic greed, the comparative treatment of European and non-European people at Versailles left a bitter legacy of conflict that continued to destabilize world politics during the 20th and early 21st centuries.

One problem was that the League had no power to enforce its decisions, and so even though international disputes were arbitrated, countries that did not want to comply did not have to. Another issue was the principle of **collective security,** or the agreement that if any of the member nations of the League were attacked, the others were bound to give it military aid. This clause was strongly opposed by Senate leaders in the United States because in their view it violated the traditional isolationist foreign policy of the United States. In his bid to gain public support for the League, Wilson embarked on a speaking tour across the country, but he tragically suffered a debilitating stroke that left him unable to defend his efforts, and the United States refused to sign the Versailles Treaty and did not join the League of Nations. Germany and Japan believed that the League served Allied needs only, and both withdrew their membership in 1933. The Soviet Union joined the organization in 1934, but it was expelled in 1940.

With all of these problems, the League was unable to stop the onset of World War II, and it collapsed as the new war began. However, the League of Nations set the precedent for a new type of international organization, and plans for its successor – the United Nations – were being made even before the older organization collapsed.

WORLD WAR I: A CULTURAL "MARKER EVENT"

World War I was clearly a political and economic "marker event," in that it so seriously wounded the economies of European countries that it resulted in their decline as imperialist powers. Although less apparent on first glance, the cultural changes brought about by the war were equally important, so that we can see distinctly different lifestyles and values after the war than before. Social restrictions loosened in Europe and the United States so that pleasure-seeking behavior unimaginable before the war – such as drinking, racy dancing, and looser sexual morality – characterized urban life during the 1920s. The changes for women were particularly notable in less modest dress styles, unescorted attendance in public places, and less deference to fathers and husbands. Secular values replaced the religious in many cities, and the rift between urban and rural lifestyles widened as the decade progressed. The reasons for these changes are complex, but the war clearly sparked them. One explanation is that the horrors of war caused many to react by seeking escape through pleasurable, immediately gratifying behaviors. Another explanation is that the war interrupted normal social patterns, separating men and women from their traditional roles, sending women into the work place and suspending breadwinner roles for men.

NEW FORCES OF REVOLUTION IN RUSSIA AND CHINA

During the early 20th century, revolutionary forces overcame traditional monarchies in both Russia and China. In Russia the last tsar abdicated in 1917, and in China the last emperor was deposed in 1911. During the period from 1914 to 1945, Russia settled into a new-style authoritarian regime, whereas different forces continued to struggle for control of China.

The Russian Revolution of 1917 and the Creation of the Union of Soviet Socialist Republics

World War I precipitated a political crisis in Russia that had been building up during the late 19th and early 20th centuries. The last Romanov tsars clung to absolutism despite the growing number of dissidents in the country, and for many, the inability of Tsar Nicholas II to manage the war was the last straw. As the Germans threatened, the Russian army lacked food and essential equipment, and officers were unable to stop the large-scale mutiny of troops. Chaos descended as street riots broke out in Petrograd (St. Petersburg) under pressure from a council of workers called a **soviet.** The tsar abdicated his throne, leaving the government up for grabs. A provisional government briefly took control under revolutionary leaders eager to institute parliamentary rule based on western liberalism. The most prominent of these leaders was **Alexander Kerensky,** who supported religious and other freedoms, but he resisted the major land redistribution expected by the peasants, and serious popular unrest continued even as the war effort faltered badly. In November (October, according to the Russian calendar), **V.I. Lenin** arrived from exile in Switzerland to lead his Bolsheviks in a second revolution that toppled the provisional government. Using his interpretation of Marxism, his **"vanguard of the revolution"** forced its way to the top by dismantling other parties and declaring the victory of the proletariat.

Lenin's assertion of power resulted in a newly named "Union of Soviet Socialist Republics," but many elements inside and outside of Russia did not support his rule. Britain, France, the United States, and Japan all sent troops to defeat the communist threat, but their efforts to reinstate the provisional government failed. Internal resistance was even more serious, with aristocrats, army generals, faithful Russian Orthodox peasants, and many minority nationalities united in their efforts to unseat the new government. Lenin's decree to redistribute land to peasants and the **nationalization** (state takeover) of industry sparked major protests from land-owning peasants, creating even more opposition to the government. Civil war raged throughout the country from 1918 to 1921 before Lenin finally regained stability through the effective use of his **Red Army,** led by his second-in-command, **Leon Trotsky**. Lenin's willingness to promote army officers from humble backgrounds and his ability to make recruits believe in the brave new regime of communism helped him to control the dissidents. He also put in place a **New Economic Policy,** which promised small business owners and land-owning peasants the retention of their rights and freedoms, while the state set basic economic policies. The economy responded, and food production recovered from its precipitous fall during the civil war period. By 1923 Lenin's **democratic centralism** – centralized policy-making for the good of the people – was firmly in place, yet each of the "soviet socialist republics" was set up in recognition of different ethnic minorities within the country's borders. The central government was controlled by ethnic Russians, and despite a new constitution and the promise to respect human rights, competitive elections were prohibited and the Communist Party established an authoritarian system under central party bureaucracy.

Lenin died fairly suddenly in 1924 without leaving a clear path for leadership succession, and a struggle among his lieutenants – mostly behind closed doors – eventually resulted in a victory for **Joseph Stalin,** who ruled the country from 1927 until his death in 1953. Stalin turned his back on the promotion of international communist revolutions, as Leon Trotsky had advocated, and instead built "socialism in one country." His policies emphasized industrialization and strengthening agriculture from within Russian borders, and for most of the 1930s, Russia remained isolated from the rest of the world, particularly the West. Although a new regime based on communist principles had swept away the old aristocratic Russia, the old dynamics of the political culture – westernization versus the preservation of Russian ways – were very much at work as Stalin settled in as an old style authoritarian Russian ruler.

China's Struggle for Stability

When Sun Yat-sen led the Revolution of 1911 that deposed the last Qing emperor, he hoped to establish a republican form of government in China. However, China's regional generals – the warlords – continued to struggle for power, even as a new generation of Chinese supported the ideals of Sun Yat-sen. His cause was hampered by the decision at the Versailles Peace Conference to allow Japan to keep the German enclaves that they had seized. Since these were traditionally Chinese lands, many educated Chinese considered the decision to be an insult, and some were inspired to look to other philosophies for answers to China's dilemma. Many within Sun's political party, called the **Guomindang** (National People's Party), found much to admire in Lenin's revolutionary tactics, and a Soviet adviser was invited to help the party organize the country. Although he was not a communist, Sun also welcomed members of the newly created Chinese Communist Party into the Guomindang.

When Sun died in 1925 – shortly after Lenin in Russia – his party's leadership fell to Jiang Jieshi, better known as **Chiang Kai-shek** in the West. Chiang was much less accommodating to the Communists than Sun had been, and he also lacked commitment to revolutionary principles. Instead he sought to crush the regional warlords with his armies, and once he did, he turned on the Communists, whom he considered a threat. By the early 1930s he had established a dictatorship that had none of the strength of the Bolsheviks who modernized Russia, nor the ability of the Meiji oligarchs who strengthened Japan. Meanwhile, the leader of the Chinese Communist Party, **Mao Zedong,** continued to attract followers, causing Chiang to try to get rid of him. However, the **Long March** – the 1934-36 pursuit of Mao's army across China by Chiang and his supporters – only served to strengthen the communist cause. Chiang was trying to depose his rival, but his attempt to find and conquer Mao had the opposite effect. Mao eluded him until finally Chiang had to turn his attentions to the invading Japanese, and the decision as to who would rule China was postponed until after World War II ended.

ECONOMIC INSTABILITY AND THE GREAT DEPRESSION

Whereas the 1920s are often seen as a time of prosperity in industrialized countries, a great deal of economic instability characterized the era. It is true that industrial productivity returned to prewar levels by the mid-1920s, but the recovery was fragile, and in 1929 stock market crashes in major western cities sparked a deep economic depression that reflected the total collapse of the old capitalist system. During the 1930s industrial production shrank, world trade dropped dramatically, and unemployment rose to unprecedented levels. Known as the **Great Depression,** the worldwide economic patterns did not change for the better until after World War II began, when demand for war production was pivotal in bringing a return to prosperity by the 1950s.

Economic Problems of the 1920s

The economies of European countries and the United States were grounded in war debts among the Allies and the flow of money from the United States to Europe. Because Germany was saddled with a huge reparations debt, the U.S. loaned Germany money and invested funds in rebuilding the German economy. Germany had to have this money to pay reparations to Britain and France, who in turn needed that money to repay money that the U.S. loaned them during the war. When the U.S. began pulling back on their investments in Europe in mid-1928, the lack of capital caused the whole repayment structure to collapse.

Germany, in particular, was on the verge of economic collapse during most of the 1920s under the direction of a new government called the **Weimar Republic,** which faced what ultimately became insurmountable problems. In early 1919 the German communists staged a coup d'etat, hoping to emulate what Lenin had achieved in Russia in 1917. The German army managed to stem the coup, but the government faced the difficult task of paying $33 billion in reparations to the Allies, an amount that equaled Germany's total gross national product for five years. Through tremendous effort, the government managed to make their payments for two years before asking for a two-year moratorium. The French responded by sending troops to occupy the Ruhr area along the Rhine River, the heart of Germany's industrial production. There they seized the iron and coal that was produced, so the German government instructed workers to go on strike, effectively shutting down all production. Without these vital industries, Germany slipped even further into economic chaos, and severe inflation drastically reduced the value of the German mark. The German middle class was virtually wiped out, and many people were reduced to begging, stealing, and selling family possessions to avoid starving. The situation was stemmed by American government loans in U.S. dollars to the German national bank, and in 1924 the U.S. sponsored the Dawes Plan, which provided for French withdrawal from the Ruhr and some reduction in reparations payments. Although these agreements held until 1929, much damage was already done to the economy, and resentments between Germany and France continued to simmer.

Although they had won the war, France and Britain were not immune to serious economic problems. France generally had a well-balanced national economy, and German reparations and the return of Alsace and Lorraine to French control helped feed post-war prosperity. However, France had lost 1.5 million people in the war, and German reparations could only gradually make up for the $23 billion in war damage to French property. Britain's economic problems were more apparent during the 1920s, partly because British economic health had actually slipped before the war began. English mines and factories out-produced consumption even within the extended British Empire, and unemployment levels became quite high as demand for workers decreased. Britain's merchant marine had suffered great losses during the war, and could no longer hold the links of empire together, and the United States had taken over as a financial center of the world. As Britain declined, capital that had once been invested by Britain around the world came to be supplied by the United States, causing British production to fall further and unemployment rates to stay high in Britain throughout the 1920s. In contrast, the United States had suffered little damage and few casualties in World War I, and its industrial power and pool of capital grew, so that it became the prime creditor nation in world trade by the early 1920s. By 1929 economies around the world were dependent on the prosperity of the United States, and when the New York Stock Exchange faltered, the depression it triggered set off a chain reaction of economic collapse that affected almost all other areas of the world.

Colonies around the world suffered as the imperialist nations experienced economic setbacks. For example, in Africa and Latin America, plantations that raised coffee, sugar, and rubber expanded their production to make up for a fall in prices, leading to overproduction and further reductions in prices and earnings. As colonial people lost the ability to buy manufactured goods, the economies of industrialized countries suffered in a situation where global interdependence reinforced problems that generally were ignored by the nations' leaders. Instead, western nations turned to **protectionism,** characterized by high tariff barriers meant to protect each country's industries and nationalistic concerns at the expense of world economic growth.

The New York Stock Market Crash and the "Great Depression"

The events that led to the economic collapse of capitalist countries were rooted in the depressed state of agriculture resulting from the war. While Europe was unable to produce crops during the war, farmers in the United States, Canada, Argentina, and Australia expanded their production. When European farmers went back to work after the war ended, it caused worldwide food surpluses and triggered falling prices. Farm families suffered and were unable to buy manufactured goods, causing factories to be left with large surplus inventories by 1929. The impact was less serious in the United States, where many urban workers and middle-class businessmen continued to earn enough to invest in speculative ventures on the stock market. One particularly damaging behavior was buying stock on the **margin** – putting up only a small fraction of a stock's price in cash and borrowing the remainder from stock brokers. As long as stock prices climbed, the speculators made money, but by 1929 so many people had borrowed heavily that when prices stumbled, a panic swept the financial markets as brokers called for their loans to be repaid. When the New York stock market crashed, United States banks collapsed because they depended heavily on their stock investments. When banks failed, depositors lost money, and the economic impact spread far beyond the financial markets.

The economic collapse became international when Americans began to call back earlier loans to Europe, resulting in key bank failures in Austria and Germany. The whole infrastructure built on repayment of war debts caved in as investment funds vanished and creditors went bankrupt or tried to call in their loans. The downward spiral continued as lack of investments caused industrial production to fall, leading to massive layoffs of workers, who in turn could not buy anything since they were unemployed. Since farmers were already in serious economic trouble, the crisis expanded to affect almost every sector of industrial societies and their colonies around the world. The situation in Europe worsened when businesses were unable to export goods to the United States because the U.S. government placed high tariffs on foreign products to protect their own industries. Also greatly affected was the Japanese economy, which was very dependent on the U.S. market. Between 1929 and 1931 the value of Japanese exports dropped by 50%, leaving workers with decreased incomes or out of work entirely.

In **primary producing economies,** such as Latin America, export of raw materials and agricultural goods plummeted as demand from industrialized countries decreased. These economies were often dependent on the export of one primary product (such as coffee, sugar, cotton, minerals, ores, or rubber), and when the market for that product disappeared, they had little to fall back on. Latin

ORIGINAL DOCUMENT: JOSEPH STALIN'S FIVE YEAR PLANS

The worldwide depression of the 1930s generally did not affect the U.S.S.R. because Joseph Stalin, the Russian leader, instituted economic policies that emphasized internal development and self-sufficiency. These policies took the shape of **Five Year Plans** in which development goals were set at the beginning of a five-year period to be met by the end. Stalin's first Five Year Plan began in 1928, and in 1933, he reported the country's progress in a report to the Central Committee of the Communist Party of the Soviet Union. The excerpts below cite some of the plan's achievements.

"We did not have an iron and steel industry, the foundation for the industrialization of the country. Now we have this industry.

We did not have a tractor industry. Now we have one.

We did not have an automobile industry. Now we have one.

We did not have a machine-tool industry. Now we have one.

We did not have a big and up-to-date chemical industry. Now we have one...

We did not have an aircraft industry. Now we have one...

In the output of oil products and coal we were last on the list. Now we rank among the first...

As a result of all this the capitalist elements have been completely and irrevocably eliminated from industry, and socialist industry has become the sole form of industry in the U.S.S.R. "

Reference: Joseph Stalin, "The Task of Business Executives" in *Problems of Leninism* (Moscow, 1940), pp. 359-360.

American countries tried to raise prices by holding supplies off the market, but these efforts failed, and unemployment rates increased rapidly. Although most imperialist countries suffered from the depression, their colonies could provide at least some of the products they needed, and as a result, some colonies – such as many in Africa – were protected from the international downturn as they continued to trade according to the dictates of their mother countries. Countries whose economies were not dependent on foreign trade felt the effects of the worldwide depression less than others. For example, Joseph Stalin emphasized the development of **"socialism in one country"** in the U.S.S.R., so no serious unemployment occurred there, and industrial production increase steadily. Also, China's large agriculture-based economy was protected, since the largest share of Chinese markets were domestic.

Despite the unevenness of the global effects of the Great Depression, the international financial and commercial network of capitalist economies was destroyed. Governments reacted by practicing economic nationalism through high tariffs and import quotas and prohibitions, which provoked retaliation from others. As a result, international trade dropped sharply, decreasing by more than 66 % between 1929 and 1932, and world production declining 38%.

Political Reactions to Economic Woes

According to Adam Smith's free enterprise theory described in his influential book, *The Wealth of Nations,* the force behind the economy should be the "invisible hand" of competition, not the forceful hand of government. According to this "laissez-faire" approach, governments should stand by while normal business cycles took place. Recessions (small market downturns) and depressions (big downturns) will happen, and if the government doesn't interfere, a natural recovery will take place. However, this theory was seriously challenged by the Great Depression that began after the stock market crash of 1929.

In the United States, President Herbert Hoover waited for the natural upturn, but instead conditions worsened, and he was voted out of office in 1932. The new president, Franklin Roosevelt, searched for a new philosophy. He found it in the writings of English economist **John Maynard Keynes,** who warned that if people do not consume enough or invest enough, the national income will fall. Keynes argued that the best way to increase national income is for the government to do the spending and investing if private enterprise can't or won't. Roosevelt reasoned that people and businesses in the United States had been so burned by terrifying experiences during the early days of the Great Depression that they were too afraid to consume or invest. Roosevelt began a great number of **New Deal** programs, which involved massive government spending aimed to prevent the collapse of the banking system, provide jobs and farm subsidies, give workers the right to organize and bargain collectively, guarantee minimum wages, and provide social security in old age.

In Japan the government first was passive, but after widespread unrest and violence, Japan's leaders intervened forcefully in the economy with programs to build public works, incentives and subsidies for selected industries, devaluation of the currency, and wage control. These measures stimulated economic recovery by 1931. In Germany, Adolf Hitler's government also intervened aggressively in the economy after 1933 with large public works projects to stimulate employment and deficit spending directed toward military preparation, bringing about economic recovery by the mid-1930s.

THE RISE OF FASCISM

Despite the fact that the Soviet Union did not suffer many of the ill effects of the Great Depression, the Soviet people had to endure the repressive, terrorist tactics of Stalin's government in the modernization of Russia. Besides industrialization, the government collectivized agriculture by consolidating small private farms into vast commonly owned fields. Each collective was expected to supply the government with a fixed amount of food to be consumed by industrial workers and distribute what was left among its members. Collectivization met resistance, especially among **kulaks,** or prosperous peasants, who stood to lose their farms to the government. Kulaks slaughtered their own livestock rather than give it to the government, and Stalin ruthlessly ordered the "liquidation of kulaks as a class." Millions were arrested or sent to labor camps, and many were executed. To prevent any further resistance or rebellion, the NKVD, Stalin's secret police force, scoured the countryside, and even members of the Communist Party elite were arrested and expelled from the party. Millions of people were sentenced to death without trial, and many were sent to gulags (labor camps) far away from their homes.

These changes in Russia frightened people all over Europe and North America, and led to a fear that communist elements would take over other countries. The Great Depression made people uncertain of their future, and the two factors together – communism and the apparent collapse of free-market capitalism – made many turn to the radical political solution of **fascism.** The name was derived from the fasces, an ancient Roman symbol of power consisting of a bundle of rods wrapped together around an axe. Fascism emphasized an extreme form of nationalism, and encouraged individuals to subordinate their will to the state. Fascist leaders promised to bring back full employment, stop communism, and conquer new territories. They condemned the communist model for abolishing private property, but they used Stalin's tactics to accomplish their goals: one-party rule of a totalitarian state with a powerful secret police that terrorized and intimidated the people.

The term fascism was first used by **Benito Mussolini**, who gained controlled of Italy in 1922 and established a one-party dictatorship. The Fascist Party took over all positions in government, the press, and public education, and it gave employers control over their workers. Known as "Il Duce" (the leader), Mussolini applied the techniques of modern mass communications to rule Italy through his oratory talents. By the 1930s fascist movements had appeared in most European countries, as well as in Latin America, China, and Japan. Fascism appealed to people who feared rapid change and economic insecurity and placed their hopes in charismatic leaders who promised to lead their countries to glory. The most notorious version of fascism grew in Germany under the **Nazi Party** led by **Adolf Hitler.**

Nazi leaders advocated an aggressive foreign policy that would reverse Germany's humiliating defeat in World War I and the terrible aftermath that plunged the country into the depths of economic depression. Hitler abolished the Weimar Republic and built a totalitarian state under his control. In flagrant violation of the terms of the Versailles Treaty, he deliberately reconstructed the German war machine under the premise that war is the main function of the state. Hitler expanded arms production, created new jobs, and rebuilt the German economy, and he advocated the doctrine that Germans were racially superior to all others, particularly to the Jewish minority that lived in the country. He referred to "**Aryans**" as a superior people who came from Europe's original racial stock that traced its ancestry to the Indo-Europeans that migrated from western Asia as early as 2000 B.C.E. Nazism appealed to the members of the lower-middle classes, many of whom had lost almost everything they had as Germany's economy had collapsed.

Hitler's new order required all to subject their will to the government in order to achieve greatness, and the rigid hierarchy that emerged included the reinforcement of traditional roles for women. Whereas communism usually had the effect of elevating the status of women through its emphasis on equality, fascist regimes generally limited women's rights. Nazis were alarmed by the declining birth rate spurred by the demographic transition (see page 383) in Germany, and they launched a campaign to increase births to strengthen the country. Abortions were outlawed, birth control centers were closed, and information about family planning became nonexistent. Women with large numbers of children were given special awards, and propaganda extolled the virtues of motherhood. Despite these efforts, birth rates remained low, since the demands of urban life made large numbers of children impractical for most families.

Nazism also drew on theories of scientific racism from the 19th century to establish its plan to suppress Germany's Jewish population. According to Hitler's theories, Jews were not from Aryan stock because their language was Semitic, and not derivative from Indo-European languages, such as Greek, Latin, Celtic, Persian, Sanskrit, or Balto-Slavonic. Starting in the early 1930s, discriminatory laws deprived German Jews of their citizenship and prohibited marriage between Jews and other Germans. Jewish civil servants lost their jobs, Jewish professionals lost their non-Jewish clients, and Jewish-owned businesses were seized by the Nazi Party. In 1938 many Jews left Germany after the notorious night of November 9-10, when Nazis destroyed thousands of Jewish stores, burned synagogues, and murdered more than 100 Jews.

PERSPECTIVES:
MEIN KAMPF BY ADOLF HITLER

After becoming the leader of the National Socialist German Workers' Party (the Nazis), Adolf Hitler was imprisoned by the German government for staging an attempted coup d'etat. During the nine months that he spent in prison he wrote the first volume of his major work, **Mein Kampf** (My Struggle). The book excerpted below, explains his racist doctrines that eventually guided his policies and actions as the German *Fuehrer* (dictator).

"All the great civilizations of the past died out because contamination of their blood caused them to become decadent...In other words, in order to protect a certain culture, the type of human who created the culture must be preserved. But such preservation is tied to the inalterable law of the necessity and the right of victory of the best and the strongest...
What we see before us today as human culture, all the yields of art, science, and technology, are almost exclusively the creative product of the Aryans. Indeed this fact alone leads to the not unfounded conclusion that the Aryan alone is the founder of the higher type of humanity, and further that he represents the proto-type of what we understand by the word: MAN...[whose spirit] has permitted humans to ascend the path of mastery over the other beings of the earth. Elimi-nate him and deep darkness will again descend on the earth after a few thousand years; human civilization will die out and the earth will become a desert...
The Jew provides the greatest contrast to the Aryan...the Jews lack the most basic characteristic of a truly cultured people, namely an idealistic spirit."

Reference: Adolf Hitler, *Mein Kampf* (Munich: F. Eher Nachfolger, 1927), trans. by J. Overfield.

In Japan, the regime turned more authoritarian as it sought to stave off the ill effects of the Great Depression. Whereas most Japanese preferred moderate po-litical parties, the country's leadership fell into the hands of a military group that advocated a "defense state" under its control. The Japanese army marched into Manchuria in 1931, proclaiming it to be independent from China. The military leadership was responsible for killing the prime minister in 1932, and by 1937 Japan's military rulers began aggressively attacking other areas of Asia.

EXAMINING THE EVIDENCE: THE NANKING MASSACRE

On December 13, 1937, the Nationalist Chinese capital of Nanking fell to an invading Japanese army, beginning a notorious occupation in which Chinese civilians experienced mass killings, systematic arson, torture, and rape. Hundreds of thousands of people were affected, but the horror may well have been worse except for the intercession of a handful of American and European residents who created the "Nanking Safety Zone," a neutral area in the center of the city that served as a refuge of those escaping the Japanese army. Below are some excerpts from the diary of John Rabe, a German businessman who witnessed the horror and headed the effort to save lives.

"The Japanese march through the city in groups of ten to twenty soldiers and loot the shops. If I had not seen it with my own eyes I would not have believed it. They smash open windows and doors and take whatever they like...Of the perhaps one thousand disarmed soldiers that we had quartered at the Ministry of Justice, between 400 and 500 were driven from it with their hands tied. We assume they were shot since we later heard several salvos of machine-gun fire ...these events have left us frozen with horror...We manage quickly to find lodging in some vacant buildings for a group of 125 Chinese refugees, before they fall into the hands of the Japanese military. Mr. Han says that three young girls of about 14 or 15 have been dragged from a house in our neighborhood.."

Reference: Edwin Wickart, ed., and John Woods, trans., *The Good Man of Nanking: The Diaries of John Rabe* (New York: Alfred A. Knopf, Inc., 1998), p. 67.

Note: "Nanking" is the British spelling of the city at the time. Later translations spell it "Nanjing."

WORLD WAR II

World War II formally began in 1939, but in many ways it resulted from a renewal of tensions from World War I that had never been resolved. The causes of the war were global, with Japanese expansion sparking conflicts in Asia and fascist movements in Europe encouraging military aggression in the name of nationalism. Germany withdrew from the League of Nations as Hitler rebuilt the military, and in 1935 Mussolini attacked Ethiopia in a nationalistic attempt to make up for Italy's failure to claim the area in the imperialist aggression of the 1890s. Fascism gained enough support in Spain to trigger a civil war between liberals and authoritarians, resulting in a fascist takeover in 1939.

The Onset of War

In 1938 Hitler invaded the Sudetenland, a German-speaking part of Czecho-slovakia, and the **Munich Conference** among European powers was called to address Czechoslovakia's protests. The response from Britain and France was weak, as they agreed on British Prime Minister Neville Chamberlain's **appease-ment policy,** which allowed Germany to keep the Sudetenland in return for Hitler's promise to cease his aggressions. However, Hitler did not keep his word, and went on to capture all of Czechoslovakia in March 1939, and his at-tack of Poland on September 1, 1939 resulted in a formal declaration of war on Germany by Britain and France. Germany and Italy joined together in an alli-ance called the **Rome-Berlin axis** as Mussolini declared that the rest of Europe would revolve around this central pact between the two countries.

By the time the war began in Europe, fighting had already started between Japan and China. Skirmishes broke out in 1937 in the Beijing area as Japanese forces occupied cities and railroads in eastern China. Although the conflict drifted into a long-lasting stalemate in China, Japan used the outbreak of war in Europe as a reason to attack other areas in Asia, seizing Indochina from French troops and attacking British Malaya and Burma. In 1940 the two main areas of fighting came together when Germany, Italy, and Japan signed the **Tripartite Pact** that united the three countries as the strongest of the **Axis Powers.** Even though Japan never cooperated closely with Germany and Italy, the alliance clearly spread the war into two major theatres: the Pacific and Europe. Whereas much of World War I was fought along fairly well-defined fronts, the areas of fight-ing were much broader in World War II, spreading from Hawaii to the South Pacific to East Asia, and from North Africa across the Mediterranean over most of Europe.

As war broke out between 1937 and 1939, Britain and France did little to pre-pare for war since both countries were still feeling the debilitating effects of World War I and had little appetite for another conflict. Only in late 1938 did Britain begin an expansion of its army and aircraft production that proved to be important in defending their island, but it took until 1942 and 1943 for the Allies to stop early German and Japanese successes.

The Nature of the War

Like World War I, World War II was a **total war** in which vast resources and emotional commitments of civilians supported massive military efforts. Mo-bilization for war was extensive and required government control of natural and labor resources. The steadily more destructive technologies of World War I – battleships, tanks, poison gas, machine guns, and long-range artillery – were used in World War II, along with airplanes, aircraft carriers, new bombing technology, rocketry, and ultimately the atomic bomb. Since the areas of fighting were so much greater in World War II, the increasingly sophisticated technology insured that this war would be far more destructive than any other in history. World War II also saw the blurring of the distinction between military and civilian, so that whole civilian populations not only supported the war, but were also subject to its destruction. Bombing raids were launched on cities, killing large numbers of civilians, and the final actions of the war – dropping atomic bombs on Nagasaki and Hiroshima – targeted civilian populations.

An important aspect of total war during World War II was the **Holocaust,** a mass extermination of targeted people by Nazi Germany. The first victims were Jews, who were sent in huge numbers to extermination camps in southern Germany and eastern Europe in what Hitler called the "final solution to the Jewish problem." This **genocide** – the wholesale murder of an entire people – took place in the camps, where modern industrial methods were used to execute people by asphyxiation with poison gas and dispose of their bodies by cremation in large ovens. Some became victims of "medical experiments" in which they were tortured or killed, and others worked in the camps until they starved to death. By the end of the war, about 6 million Jews were exterminated, and the executions extended to many others judged to threaten the purity of the Aryan race - such as gypsies, homosexuals, Polish Catholics, and the mentally and physically disabled.

War in Europe and North Africa

 In World War I, defensive fighting had characterized the Western Front, so in World War II the Germans took advantage of new motorized technology to benefit from offensive movements. Their warfare was called **blitzkrieg** ("lightning war") that involved three carefully synchronized steps. First, fighter planes scattered enemy troops and disrupted communications; secondly, tanks rolled over enemy defense lines; and third, the infantry invaded and actually occupied the targeted land. Blitzkrieg forced the surrender of Poland, Austria, Norway, Denmark, and Belgium within the early days of the war, and France quickly collapsed to German attack in mid-1940. Until 1944, France was ruled by a puppet government in German-controlled Vichy, although French Resistance troops staged guerilla attacks in the southern half of the country where German troops were less entrenched. However, the quick defeat of France in 1940 left Britain essentially alone in resisting Germany until Russia and the United States joined the war in 1941.

Britain was protected from Germany's lightning war tactics because it was an island, and under the leadership of **Winston Churchill,** Britain withstood a massive air attack from the German Luftwaffe (air force) that lasted from June

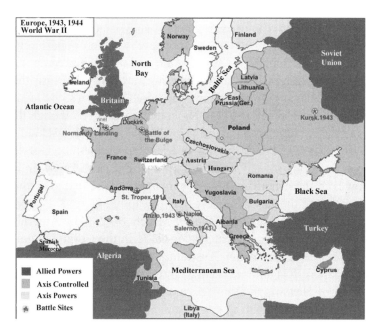

War-torn Europe, Mid-World War II. By 1942 the Axis powers controlled much of Europe, but the Allied powers began to regain lost territory by 1943 by stopping the German advance into Russia, attacking Italy from northern Africa, and invading occupied France across the English Channel. By 1945 Germany was surrounded and then dissected, as Russian armies came from the east and western armies from the west, forcing Germany's surrender in May 1945.

through September. In this **Battle of Britain,** the British Royal Air Force successfully counterattacked the German planes, using the new technology of radar to detect the enemy's approach. Unable to defeat Britain, Hitler turned eastward to Russia, even though he had signed a non-aggression pact with Stalin in 1939. In reaction to his 1941 attack – the largest in history – Russia hastily joined the war on the side of the Allies, but within five months the German army conquered the Baltic states, Ukraine, and half of European Russia. However, Hitler suffered the same fate that Napoleon had experienced more than 100 years earlier: the weather turned cold, supply lines were overextended, and his army was so seriously diminished that his 1942 attack on Stalingrad (now Volgagrad) failed. Since Russia had joined on the side of the Allies after Hitler's invasion, the victory at Stalingrad was the first major Allied victory of the war. After the United States joined the war in late 1941, the U.S. and Britain planned a strategy of striking the Axis from northern Africa, at the "soft underbelly" of Europe in Italy, clearly the weaker of the two European Axis powers. The British victory at El Alamein in northern Egypt was achieved partly because of the Allies' ability to break German codes, and the German army was finally expelled from Africa in May 1943. From there Allied armies captured Sicily and invaded Italy.

The War in Asia and the Pacific

Once France fell to Hitler's invasion in 1940 and Britain was busy defending its territory from German air attack, the Japanese saw their opportunity to seize European colonies in Southeast Asia. Britain and the United States responded by stopping shipments of steel and oil to Japan. Partly because the Americans insisted that Japan give up its newly acquired territories, the Japanese war cabinet made plans to attack the U.S. Navy in Hawaii, even though the United States was still officially neutral in the war. The December 7, 1941 attack on the American naval base at **Pearl Harbor** in Hawaii prompted the U.S. to declare war on Japan the following day, and the mobilization of the American war effort began. However, the American fleet of warships was decimated by their losses at Pearl Harbor, and the Japanese were able to capture Hong Kong, Singapore, Thailand, the Philippines, and Malaya by March 1942. The Americans were able to stop the Japanese in a great sea/air battle in the Coral Sea northeast of Australia in May 1942, protecting Australia from Japanese invasion. The next month the Japanese lost four of its six large aircraft carriers at the **Battle of Midway,** west of Hawaii, and the U.S. navy and air forces began an **"island-hopping"** campaign of capturing key islands in the Pacific while making their way slowly toward Japan.

The End of the War

The Battle of Stalingrad in 1942 was a major turning point of the war in Europe, and by 1943 the Russian army began pushing the Germans westward. In western and southern Europe, the United States, Britain, and other Allies staged two invasions: one across the Mediterranean Sea to Italy in 1943, and the other across the English Channel to the coast of Normandy in June 1944. Italy signed an armistice in 1943, and the invasion of France was successful as Allied troops landed in Normandy on **D-Day** – June 6, 1944 – and made their way to Paris by August. From there, the Allies advanced into Belgium where they decisively defeated the Germans at the **Battle of the Bulge.** As Britain and the United States – now joined by French forces – marched east across Germany, the Russians marched west, and the two armies met at the Elbe River, signifying the conquest of Germany. On May 7, 1945, a week after Hitler committed suicide, German military leaders surrendered to the Allies.

The war in the Pacific continued until August, with a formal surrender signed in early September. By early 1945, U.S. forces had "island-hopped" (or "leap-frogged") their way to Iwo Jima and Okinawa, two islands south of Japan. After bitter fighting the U.S. took the islands and prepared for an invasion of Japan. Then on August 6, 1945 the United States dropped an atomic bomb on Hiroshima, killing about 80,000 people immediately and leaving another 120,000 to die from the after-effects of burns and radiation. Three days later, a second bomb was dropped on Nagasaki, and Emperor Hirohito of Japan ordered surrender on August 14.

World War II marked the end of an important era in world history: the age of European domination. The war also was the most widespread, deadliest war in history, illustrating the powers unleashed by technologies of the industrial era. By the mid-20th century, the interdependence of the nations of the world was greater than it had ever been before, as two superpowers – the United States and the Soviet Union – emerged to compete for control of technological knowledge and assert their hegemonic power over most of the world.

MARKER EVENT:
THE ATOMIC BOMB CONTROVERSY

Should the United States have dropped the atomic bomb? The decision to drop atomic bombs on the Japanese cities of Hiroshima and Nagasaki is one of the most controversial "marker events" of the 20th century, perhaps of all times. Summarized below are arguments on both sides.

PROS	CONS
The events brought about the surrender of Japan, winning the war for the Allies.	The bombs killed civilians indiscriminantly, the ultimate cruelty of "total war."
Aggressive nations must be dealt with aggressively.	Many died slow, agonizing deaths due to radiation poisoning and burns that would not heal.
The events saved lives in the long run, since it shortened the war.	The United States opened a "Pandora's Box" of weapons that could destroy the world, making
Technological advantages win wars, and must be used to secure victory.	it a more dangerous place for all.
The bombs paved the way for a secure peace, allowing no opportunity for a revival of hostilities, as happened after World War I.	The U.S. should have warned Japan more clearly before they used the horrible new weapon; if they had, perhaps Japan would have surrendered without using the bomb.
If Germany had developed the bomb first, they would have used it against the Allies.	

CONCEPTS AND IDENTIFICATIONS

appeasement policy
Aryans
Battle of Britain
Battle of the Bulge
Battle of Midway
Brest-Litovsk Treat
Central Powers
Chiang Kai-shek
Churchill, Winston
collective security
conscription
D-Day
democratic centralism
Eastern Front
fascism
Five Year Plans
Fourteen Points
genocide
Great Depression
"Great War"
Guomindang
Hitler, Adolf
Holocaust
home front
"island-hopping"
Kemal, Mustafa (Ataturk)
Kerensky, Alexander
Keynes, John Maynard
League of Nations
Lenin, V.I.
mandate system
Mao Zedong
margin (stock)
Mein Kampf
Munich Conference
Mussolini, Benito
Nanking Massacre
nationalism
Nazi Party

CHAPTER TWENTY-ONE: THE THREE WORLDS – 1945-1991

World War II was an important marker event of the 20th century because it changed the world order, although in many cases it confirmed changes that began much earlier in the century. The two superpowers – the United States and the Soviet Union – that emerged had been building their power for some time, but in the era between 1945 and 1991, they dominated the globe. The old imperialist order collapsed as European powers granted their colonies independence, so that by 1970 very few colonies remained officially tied to their old masters. Even though colonial imperialism virtually disappeared, political, economic, and social-cultural imperialism continued on, with the world clearly divided into "have" and "have not" countries. Politically, the global struggle for power and influence between the United States and the Soviet Union divided the world into three categories: friends of the United States (The First World), friends of the Soviet Union (The Second World), and those whose support both superpowers sought (The Third World). Supranationalism had failed in the early part of the century, but new international organizations formed and strengthened during this period, continuing a trend away from organizing the world exclusively into nation-states, although nation-states remained strong. Economically, more countries continued to industrialize, but those that had industrialized earlier went into a post-industrial phase with new goals and values, including an emphasis on enhancement of the quality of life, the realization of individual rights for minorities and women, and improvement of the environment.

COLD WAR POLITICS

The rivalry between the United States and the Soviet Union began before World War II was over. Wartime cooperation between Britain and the United States was close, anchored by the friendship between **Winston Churchill** – the British prime minister – and **Franklin Roosevelt** – the president of the United States. Neither trusted **Joseph Stalin** nor approved of the Soviet Union's communist system. Stalin saw the United States and Britain as essential, but not trusted, allies in the war effort. As the defeat of Germany and Japan drew near, this divisiveness became clear, as each side vied to contain the power of the other. Tensions were apparent at three Allied conferences held during the war.

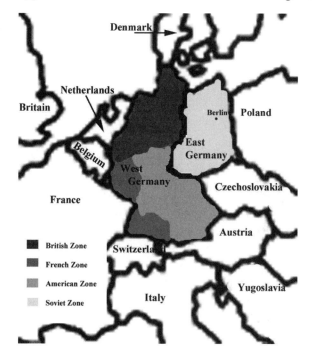

Post-World War II Germany. At the Yalta Conference in 1945, the Allies divided Germany into four occupation zones: British, French, American, and Soviet sectors. Since the capital city of Berlin was in the Soviet zone, they agreed to split the city into four zones of control as well. Once the war was over and the Cold War began, the country split into two parts: West Germany (a democratic country) and East Germany (a communist country).

Allied Conferences during World War II

Improved transportation and communications made it possible for the leaders of the Allied powers to hold meetings and conferences during the war, with some more formal than others. Three conferences – one in 1943 and two in 1945 – clearly illustrated the growing tension between the United States and the British on one side and the Soviet Union on the other. At the **Tehran Conference** in 1943, the Soviet government encouraged the western powers to open a new front in France, which they did with the D-Day invasion of Normandy in 1944. With the United States and Britain focused on France, the Soviet Union was free to occupy eastern Europe as its forces pushed the German armies back. Britain negotiated with the Soviets to maintain western dominance in Greece and influence in Yugoslavia and Hungary, but the United States asserted its support of self-determination for these small nations, as Woodrow Wilson had done at Versailles after World War I. At the **Yalta Conference** in 1945, the countries could not agree on a cooperative approach to handling post-war Germany, so they divided Germany into four occupation zones: Britain, the United States, France, and the Soviet Union. The Soviet Union wanted to eliminate German industrial power, but Britain and the United States did not agree, since they believed that Germany might ally with them against Russia. Strong arguments erupted over the status of the eastern European countries, with Stalin wishing to control their governments, and Britain and the United States wanting them to be free and democratic.

EXAMINING THE EVIDENCE: DISCUSSIONS OF THE ATOMIC BOMB AT POTSDAM

When Winston Churchill, Harry Truman, and Joseph Stalin met in July 1945 at Potsdam, Germany, Truman knew that the United States was ready to use the atomic bomb. He discussed the news with Churchill, who strongly supported the bomb's use, but he was unsure how to handle the news with Stalin, whom he did not trust. He resolved the dilemma as to whether to treat Stalin as an ally or an enemy by vaguely mentioning it to him toward the end of the conference. According to Truman's recollection,

"I casually mentioned to Stalin that we had a new weapon of unusual destructive force. All he said was that he was glad to hear it and hoped we would
make 'good use of it against the Japanese.' "

Truman did not share any specifics about the weapon, and he noted that Stalin seemed neither surprised nor the least bit curious. Stalin, however, did not need to ask because he had a spy, Klaus Fuchs (a naturalized British citizen), at the U.S. "top secret" research site in Los Alamos, New Mexico, who had been supplying the Russians with atomic secrets for some time. As a result of this intelligence, Stalin understood perfectly what Truman had said, although Truman did not know it at the time.

Reference: David McCulloch, *Truman* (New York: Simon and Schuster, 1992), pp, 442-3.

By the time of the **Potsdam Conference** in July 1945, the war in Europe was over, but was still going on in the Pacific. The Soviet Union had installed communist regimes in Romania, Bulgaria, Poland, Hungary, and Yugoslavia, and had dismantled German, Austrian, and Hungarian industrial equipment for shipment to the Soviet Union. In response to these moves, Winston Churchill and the new U.S. President, Harry Truman, met with Stalin to protest these actions, and Stalin let them know that he had no intention of keeping promises made at Yalta regarding the freedom of eastern European countries. The conference arranged further details of occupation and terms of future Japanese surrender but did not resolve the question of eastern Europe. In a further sign of growing tension between the U.S. and the Soviet Union, Truman disclosed to Churchill his plans to use the atomic bomb in Japan, but did not share the news with Stalin. Now that Hitler's threat to Europe had passed, the differences among the Allies – with capitalist, democratic Britain and the United States on one side and the communist Soviet Union on the other – became apparent, setting the stage for post-war political divisions.

Because of the rising hostility between the Soviet Union and the United States, no peace treaty was signed with Germany, and by the late 1940s a divided Germany had solidified into two countries, with West Germany supported by the United States and western Europe and East Germany supported by the Soviet Union. A similar division occurred in Asia, with the United States alone occupying Japan (since the surrender had occurred because of U.S.-developed technology – the atomic bomb) and Korea occupied half by the Soviets and half by the Americans. When no agreement could be reached between the United States and the Soviet Union on holding countrywide elections, communist North Korea and noncommunist South Korea became independent states in 1948, officially divided at the 38th parallel latitude.

The Emergence of the "Superpowers"

While tension was building between the United States and the Soviet Union, Britain gradually lost its pre-eminent role in determining world politics. When Franklin Roosevelt died in 1945, the famous Churchill/Roosevelt partnership was broken, and then, shortly after the war ended, Churchill's Conservative Party lost its majority control of Parliament, and Churchill lost his position as prime minister. Although he later regained the position, the winning Labour Party turned toward domestic affairs, leaving the United States as the pre-eminent foe of the Soviet Union. President Harry Truman asserted the new superpower's position in 1947 with a statement known as the **Truman Doctrine.** In Truman's own words, "I believe that it must be the policy of the United States to support free peoples who are resisting attempted subjugation by armed minorities or by outside pressures." When the British informed the United States that they could no longer support the Greeks in their fight against a communist insurrection supported from the outside, President Truman asked Congress for legislation in support of both Greece and Turkey. This statement clearly reflected the change in western leadership; the United States had replaced Britain as the protector of western values and authority.

The United States responded to Russia's power plays in eastern Europe not only by supporting regimes in Iran, Turkey, and Greece that were under Soviet pressure, but by proclaiming the **Marshall Plan,** a program that provided loans to aid the nations of western Europe to rebuild war-torn lands. From the Soviet point of view, the United States was trying to dominate Europe economically, and the lines between western and eastern Europe began to be drawn firmly in the sand. The Soviet drive to control eastern Europe was based partly on the belief that it was recovering lands that had been taken away from it at Versailles in 1919. However, the roots of Russian desires were much deeper. With all of their ambitions to westernize Russia, Peter the Great and Catherine the Great could never have dreamed that their "backward" country would ever hold a base so close to the heart of Europe or that Russia would eventually become a "super-power," as celebrated nations of western Europe faded from the world scene.

ORIGINAL DOCUMENT:
THE "IRON CURTAIN" SPEECH

British Prime Minister Winston Churchill was known for his rhetorical skills, and even though his country's power was fading at the end of World War II, he helped to shape the advent of the Cold War in a famous speech delivered in Fulton, Missouri in 1946. He defined the existence of what came to be known as the Cold War by identifying an "iron curtain" that divided Europe.

"From Stettin in the Baltic to Trieste in the Adriatic, an iron curtain has descended across the Continent. Behind that line lie all the capitals of the ancient states of central and eastern Europe. Warsaw, Berlin, Prague, Vienna, Budapest, Belgrade, Bucharest and Sofia; all these famous cities and the populations around them lie in the Soviet sphere and all are subject in one form or another, not only to Soviet influence but to a very high and increasing measure of control from Moscow...

...If the western democracies stand together in strict adherence to the principles of the United Nations Charter, their influence for furthering these principles will be immense and no one is likely to molest them. If however, they become divided or falter in their duty, and if these all-important years are allowed to slip away, then indeed catastrophe may overwhelm us all."

Reference: "Winston Churchill's Speech at Fulton," in *Vital Speeches of the Day,* Vol. 12 (New York: City News Publishing), March 15, 1946, pp. 331-332.

Germany was the focus of the Cold War in the early years. The Soviets took the point of view that seizing German goods and factories served as reparation for the war. The western Allies prevented Russia from intervening in their zones and gave West Germany economic support – such as in the Marshall Plan – to rebuild. In 1947 the Soviet Union blockaded the city of Berlin, so that no supplies could reach the areas under control of western countries. The United States responded with a massive airlift to keep the city supplied, and by 1948 the two Germanies were separated by heavy fortifications along their mutual borders. In 1961 Berlin's division became clearly visible when the East German government built the Berlin Wall that separated East Berlin from West Berlin, intended to prevent its citizens from fleeing to the noncommunist areas of the city. Cold War divisions spread to more countries with the formation of two military alliances: the **North Atlantic Treaty Organization (NATO),** which grouped western European countries, Canada and the United States; and the **Warsaw Pact,** in which the Soviet Union organized eastern European countries to counter NATO. In 1949 tensions escalated even further when the Soviet Union developed its own atomic bomb, starting an arms race that lasted into the 1980s. Both sides built more and more sophisticated nuclear arsenals of weapons and missile systems to deliver them. More conventional forces also expanded, with large amounts of each country's national budget allocated to military buildup.

The United Nations and Cold War Politics

Even before the United States officially entered World War II, President Roosevelt and Prime Minister Churchill signed the Atlantic Charter, which supported the establishment of a peacekeeping world organization after the war. Although the League of Nations had failed, Allied leaders continued to believe that such an organization could succeed if they corrected earlier structural and administrative mistakes and expanded their vision of what could be accomplished. In 1944 representatives from the United States, Britain, Russia, and China drafted proposals that eventually resulted in the **United Nations Charter,** ratified on October 24, 1945, only a few weeks after World War II officially ended.

The Charter created two main bodies: the **General Assembly,** with representatives from all member states, and the smaller **Security Council** dominated by the major Allied powers. The Security Council was charged with keeping world peace and with dealing with situations that threatened the national security of United Nations member states. It was composed of five permanent members – Britain, China, France, the Soviet Union, and the United States – who all had to approve any action that the United Nations took in world crises. Decisions of the Council also had to have majority consent from seven rotating members. The General Assembly voted on non-security issues, and only majority consent was necessary to pass measures there. A full-time bureaucracy headed by a Secretary General carried out the day-to-day business of the United Nations, and various agencies – such as the Food and Agriculture Organization (FAO) and United Nations Educational, Scientific and Cultural Organization (UNESCO) – were set up to address special international issues.

The United Nations was more flexible than the League of Nations had been because it did not require unanimous approval for decisions, as the League's charter had specified. However, Cold War politics often rendered the Security Council helpless, because so often the United States and the Soviet Union were on opposite sides of the issues. Other times Britain and France were at odds as they lost control of their colonies around the world. A further complication occurred when a communist government took over China in 1949, only to have the United Nations reject its legitimacy until 1972.

One crisis in the U.N.'s early years was decisively addressed by the Security Council, but only because the Soviet delegation was absent when the initial decisions were made. The Council voted to condemn the actions of communist North Korea when it invaded non-communist South Korea in 1950. United Nations troops were sent to defend South Korea, although most soldiers were either South Korean or American. The **Korean War** lasted until 1953, and even though the United Nations was directly involved, the situation reflected the fact that the real forces at work were nation-states, not this new supranational organization. The United States was the primary ally of South Korea, and the People's Republic of China (the new communist regime) gave substantial support to North Korea. Since the PRC was not recognized as a nation by the United Nations, the actions of the international organization were subsidiary to those of powerful nation-states.

"Limited War"

The Korean War represented a new style of fighting that emerged during the post-World War II era: **"limited war."** Even though the superpowers had the ability to launch global warfare, they instead faced one another in clashes that were limited to the regions where they initially broke out. Hanging over all was the threat of a "World War III" in which atomic weaponry could be used to annihilate both sides and even bring about the destruction of all civilizations on earth. As a result, every regional crisis contained the seeds of nuclear war, with each side "rattling their sabers" at the other, stepping to the brink of total war, and then retreating before absolute disaster could occur. In Korea the United States feared that launching attacks into China might bring retaliation from China's ally, the Soviet Union, and so even though both sides played it very dangerously, the war soon bogged down at the border between North and South Korea.

The fighting settled into a war with troops on either side of the 38th parallel that separated the two countries, and even though a truce was signed in 1953, both sides have continued to arm the border, so that the possibility of renewed warfare remains a threat even today.

A long-lasting "limited war" shaped by Cold War politics was fought in Vietnam, a part of French Indochina until 1954. The conflict began as a nationalist rebellion against the French, led by **Ho Chi Minh,** a Marxist trained in Moscow, who defeated the French on the battlefield and installed a communist regime in the northern half of the country in 1954. When the French left Vietnam, U.S. President Dwight Eisenhower decided to fund the government in the south, and agreed to hold free elections for a national Vietnamese government. Elections were never held because the U.S. feared that Ho would manipulate them, and President John Kennedy sent U.S. ground and air power to counter increasing guerrilla activity in the south. Then in the mid-1960s President Lyndon B. Johnson, who inherited a small-scale war, escalated it in order to bring it to a successful conclusion. By the end of 1966, 365,000 U.S. troops were engaged in the **Vietnam War,** but they were unable to defeat the Viet Cong, as Ho's supporters were called. Although China supplied the Viet Cong, Chinese soldiers never became actively involved, so the U.S. losses came at the hands of the North Vietnamese. With expenses of the war and military deaths mounting, a significant antiwar movement grew in the United States, finally bringing about a treaty between North Vietnam and the United States in 1973. In 1975 the treaty was violated when Viet Cong and North Vietnamese troops overran the South Vietnamese army and captured the southern capital of Saigon, reuniting the two parts of Vietnam in a single communist state ruled from the north.

The Nuclear Arms Race

Although "limited war" grew from a fear of nuclear warfare, both the United States and the Soviet Union continued to develop more and more powerful nuclear weapons. After the Soviet Union exploded its first atomic bomb in 1949, the U.S. developed a far more powerful weapon, the hydrogen bomb, which was tested in 1952, only to have the Soviets reveal their own version a year later. One of the most dangerous conflicts occurred in 1962 when the Soviet Union deployed nuclear missiles in Cuba, an action they took in response to U.S. efforts to overthrow Fidel Castro's government. When United States reconnaissance planes discovered the missiles, President John Kennedy prepared to invade Cuba, and for a few tense days it looked as if the U.S. and the U.S.S.R. would at last go to war. Catastrophe was avoided at the last minute, however, when the Soviet leader, Nikita Khrushchev, stopped Russian ships from breaking the U.S. quarantine that surrounded the island. Khrushchev eventually withdrew the missiles from Cuba, and the U.S. removed its missiles from Turkey.

As frightening as the **Cuban missile crisis** was, ultimately both countries acted to avoid using nuclear weapons that could spark all-out total war.

The commitment of both sides to contain the tensions of the Cold War was reflected in a series of arms limitation treaties. In 1963 Britain, the United States, and the Soviet Union agreed to ban the testing of nuclear weapons in the atmosphere, in space, and underwater in the interest of reducing the danger of radioactive fallout. The Nuclear Non-Proliferation Treaty that limited further development of nuclear weapons was signed by 137 countries in 1968, and talks between the U.S. and the Soviet Union continued for several years as they painstakingly negotiated weapons limits. By 1975 attention turned from arms limitation to an attempt to ease tensions in general. In the Helsinki Accords, western nations agreed to recognize the Soviet-dictated boundaries of eastern European nations in exchange for more liberal exchanges of people and information between East and West.

One highly competitive offshoot of the nuclear arms race was space exploration, with the two superpowers competing to build larger and more accurate missiles by launching space satellites. The U.S.S.R. successfully placed a satellite called **Sputnik** in space in 1957, and the U.S. responded with its own satellite a few months later. The **space race** continued during the 1960s as both countries strived to reach the moon first, an accomplishment claimed by the United States in 1969.

THE RISE OF COMMUNIST CHINA

Early in the development of the Cold War, the United States adopted a foreign policy of **containment,** or preventing the spread of communism beyond areas where it had already spread. The Truman Doctrine reflected this philosophy as it proclaimed the U.S. willingness to protect Greece and Turkey, and U.S. involvement in both the Korean War and the Vietnam War was stimulated by the desire to stop the spread of communism.

One of the biggest blows to U.S. efforts occurred in 1949 when communist forces under **Mao Zedong** managed to drive Chinese Nationalist forces under **Chiang Kai-shek** out of mainland China and declare the founding of the People's Republic of China. The Japanese occupied China during World War II, but after the war ended, the forces of Chiang and Mao met in civil war, and Mao prevailed. In 1949 Chiang fled to Taiwan, and Mao established the People's Republic of China under communist rule, while Chiang claimed that his headquarters in Taiwan formed the true government. The "**Two Chinas,**" then, were created, and the PRC was not to be recognized as a nation by the United Nations until 1972.

**PERSPECTIVES:
A RUSSIAN VIEW OF
THE SPACE RACE**

When the Soviet Union managed to successfully launch the first satellite into space in 1957, the event shook American pride and confidence to its core. In contrast, many people in the U.S.S.R. were overjoyed that their country had made this important leap ahead in the space race. In the excerpt below, Semyon Reznik, a Soviet journalist and author who later moved to the United States, recalled the joyous event.

"The day our satellite *Sputnik* was launched, a special voice came over the radio to announce it to us. Traditionally, in the Soviet Union a few of the radio announcers were hired to read only the most urgent news on the radio... On an October morning in 1957, we heard one of those voices announce, 'Attention. All radio stations of the Soviet Union are broadcasting...Our satellite *Sputnik* is in space.' I felt so proud. Who did it? We did it! The Soviet Union is first in space! I was in my second year of college and just couldn't imagine that this could happen in my lifetime. In my mind, space travel only existed in science fiction. We didn't even know that the project was in the works..."

Reference: Peter Jennings and Todd Brewster, *The Century.* (New York: Doubleday, 1998), p. 357.

Rule by Mao Zedong

The early development of the PRC proceeded in two phases:

1) **The Soviet model** (1949-1957) – The Soviet Union had been supporting Mao's efforts since the 1920s, and with his victory in 1949, they began pouring money and expertise into the PRC. With this help, Chairman Mao and the Chinese Communist Party (CCP) quickly turned their attention to some of the country's most glaring social problems.

   • Land reform – This campaign redistributed property from the rich to the poor and increased productivity in the countryside.

   • Civil reform – The CCP set about to free people from opium addiction, and it greatly enhanced women's legal rights. For example, it allowed women to free themselves from unhappy arranged marriages.

These measures helped to legitimize Mao's government in the eyes of the people.

- Five Year Plans – Between 1953 and 1957, the CCP launched the first of its Soviet-style Five Year Plans to nationalize industry and collectivize agriculture, implementing steps toward socialism.

2) **The Great Leap Forward** (1958-1966) – Mao changed directions in 1958, partly in an effort to free China from Soviet domination. The spirit of nationalism was a force behind Mao's policy here, and he was still unhappy with the degree of inequality in Chinese society. The Great Leap Forward was a utopian effort to transform China into a radical egalitarian society. Its emphasis was mainly economic, and it was based on four principles:

- All-around development – The emphasis was not just heavy industry (as under Stalin in the USSR), but almost equal attention was given to agriculture.

- Mass mobilization – An effort was made to turn the sheer numbers of the population into an asset – better motivation, harder work, less unemployment.

- Political unanimity and zeal – An emphasis was placed on party workers running government, not bureaucrats. Cadres – party workers at the lowest levels – were expected to demonstrate their party devotion by spurring the people on to work as hard as they could.

- Decentralization – Stronger governments on the local level was encouraged, with less central government control. The people can do it!

The Great Leap Forward did not live up to its name. Mao's efforts ran counter to the traditional political culture (bureaucratic centralism), and the people lacked skills to contribute to industrialization. Some bad harvests conjured up fears of the loss of the mandate of heaven.

Between 1960 and 1966, Mao allowed two of his faithful – Liu Shaoqi and Deng Xiaoping – to implement market-oriented policies that revived the economy, but Mao was still unhappy with China's progress toward true egalitarianism. So he instituted the **Cultural Revolution** – a much more profound reform in that it encompassed political and social change, as well as economic. His main goal was to purify the party and the country through radical transformation.

A primary goal of the Cultural Revolution was to remove all vestiges of the old China and its hierarchical bureaucracy and emphasis on inequality. Scholars

MARKER EVENT: THE CHINESE COMMUNIST REVOLUTION AND WOMEN'S RIGHTS

The important philsophical influence of Confucianism throughout China's long history encouraged a hierarchical society that assumed inequalities as basic to an orderly society with men and women playing very traditional, family-based roles. As the revolutionary spirit erupted in China during the early 20th century, women's rights became an important issue, resulting in a ban on foot binding and an increase in educational and career opportunities for women. When Mao Zedong instituted the egalitarian values of communism in China, one effect was to create more equal roles for men and women. Mao was committed to women's equality because, in his words, "women hold up half of the heavens."

Even before Mao's Communist Party took over the country, women actively advanced the revolutionary cause by serving as teachers, nurses, spies, laborers, and occasionally as soldiers on the front line. Mao's commitment to women's rights extended to his personal life as well, with his wife, Jiang Qing, playing an increasingly prominent role as an adviser and eventually implementer of his policies. Despite these changes, after Mao's death traditional values remained, with foot binding still practiced among some elites. However, the expectation that women work outside the home continued, and opportunities for educational and professional careers have remained open to women.

---

were sent into the fields to work, and universities and libraries were destroyed. Emphasis was put on elementary education – all people should be able to read and write – but any education that created inequality was targeted for destruction.

Mao died in 1976, leaving his followers divided into factions:

- Radicals – This faction was led by Mao's wife, Jiang Qing, one of the "Gang of Four," who supported the radical goals of the Cultural Revolution.

- Military - Always a powerful group because of the long-lasting 20th century struggles that required an army, the military was led by Lin Biao, who died in a mysterious airplane crash in 1971.

- Moderates – This group was led by Zhou Enlai, who emphasized economic modernization and limited contact with other countries, including the United States. Zhou influenced Mao to invite President Richard Nixon to China in 1972. He died only a few months after Mao.

Reforms Under Deng Xiaoping

The Gang of Four was arrested by the new CCP leader, Hua Guofeng, whose actions helped the moderates take control. Zhou's death opened the path for new leadership from the moderate faction. By 1978, the new leader emerged - **Deng Xiaoping.** His vision drastically altered China's direction through "Four Modernizations" invented by Zhou Enlai before his death – industry, agriculture, science, and the military. Under Deng's leadership, these policies have helped to implement the new direction:

- "Open door" trade policy – Trade with everyone was encouraged, including capitalist nations like the U.S., in order to boost China's economy.

- Reforms in education – Higher academic standards and expansion of higher education and research were emphasized (a reversal of the policy during the Cultural Revolution).

- Institutionalization of the Revolution – The legal system and bureaucracy of the Old China were restored, the government decentralized, elections modified, and capitalism infused.

DECOLONIZATION

National identities changed in many important ways during the period from 1945 to 1991. Whereas China had been transformed from an ancient empire to a new communist state, other areas of the world that had been colonized by imperialist powers asserted their identities in successful independence movements that resulted in dozens of new countries. Political scientist **Samuel Huntington** has linked this **decolonization** (former colonies becoming independent countries) to the second of what he called **"three waves" of democratization.** Democratic governments have been based on rule of law, selection of leaders by popular election, and the guarantee of individual liberties and rights. The first wave came with the revolutions in America and France during the late 18th century, developed slowly, and then hit obstacles of totalitarianism in the early 20th century that caused the number of democracies to fall from 29 to 12 in the era between the two world wars. The "second wave" started with the Allied victory in World War II and continued until about 1962, and included the formation of new countries in Africa, South Asia, and Southeast Asia. Huntington's "third wave" started in the mid-1970's when three dictatorships in southern Europe came to an end (in Greece, Portugal, and Spain), followed by countries in eastern Europe that escaped from Soviet control, and finally with the dissolution of the Soviet Union itself in 1991.

Why did these last two rapid "waves" of democracy occur in the mid-to-late 20th century, when the first wave had taken so many years to develop? According to Huntington, some factors are:

- the loss of legitimacy by both right and left wing authoritarian regimes, as illustrated by the defeat of Hitler's Germany and Mussolini's Italy;

- the expansion of an urban middle class in developing countries as the old imperialist system collapsed and industrialization took place in other parts of the world;

- a new emphasis on "human rights" by the United States and western Europe, as an alternative foreign policy to Cold War containment of communism;

- the "snowball" effect, or the fact that when one country in a region becomes democratic, it influences others to do so. An example is Poland's influence on other nations of eastern Europe during the 1980s.

As we have seen in the era 1750 and 1914, stirrings for independence movements in India and Egypt started long before World War I began, as native elites struggled to protect their lands from European domination. World War I encouraged these movements as the imperialist powers turned on one another, with each looking to its colonies for soldiers, laborers, food, and raw materials. For example, in India the British encouraged expansion of industrial production – contrary to long-standing colonial policy – to supplement the efforts of British factories to keep up with war demands. Administrative personnel in the colonies were called to fill wartime posts, requiring that the colonial jobs be filled by African and Asian administrators.

The Indian Independence Struggle

During World War I British leaders had promised Indian nationalists that if they supported the war effort, India would move toward self-government within the empire once the conflict was over. An action that pleased both the Indian National Congress and the Muslim League (independence organizations founded before World War I) was the Government of India Act passed in 1919, which transferred powers over agriculture, public works, education, local self-government, and education to Indian-elected legislators at the provincial level. However, the British waffled between treating India as a budding democratic home-ruled nation and a colony, and their mixed messages frustrated Indians. Leaders of the independence movement had heard Woodrow Wilson's expression of self-determination in his Fourteen Points, and they expected the principle to be applied to their country. Yet the British government did not support freedom of the press and assembly, and independence rallies were met with repressive control. Voices for independence became much louder as they organized under the direction of **Mohandas K. Gandhi,** known to many of his followers as "Mahatma" or "great soul."

ORIGINAL DOCUMENT: GANDHI ON PASSIVE RESISTANCE

Mohandas Gandi advocated passive resistance – a combination of civil disobedience and non-violence – for his followers in their efforts to bring about Indian independence from the Britain. In the passage below, he explains why these methods are superior to armed resistance.

"Passive resistance is a method of securing rights by personal suffering; it is the reverse of resistance by arms. When I refuse to do a thing that is repugnant to my conscience, I use soul-force. For instance, the government of the day has passed a law which is applicable to me: I do not like it, if, by using violence, I force the government to repeal the law, I am employing what may be termed body-force. If I do not obey the law and accept the penalty for its breach, I use soul-force. It involves sacrifice of self....

...Wherein is courage required – in blowing others to pieces from behind a cannon or with a smiling face to approach a cannon and to be blown to pieces? Who is the true warrior – he who keeps death always as a bosom-friend or he who controls the death of others? Believe me that a man devoid of courage can never be a passive resister...

Passive resistance is an all-sided sword; it can be used anyhow; it blesses him who uses it and him against whom it is used. Without drawing a drop of blood, it produces far-reaching results."

Reference: Mohandas Gandhi, *Indian Home Rule* (Madras, India: Ganesh & Co., 1922), pp. 90-91.

Gandhi was an English-educated Hindu who practiced law in South Africa before he returned to his native India during World War I to join the Indian National Congress. Although from a well-to-do family himself, Gandhi showed his sympathy for the poor by wearing simple peasant garb: a length of homespun cloth below his waist and a shawl to cover his torso. He attracted large numbers of admirers, and he transformed the cause of Indian independence from an elite movement of the educated into a mass movement that centered on his charismatic presence. Gandhi's ideals came to be symbolized by a spinning wheel – the traditional mechanism used by Indians to spin cotton yarn before the British began sending Indian cotton to factories in England. He sparked nationalistic feelings among his followers by advocating a return to Indian self-sufficiency and the shedding of British control. In 1929 he led a few followers on an 80-mile walk to gather salt from the sea in an act of civil disregard for the government's monopoly on salt. This famous action illustrated his belief that **civil disobedience** – peacefully breaking unjust laws – and non-violence were the best practices for bringing about change.

One conflict that Gandhi could not heal was the rift between Muslims and Hindus in India. Even though he fasted for twenty-one days in 1924 to promote Hindu-Muslim unity and he walked through violence-torn areas in 1947 to advocate peace, Muslims associated the independence movement with Hinduism. **Muhammad Ali Jinnah,** the leader of the Muslim League, who eventually led the movement for a separate Pakistan after World War II, did not trust Gandhi's Indian National Congress to deal equitably with Muslims. Gandhi also disagreed with his successor, **Jawaharlal Nehru,** who supported the creation of a modern industrial India. By the time that World War II began, Indian entrepreneurs had built plants to manufacture iron and steel, cement, paper, cotton and jute textiles, and sugar – all protected by high tariff barriers with British approval.

When World War II ended, Britain's new Labour Party government agreed to Indian independence, but the process was complicated by disagreements between Hindus, as represented by Nehru's Indian National Congress, and Muslims, as represented by Jinnah's Muslim League. Violent rioting between Hindus and Muslims broke out, even though Gandhi begged for tolerance and cooperation. Finally, in 1947 the agreement was made to partition India into two states – one secular but dominated by Hindus and the other Muslim – and the new India and Pakistan became independent countries. The Indian National Congress, led by Nehru, formed the first government of India; Jinnah and the Muslim League established a government for Pakistan.

Despite the fact that India was at last independent, the transition was chaotic, with Muslim and Hindu neighbors turning on one another in violence. For centuries Hindus and Muslims had intermingled, but now Hindus in Pakistan had to move to India to avoid attack by Muslims, and Muslims in India became refugees as they sought to escape massacre by Hindus. Within a few months some 12 million people had left their ancestral homes, and 500,000 lay dead, including Gandhi, who was killed in January 1948 by a Hindu refugee. When the violence finally settled down, one state with a Muslim majority – Kashmir – remained in India because the local maharajah was Hindu, and because the state held the headwaters of rivers that irrigated many Indian farms in the north-western part of the subcontinent. This situation contributed to continued unrest, since many Muslims in Kashmir would have preferred to join Pakistan.

COMPARISON: 20TH CENTURY NATIONALISM IN CHINA AND INDIA

By the early 20th century both China and India had experienced strong nationalistic movements that emphasized the rejection of control by Westerners. The economies of both societies were rooted in agriculture, with the majority of their populations living in rural areas. These populations were successfully organized by Mao Zedong in China and Mohandas Gandhi in India, with both leaders concerned about equity for ordinary peasants. Both movements succeeded after much loss of life in their support. By the late 20th century the two countries also had the largest populations in the world with governments that guided the countries to cumulative and growing economic expansion. The differences between these two giant countries, however, are great. China had not been colonized as India had been, and so China had no functioning central government until 1949. India's central government was controlled by the British until 1947. China's civil war that led to the establishment of the People's Republic of China was a bloody military conflict, but India's independence movement under Gandhi emphasized non-violent mass civil resistance. India's nationalist leaders - particularly Jawaharlal Nehru and his successors - welcomed businessmen in their struggle, and when independence occurred in 1947, relations with Britain remained harmonious. In contrast, Mao's new communist government spurned capitalism and contact with the West, although his successor, Deng Xiaoping, loosened restraints on both after 1978.

Decolonization in Southeast Asia

Britain gave independence to Burma – a colony east of India – in 1947, Ceylon (now Sri Lanka) in 1948, and Malaysia in 1963. The French, too, pulled out of Southeast Asia even before the battle of Dien Bien Phu in 1954, when Ho Chi Minh's forces decisively defeated the French army. Like the British, the French had been so devastated by World War II that holding onto its colonies became economically impossible. French Indo-China was carved into separate nations, and the countries of Laos and Cambodia were created in 1949 and 1954 respectively. Because of disagreements between Ho Chi Minh's communist forces in the north and the French and U.S. supported government in the south, North and South Vietnam remained as separate countries until after the Vietnam War ended in 1973. The independence wave in Southeast Asia extended to Indonesia, where the Dutch decolonized in 1949, and to the Philippines, finally released in 1946 from the United States, who had controlled it since 1898.

Decolonization in Sub-Saharan Africa

As happened in India, the African independence movements were led by men newly educated in European ideals, mainly in universities in Europe and the United States, who came to dream of democracy and nationalistic independence for colonies in Africa. During the 1930s newspapers began appearing in some British colonies, although only a small percentage of Africans were literate by 1960. Just as Indians did, Africans served in the world wars in support of their mother countries, giving soldiers exposure to lands far from home, and they too became disillusioned with the brutality of Europeans fighting Europeans. Seeds of African discontent lay in the treatment of Africans working in the mines, plantations, railroads, and docks for Europeans that controlled the economy and often projected an air of racial superiority that made Africans long for independence.

Africans from across the continent gathered in five meetings between the end of World War I and the end of World War II, although transportation limitations meant that all five congresses met in Europe or the United States. These **All-African People's Conference** meetings were led by famous men such as **W.E.B. Du Bois** – an American scholar – and **Blaise Diagne** of Senegal, but little progress was made toward independence until the Fifth Congress convened in Manchester, England, in 1945. In a world where European empires were beginning to crumble, a new generation of African leaders, most notably **Kwame Nkrumah** of Ghana and **Jomo Kenyatta** of Kenya, could more confidently demand African independence.

New African Countries

Both Britain and France came to understand that the wars had weakened their economies so severely that they could no longer afford to keep their colonies, so both countries devised plans for granting independence but also keeping the good will of the new countries. They wanted to keep profitable trade going, and so they invested in projects to support the African infrastructure, such as hydroelectric schemes on major river systems, and agricultural, veterinary, and fishing technology. Educational facilities increased, with four university colleges established by the British between 1945 and 1949. Even so, African economies remained weak, especially in the Belgian Congo, Angola, and Mozambique, where Belgium and Portugal were less willing to grant independence.

The first black African country to win independence was the Gold Coast, choosing the name Ghana to link the new country to an earlier African empire. Kwame Nkrumah, educated in the United States, led the movement in Ghana, and after independence was won in 1957, he convened the All-African People's Conference at Accra (the capital of Ghana), the first time that the conference ever met in Africa. Three years later, Britain granted independence to Nigeria, which was the most populous country in Africa with 42 million people in 1960. Like many other African nations, the borders were drawn arbitrarily, grouping many unrelated, often hostile, groups within the same country and separating groups that were related. Nigeria was composed of three regions based on ethnicity: the Hausa majority in the north, the Yoruba in the southwest, and the Ibo in the southeast. Not only were tribal affiliations different, but the people in the north – influenced by the slow cultural diffusion of Islam across the Sahara to Sub-Saharan Africa – were mainly Muslim; those in the south – influenced by missionaries coming from Britain – were mainly Christian. These differences made nationalism a serious problem for Nigeria, a common pattern experienced by many other newly-created African countries.

In 1956 France turned over local self-government to its colonies in west and central Africa, but still kept them within the French Empire. Two years later, it offered each of its colonies the choice between complete independence and more limited self-government under French protection. By 1960 Guinea and French Somaliland (Djibouti) chose independence, but in all others, strong ties continued between France and its former African colonies. For example, many currencies remained tied to the French franc, some African governmental positions were filled by French expatriates, the French military maintained a presence in some colonies, and former colonies received preferential trading rights with France.

The freeing of the Belgian colonies was accompanied by violence, with Belgium, unlike Britain and France, doing little preparation for independence. In 1959, in response to rioting and looting of Belgian shops in Leopoldsville, the capital of the Belgian Congo, Belgium suddenly decided to pull out of the country within the year, leaving it in chaos that soon turned into civil war. The colonial government had been one of the most cruel and exploitative, and the new government's prime minister, Patrice Lumumba, expressed his bitterness at the independence ceremony, only to be deposed in a coup and assassinated a few months later. In nearby Ruanda-Urundi (present-day Rwanda and Burundi), the Belgians had allowed the Tutsi minority (about 15 percent of the population) to dominate the government, and when independence came in 1962, the majority

Hutus challenged the Tutsis for control, and tensions broke out into warfare and massacres by 1972, escalated in the 1990s, and continues today.

South Africa

After 1980 South Africa was the only white-ruled country in Sub-Saharan Africa. About 1/5 of the population was white, some with Dutch ancestry called "Boers" or "Afrikaners," and some of British descent. The British and Dutch had fought the Boer War of 1899-1902, but had come together to form the Union of South Africa in 1910. The majority black and "colored" (mixed) populations were ruled harshly, with no political rights, few economic opportunities, and the right to purchase land in only specified areas. In 1913 the **African National Congress (ANC)** formed as a party of protest, but it was unable to convince the white government to liberalize its racial policies. In 1948 **apartheid** – segregation of the races – was established, and black workers in the cities could not live near their work, but were forced to live in black residential areas far away or in dormitories apart from their families.

As most colonies in Africa declared their independence and set up governments run by natives, international pressure built against the South African government to dismantle the apartheid system, but they resisted any change. The ANC then shifted to more aggressive methods, including strikes and sabotage of white property, and its leader, **Nelson Mandela,** who was already incarcerated, was sentenced to life imprisonment in 1964. These actions first brought support from surrounding countries to the ANC, and in 1976 the United Nations unanimously condemned the elevation of one of the black "homelands", Transkei, into an independent state because it remained dependent on South Africa. Not one country in the world recognized the new state, but in 1982, almost one million black South Africans were transferred to another country – Swaziland – without their having any say in the matter. Through the United Nations as well as through unilateral actions, many nations adopted sanctions against South Africa, restricting trade, or withdrawing economic investments. Enforcing the sanctions proved difficult because South Africa was wealthy with many natural resources, including diamonds and gold, and the South African military was very strong.

Ultimately, many blacks demonstrated, held strikes and rioted over the government's discriminatory practices. As a result, the sanctions did gradually work and diplomatic pressure mounted abroad for change. In 1990, Nelson Mandela finally was released from prison, and he was elected president of the African National Congress the following year. In 1993 he received the Nobel Peace Prize, and on May 10, 1994, he was elected South Africa's first black president, in that country's first truly democratic election, with all races able to vote.

EXAMINING THE EVIDENCE: NELSON MANDELA'S TRIAL STATEMENT

Nelson Mandela led the African National Congress to adopt tactics of armed resistance in the face of apartheid conditions in South Africa. After the police killed sixty-nine peaceful demonstrators in Sharpeville in 1961, Mandela became the commander of the new ANC guerilla army, was arrested, and later sentenced to life in prison. At a statement at his trial for leading the Umkonto We Sizwe, the military wing of the ANC, he explained his view of the use of violence.

"Some of the things so far told to the Court are true and some are untrue. I do not, however, deny that I planned sabotage. I did not plan it in a spirit of recklessness, nor because I have any love of violence. I planned it as the result of a calm and sober assessment of the political situation that has arisen after many years of tyranny, exploitation and oppression of my people by the Whites...
But the violence which we chose to adopt was not terrorism. We who formed Umkonto were all members of the African National Congress, and had behind us the ANC tradition of non-violence and negotation as a means of solving political disputes....We did not want an inter-racial war, and tried to avoid it to the last minute..."

Reference: From Protests to Challenge: A Documentary History of African Politics in South Africa, 1882-1964. ed. Thomas Karis and Gwendolyn M. Carter, Vol. III.

Decolonization and Change in North Africa and the Middle East

Whereas most Sub-Saharan African countries were colonized during the late 19th century, areas in northern Africa and the Middle East experienced many different patterns and time frames as nation-states were formed. The entire Arab world is included in this region, but all the inhabitants are not Arabs. Iran's heritage is more Persian than Arab, but it shares a Muslim heritage with Arab countries, as does Turkey, which inherited the mantle of the Ottoman Turks. In 1947 the founding of Israel meant that the number of Jews in the Middle East increased rapidly. The fact that this area is one of the oldest centers of civilization lends it a complexity that is reflected in different patterns of nationalism and varied responses to decolonization and the declining influence of the West.

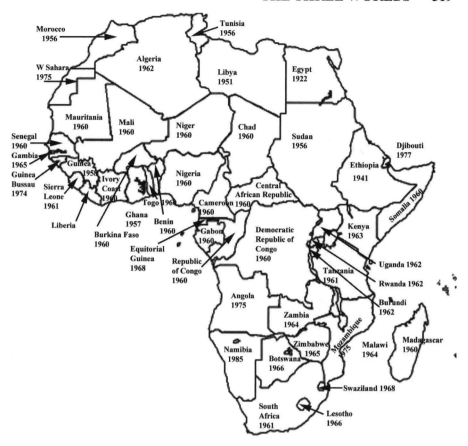

The Decolonization of Africa. The year of each country's independence is shown on the map. Ethiopia was only colonized by Italy under Mussolini for a few years, Liberia had been established as an independent state, and Egypt was granted independence in 1922, but most African states gained their independence after World War II. Each colonial power had its own pattern for granting independence, and although many experienced violence, the British and French hoped to establish friendly relations, whereas the Portuguese and Belgians left their colonies less willingly.

Turkey

After **Mustafa Kemal (Ataturk)** unified Turkey as an independent country in 1923, he set about creating a secular nationalist state. To do so, he curbed the power of Islam by abolishing shari'a law, the practice of polygamy, and the office of caliph in the government. He replaced Arabic script with the Roman alphabet, encouraged Turks to wear western clothes, and encouraged women to discontinue wearing veils. His goals were similar to those of the Ottoman Empire in earlier days – to adopt western technology customs in order to have a respected place in the world. However, his quest for modernity included the acceptance of a loan from the Soviet Union to buy Soviet equipment to use in the country's sugar and textile industries. By the time that World War II broke out, Turkey had made some amazing economic and educational strides, and true to their nationalism, they remained neutral for most of World War II, siding with the Allies only toward the end of the war.

Despite these accomplishments, Ataturk's secular nationalism was highly controversial, especially among Muslim clerics, and his actions created a rift in Turkey's political culture between those who wished to keep the state secular and those who wanted to return to a Muslim state. The presence of a large Kurdish population complicated Turkey's statehood, since the nationalistic Kurds have advocated a separate Kurdish state composed of people now spread out into six Middle Eastern countries. To add to the tensions, the armed forces have intervened periodically in politics so that the government has alternated between democratic elections and military dictatorships. As in times past, Turkey's geographic location has split its orientation between Europe and western Asia.

Iran

World events of the early 20th century led to Iran's division into three parts, with one piece for the Iranian government, but another piece occupied by Russia, and another by Britain during World War I. By 1921 Iran was in political and economic disarray, with quarreling factions polarizing the legislature into an ineffective ruling body. The country was ready for a strong leader to deliver them from complete chaos. Colonel Reza Khan, carried out a successful coup d'etat against the weakened political state in 1921, and declared himself shah in 1925, establishing his own **Pahlavi dynasty**, using the name of an ancient language from Iran's glorious past.

Under Reza Shah, the legislature lost its power, and authoritarian rule was reestablished in Iran. He ruled with absolute authority until he turned over power to his son, Muhammad Reza Shah in 1941. Despite the fact that the Pahlavis reestablished order in Iran, democratic experimentation from earlier in the century was not forgotten, and the second shah had to confront some democratic opposition. Muhammad Mosaddeq was elected prime minister in 1951, and his power grew so that the shah was forced to flee the country in 1953. Mosaddeq's career was cut short when the British and the American governments sponsored an overthrow of Mosaddeq and restored the shah to full power again. The U.S. saw the ploy as a means to keep Soviet power contained during these Cold War days. As a result, many Iranians came to see Britain and the U.S. as supporters of autocracy, and the shah as a weak pawn of foreign powers. During their rule, the two Pahlavi shahs built a highly centralized state, the first since the ancient days of the Persian Empire. Whereas Iran remained a religious state, its courts became fully secularized, with a European-style judicial system and law codes in place. The shah secularized Iran further by extending voting rights to women, restricting polygamy, and allowing women to work outside the home.

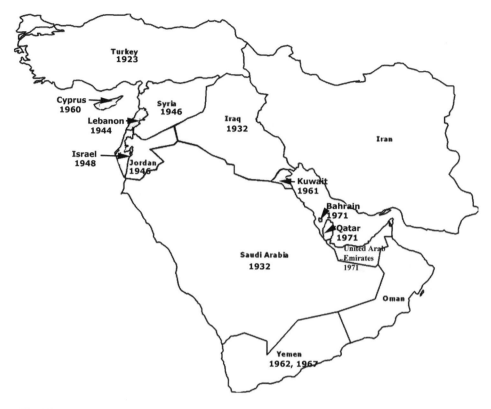

The Middle East and Independence. Independence dates for countries in the Middle East vary more than those for most of Sub-Saharan Africa. Some were never colonized – such as Iran and Oman, although Oman was a British protectorate. Others formed into nation-states after World War I – such as Turkey, Iraq, and Saudi Arabia. Most others were part of the decolonization that occurred around the world after World War II, although the dates in this category range from 1944 to 1971.

The shah's behavior disturbed Iranians largely because from many people's points of view, he overstepped the bounds of the political culture in three ways:

- He was perceived as being totalitarian, not just authoritarian, as shahs before the Pahlavis had been.

- He broke the balance between the secular and the religious state by secularizing Iran too much and too fast, certainly from the point of view of the clergy.

- His ties to the west (particularly the United States) offended Iranian nationalists as well as the clergy.

In many ways, the shah created a divide in the political culture, with one side supporting modernization in the sense of establishing closer ties to the West, and the other side staunchly defending traditional ways, in particular Shi'ism. An elite of clerics rose to oppose the shah, lead a revolution, and eventually take over the government.

Great revolutions have shaken the world in many places since the late 18th century, and the causes and consequences of Iran's 1979 revolution are in some ways very similar to those in Russia, China, and Mexico in the 20th century. However, Iran's revolution is unique in that it was almost completely religious in nature. The dominant ideology was religion, whereas revolutions in Russia and China revolved around communism. Although the Catholic Church was very much involved in the revolutionary era (early 20th century) in Mexico, the Church did not direct the military, and Mexico's ruling party quickly sidelined the Church once the party gained control of the country. In Iran, the dominant ideology was Shi'ism, and the most important revolutionary leader was a cleric, who in turned ruled Iran for ten years following the revolution. Perhaps most significantly, Iran's revolution resulted in the establishment of a theocracy, while other revolutions generally were against religious control of the government.

One more ingredient for the success of the revolution was the charisma of its leader, the **Ayatollah Ruhollah Khomeini**. He not only defended **Islamic fundamentalism**, which emphasized literal interpretation of Islamic texts, social conservatism, and political traditionalism, but he also articulated resentments against the elite and the United States. His depiction of the United States as the "Great Satan" puzzled many Americans, but resonated with frustrated people in Iran. The Ayatollah gave new meaning to an old Shi'i term *velayat-e faqih* **(jurist's guardianship)**. The principle originally gave the senior clergy (including himself) broad authority over the unfortunate people (widows, orphans, mentally unstable) in the society, but Khomeini claimed that the true meaning of jurist's guardianship gives the clergy authority over the entire Shi'ia community.

Once the reins loosened, many groups supported the revolution – political parties, labor organizations, professional associations, bazaar (merchant) guilds, college students, and oil workers. In late 1978, hundreds of unarmed demonstrators were killed in a central square in Tehran, and oil workers had gone on strike, paralyzing the oil industry. Anti-regime rallies were attracting as many as 2 million protestors. It is important to note that the rallies were organized and led by the clerics, but were broadly supported by people from many sectors of society. Although Khomeini was in exile in Paris, audiotapes of his speeches were passed out freely at the rallies, where people called for the abolition of the monarchy. The shah fled the country at the beginning of February 1979, and his government officially ended on February 11, with the founding of the Islamic Republic of Iran.

Once the new constitution was endorsed, the Shi'ite leaders launched the **Cultural Revolution** with goals that were very similar to Mao Zedong's goals as he led China's Cultural Revolution in 1966. Different beliefs lay behind the two revolutions, with Shi'ism inspiring Iran and communism fueling China. However, purification was at the heart of both revolutions. The Cultural Revolution in Iran aimed to purify the country from not only the shah's regime, but also from secular values and behaviors, particularly those with western origins. The universities were cleared of liberals and staffed with faculty who supported the new regime. The new government suppressed all opposition, and many were executed in the name of "revolutionary justice."

States in Northern Africa

Egypt had operated as an independent state since the days of Muhammad Ali in the early 19th century, even though it remained technically a part of the Ottoman Empire until World War I. However, the British held a great deal of economic control, even though independence was officially granted in 1922. During World War II, the British put the government in the hands of the Wafd, an Egyptian nationalist party, and the new government took the leadership in establishing the **League of Arab States,** a regional organization designed to strengthen and unite countries with Arab majorities. In 1952 the army drove out the Egyptian king and cut many ties with the British, paving the way for the emergence of **Gamel Abdel Nasser** as the new nationalist leader. Nasser took advantage of Cold War politics to seek and gain aid from both the United States and the Soviet Union, but joined in meetings with states that aligned with neither superpower. In 1956 he declared that the Suez Canal belonged to Egypt, and despite the protests of Britain and France in the United Nations Security Council, the United States sided with Nasser and pressured its allies to support Egypt's nationalization of the canal. Nasser's move was successful, and his bold challenge of the imperialist order was one more example of the transition from western European global hegemony to the Cold War era of "Third World" countries balancing the competition between the U.S. and U.S.S.R. in order to curry benefits for their nation.

Even before World War II, an Arab-Islamic nationalist movement had developed in Algeria, which was a French colony in northern Africa. After the war was over and France was having trouble controlling its world empire, the movement in Algeria intensified into a revolution in the mid-1950s. The Arab nationalists were united as the National Liberation Front, and they fought against those that wished to keep ties to France intact. The violence spread throughout Algeria and eventually to France, triggering the fall of the Fourth French Republic. The situation was contained by **Charles De Gaulle,** the leader of the French Resistance during World War II, who ushered in a new government in France – the Fifth Republic – and negotiated Algerian independence in 1962. The new state was limited by the exodus of virtually all the one million European residents in Algeria, some of whom had filled the most important positions in the government. The new leaders encouraged industrialization, and oil revenues financed government programs to build roads, infrastructure for industries, and the education system. Despite these efforts, many Algerians emigrated to France, and control of the country has remained fragile as the military and Islamic fundamentalists have struggled for power.

The Israeli-Palestinian Conflict

The Jewish claims for a homeland have roots that extend back to Abraham's settlement in the lands on the eastern end of the Mediterranean Sea about 4000 years ago. Over the years the Hebrew people had conflicts with many others in the region, and were finally dispelled by the Romans in the 1st century C.E. The diaspora that followed was accompanied by a strong desire among many Jews to return to the area. By the early 20th century the **Zionist Movement** succeeded in getting Britain's foreign secretary to issue the Balfour Declaration in support to their land claims. After World War I the British government took no substantial steps to realize the promise in that document, but the Zionist movement eventually realized its goal in 1948 with the creation of the state of Israel, a Jewish homeland in the area that Abraham called "the land of milk and honey." However, as welcome as this news was to Jews around the world, the Arab people in the areas – the Palestinians – who had settled there over the centuries since the diaspora were distressed because many were displaced from what they considered to be their ancestral lands.

After World War I Jewish settlement in Palestine increased in response to the Balfour Declaration, but with it came increasing conflict. Armed Arabs – who had also received promises from Britain for independence – attempted unsuccessfully to halt and drive out Jewish immigration from the 1920s onward. Nazi persecution of Jews throughout World War II and the atrocities of the Holocaust reminded Britain and the other Allies of the need for a political state for the Jewish people, who had been driven from their homes and killed, just as had happened in ancient times. In this spirit, the United Nations passed a resolution agreeing to the establishment of an independent Jewish state in Palestine on land occupied by Arabs. When Arabs tried to block the creation of Israel, many Jews interpreted their actions not as a land dispute, but as a new form of anti-Semitism that had so recently resulted in the Holocaust. Because Palestinians were mostly Muslim, the conflict came to have broader religious meanings in the land where Judaism, Christianity, and Islam originated.

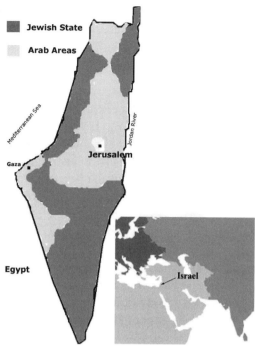

The Partition of Palestine in 1948. After World War II the United Nations agreed to form Israel from the British-controlled mandate of Palestine. Israel was a homeland for Jewish people, and Palestinians were allowed to stay in the Arab areas. The area around Jerusalem was designated as an international zone. In 1967 war erupted when Israel claimed land along the West Bank of the Jordan River and the Gaza strip that bordered Egypt.

Soon after the United Nations created Israel and partitioned Palestine into Arab and Jewish areas, all-out warfare erupted. Though heavily outnumbered, the Zionists were better armed and defended themselves quite well, and the brief but bloody war created hundreds of thousands of Palestinian Arab refugees. Ironically, many desired nothing less than reclaiming their homelands, and the bitterness between the two sides continued to grow. The **Palestine Liberation Organization (PLO)** was formed to represent the stateless people, who were often not absorbed into the neighboring Arab states, but were shuffled into refugee camps where their presence threatened the stability of the entire region. In 1967 Israel launched a military offensive to conquer the West Bank and Gaza strip, areas where Arabs had hoped to form their own state. These areas became hotbeds of conflict that eventually put Israel at odds with Egypt, whose borders touched the Gaza area, and Israeli armies inflicted a humiliating defeat of Nasser's Egyptian forces, capturing the Sinai Peninsula and even the Suez Canal. Another war occurred in 1973 when Egypt struck back under Nasser's successor, Anwar el-Sadat. A peace agreement was finally signed in 1979 through the mediation of U.S. President Jimmy Carter in which Egypt regained the Sinai Peninsula and the Suez Canal, and Israel gained U.S. assistance of more than one billion dollars. However, this agreement had dissidents on both sides, and in 1981 Anwar el-Sadat was assassinated by a splinter group of Muslims. Although his successor, Hosni Mubarak, gained control of the country, the underlying tensions between Israelis and Palestinians continued to fester.

LATIN AMERICA

Despite the fact that Latin American countries had gained their independence long before the Post World War II decolonization of Africa, Southeast Asia, and parts of the Middle East, they remained a part of the **Third World**, neither squarely aligned with the capitalist industrial nations of the First World nor the communist industrial nations of the Second World. However, Latin America demonstrated how large and diverse the category of Third World countries was, since most Latin American economies were midway between the nations of the North Atlantic and the developing countries of Asia and Africa. Although they shared many problems with other Third World countries, including authoritarian governments led by elites, those elites were often in close contact with capitalist countries, and European countries and the United States heavily invested in Latin America. As a result, Latin America was economically vulnerable when international markets collapsed during the Great Depression, and its people – especially the middle classes and elites – were very much influenced by the cultures of Europe and the United States. Decolonization took place in Latin America primarily for economic and cultural reasons, as new nations sought autonomy and control of their own destinies by escaping the dependency that had so long characterized their relationships with North Atlantic countries.

The Search for Stability in the Early 20th Century

World War I had some immediate economic effects in Latin America. Since trade with Europe and the United States seriously declined, many of the countries turned to **import substitution industrialization,** in which they produced for themselves some of what they had formerly imported. As a result, industries developed, but the end of war brought international competition into play again, and the fragile economies suffered debilitating inflation that increased political unrest, always an underlying theme since colonial days. Despite the problems, industrialization produced a growing middle class who became active in politics, particularly in Brazil, Chile, and Argentina. Industrialization also supported large numbers of urban workers, with some immigrating from Spain and Italy where radical political ideologies were already well developed. Just as in industrialized countries in Europe and North America, unions formed and workers went on strike, creating a growing sense of class conflict. Socialist and communist parties formed or grew in strength in several Latin American nations, and political parties formed that backed left-leaning candidates for public office. These groups were opposed by conservative elites, and the military remained important in keeping order. As in previous eras, personalist leaders appeared on both sides of the political aisle – some as military generals and others as populist radicals.

Post-Revolutionary Mexico

As discussed in Unit Four, Mexico had suffered a bloody revolution in 1910-11 that sent it into chaos until the 1930s. During that period, as well as earlier, Mexico had been ruled by military strongmen who were often subject to coups by other military leaders. In 1929 regional caudillos – or military leaders – united for the sake of stability under the **Party of the Institutionalized Revolution (PRI)** in 1929. During the 1930s President **Lazaro Cardenas** stabilized the country through charismatic leadership, but he also put in place a pattern common to many other Latin American countries: a socialist-leaning government that nationalized industries versus a capitalist, free market economy heavily dependent on the West. After the Cardenas presidency, in which the government leaned left, leadership of the country fell to a president who supported the free market. Because the Mexican president is limited to one six-year term, the orientation of the government switched back and forth until the 1980s, when it settled into a more predictable pattern of moderate capitalism. By the 1990s PRI still dominated the country, with all presidents chosen from within its ranks, and very few signs of democracy and instability still a very real issue in Mexican politics. Democratization finally appeared to take hold in Mexico in 2000, when Vicente Fox, a non-PRI candidate, was elected as president.

The Vargas Regime in Brazil

In Brazil **Getulio Vargas** rose to power in the same year as the New York stock market crash – 1929. In contrast to Cardenas, Vargas based his state on Mussolini's Italy, and established an authoritarian regime supported by military force. After World War II began, Vargas traded with both Allied and Axis Powers for a while, but eventually sided with the Allies in return for arms, financial aid, and trade advantages. His government was based on **corporatism,** or the authoritarian state's allowance of input from major groups outside the government, such as big businesses and labor organizations. In 1945 Vargas was deposed by a military coup, but returned again five years later, when he showed signs of incorporating views from the left. He made peace with communist elements and – like Mexico – nationalized the oil industry. His larger-than-life personality image was reinforced by his suicide in 1954, and since then he has become a national hero to many Brazilians.

Argentina: The Personalist Rule of the Perons

During the 1920s Argentina was controlled by a left-leaning political party backed by the middle class, but when the economy collapsed in 1929, a military coup installed a coalition of nationalists, fascists, and socialists – an unusual mix of people. Not surprisingly, this government did not last, and a conservative, military-backed party came to rule during the 1930s. The country's instability was apparent as it was racked by a military coup again in 1943, with a military general, **Juan Peron,** coming to power. He appealed to Argentina's growing sense of nationalism, and his goals were to industrialize and modernize Argentina to make it the dominant power of South America. Peron, like most other personalist leaders in Latin American history, gained power through his charismatic appeal, and although there were many attempts to displace him, he remained wildly popular, especially among urban workers. His popularity was aided by his iconic wife, **Eva Peron,** known affectionately by her supporters as "Evita." During World War II Peron's support for the Axis powers was widely known, but he successfully sidestepped an attempt by the United States to discredit him during the election campaign of 1946, when he was re-elected by his nationalistic supporters.

Like Vargas in Brazil, Peron learned to moderate his government through nationalization of industries and deft management of a quite diverse coalition of political forces. However, his personalist skills did not prevent a coup in 1955 by anti-Peron military officers. The Peronist party was banned, but urban workers and the strongly Peronist unions agitated in support of his programs, and he won the presidency again in 1973, this time with his new wife, Isabel, serving as vice president (Evita had died in 1952). However, this triumph was short-lived, since conflict among Peron's supporters made his government ineffectual until his death the following year. In 1976 Argentina once again fell under the sway of military dictatorship, which regained control only after brutally suppressing its opposition through terrorist tactics that resulted in the death of thousands of people.

Radical Governments in Guatemala and Cuba

The Marxist Revolution in Russia impacted most of the countries of Latin America, but in two – Guatemala and Cuba – socialist governments brought about radical changes that captured the attention of the world. The Central American country of Guatemala exemplified some of the worst of the region's problems, with a huge gap between the wealth of the elites and the large Amerindian population. Most of the land was owned by the rich and supported the cultivation of bananas and coffee for export. In 1944 a reformer, Juan Jose Arevalo, was elected as president, and under his leadership a series of socialist programs was enacted, including land reform and regulation of working conditions in factories and farms. The government became involved in Cold War politics when it turned on foreign companies operating in Guatemala, particularly the **United Fruit Company** that was targeted as an object of nationalistic anger because it controlled transportation, shipping, and large amounts of land. The president that followed Arevalo – Colonel Jacobo Arbenz – was even more radical, and he moved to nationalize many areas of the economy that were controlled by foreign companies. The United States backed United Fruit's opposition to the plans, largely out of fear of communist influences at work within the government, and imposed economic and diplomatic restrictions on Guatemala. Socialists in other Latin American countries sided with the Guatemalan government, and old resentments of the "Bully of the North" came to the fore, particularly after the U.S. Central Intelligence Agency helped to organize a military force to invade Guatemala in 1954. The government fell and was replaced by a pro-American regime that ruled by military force. Throughout the remainder of the 1950s and the 1960s the military governments did not address the poverty of Amerindians, and politics were controlled by a coalition of coffee growers, foreign investors, and the military.

The intervention of the United States in Guatemala was seen by leftist forces in Latin America as outside interference with the internal workings of a government that was trying to help the people. The United States in turn was concerned that socialist governments would come under the sway of the Soviet Union, a situation that could weaken the U.S. position in the Cold War. These tensions had roots in the 19th and early 20th centuries when the industrializing United States was seen by poorer Latin American countries as overbearing. However, the international Cold War atmosphere deepened these divides and created a confrontation in the Caribbean that came to represent the worldwide struggle for power between the United States and the Soviet Union.

Like Guatemala, Cuba was dependent on foreign investments for its well being, but its geographic location just south of Florida gave it even more connections to the U.S. economy. Just as Guatemala's economy was dependent on bananas and coffee for export, Cuba's economy was based on the production of sugar for export. Living conditions in Cuba, however, were generally better than they were in Guatemala, and the American investments in the island helped to create businesses that employed a large middle class. On and off between 1934 and 1959 Cuba was ruled by **Fulgencio Batista,** an authoritarian strongman who promised reforms in his earlier years, but had become an entrenched dictator by the 1950s. Concerned about the corruption and favoritism of the regime, a lawyer named **Fidel Castro** organized an army composed of students, intellectuals, laborers, and rural workers to depose Batista from office in 1959.

The United States government had mixed feelings about the coup at first, since Batista's excesses had already lost U.S. support. However, Castro's actions after he took control brought Cuba front and central to Cold War politics. Instead of enacting moderate reforms as most observers expected him to do, Castro nationalized virtually all foreign properties, most belonging to United States citizens. He instituted a centralized socialist economy based on Marxist principles of eliminating all private property, and his foreign policy was expressed in a great deal of anti-imperialist rhetoric. Relations with the United States were broken in 1961, and Cuba became increasingly dependent on foreign aid from the Soviet Union. This situation developed into exactly what the United States feared would happen all over Latin America: Soviet intrusion into the Western Hemisphere.

PERSPECTIVES: WHO WAS "CHE" GUEVARA?

Ernesto ("Che") Guevara is a legendary figure from the Cold War era in Latin America when leftist forces battled against dictatorships and the capitalist influence of the United States. Che first came to world attention as the militant Argentine revolutionary who came to Fidel Castro's aid in defeating Fulgencio Batista in Cuba in 1959. He spent years fighting with Castro in Cuban swamps and mountains, and when their struggle resulted in success, he returned to South America to sponsor other revolutions.

Che was originally a doctor who abandoned his profession to support the Cuban cause, which he saw as a movement to promote the rights of the poor and powerless. His bravery and skill during the Cuban Revolution inspired his appointment as commandant of the forces, and he emerged as the hero that fearlessly stood up to the "Yanquis."

Che Guevara was captured and executed in 1967 in Bolivia, but his death magnified his fame through his last words, "Shoot, coward, you're only going to kill a man." People in the streets of cities all across Latin America responded with their cry, " ¡No lo vamos a olvidar!" (We won't let him be forgotten!)

Over the years his fame has resulted in the appearance of his likeness on coffee mugs, posters, and tee shirts, and his name is universally known today as the spirit of the revolutionist and the symbol of rebellion.

As Castro's communist sentiments became apparent, Cubans that disagreed with his policies fled the country or were exiled by the government, and they conspired to overthrow the new regime. In reaction to the Soviet foothold in Cuba, the U.S. government sponsored an external invasion of the island in 1961 by the exiles through funding and training, and it helped them with strategic planning. The invasion turned into a disastrous failure as the dissidents landed at the Bay of Pigs in southwest Cuba, where Castro's forces met and crushed them. The Soviet Union responded by placing nuclear missiles in Cuba pointed toward the United States. The Cuban Missile Crisis occurred in 1962 when the U.S. demanded that the missiles be removed, the Soviets balked, and the U.S. sent ships to quarantine the island. Soviet ships headed toward Cuba, but turned back at the last minute before encountering U.S. ships, and the missiles were eventually removed. However, Cuba remained a dangerous "hot spot" in the Cold War that threatened to explode during the decades that followed. The Soviets continued to support the Cuban economy and government with massive amounts of foreign aid, and Cuban citizens supportive of U.S. capitalism left the country to live in the United States.

Chile: The Clash of Socialism and Militarism

In the 1960s Latin American military governments were alarmed by the Cuban success, and they greatly feared the popularity of leftist politics in many countries. In Chile, the socialist government of **Salvador Allende** was overthrown in 1973 by the military, which generally had not been active in politics before. Allende had nationalized industries and banks and had worked to promote land redistribution plans to favor the peasants. As in other Latin American countries business interests, foreign companies, and the military opposed the reforms, and when the economy suffered, these forces joined together to take over the government in a military coup led by **Augusto Pinochet** and supported by the United States. President Allende and thousands of Chileans died in the uprising, and others were tortured and illegally imprisoned. Pinochet's government rolled back the social reforms, encouraged foreign investment, and controlled the country until 1990, when a civilian government was elected.

In the time period between 1945 and 1991 many parts of the globe were affected by the fierce competition between the United States and the Soviet Union. At the conclusion of World War II, the Soviet Union seized countries of eastern Europe as satellites to protect them from the aggressions of capitalism, and the United States sponsored the Marshall Plan to shore up western European nations so they would not be vulnerable to communism. The U.S. aided Turkey and Greece in their fight against Soviet military pressure and subversion. Wars were fought in Korea and Vietnam that, though limited in scope, pitted the communist world versus the non-communist. Shrewd leaders of Third World countries, such as Nasser of Egypt, played one side against the other by getting aid from both. In Latin America, the United States reacted to socialist movements in Chile and Guatemala through fear that the Soviets would win their favor, a fear that was realized in Cuba with the installation of Fidel Castro's new regime in 1959. During this same time period, rapid decolonization in Africa, Asia, and the Middle East left European countries much less in control of world affairs than they had been during the 19th and early 20th century. New countries were left vulnerable after years of dependency on imperialist powers. These two forces – Cold War politics and decolonization – together shaped the world until 1991, when the collapse of the Soviet Union produced major changes as the 20th century entered its last decade.

CONCEPTS AND IDENTIFICATIONS

African National Congress
All-African People's Conference
Allende, Salvador
apartheid
Batista, Fulgencio
Cardenas, Lazaro
Castro, Fidel
Chiang Kai-shek
Chinese Cultural Revolution
Churchill, Winston
civil disobedience
containment
corporatism
Cuban missile crisis
decolonization
De Gaulle, Charles
Diagne, Bliase
DuBois, W.E.B.
General Assembly (of UN)
Gandhi, Mohandas K.
Great Leap Forward
Guevara, Chi
Ho Chi Minh
Huntington, Samuel
import substitution industrialization
Iranian Cultural Revolution
iron curtain
Islamic fundamentalism
Jinnah, Muhammad Ali
Kemal, Mustafa (Ataturk)
Kenyatta, Jomo
Khomeini, Ruhollah
Korean War
League of Arab States
"limited war"

Mandela, Nelson
Mao Zedong
Marshall Plan
Nasser, Gamel Abdel
NATO
Nehru, Jawaharlal
Nkrumah, Kwame
Pahlavi dynasty
Palestinian Liberation Organization (PLO)
Party of the Institutionalized Revolution (PRI)
Peron, Juan
Peron, Eva
Potsdam Conference
Pinochet, Augusto
Roosevelt, Franklin
Security Council (of UN)
space race
Sputnik
Stalin, Joseph
Tehran Conference
Third World
"three waves" of democratization
Truman Doctrine
"Two Chinas"
United Fruit Company
United Nations Charter
Vargas, Getulio
Vietnam War
Warsaw Pact
Yalta Conference
Zionist Movement

CHAPTER TWENTY-TWO:
1991-PRESENT –
A GLOBALIZED OR FRAGMENTED
NEW WORLD?

As the last decade of the 20th century began, almost everyone – experts and ordinary people alike – assumed that Cold War politics would continue indefinitely, so the collapse of the Soviet Union in 1991 was an astonishing, unanticipated event. Although the repercussions of this abrupt end to the Cold War are far from complete, it is clear that 1991 marks a new era in world history. No one knows how important the change actually was because, after all, the Cold War itself lasted less than forty years – a microcosm of time in the ongoing story of the world. Even the longer trend of declining power of Europe may be changing, as the European Union has become a major international force since 1991. It is too early to know which trends will last and which will prove to be only brief intervals that have little impact on the future. However, this chapter analyzes various current economic, technological, political, social, and cultural trends, and only the passage of time will reveal which are the true harbingers of the future.

THE BREAK-UP OF THE SOVIET UNION

After Stalin died in 1953, a power struggle among top Communist Party leaders resulted in **Nikita Khrushchev** being chosen as party secretary and premier of the USSR. In 1956 he gave his famous secret speech, in which he revealed the existence of a letter written by Lenin before he died. The letter was critical of Stalin, and Khrushchev used it to denounce Stalin's rules and practices, particularly the purges that he sponsored. This denouncement led to **deStalinization,** a process that led to reforms, such as loosening government censorship of the press, decentralization of economic decision-making, and restructuring of the collective farms. In foreign policy, Khrushchev advocated "peaceful coexistence," or relaxation of tensions between the United States and the Soviet Union. Other members of the Politburo (the governing body of the Soviet Union) criticized him from the beginning for the suggested reforms, and his diplomatic and military failure in the Cuban Missile Crisis led to his removal from power. Furthermore, most of his reforms did not appear to be working by the early 1960s. He was replaced by the much more conservative Leonid Brezhnev, who ended the reforms and tried to cope with the increasing economic problems that were just under the surface of Soviet power.

The Gorbachev Reforms

When Brezhnev died in 1982, he was replaced by a reformer from a younger generation, **Mikhail Gorbachev**. Gorbachev was unlike any previous Soviet leader in that he not only looked and acted more "western," but he also was more open to western-style reforms than any other, including Khrushchev. Gorbachev inherited far more problems than any outsider realized at the time, and many of his reforms were motivated by shear necessity to save the country from economic disaster. His program was three-pronged:

- **Glasnost** – This term translates from the Russian as "openness," and it allowed more open discussion of political, social and economic issues as well as open criticism of the government. Although this reform was applauded by western nations, it caused problems for Gorbachev. After so many years of repression, people vented hostility toward the government that encouraged open revolt, particularly among some of the republics that wanted independence from Soviet control.

- **Democratization** – Gorbachev believed that he could keep the old Soviet structure, including Communist Party control, but at the same time insert a little democracy into the system. Two such moves included the creation of a Congress of People's Deputies with directly elected representatives and a new position of "President" that was selected by the Congress. The reforms did bring a bit of democracy. However, many of the new deputies were critical of Gorbachev, increasing the level of discord within the government.

- **Perestroika** – This economic reform was Gorbachev's most radical, and also his least successful. Again, he tried to keep the old Soviet structure, and modernize from within. Most significantly, it transferred many economic powers held by the central government to private hands and the market economy. Specific reforms included authorization of some privately owned companies, penalties for under-performing state factories, farm leases outside the collective farms, price reforms, and encouragement of joint ventures with foreign companies.

None of Gorbachev's reforms were ever fully carried out because the Revolution of 1991 swept him out of office.

A Failed Coup and the Revolution of 1991

In August 1991 "conservatives" (those that wanted to abandon Gorbachev's reforms) from within the Politburo led a coup d'etat that tried to remove Gorbachev from office. The leaders included the vice-president, the head of the KGB (Russian secret police), and top military advisers. The coup failed when popular protests broke out, and soldiers from the military defected rather than support their leaders. The protesters were led by **Boris Yeltsin**, the elected president of the Russian Republic and former Politburo member. Yeltsin had been removed from the Politburo a few years earlier because his radical views offended the conservatives. Yeltsin advocated more extreme reform measures than Gorbachev did, and he won his position as president of the Russian Republic as a result of new voting procedures put in place by Gorbachev. Gorbachev was restored to power, but the U.S.S.R. only had a few months to live. By December 1991 eleven republics had declared their independence, and eventually Gorbachev was forced to announce the end of the union, which put him out of a job. The fifteen republics went their separate ways, but **Boris Yeltsin** emerged as the president of the largest and most powerful republic, now renamed the Russian Federation.

A NEW WORLD ORDER

The Soviet Union held hegemony over huge portions of the world for much of the 20th century, and when it fell apart in 1991, that dominance was broken. The 1990s were a time of chaos and humiliation, as Yeltsin had to rely on loans from Russia's old nemesis, the United States, to help shake its economic doldrums. As the 21st century began, the new president, **Vladimir Putin,** set out to redefine Russia's place in the world, a two-dimensional task that required a new interpretation of the country's relationship with the West, as well as its role among the former Soviet States. The biggest adjustment for Russia has been the loss of its superpower status from the Cold War era. The United States emerged as the lone superpower in 1991, and the two old enemies – Russia and the United States – had to readjust their attitudes toward one another. U.S. Presidents George H. Bush and Bill Clinton both believed that it was important to maintain a good working relationship with Russia, and they also knew that the economic collapse of Russia would have disastrous results for the world economy. Both presidents sponsored aid packages for Russia, and they also encouraged foreign investment in the country's fledgling market economy.

The United States: A Lone Superpower?

With the sudden fall of the Soviet Union in 1991, the United States unexpectedly found itself the winner of the Cold War. The country's foreign policy had been guided first by **containment** (keeping communism from spreading) and

The Commonwealth of Independent States. The fifteen countries of the CIS are divided by the solid black line from neighboring states. When the Soviet Union broke apart in 1991, it split into fifteen separate countries – the former Soviet Republics that made up the U.S.S.R. The fifteen former republics are Estonia, Latvia, Lithuania, Belarus, Ukraine, Moldavia, Armenia, Georgia, Azerbaijan, Turkmenistan, Uzbekistan, Kazakhstan, Tajikistan, Kyrgzstan, and Russia.

then by **detente** (peaceful coexistence with the Soviet Union), but without the Soviet Union, foreign policy had to change significantly. The attacks on the World Trade Towers and the Pentagon on September 11, 2001, shaped the country's direction significantly, as the government under President George W. Bush spearheaded an international "war on terrorism." The war was directed first at finding **Osama bin Laden,** the head of **Al-Qaeda,** the international terrorist organization that claimed responsibility for the attacks. In 2003, the United States government decided to invade Iraq to remove **Saddam Hussein** from power based on the premise that he was harboring Al-Qaeda operatives and constructing **Weapons of Mass Destruction (WMDs)** to use against the United States. To justify the war, President Bush used a foreign policy of **preemption**, or the principle of attacking before being attacked. As of 2008 no WMDs have been found, so the United States was widely criticized for its actions, and its credibility as a "superpower" was questioned because of its inability to bring stability to Iraq in the post-Hussein era.

The Rise of China

During the late 20th century and the early 21st century, China re-emerged as one of the most powerful countries in the world, with an economy that rapidly expanded after the death of Mao Zedong in 1976. From 1949 to 1978, China followed a communist political economic model: a **command economy** (no private ownership of property) directed by a central government based on democratic centralism. Mao Zedong called this policy the "iron rice bowl," or cradle-to-grave health care, work, and retirement security. The state set production quotas and distributed basic goods to consumers. When this model failed, **Deng Xiaoping** began a series of economic reforms that make up the **socialist market economy** – gradual infusion of capitalism while still retaining state control.

In the early 1980s, Deng dismantled the people's communes that had been created during the 1950s, and replaced them with a **household responsibility system**, which is still in effect today. In this system individual families take full charge of the production and marketing of crops. After paying government taxes and contract fees to the villages, families may consume or sell what they produce. Food production improved dramatically, and villages developed both private farming and industry. In 1988 the National People's Congress officially created a new category of **"private business"** under the control of the party. It included urban co-ops, service organizations, and rural industries that largely operate as capitalist enterprises. The importance of China's state sector has gradually diminished, although private industry remains heavily regulated by the government. Price controls have been lifted, and private businesses have grown by leaps and bounds since the 1980s, and today are far more profitable and dynamic than are the state-owned ones.

Another integral part of the economic reform of the past quarter century has been the opening of the Chinese economy to international forces. Four **Special Economic Zones (SEZs)** were established in 1979. In these regions, foreign investors were given preferential tax rates and other incentives. Five years later fourteen more areas became SEZs, and today foreign investments and free market mechanisms have spread to most of the rest of urban China. Since 1978 China's trade and industry have expanded widely. With this expansion has come a rapid growth in production, entrepreneurship, and trade with many nations. A wealthy class of businessmen has emerged, and Chinese products have made their way around the world. China is now a member of the World Trade Organization, as well as "most favored nation status" for trading with the U.S. A monumental recognition of China's new economic power came in 1997, when the British officially "gave" the major trading city of Hong Kong back to Chinese control.

Since 1998 Chinese foreign policy has undergone profound changes that have brought the country closer into the mainstream of international politics. Especially in the areas of trade, China has integrated itself into the world community in almost unprecedented ways. It is quickly replacing Japan as the most

**CHANGE OVER TIME:
CHINA
1750-PRESENT**

After centuries of following dynastic cycles, China has undergone some important changes since 1750, although continuities bind the civilization together over time.

1750-1914 – In 1750 China was prospering under the strong leadership of the Qing Dynasty. As always, Chinese products, such as pottery, silk, tea, and decorative items were in high demand, and China had good reason to think of itself as the "Middle Kingdom." However, the Qing Dynasty began to weaken after the death of Emperor Qinglong at the end of the 18th century, just in time for British traders to begin trading opium in Canton. The Opium Wars during the 1830s resulted in the first of a series of "unequal treaties" between Europeans and the Qing government that led to the economic carving of China into "spheres of influence." Efforts to "self-strengthen" failed, but Chinese nationalism grew and influenced the overthrow of the Qing Dynasty in the Revolution of 1911 led by Sun Yat-sen. (pp. 407-413)

1914-Present – The Revolution of 1911 led to decades of instability in China, characterized by a struggle for power between Chiang Kai-shek, the president of China, and Mao Zedong, the leader of the Chinese Communist Party. In 1949 Mao drove Chiang's army to the island of Taiwan, and Mao established the People's Republic of China, a communist state, on the Chinese mainland. Until Mao's death in 1976 the country followed a communist model with a command economy (centralized and controlled by the government). Mao's successor, Deng Xiaoping, changed the direction of the country by establishing a "socialist market economy" that gradually infused capitalism. By the early 20th century, the Chinese economy was growing rapidly at the same time that the government remained highly authoritarian. China's rapid economic growth coupled with its huge population (1.2 billion people) led many to believe that China was becoming one of the most powerful countries in the world, a status that it enjoyed during most of the eras before the decline it suffered during the 19th century. (pp. 480-481, 506-510, 537-540)

powerful economy in Asia, and is now Asia's central economy that affects all others. Deng Xiaoping emphasized economic reform, but he continued to believe that the Party should be firmly in command of the country. In general, he did not support political reforms that included democracy and/or more civil liberties for citizens.

Since the **Tiananmen Crisis** of 1989, China has been under a great deal of pressure from international human rights organizations to democratize its political process and to abide by human rights standards advocated by the groups. The crisis began as a demonstration in Tiananmen Square in Beijing. Most of the original demonstrators were students and intellectuals, but other groups participated. They criticized corruption and demanded democratic reforms, and hundreds of thousands joined in. Protests erupted all over China, and Tiananmen became the center of international attention for almost two months. The government responded by sending in the army to shut down the protests, using whatever means necessary. The army shot its way to the square, killing hundreds of protesting citizens. They recaptured control, but the fatalities and arrests began a broad new wave of international protests from human rights advocates. Unofficial estimates of fatalities range from 700 to several thousand.

SUPRANATIONALISM AND GLOBALIZATION

The new world order since 1991 is still taking shape, and the roles that Russia, the United States, and China play in international affairs are very much in flux. All countries exist within an interactive environment with other governments, but more and more they are affected by **supranational organizations** that go beyond national boundaries. These organizations reflect a trend toward **integration**, a process that encourages states to pool their sovereignty (right to rule themselves) in order to gain political, economic, and social clout. Integration binds states together with common policies and shared rules. In the 20th century, many national governments established relationships with regional organizations – such as NATO, the European Union, NAFTA, and OPEC – and with international organizations, such as the United Nations.

These supranational organizations reflect the phenomenon of **globalization** – an integration of social, environmental, economic, and cultural activities of nations that has resulted from increasing international contacts. Globalization has changed the nature of world politics, largely because it breaks down the distinction between international relations and domestic politics, making many aspects of domestic politics subject to global forces. Likewise, it also internationalizes domestic issues and events. Because globalization deepens and widens international connections, local events, even small ones, can have ripple effects throughout the world. Perhaps most apparent is the effect of technology and its ability to ignore national boundaries. The internet allows news from every corner of the globe to rapidly spread to other areas, so that what happens in one place affects others around the world. On the other hand, many scholars and journalists point out a counter trend – **fragmentation** – a tendency for people to base their loyalty on ethnicity, language, religion, or cultural identity. Although globalization and fragmentation appear to be opposite concepts, they both transcend political boundaries between individual countries.

World-Wide Organizations

The United Nations continues to function as a major peacekeeping organization, although its authority is limited and its challenges are many. The organization's goals have broadened over the years, so that many international organizations are sponsored and funded under its umbrella. Two other important supranational organizations of the late 20th and early 21st centuries include:

- **The World Trade Organization** – Established in 1995, the WTO is an organization of member states who have agreed to rules of world trade among nations. It is responsible for negotiating and implementing new trade agreements. The WTO serves as a forum for settling trade disputes, and it supervises members to be sure that they follow the rules that the organization sets. Most of the world's trading nations belong to the WTO, although Russia is a major exception. The WTO oversees about 60 different agreements which have the status of international legal texts that bind its 151 members. The process of becoming a WTO member is unique to each applicant country, and the terms of membership are dependent upon the country's stage of economic development and current trade regime. The process takes about five years, but it can last more if the country's economic status is questionable or if political issues make it objectionable. For example, China was denied WTO status for many years because of questions about human rights abuses, but its growing economic prowess finally influenced member states to approve it.

- **The World Bank** – Although the World Bank was created in 1944 to aid countries rebuild after World War II, its focus today in on loaning money to low and middle-income countries at modest interest rates. The Bank's goals are to eliminate poverty in these countries and to support economic development through investment in projects that build businesses, improve transportation and communications, provide jobs, and eliminate corruption in government. The Bank has also supported health initiatives – such as vaccination programs for disease and research to combat AIDs – and efforts to reduce greenhouse gases that contribute to global warming.

Regional Organizations

During the Cold War era, regional military alliances appeared, and countries joined them based on their affiliation either with the United States or Russia.

The North Atlantic Treaty Organization (NATO) formed in the late 1940s with fourteen European members, the United States, and Canada, with the purpose of providing mutual defense in case of attack. An opposing alliance – the Warsaw Pact – began in 1955, and was composed of the Soviet Union and six Eastern European countries. Together the two organizations were designed to maintain a bipolar balance of power in Europe. The Warsaw Pact disbanded with the breakup of the Soviet Union, and NATO expanded to include many of its former members. Other regional organizations include the Organization of American States (OAS) to promote social, cultural, political, and economic links among member states in the Western Hemisphere, and the Organization for African Unity (OAU) that has promoted the elimination of minority white-ruled governments in southern Africa.

The European Union

A regional organization that promises to redefine the meaning of sovereignty is the **European Union.** All the countries of Europe are deeply affected by the trend toward **integration,** a process that encourages states to pool their sovereignty in order to gain political, economic, and social clout. Integration binds states together with common policies and shared rules, and the supranational organization that integrates the states of Europe is called the European Union. The organization began in an effort to revitalize a war-torn Europe after World War II ended. The most immediate need was to repair the nations' broken economies, so the initial goals were almost completely economic in intent. In 1949 the Council of Europe was formed, which had little power, but did provide an opportunity for national leaders to meet. The following year a supranational authority was formed to coordinate the coal and steel industries, both damaged heavily in the war.

The organization went through several name changes, but until 1991 its goals were exclusively economic. The Maastricht Treaty created the modern organization, and gave it authority in new areas, including monetary policy, foreign affairs, national security, transportation, the environment, justice, and tourism. The treaty established the three pillars, or spheres of authority:

- Trade and other economic matters, including economic and monetary union into a single currency, and the creation of the European Central Bank

- Justice and home affairs, including policy governing asylum, border crossing, immigration, and judicial cooperation on crime and terrorism

- Common foreign and security policy, including joint positions and actions, and common defense policy

EU 15

NEW
COUNTRIES
2004-07

The European Union. Ongoing expansion is a major characteristic of the European Union, with a total membership of 27 countries as of 2008. The European Union began with six members in 1957: Belgium, France, Germany, Italy, Luxembourg, and the Netherlands. Denmark, Great Britain, and Ireland joined in the early 1970s; Greece in 1981; Portugal and Spain in 1986; and Austria, Finland, and Sweden in 1995. Ten countries joined on May 2, 2004: Cyprus (Greek part), the Czech Republic, Estonia, Hungary, Latvia, Lithuania, Malta, Poland, Slovakia and Slovenia. Bulgaria and Romania joined on January 1, 2007.

The EU has made remarkable strides in its ability to set European monetary policy, or the control of the money supply. Today the euro has replaced the old national currencies, which are well on their way to being phased out. Also, the power to set basic interest rates and other fiscal policies is being passed from national banks and governments to the European Monetary Union and its new central bank. Today, in twelve of the member countries, the euro is accepted as a common currency both in banking and for everyday business transactions. Two exceptions to the rule are Britain and Sweden, which as of 2008 still refuse to give up their national currencies in favor of a common European currency.

NAFTA

The **North American Free Trade Agreement (NAFTA)** was signed in 1995 by Mexico, Canada, and the United States. Its goal is to more closely integrate the countries' economies by eliminating tariffs and reducing restrictions so that companies can expand into all countries freely. Mexico hopes to stimulate its overall growth, enrich its big business community, and supply jobs for Mexicans in new industries. On the other hand, American firms gain from access to inexpensive labor, raw materials, series and tourism, as well as new markets to sell and invest in. Mexico runs the risk of again being overshadowed by the United States, but hopes that the benefits will outweigh the problems. Many in the United States have criticized NAFTA for taking jobs from Americans when factories move south to Mexico. Unlike the agreement among member nations of the European Union, the NAFTA agreement currently does not allow free flow of labor across borders.

ECONOMIC TRENDS

During the late 20th and early 21st centuries two important economic trends may be identified: the continuation of the large gap in economic development between rich and poor countries and the preference of more and more countries for free market economies based on capitalism.

Inequalities in Economic Development

Countries of the world may be categorized by the evolution of their economic activities. Those that have experienced industrialization may be called **more developed countries (MDCs)**, and those that have not may be categorized as **less developed countries (LDCs).** More countries in today's world belong to the latter category, but some may be subcategorized as newly industrializing countries. During the last few decades, some countries, mostly in Asia and parts of Latin America, have experienced economic growth, so that they appear to be somewhere in between MCD and LDC status. An example is South Korea, a country that only fifty years ago was a relatively poor agricultural country. During the late 20th and early 21st century, South Korea developed into one of the world's largest economies and also experimented with democratic institutions. The process that it experienced is sometimes called **compressed modernity** – rapid economic and political change that transformed the country into a stable nation with democratizing political institutions, a growing economy, and an expanding web of nongovernmental institutions. Mexico is often cited as newly industrializing, with its dramatic economic growth that began in the 1980s based on its abundance of oil.

What factors explain differences in levels of economic development? Two conflicting theories guided social scientists in the 20th century in answering these questions:

- **Modernization model** – According to this theory (also called the westernization model), Britain was the first country to begin to develop its industry. The Industrial Revolution was spurred by a combination of prosperity, trade connections, inventions, and natural resources. Max Weber explained that the cultural environment of western Europe favored change. Wealth was regarded as a sign of personal virtue, and the growing importance of individualism steadily replaced the traditional emphasis on kinship and community. Once started, the British model spread to other European nations and the United States, who prospered because they built on British ingenuity and economic practices. By extension, any country that wants its economy to grow should study the paths taken by the industrial nations, and logically they too can reap the benefits of modernization, or "westernization." Modernization theory identifies tradition as the greatest barrier to economic development. In societies with strong family systems and a reverence for the past, the culture discourages people from adopting new technologies that would raise their standards of living.

- **Dependency theory** – This analysis puts primary responsibility for global poverty on rich nations. In contrast to the modernization model, dependency theory holds that economic development of many countries in the world is blocked by the fact that industrialized nations exploit them. How can a country develop when its resources (natural and human) are controlled by a handful of prosperous industrialized countries? Inequality has its roots in the colonial era when European nations colonized and exploited the resources of other areas around the world. Although virtually all colonies gained independence by the late 20th century, political liberation has not translated into economic health. Dependency theory is an outgrowth of Marxism, which emphasizes exploitation of one social class by another. The same dynamic is at work in assessing relationships among countries. Problems, then, cannot be solved by westernization, but must be addressed by establishing independence. In reaction to this theory, many LDCs have experimented with forms of socialism, with the intent of nationalizing industry and narrowing the gap between the rich and the poor.

The two theories may be combined to explain that a country's problems have many sources, and LDCs often react by mixing elements of capitalism and socialism to address them. Political leaders are influenced by both theories, with left-leaning governments usually preferring dependency theory, and more conservative governments looking to westernization as a model.

Movement toward Market Economies

A second economic trend of the 20th and early 21st centuries is a movement toward market economies. Many political economists today declare that the economic competition between capitalism and socialism that dominated the 20th century is now a part of the past. The old **command economies**, with socialist principles of centralized planning and state ownership are fading from existence, except in combination with **market economies** that following free market principles without government control. The issue now is what type of market economy will be most successful: one that allows for significant control from the central government – a "**mixed economy**" – or one that does not – a pure market economy. For example, modern Germany has a "social market economy" that is team-oriented and emphasizes cooperation between management and organized labor. In contrast, the United States economy tends to be more individualistic and anti-government control.

Two factors that have promoted the movement toward market economies are:

- Belief that government is too big – Command economies require an active, centralized government that gets heavily involved in economic issues. Anti-big government movements began in the 1980s in the United States and many western European nations, where economies had experienced serious problems of inefficiency and stagnation. Margaret Thatcher in Britain and Ronald Reagan in the United States rode to power on waves of public support for reducing the scale of government.

- Lack of success of command economies – The collapse of the Soviet Union is the best example of a failed command economy that reverberated around the world. This failure was accompanied by changes among the eastern European satellite states from command to market economies. Meanwhile, another big command economy – China – had been slowly infusing capitalism into its system since its near collapse in the 1970s. Today China is a "socialist market economy" that is fueled by ever growing doses of capitalism.

Marketization is the term that describes the state's creation of a market in which property, labor, goods, and services can all function in a competitive environment to determine their value. **Privatization** is the transfer of state-owned property to private ownership. Good examples of both processes may be found in the phenomenal growth of the Chinese economy since 1978. Although the government retains the right to centrally control the economy, political leaders have allowed marketization and privatization to take place, at first gradually and then much more rapidly so that by the early 21st century China was experiencing rapid economic growth.

The trend toward market economies has reinforced globalization in many ways as markets transcend national boundaries and encourage trade to be free, currencies readily convertible, and banking open. In Europe, Asia, Africa, the South Pacific, and the Americas, international banks and multinational corporations have encouraged standardization of trade practices. The quest for international profits makes businesses less likely to restrict their hours and practices according to local customs, and common markets are facilitated by a common language, currency, laws, and business behaviors.

TECHNOLOGICAL TRENDS

Many technological inventions changed people's lives during the period from 1914 to the present and greatly increased the interconnectedness of the world. During the early part of the era the wide use of telephones changed the nature of communication, and the extension of the technology to cell phones by the late 20th century made contacts much faster and more efficient. Electricity has allowed people to work or play at whatever time of day or night suits them, and has enabled the use of electric-powered inventions. Communications expanded with the invention and spread of radio, film, and television technology, first in the United States within limited areas, but eventually it permeated national borders to spread American culture to many parts of the globe.

During the late 20th and early 21st centuries computer technology encouraged information sharing around the globe, particularly with the advent of the internet. The hardware of the new technologies is systemic and integrated – computer, television, cable satellite, laser, fiber-optic, and microchip technologies combine to create a vast interactive communications and information network that can potentially give every person on earth access to every other person, and make all data available to every set of eyes. Movies, music, videos, and television shows may be downloaded to individual computers so that geographical distances are no longer the barriers they once were. However, access to technology is still unequal, with people in less developed countries much less likely to be internationally connected than those is more developed countries.

SOCIAL AND DEMOGRAPHIC TRENDS

Recent social trends include rapid urbanization of many areas of the globe, population growth due to increased agricultural productivity, changes in the basis for social status, more equality for women, and recognition of human rights.

Rural-Urban Migration and Urban Growth

Urbanization accelerated in the 1800s in the countries of Europe and North America largely because of industrial development. For example, the proportion of people living in urban areas in the United States increased from 5 % in 1800 to 50% in 1920. Today about three-fourths of people in developed countries live in urban areas.

In more recent years migration from rural to urban areas has rapidly increased in less developed countries in Africa, Asia, and Latin America. This migration has meant that the percentage of people in poor countries that live in cities has risen from 25% in 1950 to an estimated 50% by 2010. By 2000, 48 cities in the world had passed the 5 million population mark, and 32 of them were in less developed nations. Part of the reason for the growth of cities in poor countries is that longevity has increased, but much of it results from a migration from rural to urban areas by people looking for jobs, education, and conveniences, such as electricity and running water. As countries begin to industrialize, opportunities shift from rural to urban areas, and the pull of the city stimulates migration.

The amount of urban growth differs from continent to continent and from region to region, but nearly all countries have two things in common: the proportion of their people living in cities is rising, and the cities themselves are large and growing. The United Nations now projects that the majority of the world's people today live in cities, and the trend toward urbanization is holding strong today.

By 2000 nineteen metropolises in the world had populations of more than 10 million, earning them the title, **"megacities,"** a term created by the United Nations in the 1970s. Today another six cities are estimated to have reached that mark, bringing the total to 25. In 1900, no cities were that large. Just how large they will grow in the future is debatable, but rapid expansion of many megacities seems to be slowing today.

Population Growth

By the early 21st century the population of the world had increased to about 6 ½ billion, although growth rates were much less in more industrialized countries that experienced the **demographic transition** (see p 383) during the 19th and 20th centuries. One reason for population increase was overall improvements in health care in many parts of the world. Another boost to world population was a revolution in food production that occurred during the late 20th century and continues in today's world. By the 1970s the collection of new agricultural techniques was called the **Green Revolution**, which involved two important practices: the use of new higher-yield seeds and the expanded use of fertilizers. New miracle seeds diffused rapidly around the world, with many countries recording dramatic productivity increases. Biotechnology doesn't just cross two varieties of plant or animal, hoping for the best. Instead, they identify the

EXAMINING THE EVIDENCE:
THE GROWTH OF "MEGACITIES"

Ten Largest Megacities in the World

Tokyo, Japan	34,000,000
Mexico City, Mexico	22,800,000
Seoul, South Korea	22,300,000
New York City, USA	21,900,000
São Paulo, Brazil	20,200,000
Mumbai (Bombay), India	19,800,000
Delhi, India	19,700,000
Shanghai, China	18,150,000
Los Angeles, USA	18,000,000
Osaka, Japan	16,800,000

Other megacities are Beijing, Buenos Aires, Cairo, Dhaka, Istanbul, Jakarta, Karachi, Kolkata (Calcutta), Lagos, London, Manila, Moscow, Rio de Janeiro, Shenzhen, and Tehran.

Source: Th. Brinkhoff: The Principal Agglomerations of the World, 2006-01-28

particular genes on the DNA molecules that produce the desirable characteristic and splice the genes directly into the chromosomes of the other plant or animal. During the 19th century scientists identified the critical elements in natural fertilizers (manure, bones, and ashes) as nitrogen, phosphorus, and potassium. Today these three elements form the basis for fertilizers that have boosted crop productivity even further. The Green Revolution resulted in agricultural production outpacing population growth by the late 20th century.

Whereas the Green Revolution appears to be contributing to the good health of many people around the world, it has failed to provide famine relief for people in Sub-Saharan Africa. Seriously affected countries include Somalia, Ethiopia, Sudan, Gambia, Senegal, Mali, Mauritania, Burkina Faso, Niger, and Chad. Part of the problem is lack of resources to buy seed, fertilizer, and machinery,

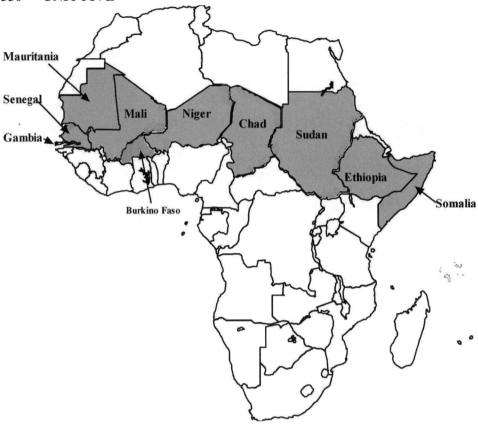

Food Supply Crisis in Africa. Production of most food crops is lower today in Africa than it was forty years ago, whereas populations are increasing. Particularly hard hit are the countries that formerly were inhabited by nomadic herders shown in gray shading on the map above. The problem has been worsened not only by increasing population, but also by desertification, as the Sahara Desert continues to spread southward.

but the situation is worsened by rapid population growth. Traditionally, this region supported limited agriculture, with pastoral nomadism prevailing. The land has now been overgrazed by animals, and soils have been exhausted from over planting. Soil erosion has become a problem, with the limited number of trees cut for wood and charcoal for urban cooking and heating. Government policies have traditionally favored urban populations by keeping food prices low, giving farmers little incentive to increase their productivity.

The Changing Nature of Social Class

During most of the history of the world after the Neolithic Revolution, social status has generally been based on land ownership. The Industrial Revolution began to change that long-time tradition by tying social status to ownership of capital (money), and by the late 20th century it was clear that aristocracies and landlord classes were much less important than they had ever been since the dawn of civilization. Urbanized societies tend to place emphasis not just on ownership of capital, but also on knowledge and managerial control within large organizations. This has been the clear pattern in the West and in eastern Europe even under communism, and the pattern seems to be emerging in Africa and Asia as well. Divisions between wealthy classes and laboring groups are not just based on ownership of property, but also on levels of education and ability to direct the actions of others.

Tensions between social classes in the West declined during the mid-to-late 20th century as workers came to own many consumer goods, such as home appliances, electronics, and cars. Social lines were blurred by social mobility based on educational opportunities that became more accessible to ordinary people in many western countries in the years after World War II ended. Yet during the early 21st century income inequality increased in many western countries, particularly in the United States, where the income and wealth of those at the top grew dramatically.

Equality between Men and Women

By the early 21st century, some clear signs pointed to a narrowing of the gap in the social status of men and women. After the success of suffrage movements in Europe, North America, and Latin America during the early 20th century, many feminists (advocates for equality between men and women) had reason to believe that greater equality in the West would influence other areas of the world to move in the same direction. Just as in World War I, women went to work outside the home during World War II, and even though many left their jobs when the war was over, the impact was a reinforcement of the movement toward equality. The emphasis on overall equality in communist countries supported that trend, not only for political rights but for economic and social status as well. In many countries today women are gaining more education, birth rates are falling, and voting rights are fairly common.

During the last decades of the 20th century, a new women's movement began in the West that emphasized economic gains for women and a rejection of purely domestic roles. In the United States the movement gained momentum as a result of the civil rights movement for Black Americans of the 1950s and 1960s, and it resulted in increasing rates of employment of women in most western countries. Although by the early 21st century most women remained in clerical jobs and other traditional "women's jobs" (such as nursing and teaching), a growing number of middle-class women were entering professional and management occupations previously reserved for men. A brief increase in the western birth rate after World War II ended in the early 1960s, and a rapid decline continued throughout the century, allowing more women to pursue interests outside the home.

Although the women's rights movements in western countries did encourage the founders of new nations during the 20th century to write female suffrage into their constitutions, women in Africa and Asia made only limited political and economic gains. Women – such as Indira Gandhi in India, Corazon Aquino in the Philippines, and Benazir Bhutto in Pakistan – emerged as heads of states in less developed and developing countries, but the majority of elected officials and government administrators were still men by the early 21st century. However, a number of countries have passed legislation or written provisions into their constitutions that require political parties to run a minimum percentage of women as candidates for office or set minimum levels of female representation in legislatures. Most of these laws and provisions have succeeded in their goals, and even though most females that have held high political positions have had powerful male relatives, the trend appears to be toward more active participation by women in politics.

Economic barriers to female equality are still overwhelming in most emerging nations of the world. Early marriage ages for women and large families are still the norm in most African and Asian societies, limiting the ability of women to receive higher education or follow a career outside the home. Low levels of nutrition often affect women more adversely than men in societies where tradition dictates that men should be served the best food and women should have the leftovers, if any remain. These customs, along with high death rates in childbirth, result in lower overall life expectancies for women than men in many less developed countries, in contrast to the pattern in industrial societies, where women outlive men on the average. Despite these indications of lingering inequalities, the United Nations has actively supported an international women's movement by first adopting the Convention on the Elimination of All Forms of Discrimination against Women in 1979, and then sponsoring two international conferences on the status of women, one in 1985 in Nairobi, Kenya, and another ten years later in Beijing. Women at these conferences revealed differing views of gender equality, and participated in debates regarding the meaning of head-coverings and loose-fitting garments for Muslim women, the quality of family life in the West, and issues of poverty and disease.

Human Rights

The formal recognition of individual rights began with Enlightenment documents of the late 18th century, such as the U.S. Declaration of Independence (1776), the U.S. Constitution (1788), the French Declaration of the Rights of Man (1789), and the U.S. Bill of Rights (1791). During the 19th century anti-slavery movements argued that the practice of slavery violated these guarantees of individual rights, and in the mid-20th century the black civil rights movement in the United States sought to gain equal political, economic, and social treat-

COMPARISONS:
WOMEN IN NATIONAL PARLIAMENTS

One way to measure political equality of men and women in different countries of the world is to examine the percentage of women that serve in their legislatures. Below are a sampling of percentages for comparison. Some countries with high percentages of female legislators have laws that require minimum numbers of women to be represented. Others have cultural and ideological norms that support female equality.

Rank	Country	% of women in lower house	Rank	Country	% of women in lower house
1	Rwanda	48.8%	51	Pakistan	21.1%
2	Sweden	47%	54	China	20.6%
4	Argentina	40%	61	United Kingdom	19.5%
8	Spain	36.6%	70	Bolivia	16.9%
17	Germany	31.6%	71	United States	16.8%
18	Uganda	30.7%	80	Greece	14.7%
21	Peru	29.2%	85	Cameroon	13.9%
27	Afghanistan	27.7%	97	Thailand	11.7%
33	Iraq	25.5%	107	Turkey	9.1%
41	Mexico	23.2%	125	Haiti	4%
50	Canada	21.3%	135	Eight Way Tie*	0%

* Tied at the bottom are Micronesia, Nauru, Oman, Palau, Qatar, Saudi Arabia, Solomon Islands, and Tuvalu.

Source: "Women in National Parliaments: Situation as of 31 December 2007," www.ipu.org.

ment of minorities. By the late 20th century these beliefs were internationalized through a **human rights movement,** articulated in the **Universal Declaration of Human Rights,** a document sponsored by the United Nations and signed by the UN General Assembly in 1948. In Article 2, the declaration affirms the principle of equality with these words:

> Everyone is entitled to all the rights and freedoms set forth in this Declaration, without distinction of any kind, such as race, colour, sex, language, religion, political or other opinion, national or social origin, property, birth or other status. Furthermore, no distinction shall be made on the basis of the political,

jurisdictional or international status of the country or territory to which a person belongs, whether it be independent, trust, non-self-governing or under any other limitation of sovereignty.

(Reference: The United Nations website, http://www.un.org/Overview/rights.html)

In other articles, the declaration condemns slavery, torture, cruel and inhuman punishment, arbitrary arrest, detention, and exile. While many have praised the efforts of the United Nations to create a universal standard for human rights, others have questioned the right of western countries to impose their values on the rest of the world whose traditional cultures or religion may emphasize other beliefs as more important than individual rights. Despite these objections, **non-governmental organizations (NGOs)** have joined the United Nations in promoting human rights. Examples are Amnesty International, which concentrates on gaining the freedom of people tortured or imprisoned without trial by their governments, and Doctors Without Borders, which provides medical assistance for people caught in crisis situations around the world.

CULTURAL TRENDS

Globalization has promoted the spread of western values through new technologies – such as radio, television, movies, and the internet – to many people in various cultures around the world. During the 19th century industrialization impacted much more than the way economies operated; it was accompanied by a set of values called **modernism.** These values included secularism (an emphasis on non-religious aspects of life), an emphasis on reason (rationalism), materialism (valuing concrete objects and possessions), technology, bureaucracy, and an emphasis on freedom rather than collective equality. In other words, industrialization encouraged making money and gaining economic success. During the 20th century, the economies of many western nations went into post-industrialism, in which the majority of people are employed in the service sector, or jobs that do not produce goods directly but instead provide services in technology, health care, business and legal services, finance, and education. These contrast to the most common type of job created earlier by industrialization, the industry sector, which employs people to create tangible goods, such as cars, clothing, or machinery. Post-industrialism has been accompanied by **post-modernism,** a set of values that emphasizes quality of life over concern with material gain. Some examples of post-modern values are the preservation of the environment and the promotion of health care and education.

Global Culture

Technological innovations and international marketization and privatization have encouraged **cultural globalization,** or the spread of western – particularly American – culture to other parts of the globe. Because so many global cultural influences have their origins in the West, many criticize them as a form of **cultural imperialism** that dominates the world's movie theaters, televisions, and computer screens with image of western goods and styles. Just as in the 19th century, the West is still seeking markets, and sophisticated advertising techniques promote consumption of U.S. products and values that undercut traditional cultures and alternative ideologies.

EXAMINING THE EVIDENCE: POST-MODERNISM – CONCERN FOR GLOBAL WARMING

As western countries have moved into post-industrialism, values have changed to post-modernism, which reflects a concern for quality of life issues. One concern that has gained a growing amount of international attention is global warming, or the so-called "greenhouse effect." The warming is caused by a layer of atmospheric gases that allows solar radiation to reach earth and warm it but keeps heat from radiating from earth's surface into space. Increases in greenhouse-gas emissions from the burning of fossil fuels in industry and transportation have threatened to elevate earth's temperatures so intensely that glaciers and Arctic Ocean sea ice are melting. Many are predicting an elevation in sea waters that could flood coastal areas and bring disaster worldwide.

The first international Earth Summit was held in Rio de Janeiro in 1992, where representatives from 178 countries pledged to limit their increases in greenhouse gas emissions. Although these pledges proved to be ineffective, many nations signed the 1997 Kyoto Protocol, which imposed penalities on countries that failed to cut greenhouse-gas emissions. The United States did not sign the agreement, with President George W. Bush remaining unconvinced by the scientific evidence that supports the argument that global warming is taking place.

New technologies associated with more sophisticated and powerful television broadcasting and the growing dimensions of internet use have had cultural consequences that almost no one could have foreseen. One area of influence is **global pop culture,** which allows many ordinary people access to dress, food, music, movies, and television shows that reflect American culture. Many American entertainers have become well-known in other parts of the world, and the transmission of their performances in English has also had a globalizing effect as more people are encouraged to access pop culture through a common language. Although American culture has clearly dominated the global pop culture, cultural influences from other countries have also traveled the global circuit. For example, the Indian movie industry, nicknamed "Bollywood," has grown tremendously, and Indian films are viewed by millions of people, including many who live outside the Indian subcontinent.

Another cluster of cultural influences has created a **global elite culture** that directly reaches far fewer people than the global pop culture does, but it links influential people in many walks of life across cultures. One component of these networks of elites is the use of English as a common language, a process that began when Britain established its worldwide empire and exposed far-flung colonies to its language. After independence during the 20th century, many former colonies continued to use English as their official language, a practice that enabled elites who spoke different local languages within a country to communicate with one another. When the United States emerged as a superpower after World War II, the use of English as a second language was promoted as a necessity for conducting business, diplomatic relationships, and military coordination with U.S. elites. After the collapse of the Soviet Union, even more international students flocked to learn English as a second language. Today English is more commonly used than any other language in conducting international academic and diplomatic conferences and business meetings. Another factor in the creation of a global elite culture is the sharing of modern science. Science has long had a globalizing effect as people from different cultures have shared knowledge of biology, chemistry, and physics, but the growing ease of contacting fellow scientists in other countries has magnified its importance. Because the structures of studying modern science are western in origin, this pillar of global elite culture is dominated by the U.S. and Europe. Western universities now welcome increasing numbers of international students who study their disciplines through western eyes and after graduation carry their knowledge to all parts of the globe.

Fragmentation: Counter-Influence to Globalization

Until recently, few people predicted that **fragmentation** – divisions based on ethnic or cultural identity – would become increasingly important in world interactions. A few years ago **nationalism** – identities based on nationhood – seemed to be declining in favor of increasing globalization. However, nationality questions almost certainly did block Mikhail Gorbachev's attempts to resuscitate the Soviet Union, and national identities remain strong in most parts of the world. Perhaps most dramatically, the **politicization of religion** has dominated world politics of the early 21st century. Most westerners have been caught off guard by this turn of events, especially in the United States, where separation of church and state has been a basic political principle since the founding of the country.

Political scientist Samuel Huntington argued in the early 1990s that our most important and dangerous future conflicts would be based on clashes of civilizations, not on socioeconomic or even ideological differences. He divided the world into several different cultural areas that may already be poised to threaten world peace: the West, the Orthodox world (Russia), Islamic countries, Latin American, Africa, the Hindu world, the Confucian world, the Buddhist world, and Japan. Some scholars criticize Huntington by saying that he distorts cultural divisions and that he underestimates the importance of cultural conflicts within nations. In either case – a world divided into cultural regions or a world organized into multicultural nations – the revival of ethnic or cultural politics tends to emphasize differences among nations rather than commonalities.

The two forces – globalization and fragmentation – may operate within one country at one time. For example, India has organized into the world's largest democracy, and it has developed information technology centers that collaborate extensively with westerners in international business and trade. However, India still has tendencies toward fragmentation based on the historical conflict between Hindus and Muslims. Tensions that created such havoc after Indian independence was announced in 1947 erupt from time to time, affecting the government's authority to rule and its citizens' ability to lead peaceful private lives.

A Stateless Nation. The Kurds have had a national identity for many centuries, but they have never had a state. Instead, 20 million Kurds are spread in an area that crosses the formal borders of six countries: Turkey, Syria, Iraq, Iran, Armenia, and Azerbaijan.

Evidence that fragmentation is at work in today's world may be found in the number of **stateless nations** – people of a common identity without a corresponding state organized by a central government – that make their way into today's headlines. Examples include Basques, who are a minority people in northern Spain; Québécois, who are a minority French-speaking people in Canada; the Catholics of Northern Ireland, who are part of the United Kingdom; Palestinians, who seek a state in the Middle East; and Kurds, who are a nation of some 20 million people divided among six states in the Middle East but dominant in none.

The attack on the World Trade Towers in New York City and the Pentagon in Washington, D.C., on September 11, 2001 was clearly a "marker event" in recent history, although we don't know the full impact that the events of that day will have on the course of history. One interpretation is that the attack was a demonstration of the importance of conflicting cultural identities in the modern world. From the point of view of many in the United States, the actions were heinous crimes carried out by extremists who acted out of hatred for and jealousy of a powerful yet blessed country. From the point of view of the hijackers and their supporters, they were engaged in a holy struggle against a culture that they considered an evil force in the world. Other events of the early 21st century, including the American invasion of Iraq and subsequent terrorist actions in many different countries, may be interpreted as signs of powerful fragmenting forces that are tearing the world apart. On the other hand, the unifying forces of globalization are undeniable, and perhaps the fragmenting events of today's world are the last vestiges of the old divisions created during the age of imperialism. The patterns are still taking shape, and the answers will be written in the next chapter of the interrelated and ever unfolding story of the world.

CONCEPTS AND IDENTIFICATIONS

Al-Qaeda
command economy
compressed modernity
containment
cultural globalization
cultural imperialism
dependency theory
European Union
fragmentation
glasnost
global elite culture
global pop culture
globalization

Green Revolution
household responsibility system
human rights movement
Hussein, Saddam
integration
Khrushchev, Nikita
LDCs, MDCs
market economy
marketization
megacities
mixed economy
modernism
modernization model
NAFTA
NGOs
perestroika
preemption
"private business"
privatization
politicization of religion
post-modernism
Putin, Vladimir
socialist market economy
SEZs
stateless nations
supranational organizations
Tiananmen crisis
Universal Declaration of Human Rights
WMDs
World Bank
WTO
Yeltsin, Boris

UNIT FIVE QUESTIONS

Multiple-Choice Questions:

1. After the founding of the People's Republic of China, Mao Zedong based his first model for economic development most closely on the model provided by

    a) Taiwan
    b) Japan
    c) the Soviet Union
    d) the Qing Dynasty
    e) India

2. After independence in 1947 the Indian subcontinent was partitioned into different countries based primarily on

    a) natural geographic boundaries
    b) economic development
    c) political differences
    d) religious identities
    e) language groups

3. Which of the following was NOT established as a communist country during the 20th century?

    a) People's Republic of China
    b) Cuba
    c) U.S.S.R.
    d) Brazil
    e) Vietnam

4. In the years just prior to World War I the spirit of nationalism that inspired many people in eastern Europe to fight for their independence expressed itself as

    a) self-determination
    b) entangling alliances
    c) protectionism
    d) appeasement
    e) containment

5. Which of the following is the BEST single reason why women in many western nations were granted suffrage rights in 1918 and the years that followed?

    a) the election of large numbers of women to national legislatures
    b) the defeat of authoritarian governments during World War I
    c) the large number of women who worked in traditional male jobs during World War I
    d) the growing influence of socialism
    e) the conscription of women into the armed services during World War I

(Questions 6 and 7 are based on the following quote):

"His Majesty's Government view with favor the establishment in Palestine of a national home for the Jewish people and will use their best endeavors to facilitate the achievement of that object, it being clearly understood that nothing shall be done which may prejudice the civil and religious rights of existing non-Jewish communities in Palestine."

6. The government that is making promises in the document is

    a) France
    b) Russia
    c) Iran
    d) China
    e) Britain

7. Although the promises were not immediately kept, they eventually resulted in the establishment of

    a) Palestine
    b) Israel
    c) Lebanon
    d) Syria
    e) Iraq

8. The provisions of the Versailles treaties that followed World War I treated eastern Europe and the Middle East differently in that

   a) eastern European countries were made mandates of the League of Nations, but most of the areas of the Middle East were kept as colonies
   b) new eastern European countries were created based on the principle of self-determination, but all Middle Eastern countries were designated as mandates
   c) eastern European ethnic groups were kept under the control of large empires, but Middle Eastern countries were split up based on ethnicities
   d) countries in both areas were governed under the mandate system, but Eastern European nationalities had more hope of someday becoming independent countries
   e) new eastern European countries were created based on the principle of self-determination, but Middle Eastern nationalities either had to struggle for their independence or were designated as mandates

9. The Russian Revolution of 1917 and the Chinese regime change in 1949 both resulted in the

   a) creation of a communist state
   b) restoration of a hereditary monarchy
   c) purification of an existing dominant ideology
   d) transfer of power to leaders from other countries
   e) almost immediate improvement in the countries' economies

10. Which of the following countries was LEAST negatively impacted by the Great Depression?

   a) Germany
   b) the United States
   c) France
   d) Mexico
   e) the U.S.S.R.

11. Which of the following is the BEST description of political trends in the era between World War I and World War II?

a) Many more countries became democratic.
b) A number of political systems in industrialized nations became decidedly more authoritarian.
c) Communist social movements weakened considerably.
d) Many countries returned to rule by hereditary monarchies.
e) The international influence of European imperialist powers increased significantly.

12. World War II was different from most previous wars because it

a) was the first total war
b) made use of limited warfare
c) was fought primarily in trenches
d) blurred the distinction between military and civilian
e) was the first to use machine gun and tank technology

13. The Truman Doctrine was an expression of the U.S. foreign policy of

a) isolationism
b) containment
c) détente
d) preemption
e) appeasement

14. In 1978 Deng Xiaoping began a gradual but dramatic change in China by introducing

a) communism
b) the Great Leap Forward
c) the socialist market economy
d) the Cultural Revolution
e) military rule

15. What did all of the areas north and east of the heavy black line have in common between 1917 and 1991?

a) They were all part of the Soviet Union.
b) They were all a part of the Commonwealth of Independent States.
c) They were separated from countries on the other side of the line by the "iron curtain."
d) They all shared a common majority ethnicity.
e) The Russian Orthodox Church was the official religion in all areas.

16. Which of the following was an important difference between 20th-century nationalist movements in China and India?

a) China's nationalism was more focused on equity for ordinary peasants.
b) India's leaders put more emphasis on the use of violence to achieve their goals.
c) India's leaders rejected capitalism; China's leaders did not.
d) China's government was more centralized than India's especially during the early part of the century.
e) Communism was a central feature of Chinese struggles but not for nationalist assertions in India.

17. Which of the following countries in Africa received its independence BEFORE the post-World War II decolonization period?

a) Libya
b) Nigeria
c) Egypt
d) Kenya
e) Ghana

18. Which of the following did Latin American countries have in common with Third World countries of Asia and Africa during the mid-to-late 20th century?

a) European countries and the United States had few investments in any of the areas.
b) All experienced successful democratization movements.
c) Elites in all places were often in close contact with capitalist countries.
d) Most had authoritarian governments led by elites.
e) All areas experienced rapid decolonization.

19. Which of the following areas of the world was LEAST impacted by the Green Revolution of the late 20th century?

a) China
b) Southeast Asia
c) The Middle East
d) Latin America
e) Sub-Saharan Africa

20. In the early 21st century the foreign policy of the United States most often criticized by other countries was that used in the

a) invasion of Iraq
b) determination of aid packages to Russia
c) designation of China as "most favored nation" for trade purposes
d) support of Palestinians in their conflict with Israel
e) failure to form a supranational organization to match the European Union in power

COMPARISONS:
WOMEN IN NATIONAL PARLIAMENTS

One way to measure political equality of men and women in different countries of the world is to examine the percentage of women that serve in their legislatures. Below are a sampling of percentages for comparison. Some countries with high percentages of female legislators have laws that require minimum numbers of women to be represented. Others have cultural and ideological norms that support female equality.

Rank	Country	% of women in lower house	Rank	Country	% of women in lower house
1	Rwanda	48.8%	51	Pakistan	21.1%
2	Sweden	47%	54	China	20.6%
4	Argentina	40%	61	United Kingdom	19.5%
8	Spain	36.6%	70	Bolivia	16.9%
17	Germany	31.6%	71	United States	16.8%
18	Uganda	30.7%	80	Greece	14.7%
21	Peru	29.2%	85	Cameroon	13.9%
27	Afghanistan	27.7%	97	Thailand	11.7%
33	Iraq	25.5%	107	Turkey	9.1%
41	Mexico	23.2%	125	Haiti	4%
50	Canada	21.3%	135	Eight Way Tie*	0%

* Tied at the bottom are Micronesia, Nauru, Oman, Palau, Qatar, Saudi Arabia, Solomon Islands, and Tuvalu.

21. The best explanation for Rwanda's rank in the chart above is that

    a) the Belgians encouraged equality for women when they colonized the area

    b) the country's limited economic development means that men and women have roughly equal social statuses

    c) Rwanda has a national law requiring a minimum number of women in the legislature

    d) Rwanda's native religion sanctions women as political leaders

    e) the country's birth rate has declined rapidly in recent years

22. The creation of the household responsibility system, "private business," and Special Economic Zones were all programs adopted during the late 20th century in

    a) Russia
    b) China
    c) Brazil
    d) South Africa
    e) India

23. In the years after it was created in 1991, the European Union brought about the most change in Europe in regard to its

    a) ability to coordinate international security
    b) creation of an international judicial system
    c) ability to control border crossings and immigration
    d) creation of a common currency for most of its members
    e) coordination of common agricultural policies

24. According to modernization theory, a country's greatest barrier to economic development is usually

    a) lack of educational opportunities for ordinary citizens
    b) tradition
    c) exploitation by more developed countries
    d) high levels of corruption among political leaders
    e) a weak infrastructure to support economic activities

25. By the early 21st century, "megacities" existed in

    a) North America, Europe, and Japan only
    b) most areas of the world
    c) Asia only
    d) the Western Hemisphere only
    e) in India and China only

Free-Response Questions:

For all essays, be sure that you have a relevant thesis that is supported by historical evidence.

Document-Based Question (DBQ): (suggested reading time – 10 minutes; suggested writing time – 40 minutes)

For the DBQ, be sure that you

- **Use all of the documents**

- **Use evidence from the documents to support your thesis**

- **Analyze the documents by grouping them in at least two or three appropriate ways**

- **Consider the source of the document and analyze the author's point of view**

- **Explain the need for at least one additional document**

1. Using the documents, analyze the arguments for and against the U.S. decision to use the atomic bomb on Hiroshima and Nagasaki in 1945. Identify one additional type of document and explain briefly how it would help your analysis.

DOCUMENT 1

"The idea of the destruction of civilization is not melodramatic hysteria or crackpot raving. It is a very real and, I submit, almost inevitable result...

I do not of course want to propose anything to jeopardize the war with Japan but, horrible as it may seem, I know it would be better to take greater casualties now in conquering Japan than to bring upon the world the tragedy of unrestrained competitive production of this material...In the name of the future of our country and of the peace of the world, I beg you, sir, not to pass this off because I happen to be unknown, without influence or name in the public eye..."

> Letter to Harry Truman from an engineer who had worked on uranium isotope separation in developing the bomb, 1945

DOCUMENT 2

"For the first time is history there was a nuclear explosion. And what an explosion...For a brief period there was a lighting effect within a radius of 20 miles equal to several suns in midday; a huge ball of fire was formed which lasted for several seconds. This ball mushroomed and rose to a height of over ten thousand feet before it dimmed. The light from the explosion was seen clearly at...points generally to about 180 miles away....A massive cloud was formed which surged and billowed upward with tremendous power, reaching the substratosphere at an elevation of 41,000 feet...

One-half mile from the explosion there was a massive steel test cylinder weighting 220 tons. The base of the cylinder was solidly encased in concrete. Surrounding the cylinder was a strong steel tower 70 feet high, anchored to concrete foundations...The blast tore the tower from its foundations, twisted it, ripped it apart and left it flat on the ground...None of us had expected it to be damaged."

> An eyewitness to the atomic
> bomb test
> New Mexico, July 21, 1945

DOCUMENT 3

"My own knowledge of these [atomic] developments had come about only after I became President...that the project was nearing completion, and that a bomb could be expected within another four months...I had then set up a committee of top men and had asked them to study with great care the implications the new weapon might have for us...

It was their recommendation that the bomb be used against the enemy as soon as it could be done. They recommended further that it should be used without specific warning...'We can propose no technical demonstration likely to bring an end to the war; we see no...alternative to direct military use.' It was their conclusion that no technical demonstration they might propose, such as over a deserted island, would be likely to bring the war to an end. It had to be used against an enemy target."

> Harry Truman, 1955
> Comments in his memoirs

DOCUMENT 4

"Suddenly from outside the front entrance an indescribable color and light – an eerie greenish-white flash – came thrusting in.

After a little while I regained consciousness. Everything around me was pitch dark...I was buried under the wreckage of the two-story building...I couldn't move my body...I called for Mother as loudly as I could. Mother pulled aside the boards and beams which were already on fire and pulled me out to safety...But at once I was stunned by the completeness of the change which had taken place in my surroundings. Everything in sight which can be called a building is crushed to the ground and sending out flames. People who are burned so badly that the skin of their bodies is peeling off in red strips are raising shrieking cries that sound as though the victims would die the next minute...The street is so covered with dead people and burned people stretched out and groaning, and with fallen houses and things, that we can't get through...Looking at this pitiable scene, I wondered why human beings, who ought to be of the same mind, have to make wars; why they have to kill each other like this."

Account from a school composition of a boy that lived through the Hiroshima blast

DOCUMENT 5

"The Japanese had demonstrated in each case [the defense of Okinawa and Iwo Jima, two islands south of Japan] they would not surrender and they fight to the death...It was to be expected that resistance in Japan, with their home ties, could be even more severe. We had one hundred thousand people killed in Tokyo in one night of bombs, and it had seemingly no effect whatsoever. It destroyed the Japanese cities, yes, but their morale was affected, so far as we could tell, not at all. So it seemed quite necessary, if we could, to shock them into action...We had to end the war; we had to save American lives."

George C. Marshall
Chief of Staff, U.S. Armed
Services during World War II

DOCUMENT 6

"At the time the Army felt it would be a great shame for them if they were to surrender unconditionally as a military force, even if it was not a national surrender. They felt it was impossible. Therefore it was necessary to work out a suitable pretext which would make the Army feel they could not do anything else but just follow it…The A-Bomb provided an excellent help, because the A-Bomb sacrificed many people other than Japanese military men. This provided us with an excuse that America would not refrain from doing such evils, that therefore there would be no other choice but to cease the war to save many innocent Japanese citizens. If the A-Bomb had not been dropped, we would have had great difficulty to find a good reason to end the war."

> Hisatune Sakomizu
> Secretary to the Japanese
> cabinet 1945

DOCUMENT 7

"[It is] folly to argue whether one weapon is more immoral than another. For, in a larger sense, it is war itself which is immoral, and the stigma of such immorality must rest upon the nation which initiates hostilities."

> General Omar Bradley
> Comments concerning the
> controversy over building the
> hydrogen bomb, 1950

DOCUMENT 8

"If we let Russia get the Super [hydrogen bomb] first, catastrophe becomes all but certain – whereas if we get it first, there exists a chance of saving ourselves."

> Senator Brien McMahon
> Chairman of the Joint Committee
> on Atomic Energy, 1950

Change Over Time Essay (Suggested writing time: 40 minutes)

2. Analyze changes and continuities in the development of supranational organizations from 1914 to the present. Be sure to use examples of specific organizations to illustrate your analysis.

Comparative Essay (suggested writing time: 40 minutes)

3. Within the time period from 1914 to the present, compare the impacts of globalization AND fragmentation in Russia with ONE of the following.

Western Europe

OR

The Middle East

AP WORLD HISTORY PRACTICE EXAM

Directions: Each of the questions or incomplete statements below is followed by five suggested answers or completions. Select the one that is best in each case.

1. Which of the following is a basic belief of Hinduism?

   a) The Eightfold Path leads to Enlightenment.
   b) When an individual dies, his or her soul may be reborn in another living being.
   c) The perfect society is one in which all people are equal.
   d) Bodhisattvas are spiritual beings sent to help people on earth learn to overcome suffering.
   e) Pork is unclean and should not be eaten by those that adhere to the Hindu faith.

2. Which of the following ancient civilizations put government bureaucrats at the top of its social hierarchy?

   a) Ancient Greece
   b) Gupta Empire of India
   c) Han Empire of China
   d) the New Kingdom of Egypt
   e) Ancient Rome

3. Which of the following did all of the earliest civilizations in the Middle East and south Asia have in common?

   a) They were all in areas with abundant rainfall.
   b) All were self-sufficient with little trade with other civilizations.
   c) All had strong central governments.
   d) None had well-developed writing systems.
   e) All practiced polytheism.

4. The ruin in southern France, shown above, exemplifies the

    a) influence of Islamic architecture
    b) incorporation of architectural techniques of the Ancient Egyptians
    c) influence of Gothic architecture
    d) craftsmanship of Ancient Persians
    e) Roman architectural style

5. The belief system that is based on the notion that people give and take within the context of five basic relationships of society is

    a) Confucianism
    b) Buddhism
    c) Hinduism
    d) Daoism
    e) Shamanism

6. Which of the following was a significant difference between the Roman Empire and the Han Empire?

    a) The Han Empire had more difficulty defending its borders.
    b) The Roman Empire was more heavily dependent on slave labor.
    c) The Han economy was based mainly on agriculture; the Roman economy was based mainly on trade.
    d) Peasant rebellions were more problematic for the Han than for the Romans.
    e) The Roman Empire encompassed many more diverse peoples than the Han did.

7. Which of the following religions originated AFTER 600 C.E.?

    a) Islam
    b) Judaism
    c) Hinduism
    d) Buddhism
    e) Daoism

8. Which of the following best describes Sub-Saharan trade in the period between 1000 and 1450?

    a) Sub-Saharan people traded with one another but not with people in other areas of the world.
    b) Sub-Saharan people traded with Europeans from trading posts along Africa's western coast.
    c) The area was isolated from other areas of the world, and most tribes were self-sufficient.
    d) Sub-Saharan people conducted a limited trade with people in the Middle East.
    e) The area was strongly connected to major long-distance trade routes of the Eastern Hemisphere.

9. The religion that requires a once-in-a-lifetime pilgrimage to its founding city is

    a) Judaism
    b) Islam
    c) Hinduism
    d) Buddhism
    e) Daoism

10. Which of the following groups invaded China in the 13th century and established the Yuan Dynasty?

a) Seljuk Turks
b) Tibetans
c) Mongols
d) Japanese
e) Jurchens

(Questions 11and 12 are based on the following chart)

The Americas	**The Eastern Hemisphere**
beans, squash, tomatoes, sweet potatoes, peanuts, chilis, ⟷ chocolate, maize (corn), potatoes, avocados, pineapple, manioc	wheat, rice, olives, grapes, bananas, rice, citrus fruits, melons, figs, sugar, coconuts horses, cattle, pigs, sheep, goats, chickens, rabbits, rats

11. The diffusion of crops, other plants, and animals illustrated on the chart above was called

a) the Indian Ocean Exchange
b) the Socialist Market System
c) the Putting Out System
d) mercantilism
e) the Columbian Exchange

12. The diffusion identified in # 11 first began to impact world trade patterns during the

a) 12th century
b) 14th century
c) 16th century
d) 18th century
e) 20th century

13. The spread of the bubonic plague from Asia to Europe during the 14th century is directly attributable to the

a) Mongol unification of Eurasia
b) invasion of eastern Europe by the Seljuk Turks
c) Portuguese involvement in the Indian Ocean trade
d) movement of people during the Crusades
e) development of the Great Circuit trade

14. Under the rule of which of the following dynasties was China MOST wary of contact with outsiders?

a) Tang
b) Song
c) Yuan
d) Ming
e) Qing

15. During the era from 1450 to 1750, which of the following areas of Asia was the most isolated from foreign influences?

a) China
b) Vietnam
c) Korea
d) Japan
e) India

16. Which of the following was NOT a major cultural movement in Europe in the era between 1450 and 1800?

a) Renaissance
b) Reformation
c) Enlightenment
d) Scholasticism
e) Deism

17. The existence of "Africanity", or widely shared customs across many parts of Africa by 1450, is probably best explained by

   a) the lack of geographic obstacles to travel across the continent
   b) powerful centralized kingdoms in early African history
   c) the Bantu migrations
   d) early trade contacts across the Sahara Desert
   e) strong native religions

18. Ibn Battuta's detailed 14th-century written account is an important source of information about

   a) China during the rule of Kubilai Khan
   b) life in Islamic lands
   c) the lives of ordinary peasants in central Asia and the Middle East
   d) demographic changes in Eurasia as the result of the spread of disease
   e) technological innovations that spread from east Asia to Europe along the Silk Road

19. Which of the following characterized political systems in Sub-Saharan Africa and Southeast Asia during the late 19th century?

   a) They were almost all ruled by hereditary monarchs.
   b) Most had established democracies.
   c) Most were authoritarian, but had legislatures that shared some powers with the chief executive.
   d) Most were under colonial rule.
   e) They were characterized by weak central governments that tried to exert power over fragmented groups.

20. One characteristic that the American Declaration of Independence and the French Declaration of the Rights of Man and the Citizen had in common was that both

   a) emphasized liberty more than equality
   b) denounced nationalism
   c) affirmed the natural rights of citizens
   d) affirmed the rights of hereditary monarchs
   e) endorsed equal rights for women

21. The map above shows Europe during the time of

    a) the Crusades
    b) the Protestant Reformation
    c) the Napoleonic Wars
    d) World War I
    e) World War II

22. The 19th-century independence movement in Brazil was different from independence movements in Mexico and Gran Colombia because

    a) Brazilian elites were more afraid of slave revolts than were the elites in Mexico and Gran Colombia
    b) few elites in Brazil were influenced by Enlightenment ideas
    c) Brazil did not have a well-developed class of elites
    d) the movement was ultimately unsuccessful in Brazil
    e) Brazilians did not have a written constitution; Gran Colombia and Mexico did

23. Which of the following was NOT an innovation associated with the Industrial Revolution in the 19th century?

   a) mass production
   b) the cotton gin
   c) movable type
   d) the spinning jenny
   e) the steam engine

24. A 19th-century movement in arts and literature that was a reaction to the Enlightenment's emphasis on rational thought was called

   a) secularism
   b) isolationism
   c) socialism
   d) romanticism
   e) Marxism

25. "The cult of domesticity" is a 19th-century phrase that describes the

   a) insulated world of middle-class women in industrialized societies
   b) home life of European peasants
   c) urban working class in industrialized societies
   d) traditional values of women in east Asia
   e) system of producing goods by hand at home

26. Which broad ideology in 19th-century Europe was reinforced by the action of the Congress of Vienna in 1815?

   a) liberalism
   b) Marxism
   c) nationalism
   d) regionalism
   e) conservatism

27. "The Young Turks" were motivated to form and take action by their belief in

   a) a religious state in Turkey
   b) Turkish nationalism
   c) the need to restore the power of the Ottoman sultan
   d) Turkey's need to join the European Union
   e) non-violent resistance to European domination

28. After World War II the hegemony of western Europe was broken and replaced by

   a) hegemony of supranational organizations
   b) hegemony of Japan and China
   c) competition between Russia and countries of the Middle East for control
   d) competition between the United States and the Soviet Union
   e) cooperative hegemony of the United States and Great Britain

29. One important impact of World War II on the African continent was

   a) colonization by European powers
   b) a substantial reduction in overall population
   c) the establishment of many new communist countries
   d) decolonization
   e) the strengthening of national militaries

30. The policies of Soviet leader Joseph Stalin emphasized

   a) the spread of international communism
   b) collectivization of agriculture and industrialization
   c) more equal opportunities for peasants and city workers
   d) the purification of Marxist doctrines
   e) westernization and cooperation with international organizations

31. Which of the following 20ᵗʰ-century ideologies was directly supportive of equality between men and women?

    a) communism
    b) fascism
    c) self-determination
    d) protectionism
    e) appeasement

32. Post-modernist values contrast with modernist values in that post-modernist values emphasize

    a) materialism
    b) rationalism
    c) freedom
    d) technology
    e) quality of life

33. Which of the following explanations for the lack of development in a modern country is most likely based on dependency theory?

    a) The political and economic leaders are corrupt.
    b) Traditional values hamper development.
    c) The country has not enlisted the aid of a more developed country.
    d) The country has been blocked by the greed of more developed countries.
    e) The country has few natural resources, and those that it has are poorly used.

34. Which of the following did NOT live during the 19ᵗʰ century?

    a) Peter the Great
    b) Napoleon Bonaparte
    c) James Watt
    d) Charles Darwin
    e) Cixi

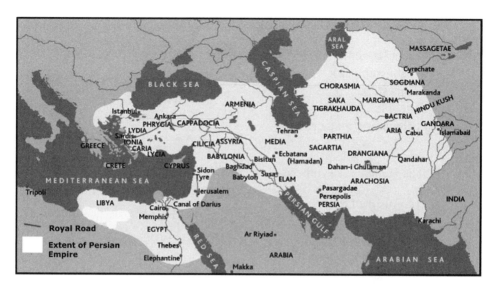

35. The map above shows which of the following empires at its greatest extent?

    a) Ancient Rome
    b) Ancient Greece
    c) Assyrian Empire
    d) Byzantine Empire
    e) Persian Empire

36. The concept of private property first came about as a result of the

    a) Neolithic Revolution
    b) development of the first cities
    c) organization of the earliest civilizations
    d) feudalistic ties in medieval Europe
    e) development of capitalism

37. The philosophies of the Ancient Greeks, such as Aristotle and Plato, were based most directly on their

    a) belief in a polytheistic religion
    b) fear of dangers in the natural world
    c) emphasis on secularism
    d) support of military power
    e) reliance on feelings and emotions

38. In Ancient China, the mandate of heaven belonged to the

a) scholar-gentry
b) ruling emperor
c) ancestors
d) people
e) emperor's mother

39. The Hellenistic synthesis was created most directly by

a) Cyrus the Great
b) Pericles
c) Julius Caesar
d) Alexander the Great
e) Ashoka

40. Which of the following is an accurate comparison of the Roman Republic and the Roman Empire?

a) Agriculture was a more important component of the economy during the Empire.
b) The Senate had more real governing power during the Republic.
c) Military success was more important during the Empire.
d) Peasants come into conflict with wealthy aristocrats over land ownership during the time of the Republic, but not during the Empire period.
e) The succession to leadership was determined by heredity under the Empire but not during the time of the Republic.

41. In the period between 600 and 1450 C.E., the interregional impact of nomadic movements

a) was not as great as it had been during the Classical Era
b) was significant, but not as great as in later eras
c) was important in the Western Hemisphere, but not in the Eastern Hemisphere
d) reached its greatest extent in world history
e) was minimal, as it has generally been throughout world history

42. The lateen sail was an important technology for travelling across the Indian Ocean because

    a) its square shape meant that it picked up more ocean breezes
    b) it was more durable than most other sails
    c) it worked best when combined with tiers of oars
    d) it was especially suited for short distance travel
    e) its shape made maneuvering the monsoon winds possible

SLAVE TRADE STATISTICS, 1521-1773

DESTINATION	NUMBERS OF SLAVES
Brazil	3,646,800
British West Indies	1,665,000
French West Indies	1,600,200
Spanish America	1,552,000 (702,000 to Cuba alone)
Dutch West Indies	500,000
United States and pre-1776 North America	399,000
Danish West Indies (now the Virgin Islands)	28,000

43. The table above supports the fact that the vast majority of slaves were traded to areas where the economy was dominated by

    a) gold and silver mines
    b) tobacco
    c) corn and beans
    d) cotton
    e) sugar

44. Although the political organization of early medieval Europe was decentralized and fragmented, the most important "glue" that provided structure and order was

    a) the code of honor among nobles and knights
    b) an extensive trade system
    c) parliamentary organization
    d) the Roman Catholic Church
    e) a common language and culture

45. Despite the differences between them, which of the following did the Byzantine Empire and the early Islamic caliphates have in common?

   a) All were Islamic.
   b) None had strong centralized governments.
   c) None relied on a strong military to keep their empires strong.
   d) All had only limited literary and artistic accomplishments.
   e) In all, both political and religious power was concentrated in the ruler's hands.

46. The Inca and Aztec societies were different in that

   a) the Inca had a large army; the Aztecs did not
   b) the Aztecs had a written language; the Inca did not
   c) the Inca diet was based on corn and beans; the Aztec diet was based on potatoes and tomatoes
   d) the Aztecs built sophisticated public buildings; the Inca did not
   e) the Aztecs used animals as beasts of burden; the Inca did not

47. Neo-Confucianism was created during the Song Era in China to ease the growing tension between Confucianism and

   a) Daoism
   b) Shintoism
   c) Buddhism
   d) Hinduism
   e) Legalism

48. For its subject matter, *The Tale of Genji*, the first novel to be written in Japanese, focused on

   a) the lives of the nobility in the emperor's court
   b) ordinary Japanese peasants
   c) the adventures of the shogun and samurai
   d) Japanese encounters with westerners
   e) life inside a Buddhist monastery

49. Which of the following is an accurate statement regarding the long-term influence of the Byzantine Empire after it fell?

    a) Its religion and many customs influenced the development of Russia.
    b) Constantinople remained as a primarily Christian city.
    c) Its territories remained united for many centuries.
    d) It set the example for later civilizations of separation of church and state.
    e) It provided a long-lasting common language for all eastern Europeans.

50. The structure pictured above was built by the people of

    a) Ancient Egypt
    b) Teotihuacan
    c) the Inca Empire
    d) Han China
    e) the Mauryan Empire

51. One difference in the relationships between European settlers and Amerindians in Latin America and North America was that in Latin America

    a) Amerindians were usually pushed out of places Europeans wanted for settlement
    b) social classes were generally less hierarchical
    c) few efforts were made to convert natives to Christianity
    d) Europeans were more likely to settle in rural areas
    e) many more Amerindians were forced into labor by Europeans

52. The hold that the Roman Catholic Church had on European society was significantly weakened during the 16th century by

    a) the Mongol invasions
    b) the Protestant Reformation
    c) Islamic invasions of Spain and France
    d) the Italian Renaissance
    e) a loss of church lands due to financial mismanagement

53. During what period in world history did sea-based powers rise in influence in contrast to most land-based powers, which either lost influence or stayed the same?

    a) the Classical Era (1000 B.C.E. – 600 C.E.)
    b) 600-1450 C.E.
    c) 1450-1750 C.E.
    d) 1750-1914 C.E.
    e) 1914 C.E. – Present

54. Which of the following people was most likely to serve as a viceroy in the Spanish colonies in the Americas?

    a) a mestizo
    b) a creole
    c) a peninsulare
    d) a mulatto
    e) an Amerindian

(Question 55 and 56 are based on the following map):

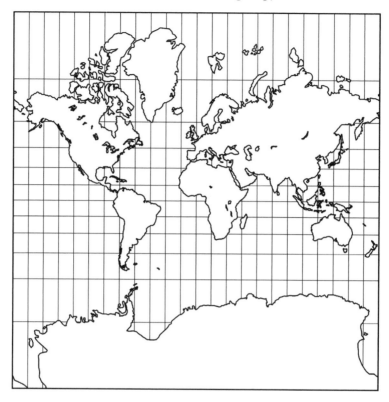

55. The Mercator projection map pictured above was tailored to aid

    a) explorers as they circumnavigated the globe by going south from Europe
    b) traders on the Indian Ocean trade circuits
    c) overland travelers on the Silk Road
    d) European traders on the Atlantic Ocean
    e) inland explorers of North and South America

56. One disadvantage of the Mercator projection is that it distorts the

    a) size of land masses, particularly those far away from the equator
    b) shapes of land masses
    c) distance between two different points on the globe
    d) size of the oceans, particularly the areas close to the equator
    e) shapes of oceans

57. One purpose of Zheng He's voyages in the early 15th century was to

    a) find a trading route to the Western Hemisphere
    b) reassert China's power after the demise of the Yuan Dynasty
    c) conquer lands around the Indian Ocean basin
    d) find and sink the Portuguese ships that were stealing Chinese trade
    e) find new converts to Confucianism

58. One reason that personalist leaders have had more political influence in Latin America than in North America is that

    a) Latin American leaders generally have been more charismatic than North American leaders
    b) Latin American leaders are not directly elected by the people; North American leaders are
    c) Latin American leaders were more likely to come from ordinary backgrounds than North American leaders
    d) Latin American leaders were more likely to be both political AND religious leaders
    e) Latin America was slower to develop stable political institutions than North America

59. Ever since Canada became a self-governing political system, an important problem for establishing and maintaining Canadian identity has been

    a) the significant French minority living primarily in Quebec
    b) the inability of the British government to stay out of Canadian affairs
    c) lack of transportation systems to tie people on the East Coast to those on the West Coast
    d) a centralized government that gives little authority to the provinces
    e) its open immigration policy that allows almost anyone to settle in Canada

60. Which of the following was a common goal of both Peter the Great and Catherine the Great for Russia?

a) freeing the serfs
b) expanding the country's borders
c) preserving Slavic customs above all others
d) breaking the power of Russian army and naval leaders
e) recognizing the rights of ethnic minorities to self-rule

"...this poison has spread far and wide in all the provinces. You, I hope, will certainly agree that people who pursue material gains to the great detriment of the welfare of others can be neither tolerated by Heaven nor endured by men...
Heaven is furious with anger, and all the gods are moaning with pain!"

61. The "poison" that Lin Zexu refers to in his 1838 letter to Queen Victoria excerpted above was

a) the plague
b) toxic gases
c) opium
d) food from the Americas
e) lead

62. "The cult of the emperor" was a campaign to glorify the Japanese emperor by the

a) Fujiwara family during the Heian Era
b) shogun during the Tokugawa Shogunate
c) oligarchs during the Meiji Restoration
d) military leaders during World War I
e) military leaders during World War II

63. The breakup of the Soviet Union in 1991 may be most directly linked to the 20th-century process of

a) the politicization of religion
b) globalization
c) post-modernism
d) fragmentation
e) integration

(Questions 64 and 65 are based on the following map)

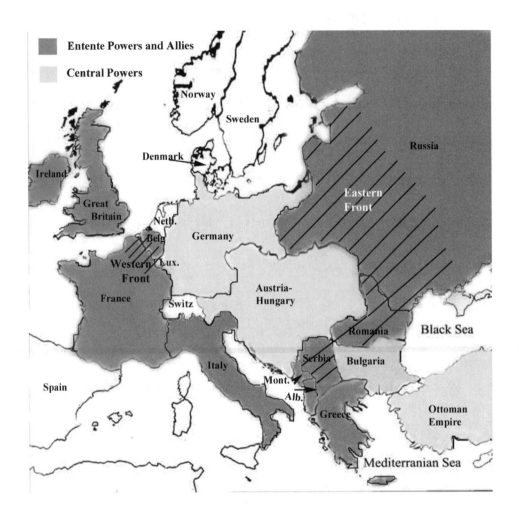

64. The map above shows Europe while countries were fighting

    a) the Napoleonic War
    b) the Crimean War
    c) World War I
    d) World War II
    e) the Cold War

65. The nature of the warfare fought in the area called the "Western Front" is best described as

a) trench warfare
b) blitzkrieg
c) a combination of infantry and horse brigades
d) a combination of submarine and tank warfare
e) scorched earth warfare

66. Which of the following regional organizations has most successfully come to control the money supply of its member states?

a) European Union (EU)
b) North American Free Trade Agreement (NAFTA)
c) North Atlantic Treaty Organization (NATO)
d) Organization of American States (OAS)
e) Organization for African Unity (OAU)

67. Which of the following is the BEST explanation for why Germany remained divided into two countries from 1945 till 1989?

a) Germans could not agree on the type of democracy they would form.
b) The cost of rehabilitating Germany after World War II was so great that it made sense to split the responsibility between the two superpowers.
c) Disagreements erupted between the U.S. and the Soviet Union over Germany's new capital city.
d) France insisted that West Germany should fall under its control since Germany had occupied France during World War II.
e) Cold War politics settled in, with West Germany establishing a democratic government, and East Germany establishing a communist government.

68. Passive resistance is a method employed in a 20ᵗʰ-century independence movement by

a) Ho Chi Minh
b) Mohandas Gandhi
c) Gamel Abdel Nasser
d) Fidel Castro
e) Salvador Allende

(Questions 69 and 70 are based on the following excerpt):

> "All the great civilizations of the past died out because contamination of their blood caused them to become decadent...
> In other words, in order to protect a certain culture, the type of human who created the culture must be preserved. But such preservation is tied to the inalterable law of the necessity and the right of victory of the best and the strongest..."

69. The excerpt above was written by

    a) Winston Churchill
    b) Mustafa Kemal
    c) V.I. Lenin
    d) Joseph Stalin
    e) Adolf Hitler

70. The philosophy expressed in the excerpt was used to justify the

    a) urge of kulaks
    b) Russian Revolution of 1917
    c) independence movements of the 1950s and 60s
    d) Holocaust
    e) use of the atomic bomb in 1945

FREE-RESPONSE QUESTIONS

For all essays, be sure that you have a relevant thesis that is supported by historical evidence.

Document-Based Question (DBQ): (suggested reading time – 10 minutes; suggested writing time – 40 minutes)

For the DBQ, be sure that you

- Use all of the documents

- Use evidence from the documents to support your thesis

- Analyze the documents by grouping them in at least two or three appropriate ways

- Consider the source of the document and analyze the author's point of view

- Explain the need for at least one additional document

1. Based on the following documents, analyze the responses to the spread of Islam from its origins on the Arabian Peninsula in the 7th century until 1450. Explain how another type of document would help you analyze the effects of the spread of Islam.

Document 1

"Mahmud marched into India during a period of thirty years and more....Mahmud utterly ruined the prosperity of the country, and performed there wonderful exploits, by which the Hindus became like atoms of dust scattered in all directs, and like a tale of old in the mouth of the people. Their scattered remains cherish, or course, the most inveterate aversion towards all Muslims…

…the Hindus believe that there is no country but theirs, no nation like theirs, no kings like theirs, no religion like theirs, no science like theirs. They are haughty, foolishly vain, self conceited, and stolid."

> Abu'l Raihan al-Birun, an Iranian
> scholar describing Sultan Mahmud's
> 11th-century invasions of India

Document 2

"In the name of Allah, the compassionate, the merciful. This is a statement from Habib ibn-Muslama to the inhabitants of Tiflis....securing them safety for their lives, churches, convents, religious services and faith, provided they acknowledge their humiliation and pay tax to the amount of one *dinar* on every household....You owe us counsel and support against the enemies of Allah and his Prophet to the utmost of your ability, and are bound to entertain the needy Muslim for one night and provide him with that food used by "the people of the Book" and which it is legal for us to partake of. If a Muslim is cut off from his companions and falls into your hands, you are bound to deliver him to the nearest body of the "Believers," unless something stands in the way. If you return to the obedience of Allah and observe prayer, you are our brethren in faith, otherwise poll-tax is incumbent on you..."

> The Pact of Ibn Muslama, about 650 C.E., with the Christians of Tiflis (in the Caucasus) defeated by him in battle

Document 3

"From the confines of Jerusalem and from the city of Constantinople a grievous report has gone forth and has been brought repeatedly to our ears; namely, that a race from the kingdom of the Persians, an accursed race, a race wholly alienated from God...has violently invaded the lands of those Christians and has depopulated them by pillage and fire....This royal city [Jerusalem]...situated at the center of the earth, is now held captive by the enemies of Christ and is subjected, by those who do not know God, to the worship of the heathen...When an armed attack is made upon the enemy, let this one cry be raised by all the soldiers of God: 'It is the will of God! It is the will of God!'"

> Pope Urban II, 1095
> Call to the Crusade, describing the Muslim Seljuk Turks

Document 4

"In Baghdad there are about forty thousand Jews, and they dwell in security, prosperity, and honor under the great Caliph, and among them are great sages, the heads of academies engaged in the study of the Law…there are twenty-eight Jewish Synagogues, situated either in the city itself or in al-Karkh on the other side of the Tigris…The great synagogue of the Head of the Captivity has columns of marble of various colors overlaid with silver and gold…And in front of the ark are about ten steps of marble; on the topmost step are the seats of the Head of the Captivity and of the Princes of the House of David."

> Benjamin of Tudela, a Jewish traveler from northern Spain, describing Baghdad (the capital of the Abbasid caliphate) in the 12th century

Document 5

…"the hospital shall keep all patients, men and women, until they are completely recovered. All costs are to be borne by the hospital, whether the people come from afar or near, whether they are residents or foreigners, strong or weak, low or high, rich or poor, employed or unemployed, blind or sighted, physically or mentally ill, learned or illiterate. There are no conditions or consideration of payment; none is objected to even indirectly, for non-payment. The entire service is through the magnificence of Allah, the generous one."

> Emur Mansur, the Mamluk governor of Egypt,
> 13th century bequest to his subjects

Document 6

"The Hindus and idol-worshipers had agreed to pay the money for toleration, and had consented to the poll tax, in return for which they and their families enjoyed security. These people now erected new idol temples in the city and the environs in opposition to the Law of the Prophet which declares that such temples are not to be tolerated. Under Divine guidance I destroyed these edifices, and I killed those leaders of infidelity who seduced others into error, and the lower orders I subjected to stripes and chastisement, until this abuse was entirely abolished."

> Firez Shah Tughluq, ruler of
> the Delhi Sultanate from 1351
> to 1388

Document 7

"Another of their good properties is…their constant custom of attending prayers with the congregation; for unless one makes haste, he will find no place left to say his prayers in. Another is, their insisting on the Koran's being committed to memory: for if a man finds his son defective in this, he will confine him till he is quite perfect, nor will he allow him his liberty until he is so."

> Ibn Battuta, describing his
> impressions of the subjects
> of Mansa Suleiman of Mali,
> 1353

Change Over Time Essay (suggested writing time: 40 minutes)

2. Choose TWO of the areas listed below and analyze how each area's relationship to western countries changed from 1750 to the present. Be sure to describe each area's involvement with western countries around 1750 as your starting point.

    •   Russia

    •   China

    •   Sub-Saharan Africa

    •   Latin America

Comparative Essay (suggested writing time: 40 minutes)

3. Compare and contrast the social and political organization of TWO of
    the following classical civilizations in the era between 200 B.C.E. and
    600 C.E.

    •   Gupta India

    •   Han China

    •   The Roman Empire

INDEX

ORDER INFORMATION

Five ways to order:

1) Fill out and send this form to:
   WoodYard Publications
   P.O. Box 3856
   Reading, PA 19606

Full payment must accompany the order. Make checks payable to WoodYard Publications.

2) Purchase Orders (for schools only) - Send purchase order to the above address or Fax to 610-372-8401.

3) Order from Amazon. Go to www.amazon.com for order information.

4) Pay for one student book through Pay Pal. Go to the website (http://worldhistap.home.comcast.net), click on "Order Form," and order.

5) Use your credit card by phoning 610-207-1366. Visa, Mastercard, American Express, and Discover cards accepted.

Questions? Call 610-207-1366 or e-mail at worldhistap@comcast.net

Please use order form on the reverse side.

Order Form

Please send _____copies of AP World History: An Essential Coursebook to:

Name_____

Mailing Address_____

City, State, Zip_____

Phone_____

E-mail Address_____

School_____

School Address_____

City, State, Zip_____

Please check one: Please send book(s) to _____Home Address

or

_____School Address

Prices:

> **1 book - $24.95 + $4.60 Priority Mail shipping = $29.55**
>
> **2-4 books - $19.95 each + 8% shipping**
>
> **5-49 books - $16.95 each + 8% shipping**
>
> **50+ books - $14.95 each + 8% shipping**

Mail this form with check payable to WoodYard Publications, P.O. Box 3856, Reading, Pennsylvania 19606. School purchase orders also accepted.